SpringBoard®
English
Language Arts

STUDENT EDITION   ENGLISH III

About The College Board

The College Board is a mission-driven not-for-profit organization that connects students to college success and opportunity. Founded in 1900, the College Board was created to expand access to higher education. Today, the membership association is made up of over 6,000 of the world's leading educational institutions and is dedicated to promoting excellence and equity in education. Each year, the College Board helps more than seven million students prepare for a successful transition to college through programs and services in college readiness and college success—including the SAT® and the Advanced Placement Program®. The organization also serves the education community through research and advocacy on behalf of students, educators, and schools. For further information, visit collegeboard.org.

ISBN: 978-1-4573-1297-7

1 2 3 4 5 6 7 8   20 21 22 23 24 25 26

Printed in the United States of America

Acknowledgements

The College Board gratefully acknowledges the outstanding work of the classroom teachers who have been integral to the development of this program. The end product is testimony to their expertise, understanding of student learning needs, and dedication to rigorous and accessible English Language Arts instruction.

Lance Balla
Everett School District
Everett, Washington

Carisa Barnes
San Diego Unified School District
San Diego, California

Leia Bell
Hillsborough County Public Schools
Tampa, Florida

Alysa Broussard
Lafayette Parish School System Lafayette, Louisiana

Robert J. Caughey
San Dieguito Union High School District
San Diego, California

Susie Challancin
Bellevue School District 405
Bellevue, Washington

Doug Cole
Cherry Creek School District
Greenwood Village, Colorado

Cari Davis
Rio Rancho Public School District
Rio Rancho, New Mexico

Paul De Maret
Poudre School District
Fort Collins, Colorado

Sylvia Ellison
Hillsborough County Public Schools Hillsborough, Florida

Karen Fullam
Hillsborough County Public Schools Tampa, Florida

Michael Gragert
Plano Independent School District Plano, Texas

Nancy Gray
Brevard County Schools
Viera, Florida

Charise Hallberg
Bellevue School District 405
Bellevue, Washington

T.J. Hanify
Bellevue School District 405
Bellevue, Washington

Jessi Hupper
Peninsula School District
Gig Harbor, Washington

Nimat Jones
ICEF Public Schools, Los Angeles, California

Karen Kampschmidt
Fort Thomas Independent School District
Fort Thomas, Kentucky

Karen Kennedy
Peninsula School District
Peninsula, Washington

LeAnn Klepzig
Bradley County Schools
Cleveland, Tennessee

Susie Lowry
Volusia County School District Deland, Florida

Michelle Lewis
Spokane Public School
Spokane, Washington

John Marshall
Mead School District
Mead, Washington

Cassandra Mattison
Hillsborough County Public Schools Tampa, Florida

Glenn Morgan
San Diego Unified School District San Diego, California

John Murray
Garland Independent School District Sachse, Texas

Kristen J. Ohaver
Charlotte-Mecklenburg Schools Charlotte, North Carolina

Amanda Olinger
Harrisburg School District
Harrisburg, South Dakota

Julie Pennabaker
Quakertown Community School District
Quakertown, Pennsylvania

Bryan Sandala
School District of Palm Beach County
West Palm Beach, Florida

Angela Seiler
Rio Rancho Public School District Rio Rancho, New Mexico

Amanda Shackelford
Lafayette Parish School System Lafayette, Louisiana

Kimberlyn Slagle
Lafayette Parish School System Lafayette, Louisiana

Sarah Smith Arceneaux
Lafayette Parish School System
Lafayette, Louisiana

Holly Talley
Hillsborough County Public Schools
Ruskin, Florida

Derek Thomas
Hillsborough County Public Schools
Tampa, Florida

Maria Torres-Crosby
Hillsborough County Public Schools Tampa, Florida

Susan Van Doren
South Lake Tahoe, California

JoEllen Victoreen
San Jose Unified School District
San Jose, California

Rebecca Wenrich
Peninsula School District
Gig Harbor, Washington

Research and Planning Advisors

We also wish to thank the members of our SpringBoard Advisory Council and the many educators who gave generously of their time and their ideas as we conducted research for both the print and online programs. Your suggestions and reactions to ideas helped immeasurably as we created this edition. We gratefully acknowledge the teachers and administrators in the following districts.

ABC Unified School District
Cerritos, California

Allen Independent School
District
Allen, Texas

Bellevue, School District 405
Bellevue, Washington

Burnet Consolidated
Independent School District
Burnet, Texas

Community Unit School
District 308
Oswego, Illinois

Fresno Unified
School District
Fresno, California

Frisco Independent
School District
Frisco, Texas

Garland Independent
School District
Garland, Texas

Grapevine-Colleyville
Independent School District
Grapevine, Texas

Hamilton County Schools
Chattanooga, Tennessee

Hesperia Unified
School District
Hesperia, California

Hillsborough County Public
Schools
Tampa, Florida

ICEF Public Schools
Los Angeles, California

IDEA Public Schools
Weslaco, Texas

Irving Independent
School District
Irving, Texas

Keller Independent
School District
Keller, Texas

KIPP Houston
Houston, Texas

Lafayette Parish Schools
Lafayette Parish, Louisiana

Los Angeles Unified
School District
Los Angeles, California

Lubbock Independent
School District
Lubbock, Texas

Mansfield Independent
School District
Mansfield, Texas

Midland Independent
School District
Midland, Texas

Milwaukee Public Schools
Milwaukee, Wisconsin

New Haven School District
New Haven, Connecticut

Ogden School District
Ogden, Utah

Rio Rancho Public Schools
Rio Rancho, New Mexico

San José Unified
School District
San José, California

Scottsdale Unified
School District
Scottsdale, Arizona

Spokane Public Schools
Spokane, Washington

Tacoma Public Schools
Tacoma, Washington

SpringBoard English Language Arts

Lori O'Dea
Executive Director
Content Development

Natasha Vasavada
Executive Director,
Pre-AP & SpringBoard

Doug Waugh
VP, SpringBoard &
Pre-AP Programs

Sarah Balistreri
Senior Director
ELA Content Development

Florencia Duran Wald
Senior Director
ELA Content Development

Julie Manley
Senior Director
Professional Learning

Joely Negedly
Senior Director
Pre-AP Humanities

Jessica Brockman
Product Manager
English Language Arts

Suzie Doss
Director
SpringBoard Implementation

Jennifer Duva
Director
English Language Arts

Spencer Gonçalves
Director
Digital Content Development

Rebecca Grudzina
Senior Editor
English Language Arts

Georgia Scurletis
Senior Instructional Writer
Pre-AP English Language
Arts

Abigail Johnson
Editor
English Language Arts

Casseia Lewis
Assistant Editor
English Language Arts

Natalie Hansford
Editorial Assistant
English Language Arts

Table of Contents

ACTIVITY	Unit 1: The American Dream	

CONTENTS

ACTIVITY   Unit 2: The Power of Persuasion

CONTENTS

ACTIVITY **Unit 3: American Forums: The Marketplace of Ideas**

CONTENTS

CONTENTS

Resources

Texts not included in these materials.

Introduction to SpringBoard English Language Arts

About SpringBoard ELA

SpringBoard was built around a simple belief: if you give students and teachers the best materials, engaging methods, and ongoing support, then student success will surely follow. Developed by teachers, SpringBoard brings your classroom to life with materials that help you practice the skills and learn the knowledge you need to excel in high school and beyond. Read on to find out how SpringBoard will support your learning.

Instructional Materials

SpringBoard English Language Arts supplies a Student Edition and Teacher Edition, in print and digital form, for grades 6–12. In addition to using the English Language Arts curriculum, you can sharpen your reading, writing, and language skills with materials including Language Workshop, Close Reading Workshop, and Writing Workshop.

Design that Begins with the End in Mind

- Based on the Understanding by Design model, SpringBoard teaches the skills and knowledge that matter most to meet AP and college and career readiness standards.

- You will start each unit by unpacking the assessment, so you know where you're heading and why the skills you're developing matter.

- Each activity starts with clear, standards-aligned learning targets.

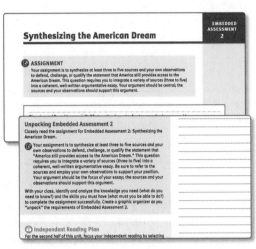

EMBEDDED ASSESSMENT 2

Synthesizing the American Dream

ASSIGNMENT
Your assignment is to synthesize at least three to five sources and your own observations to defend, challenge, or qualify the statement that America still provides access to the American Dream. This question requires you to integrate a variety of sources (three to five) into a coherent, well-written argumentative essay. Your argument should be central; the sources and your observations should support this argument.

Unpacking Embedded Assessment 2
Closely read the assignment for Embedded Assessment 2: Synthesizing the American Dream.

Your assignment is to synthesize at least three to five sources and your own observations to defend, challenge, or qualify the statement that "America still provides access to the American Dream." This question requires you to integrate a variety of sources (three to five) into a coherent, well-written argumentative essay. Be sure to refer to the sources and employ your own observations to support your position. Your argument should be the focus of your essay; the sources and observations should support this argument.

With your class, identify and analyze the knowledge you need (what do you need to know?) and the skills you must have (what must you be able to do?) to complete the assignment successfully. Create a graphic organizer as you "unpack" the requirements of Embedded Assessment 2.

Independent Reading Plan
For the second half of this unit, focus your independent reading by selecting

---

The Practice of Reading Closely

- SpringBoard puts a special focus on close reading, giving you strategies and structure for developing this key skill.

- You will encounter compelling texts—fiction, nonfiction, poetry, drama, visuals, and film.

UNIT 1

THE AMERICAN DREAM

VISUAL PROMPT
From 1892 until 1954, Ellis Island was the gateway to the United States for over 12 million immigrants in search of the American Dream. What do you think the American Dream is?

America! From the other end of the earth from where I came, America was a land of living hope, woven of dreams, aflame with longing and desire.

—from "America and I" by Anzia Yezierska

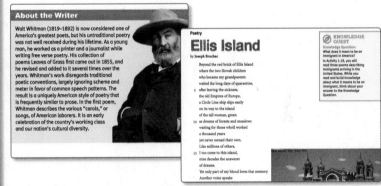

About the Writer

Walt Whitman (1819–1892) is now considered one of America's greatest poets, but his untraditional poetry was not well received during his lifetime. As a young man, he worked as a printer and a journalist while writing free verse poetry. His collection of poems Leaves of Grass first came out in 1855, and he revised and added to it several times over the years. Whitman's work disregards traditional poetic conventions, largely ignoring scheme and meter in favor of common speech patterns. The result is a uniquely American style of poetry that is frequently similar to prose. In the first poem, Whitman describes the various "carols," or songs, of American laborers. It is an early celebration of the country's working class and our nation's cultural diversity.

Poetry

Ellis Island
by Joseph Bruchac

Beyond the red brick of Ellis Island
where the two Slovak children
who became my grandparents
waited the long days of quarantine,
after leaving the sickness,
the old Empires of Europe,
a Circle Line ship slips easily
on its way to the island
of the tall woman, green
as dreams of forests and meadows
waiting for those who'd worked
a thousand years
yet never owned their own.
Like millions of others,
I too come to this island,
nine decades the answerer
of dreams.
Yet only part of my blood loves that memory.
Another voice speaks

KNOWLEDGE QUEST
Knowledge Question:
What does it mean to be an immigrant in America?
In Activity 1.19, you will read three poems describing immigrants arriving in the United States. While you read and build knowledge about what it means to be an immigrant, think about your answer to the Knowledge Question.

A Living System of Learning

- SpringBoard puts you and your classmates in charge of your learning to create a more dynamic classroom experience.

- With a flexible design and rich library of tools and resources, SpringBoard helps your teacher personalize instruction for your class.

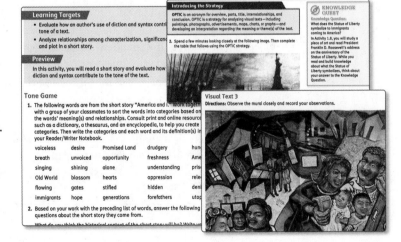

Learning Targets
- Evaluate how an author's use of diction and syntax contribute to the tone of a text.
- Analyze relationships among characterization, significance, and plot in a short story.

Preview
In this activity, you will read a short story and evaluate how diction and syntax contribute to the tone of the text.

Introducing the Strategy
OPTIC is an acronym for overview, parts, title, interrelationships, and conclusion. OPTIC is a strategy for analyzing visual texts—including paintings, photographs, advertisements, maps, charts, or graphs—and developing an interpretation regarding the meaning or theme(s) of the text.

2. Spend a few minutes looking closely at the following image. Then complete the table that follows using the OPTIC strategy.

KNOWLEDGE QUEST
Knowledge Question:
What does the Statue of Liberty symbolize to immigrants coming to America?
In Activity 1.8, you will study a piece of art and read President Franklin D. Roosevelt's address on the anniversary of the Statue of Liberty. While you read and build knowledge about what the Statue of Liberty symbolizes, think about your answer to the Knowledge Question.

Tone Game
1. The following words are from the short story "America and I." Work together with a group of your classmates to sort the words into categories based on the words' meaning(s) and relationships. Consult print and online resources such as a dictionary, a thesaurus, and an encyclopedia, to help you create categories. Then write the categories and each word and its definition(s) in your Reader/Writer Notebook.

voiceless	desire	Promised Land	drudgery	hun
breath	unvoiced	opportunity	freshness	Ame
singing	shining	alone	understanding	pris
Old World	blossom	hearts	oppression	rele
flowing	gates	stifled	hidden	den
immigrants	hope	generations	forefathers	uto

2. Based on your work with the preceding list of words, answer the following questions about the short story they come from.

What do you think the historical context of the short story will be? Write u

Visual Text 3
Directions: Observe the mural closely and record your observations.

Bringing the Classroom to Life

When you enter a SpringBoard classroom you don't hear a teacher talking in the front of the room. You hear a buzz of excitement, with students working together and taking charge of how they learn. That's what the teachers who designed SpringBoard wanted for their classrooms, so they created a curriculum and materials that are focused on real classroom needs, encouraging teacher and student involvement.

SpringBoard translates the expectations of state standards into engaging daily lessons. We believe that reading, writing, speaking, and listening should all be learned together. You'll see examples of our integrated approach throughout our materials. And we put a special focus on close reading, giving you strategies and structure for developing this key skill.

Our Approach to Reading

In SpringBoard ELA, we move right into compelling texts—fiction, nonfiction, poetry, drama, visuals, and film—and offer the tools, supports, and approaches that will help you get the most out of every reading.

The Practice of Reading Closely

Texts take center stage in the SpringBoard ELA classroom, where you will prepare for close, critical reading of a wide range of materials. With guidance from your teacher, you will develop the habits of close reading that will serve you for a lifetime.

- **As You Read:** You prepare to read and annotate the text for notable elements like genre characteristics, important use of words, and text structures.

- **First Reading:** You read on your own, with a partner, in a group, or with the class. You annotate the text as you begin to uncover its meaning.

- **Making Observations:** Your teacher guides you to pause during or right after the first reading to observe the small details within a text in order to arrive at a deeper understanding of the whole.

- **Returning to the Text:** You continue to deepen your understanding of the text by responding to a series of text-dependent questions. You will use text evidence, speak with new vocabulary words, reflect on your classmates' ideas, and make connections among texts, ideas, and experiences.

- **Working from the Text:** You use the text as a source as you move from reading and analysis to productive work, including academic discussion and writing.

Reading Independently

As a SpringBoard student, you'll practice good reading habits in class so that you can read challenging texts in other classes and on your own. Independent reading is an integral part of every SpringBoard English Language Arts unit. At the beginning of the year, you will learn how to make a plan for independent reading. **Independent Reading Lists** for each unit give you a jump-start on selecting texts by offering a list of suggested titles, including a number of Spanish-language titles, that connect to the themes, genres, and concepts of the SpringBoard unit.

While you work your way through each unit, you will respond to **Independent Reading Links** that lead you to make connections between the reading you're doing on your own and the skills and knowledge you're developing in class. Twice per unit, **Independent Reading Checkpoints** give you a chance to reflect on and synthesize your independent reading in an informal writing assignment or discussion.

Reading to Build Knowledge

SpringBoard units are designed so that you can delve deeply into an overarching topic, theme, or idea. Each unit will pose essential questions that relate to the ideas and texts within the unit, and you will return to these questions again and again, each time refining your responses with new understanding and new evidence to support your point of view. You will also deepen your knowledge of key topics by conducting both on-the-spot and extended research, asking and answering questions, evaluating multiple sources, and synthesizing your findings.

Twice a unit, you will go on a **Knowledge Quest**. Each Knowledge Quest begins with a Knowledge Question and supporting questions to focus your reading. After reading several texts that explore a topic, theme, or idea, you will get to return to the Knowledge Question and show your growing understanding of the topic by responding to a writing prompt or engaging in a discussion.

At the end of a Knowledge Quest, you will be encouraged to continue building your knowledge of the topic by going to **Zinc Reading Labs** and finding related texts to read. Zinc Reading Labs offers a variety of informational and literary texts that you can choose based on your interests. Vocabulary sets for each text let you learn new words and practice using them.

Your independent reading can also enhance your understanding of the topics you are studying in class if you want it to. SpringBoard's **Independent Reading Lists** include suggested books that relate to the topics and themes from each unit. By choosing those books you can see a different side of the topic, learn new words, and find other topics you want to learn more about.

Reading to Gain Perspectives

Gaining Perspectives features use a text as a jumping off point for examining an issue relevant to you. You will be asked to consider the perspectives of others and to empathize with others who have different points of view. You will also be asked to think about social and ethical norms and to recognize the family, school, and community resources available to you. Each Gaining Perspectives feature concludes with a writing task in which you will summarize the discussion you have with your classmates.

Our Approach to Writing

SpringBoard English Language Arts provides you with the support you need to write in all the major modes, emphasizing argumentative, informational, and narrative. You will write often, and you will learn to become a critical reviewer of your own and your peers' work through frequent opportunities for revision and editing. You will learn to plan with purpose, audience, topic, and context in mind; develop drafts with engaging ideas, examples, facts and commentary; revise for clarity, development, organization, style, and diction; and edit using the conventions of the English language.

The Craft of Writing

As you read texts by skilled authors, you will observe the many choices those authors make. You'll tune in to the ways authors purposefully use words, sentences, and structures to convey meaning. After analyzing and critiquing others' work, you will learn to apply your understanding of author's craft to your own writing. A few SpringBoard features help you do just that:

- **Writing prompts** lead up to the Embedded Assessments and give you practice with writing texts in multiple genres, including personal narratives, argumentative essays, letters, research papers, and more. Writing to Sources writing prompts drive you back to texts you have read or viewed to mine for evidence.

- **Focus on the Sentence** tasks help you process content while also practicing the craft of writing powerful sentences.

- **Grammar & Usage** features highlight interesting grammar or usage concepts that appear in a text, both to improve your reading comprehension and to help you attend to these concepts as you craft your own texts.

- **Language & Writer's Craft** features address topics in writing such as style, word choice, and sentence construction.

- **Language Checkpoints** offer in-depth practice with standard English conventions and guide you to develop an editor's checklist to use as a reference each time you check your own or a peer's written work.

Modes of Writing

SpringBoard helps you become a better academic writer by giving you authentic prompts that require you to use sources, and showing you how to work through the writing process. Over the course of the year you will have the chance to write narratives, arguments, and informational texts, and you will develop a wide range of writing skills:

- Consider task, audience, and purpose when structuring and organizing your writing.

- Incorporate details, reasons, and textual evidence to support your ideas.

- Generate research questions, evaluate sources, gather relevant evidence, and report and cite your findings accurately.

- Use research-based strategies that will guide you through the writing process.

Writing with a Focus on the Sentence

SpringBoard English Language Arts leverages sentence writing strategies that were developed by The Writing Revolution. These evidence-based strategies are part of the Hochman Method, the Writing Revolution's system for helping students learn to write across all content areas and grades. The Writing Revolution emphasizes the importance of embedding writing and grammar instruction into content. That's why SpringBoard's Focus on the Sentence tasks integrate sentence-level writing into the curriculum. These tasks not only help you learn and practice important grammar concepts and sentence forms, but they also provide a chance for you to process and demonstrate your understanding of texts, images, class discussions, and other content.

Our Approach to Vocabulary

Vocabulary is threaded throughout each unit and developed over the course of the SpringBoard English Language Arts year. You will have ample opportunities to read and hear new words, explore their meanings, origins, and connotations, and use them in written and oral responses.

- Important academic and literary terms that you will need to actively participate in classroom discussions are called out in your book.

- Challenging vocabulary terms found in reading passages are glossed at the point of use.

- Periodic Word Connections boxes guide you through the process of exploring a word with multiple meanings and nuances, an interesting etymology, a telling root or affix, a helpful Spanish cognate, a relationship to another word, or a connection to another content area.

Zinc Reading Labs

Zinc Reading Labs combines the best features of a typical vocabulary program with those of a typical reading program and makes reading and learning new words a game. Zinc offers a variety of nonfiction and fiction texts that you can choose from based on individual needs and interest. Each article has a corresponding vocabulary set that pre-teaches challenging words through spaced repetition, to help you genuinely learn and internalize the vocabulary. Additional vocabulary games focus on SAT/ACT power words and foundational words for English language learners.

Pre-AP Connections

SpringBoard shares Pre-AP's core principles and encourages you to build skills that you will use in high school and beyond. These principles are evident in every SpringBoard activity.

Close Observation and Analysis
... to notice and consider

When reading, your teacher will guide you to pause to make observations and notice details in the text before analyzing or explaining. Only after you have noticed and enjoyed elements of the text do you then return to the text for deeper analysis and inferential thinking. This close reading sequence helps you interact and engage with the text in increasingly meaningful ways.

Evidence-Based Writing
... with a focus on the sentence

SpringBoard offers varied and frequent writing opportunities, with specific attention to developing complex and precise sentences as the building block to sophisticated paragraph and essay length writing. Instead of being isolated from reading, sentence-level grammar and writing exercises are integrated into the curriculum to enhance your comprehension and your ability to compose a variety of texts.

Higher-Order Questioning
... to spark productive lingering

Each unit opens with two essential questions that relate to the topics, themes, and texts within that unit. You return to these questions throughout the unit and refine your answers as new evidence is presented. SpringBoard also encourages you to craft your own questions, and to dig deeply into the texts you read. After each reading passage, you evaluate the meaning of the text and examine the choices that the author made when writing it.

Academic Conversations
... to support peer-to-peer dialogue

SpringBoard classrooms are places where students like you engage in collaborative learning. You will participate in discussion groups, writing groups, debates, Socratic seminars, literature circles, and oral interpretations and performances. These activities create an environment where you can share, compare, critique, debate, and build on others' ideas to advance your learning.

PSAT/SAT Connections

We want you to be rewarded for the hard work you do in your English Language Arts courses, including when you sit down to take important assessments. Therefore, SpringBoard English Language Arts focuses on the same essential knowledge and skills that are the center of the Evidence-Based Reading and Writing sections of the SAT Suite of Assessments (SAT, PSAT/NMSQT, PSAT™ 10, and PSAT™ 8/9). To make our alignment transparent, we conducted a research study, the results of which showed strong to exemplary alignment between the SpringBoard ELA courses and the corresponding SAT Suite tests. This means that you are getting ready for the SAT, PSAT/NMSQT, PSAT™ 10, and PSAT™ 8/9 in the classroom every day.

Tools and Supports

SpringBoard Digital

SpringBoard puts you in charge of what you learn and gives students and teachers the flexibility and support they need. SpringBoard Digital is an interactive program that provides always-available online content that's accessible from any device—desktop computer, laptop, tablet, or interactive whiteboard. The student edition allows you to interact with the text, respond to prompts, take assessments, and engage with a suite of tools, all in the digital space. Teachers get access to a correlations viewer that embeds correlations at point of use, a lesson planner, progress reports, grading, messaging, and more.

Zinc Reading Labs

All SpringBoard users have access to Zinc Reading Labs, where you can find a huge library of reading material chosen specifically to align with the SpringBoard English Language Arts curriculum.

Zinc offers:

- Fresh and engaging nonfiction and fiction content for independent reading.
- Interactive games, quizzes, and tasks that build skills and confidence.
- Freedom of choice: Zinc's massive and ever-growing library means that all students should find texts they want to read.

Turnitin Revision Assistant

When you develop drafts of an available Embedded Assessment through SpringBoard Digital, you can use a tool called Turnitin Revision Assistant. This online tool gives instant feedback to students as they write so they can polish their drafts and practice their revision skills. The feedback model Revision Assistant uses is based on scoring by SpringBoard teachers, and it's trained to assess the same rubric areas that they assess.

Revision Assistant offers:

- A template to help you create an outline.
- Actionable, instant feedback in specific areas such as structure, use of language, and ideas.
- Identification of strengths and weakness in your writing.

A Letter to the Student

Dear Student,

Welcome to the SpringBoard program! We created this program with you in mind: it puts you and your classmates at the center of your learning and equips you with the skills and knowledge you need to excel in high school and beyond.

The energy and excitement you bring to class helps you and your classmates learn. You will explore compelling themes through readings, classroom discussions, and projects. You will dive into fascinating texts—some of which you'll choose on your own—from different genres including myths, poems, biographies, plays, and films. You will engage in lively discussions, debates, and performances so that you become confident sharing and presenting your ideas. You will write frequently to sharpen your ability to craft effective sentences, paragraphs, and longer texts. And you'll start each unit with a clear understanding of where you're headed by unpacking the skills and knowledge you'll need to do well on the assessment at the end.

SpringBoard helps you make connections between the concepts you're reading and writing about in class and the real world. Instead of just memorizing how to do things, you'll draw on your own and your classmates' experiences and knowledge to come to new and deeper understandings. When questions arise from the materials you're studying in class, you'll learn how to do both quick and longer-term research to find answers. Plus, you'll have access to tools and resources that are built right into the program, including powerful learning strategies, independent reading lists to help you select texts to read outside of class, and digital tools that you can access any time from any device—desktop computer, laptop, or tablet.

We want students to be rewarded for the hard work they do in their English Language Arts course. That's why the SpringBoard program focuses on the essential knowledge and skills that will prepare you for the challenging work you'll do in your high school classes, in AP courses, and in college.

Students from around the country are talking about how much they like the SpringBoard approach to learning. We hope you enjoy learning with SpringBoard, too.

Sincerely,

The SpringBoard Team

VISUAL PROMPT
From 1892 until 1954, Ellis Island was the gateway to the United States for over 12 million immigrants in search of the American Dream. What do you think the American Dream is?

THE AMERICAN DREAM

America! From the other end of the earth from where I came, America was a land of living hope, woven of dreams, aflame with longing and desire.

—from "America and I" by Anzia Yezierska

GOALS

- To synthesize information from a variety of sources to define what it means to be an American and to argue whether the American Dream is attainable for all
- To analyze how writers in various genres use language and structure to convey meaning and influence readers
- To read, analyze, and compare works of American literature by authors of various backgrounds and different periods
- To monitor comprehension while reading and use strategies to make adjustments when needed
- To plan, draft, revise, edit, and publish informational and argumentative texts using genre characteristics and craft

VOCABULARY

ACADEMIC
challenge
defend
plagiarism
qualify
rhetoric
rhetorical devices

LITERARY
diction
imagery
syntax
tone

ACTIVITY   CONTENTS

My Independent Reading List

My Independent
Reading List

Previewing the Unit

Learning Targets

- Preview the big ideas for the unit.
- Create a plan for reading independently.

Preview

In this activity, you will explore the big ideas and tasks of the unit to come and make plans for your own independent reading.

About the Unit

In this unit, you will read a variety of texts and be asked to think about ideas and concepts that are "American." For the first embedded assessment, you will define what it means to be an American. Some words, concepts, and ideas are too complex for a simple definition and require a multi-paragraph essay to define. Definitions also provide a writer the opportunity to clear up misconceptions about a concept or idea. You will learn to define a word or concept using four definition strategies: by example, by classification, by function, and by negation.

Essential Questions

Based on your current thinking, how would you answer these questions?

1. What does it mean to be an American?

2. What is the "American Dream"?

3. Does America still provide access to the "American Dream"?

Unpacking Embedded Assessment 1

Closely read the assignment for Embedded Assessment 1: Writing a Definition Essay.

Your assignment is to write a multi-paragraph essay that defines your interpretation of what it means to be an American. This essay should use the strategies of definition and different perspectives from the unit to help you develop a complex and thoughtful definition. If possible, incorporate an iconic image in your essay.

Find the Scoring Guide and work with your class to paraphrase the expectations for the assignment. Create a graphic organizer to use as a visual reminder of the required skills and concepts. Copy the graphic organizer into your Reader/Writer Notebook and revisit it after each activity to check your progress.

My Notes

Planning Independent Reading

To enhance this unit's focus, look for nonfiction essays, memoirs, autobiographies, or biographies that that will help you understand how others define the American Dream. Consider how these readings connect to what you read in the unit and to your own perspectives. Choose exceptional readings to recommend to and discuss with your peers. To help you choose the right book, use the following questions as a guide.

1. What have you enjoyed reading in the past? What is your favorite book or favorite type of book? Who is your favorite author?

2. When you select a potential book, preview it. What do you notice about the front cover design? What type of visual is shown? What types of fonts and colors are used? What information is on the back cover? Are there awards or brags that tell you about the book?

3. Read the first few pages. Are they interesting? How does the author try to hook you to keep reading? What can you tell about the characters and setting so far? Are there any connections that you can make to personal experiences, ideas in other texts, or society? Does this seem too hard, too easy, or just right?

Reading Discussion Groups

Listen carefully as your teacher guides you through a book pass and group discussion. Practice previewing each book by looking at the covers and reading the first few pages.

1. In your Reader/Writer Notebook, record each book's title and author, something from your previewing that stands out to you, and your rating of the book.

2. After previewing each book and thinking about the goals of this unit, do you want to continue reading the book you brought to the group or choose something else?

3. Create an Independent Reading Plan to help you set personal reading goals. Keep this plan in your Reader/Writer Notebook.

I have chosen to read _____

by (author) _____

because (reason from previewing) _____

_____

I will set aside time to read at (time, place) _____

I should finish this text by (date) _____

4. Record your daily reading pace in your Independent Reading Log. Write a brief daily report in your log responding to what you have read. Include in your report questions, connections, or predictions about what you have read.

5. Respond to the Independent Reading Links you encounter throughout the unit.

Analyzing Visual Texts

Learning Strategies

Making Inferences
Note-taking

Learning Targets

- Use details in a series of visual texts to make inferences about the creators' perspectives on the American Dream.
- Reflect on and adjust responses based on research.
- Describe personal connections to visual texts.

Preview

In this activity, you will read a series of visual texts to observe the details they contain and use your observations to make inferences about the creators' perspective on the American Dream.

My Notes

The American Dream

On July 4, 1776, the founders of the United States signed the Declaration of Independence. Early in that document, we find the sentence "We hold these truths to be self-evident, that all men are created equal, that they are endowed by their Creator with certain unalienable Rights, that among these are Life, Liberty and the pursuit of Happiness." Those last words in particular are a direct statement of the American Dream—the idea that people have the right to live in ways that makes them happy.

Think for a moment about your own potential. What kinds of things interest you? What pursuits bring you happiness? What kinds of accomplishments do you find worthwhile? Imagine the life you want to live and think about ways to build that life. That is your American Dream.

Quickwite: After spending a few minutes considering the preceding questions, use the following lines to describe your perspective on the American Dream.

Visual Text 1

Directions: Observe the illustration closely and record your observations.

This color lithograph by J. Keppler titled "Welcome to All!" was originally published in *Puck* magazine in 1880. *Puck* magazine was a weekly humor magazine in the United States in circulation from 1871 to 1918.

What details do you observe in this illustration?

_____

_____

What details in this illustration could be significant clues about how the creator perceives the American Dream?

_____

_____

_____

Visual Text 2

Directions: Observe the photograph closely and record your observations.

This photograph titled, "World's Highest Standard of Living," was taken by photographer Margaret Bourke-White and was featured in *Life* magazine's February 1937 issue.

What details do you observe in this visual text?

_____

_____

What details in this visual could be significant clues about how the creator perceives the American Dream?

_____

_____

Visual Text 3

Directions: Observe the mural closely and record your observations.

Xavier Cortada's painted his 96" x 96" mural "Stepping into the American Dream" for the White House Conference on Minority Home Ownership in 2002.

What details do you observe in this mural?

_____

_____

What details in this mural could be significant clues about how the creator perceives the American Dream?

_____

_____

Returning to the Images

- Return to the visual texts as you respond to the following questions. Use evidence from the texts to support your responses.
- Write any additional questions you have about the visual texts in your Reader/Writer Notebook.

1. The people depicted in both "Welcome to All!" and "World's Highest Standard of Living" are standing in lines. Use details from the visual texts to make inferences about how their experiences are different.

_____
_____
_____
_____
_____
_____
_____

2. What can you infer through the juxtaposition the artist creates in Visual Text 2? What message does it send to the viewer?

_____
_____
_____
_____
_____
_____
_____

3. Look closely at the mural "Stepping into the American Dream." Describe the expressions on the people's faces. Name some of the objects in the mural. Based on these details, what do you think the title means?

_____
_____
_____
_____
_____
_____
_____

On the Spot Research

Choose one of the visual texts to reexamine. Do some research about the creator or the context in which the text was created and use that information to reflect on your previous response and adjust it as needed. Decide which of the text's details are particularly revealing about the creator's perspective on the American Dream. Write three sentences that connect those details to the information you learned.

You can use the following sentence frame to help you write each of your sentences:

The_____ is a detail that reveals _____.

_____

_____

_____

4. **Collaborative Discussion:** In a small group, share the information you learned about the visual text you chose to reexamine. Then expand the conversation to discuss how the text is similar to or different from your own perception of the American Dream. Are there details in the text that are opposed to or supportive of your ideas? What personal connections can you make?

☑ Check Your Understanding

Create a visual text that reflects your current perception of the American Dream using the art supplies provided by your teacher. You will present your visual text to a small group. Use the On the Spot Research sentence frame to help you express how the details in the visual text support your ideas about the American Dream.

An American Story

Learning Targets

- Evaluate how an author's use of diction and syntax contributes to the tone of a text.
- Analyze relationships among characterization, significance of setting, and plot in a short story.

Preview

In this activity, you will read a short story and evaluate how the author's diction and syntax contribute to the tone of the text.

My Notes

Tone Game

1. The following words are from the short story "America and I." Work together with a group of your classmates to sort the words into categories based on the words' meaning(s) and relationships. Consult print and online resources, such as a dictionary, a thesaurus, and an encyclopedia, to help you create categories. Then write the categories and each word and its definition(s) in your Reader/Writer Notebook.

voiceless	desire	Promised Land	drudgery	hunger
breath	unvoiced	opportunity	freshness	America
singing	shining	alone	understanding	prison
Old World	blossom	hearts	oppression	release
flowing	gates	stifled	hidden	denied
immigrants	hope	generations	forefathers	utopia

2. Based on your work with the preceding list of words, answer the following questions about the short story they come from.

   What do you think the historical context of the short story will be? Write your answer and explain which words support your response.

   _____

   _____

   _____

   _____

3. What do you think the tone of the short story is most likely to be?

   _____

   _____

   _____

   _____

LITERARY

Tone is a writer's or speaker's attitude toward a subject, character, or audience. A writer's diction and syntax contribute to the tone of their work. **Diction** is the writer's choice or words and **syntax** is the arrangement of words and the order of grammatical elements in a sentence; the way in which words are put together to make meaningful elements, such as phrases, clauses, and sentences.

VOCABULARY

Check Your Understanding

Make a prediction about the story based on what you have inferred from the words that come from it. Use the following sentence frame to help you write your prediction. Include vocbulary from the text in your response.

I predict that the short story will be about _____ because _____.

> **Opening Writing Prompt**
>
> Listen as your teacher reads aloud the excerpt from "America and I." Then respond to the following question in a quickwrite. Later you will discuss your response in a class discussion.
>
> Based on the **diction** and **syntax** in the excerpt, what is the author's tone toward America and the American Dream? What details about word choice and syntax support your answer?

As one of the dumb, voiceless ones I speak. One of the millions of immigrants beating, beating out their hearts at your gates for a breath of understanding.

Ach! America! From the other end of the earth from where I came, America was a land of living hope, woven of dreams, aflame with longing and desire.

Choked for ages in the airless oppression of Russia, the Promised Land rose up—wings for my stifled spirit—sunlight burning through my darkness—freedom singing to me in my prison—deathless songs tuning prison-bars into strings of a beautiful violin.

I arrived in America. My young, strong body, my heart and soul pregnant with the unlived lives of generations clamoring for expression.

What my mother and father and their mother and father never had a chance to give out in Russia, I would give out in America. The hidden sap of centuries would find release; colors that never saw light—songs that died unvoiced—romance that never had a chance to blossom in the black life of the Old World.

In the golden land of flowing opportunity I was to find my work that was denied me in the sterile village of my forefathers. Here I was to be free from the dead drudgery for bread that held me down in Russia. For the first time in America, I'd cease to be a slave of the belly. I'd be a creator, a giver, a human being! My work would be the living job of fullest self-expression.

But from my high visions, my golden hopes, I had to put my feet down on earth. I had to have food and shelter. I had to have the money to pay for it.

I was in America, among the Americans, but not of them. No speech, no common language, no way to win a smile of understanding from them, only my young, strong body and my untried faith. Only my eager, empty hands, and my full heart shining from my eyes!

As You Read

- As you read, pause after each chunk and summarize what you just read. Ask question to make sure that you are comprehending what you are reading.
- Circle unknown words and phrases. Try to determine the meaning of the words by using context clues, word parts, or a dictionary.

About the Author

Anzia Yezierska (mid-1880s–1970) was a Jewish-American writer who emigrated from Poland with her family as a child. Her writing first appeared in the early 1920s in general interest magazines. Yezierska's realism and emotional openness, combined with her frequent use of first-person narration, are so convincing that many readers mistakenly believe all of her stories to be literally autobiographical. "America and I" first appeared in a 1923 collection of short stories called *Children of Loneliness*. Like much of Yezierska's work, it explores the changes and challenges immigrants face as they assimilate into the United States.

Short Story

America and I

by Anzia Yezierska

Chunk 1

1   As one of the dumb, voiceless ones I speak. One of the millions of immigrants beating, beating out their hearts at your gates for a breath of understanding.

2   Ach! America! From the other end of the earth from where I came, America was a land of living hope, woven of dreams, aflame with longing and desire.

3   Choked for ages in the airless oppression of Russia, the Promised Land rose up—wings for my stifled spirit—sunlight burning through my darkness—freedom singing to me in my prison—deathless songs tuning prison-bars into strings of a beautiful violin.

4   I arrived in America. My young, strong body, my heart and soul pregnant with the unlived lives of generations clamoring for expression.

5   What my mother and father and their mother and father never had a chance to give out in Russia, I would give out in America. The hidden **sap** of centuries would find release; colors that never saw light—songs that died unvoiced—romance that never had a chance to blossom in the black life of the Old World.

My Notes

sap: energy, vitality

My Notes

6   In the golden land of flowing opportunity I was to find my work that was denied me in the **sterile** village of my forefathers. Here I was to be free from the dead **drudgery** for bread that held me down in Russia. For the first time in America, I'd cease to be a slave of the belly. I'd be a creator, a giver, a human being! My work would be the living job of fullest self-expression.

7   But from my high visions, my golden hopes, I had to put my feet down on earth. I had to have food and shelter. I had to have the money to pay for it.

8   I was in America, among the Americans, but not of them. No speech, no common language, no way to win a smile of understanding from them, only my young, strong body and my untried faith. Only my eager, empty hands, and my full heart shining from my eyes!

Chunk 2

9   God from the world! Here I was with so much richness in me, but my mind was not wanted without the language. And my body, unskilled, untrained, was not even wanted in the factory. Only one of two chances was left open to me: the kitchen, or minding babies.

10   My first job was as a servant in an Americanized family. Once, long ago, they came from the same village from where I came. But they were so well-dressed, so well-fed, so successful in America, that they were ashamed to remember their mother tongue.

11   "What were to be my wages?" I ventured timidly, as I looked up to the well-fed, well-dressed "American" man and woman.

12   They looked at me with a sudden coldness. What have I said to draw away from me their warmth? Was it so low for me to talk of wages? I shrank back into myself like a low-down bargainer. Maybe they're so high up in well-being they can't any more understand my low thoughts for money.

13   From his rich height the man preached down to me that I must not be so grabbing for wages. Only just landed from the ship and already thinking about money when I should be thankful to associate with "Americans." The woman, out of her smooth, smiling fatness assured me that this was my chance for a summer vacation in the country with her two lovely children.

14   My great chance to learn to be a civilized being, to become an American by living with them.

15   So, made to feel that I was in the hands of American friends, invited to share with them their home, their plenty, their happiness, I pushed out from my head the worry for wages. Here was my first chance to begin my life in the sunshine, after my long darkness. My laugh was all over my face as I said to them: "I'll trust myself to you. What I'm worth you'll give me." And I entered their house like a child by the hand.

16   The best of me I gave them. Their house cares were my house cares. I got up early. I worked till late. All that my soul hungered to give I put into the passion with which I scrubbed floors, scoured pots, and washed clothes.

GRAMMAR & USAGE

Quotation Marks for Effect
Writers sometimes place quotation marks around a word to suggest irony or sarcasm. Yezierska does this with the word American in paragraph 11. By using quotation marks, she implies that her new employers are not really American. Overuse of ironic quotation marks, however, makes them lose their effect.

Study the author's uses of quotation marks around American and Americans in paragraphs 39 and 40. What new tone do these words in quotations help to express?

sterile: unable to grow or develop
drudgery: dull, boring work

My Notes

I was so grateful to mingle with the American people, to hear the music of the American language, that I never knew tiredness.

17   There was such a freshness in my brains and such a willingness in my heart I could go on and on—not only with the work of the house, but work with my head—learning new words from the children, the grocer, the butcher, the iceman. I was not even afraid to ask for words from the policeman on the street. And every new word made me see new American things with American eyes. I felt like a Columbus, finding new worlds through every new word.

18   But words alone were only for the inside of me. The outside of me still branded me for a steerage immigrant. I had to have clothes to forget myself that I'm a stranger yet. And so I had to have money to buy these clothes.

19   The month was up. I was so happy! Now I'd have money. *My own*, *earned* money. Money to buy a new shirt on my back—shoes on my feet. Maybe yet an American dress and hat!

20   Ach! How high rose my dreams! How plainly I saw all that I would do with my visionary wages shining like a light over my head!

21   In my imagination I already walked in my new American clothes. How beautiful I looked as I saw myself like a picture before my eyes! I saw how I would throw away my immigrant rags tied up in my immigrant shawl. With money to buy—free money in my hands—I'd show them that I could look like an American in a day.

22   Like a prisoner in his last night in prison, counting the seconds that will free him from his chains, I trembled breathlessly for the minute I'd get the wages in my hand.

23   Before dawn I rose.

24   I shined up the house like a jewel-box.

25   I prepared breakfast and waited with my heart in my mouth for my lady and gentleman to rise. At last I heard them stirring. My eyes were jumping out of my head to them when I saw them coming in and seating themselves by the table.

26   Like a hungry cat rubbing up to its boss for meat, so I edged and simpered around them as I passed them the food. Without my will, like a beggar, my hand reached out to them.

27   The breakfast was over. And no word yet from my wages.

28   "*Gottuniu!*" I thought to myself. "Maybe they're so busy with their own things, they forgot it's the day for my wages. Could they who have everything know what I was to do with my first American dollars? How could they, soaking in plenty, how could they feel the longing and the fierce hunger in me, pressing up through each visionary dollar? How could they know the gnawing ache of my **avid** fingers for the feel of my own, earned dollars? *My* dollars that I could spend like a free person. *My* dollars that would make me feel with everybody alike!"

avid: very eager, desirous

My Notes

_____
_____
_____
_____
_____
_____
_____
_____
_____
_____
_____
_____
_____
_____
_____
_____
_____
_____
_____
_____
_____

WORD CONNECTIONS

Etymology
In modern history, the word **ghetto** refers to crowded urban areas of minority groups. In seventeenth-century Italy, the ghetto was the part of a city in which Jews were required to live. The word's origin is uncertain, but it may come from the Yiddish word *get*, meaning "deed of separation." A similar Italian word, *borghetto*, means "a small section of town."

29 Lunch came. Lunch passed.

30 Oi-i weh! Not a word yet about my money.

31 It was near dinner. And not a word yet about my wages.

32 I began to set the table. But my head—it swam away from me. I broke a glass. The silver dropped from my nervous fingers. I couldn't stand it any longer. I dropped everything and rushed over to my American lady and gentleman.

33 "Oi weh! The money—my money—my wages!" I cried breathlessly.

34 Four cold eyes turned on me.

35 "Wages? Money?" The four eyes turned into hard stone as they looked me up and down. "Haven't you a comfortable bed to sleep, and three good meals a day? You're only a month here. Just came to America. And you already think about money. Wait till you're worth any money. What use are you without knowing English? You should be glad we keep you here. It's like a vacation for you. Other girls pay money yet to be in the country."

36 It went black for my eyes. I was so choked no words came to my lips. Even the tears went dry in my throat.

Chunk 3

37 I left. Not a dollar for all my work.

38 For a long, long time my heart ached and ached like a sore wound. If murderers would have robbed me and killed me it wouldn't have hurt me so much. I couldn't think through my pain. The minute I'd see before me how they looked at me, the words they said to me—then everything began to bleed in me. And I was helpless.

39 For a long, long time the thought of ever working in an "American" family made me tremble with fear, like the fear of wild wolves. No—never again would I trust myself to an "American" family, no matter how fine their language and how sweet their smile.

40 It was blotted out in me all trust in friendship from "Americans." But the life in me still burned to live. The hope in me still craved to hope. In darkness, in dirt, in hunger and want, but only to live on!

41 There had been no end to my day—working for the "American" family.

42 Now rejecting false friendships from higher-ups in America, I turned back to the Ghetto. I worked on a hard bench with my own kind on either side of me. I knew before I began what my wages were to be. I knew what my hours were to be. And I knew the feeling of the end of the day.

43 From the outside my second job seemed worse than the first. It was in a sweatshop of a Delancey Street basement, kept up by an old, wrinkled woman that looked like a black witch of greed. My work was sewing on buttons. While the morning was still dark, I walked into a dark basement. And darkness met me when I turned out of the basement.

44   Day after day, week after week, all the contact I got with America was handling dead buttons. The money I earned was hardly enough to pay for bread and rent. I didn't have a room to myself. I didn't even have a bed. I slept on a mattress on the floor in a rat-hole of a room occupied by a dozen other immigrants. I was always hungry—oh, so hungry! The scant meals I could afford only sharpened my appetite for real food. But I felt myself better off than working in the "American" family where I had three good meals a day and a bed to myself. With all the hunger and darkness of the sweatshop, I had at least the evening to myself. And all night was mine. When all were asleep, I used to creep up on the roof of the tenement and talk out my heart in silence to the stars in the sky.

45   "Who am I? What am I? What do I want with my life? Where is America? Is there an America? What is this wilderness in which I'm lost?"

46   I'd hurl my questions and then think and think. And I could not tear it out of me, the feeling that America must be somewhere, somehow—only I couldn't find it—*my America*, where I would work for love and not for a living. I was like a thing following blindly after something far off in the dark!

47   "*Oi weh.*" I'd stretch out my hand up in the air. "My head is so lost in America. What's the use of all my working if I'm not in it? Dead buttons is not me."

48   Then the busy season started in the shop. The mounds of buttons grew and grew. The long day stretched out longer. I had to begin with the buttons earlier and stay with them till later in the night. The old witch turned into a huge greedy maw for wanting more and more buttons.

49   For a glass of tea, for a slice of herring over black bread, she would buy us up to stay another and another hour, till there seemed no end to her demands. One day, the light of self-assertion broke into my cellar darkness. "I don't want the tea. I don't want your herring," I said with terrible boldness "I only want to go home. I only want the evening to myself!"

50   "You fresh mouth, you!" cried the old witch. "You learned already too much in America. I want no clock-watchers in my shop. Out you go!"

Chunk 4

51   I was driven out to cold and hunger. I could no longer pay for my mattress on the floor. I no longer could buy the bite in my mouth. I walked the streets. I knew what it is to be alone in a strange city, among strangers.

52   But I laughed through my tears. So I learned too much already in America because I wanted the whole evening to myself? Well America has yet to teach me still more: how to get not only the whole evening to myself, but a whole day a week like the American workers.

53   That sweatshop was a bitter memory but a good school. It fitted me for a regular factory. I could walk in boldly and say I could work at something, even if it was only sewing on buttons.

 INDEPENDENT READING LINK

Read and Respond

For many authors in this unit, the American Dream is found in daily life and work. Select a moment in your independent reading that reflects this idea. Write how the American Dream is reflected in small details.

My Notes

54 Gradually, I became a trained worker. I worked in a light, airy factory, only eight hours a day. My boss was no longer a sweater and a blood-squeezer. The first freshness of the morning was mine. And the whole evening was mine. All day Sunday was mine.

55 Now I had better food to eat. I slept on a better bed. Now, I even looked dressed up like the American-born. But inside of me I knew that I was not yet an American. I choked with longing when I met an American-born, and I could say nothing.

56 Something cried dumb in me. I couldn't help it. I didn't know what it was I wanted. I only knew I wanted. I wanted. Like the hunger in the heart that never gets food.

57 An English class for foreigners started in our factory. The teacher had such a good, friendly face, her eyes looked so understanding, as if she could see right into my heart. So I went to her one day for an advice:

58 "I don't know what is with me the matter," I began. "I have no rest in me. I never yet done what I want."

59 "What is it you want to do, child?" she asked me.

60 "I want to do something with my head, my feelings. All day long, only with my hands I work."

61 "First you must learn English." She patted me as if I was not yet grown up. "Put your mind on that, and then we'll see."

62 So for a time I learned the language. I could almost begin to think with English words in my head. But in my heart the emptiness still hurt. I burned to give, to give something, to do something, to be something. The dead work with my hands was killing me. My work left only hard stones on my heart.

63 Again I went to our factory teacher and cried out to her: "I know already to read and write the English language, but I can't put it into words what I want. What is it in me so different that can't come out?"

64 She smiled at me down from her calmness as if I were a little bit out of my head.

65 "What *do you want* to do?"

66 "I feel. I see. I hear. And I want to think it out. But I'm like dumb in me. I only know I'm different—different from everybody."

67 She looked at me close and said nothing for a minute. "You ought to join one of the social clubs of the Women's Association," she advised.

68 "What's the Women's Association?" I implored greedily.

69 "A group of American women who are trying to help the working-girl find herself. They have a special department for immigrant girls like you."

Chunk 5

70 I joined the Women's Association. On my first evening there they announced a lecture: "The Happy Worker and His Work," by the Welfare director of the United Mills Corporation.

71 "Is there such a thing as a happy worker at his work?" I wondered. Happiness is only by working at what you love. And what poor girl can ever find it to work at what she loves? My old dreams about my America rushed through my mind. Once I thought that in America everybody works for love. Nobody has to worry for a living. Maybe this welfare man came to show me the *real* America that till now I sought in vain.

72 With a lot of polite words the head lady of the Women's Association introduced a higher-up that looked like the king of kings of business. Never before in my life did I ever see a man with such a sureness in his step, such power in his face, such friendly positiveness in his eye as when he smiled upon us.

73 "Efficiency is the new religion of business," he began. "In big business houses, even in up-to-date factories, they no longer take the first comer and give him any job that happens to stand empty. Efficiency begins at the employment office. Experts are hired for the one purpose, to find out how best to fit the worker to his work. It's economy for the boss to make the worker happy." And then he talked a lot more on efficiency in educated language that was over my head.

74 I didn't know exactly what it meant—efficiency—but if it was to make the worker happy at his work, then that's what I had been looking for since I came to America. I only felt from watching him that he was happy by his job. And as I looked on the clean, well-dressed, successful one, who wasn't ashamed to say he rose from an office-boy, it made me feel that I, too, could lift myself up for a person.

75 He finished his lecture, telling us about the Vocational Guidance Center that the Women's Association started.

76 The very next evening I was at the Vocational Guidance Center. There I found a young, college-looking woman. Smartness and health shining from her eyes! She, too, looked as if she knew her way in America. I could tell at the first glance: here is a person that is happy by what she does.

77 "I feel you'll understand me," I said right away.

78 She leaned over with pleasure in her face: "I hope I can."

79 "I'm different."

80 She gave me a quick, puzzled look from the corner of her eyes. "What are you doing now?"

81 "I'm the quickest **shirtwaist** hand on the floor. But my heart wastes away by such work. I think and think, and my thoughts can't come out."

shirtwaist: a tailored blouse worn by women

82 "Why don't you think out your thoughts in shirtwaists? You could learn to be a designer. Earn more money."

83 "I don't want to look on waists. If my hands are sick from waists, how could my head learn to put beauty into them?"

84 "But you must earn your living at what you know, and rise slowly from job to job."

85 I looked at her office sign: "Vocational Guidance." "What's your vocational guidance?" I asked. "How to rise from job to job—how to earn more money?"

86 The smile went out from her eyes. But she tried to be kind yet. "What *do* you want?" she asked, with a sigh of last patience.

87 "I want America to want me."

88 She fell back in her chair, thunderstruck with my boldness. But yet, in a low voice of educated self-control, she tried to reason with me:

89 "You have to *show* that you have something special for America before America has need of you."

90 "But I never had a chance to find out what's in me, because I always had to work for a living. Only, I feel it's efficiency for America to find out what's in me so different, so I could give it out by my work."

91 Her eyes half closed as they bored through me. Her mouth opened to speak, but no words came from her lips. So I flamed up with all that was choking in me like a house on fire:

92 "America gives free bread and rent to criminals in prison. They got grand houses with sunshine, fresh air, doctors and teachers, even for the crazy ones. Why don't they have free boarding-schools for immigrants—strong people—willing people? Here you see us burning up with something different, and America turns her head away from us."

93 Her brows lifted and dropped down. She shrugged her shoulders away from me with the look of pity we give to cripples and hopeless lunatics. "America is no Utopia. First you must become efficient in earning a living before you can indulge in your poetic dreams."

Chunk 6

94 I went away from the vocational guidance office with all the air out of my lungs. All the light out of my eyes. My feet dragged after me like dead wood.

95 Till now there had always lingered a rosy veil of hope over my emptiness, a hope that a miracle would happen. I would open up my eyes some day and suddenly find the America of my dreams. As a young girl hungry for love sees always before her eyes the picture of lover's arms around her, so I saw always in my heart the vision of Utopian America.

96 But now I felt that the America of my dreams never was and never could be. Reality had hit me on the head as with a club. I felt that the America that I sought was nothing but a shadow—an echo—a chimera of lunatics and crazy immigrants.

97 Stripped of all illusion, I looked about me. The long desert of wasting days of drudgery stared me in the face. The drudgery that I had lived through, and the endless drudgery still ahead of me rose over me like a withering wilderness of sand. In vain were all my cryings, in vain were all frantic efforts of my spirit to find the living waters of understanding for my perishing lips. Sand, sand was everywhere. With every seeking, every reaching out I only lost myself deeper and deeper in a vast sea of sand.

98 I knew now the American language. And I knew now, if I talked to the Americans from morning till night, they could not understand what the Russian soul of me wanted. They could not understand *me* any more than if I talked to them in Chinese. Between my soul and the American soul were worlds of difference that no words could bridge over. What was that difference? What made the Americans so far apart from me?

99 I began to read the American history. I found from the first pages that America started with a band of Courageous Pilgrims. They had left their native country as I had left mine. They had crossed an unknown ocean and landed in an unknown country, as I.

100 But the great difference between the first Pilgrims and me was that they expected to make America, build America, create their own world of liberty. I wanted to find it ready made.

101 I read on. I delved deeper down into the American history. I saw how the Pilgrim Fathers came to a rocky desert country, surrounded by Indian savages on all sides. But undaunted, they pressed on—through danger—through famine, pestilence, and want—they pressed on. They did not ask the Indians for sympathy, for understanding. They made no demands on anybody, but on their own indomitable spirit of persistence.

102 And I—I was forever begging a crumb of sympathy, a gleam of understanding from strangers who could not understand.

103 I, when I encountered a few savage Indian scalpers, like the old witch of the sweatshop, like my "Americanized" countryman, who cheated me of my wages—I, when I found myself on the lonely, untrodden path through which all seekers of the new world must pass, I lost heart and said: "There is no America!"

104 Then came a light—a great revelation! I saw America—a big idea—a deathless hope—a world still in the making. I saw that it was the glory of America that it was not yet finished. And I, the last comer, had her share to give, small or great, to the making of America, like those Pilgrims who came in the *Mayflower*.

WORD CONNECTIONS

Roots and Affixes
The word **persistence** comes from the Latin prefix *per*, meaning "through, completely"; the root *sist*, meaning "to stand"; and the suffix *-ence*, meaning "the quality of." *Persistence* is therefore "the quality of standing or lasting completely."

chimera: illusion
indomitable: incapable of defeat

105 Fired up by this revealing light, I began to build a bridge of understanding between the American-born and myself. Since their life was shut out from such as me, I began to open up my life and the lives of my people to them. And life draws life. In only writing about the Ghetto I found America.

106 Great chances have come to me. But in my heart is always a deep sadness. I feel like a man who is sitting down to a secret table of plenty, while his near ones and dear ones are perishing before his eyes. My very joy in doing the work I love hurts me like secret guilt, because all about me I see so many with my longings, my burning eagerness, to do and to be, wasting their days in drudgery they hate, merely to buy bread and pay rent. And America is losing all that richness of the soul.

107 The Americans of tomorrow, the America that is every day nearer coming to be, will be too wise, too open-hearted, too friendly-handed, to let the least lastcomer at their gates knock in vain with his gifts unwanted.

In the late 1800s and early 1900s, young women worked in the textile industry in unsafe conditions for sometimes more than 80 hours a week. This photograph was taken in January 1917 of 15-year-old Bessie Blitch sewing curtains on a sewing machine at Boutwell, Fairclough & Gold in Boston, Massachusetts.

Making Observations

- What have we learned about the narrator so far?
- What emotions do you feel as you read the narrator's experiences?
- Were your predictions about the story correct?

Returning to the Text

- Return to the story as you respond to the following questions. Use text evidence to support your responses.
- Write any additional questions you have about the text in your Reader/Writer Notebook.

4. Reread paragraphs 1–6 and summarize how the narrator feels about leaving Russia and immigrating to the United States. How does she expect her life to be better in America? Use text evidence to support your response.

_____

_____

_____

_____

5. Summarize the way in which the narrator builds suspense about her wages in paragraphs 19–33.

_____

_____

_____

_____

_____

6. How has the author been affected by her experience working for an American family? What decision does the experience lead her to make in paragraph 42?

_____

_____

_____

_____

_____

_____

7. What theme or central idea is suggested by the author's response in paragraph 71 to the factory lecture "The Happy Worker and His Work"? Does it prove to be true for her?

_____

_____

_____

_____

8. How do the narrator's exposure and reaction to American history in paragraphs 99–105 change her outlook toward her new country?

_____

_____

_____

_____

Appreciating the Author's Craft

Now that you have completed a second reading of the text, return to it again to underline words, phrases, and sentences that show the tone of the text. Answer the following questions based on your annotations.

9. Name five examples of images or diction that evoke the American Dream in the first three paragraphs of "America and I."

_____

_____

_____

_____

10. Cite two or three examples of the narrator's use of some form of the word _America_ in paragraphs 10–13. What idea does each use communicate?

_____

_____

_____

_____

_____

11. Describe the tone created by the syntax of this sentence in paragraph 53: "That sweatshop was a bitter memory but a good school." What does the narrator mean by this sentence?

_____

_____

_____

_____

12. Describe how the tone of Yezierska's writing differs between the first five paragraphs of Chunk 1 and the first five paragraphs of Chunk 6. Include examples of the author's word choice and syntax.

_____

_____

_____

_____

_____

☑ Check Your Understanding

Explain how the author's diction and syntax in the final paragraph convey her hope for America.

📝 Writing Prompt: Literary

Think about the experience of the narrator you read about in "America and I" and how she describes a difficult experience in her life. Write a three- to five-paragraph narrative about a difficult moment from your own life. Be sure to:

- Develop the events using well-chosen details and a well-structured sequence of events with a clear problem that is solved.
- Use narrative techniques, such as dialogue, description, or reflection, to develop the events. The events should build toward a particular tone and outcome.
- Use precise sensory details and figurative language to convey a vivid picture of the events, settings, and characters.
- Include a conclusion that reflects on what is experienced, observed, or resolved over the course of the narrative.

Writing a Literary Analysis and Revising for Sentence Fluency

My Notes

Learning Targets

- Use summarized, paraphrased, or directly quoted text evidence along with original commentary to develop a draft of a literary analysis in a timed writing situation.
- Analyze an author's syntax to help you revise drafts to improve fluency both within and between sentences.

Preview

In this activity, after completing a timed writing prompt, you will reexamine Anzia Yezierska's syntax in "America and I" to learn more about fluency both within and between sentences and revise your own writing to demonstrate what you have learned.

Planning to Write

1. Read and annotate the following writing prompt. In small groups, share your annotations. Work together to create a thesis statement and decide which details you noted are most relevant in supporting your thesis.

✒️ Writing Prompt: Literary Analysis

Timed Prompt: The tone of "America and I" changes and develops over the course of the narrative as Anzia Yezierska has new experiences. Draft an essay evaluating how Yezierska's use of diction and syntax affects the evolution of tone in the narrative. Be sure to:

- Include a clear thesis that states how the tone changes over the course of the narrative and evaluates the author's use of diction and syntax to create those changes.
- Support your evaluation by citing specific examples and details from the story, including the author's use of diction syntax, and add original commentary.
- Use summaries, paraphrases, and direct quotations, as appropriate, to support your thesis and introduce and punctuate all quotations correctly.
- Include clear transitions as you describe changes in tone over time and a clear and strong conclusion.

LANGUAGE & WRITER'S CRAFT:
Using Text Evidence in Your Writing

There are three correct ways to use someone else's words in your own writing: quoting, paraphrasing, and summarizing.

Quoting is using a text's exact words.

Example: Toward the end of Yezierska's story, the narrator states, "But the great difference between the first Pilgrims and me was that they expected to make America, build America, create their own world of liberty. I wanted to find it ready made."

Paraphrasing is restating a text's ideas in your own words. A paraphrase is usually slightly shorter than the original text.

Example: Yezierska's narrator tells herself that, like the Pilgrims, she must assert herself and create her own path to success.

Summarizing is similar to paraphrasing, but it includes only a text's main point.

Example: Yezierska's narrator realizes that she must work for her own success.

Always use text evidence in a way that preserves its original meaning and the order of its events or points. It is also important to make certain that your source is clearly cited; otherwise you are guilty of plagiarism, or claiming the work of others as your own.

PRACTICE Write three separate sentences quoting, paraphrasing and summarizing the story excerpt.

> "Now I had better food to eat. I slept on a better bed. Now, I even looked dressed up like the American-born. But inside of me I knew that I was not yet an American."

Drafting

2. Use what you learned about the three ways to incorporate text evidence in your writing and the planning work you completed in groups to write a draft response to the writing prompt.

ACADEMIC

By citing text evidence, you avoid the mistake of plagiarism, which is using or imitating another person's words or ideas without giving proper credit. Whether intentional or accidental, plagiarism is not ethical and must be avoided in all writing.

VOCABULARY

Analyzing Sentences for Fluency

This advice for writing with **fluency** comes from Steve Peha, an award-winning writer of young adult nonfiction: "When we write, we write in sentences. Beginning with a capital letter, we wind our way over words and phrases until we've expressed a complete thought, and then we mark the endpoint with a period, question mark, or exclamation mark."

Readers read the same way. They follow the shape of each sentence from beginning to end trying to understand the single complete thought the writer is expressing. In order for readers to do that, your writing needs to flow smoothly from word to word, phrase to phrase, and sentence to sentence. **Sentence fluency** refers to the flow between words in a sentence and between sentences in a text. Fluent writing reads smoothly, with an easy movement between words, sentences, paragraphs, and ideas. Notice the ways the two following paragraphs vary.

Example Text:

Sometimes a musical act gives something new to the world. The Beatles were from Liverpool, England. They formed in 1957 and lasted about 13 years until their breakup in 1970. There were four of them. Their name was a pun using the musical term "beat." A lot of their music was traditional, but some of it was experimental. They were hugely popular while they were together. They are still very famous and popular today.

Text Revised for Fluency:

Sometimes something special comes along at the right time and creates an influence that's felt everywhere. In 1957, four young men from Liverpool, England, formed a local band. By the time they broke up in 1970, they'd become a household word. Their name was a play on words, blending the musical term "beat" with the image of a funny little bug. Their music was amazingly varied. Some of it sounded Elizabethan; other tunes seemed to have come from the distant future. Today, their work remains among the most famous and influential ever created. As you read this, someone, somewhere, is listening (and probably singing along) to the Beatles.

Revising for Sentence Fluency

When revising sentences for fluency, examine them for:

Word choice: Sometimes complicated words are necessary, but in general it is better to express an idea in simpler, more straightforward language. Clear, plain diction makes ideas more accessible to the reader.

- **Instead of:** Yezierska's narrator came to America anticipating an enhancement in the fabric of her existence.
- **Try:** Yezierska's narrator came to America hoping for a better life.

Appropriate length and variety of sentences: Using very long sentences, especially in a short text, creates the risk of boring or confusing the reader. It is often a good idea to divide long sentences into shorter ones. Keep in mind, though, that using *too many* short sentences will make your writing choppy and irritating to read. Fluency includes a variety of sentence lengths while avoiding sentences that are so long they become dull or lose their point altogether.

- **Instead of:** Yezierska's narrator had a fear of how she would be regarded as an immigrant by those who had assimilated into the culture of America, leading her to dream of going out with her first wages and replacing her "immigrant rags" with a wardrobe worthy of one who had fully adopted the American lifestyle.
- **Try:** Yezierska's narrator disliked her "immigrant rags." She feared being looked down upon because of how she dressed. Once she was paid, she would buy new clothes. She hoped that doing so would make her look truly American.

Redundancy: Sometimes writers repeat themselves in an effort to make a point. This is almost always unnecessary and an obstacle to fluency. Deleting redundant language improves fluency without changing meaning.

- **Instead of:** Yezierska's narrator was a novice when it came to housekeeping, a beginner who lacked experience.
- **Try:** Yezierska's narrator lacked experience in housekeeping.

Self-reference: It Is seldom necessary to point out that a text is expressing its writer's point of view. Phrases like "I think" or "in my opinion" are usually distractions that can be safely omitted.

- **Instead of:** It's obvious to me that Yezierska's narrator had much to learn about being American.
- **Try:** Yezierska's narrator had much to learn about being American.

Voice: Sometimes writers rely too strongly on passive voice. While it might be appropriate in specific instances, its repeated use creates unnecessary wordiness and detracts from a text's fluency.

- **Instead of:** Buttons were sewed on for little pay by Yezierska's narrator.
- **Try:** Yezierska's narrator sewed on buttons for little pay.

Flow between sentences: A fluent text is more than a series of smoothly composed sentences. Those sentences as a whole must "flow" in a clear, logical order. Writers revise how their thoughts are presented in order to establish that order. Good writing requires a coherent text structure, which can be chronological, sequential, cause-and-effect, order of importance, or compare-and-contrast depending on which is best for presenting the idea.

- **Instead of:** Yezierska's narrator eventually worked out her own vision of the "American Dream." Her worst job was sewing on buttons for a factory. She came from Russia to find a better life. At first, she worked for a family who came from Russia for only room and board. It took her a while to understand what was required of her in her new home. She had been poor and unemployed in her native land.
- **Try:** Yezierska's narrator had come from Russia to find a better life. She had been poor and unemployed in her native land. Her first job was working for a Russian family for room and board. From there, she went to a terrible job sewing on buttons at a factory. It took a while for her to understand what would be required of her in her new home. Eventually, she worked out her own vision of the "American Dream."

3. Analyzing sentences for fluency when reading can help you improve your writing. Practice looking for fluency by analyzing a portion of the narrative you just read. Complete the following chart as your teacher directs.

Sentence Number	Sentence Beginning (First Four to Six Words)	Structure of Sentence (Simple, Compound, Complex, Compound/Complex, Fragment, etc.)	Words in Sentence
1	As one of the dumb, voiceless	complex	9

4. Afterward, reflect on what the chart tells you about the fluency of this particular text. What might using this chart teach you about your own writing?

☑ Check Your Understanding

After completing the table and reviewing the various ways to improve fluency, review your Timed Writing with a partner. Analyze your sentences, looking specifically at their flow and ease of understanding. Select a few sentences and revise them by changing their beginnings, length, and structure.

Questioning the Text

Learning Targets

- Use the strategy questioning the text, before, during, and after reading.
- Generate questions about a text to deepen understanding and gain information.

Preview

In this activity, you will generate levels of questions before, during, and after reading the essay "The Two Clashing Meanings of 'Free Speech'" by Teresa M. Bejan to deepen your understanding and to gain information about the freedom of speech guaranteed by the First Amendment and how it is being interpreted or misinterpreted on some college campuses today.

My Notes

Introducing the Strategy

Questioning the Text

A strategy for thinking actively and interpretively about your reading is to ask questions before, during, and after reading. As you read any text, you can ask questions that aid your understanding with different levels of ideas. Questioning helps you experience a text in depth, gain information, and monitor your understanding.

Level 1, Literal: Literal questions can be answered by referring to the text or consulting references.

> **Example:** In Anzia Yezierska's "America and I," what was the narrator's first job in her new country?

Level 2, Interpretive: Interpretive questions call for inferences because the answers cannot be found directly in the text, but textual evidence points to and supports the answers.

> **Example:** By the end of the story, how does the narrator's view of the "American Dream" align with the commonly held conception of that idea?

Level 3, Universal: Universal questions go beyond the text. What are the larger issues or ideas raised by the text?

> **Example:** What do people everywhere require to be happy?

1. Write two questions about the text you are about to read.

As You Read

- Jot down any questions you have about the essay as you read.
- Circle unknown words and phrases. Try to determine the meaning of the words by using context clues, word parts, or a dictionary.

About the Author

Teresa M. Bejan (b. 1984) received her PhD in political philosophy from Yale University in 2013 and is an associate professor of political theory at Oxford University in England. Her writing focuses on present-day issues while drawing upon the work of Enlightenment thinkers such as John Locke and Thomas Hobbes. Her essay "The Two Clashing Meanings of 'Free Speech'" appeared in *The Atlantic* on December 2, 2017.

Essay

The Two Clashing Meanings of "Free Speech"

Today's campus controversies reflect a battle between two distinct conceptions of the term—what the Greeks called *isegoria* and *parrhesia*.

by **Teresa M. Bejan**

1   Little distinguishes democracy in America more sharply from Europe than the primacy—and **permissiveness**—of our commitment to free speech. Yet ongoing controversies at American universities suggest that free speech is becoming a partisan issue. While conservative students defend the importance of inviting controversial speakers to campus and giving offense, many self-identified liberals are engaged in increasingly disruptive, even violent, efforts to shut them down. Free speech for some, they argue, serves only to silence and exclude others. Denying hateful or historically "privileged" voices a platform is thus necessary to make *equality* effective, so that the **marginalized** and vulnerable can finally speak up—and be heard.

2   The reason that appeals to the First Amendment cannot decide these campus controversies is because there is a more fundamental conflict between two, very different concepts of free speech at stake. The conflict between what the ancient Greeks called *isegoria*, on the one hand, and *parrhesia*, on the other, is as old as democracy itself. Today, both terms are often translated as "freedom of speech," but their meanings were and are importantly distinct. In ancient Athens, *isegoria* described the equal right of citizens to participate in public debate in the democratic assembly; *parrhesia*, the license to say what one pleased, how and when one pleased, and to whom.

3   When it comes to private universities, businesses, or social media, the would-be censors are our fellow-citizens, not the state. Private entities like Facebook or Twitter, not to mention Yale or Middlebury, have broad rights to

permissiveness: tolerance
marginalized: those kept in a powerless position within society

regulate and exclude the speech of their members. Likewise, online mobs are made up of outraged individuals exercising their own right to speak freely. To invoke the First Amendment in such cases is not a knock-down argument, it's a non sequitur. | Negation

4   John Stuart Mill argued that the chief threat to free speech in democracies was not the state, but the "social tyranny" of one's fellow citizens. And yet today, the civil libertarians who style themselves as Mill's inheritors have for the most part failed to refute, or even address, the arguments about free speech and equality that their opponents are making.

5   The two ancient concepts of free speech came to shape our modern liberal democratic notions in fascinating and forgotten ways. But more importantly, understanding that there is not one, but *two* concepts of freedom of speech, and that these are often in tension if not outright conflict, helps explain the frustrating shape of contemporary debates, both in the U.S. and in Europe—and why it so often feels as though we are talking past each other when it comes to the things that matter most.

6   Of the two ancient concepts of free speech, *isegoria* is the older. The term dates back to the fifth century BCE, although historians disagree as to when the democratic practice of permitting any citizen who wanted to address the assembly actually began. Despite the common translation "freedom of speech," the Greek literally means something more like "equal speech in public." The verb *agoreuein*, from which it derives, shares a root with the word *agora* or marketplace—that is, a public place where people, including philosophers like Socrates, would gather together and talk.

7   In the democracy of Athens, this idea of addressing an informal gathering in the *agora* carried over into the more formal setting of the *ekklesia* or political assembly. The herald would ask, "Who will address the assemblymen?" and then the volunteer would ascend the *bema*, or speaker's platform. In theory, *isegoria* meant that any Athenian citizen in good standing had the right to participate in debate and try to persuade his fellow citizens. In practice, the number of participants was fairly small, limited to the practiced rhetoricians and elder statesmen seated near the front. (Disqualifying offenses included prostitution and taking bribes.)

8   Although Athens was not the only democracy in the ancient world, from the beginning the Athenian principle of *isegoria* was seen as something special. The historian Herodotus even described the form of government at Athens not as *demokratia*, but as *isegoria* itself. According to the fourth-century orator and patriot Demosthenes, the Athenian constitution was based on speeches (*politeia en logois*) and its citizens had chosen *isegoria* as a way of life. But for its critics, this was a bug, as well as a feature. One critic, the so-called 'Old Oligarch,' complained that even slaves and foreigners enjoyed *isegoria* at Athens, hence one could not beat them as one might elsewhere.

Harvard University students chant slogans as they protest a scheduled speaking appearance of author Charles Murray on the campus of Harvard University, Wednesday, Sept. 6, 2017, in Cambridge, Mass. Murray, who co-wrote a book discussing racial differences in intelligence, touched off a boisterous protest earlier in 2017 at Vermont's Middlebury College.

My Notes

_____

_____

_____

_____

_____

_____

_____

_____

_____

_____

_____

_____

_____

_____

_____

_____

_____

_____

9 Critics like the Old Oligarch may have been exaggerating for comic effect, but they also had a point: as its etymology suggests, *isegoria* was fundamentally about equality, not freedom. As such, it would become the hallmark of Athenian democracy, which distinguished itself from the other Greek city-states not because it excluded slaves and women from citizenship (as did every society in the history of humankind until quite recently), but rather because it included the poor. Athens even took positive steps to render this equality of public speech effective by introducing pay for the poorest citizens to attend the assembly and to serve as jurors in the courts.

10 As a form of free speech then, *isegoria* was essentially political. Its competitor, *parrhesia*, was more expansive. Here again, the common English translation "freedom of speech" can be deceptive. The Greek means something like "all saying" and comes closer to the idea of speaking freely or "frankly." *Parrhesia* thus implied openness, honesty, and the courage to tell the truth, even when it meant causing offense. The practitioner of *parrhesia* (or *parrhesiastes*) was, quite literally, a "say-it-all."

11 *Parrhesia* could have a political aspect. Demosthenes and other orators stressed the duty of those exercising *isegoria* in the assembly to speak their minds. But the concept applied more often outside of the *ekklesia* in more and less informal settings. In the theater, *parrhesiastic* playwrights like Aristophanes offended all and sundry by skewering their fellow citizens, including Socrates, by name. But the paradigmatic *parrhesiastes* in the ancient world were the Philosophers, self-styled "lovers of wisdom" like Socrates himself who would confront their fellow citizens in the *agora* and tell them whatever hard truths they least liked to hear. Among these was Diogenes the Cynic, who famously lived in a barrel […] and told Alexander the Great to get out of his light—all, so he said, to reveal the truth to his fellow Greeks about the arbitrariness of their customs.

12 The danger intrinsic in parrhesia's offensiveness to the powers-that-be—be they monarchs like Alexander or the democratic majority—fascinated Michel Foucault, who made it the subject of a series of lectures at Berkeley (home of the original campus Free Speech Movement) in the 1980s. Foucault noticed that the practice of *parrhesia* necessarily entailed an asymmetry of power, hence a "contract" between the audience (whether one or many), who pledged to tolerate any offense, and the speaker, who agreed to tell them the truth and risk the consequences.

13 If *isegoria* was fundamentally about equality, then, *parrhesia* was about liberty in the sense of license—not a right, but rather an unstable privilege enjoyed at the pleasure of the powerful. In Athenian democracy, that usually meant the majority of one's fellow citizens, who were known to shout down or even drag speakers they disliked (including Plato's brother, Glaucon) off the *bema*. This ancient version of "no-platforming" speakers who offended popular sensibilities could have deadly consequences—as the trial and death of Socrates, Plato's friend and teacher attests.

paradigmatic: model example

My Notes

14   Noting the lack of success that Plato's loved ones enjoyed with both *isegoria* and *parrhesia* during his lifetime may help explain why the father of Western philosophy didn't set great store by either concept in his works. Plato no doubt would have noticed that, despite their differences, *neither* concept relied upon the most famous and distinctively Greek understanding of speech as *logos*—that is, reason or logical argument. Plato's student, Aristotle, would identify *logos* as the capacity that made human beings essentially political animals in the first place. And yet neither *isegoria* nor *parrhesia* identified the reasoned speech and arguments of *logos* as uniquely deserving of equal liberty or license. Which seems to have been Plato's point—how was it that a democratic city that prided itself on free speech, in all of its forms, put to death the one Athenian ruled by *logos* for speaking it? […]

***

15   Debates about free speech on American campuses today suggest that the rival concepts of *isegoria* and *parrhesia* are alive and well. When student protesters claim that they are silencing certain voices—via no-platforming, social pressure, or outright censorship—in the name of free speech itself, it may be tempting to dismiss them as insincere, or at best confused. As witnessed at an event at Kenyon College in September, when confronted with such arguments the response from gray-bearded free-speech fundamentalists like myself is to continue to preach to the converted about the First Amendment, but with an undercurrent of solidaristic despair about "kids these days" and their failure to understand the fundamentals of liberal democracy.

16   No wonder the "kids" are unpersuaded. While trigger warnings, safe spaces, and no-platforming grab headlines, poll after poll suggests that a more subtle, shift in mores is afoot. To a generation convinced that hateful speech is itself a form of violence or "silencing," pleading the First Amendment is to miss the point. Most of these students do not see themselves as standing against free speech at all. What they care about is the *equal right* to speech, and equal access to a public forum in which the historically marginalized and excluded can be heard and count equally with the privileged. This is a claim to *isegoria*, and once one recognizes it as such, much else becomes clear—including the contrasting appeal to *parrhesia* by their opponents, who sometimes seem determined to reduce "free speech" to a license to offend.

17   Recognizing the ancient ideas at work in these modern arguments puts those of us committed to America's *parrhesiastic* tradition of speaking truth to power in a better position to defend it. It suggests that to defeat the modern proponents of *isegoria*—and remind the modern *parrhesiastes* what they are fighting for—one must go beyond the First Amendment to the other, orienting principle of American democracy behind it, namely equality. After all, the genius of the First Amendment lies in bringing *isegoria* and *parrhesia* together, by securing the equal right and liberty of citizens not simply to "exercise their reason" but to speak their minds. It does so because the alternative is to allow the powers-that-happen-to-be to grant that liberty as a license to some individuals while denying it to others.

My Notes

18 In contexts where the Constitution does not apply, like a private university, this opposition to **arbitrariness** is a matter of culture, not law, but it is no less pressing and important for that. As the evangelicals, protesters, and provocateurs who founded America's *parrhesiastic* tradition knew well: When the rights of all become the privilege of a few, neither liberty nor equality can last.

Making Observations
- What ideas in the text capture your attention?
- What about freedom of speech do you know now that you didn't before?
- What questions did you have while reading this text?

arbitrariness: not being based on any principle, plan, or system

7. Use your research and notes to write a topic sentence for a rhetorical analysis paragraph. The sentence should contain a claim pertaining to how the author uses a particular rhetorical device in her essay. You can use this sentence frame to help you construct your topic sentence:

Bejan uses the rhetorical device (classification/exemplification/function/negation) in order

to _____.

✍ Writing Prompt: Rhetorical Analysis

Write a paragraph that analyzes the author's use of a rhetorical device (classification, exemplification, function, or negation). Be sure to:

- Include a topic sentence that states the rhetorical device.
- Provide textual evidence for support.
- Describe the effect the author achieves with the use of that rhetorical device.

My Notes

Learning Targets

- Read historical documents to analyze the author's purpose, audience, and message.
- Evaluate the use of text structure to achieve the author's purpose.
- Participate collaboratively in a mock Constitutional Convention.

Preview

In this activity, you will read the Preamble to the Constitution and the Bill of Rights to analyze the framers' purpose, audience, and message and evaluate the use of text structure to achieve their purpose.

Introducing the Strategy

Metacognitive Markers

Metacognition refers to the thinking you do about your own learning. Using metacognitive markers involves marking the text with symbols to reflect the thinking you are doing as you read. After reading, you can scan the text and use your metacognitive markers to quickly find evidence when you are talking or writing about a text. Here are the markers:

?   Use a question mark for questions you have about the text.

!   Use an exclamation point for a reaction to what you are reading.

*   Use an asterisk for a comment about the text.

_   Use an underline to identify a key idea or detail in the text.

As You Read

- Use metacognitive markers as you read.
- Circle unknown words and phrases. Try to determine the meaning of the words by using context clues, word parts, or a dictionary.

About the Document

The Preamble to the Constitution of the United States was a part of the original document that was ratified on June 1, 1788. Almost immediately after that ratification, Congress approved 12 proposed amendments called the Bill of Rights and sent them to the individual states for ratification. Nine states approved 10 of the amendments within six months. The endorsement of 11 states was necessary before anything could take effect, however. Vermont and Virginia finally accepted the 10 amendments in 1791, and the Bill of Rights became part of the Constitution that same year.

Historical Document

The Preamble to the Constitution of the United States

We the People of the United States, in Order to form a more perfect Union, establish Justice, insure domestic Tranquility, provide for the common defence, promote the general Welfare, and secure the Blessings of Liberty to ourselves and our Posterity, do ordain and establish this Constitution for the United States of America.

Historical Document

The Bill of Rights: A Transcription

Note: The following text is a transcription of the first ten amendments to the Constitution in their original form. These amendments were ratified December 15, 1791, and form what is known as the "Bill of Rights."

Amendment I

Congress shall make no law respecting an establishment of religion, or prohibiting the free exercise thereof; or **abridging** the freedom of speech, or of the press; or the right of the people peaceably to assemble, and to petition the Government for a **redress** of grievances.

Amendment II

A well regulated Militia, being necessary to the security of a free State, the right of the people to keep and bear Arms, shall not be infringed.

Amendment III

No Soldier shall, in time of peace be quartered in any house, without the consent of the Owner, nor in time of war, but in a manner to be prescribed by law.

Amendment IV

The right of the people to be secure in their persons, houses, papers, and effects, against unreasonable searches and seizures, shall not be violated, and no Warrants shall issue, but upon probable cause, supported by Oath or affirmation, and particularly describing the place to be searched, and the persons or things to be seized.

Amendment V

No person shall be held to answer for a capital, or otherwise infamous crime, unless on a presentment or indictment of a Grand Jury, except in cases arising in the land or naval forces, or in the Militia, when in actual service in time of War or public danger; nor shall any person be subject for the same offence to be twice put in jeopardy of life or limb; nor shall be compelled in any criminal case to be a witness against himself, nor be deprived of life, liberty, or property, without due process of law; nor shall private property be taken for public use, without just compensation.

My Notes

abridging: shortening, curtailing
redress: remedy, correction

Amendment VI

In all criminal prosecutions, the accused shall enjoy the right to a speedy and public trial, by an impartial jury of the State and district wherein the crime shall have been committed, which district shall have been previously ascertained by law, and to be informed of the nature and cause of the accusation; to be confronted with the witnesses against him; to have **compulsory** process for obtaining witnesses in his favor, and to have the Assistance of Counsel for his defence.

Amendment VII

In Suits at common law, where the value in controversy shall exceed twenty dollars, the right of trial by jury shall be preserved, and no fact tried by a jury, shall be otherwise re-examined in any Court of the United States, than according to the rules of the common law.

Amendment VIII

Excessive bail shall not be required, nor excessive fines imposed, nor cruel and unusual punishments inflicted.

Amendment IX

The **enumeration** in the Constitution, of certain rights, shall not be construed to deny or disparage others retained by the people.

Amendment X

The powers not delegated to the United States by the Constitution, nor prohibited by it to the States, are reserved to the States respectively, or to the people.

Created by Howard Chandler Christy in 1940, this oil on canvas painting titled "The Signing of the Constitution of the United States in 1787" depicts the Constitutional Convention at Independence Hall in Philadelphia on September 17, 1787. Do you recognize any of the historical figures in the image?

compulsory: required by law
enumeration: complete and ordered listing

Making Observations

- What catches your attention about the amendments?
- Which amendments have you heard of before?

Returning to the Text

- Return to the historical documents as you respond to the following questions. Use text evidence to support your responses.
- Write any additional questions you have about the text in your Reader/Writer Notebook.

1. For whom did those who ratified the U.S. Constitution claim to speak, and on what authority did they make that claim?

_____

_____

_____

_____

2. What is a word that accurately describes the government's proper relationship to religion, the press, and public assembly according to Amendment I of the Bill of Rights?

_____

_____

_____

_____

3. Who does Amendment VI guarantee must participate in a trial on behalf of the person being tried?

_____

_____

_____

_____

4. Why do you think the framers of the Constitution felt they had to include Amendment VIII in the Bill of Rights?

_____

_____

_____

_____

5. Explain how Amendments IX and X affirm the rights of states and individual citizens.

_____

_____

_____

_____

Author's Purpose

Remember that an author's purpose is the reason that an author or group of authors writes about a specific topic. Nearly all texts are written to either inform, entertain, or explain something to an audience.

Reread the About the Document section at the beginning of this activity, along with the historical documents that follow. Like any text, the Preamble and Bill of Rights can be analyzed in terms of author's purpose, audience, and message. To discern that information, examine the text while applying what you know about the early history of our country. Ask yourself:

- Why did the founders of the United States write and ratify a constitution?
- For whom was the information in the Constitution intended?
- What is the message of each of the Constitution's first 10 amendments?

6. With a partner, complete the following graphic organizer.

The Constitution's Preamble and Bill of Rights	
Author's Purpose:	
Audience:	

Amendment	Message Within the Text
Amendment I	
Amendment II	
Amendment III	
Amendment IV	
Amendment V	
Amendment VI	
Amendment VII	
Amendment VIII	
Amendment IX	
Amendment X	

7. How does the presentation of the Bill of Rights as a list support the author's purpose?

_____

_____

☑ Focus on the Sentence

Turn the following fragments into complete sentences, using what you know about the Constitution. Use correct punctuation and capitalization.

the Constitution

_____

founders wanted

_____

guaranteeing basic rights

_____

 Gaining Perspectives

With the creation of the Preamble and the Bill of Rights, citizens of the United States were given certain rights and liberties. The founding fathers were wise enough to know that they could not predict what rights and liberties would need defining as the country grew. Therefore, they created amendments. Adding an amendment to the Constitution is a lengthy process that underscores the importance of the right being added. With a partner, think about the amendments you know of that have not been mentioned in this activity and discuss how these amendments expanded civil rights and liberties. When you are done, present the ideas you discussed with another pair.

Governing Your Island

8. Imagine that on a school trip sailing to a small and remote island, you and all of your classmates become stranded without the ability to communicate with the outside world and with little hope of being rescued in the foreseeable future. The island that you are stranded on can provide the basic necessities of food, water, and shelter, but you must work together to survive. Working in small groups, brainstorm a list of recommendations to consider when developing a new government following these guiding questions:

- How will you make sure that everyone works toward common goals?
- How will you make sure that everyone has the opportunity to speak and be heard?
- How will you make sure that everyone will take part in protecting the island?
- How will you make sure that resources are used fairly among the people?
- How will you ensure that all people are free to do what they want as long as others are not hurt?
- How will you make sure that your rules and laws are protected for future generations?

9. Per directions from your teacher, work with your classmates to participate in a mock Constitutional Convention. Work as a group to establish roles, set goals, and create deadlines.

America's Promise

Learning Strategies

Marking the Text
OPTIC
Previewing
Think-Pair-Share
SOAPSTone

My Notes

Learning Targets

- Synthesize information presented in two primary sources: an illustration and a speech to create a new understanding about America's promise to new immigrants.
- Cite evidence from multiple texts to define a concept.
- Integrate ideas from multiple texts to build knowledge and vocabulary about what the Statue of Liberty symbolizes.

Preview

In this activity, you will look at an illustration and read a speech that both describe the immigrant experience in the United States of America.

1. **Quickwrite:** Based on what you already know about immigration, how would you define America's promise to immigrants entering the United States?

Introducing the Strategy

OPTIC is an acronym for overview, parts, title, interrelationships, and conclusion. OPTIC is a strategy for analyzing visual texts—including paintings, photographs, advertisements, maps, charts, or graphs—and developing an interpretation regarding the meaning or theme(s) of the text.

KNOWLEDGE QUEST

Knowledge Question:

What does the Statue of Liberty symbolize to immigrants coming to America?

In Activity 1.8, you will study a piece of art and read President Franklin D. Roosevelt's address on the anniversary of the Statue of Liberty. While you read and build knowledge about what the Statue of Liberty symbolizes, think about your answer to the Knowledge Question.

2. Spend a few minutes looking closely at the following image. Then complete the table that follows using the OPTIC strategy.

This image was originally printed on July 2, 1887, in *Frank Leslie's Illustrated Newspaper* and is titled "New York—Welcome to the land of freedom—An ocean steamer passing the Statue of Liberty: Scene on the steerage deck / from a sketch by a staff artist."

My Notes

O (Overview): Write notes on what the visual appears to be about.	
P (Parts): Zoom in on the parts of the visual and describe any elements or details that seem important.	
T (Title): Highlight the words of the title of the visual (if one is available).	
I (Interrelationships): Use the title as the theory and the parts of the visual as clues to detect and specify how the elements of the graphic are related.	
C (Conclusion); Draw a conclusion about the visual as a whole. What does the visual mean? Summarize the message of the visual in one or two sentences.	

☑ Focus on the Sentence

Use your OPTIC analysis of the illustration to answer the questions that follow. Then use what you know about ordering clauses to expand the kernel sentence into an informative caption.

Kernel: An ocean steamer carries immigrants _____

When? _____

Where? _____

Why? _____

Expanded Sentence: _____

_____

As You Read

- Underline phrases that help you create mental images about America.
- Highlight phrases that describe the immigrants Roosevelt is referring to.
- Circle unknown words and phrases. Try to determine the meaning of the words by using context clues, word parts, or a dictionary.

Speech

Address on the Occasion of the Fiftieth Anniversary of the Statue of Liberty, October 28, 1936

by **President Franklin D. Roosevelt**

1   " … It is the memory of all these eager seeking millions that makes this one of America's places of great romance. Looking down this great harbor I like to think of the countless numbers of inbound vessels that have made this port. I like to think of the men and women who, with the break of dawn off Sandy Hook, have **strained** their eyes to the west for a first glimpse of the New World.

2   They came to us—most of them—in **steerage**. But they, in their humble quarters, saw things in these strange horizons which were denied to the eyes of those few who traveled in greater luxury.

3   They came to us speaking many tongues—but a single language, the universal language of human aspiration.

4   How well their hopes were justified is proved by the record of what they achieved. They not only found freedom in the New World, but by their effort and **devotion**, they made the New World's freedom safer, richer, more far-reaching, more capable of growth.

5   Within this present generation, that stream from abroad has largely stopped. We have within our shores today the materials out of which we shall continue to build an even better home for liberty.

6   We take satisfaction in the thought that those who have left their native land to join us may still **retain** here their **affection** for some things left behind—old customs, old language, old friends. Looking to the future, they wisely choose that their children shall live in the new language and in the new

customs of this new people. And those children more and more realize their common **destiny** in America. That is true whether their forebears came past this place eight generations ago or only one.

7   The realization that we are all bound together by hope of a common future rather than by reverence for a common past has helped us to build upon this continent a unity unapproached in any similar area or population in the whole world. For all our millions of square miles, for all our millions of people, there is a unity in language and speech, in law and in economics, in education and in general purpose, which nowhere finds its match.

8   It was the hope of those who gave us this Statue and the hope of the American people in receiving it that the Goddess of Liberty and the Goddess of Peace were the same.

9   The grandfather of my old friend the French Ambassador and those who helped him make this gift possible, were citizens of a great sister Republic established on the principle of the democratic form of government. Citizens of all democracies unite in their desire for peace. Grover Cleveland recognized that unity of purpose on this spot fifty years ago.

10   He suggested that liberty enlightening the world would extend her rays from these shores to every other Nation.

11   Today that symbolism should be broadened. To the message of liberty which America sends to all the world must be added her message of peace.

12   Even in times as troubled and uncertain as these, I still hold to the faith that a better civilization than any we have known is in store for America and by our example, perhaps, for the world. Here destiny seems to have taken a long look. Into this continental reservoir there has been poured untold and untapped wealth of human resources. Out of that reservoir, out of the melting pot, the rich promise which the New World held out to those who came to it from many lands is finding fulfillment.

13   The richness of the promise has not run out. If we keep the faith for our day as those who came before us kept the faith for theirs, then you and I can smile with confidence into the future. It is fitting therefore, that this should be a service of rededication, rededication to the liberty and the peace which this statue symbolizes.

WORD CONNECTIONS

Content Connections

Historically, the term **melting pot** referred to the viewpoint that the immigrants who came to the United States from many countries and cultures would combine, or melt, into one American people and culture.

The term can be traced back to 1782, but a 1908 play called *The Melting Pot* popularized it. The playwright, Israel Zangwill, was a Jewish immigrant from Great Britain.

destiny: an experience in the future

⊘ Knowledge Quest

- What is symbolism?
- Which details about the Statue of Liberty from the speech are the most interesting to you?

Returning to the Text

- Return to the speech as you respond to the following questions. Use text evidence to support your responses.
- Write any additional questions you have about the text in your Reader/Writer Notebook.

1. **KQ** In paragraph 3, what does Roosevelt mean by *universal* when he refers to "the universal language of human aspiration"?

_____

_____

_____

_____

2. Summarize Roosevelt's description of the Statue of Liberty's significance in the first five paragraphs of his speech. What has prompted his oratory on this occasion?

_____

_____

_____

_____

_____

3. Reread paragraph 7. What does Roosevelt believe binds Americans together? What does he cite as evidence for that assertion?

_____

_____

_____

_____

4. In paragraph 11, how does Roosevelt describe the Statue of Liberty's symbolism?

_____

_____

_____

5. What imagery does Roosevelt use in paragraph 12 of his speech? What does it mean?

_____

_____

_____

_____

_____

6. What comparison does Roosevelt make as he concludes his speech? What is his point in doing so?

_____

_____

_____

7. **KQ** How does Roosevelt's speech convey what the Statue of Liberty symbolizes?

_____

_____

_____

_____

_____

INDEPENDENT READING LINK

Read and Discuss

You can continue to build your knowledge about what the Statue of Liberty symbolizes by reading other articles at ZINC Reading Labs. Search for keywords such as *American Dream* or *American symbols*.

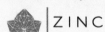

🖉 Knowledge Quest

Think about the Statue of Liberty. With a small group, discuss what the Statue of Liberty symbolizes to immigrants coming to America. Does the Statue of Liberty symbolize the same things for someone born in the United States? Be sure to:

- Set rules with your classmates to facilitate a collegial discussion of the topic.
- Ask and respond to questions to broaden the discussion, connect ideas, and draw others in to the conversation.
- Respond thoughtfully to the various perspectives that classmates offer and summarize points of agreement and disagreement.

Working from the Text

Introducing the Strategy

SOAPSTone stands for Speaker, Occasion, Audience, Purpose, Subject, and Tone. It is a reading and writing tool for analyzing the relationship among a writer, his or her purpose, and the target audience of the text. SOAPSTone guides you in asking questions to analyze a text or to plan for writing a composition.

- **Speaker:** The speaker is the voice that tells the story.
- **Occasion:** The occasion is the time and place of the story; it is the context that prompted the writing.
- **Audience:** The audience is the person or persons to whom the piece is directed.
- **Purpose:** The purpose is the reason behind the text or what the writer wants the audience to think as a result of reading the text.
- **Subject:** The subject is the focus of the text.
- **Tone:** Tone is the speaker's attitude toward the subject.

8. Complete a SOAPSTone graphic organizer to analyze President Franklin D. Roosevelt's speech given to celebrate the 50th anniversary of the Statue of Liberty.

☑ Focus on the Sentence

Use your SOAPSTone analysis of Roosevelt's speech to compose fragments that name each part of that analysis. Then combine those fragments into a one- or two-sentence summary of the speech.

Speaker: _____

Occasion: _____

Audience: _____

Purpose: _____

Subject: _____

Tone: _____

Summary: _____

_____

_____

_____

Synthesizing Information

Review the notes you made using your OPTIC and SOAPSTone analyses of the illustration and speech. Consider how the image and speech both present a view of America's promise. Then synthesize the information from both sources, using and combining ideas from each one, to complete the following sentences.

9. In both the speech and the illustration, immigration is presented as

10. In the speech and the illustration, the Statue of Liberty symbolizes a promise to new Americans of

11. The illustration connects to Roosevelt's reference to a "melting pot" by

12. Roosevelt's references to the "Goddess of Liberty" and the "Goddess of Peace" are relevant to the illustration because

Writing Prompt: Informational

Write a short essay that draws on details in both the illustration and the speech to create a definition of America's promise. Use definition strategies that will help you support your thesis. Be sure to:

- Begin with a clear thesis that defines the promise of America.
- Use the most significant and relevant details from the illustration and the speech to support your thesis on what that promise means.
- Include rhetorical strategies that help support your definition.
- Include transitions between points and a concluding statement that ties together your essay.

Language Checkpoint: Placing Modifiers

Learning Targets

- Place phrases and clauses correctly in sentences.
- Recognize and correct misplaced and dangling modifiers.

Preview

In this activity, you will learn about how to place phrases and clauses correctly in sentences and correct misplaced and dangling modifiers in your writing.

Placing Modifiers Correctly

Part of being an effective writer is placing modifiers so that your meaning is clear and knowing how to revise misplaced and dangling modifiers.

A **modifier** is a word, phrase, or clause that makes the meaning of another word or word group more specific. For example, the boldfaced words and word groups in the following phrases are all modifiers:

an **immense** statue

the statue **in New York Harbor**

a statue **that symbolizes freedom**

Modifiers should be placed near the word or word group they modify. A **misplaced modifier** can create confusion or accidental humor.

Modifier placement is particularly important in speeches, when the audience is listening and can't reread to figure out the speaker's meaning. For example, in the speech "Address on the Occasion of the Fiftieth Anniversary of the Statue of Liberty," President Franklin D. Roosevelt says this:

We have **within our shores** today the materials out of which we shall continue to build an even better home for liberty.

Notice that Roosevelt places the modifying adverb phrase *within our shores* and the adverb *today* directly after the verb *have*.

1. Read the following sentences and underline the misplaced modifiers. Then rewrite the sentence, placing the modifier correctly. The first one has been done for you.

   a. Franklin Delano Roosevelt was the 32nd president of the United States, <u>who was a fifth cousin of President Theodore Roosevelt.</u>

   Franklin Delano Roosevelt, who was a fifth cousin of President Theodore Roosevelt, was the 32nd president of the United States.

b. We read about First Lady Eleanor Roosevelt's work championing human rights <u>during our social studies class</u>.

c. I wonder how immigrants on ships in New York Harbor <u>passing the Statue of Liberty felt when they saw the statue</u>.

d. "The New Colossus," a famous poem, is inscribed on a plaque inside the base of the statue <u>by Emma Lazarus</u>.

2. Revisit each of the sentences you just revised. Pick two and describe what the original sentence literally meant.

Correcting Dangling Modifiers

A modifier that does not clearly modify any word or word group in a sentence is a **dangling modifier**. While you usually can correct a misplaced modifier by rearranging the sentence, in the case of a dangling modifier, you may need to add or replace words to clarify your meaning.

Dangling: After reading the speech, a discussion took place.

In this example, the phrase does not clearly modify anything in the sentence. After all, the discussion did not read the speech.

Revised: After reading the speech, we discussed it.

Now, the phrase modifies *we*.

Dangling: Holding her torch for more than 120 years now, we marvel at the sculptor's achievement.

The phrase seems to modify *we*, but that doesn't make sense.

Revised: The statue has been holding her torch for more than 120 years now, and we marvel at the sculptor's achievement.

Adding words to the modifier and following the comma with and has clarified the sentence's meaning.

3. Read the following sentences and underline the dangling modifiers. Then rewrite each sentence to make it clear.

a. <u>Listening to the speech</u>, eyes filled with tears, and hearts filled with hope.

b. <u>Studying the statue</u>, it was surprising to learn that it was engineered by Gustave Eiffel, who also designed the Eiffel Tower.

c. Weary from the long voyage, the boat pulled into the harbor.

Revising

Read the paragraph from a student's essay about the Statue of Liberty. Work with a partner to check whether modifiers are placed correctly and whether each clearly modifies a word or word group. Underline any mistakes you notice and rewrite the paragraph, correcting the mistakes. Not all sentences include errors.

[1] Wanting to honor the abolition of slavery and to celebrate liberty, the statue was first envisioned in 1865 by Edouard de Laboulaye. [2] His friend, the sculptor Frederic Bartholdi, helped make Laboulaye's vision a reality. [3] French citizens and U.S. citizens donated to help pay for the immense sculpture who loved the idea of commemorating the friendship between their countries. [4] Taking years to complete the work, the statue would eventually stand over 151 feet high. [5] Like a beacon of hope, we appreciate how immigrants must have felt as they crossed New York Harbor.

☑ Check Your Understanding

Imagine you are editing a classmate's writing and you notice these sentences:

Astonished, our studies showed that the 225-ton statue was built in France. The pieces were packed into hundreds of boxes to be assembled by workers delivered by ship.

In your own words, write an explanation so that your classmate understands the mistakes and how to correct them. Then add a question to your Editor's Checklist to remind yourself to check for correct use and placement of modifiers.

Practice

Return to the essay you wrote in Activity 1.3 and check it for correct use and placement of modifiers. Work with a partner to follow these steps:

   a. Underline any modifying words, phrases, and clauses.

   b. Check for correct placement and use of modifiers.

   c. Rewrite sentences to correct any misplaced or dangling modifiers.

Defining an American

Learning Targets

- Analyze how authors use definition strategies to support their thesis.
- Summarize text clearly and accurately.
- Use brainstorming and collaboration to plan a definition essay.

Preview

In this activity, you will read a letter that explores what it meant to be American when the country was newly formed.

Beginning a Definition

What does it mean to be an American? What makes Americans unique? What characteristics or traits do Americans share? With a partner, review the texts and images you have read in this unit to create a vocabulary tree in your Reader/Writer Notebook. Use your tree to keep track of the multiple aspects of a definition of an American. As you continue through the first part of this unit, add details and examples to your tree.

As You Read

- Underline words and phrases you could add to your vocabulary tree.
- After reading each paragraph, jot down what you think the key idea is based on the details in the margin.
- Circle unknown words and phrases. Try to determine the meaning of the words by using context clues, word parts, or a dictionary.

About the Author

J. Hector St. John de Crèvecoeur (1735–1813) was born in France about 40 years before the American Revolution. He lived in New York during the Revolution and was jailed by the British for his support of colonial independence. Upon his release, he returned to France and wrote the highly successful *Letters from an American Farmer*, a work of fiction that he eventually expanded into a three-volume set. His writing is noted for its charm and optimism, and he is credited with coining the term *melting pot* as a description of American culture.

My Notes

Letter

What Is an American?

from *Letters from an American Farmer (1781)*

by J. Hector St. John de Crèvecoeur

1   In this great American asylum, the poor of Europe have by some means met together, and in consequence of various causes; to what purpose, should they ask one another, what countrymen they are? Alas, two thirds of them had no country. Can a wretch who wanders about, who works and starves, whose life is a continual scene of sore affliction or pinching **penury**; can that man call England or any other kingdom his country? A country that had no bread for him, whose fields **procured** him no harvest, who met with nothing but the frowns of the rich, the severity of the laws, with jails and punishments; who owned not a single foot of the extensive surface of this planet? No! Urged by a variety of **motives**, here they came. Every thing has tended to regenerate them; new laws, a new mode of living, a new social system; here they are become men: in Europe they were as so many useless plants, wanting vegetative mould, and refreshing showers; they withered, and were mowed down by want, hunger and war: but now, by the power of transplantation, like all other plants, they have taken root and flourished! Formerly they were not numbered in any civil list of their country, except in those of the poor; here they rank as citizens. By what invisible power has this surprising **metamorphosis** been performed? By that of the laws, and that of their industry. The laws, the indulgent laws, protect them as they arrive, stamping on them the symbol of adoption; they receive ample rewards for their labours; these accumulated rewards procure them lands; those lands confer on them the title of freemen; and to that title every benefit is affixed which men can possibly require. This is the great operation daily performed by our laws. From whence proceed these laws? From our government. Whence that government? It is derived from the original genius and strong desire of the people ratified and confirmed by government. This

penury: extreme poverty
procured: gained
motives: reasons
metamorphosis: change

s the great chain which links us all, this is the picture which every **province** exhibits, Nova Scotia excepted. There the crown has done all; either there were no people who had genius, or it was not much attended to: the consequence is, that the province is very thinly inhabited indeed; the power of the crown, in conjunction with the musketos, has prevented men from settling there. Yet some part of it flourished once, and it contained a mild harmless set of people. But for the fault of a few leaders the whole were banished. The greatest political error the crown ever committed in America, was to cut off men from a country which wanted nothing but men!

2   What attachment can a poor European **emigrant** have for a country where he had nothing? The knowledge of the language, the love of a few kindred as poor as himself, were the only cords that tied him: his country is now that which gives him land, bread, protection, and consequence: Ubi panis ibi patria,1 is the motto of all emigrants. What then is the American, this new man? He is either an European, or the descendant of an European; hence that strange mixture of blood, which you will find in no other country. I could point out to you a man, whose grandfather was an Englishman, whose wife was Dutch, whose son married a French woman, and whose present four sons have now four wives of different nations. He is an American, who, leaving behind him all his ancient prejudices and manners, receives new ones from the new mode of life he has embraced, the new government he obeys, and the new rank he holds. He becomes an American by being received in the broad lap of our great Alma Mater.

3   Here individuals of all nations are melted into a new race of men, whose labours and posterity will one day cause great change in the world. Americans are the western pilgrims, who are carrying along with them that great mass of arts, sciences, vigour, and industry, which began long since in the East; they will finish the great circle. The Americans were once scattered all over Europe; here they are incorporated into one of the finest systems of population which has ever appeared, and which will hereafter become distinct by the power of the different climates they inhabit. The American ought, therefore, to love this country much better than that wherein either he or his forefathers were born. Here the rewards of his industry follow with equal steps the progress of his labour; his labour is founded on the basis of nature, self-interest; can it want a stronger allurement? Wives and children, who before in vain demanded of him a morsel of bread, now, fat and frolicsome, gladly help their father to clear those fields whence exuberant crops are to arise to feed and to clothe them all; without any part being claimed, either by a **despotic** prince, a rich **abbot**, or a mighty lord. Here religion demands but little of him; a small voluntary salary to the minister, and gratitude to God; can he refuse these? The American is a new man, who acts upon new principles; he must therefore entertain new ideas, and form new opinions. From involuntary idleness, servile dependence, penury, and useless labour, he has passed to toils of a very different nature, rewarded by ample **subsistence**. This is an American.

---

1 Where there is bread there is my country.

province: part of a country
emigrant: a person leaving his homeland
despotic: authoritarian, oppressive
abbot: head of a monastery
subsistence: livelihood, earnings

Making Observations

- What images come to mind as your read this text?
- What details about an American stayed with you after reading the text?

Returning to the Text

- Return to the letter as you respond to the following questions. Use text evidence to support your responses.
- Write any additional questions you have about the text in your Reader/Writer Notebook.

1. In paragraph 1, what opinion does the author express about a poor "countryman's" place in Europe versus his place in America?

_____

_____

_____

_____

2. Use print or digital resources to determine possible meanings of the word *asylum*. List those meanings and then use context clues to determine which meaning applies to the word in the first sentence of paragraph 1.

_____

_____

_____

_____

3. What does the word *kindred* mean in paragraph 2? What point is the author making with its use?

_____

_____

_____

_____

4. Summarize the author's main point in paragraph 2.

_____

_____

_____

_____

5. What are some attributes that define the "new race of men" as the author describes them in paragraph 3?

_____

_____

_____

_____

6. In paragraph 3, how does the author compare the life of a father before and after moving his wife and children to America?

_____

_____

_____

_____

Analyzing the Characteristics and Structural Elements of a Definition Essay

7. With a partner, use the chart to record specific evidence of the thesis, definition strategies, and conclusion from de Crèvecoeur's text. Discuss how each contributes to your understanding of de Crèvecoeur's definition of an American.

Characteristic of Definition Essay	Examples from "What Is an American?" by J. Hector St. John de Crèvecoeur
Thesis	
Exemplification	
Negation	
Function	
Classification	
Conclusion	

Writing Prompt: Informational

Write a short summary of de Crèvecoeur's definition of an American using details from his letter to support your summary. Be sure to:

- Include a clear statement of de Crèvecoeur's main idea.
- Provide an objective summary of his thinking, following his organization but stating his points in your own words.
- Include at least one quote with original commentary. Punctuate the quote correctly.

 INDEPENDENT READING LINK

Read and Research

In this unit and perhaps in your independent reading, you discovered how the idea and experience of the American Dream changed lives. Extend what you learned by researching the subject of your independent reading to find out what happened later in his or her life. Did the author or subject's view of the American Dream change? If so, how? Share your findings with a partner.

Whitman's America

My Notes

Learning Targets

- Analyze how an author's use of language in poetry shapes reader perceptions.
- Compare similar ideas as explored in different poems.

Preview

In this activity, you will read two poems by celebrated American poet Walt Whitman and write an analytical response that compares them.

As You Read

- Create an image in your mind of the sights, smells, or sounds that the poet describes.
- Circle unknown works and phrase. Try to determine the meaning of the words by using context clues or a dictionary.

About the Writer

Walt Whitman (1819–1892) is now considered one of America's greatest poets, but his untraditional poetry was not well received during his lifetime. As a young man, he worked as a printer and a journalist while writing free verse poetry. His collection of poems Leaves of Grass first came out in 1855, and he revised and added to it several times over the years. Whitman's work disregards traditional poetic conventions, largely ignoring scheme and meter in favor of common speech patterns. The result is a uniquely American style of poetry that is frequently similar to prose. In the first poem, Whitman describes the various "carols," or songs, of American laborers. It is an early celebration of the country's working class and our nation's cultural diversity.

Poetry

My Notes

America

by Walt Whitman

Center of equal daughters, equal sons,

All, all alike endear'd, grown, ungrown, young or old,

Strong, ample, fair, enduring, capable, rich

Perennial with the Earth, with Freedom, Law and Love,

A grand, sane, towering, seated Mother,

Chair'd in the adamant of Time.

Making Observations
- What emotions does this poem make you feel?
- What details or images do you find striking?

Poetry

I Hear America Singing

by Walt Whitman

I hear America singing, the varied carols I hear,

Those of mechanics, each one singing his as it should be **blithe** and strong,

The carpenter singing his as he measures his plank or beam,

The **mason** singing his as he makes ready for work, or leaves off work,

5   The boatman singing what belongs to him in his boat, the deckhand singing on the steamboat deck, The shoemaker singing as he sits on his bench, the hatter singing as he stands,

The woodcutter's song, the plowboy's on his way in the morning, or at noon intermission or at sundown.

The delicious singing of the mother, or of the young wife at work, or of the girl sewing or washing, Each singing what belongs to him or her and to none else.

10   The day what belongs to the day—at night the party of young fellows, robust, friendly, Singing with open mouths their strong melodious songs.

> **perennial:** lasting or existing for a long or apparently infinite time
> **blithe:** happy, carefree
> **mason:** a person who builds with brick or stone

Making Observations

- What references to music do you notice?
- What details or images do you find striking?

Returning to the Text

- Return to the poems as you respond to the following questions. Use evidence from the poems to support your responses.
- Write any additional questions you have about the photographs in your Reader/ Writer Notebook.

"America"

1. Describe the tone created by Whitman. What words does he use to contribute to the tone he creates?

_____

_____

_____

_____

2. How does the use of commas impact the images Whitman creates?

_____

_____

_____

_____

3. What is Whitman's message about America? Support your answer with words and phrases from the poem.

_____

_____

_____

_____

"I Hear America Singing"

4. Describe the central image Whitman uses to evoke the people of America throughout the poem.

_____

_____

_____

_____

5. What is unique about the characters in line 8 of Whitman's poem?

_____

_____

_____

_____

6. What is Whitman's message about America in this poem? Support you answer with words and phrases from the poem.

_____

_____

_____

_____

☑ Check Your Understanding

Consider the messages in both poems. What is Whitman saying about being American in the 19th century? How do the poems treat this message similarly and differently? How does Whitman's 19th-century America compare with America today?

✐ Writing Prompt: Literary

Think about what you think it means to be American today. Write a short essay on an experience or observation that led you to this personal definition. In your writing, be sure to:

- Develop the events described using well-chosen details and a well-structured sequence.
- Use narrative techniques, such as dialogue, description, or reflection, to develop the events. The events should build toward a particular tone and outcome.
- Use precise sensory details and figurative language to convey a vivid picture of the events, settings, and characters.
- Include a conclusion that follows from and reflects on what is experienced, observed, or resolved over the course of the narrative.

America's Voices

INDEPENDENT READING LINK

Read and Connect

Select a person in your independent reading who identifies an important symbol that keeps the American Dream alive. Compare this symbol to a symbol selected by an author of a reading in this unit. In your Reader/Writer Notebook, note similarities and differences.

My Notes

Learning Targets

- Analyze how an author's use of language in poetry shapes reader perceptions.
- Compare similar ideas as explored in different poems.

Preview

In this activity, you will read two poems by celebrated American writers and write a response that compares them.

As You Read

- While you read each poem, create an image in your mind of the sights, smells, or sounds that the poet describes.
- Circle unknown words and phrases. Try to determine the meaning of the words by using context clues, word parts, or a dictionary.

About the Author

Langston Hughes (1902–1967) began his writing career early. By eighth grade, he was named the class poet. He regularly wrote verse for his high school magazine. Hughes entered Columbia University in 1921 and discovered the arts scene in Harlem. He became a prominent figure in the Harlem Renaissance. His poetry, plays, and stories frequently focus on the African American experience, particularly on the struggles and feelings of people in a segregated society. His poetry was especially informed by the jazz and blues rhythms of African American music.

Poetry

I, Too

by **Langston Hughes**

> I, too, sing America.
>
> I am the darker brother.
>
> They send me to eat in the kitchen
>
> When company comes,

My Notes

5 But I laugh,

And eat well,

And grow strong.

Tomorrow,

I'll be at the table

10 When company comes.

Nobody'll dare

Say to me,

"Eat in the kitchen,"

Then.

15 Besides,

They'll see how beautiful I am

And be ashamed—

I, too, am America.

Making Observations

- Who is speaking in the poem?
- What emotions are named in the poem?

About the Author

Julia Alvarez was born in 1950 in New York City but spent her early youth in the Dominican Republic. When she was 10, her family returned to the United States and settled in Brooklyn, New York. In 1991, she published her first novel, the critically acclaimed best seller *How the Garcia Girls Lost Their Accents*. Since then, she has written fiction for adults, young adults, and children along with essays and poetry. Much of her work explores the theme of being caught between two cultures.

My Notes

Poetry

I, Too, Sing América

by **Julia Alvarez**

I know it's been said before

but not in this voice

of the plátano[1]

and the mango,

5   marimba y bongó,[2]

not in this sancocho

of inglés

con español.[3]

Ay sí,[4]

10   it's my turn

to oh say

what I see,

I'm going to sing America!

with all América

15   inside me:

from the soles

of Tierra del Fuego[5]

to the thin waist

of Chiriquí[6]

20   up the spine of the Mississippi

through the heartland

of the Yanquis[7]

to the great plain face of Canada —

all of us

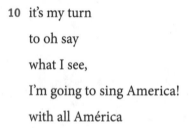

[1] *plátano:* a plantain, starchier and less sweet than a banana and often cooked before eating

[2] *marimba y bongo:* The marimba and the bongo are musical instruments often heard in Latin American music.

[3] *sancocho* of *inglés con español:* a mixture (*sancocho* = "stew") of English with Spanish

[4] *Ay si:* "Oh, yes!"

[5] *Tierra del Fuego:* an archipelago at the very southern tip of South America.

[6] *Chiriquí:* a province in Panama

[7] *Yanquis:* white Americans ("Yankees")

My Notes

25 singing America,

the whole hemispheric

familia[8]

belting our canción,[9]

singing our brown skin

30 into that white

and red and blue song —

the big song

that sings

all America,

35 el canto

que cuenta

con toda América:[10]

un new song![11]

Ya llegó el momento,[12]

40 our moment

under the sun—

ese sol[13] that shines

on everyone.

So, hit it maestro!

45 give us that Latin beat,

¡Uno-dos-tres![14]

One-two-three!

Ay sí,

(y bilingually):[15]

50 Yo también soy América[16]

I, too, am America.

---

[8] *familia*: family
[9] *canción*: song
[10] *el canto que cuenta con toda América*: the singing that includes all of America
[11] *un* new song!: a new song!
[12] *Ya llegó el momento*: The time has come.
[13] *ese sol*: that sun
[14] *¡Uno-dos-tres!*: one, two, three!
[15] *(y bilingually)*: (and in two languages)
[16] *Yo también soy América*: I, too, am America.

Making Observations

- What images come to your mind as you read the poem?
- What do you notice about the mixture of Spanish and English in the poem?

Returning to the Text

- Return to the poems as you respond to the following questions. Use text evidence to support your responses.
- Write any additional questions you have about the texts in your Reader/Writer Notebook.

Hughes

1. What effect does the word *too* in the first line of the Hughes poem have on the poem's voice?

   _____

   _____

   _____

   _____

2. What effect do the short lines in Hughes's poem have on its rhythm, as compared to the long lines in Whitman's poem?

   _____

   _____

   _____

   _____

3. What change does the speaker hint at in lines 8–10? How will life be different for the speaker after "Tomorrow"?

   _____

   _____

   _____

   _____

Alvarez

4. Who is the intended audience for Julia Alvarez's "I, Too, Sing América"?

_____

_____

_____

_____

5. In lines 16–27, what imagery does Alvarez use to reference the history and heritage of those who live in "América"? What is that imagery's purpose? Explain.

_____

_____

_____

_____

_____

6. What effect is created by the bilingual content of Alvarez's poem?

_____

_____

_____

_____

Working from the Text

7. The two poems in this activity and Walt Whitman's "I Hear America Singing" from Activity 1.10 all reflect a unique experience of what it means to be an American. Use the chart to record examples of the language each author uses to inform readers of their experience, as well as the tone the author uses.

Title	Description of Experience	Tone	Evidence
"I Hear America Singing"			
"I, Too"			
"I, Too, Sing América"			

8. Reread Whitman's poems from Activity 1.10. How might Whitman's poems have inspired Alvarez's and Hughes's works? Cite similar words or phrases that connect the central ideas of all three poets.

✅ Check Your Understanding

Consider what the speakers in "I Hear American Singing," "I, Too" and "I, Too, Sing América" want us to know about the American Dream. Write a sentence stating what their visions have in common. Write another sentence or two stating how the vision of each is unique.

✎ Writing to Sources: Informational Text

Write a short essay comparing and contrasting how the three poems "I Hear America Singing," "I, Too" and "I, Too, Sing América" use the image of singing. Think about both the denotative and connotative meanings of the word *sing*. In your writing, be sure to:

- Begin with a clear thesis that states your position about what the three poems mean by the word *sing*.
- Include examples of diction and imagery from both texts to support each claim you make about similarities and differences in meaning.
- Include clear transitions between points and a concluding statement that reinforces your thesis.

A Hyphenated American

My Notes

Learning Targets

- Support the analysis of a text with appropriate evidence.
- Analyze and evaluate the effectiveness of the structure of an informational text.

Preview

In this activity, you will read an essay about being a "hyphenated American."

As You Read

- Underline details that vividly indicate the author's feelings about her Japanese heritage.
- Draw a dotted line under details that vividly indicate the author's feelings about her American reality.
- Circle unknown words and phrases. Try to determine the meaning of the words by using context clues, word parts, or a dictionary.

About the Author

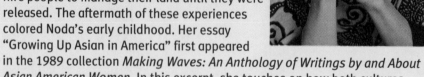

Kesaya E. Noda (b. 1950) was born in California and grew up in New Hampshire as the grandchild of Japanese immigrants. Her first book, *The Yamato Colony*, describes the history of the California farming community in which her parents grew up, married, and gave birth to her. (*Yamato* is an ancient word for "Japanese.") That community was founded in 1910 by a group of people of Japanese ancestry. When Japanese-Americans were sent to internment camps 30 years later during World War II, the residents of Yamato had to hire people to manage their land until they were released. The aftermath of these experiences colored Noda's early childhood. Her essay "Growing Up Asian in America" first appeared in the 1989 collection *Making Waves: An Anthology of Writings by and About Asian American Women*. In this excerpt, she touches on how both cultures have shaped her beliefs and character.

Essay

Growing Up Asian in America

by **Kesaya E. Noda**

1   Sometimes when I was growing up, my identity seemed to hurtle toward me and paste itself right to my face. I felt that way, encountering the stereotypes of my race **perpetuated** by non-Japanese people (primarily white) who may or may not have had contact with other Japanese in America. "You don't like cheese, do you?" someone would ask. "I know your people don't like cheese." Sometimes questions came making allusions to history. That was another aspect of the identity. Events that had happened quite apart from the me who stood silent in that moment connected my face with an incomprehensible past. "Your parents were in California? Were they in those camps during the war?" And sometimes there were phrases or nicknames: "Lotus Blossom." I was sometimes addressed or referred to as racially Japanese, sometimes as Japanese-American, and sometimes as an Asian woman. Confusions and distortions abounded.

2   How is one to know and define oneself? From the inside—within a context that is self-defined, from a grounding in a community and a connection with culture and history that are comfortably accepted? Or from the outside—in terms of messages received from the media and people who are often ignorant? Even as an adult I can still see two sides of my face and past. I can see from the inside out, in freedom. And I can see from the outside in, driven by the old voices of childhood and lost in anger and fear.

I AM RACIALLY JAPANESE

3   A voice from my childhood says: "You are other. You are less than. You are unalterably alien." This voice has its own history. We have indeed been seen as other and alien since the early years of our arrival in the United States. The very first immigrants were welcomed and sought as laborers to replace the dwindling numbers of Chinese, whose influx had been cut off by the Chinese Exclusion Act of 1882. The Japanese fell natural heir to the same anti-Asian prejudice that had arisen against the Chinese. As soon as they began striking for better wages, they were no longer welcomed.

4   I can see myself today as a person historically defined by law and custom as being forever alien. Being neither "free white," nor "African," our people in California were deemed "aliens, ineligible for citizenship," no matter how long they intended to stay here. Aliens ineligible for citizenship were prohibited from owning, buying, or leasing land. They did not and could not belong here. The voice in me remembers that I am always a *Japanese*-American in the eyes of many. A third-generation German-American is an American. A third-generation Japanese-American is a Japanese-American. Being Japanese means being a danger to the country during the war and knowing how to use chopsticks. I wear this history on my face.

GRAMMAR & USAGE

Hyphens

Writers often use **hyphens** to join two or more words into a single adjective or concept called a **compound adjective**. Hyphens in a compound adjective help readers see that two or more words are being linked together to function as one adjective: *third-generation, 90-year-old*. Hyphens also allow writers to combine the meanings of two or more words to create a new word that conveys a specific concept or idea. These words are usually used as nouns or adjectives and often include proper nouns: *Japanese-American, anti-Asian*. What different meanings does the author bring to the hyphenated word *Japanese-American*?

---

perpetuated: continued, sustained

5 I move to the other side. I see a different light and claim a different context. My race is a line that stretches across ocean and time to link me to the shrine where my grandmother was raised. Two high, white banners lift in the wind at the top of the stone steps leading to the shrine. It is time for the summer festival. Black characters are written against the sky as boldly as the clouds, as lightly as kites, as sharply as the big black crows I used to see above the fields in New Hampshire. At festival time there is liquor and food, ritual, discipline, and abandonment. There is music and drunkenness and **invocation**. There is hope. Another season has come. Another season has gone.

6 I am racially Japanese. I have a certain claim to this crazy place where the prayers **intoned** by a neighboring Shinto[1] priest (standing in for my grandmother's nephew who is sick) are drowned out by the rehearsals for the pop singing contest in which most of the villagers will compete later that night. The village elders, the priest, and I stand respectfully upon the immaculate, shining wooden floor of the outer shrine, bowing our heads before the hidden powers. During the patchy intervals when I can hear him, I notice the priest has a stutter. His voice flutters up to my ears only occasionally because two men and a woman are singing gustily into a microphone in the compound, testing the sound system. A pre-recorded tape of guitars, **samisens**, and drums accompanies them. Rock music and Shinto prayers. That night, to loud applause and cheers, a young man is given the award for the most netsuretsu— passionate, burning—rendition of a song. We roar our approval of the reward. Never mind that his voice had wandered and slid, now slightly above, now slightly below the given line of the melody. Netsuretsu. Netsuretsu.

7 In the morning, my grandmother's sister kneels at the foot of the stone stairs to offer her morning prayers. She is too crippled to climb the stairs, so each morning she kneels here upon the path. She shuts her eyes for a few seconds, her motions as matter of fact as when she washes rice. I linger longer than she does, so reluctant to leave, savoring the connection I feel with my grandmother in America, the past, and the power that lives and shines in the morning sun.

8 Our family has served this shrine for generations. The family's need to protect this claim to identity and place outweighs any individual claim to any individual hope. I am Japanese.

I AM A JAPANESE-AMERICAN

9 "Weak." I hear the voice from my childhood years. "Passive," I hear. Our parents and grandparents were the ones who were put into those camps. They went without resistance; they offered cooperation as proof of loyalty to America. "Victim," I hear. And, "Silent."

10 Our parents are painted as hard workers who were socially uncomfortable and had difficulty expressing even the smallest opinion. Clean, quiet, motivated, and determined to match the American way; that is us, and that is the story of our time here.

invocation: calling upon spirits

intoned: uttered in a singing voice

samisens: a guitar-like Japanese musical instrument

[1] traditional religion of Japan

11 "Why did you go into those camps," I raged at my parents, frightened by my own inner silence and timidity. "Why didn't you do anything to resist? Why didn't you name it the injustice it was?" Couldn't our parents even think? Couldn't they? Why were we so passive?

12 I shift my vision and my stance. I am in California. My uncle is in the midst of the sweet potato harvest. He is pressed, trying to get the harvesting crews onto the field as quickly as possible, worried about the flow of equipment and people. His big pickup is pulled off to the side, motor running, door ajar. I see two tractors in the yard in front of an old shed; the flat bed harvesting platform on which the workers will stand has already been brought over from the other field. It's early morning. The workers stand loosely grouped and at ease, but my uncle looks as **harried** and tense as a police officer trying to unsnarl a New York City traffic jam. Driving toward the shed, I pull my car off the road to make way for an approaching tractor. The front wheels of the car sink luxuriously into the soft, white sand by the roadside and the car slides to a dreamy halt, tail still on the road. I try to move forward. I try to move back. The front bites contentedly into the sand, the back lifts itself at a jaunty angle. My uncle sees me and storms down the road, running. He is shouting before he is even near me.

13 "What the matter with you," he screams. "What the hell are you doing?" In his frenzy, he grabs his hat off his head and slashes it through the air across his knee. He is beside himself. "You've blocked the whole roadway. How am I supposed to get my tractors out of here? Can't you use your head? You've cut off the whole roadway, and we've got to get out of here."

14 I stand on the road before him helplessly thinking, "No, I don't know how to drive in sand. I've never driven in sand."

15 "I'm sorry, uncle," I say, burying a smile beneath a look of sincere apology. I notice my deep amusement and my affection for him with great curiosity. I am usually devastated by anger. Not this time.

16 During the several years that follow I learn about the people and the place, and much more about what has happened in this California village where my parents grew up. The issei, our grandparents, made this settlement in the desert. Their first crops were eaten by rabbits and ravaged by insects. The land was so barren that men walking from house to house sometimes got lost. Women came here too. They bore children in 114 degree heat, then carried the babies with them into the fields to nurse when they reached the end of each row of grapes or other truck farm crops.

17 I had had no idea what it meant to buy this kind of land and make it grow green. Or how, when the war came, there was no space at all for the subtlety of being who we were—Japanese-Americans. Either/or was the way. I hadn't understood that people were literally afraid for their lives then, that their money had been frozen in banks; that there was a five-mile travel limit; that when the early evening curfew came and they were inside their houses, some of them watched helplessly as people they knew went into their barns to

My Notes

harried: anxious, worried

My Notes

steal their belongings. The police were patrolling the road, interested only in violators of curfew. There was no help for them in the face of thievery. I had not been able to imagine before what it must have felt like to be an American—to know absolutely that one is an American—and yet to have almost everyone else deny it. Not only deny it, but challenge that identity with machine guns and troops of white American soldiers. In those circumstances it was difficult to say, "I'm a Japanese-American." "American" had to do.

18 But now I can say that I am a Japanese-American. It means I have a place here in this country, too. I have a place here on the East Coast, where our neighbor is so much a part of our family that my mother never passes her house at night without glancing at the lights to see if she is home and safe; where my parents have hauled hundreds of pounds of rocks from fields and arduously planted Christmas trees and blueberries, lilacs, asparagus, and crab apples; where my father still dreams of angling a stream to a new bed so that he can dig a pond in the field and fill it with water and fish. "The neighbors already came for their Christmas tree?" he asks in December. "Did they like it? Did they like it?"

19 I have a place on the West Coast where my relatives still farm, where I heard the stories of feuds and backbiting, and where I saw that people survived and flourished because fundamentally they trusted and relied upon one another. A death in the family is not just a death in a family; it is a death in the community. I saw people help each other with money, materials, labor, attention, and time. I saw men gather once a year, without fail, to clean the grounds of a ninety-year-old woman who had helped the community before, during, and after the war. I saw her remembering them with birthday cards sent to each of their children.

20 I come from a people with a long memory and a distinctive grace. We live our thanks. And we are Americans. Japanese-Americans. ...

Making Observations
- Whom do we meet in the essay?
- What emotions do you feel while reading the essay?

angling: turn in a different direction

Returning to the Text

- Return to the essay as you respond to the following questions. Use text evidence to support your responses.
- Write any additional questions you have about the text in your Reader/Writer Notebook.

1. In paragraphs 3 and 4, the author uses the word *alien* to describe how she feels other people view her and how she has come to view herself. Consult a print or online dictionary to examine the possible meanings of that word. How might the word convey the author's discomfort with herself?

_____

_____

_____

_____

2. In paragraph 4, what inference can you make about the author's feelings when she states, "A third-generation Japanese-American is a Japanese-American"?

_____

_____

_____

_____

3. How do the essay's two headings relate to the author's purpose?

_____

_____

_____

_____

4. By the end of the essay, the author "can say that I am Japanese-American." What change has brought this decision about?

_____

_____

_____

_____

5. Each section of this essay is based upon a different central idea. What is the central idea of each?

_____

_____

_____

_____

_____

Working from the Text

6. What is the author's purpose in this essay?

_____

_____

_____

_____

7. With a partner, review and discuss the text structure of "Growing Up Asian in America." Outline that text structure, noting subtitles and providing a brief summary of each part's content.

First Part:

Second Part:

Third Part:

8. What type of text structure (chronological, sequential, cause-and-effect, order of importance, or compare-and-contrast) does Noda use to structure her essay? How does the division of the text into three parts serve the author's purpose?

_____

_____

_____

_____

9. Describe the process the author undergoes as the story progresses.

_____

_____

_____

_____

10. How did the author's environment play a role in how she viewed herself and her race?

_____

_____

_____

_____

11. Discuss as a group the different aspects of being American. Then write a definition of the term _American_. You may wish to consult your vocabulary tree from Activity 1.9 to help you compose your definition. Include details from the essay to support your definition.

_____

_____

_____

_____

☑ Check Your Understanding

In a few sentences, explain how the text structure of "Growing Up Asian in America" supports understanding of the information it presents.

Drafting Your Definition Essay

Learning Strategies

Brainstorming
Drafting

My Notes

Learning Targets

- Synthesize information from a variety of text types.
- Plan a piece of writing appropriate for a purpose and audience by generating ideas using brainstorming, discussion, and a graphic organizer.
- Develop drafts into a focused, structured, and coherent piece of writing.

Preview

In this activity, you will plan and develop a draft of your definition essay.

Planning Your Definition Essay

1. Return to your vocabulary tree where you began to record the multiple aspects of a definition of an American and refine or add to any of your ideas as needed.

2. **Collaborative Discussion:** Turn and talk to your neighbors about each other's vocabulary trees. What details and examples do you have in common? What new ideas have been generated from the conversation that you could include in your essay?

3. How would you define the concept of an American? Think about the definition strategies you have learned—negation, function, exemplification, and classification—that will help you prove or support your thesis or definition of what it means to be an American. Use the following graphic organizer to record your responses. Remember to keep in mind your purpose and audience as you plan your essay.

The Definition of an American	
Rhetorical Strategies for Defining a Concept	**Supporting Evidence, Pertinent Examples, Commentary, and Summary**
Negation (What is not an American?)	
Function (What does an American do?)	
Exemplification (Who are some examples of Americans?)	
Classification (What are types of Americans?)	

Developing Your Definition Essay

Use the following outline to help you develop your essay defining the word American. As you execute your essay-writing process, remember to focus on your topic, your purpose (to inform), and your audience (your teacher and fellow students).

Part One: Introductory Paragraph

Begin with a dictionary definition of the word *American*. This will give your reader a familiar focus from which you can proceed. Follow the definition with your thesis statement, which should present your own definition broken down according to the rhetorical device or devices you have chosen to use (classification, exemplification, negation, function). Keep your thesis as short as you can while still maintaining completeness. You will elaborate on the individual pieces of your definition in your body paragraphs.

Introductory Paragraph:

_____

_____

_____

_____

_____

Part Two: Body Paragraphs

For this activity, restrict your number of body paragraphs to three or four at the very most. Each body paragraph will explore a piece of your definition as you broke it down in your introduction. State each piece in a topic sentence that begins a paragraph. This is the place for details and commentary that support your definition. As you compose your individual body paragraphs, remember that you are free to make further use of any rhetorical device that helps place your information in a useful context.

Body Paragraphs:

_____

_____

_____

_____

_____

_____

_____

_____

_____

_____

_____

_____

_____

Part Three: Conclusion Paragraph

Your final paragraph should be mostly a simple summary of the main points of your essay (without directly repeating your introduction or topic sentences). If you find yourself inserting new information, examine your body paragraphs. If the information is relevant, it should fit into one of your body topics. If not, either revisit your definition or discard the information.

Avoid an overly dramatic or forced final sentence. At the same time, your conclusion should leave your reader with a sense that you have fully explained your definition. No vague ideas or unanswered questions should remain in the reader's mind when he or she is done with your text.

Conclusion Paragraph:

_____

_____

_____

_____

_____

Revising and Editing

Learning Targets

- Revise drafts to improve clarity, development, organization, style, diction, and sentence fluency both within and between sentences.
- Edit drafts to demonstrate a command of standard English convention using a style guide.
- Publish written work for appropriate audiences.

Preview

In this activity, you will revise and edit your definition essay in preparation for publication.

Revising and Editing Your Essay

Once you have completed the first draft of your essay, you may be tempted to consider your work finished. Good writers rarely assume that their first effort is the best they can do. They subject their text to a two-part process called revision and editing (sometimes many, many times over).

- **Revision** is the process of taking a second look at your ideas. Reread the text as though someone else has written it. With an eye on clarity, development, style, diction, and fluency, ask yourself: *What would make these ideas clearer and more convincing?* Sometimes it's a matter of rewording them; other times changing the order of the text, adding a supporting detail, or choosing a more powerful word will create improvement. If a sentence feels like it was grafted in from another essay, it's best to either rewrite it or remove it. As you revise, be sure to look closely at the rhetorical devices you use in your analysis.

1. Reexamine the first draft of your essay. Use what you have learned about the revision process to improve the clarity and fluency of your text. Describe what you revised and why.

_____

_____

_____

_____

- **Editing** is a look at the "nuts and bolts" of your text. It is where you correct misspelled words, fix punctuation errors, and resolve any problems with sentence structure. This is a process for which a style guide often comes in handy. A style guide is a collection of rules for writing. Popular style guides for general writing include *The Elements of Style, The Associated Press Stylebook*, and *The Chicago Manual of Style*. Other good style guides exist for writing in specific fields (science, medical, etc.).

2. Edit your first draft, using an online or print style guide. Describe your edits.

_____

_____

_____

My Notes

It's best to treat revision and editing as two separate processes. That lets you focus exclusively on several equally important areas. Because revision deals with the "big picture"—clarity and development of your ideas—it's important to revise first and then edit, as you may add, delete, or rewrite sentences in the revising stage.

Peer Revising and Editing

After you have revised and edited your first draft, it is often a good idea to get feedback from another writer. Choose a partner or have your teacher choose one for you. Swap your definition essays with each other and politely critique (evaluate and analyze) them. Point out the strengths you notice in your partner's essay and suggest changes that might improve the essay if they seem appropriate. Review any concerns or suggestions from your partner and consider how you can use that feedback to make your own essay better.

You might consider repeating this process until your text reads just the way you'd like it to. At that point, it's time to publish your work, or distribute it to your audience.

Setting a Purpose for Viewing

Some images have become a part of the story of the United States. Photographs from an event or of a person often capture some of the essence of what it is to be an American. What makes some images more iconic than the rest is the impact they have on the person viewing the image. There is a point at which an image has a strong enough impact that it becomes a part of our national story and collective memory.

Robert Hariman and John Louis Lucaites define the term *iconic image* in their article "Performing Civic Identity: The Iconic Photograph of the Flag Raising on Iwo Jima": "Iconic photographs are widely recognized as representations of significant historical events, activate strong emotional response, and are reproduced across a range of media, genres, or topics."

American Marines raising flag on Mount Suribachi, Iwo Jima, 1945, taken by Joe Rosenthal on February 23, 1945.

Working from the Text

3. Explain the strong emotional response that this image activates. What makes it an iconic American image?

4. Revisit your vocabulary tree and add details to your working definition of what it means to be an American.

Research Review

Review your familiarity with primary and secondary sources. For the essay you will write for Embedded Assessment 1, explaining your definition is central; the sources should support your explanation.

Primary sources are original documents containing firsthand information about a subject (e.g., letters or diaries). A secondary source is a discussion or commentary about primary sources, offering an interpretation about information gathered from a primary source (e.g., history books or encyclopedias).

To help ensure that you use substantial, accurate, and timely sources to support your position, it is important to consider each source's validity, reliability, and relevancy.

Validity: Does the information appear to be accurate and well documented? Is there a bibliography or list of sources? Does the information appear to be free from bias, or does it present only a single position?

Reliability: Are the author's name and qualifications clearly identified? Is the information from a respected institution (e.g., a university)? If it is an online resource, is the site listed as .gov, .edu, or .org rather than .com?

Relevance: Is the information closely related to your topic? Does it offer support with facts or other information you can quote to support your position?

Researching Iconic American Images

Research and find your own idea of an iconic American image. You will submit an image for your classroom's Gallery of America and provide an explanation of your choice to share with your fellow students.

5. As you think about what iconic American image you will add to the classroom gallery, revisit your vocabulary tree and the images you highlighted in the poem. With a partner, brainstorm a list of significant events that you can remember from history, news, or life.

   As you research your iconic American image, keep in mind the three elements of significant images:

   • The image is widely recognized as representative of a significant historical event.
   • The image evokes strong emotional response.
   • The image has been reproduced across a range of media, genres, or topics.

Selecting a Topic

6. Select one or two items on your list and expand your thinking with some notes on what you already know about the topic. Consider these questions as you think about your topics: How is this topic historically relevant for most Americans? What key words are associated with this topic?

   Select one topic as the subject of your gallery submission and begin your research.

Researching Your Image

7. Pictures are everywhere: on the Internet, in print media, and in history books. Internet image searches can be refined to locate black-and-white images, color images, fine art, and so on. Where will you find the most useful information? Use the ideas and the key words that you generated to guide your review of reliable sources. Print a copy of your iconic image and create a plaque with a description, title, and photographic credit.

Your image:

When it was created:

Why it is iconic:

Why you chose it:

Presenting Your Image

After all images and descriptions have been added to the Gallery of America, prepare a brief presentation of your image for your peers. This presentation should introduce the image, provide some background knowledge, and explain the significance of the image and why you chose it.

In pairs, go through the exhibit, listening to each presenter's brief explanation of his or her iconic image. After you have seen and heard all of the presentations, add additional thoughts and details to your vocabulary tree for defining the term *American*.

☑ Check Your Understanding

Review the presentations that you have seen and select two images you would add to the permanent exhibit of iconic American images. Write your choices and the reasons for your selection on a feedback card.

🔒 Independent Reading Checkpoint

Review the text or texts you have read independently so far in this unit and the different viewpoints expressed. Then write a statement that summarizes your impressions of how the authors or subjects experienced the American Dream.

Writing a Definition Essay

ASSIGNMENT

Your assignment is to write a multi-paragraph essay that defines your interpretation of what it means to be an American. This essay should use the strategies of definition and different perspectives from the unit to help you develop a complex and thoughtful definition. If possible, incorporate an iconic image into your essay.

Planning and Prewriting	■ What prewriting strategy will help you define what it means to be an American (free writing, webbing, graphic organizer)?
	■ What pieces of writing from this unit did you connect strongly with? How can they help to add depth and dimension to your definition?
	■ How can you share your ideas with a peer to help you select the strongest material to include in your draft?
Drafting	■ How will you take the complex elements of your definition and work them into a clear, focused thesis statement?
	■ How can you sequence your ideas so that they work together to build a clear and convincing definition?
	■ What strategies of definition work well with your selected evidence and ideas?
Evaluating and Revising	■ Does your essay have coherence? Does it present ideas that tie together and flow smoothly, making the essay easy to follow for the reader?
	■ Does your essay have specific, varied diction and a variety of sentence patterns?
	■ Where can you add or revise transitions so that one idea smoothly leads to another?
	■ How can you use the Scoring Guide as a tool to evaluate your draft or to seek out feedback from others?
Editing and Publishing	■ How will you check your writing for grammatical and technical accuracy?
	■ What sort of outside resources can help you to check your draft (e.g., a format guide, a dictionary)?
	■ What is an effective way to use the last read-through of your essay to make final adjustments (e.g., read it out loud or have a peer read it to you)?

Reflection

After completing this Embedded Assessment, think about how you went about accomplishing this assignment and respond to the following:

- In what ways did the process of defining what it means to be an American cause you to rethink or reevaluate your own ideas?
- Did the material that you read in this unit have a role in this? Why or why not?

Scoring Criteria	Exemplary	Proficient	Emerging	Incomplete
Ideas	The essay • asserts a focused, clearly stated thesis • develops and supports the thesis thoroughly with relevant, significant, and substantial facts and quotations • synthesizes information on multiple, relevant perspectives	The essay • asserts a clear thesis • develops and supports the thesis with relevant facts and quotations • incorporates information on various perspectives	The essay • presents an unfocused or limited thesis • attempts to develop and support the thesis with weak evidence that may not be appropriate • inconsistently incorporates information on various perspectives	The essay • asserts a weak thesis • contains facts, quotations, or other information that may not develop or support the topic • contains insufficient information on various perspectives
Structure	The essay • organizes complex ideas so that new elements build to create a unified whole • creates an effective and engaging introduction and conclusion that articulate the significance of the topic • uses a variety of definition strategies with skill and purpose • uses a variety of meaningful transitions	The essay • organizes ideas so that each new element builds on that which preceded it to create cohesion • presents a clear and focused introduction and conclusion • uses a variety of definition strategies effectively • uses transitions to connect the larger ideas of the essay	The essay • creates limited cohesion with inconsistent connections among the elements • contains an underdeveloped or unfocused introduction and/or conclusion • attempts to use definition strategies with limited success • inconsistently uses transitions to connect ideas	The essay • demonstrates limited cohesion; expected elements may be missing • lacks an introduction and/or conclusion • uses few or no definition strategies • presents limited use of transitions
Use of Language	The essay • chooses precise diction and a variety of sentence types and structures to enhance the reader's understanding • demonstrates superior command of conventions • integrates and cites textual evidence smoothly	The essay • uses diction and a variety of sentence types or structures that appropriately manage the topic • demonstrates a command of conventions so that minor errors do not interfere with meaning • integrates and cites textual evidence correctly	The essay • uses diction that is inconsistent and provides little variety in sentence structure • attempts to follow conventions, but errors in usage may cause some confusion • uses textual evidence without smooth or correct integration	The essay • uses diction that is inappropriate at times; shows little or no variety in sentence structure • contains errors in grammar, punctuation, capitalization, or spelling that interfere with meaning • contains little or no integrated textual evidence

Unpacking Embedded Assessment 2

Learning Targets

- Reflect on concepts, essential questions, and vocabulary.
- Identify and analyze the knowledge and skills needed to complete Embedded Assessment 2 successfully.
- Compose a reaction statement that takes a specific position.

Preview

In this activity, you will explore the ideas and tasks involved in Embedded Assessment 2.

Making Connections

An important task of every critical thinker is to be able to read and understand the thinking of others. More importantly, as a critical thinker you must be able to gather together many ideas and sort through them to find what you can use and what you can discard in formulating your own thinking. This act of synthesis, or combining, often entails the creative act of constructing your own definitions. Synthesizing your own thoughts, your reading, and your research will lead to your own personal understanding of a complex idea such as the "American Dream."

Essential Questions

You have constructed a personal definition of an American. Now write about your understanding of Essential Question 2: What is the American Dream?

Unpacking Embedded Assessment 2

Closely read the assignment for Embedded Assessment 2: Synthesizing the American Dream.

Your assignment is to synthesize at least three to five sources and your own observations to defend, challenge, or qualify the statement that "America still provides access to the American Dream." This question requires you to integrate a variety of sources (three to five) into a coherent, well-written argumentative essay. Be sure to refer to the sources and employ your own observations to support your position. Your argument should be the focus of your essay; the sources and your observations should support this argument.

With your class, identify and analyze the knowledge you need (what do you need to know?) and the skills you must have (what must you be able to do?) to complete the assignment successfully. Create a graphic organizer as you "unpack" the requirements of Embedded Assessment 2.

Independent Reading Plan

For the second half of this unit, focus your independent reading by selecting texts that reflect either the immigrant experience or growing up in America. Consider how your reading connects to your personal definition of the American Dream. Note examples that will help you support your ideas in your argumentative essay.

My Notes

Survey

As you read each of the following statements, use a scale from 1 to 10 and decide to what extent these ideas are prevalent today. If the idea presented in the statement is something you are exposed to on a regular basis, rate it a 10. If you do not see evidence of the statement at all, rate it a 1 (and remember there are plenty of numbers in between).

_____ 1. Education is the foundation of a free society.

_____ 2. Individuals' rights are superior to the needs of society.

_____ 3. All religious beliefs are protected.

_____ 4. Our government was created to guarantee freedoms.

_____ 5. Education is important primarily to get a job.

_____ 6. Community provides strength and support to individuals.

_____ 7. Human beings are basically good and getting better.

_____ 8. Individual liberties must always be controlled by government authority.

_____ 9. Self-reliance and independence are important to a good life.

_____ 10. Science and progress are closely related.

_____ 11. The American Dream means making lots of money.

_____ 12. Hard work equals success.

_____ 13. Everyone can achieve the American Dream.

_____ 14. The American Dream includes freedom from want.

_____ 15. Sacrifice is part of achieving success and prosperity.

Quickwrite: Reflect on your ratings. Share your responses with a partner or a small group. You might choose to share your responses with the whole class. After discussing, select one statement that you and your partners think is an important part of the American Dream. Defend your position and explain the rationale for your thinking.

The Structure of an Argument

Learning Targets

- Analyze the characteristics and structural elements of argumentative texts.
- Evaluate the effectiveness of an argument.
- Analyze how English usage has changed since the 18th century.

Preview

In this activity, you will read the Declaration of Independence and analyze its effectiveness as a piece of argumentative writing.

Vocabulary of the Declaration of Independence

1. When reading a text from a specific historical period, you will see unfamiliar words that may no longer be used in modern English or had a different meaning when the text was originally written. The Declaration of Independence can be a difficult text to comprehend as it contains both difficult words and unfamiliar words. Familiarize yourself with some of these difficult words by using the definitions in the sidebars of the text to help you complete the sentences.

abdicated	arbitrary	consanguinity	despotism	magnanimity
perfidy	redress	rectitude	unalienable	usurpations

a. The king ruled the land with absolute _____ that no one could question.

b. Robert became king through _____, not through legitimate inheritance.

c. The queen's subjects were in awe of her _____.

d. The harsh punishment for the crime seemed _____ since others received a lighter sentence.

e. The king _____ his position as ruler when he failed to send the troops to protect the gates.

f. The shop owner offered a refund as _____ to customers who bought the faulty merchandise.

g. The crooked queen was guilty of _____ when she refused to obey the treaty.

h. Life, liberty, and the pursuit of happiness are _____ rights in the United States.

i. The _____ of the distant cousins was well known thanks to family records that were kept.

j. Because of her _____, I am certain she is innocent

My Notes

Characteristics and Structural Elements of an Argument

Read through the explanations of the structural elements of arguments with a partner. Discuss each element to ensure you know its purpose and characteristics so you can recognize and use these elements.

Hook

- The hook grabs the reader's attention and interest.
- It establishes a connection between the writer and a specific, identifiable audience, using information about that audience (its concerns, characteristics, and background knowledge) to do so.
- The hook can be but is not limited to an anecdote, an image, a definition, or a quotation.

Arguable Thesis

- The thesis clearly states the writer's **claim** by telling readers what the writer wishes to argue.
- It concisely states the claim in a well-conceived complex sentence.
- It usually comes in the opening paragraph of the text.

Concessions, Refutations, and Rebuttals

- Concessions are used to recognize counterclaims made by the other side.
- Concessions acknowledge counterclaims fairly and thoroughly.
- Refutations are when a writer argues at length against the opposing viewpoint by proving that his or her claim has more validity.
- Rebuttals are when the writer grants that the other side has some validity and then explains why his or her argument is better.
- All three of these techniques build credibility by discussing strengths and limitations with fairness and objectivity.
- Concessions, refutations, and rebuttals are strongest when they anticipate the concerns, characteristics, background knowledge, and position(s) of the audience.

Support

- Support presents facts to convince the audience of the writer's claim.
- It sets out the reasoning behind the writer's argument.
- It provides supporting evidence of the writer's claim (data, quotes, anecdotes, etc.).
- It blends together logical and emotional appeals and takes into account the kinds of appeals that will have the most impact on the audience.

Convincing Conclusion

- A convincing conclusion restates the main claim of the thesis and provides readers with a call to action.
- A convincing conclusion makes a final new appeal to values.
- A convincing conclusion tries not to repeat information but sums up the argument with a few final facts and appeals.
- The **call to action** is a plea to readers to take a specific action that furthers the cause of the argument being made. It gives readers an action item that they can carry out after the writer has convinced them to support the cause.

As You Read

- Underline strong words and phrases that could appeal to a reader's emotions.
- Circle unknown words and phrases. Try to determine the meaning of the words by using context clues, word parts, or a dictionary.

About the Document

The Declaration of Independence, written primarily by Thomas Jefferson, was adopted by the Continental Congress on July 4, 1776. It announced to King George III of Great Britain that the 13 British colonies in North America had decided to become an independent nation. The colonies had been at war with Great Britain for over a year, fighting for their rights under the British Empire. By the summer of 1776, however, the colonists had decided that reconciliation would be impossible and that they needed to be entirely independent from Great Britain. Today, the declaration is considered a foundational document of the United States because it outlines the beliefs of the people who gave birth to the idea of America.

Historical Document

The Declaration of Independence

Chunk 1

1   When in the Course of human events, it becomes necessary for one people to dissolve the political bands which have connected them with another, and to assume among the powers of the earth, the separate and equal station to which the Laws of Nature and of Nature's God entitle them, a decent respect to the opinions of mankind requires that they should declare the causes which impel them to the separation.

2   We hold these truths to be self-evident, that all men are created equal, that they are endowed by their Creator with certain unalienable Rights, that among these are Life, Liberty and the pursuit of Happiness.—That to secure these rights, Governments are instituted among Men, deriving their just powers from the consent of the governed,—That whenever any Form of Government becomes destructive of these ends, it is the Right of the People to alter or to abolish it, and to institute new Government, laying its foundation on such principles and organizing its powers in such form, as to them shall seem most likely to effect their Safety and Happiness. Prudence, indeed, will dictate that Governments long established should not be changed for light and transient causes; and accordingly all experience hath shewn, that mankind are more disposed to suffer, while evils are sufferable, than to right themselves by

> impel: to drive forward, force
> unalienable: unable to be taken away

My Notes

abolishing the forms to which they are accustomed. But when a long train of abuses and **usurpations**, pursuing invariably the same Object evinces a design to reduce them under absolute **Despotism**, it is their right, it is their duty, to throw off such Government, and to provide new Guards for their future security. Such has been the patient sufferance of these Colonies; and such is now the necessity which constrains them to alter their former Systems of Government. The history of the present King of Great Britain is a history of repeated injuries and usurpations, all having in direct object the establishment of an absolute Tyranny over these States. To prove this, let Facts be submitted to a candid world.

Chunk 2

3   He has refused his Assent to Laws, the most wholesome and necessary for the public good.

4   He has forbidden his Governors to pass Laws of immediate and pressing importance, unless suspended in their operation till his Assent should be obtained; and when so suspended, he has utterly neglected to attend to them.

5   He has refused to pass other Laws for the accommodation of large districts of people, unless those people would relinquish the right of Representation in the Legislature, a right inestimable to them and formidable to tyrants only.

6   He has called together legislative bodies at places unusual, uncomfortable, and distant from the depository of their public Records, for the sole purpose of fatiguing them into compliance with his measures.

7   He has dissolved Representative Houses repeatedly, for opposing with manly firmness his invasions on the rights of the people.

8   He has refused for a long time, after such dissolutions, to cause others to be elected; whereby the Legislative powers, incapable of Annihilation, have returned to the People at large for their exercise; the State remaining in the mean time exposed to all the dangers of invasion from without, and convulsions within.

9   He has endeavoured to prevent the population of these States; for that purpose obstructing the Laws for Naturalization of Foreigners; refusing to pass others to encourage their migrations hither, and raising the conditions of new Appropriations of Lands.

10   He has obstructed the Administration of Justice, by refusing his Assent to Laws for establishing Judiciary powers.

11   He has made Judges dependent on his Will alone, for the tenure of their offices, and the amount and payment of their salaries.

12   He has erected a multitude of New Offices, and sent hither swarms of Officers to harrass our people, and eat out their substance.

usurpations: acts of wrongfully taking over a right or power that belongs to someone else

despotism: a political system where the ruler holds absolute power

13 He has kept among us, in times of peace, Standing Armies without the Consent of our legislatures.

14 He has affected to render the Military independent of and superior to the Civil power.

15 He has combined with others to subject us to a jurisdiction foreign to our constitution, and unacknowledged by our laws; giving his Assent to their Acts of pretended Legislation:

Chunk 3

16 For Quartering large bodies of armed troops among us:

17 For protecting them, by a mock Trial, from punishment for any Murders which they should commit on the Inhabitants of these States:

18 For cutting off our Trade with all parts of the world:

19 For imposing Taxes on us without our Consent:

20 For depriving us in many cases, of the benefits of Trial by Jury:

21 For transporting us beyond Seas to be tried for pretended offences

22 For abolishing the free System of English Laws in a neighbouring Province, establishing therein an Arbitrary government, and enlarging its Boundaries so as to render it at once an example and fit instrument for introducing the same absolute rule into these Colonies:

23 For taking away our Charters, abolishing our most valuable Laws, and altering fundamentally the Forms of our Governments:

24 For suspending our own Legislatures and declaring themselves invested with power to legislate for us in all cases whatsoever.

Chunk 4

25 He has abdicated Government here, by declaring us out of his Protection and waging War against us.

26 He has plundered our seas, ravaged our Coasts, burnt our towns, and destroyed the lives of our people.

27 He is at this time transporting large Armies of foreign Mercenaries to compleat the works of death, desolation and tyranny, already begun with circumstances of Cruelty & perfidy scarcely paralleled in the most barbarous ages, and totally unworthy the Head of a civilized nation.

28 He has constrained our fellow Citizens taken Captive on the high Seas to bear Arms against their Country, to become the executioners of their friends and Brethren, or to fall themselves by their Hands.

29 He has excited domestic insurrections amongst us, and has endeavoured to bring on the inhabitants of our frontiers, the merciless Indian Savages, whose known rule of warfare, is an undistinguished destruction of all ages, sexes and conditions.

WORD CONNECTIONS

Roots and Affixes
The word jurisdiction contains two Latin roots. The first is *jur-*, which means "right, law." The second is *dic-* or *dict-*, which means "to say." The suffix *-ion* means "act of." What then does *jurisdiction* mean?

My Notes

arbitrary: based on unpredictable decisions rather than law
abdicated: failed to fulfill a responsibility or duty
perfidy: deceitfulness, treachery

My Notes

_____
_____
_____
_____
_____
_____
_____
_____
_____
_____
_____

30 In every stage of these Oppressions We have Petitioned for Redress in the most humble terms: Our repeated Petitions have been answered only by repeated injury. A Prince whose character is thus marked by every act which may define a Tyrant, is unfit to be the ruler of a free people.

Chunk 5

31 Nor have We been wanting in attentions to our British brethren. We have warned them from time to time of attempts by their legislature to extend an unwarrantable jurisdiction over us. We have reminded them of the circumstances of our emigration and settlement here. We have appealed to their native justice and magnanimity, and we have conjured them by the ties of our common kindred to disavow these usurpations, which would inevitably interrupt our connections and correspondence. They too have been deaf to the voice of justice and of consanguinity. We must, therefore, acquiesce in the necessity, which denounces our Separation, and hold them, as we hold the rest of mankind, Enemies in War, in Peace Friends.

32 We, therefore, the Representatives of the United States of America, in General Congress, Assembled, appealing to the Supreme Judge of the world for the rectitude of our intentions, do, in the Name, and by Authority of the good People of these Colonies, solemnly publish and declare, That these United Colonies are, and of Right ought to be Free and Independent States; that they are Absolved from all Allegiance to the British Crown, and that all political connection between them and the State of Great Britain, is and ought to be totally dissolved; and that as Free and Independent States, they have full Power to levy War, conclude Peace, contract Alliances, establish Commerce, and to do all other Acts and Things which Independent States may of right do. And for the support of this Declaration, with a firm reliance on the protection of divine Providence, we mutually pledge to each other our Lives, our Fortunes and our sacred Honor.

Making Observations
- What emotions did you feel while reading this text?
- Which "injuries and usurpations" stand out most to you?

redress: the correction of wrong, compensation

magnanimity: the condition of being high-minded, noble

consanguinity: having the same origin or ancestry

rectitude: morally correct behavior or thinking

Returning to the Text

- Return to the historical document as you respond to the following questions. Use text evidence to support your responses.
- Write any additional questions you have about the text in your Reader/Writer Notebook.

2. According to the text, what five truths are held to be "self-evident"?

_____
_____
_____
_____

3. In paragraph 2, why does the author include the line "To prove this, let the Facts be submitted to a candid world"?

_____
_____
_____
_____

4. What does the word *assent* mean, based on how it is used in paragraph 3?

_____
_____
_____
_____

5. What function do the grievances against the king listed in Chunks 2–4 serve in the argument?

_____
_____
_____
_____

6. What rhetorical appeals does this foundational U.S. document make in paragraph 29? What effect do they have on the audience?

_____
_____
_____
_____

7. How does the author's use of the term *unwarrantable jurisdiction* in paragraph 31 affect the reader's perception of the English's treatment of the Americans?

_____

_____

_____

_____

8. What effect does the authors' use of enumeration have on their argument?

_____

_____

_____

_____

_____

 Gaining Perspectives

The Declaration of Independence is considered one of the foundational documents of the United States. In it, the founding fathers laid out the wrongs King George inflicted on his colonial subjects and also created a new way for a government to function. With a partner, discuss the reasons why the colonies wanted to form their own nation as well as the following questions:

- What would it have been like to be a creator and signer of the Declaration of Independence?
- What risks were these men taking?
- What do you think the creators would say of our modern application of the principles of American democracy?

When you are done, summarize your discussion in your Reader/Writer Notebook.

Working from the Text

9. Reread the text with a partner and note the characteristics and structural elements of argumentation in the following graphic organizer.

Characteristics and Structural Elements of an Argument	Details from the Declaration of Independence
Audience	
The Hook	
The Claim	
Concessions and Refutations	
Support	
Call to Action	

INDEPENDENT READING LINK

Read and Discuss

Meet with a partner or small group to discuss the independent reading you have completed so far. How do your readings challenge or support your definition of the American Dream? Do the subjects or narrators in your readings believe the American Dream is worth fighting for or no longer exists?

10. **Discussion Prompt:** In what ways did declaring independence protect the unalienable rights of the people of the United States? With a partner, create a list of ways unalienable rights will be protected.

☑ Check Your Understanding

Choose a sentence from the document that struck you as particularly important or strong. Rewrite the sentence using modern English. Briefly note whether the new version carries the same weight and meaning.

 Writing to Sources: Informational Text

What is the modern American Dream? How do the foundational documents of American life still support the American Dream today? Write an explanatory essay in which you explain how you think the ideas in this document, as well as those in the Preamble to the Constitution of the United States and the Bill of Rights, contribute to the idea of the American Dream. Be sure to:

- Introduce your thesis that clearly defines the American Dream and how the foundational documents support the modern evolution of that dream. Explain how the foundational documents are still relevant today.

- Use significant elements from the founding documents as support of your ideas. Maintain a formal and objective tone while using appropriate vocabulary to develop the body of your essay.

- Vary your transitions from your points and support to create a cohesive essay.

Annotating an Argumentative Text

Learning Strategies

Marking the Text
Paraphrasing
Quickwrite

Learning Targets

- Recognize and analyze characteristics and structural elements of an argument.
- Defend or challenge the author's claims using relevant text evidence and appeals to logic and emotion.

Preview

In this activity, you will read an article to evaluate the author's argument.

About the Author

David Wallechinsky (b. 1948) is a historian and author. In 1975, he published *The People's Almanac*, a collection of facts and general interest articles on a wide range of subjects. While informative, it was written as a book that people could read for pleasure. Wallechinsky was a founding member of the International Society of Olympic Historians (ISOH) and is founder and editor-in-chief of AllGov.com, a website that provides news updates about departments and agencies of the federal government. His personal library contains about 35,000 volumes.

As You Read

- Put a star next to the author's main arguments.
- Underline key evidence that supports those arguments.
- Use the margin to ask questions that clarify your understanding or challenge the author's position or evidence.

My Notes

Article

Is the American Dream Still Possible?

by **David Wallechinsky,** *Parade,* **October 2014**

1   *To be "middle class" in America once meant living well and having financial security. But today that comfortable and contented lifestyle is harder to achieve and maintain. PARADE commissioned Mark Clements Research Inc. to survey Americans nationwide about their finances and outlook for the future. Contributing Editor David Wallechinsky—author of recent articles on where your tax dollars go and on pork-barrel spending—interprets the results.*

2   The traditional American Dream is based on the belief that hardworking citizens can better their lives, pay their monthly bills without worry, give their children a start to an even better life and still save enough to live comfortably after they retire. But many average Americans are struggling—squeezed by rising costs, declining wages, credit-card debt and diminished benefits, with little left over to save for retirement. (See the following statistics.)

3   Does the dream survive? Do most Americans still believe they can forge better lives for themselves?

4   PARADE surveyed more than 2,200 Americans, of whom fully 84% described themselves as belonging to the middle class, regardless of where they live (living costs are higher in some regions) or the size of their household.

5   For this report, we focused on U.S. households earning between $30,000 and $99,000 a year. Most of those surveyed describe themselves as married and having a family. More than 64% say they are employed full-time or part-time. Most say they are in reasonably good health and have a satisfying religious or spiritual life. They own a home and at least two cars, and they are able to take vacations. By international standards, they live a life of prosperity.

6   Yet behind this prosperity is a growing unease. Half of the employed respondents say that they've experienced either increased health-care costs or a cut in health benefits over the last three years, and 39% have had cuts in their overtime, raises or bonuses. Almost two-thirds say they live from paycheck to paycheck, and 47% say that no matter how hard they work, they cannot get ahead. More than a third worry about job loss.

7   Richard Oden of Conyers, Ga.—married, with five children—worked in the beer industry for 23 years. Last year, he developed pneumonia and required major surgery. When he was unable to return to work by a given date, he says, his company terminated him at age 54—even though he had a perfect attendance record and no performance problems.

8   To help support his family, Oden had to dip into his 401(k) fund, paying a penalty for premature withdrawal. "This was very stressful," he says. "Everything had gone up—except wages."

9   Oden has since started his own business, a "leadership and personal development" consulting firm. His wife, Josett, works as a representative in the health-care field. "I do believe I will recover financially," Oden says, "and that I will realize a decent retirement. But the traditional American Dream? For most Americans, it's still a dream—a pipe dream."

10   Having drawn on his own retirement fund, Oden knows that saving can be a big problem. In the survey, nearly 83% say that there is not much left to save after they've paid their bills. Statistics from the Commerce Department bear this out: The savings rate for Americans is the lowest it has been in 73 years.

11   Self-reliance and sacrifice. Most of those interviewed display qualities common to American success stories: determination, flexibility, pragmatism, willingness to work hard and especially self-reliance. Almost three-quarters of the middle-class respondents surveyed say they take responsibility for their own financial destiny and believe that they will succeed or fail based on their own efforts. Still, many are downsizing their dreams.

12   Shelly Comer, 43, of Dos Palos, Calif., is a divorced mother of three who also takes care of a friend of her oldest child, Michelle. She is going into debt so that Michelle can go to college. Shelly has worked her whole life—as a receptionist, janitor, preschool teacher and activities director at a hospital. Recently, she became a registered nurse and now works the night shift in obstetrics at another hospital. Her annual income is $70,377.

13   Michelle, 19, is a freshman at the University of California at Merced. She says she is concerned about the financial burden her education is placing on her family: "In order to meet our expected family contribution, my mother had to borrow the entire amount of her share." For her part, Michelle earned six small scholarships, two of which are renewable for next year, and took out a federal loan. She also works 16 hours a week in the financial-aid office at the university.

14   Shelly has a retirement plan through the hospital. "But I have nothing saved for me," she says. "I'm putting it all into the kids, so that they can succeed in school. Our parents did everything for us, and I hope to do the same for my kids. I don't count on anyone else to help us get to where we want to go. It's all up to me and my family. And I trust in God to help us."

15   Who is responsible? One of the most intriguing results of the Parade survey is that 89% of the middle class believes that businesses have a social responsibility to their employees and to the community. Yet 81% believe that, in fact, American businesses make decisions based on what is best for their shareholders and investors, not what's best for their employees.

16   Randy Omark, 55, and Cherie Morris, 58, of Stroudsburg, Pa., husband and wife, are former flight attendants for TWA. Cherie took a buyout in the late

My Notes

pragmatism: a practical approach to thinking about problems

My Notes

1990s—before American Airlines bought TWA in 2001. After the acquisition, Randy was put on "**furlough**" (as were about 4,000 other former TWA flight attendants) and never rehired. After 26 years with the two airlines, his pension was frozen and then taken over by the government. Now he gets $324 a month in payments.

17 Today, despite having a college education, Randy works for $9 an hour finding community jobs for mentally challenged adults. Cherie works for a greeting-card company for $7.25 an hour.

18 "It used to be that if you stayed with your job, you would be rewarded," says Cherie. "Now there is no guarantee." As for retirement, Randy says, "Eventually, we will just downsize everything, sell our house and move into a smaller one."

19 Is the dream changing? Simone Luevano, 46, and Miguel Gutierrez, 44, run a garage-door installation and repair business in Albuquerque, N.M. While the business grossed $453,000 last year, they took home just $50,000 net to live on. They have a daughter—Marilyn, age 7—who is deaf in one ear and goes to a private school that costs $3600 a year.

20 Simone says that financial stress is part of their lives: "It comes from the 'maybe, could be, should be' nature of our business." When the economy is down, people don't buy a new garage-door system. The cost of gas at the pump is a major factor, she adds: "When the price of gasoline goes down, business goes up."

21 Have they prepared for retirement? Simone laughs, then replies, "The words 'retirement' and ' vacation' are not in our vocabulary. You know that old Tennessee Ernie Ford song: 'I owe my soul to the company store'? We don't think about retirement. They'll have to take me out of here with my high-top tennies on.

22 "The American Dream is a bygone thing," she adds. "It's not the way life is anymore. I used to believe I was responsible for my own destiny. But it's not that simple. Now it's faith and **fortitude**."

What Can You Do?

23 In this (and every) election year, many politicians rev up emotions that keep voters from focusing on the pocketbook and daily-life issues that truly matter. You know what really touches your family and life: The cost of milk, gas and prescription drugs. The quality of schools. The hope that the government will step in fully prepared to keep you safe and secure if a disaster hits your neighborhood.

24 Don't leave decision-making and priority-setting to **zealots** who have an ax to grind—or to the blindly ambitious people who emerge in every generation. For more than 200 years, our system of government has encouraged power to the people. Be an active citizen.

furlough: a period of time when an employee is told not to come to work and is not paid

fortitude: mental strength and courage

zealots: people who are fanatical in pursuing political, religious, or other ideals

Making Observations

- What words does the author use to describe the American Dream?
- What details from the text do you agree or disagree with?
- What questions did you have while reading the text?

Returning to the Text

- Return to the article as you respond to the following questions. Use text evidence to support your responses.
- Write any additional questions you have about the text in your Reader/Writer Notebook.

1. Why does the author spend time in the opening paragraphs detailing the extent of the study? How does this affect the perception of his readers?

_____

_____

_____

_____

2. Who is the author's target audience? Support your answer with evidence from the text.

_____

_____

_____

_____

_____

_____

3. What is the author's main claim? What details of the text help to identify the claim?

_____

_____

_____

_____

_____

_____

4. Is the author successful at making concessions and directly addressing counterarguments? Explain your answer.

_____

_____

_____

_____

5. Notice the author's choice to change the focus and tone in the final two paragraphs. How do the ideas in those paragraphs affect the thesis and conclusion of the argument?

_____

_____

_____

_____

6. Does the author successfully prove his claim? Support your answer with text evidence.

_____

_____

_____

_____

Appreciating the Author's Craft

7. How does the author express his purpose in this article? Provide evidence to support your answer.

_____

_____

_____

_____

8. Did the structure of the article lead to the author successfully achieving his purpose, or did it contribute to its failure? Explain your answer.

_____

_____

_____

_____

9. For what purpose did the author include the heading "What Can You Do?" Was its inclusion successful in achieving the purpose?

_____

_____

_____

_____

10. In paragraph 17, the author includes the phrase "despite having a college education" to describe Randy. How does the use of this phrase shape the readers' perception of Randy's income?

_____

_____

_____

_____

11. Based on the evidence presented in paragraph 5, what logical fallacy is present, and what is its effect on the way the text is read and understood?

_____

_____

_____

_____

☑ Check Your Understanding

Quickwrite: In the first paragraph of the article, the author begins by defining the American Dream. How does it compare to your definition? How does Wallechinsky's "call to action" show another basic tenet of the American Dream?

Defend or Challenge the Author's Claim

The author gives evidence that supports his claim. Identifying evidence and analyzing how it supports his claim will help you write an analysis of the claim.

12. Begin by restating Wallechinsky's claim. Then use the chart to analyze and explain how the text in the first column supports his claim.

_____

_____

Text	Analysis of How Text Relates to Claim
"By international standards, they live a life of prosperity. Yet behind this prosperity is a growing unease. Half of the employed respondents say that they've experienced either increased health-care costs or a cut in health benefits over the last three years, and 39% have had cuts in their overtime, raises or bonuses."	
"Shelly has a retirement plan through the hospital. 'But I have nothing saved for me,' she says. 'I'm putting it all into the kids, so that they can succeed in school.'"	
"Today, despite having a college education, Randy works for $9 an hour finding community jobs for mentally challenged adults."	
"While the business grossed $453,000 last year, they took home just $50,000 net to live on. They have a daughter—Marilyn, age 7—who is deaf in one ear and goes to a private school that costs $3600 a year."	

13. Transition words and phrases are important for argumentative writing. As in other writing, transitions help the reader navigate the text. Transitions like *however, still, despite,* and *yet* can signal that the writer is refuting opposing arguments.

In the preceding examples, identify a transition word the author uses and briefly explain how the transition word signals a relationship between ideas.

_____

_____

_____

_____

14. Write a paragraph that defends or challenges the author's claim that the American Dream is a bygone thing. Use relevant text evidence to support your answer. Be sure to use transitions to help signal purpose and the relationship between ideas in your sentences.

Explain How an Author Builds an Argument

Write an essay that explains how Wallechinsky builds an argument to persuade his readers that the American Dream is a bygone concept. Analyze how Wallechinsky uses evidence, reasoning, and stylistic or persuasive elements to strengthen the logic and persuasiveness of his argument. In your essay, be sure to:

- Identify and write to a specific target audience.
- Write a thesis that identifies Wallechinsky's claim and analyzes how he persuades his readers that his claim is valid.
- Explain what supporting evidence Wallechinsky uses and how counterclaims are addressed. Evaluate the effectiveness of the reasons, evidence, and refutations of counterclaims he provides.
- Consider how Wallechinsky uses reasoning and stylistic or rhetorical appeals.
- Include multiple direct quotations from the text as text evidence, introducing and punctuating them correctly.
- Include transitions between your points and a statement that provides a conclusion.

VOCABULARY

LITERARY

Imagery is the descriptive language authors use to create word pictures. Writers create imagery through words and details that appeal to one or more of the five senses.

Learning Targets

- Analyze the context of imagery to draw conclusions about suggested meanings.
- Analyze how authors use paradoxes and calls to action to influence readers.

Preview

In this activity, you will read and analyze a poem in order to understand how an author uses imagery and paradox to convey ideas.

Drawing Conclusions About Imagery

Often in poetry, authors use imagery to convey an idea. Based on the context, the idea will have a different interpretation than the literal interpretation of the words. You must analyze the context of the imagery and use that information to draw a conclusion about the concept the author is trying to convey through the imagery. Sometimes, the imagery may have multiple interpretations. The imagery may invoke different feelings in different readers.

For example, the phrase *it's a dog-eat-dog world* creates a specific image that has nuanced meaning, or connotation. The literal interpretation of the words, or denotation, would lead you to believe that dogs are eating dogs. But this phrase is often used to describe a fiercely competitive situation in which people are willing to do anything in order to succeed. Saying "It was a dog-eat-dog world at the cheerleading competition" also creates a more effective image than just saying "The cheerleading competition was fiercely competitive."

1. Discuss with a partner the literal meaning of each of the following underlined phrases. Then discuss a potential nuanced meaning of the imagery based on the context.

It was the end of summer camp, and it was time to go back to school, so we <u>closed the shade on our bright sunshine</u> of summer.

Denotation:

Connotation:

In the world of competitive soccer, <u>the mouse can sometimes outwit the lion.</u>
Denotation:

Connotation:

After being promoted to vice president, Jaina <u>felt trapped by the weight of her success.</u>
Denotation:

Connotation:

As You Read

- While you read the poem, create an image in your mind of the sights the author describes.
- Circle unknown words and phrases. Try to determine the meaning of the words by using context clues, word parts, or a dictionary.

Poetry

Let America Be America Again

by **Langston Hughes**

Let America be America again.

Let it be the dream it used to be.

Let it be the pioneer on the plain

Seeking a home where he himself is free.

5 (America never was America to me.)

Let America be the dream the dreamers dreamed—

Let it be that great strong land of love

Where never kings connive nor tyrants scheme

That any man be crushed by one above.

10 (It never was America to me.)

O, let my land be a land where Liberty

Is crowned with no false patriotic wreath,

But opportunity is real, and life is free,

Equality is in the air we breathe.

15 (There's never been equality for me,

Nor freedom in this "homeland of the free.")

Say, who are you that mumbles in the dark?

And who are you that draws your veil across the stars?

I am the poor white, fooled and pushed apart,

20 I am the Negro bearing slavery's scars.

I am the red man driven from the land,

I am the immigrant clutching the hope I seek—

And finding only the same old stupid plan

My Notes

_____
_____
_____
_____
_____
_____
_____
_____
_____
_____
_____
_____

Jacob Lawrence was one of the most important artists of the 20th century, widely renowned for his modernist depictions of everyday life as well as epic narratives of African American history and historical figures. In this silk-screen print titled "Carpenters," Lawrence celebrates the creative process of the carpenter.

My Notes

_____
_____
_____
_____
_____
_____
_____
_____
_____
_____
_____
_____
_____
_____

bondsman: serf or slave
bartered: traded, exchanged

Of dog eat dog, of mighty crush the weak.

25 I am the young man, full of strength and hope,

Tangled in that ancient endless chain

Of profit, power, gain, of grab the land!

Of grab the gold! Of grab the ways of satisfying need!

Of work the men! Of take the pay!

30 Of owning everything for one's own greed!

I am the farmer, **bondsman** to the soil.

I am the worker sold to the machine.

I am the Negro, servant to you all.

I am the people, humble, hungry, mean—

35 Hungry yet today despite the dream.

Beaten yet today—O, Pioneers!

I am the man who never got ahead,

The poorest worker **bartered** through the years.

Yet I'm the one who dreamt our basic dream

40 In the Old World while still a serf of kings,

Who dreamt a dream so strong, so brave, so true,

That even yet its mighty daring sings

In every brick and stone, in every furrow turned

That's made America the land it has become.

45 O, I'm the man who sailed those early seas

In search of what I meant to be my home—

For I'm the one who left dark Ireland's shore,

And Poland's plain, and England's grassy lea,

And torn from Black Africa's strand I came

50 To build a "homeland of the free."

The free?

Who said the free? Not me?

Surely not me? The millions on relief today?

The millions shot down when we strike?

55 The millions who have nothing for our pay?

For all the dreams we've dreamed

And all the songs we've sung

And all the hopes we've held

And all the flags we've hung,

60 The millions who have nothing for our pay—

Except the dream that's almost dead today.

O, let America be America again—

The land that never has been yet—

And yet must be—the land where *every* man is free.

65 The land that's mine—the poor man's, Indian's, Negro's, ME—

Who made America,

Whose sweat and blood, whose faith and pain,

Whose hand at the foundry, whose plow in the rain,

Must bring back our mighty dream again.

70 Sure, call me any ugly name you choose—

The steel of freedom does not stain.

From those who live like leeches on the people's lives,

We must take back our land again,

America!

75 O, yes,

I say it plain,

America never was America to me,

And yet I swear this oath—

America will be!

80 Out of the rack and ruin of our gangster death,

The rape and rot of graft, and stealth, and lies,

We, the people, must redeem

The land, the mines, the plants, the rivers.

The mountains and the endless plain—

85 All, all the stretch of these great green states—

And make America again!

Making Observations
- What captures your attention?
- What emotions might someone feel while reading the poem?
- What do you notice about the speakers in the poem?

graft: gain by corruption
stealth: secret means
redeem: liberate, rescue, save

My Notes

Returning to the Text

- Return to the poem as you respond to the following questions. Use text evidence to support your responses.
- Write any additional questions you have about the text in your Reader/Writer Notebook.

2. What do kings and tyrants symbolize in line 8? How is this significant?

_____

_____

_____

_____

_____

3. Two voices speak in lines 1–18. Who is speaking the words in the parentheses (lines 5, 10, 15–16)? How is that voice different from the voice speaking in lines 1–18? What points of view are expressed by the two voices?

_____

_____

_____

_____

4. Several times throughout the poem, the speaker ends a pair of lines with the rhyming words "free" and "me." What is the effect of this pairing and repetition on the reader, and how does it help convey the theme?

_____

_____

_____

_____

_____

_____

5. What is the author trying to achieve by including the descriptions in lines 65–69?

_____

_____

_____

_____

6. What idea about America is Hughes trying to convey by including the images of the "steel of freedom" and "leeches on the people's lives" (lines 71–72)?

_____

_____

_____

_____

7. How does author's choice of language in lines 80–86 shape the reader's perception? How is the author's choice to end the poem this way similar to a call to action?

_____

_____

_____

_____

Paradox

A **paradox** is a literary device in which the author juxtaposes a set of seemingly contradictory concepts. The author does so to reveal a hidden or unexpected truth. A simple example is _less is more_. This is a paradox because it uses two opposite words that contradict one another. An example from literature is the first line of _A Tale of Two Cities_ by Charles Dickens: "It was the best of times. It was the worst of times."

8. What is the purpose of the paradox in lines 13–16? Explain whether this paradox is successful in achieving its purpose.

_____

_____

_____

_____

9. What is the paradox the author uses in lines 25–26? What effect does the paradox have?

_____

_____

_____

_____

☑ Check Your Understanding

For you, what was the most powerful image in the poem? What made it powerful? What point was Hughes trying to make by using the image?

Coming to America

Learning Strategies

Brainstorming
Graphic Organizer
Marking the Text
Quickwrite

My Notes

Learning Targets

- Analyze the use of language to explain the impact of a poet's choices on a reader.
- Write responses that compare texts within genres.
- Synthesize information from multiple texts to support a thematic interpretation.
- Integrate ideas from multiple texts to build knowledge and vocabulary about a topic.

Preview

In this activity, you will read three poems and analyze their diverse perspectives on immigration and the attainment of the American Dream.

Making Adjustments While Reading

While reading complex texts, readers sometimes need to pause and make adjustments when their understanding breaks down. When you don't understand something you are reading, try the following adjustments:

- Reread the word, phrase, or sentence you do not understand. Reread out loud to see if hearing the sentence helps you understand it.
- Use your background knowledge to make sense of what you are reading.
- Ask questions about the text. Jot down questions in the My Notes section and return to them later to see if you know the answer after reading more of the text.
- Use annotations, like metacognitive markers, to note the parts of the text where you have questions or comments.

As You Read

- As you read the poems, circle contrasting words and phrases.
- Pause when you do not understand something in the text and try rereading, using background knowledge, asking questions, or annotating to deepen your understanding.
- Circle any unfamiliar words or phrases. Then use context and print or digital dictionary to determine the meanings.

About the Author

Joseph Bruchac (b. 1942) is an award-winning writer and professional storyteller. He grew up in a small town in the foothills of the Adirondack Mountains. As a child of Abenaki Indian ancestry, Bruchac wanted to tell his children the tales of his tribe and others and sought out Native elders to learn more about Native American storytelling. His first book of stories was published in 1975. Bruchac has since written dozens of books for children and adults that seek to promote and preserve Native American stories and culture.

Poetry

Ellis Island

by Joseph Bruchac

Beyond the red brick of Ellis Island
where the two Slovak children
who became my grandparents
waited the long days of quarantine,
5 after leaving the sickness,
the old Empires of Europe,
a Circle Line ship slips easily
on its way to the island
of the tall woman, green
10 as dreams of forests and meadows
waiting for those who'd worked
a thousand years
yet never owned their own.
Like millions of others,
15 I too come to this island,
nine decades the answerer
of dreams.
Yet only part of my blood loves that memory.
Another voice speaks
20 of native lands
within this nation.
Lands invaded
when the earth became owned.
Lands of those who followed
25 the changing Moon,
knowledge of the seasons
in their veins.

Ellis Island. New York City.

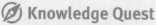
Knowledge Quest

- What details about the place Ellis Island stand out to you?
- What do you notice about the speaker of the poem's family background?

Returning to the Text

- Return to the poem as you respond to the following questions. Use text evidence to support your responses.
- Write any additional questions you have about the text in your Reader/Writer Notebook.

1. KQ In line 4 of the poem, what might the word *quarantine* mean in the context of the opening lines?

   _____

   _____

   _____

   _____

2. What image is described in lines 9–10? How does the decision to have the line break after the word *green* in line 9 affect the imagery?

   _____

   _____

   _____

   _____

3. How are the first stanza and the second stanza different? What two points of view does the author develop in each stanza?

   _____

   _____

   _____

   _____

4. How does the author's choice of the word *invaded* (line 22) help the perception of the reader?

   _____

   _____

   _____

   _____

5. KQ How does the speaker convey what it means to be an immigrant in America?

   _____

   _____

   _____

   _____

   _____

About the Author

David Ignatow was born in Brooklyn, New York, in 1914 to Russian immigrants. His poetry, which is written in straightforward language, often portrays urban life and the lives of the working poor. Ignatow won many prestigious awards for his poetry before he died in 1997.

Poetry

Europe and America

by **David Ignatow**

My father brought the emigrant bundle

of desperation and worn threads,

that in anxiety as he stumbles

tumble out distractedly;

5 while I am bedded upon soft green money

that grows like grass.

Thus, between my father

who lives on a bed of anguish for his daily bread,

and I who tear money at leisure by the roots,

10 where I lie in sun or shade,

a vast continent of breezes, storms to him,

shadows, darkness to him, small lakes, rough channels

to him, and hills, mountains to him, lie between us.

My father comes of a small hell

15 where bread and man have been kneaded and baked

together.

You have heard the scream as the knife fell;

while I have slept

as guns pounded offshore.

 **Knowledge Quest**

• What impression do you have of the speaker of the poem's father?

• What contrast do you notice in the poem?

WORD CONNECTIONS

Roots and Affixes

Knowing the meaning of Latin prefixes and roots can show the difference between immigrant and emigrant. The prefix *im-* means "in or into." The prefix *e-* means "out or from." The root *migr* in both words means "to move from one place to another." So an *emigrant* moves out of a country and becomes an *immigrant* by moving into a new country.

KNOWLEDGE QUEST

Knowledge Question:

What does it mean to be an immigrant in America?

My Notes

Returning to the Text

- Return to the poem as you respond to the following questions. Use text evidence to support your responses.
- Write any additional questions you have about the text in your Reader/Writer Notebook.

6. KQ In line 1 of the poem, how does the author use the word *bundle* in context?

_____

_____

_____

_____

7. What does "while I am bedded upon soft green money" (line 5) mean? What does this idea represent?

_____

_____

_____

_____

8. How do the words *bed of anguish* in line 8 shape the reader's perception?

_____

_____

_____

_____

9. How does the poet use imagery to show the differences between life in America and life in Europe? Use text evidence to support your answer.

_____

_____

_____

_____

10. KQ How does the speaker convey what it means to be an immigrant in America?

_____

_____

_____

About the Author

Naomi Shihab Nye (b. 1952) was born in St. Louis, Missouri but moved between Jerusalem and San Antonio, Texas, as an adolescent. Her father was a Palestinian refugee, and her mother was an American citizen. She has spoken out against the prejudice that Arab Americans face. Her experiences of living in multiple cultures can be seen in her work. In an interview with the Poetry Foundation, Nye said, "The primary source of poetry has always been local life, random characters met on the streets, our own ancestry sifting down to us through small essential daily tasks."

Poetry

My Uncle's Favorite Coffee Shop

by Naomi Shihab Nye

⊘ **KNOWLEDGE QUEST**

Knowledge Question:
What does it mean to be an immigrant in America?

Serum of steam rising from the cup,

what comfort to be known personally by Barbara,

her perfect pouring hand and starched ascot,

known as the two easy eggs and the single pancake,

5 without saying.

What pleasure for an immigrant—

anything without saying.

My uncle slid into his booth.

I cannot tell you—how I love this place.

10 He drained the water glass, noisily clinking his ice.

My uncle hailed from an iceless region.

He had definite ideas about water drinking.

I cannot tell you—all the time. But then he'd try.

My uncle wore a white shirt every day of his life.

15 He raised his hand against the roaring ocean

and the television full of lies.

He shook his head back and forth

from one country to the other

and his ticket grew longer.

20 Immigrants had double and nothing all at once.

Immigrants drove the taxis, sold the beer and Cokes.

When he found one note that rang true,

he sang it over and over inside.

Coffee, honey.

25 His eyes roamed the couples at other booths,

their loose banter and casual clothes.

But he never became them.

Uncle who finally left in a bravado moment

after 23 years, to live in the old country forever,

30 to stay and never come back,

maybe it would be peaceful now,

maybe for one minute,

I cannot tell you—how my heart has settled at last.

But he followed us to the sidewalk

35 saying, Take care, Take care,

as if he could not stand to leave us.

I cannot tell—

how we felt

to learn that the week he arrived,

40 he died. Or how it is now,

driving his parched streets,

feeling the booth beneath us as we order,

oh, anything, because if we don't,

nothing will come.

Ø Knowledge Quest

• What stands out to you about the speaker's uncle?

• What surprises you about the poem?

Returning to the Text

- Return to the poem as you respond to the following questions. Use text evidence to support your responses.
- Write any additional questions you have about the text in your Reader/Writer Notebook.

1. KQ In line 11 of the poem, what does the word *hailed* mean in context?

_____

_____

_____

_____

2. What conclusion can you draw about the meaning of the imagery of the clinking of the ice in lines 10–11?

_____

_____

_____

_____

3. How does the use of the word *bravado* in line 28 shape the perception of the reader about the uncle's choice to move back to the old country?

_____

_____

_____

_____

4. How is the uncle in "My Uncle's Favorite Coffee Shop" portrayed differently than the immigrants portrayed in "Ellis Island"?

_____

_____

_____

_____

15. **KQ** How does the speaker convey what it means to be an immigrant in America?

_____

_____

_____

_____

_____

 INDEPENDENT READING LINK

You can continue to build your knowledge about this theme by reading related **fiction and poetry** at ZINC Reading Labs.

Select the fiction and poetry filters and type keywords such as *immigration* in the **Search all ZINC articles** field.

 ZINC

Knowledge Quest

Use your knowledge about "Ellis Island," "Europe and America," and "My Uncle's Favorite Coffee Shop" to discuss what it means to be an immigrant in America. Be sure to:

- Discuss how the experiences are similar and different by referring to evidence in the texts.
- Take turns speaking, listening, and agreeing or disagreeing respectfully.
- Ask each other to expand on ideas or statements for clarification and to promote discussion.
- Conduct any additional research on the topic as necessary.

Working from the Text

16. Images often have a powerful connotative effect. Identify the denotation and connotation of key images from the three poems you just read. Discuss the effect that those particular words have on the reader.

Word or Phrase	Denotation	Connotation	Effect on the Reader
Ellis Island "knowledge of the seasons in their veins"			
My Uncle's Favorite Coffee Shop "hand against the roaring ocean"			
Europe and America "emigrant bundle of desperation"			

☑ Focus on the Sentence

Turn the following poetic fragments into complete sentences based on a reexamination of the poet's language choices and use of connotation. Add subjects, verbs, punctuation, and capitalization as needed.

bedded upon soft green money

_____

_____

bed of anguish

_____

_____

_____

where bread and man have been kneaded and baked together

_____

_____

_____

Comparison and Contrast

Use the following modified Venn diagram to compare and contrast the themes of the three poems. Write any similarities in themes among the three poems in the middle section of the Venn diagram where all three circles overlap. Record differences in the outer areas. You can also record similarities between two poems, but not three, in the overlapping spaces.

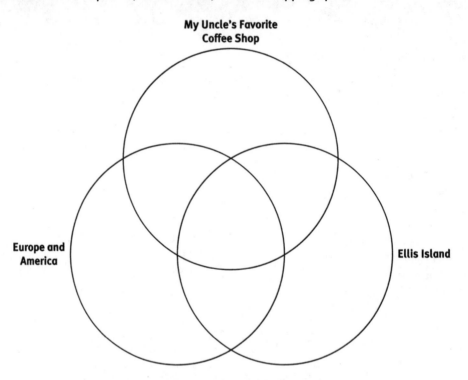

My Uncle's Favorite
Coffee Shop

Europe and
America

Ellis Island

📖 Writing Prompt: Literary Analysis

Consider the three poems you have read, in particular the connections between the speakers and how they present their experiences. Write an essay in which you use the poems to identify and analyze a common theme connecting the speakers' experiences. What contradictions between their experiences and the American Dream do the writers present, and how do they resolve the conflict—if at all? How are those responses to these contradictions similar or different? Be sure to:

- Include a thesis that connects the experiences in all three poems and the speakers' responses to those experiences.
- Provide direct quotations and specific examples from all three poems to support your analysis. Introduce and punctuate all quotations correctly.
- Use a variety of sentence beginnings.

The Sonnet and the American Dream

Learning Strategies
Close Reading
Graphic Organizer
Note-taking
TP-CASTT

Learning Targets
- Analyze a poet's message about the American Dream.
- Analyze context to draw conclusions about the meaning of imagery in a sonnet.

Preview
In this activity, you will analyze a poet's message about the American Dream using the TP-CASTT strategy.

Poetic Forms: The Sonnet
A **sonnet** is a 14-line poem. The word *sonnet* comes from the Italian word *sonnetto* meaning "little sound or song." Sonnets typically use a rhythm and rhyme scheme that give them a singsong quality. Sonnets usually focus on a single topic but then have a shift—for example, in plot or tone—in the final lines.

As You Read
- Use the My Notes section to note any mental images the author creates with her language.
- Mark the characteristics of a sonnet that you observe while reading.
- Circle any unfamiliar words or phrases. Then use context and a print or digital dictionary to determine the meanings.

About the Author
Sandra Gilbert (b. 1936) was born in New York City. She has been an author, a professor at the University of California, Davis, and a political activist. She has served as president of the Modern Language Association and has received numerous accolades for her writing. Her poetry is known for its grace and adherence to formal structures. A leading feminist literary critic and coauthor of the classic *The Madwoman in the Attic,* Gilbert infuses her feminist views in much of her writing. She now divides her time between living in Berkeley, California, and Paris, France.

INDEPENDENT READING LINK
Read and Connect

How is the American Dream portrayed in the book you are reading independently? Compare how the American Dream is shown in your book and the poem. What are the similarities and differences? How has reading about the American Dream changed your thinking about what the American Dream is?

My Notes

Poetry

Sonnet: The Ladies' Home Journal

by **Sandra Gilbert**

The brilliant stills of food, the cozy

glossy, bygone life—mashed potatoes

posing as whipped cream, a neat mom

conjuring shapes from chaos, trimming the flame—

5 how we ached for all that,

that dance of love in the living room,

those paneled walls, that kitchen golden

as the inside of a seed: how we leaned

on those shiny columns of advice,

10 stroking the thank yous, the firm thighs, the wise

closets full of soap.

      But even then

we knew it was lies we loved, the lies

we wore like Dior coats, the clean-cut airtight

15 lies that laid out our lives in black and white.

Making Observations
- What is your initial reaction to the poem?
- What imagery stands out for you?

On the Spot Research
With a partner, research the history of the *Ladies' Home Journal*. Find out the following information:

- In what year was the magazine created?
- What is the historical significance of the magazine?
- How has the magazine influenced women?

Share your findings with another set of partners.

Returning to the Text

- Return to the poem as you respond to the following questions. Use text evidence to support your responses.
- Write any additional questions you have about the text in your Reader/Writer Notebook.

1. In lines 2–3, what conclusion can be drawn about the imagery created by the mashed potatoes posing as whipped cream?

_____

_____

_____

_____

2. Which line of the poem begins the shift? What kind of change happens in the shift?

_____

_____

_____

_____

3. What message is the author trying to convey in lines 12–13?

_____

_____

_____

_____

4. In lines 13–14, why does the author describe the lies as "clean-cut" and "airtight"?

_____

_____

_____

_____

Introducing the Strategy

TP-CASTT This reading strategy is used to analyze a poetic text by identifying and discussing each element in the acronym Title, Paraphrase, Connotation, Attitude, Shift, Title again, and Theme. The strategy is a guide designed to lead you in an analysis of a literary text. It is most effective if you begin at the top and work your way down the elements. However, you will find that as you study one element, you will naturally begin to explore others. For example, a study of connotation often leads to a discussion of tone and shifts. Revisiting the title often leads to a discussion of the theme.

Working from the Text

5. Analyze the poem "Sonnet: The Ladies' Home Journal" using the following TP-CASTT graphic organizer.

Title	What does the title mean?	
Paraphrase	Paraphrase parts of the poem.	
Connotation	What is the implied meaning of some of the words?	
Attitude	What is the author's attitude about the subject?	
Shift	What is the shift in tone in the poem?	
Title Again	What new meaning does the title offer?	
Theme	What is the theme of the poem?	

Check Your Understanding

Based on your analysis of the poem "Sonnet: The Ladies' Home Journal," what does the author think about the American Dream shown in the magazine the *Ladies' Home Journal*?

Money and the American Dream

Learning Targets

- Analyze how the economic context and dramatic elements affect the theme and plot of a play.
- Compose a literary analysis of a play and evaluate how the use of language affects readers.

Preview

In this activity, you will analyze quotations about the American Dream. Then you will read, analyze, and write about a drama whose theme centers on the American Dream.

My Notes

Money and the American Dream

1. Read and review the following quotations about money and in your Reader/ Writer Notebook write a brief explanation of each one in your own words. Think of a visual to go with each one.

   a. "The love of money is the root of all evil." (from the Bible)

   b. "Money is only a tool. It will take you wherever you wish, but it will not replace you as the driver." (Ayn Rand)

   c. "Put not your trust in money, but your money in trust." (Oliver Wendell Holmes)

   d. "He who knows he has enough is rich." (Vicki Robin)

   e. "If money be not thy servant, it will be thy master." (Sir Francis Bacon)

   f. "The safest way to double your money is to fold it over twice and put it in your pocket." (Frank McKinney Hubbard)

   g. "Those who believe money can do everything are frequently prepared to do everything for money." (George Savile)

   h. "There's no money in poetry, but then there's no poetry in money, either." (Robert Graves)

   i. "Money, if it does not bring you happiness, will at least help you be miserable in comfort." (Helen Gurley Brown)

j. "A fool and his money are soon parted." (Benjamin Franklin)

k. "A penny saved is a penny earned." (Benjamin Franklin)

Dramatic Elements

2. Plays are written to be acted out on stage. As a result, they have a unique format when compared with other types of writing. Read through the chart to learn about the elements of dramatic writing.

Dramatic Elements	
Characters	• Characters are listed at the beginning of the play. • Character names will appear before each line to indicate who is speaking. • Some dramas have a character called a narrator who provides additional information to the reader/audience.
Format	• Plays are broken into **acts** and **scenes**. • There are typically five acts in a drama. • Each act is broken into smaller scenes. • The text is largely made of **dialogue** between characters called **lines**.
Stage Directions	• Stage directions appear throughout in parentheses and italic font. • Stage directions explain the setting, give special directions to the speaker/actor, and may provide additional information about where the actor should be on stage. • Stage directions can help establish tone and mood. • Stage directions can help advance the plot, build tension, or aid the timing of the delivery of the lines.
Monologues	• Monologues are long speeches made by a single character in a drama.
Plot	• Like a narrative story, a play has a plot with a **rising action**, **climax**, and **resolution**.

3. With a partner, discuss how drama is different from narrative writing. Create a T-chart in your Reader/Writer notebook describing the characteristics of and differences between both kinds of writing. When you are done, compare your pair's with another pair's chart.

As You Read

- Write down any questions you have about the economic contexts referenced in the play in My Notes.
- Mark the text by putting a star beside the different dramatic elements that you notice as you read.
- Circle any unfamiliar words or phrases. Then use context and print or digital dictionary to determine the meanings.

About the Author

Lorraine Hansberry (1930–1965) was born in Chicago, where she grew up in an educated and successful activist family. Her father moved the family into a white neighborhood to challenge discriminatory housing practices. *A Raisin in the Sun* was written with that experience in mind. She later moved to New York City, where she committed to writing full time and where she wrote *A Raisin in the Sun*. The play became a huge success on Broadway and was made into a film. She was the first African American playwright and the youngest American to win a New York Critics' Circle award.

Play

from A Raisin in the Sun

by **Lorraine Hansberry**

Characters:

> Walter and Ruth Younger (husband and wife)
>
> Lena Younger (Mama—Walter's mother)

MAMA: What was they fighting about?

RUTH: Now you know as well as I do.

MAMA (*shaking her head*): Brother still worrying hisself sick about that money?

RUTH: You know he is.

5   MAMA: You had breakfast?

RUTH: Some coffee.

MAMA: Girl, you better start eating and looking after yourself better. You almost thin as Travis.

RUTH: Lena—

MAMA: Un-hunh?

10   RUTH: What are you going to do with it?

MAMA: Now don't you start, child. It's too early in the morning to be talking about money. It ain't Christian.

RUTH: It's just that he got his heart set on that store—

MAMA: You mean that liquor store that Willy Harris want him to invest in?

RUTH: Yes—

15 MAMA: We ain't no business people, Ruth. We just plain working folks.

RUTH: Ain't nobody business people till they go into business. Walter Lee say colored people ain't never going to start getting ahead till they start gambling on some different kinds of things in the world—investments and things.

MAMA: What done got into you, girl? Walter Lee done finally sold you on investing.

RUTH: No. Mama, something is happening between Walter and me. I don't know what it is—but he needs something—something I can't give him any more. He needs this chance, Lena.

MAMA *(frowning deeply)*: But liquor, honey—

20 RUTH: Well—like Walter say—I spec people going to always be drinking themselves some liquor.

MAMA: Well—whether they drinks it or not ain't none of my business. But whether I go into business selling it to 'em is, and I don't want that on my ledger this late in life. *(stopping suddenly and studying her daughter-in-law)* Ruth Younger, what's the matter with you today? You look like you could fall over right there.

RUTH: I'm tired.

MAMA: Then you better stay home from work today.

RUTH: I can't stay home. She'd be calling up the agency and screaming at them, "My girl didn't come in today—send me somebody! My girl didn't come in!" Oh, she just have a fit ...

25 MAMA: Well, let her have it. I'll just call her up and say you got the flu—

RUTH *(laughing)*: Why the flu?

MAMA: 'Cause it sounds respectable to 'em. Something white people get, too. They know 'bout the flu. Otherwise they think you been cut up or something when you tell 'em you sick.

RUTH: I got to go in. We need the money.

MAMA: Somebody would of thought my children done all but starved to death the way they talk about money here late. Child, we got a great big old check coming tomorrow.

30 RUTH *(sincerely, but also self-righteously)*: Now that's your money. It ain't got nothing to do with me. We all feel like that—Walter and Bennie and me—even Travis.

MAMA *(thoughtfully, and suddenly very far away)*: Ten thousand dollars—

RUTH: Sure is wonderful.

My Notes

MAMA: Ten thousand dollars.

RUTH: You know what you should do, Miss Lena? You should take yourself a trip somewhere. To Europe or South America or someplace—

35 MAMA (*throwing up her hands at the thought*): Oh, child!

RUTH: I'm serious. Just pack up and leave! Go on away and enjoy yourself some. Forget about the family and have yourself a ball for once in your life—

Making Observations
- What characters are mentioned who do not have speaking lines?
- Which character is most obsessed about money? Why?
- Which character do you most relate to? Why?

Returning to the Text

- Return to the play excerpt as you respond to the following questions. Use text evidence to support your responses.
- Write any additional questions you have about the text in your Reader/Writer Notebook.

4. In line 3 of the play, how does the stage direction of *"shaking her head"* help establish Mama's opinions?

_____

_____

_____

_____

_____

5. In line 21, how does the stage direction of *"stopping suddenly and studying her daughter-in-law"* affect the flow of the plot?

_____

_____

_____

_____

_____

6. What is the significance of Mama's use of the word *ledger* when she says, "I don't want that [selling alcohol] on my ledger this late in life"?

_____

_____

_____

_____

_____

7. How do Mama and Ruth view money differently? Support your answer with evidence from the text.

_____

_____

_____

_____

_____

8. The author has Mama describe two groups of people as "business people" and "plain working folks." How does her language choice affects the reader's perception of these two groups of people?

_____

_____

_____

_____

9. What message does the author convey about the power of money?

_____

_____

_____

_____

On the Spot Research

The play *A Raisin in the Sun* is set in Chicago in the 1950s. With a partner, research the economic situation of African Americans in Chicago in the 1950s. Topics to research include:

• Second Great Migration
• *The Chicago Defender*
• Employment discrimination
• Chicago Housing Authority

Discuss your findings with another pair.

10. What does money mean to Ruth? How does the economic context of the time influence her view of money?

_____

_____

_____

_____

☑ Check Your Understanding

Look back at the quotes you read at the beginning of this activity. Which quotes relate to characters in the drama? Make a chart in your Reader/Writer Notebook to show your answers.

✍ Writing Prompt: Literary Analysis

Write a paragraph that analyzes the theme of the American Dream in *A Raisin in the Sun*. Be sure to:

- Analyze the historical and economic context of the setting and how it influences the theme.
- Use examples from the text to support your analysis.
- Use content and academic vocabulary, as appropriate.

INDEPENDENT READING LINK

Read and Connect

Review the time periods in which your independent reading and the unit readings were written. Compare and contrast how views of the American Dream were expressed in different time periods.

Working Toward the Dream

Learning Strategies

Graphic Organizer
Marking the Text
Quickwrite
Read Aloud
SOAPSTone
TP-CASTT

Learning Targets

- Analyze multiple texts to identify the development of a recurring idea or theme.
- Synthesize information to make text-to-text connections.

Preview

In this activity, you will read a poem and an essay to expand your thinking about the relationship between work and the American Dream.

My Notes

Making Connections

When analyzing texts, you can increase you understanding by connecting the ideas in texts to something you already know. Make connections to:

- **Personal experiences** by thinking about something similar that happened to you.

  Example: I can relate to how the person is feeling. I know what it feels like to lose a big game because my team lost in the championship game last week.

- **Ideas in other texts** by remembering ideas, concepts, and facts you learned about in texts you have read or the style or structure of those texts.

  Example: I know about the Great Migration because we read about it in our history text book last month.

- Things that are happening or have happened in **society**.

  Example: This text talks about the American Dream being connected to people having jobs and making money. The other day officials announced that a major distribution center would be opening in our town and people were really happy about the number of jobs it would bring. This shows me a real-world example of how jobs are tied to the American Dream.

As You Read

- Underline words and phrases that indicate the narrator's attitude toward his work (tone).
- Make connections to personal experiences, ideas in other texts, or society and record them in the My Notes section.

About the Author

Martín Espada (b. 1957) was born in Brooklyn, New York. He is a former lawyer who is now an English professor at the University of Massachusetts in Amherst. In 2018, he was awarded the Ruth Lilly Prize in Poetry—an award given annually to honor a living U.S. poet whose lifetime achievements warrant extraordinary recognition. In his poetry, Espada writes about the working-class experience, including immigrant struggles in America.

Poetry

Who Burns for the Perfection of Paper

by **Martín Espada**

At sixteen, I worked after high school hours
at a printing plant
that manufactured legal pads:
Yellow paper
5 stacked seven feet high
and leaning
as I slipped cardboard
between the pages,
then brushed red glue
10 up and down the stack.
No gloves: fingertips required
for the perfection of paper,
smoothing the exact rectangle.
Sluggish by 9 PM, the hands
15 would slide along suddenly sharp paper,
and gather slits thinner than the crevices
of the skin, hidden.
Then the glue would sting,
hands oozing
20 till both palms burned
at the punchclock.
Ten years later, in law school,
I knew that every legal pad
was glued with the sting of hidden cuts,
25 that every open lawbook
was a pair of hands
upturned and burning.

My Notes

_____
_____
_____
_____
_____
_____
_____
_____
_____
_____
_____
_____
_____
_____
_____
_____
_____
_____
_____
_____
_____
_____
_____
_____
_____
_____
_____
_____
_____
_____
_____
_____
_____
_____
_____
_____
_____
_____
_____

Making Observations

- What words or images stand out for you? How did the descriptions make you feel?
- Would you like to work the job described in the poem? Why or why not?

As You Read

- Underline words and phrases that indicate Acuna's attitude toward his work (tone).
- Make connections to personal experiences, ideas in other texts, or society and record them in My Notes.
- Circle any unfamiliar words or phrases. Then use context and print or digital dictionary to determine the meanings.

About the Author

Studs Terkel (1912–2008) was a legendary radio broadcaster, interviewer, and writer. Born Louis Terkel, he officially adopted the nickname of Studs as a young actor in Chicago. Best known as an oral historian, he interviewed both celebrities and regular people. He turned some of these oral histories into books. He won the Pulitzer Prize for his book *The Good War: An Oral History of World War II*. According to NPR, Terkel said that his books "deal with the lives of ordinary people, not celebrities. What is it like to be a certain kind of person, at a certain circumstance, at a certain time?" His 1974 best seller *Working* chronicles the work life of everyday Americans, from welders and waitresses to farm workers and pharmacists.

Nonfiction

Roberto Acuna Talks About Farm Workers
from *Working*

by **Studs Terkel**

1   I walked out of the fields two years ago. I saw the need to change the California feudal system, to change the lives of farm workers, to make these huge corporations feel they're not above anybody. I am thirty-four years old and I try to organize for the United Farm Workers of America. ...

2   If you're picking lettuce, the thumbnails fall off 'cause they're banged on the box. Your hands get swollen. You can't slow down because the foreman sees you're so many boxes behind and you'd better get on. But people would help each other. If you're feeling bad that day, somebody who's feeling pretty good would help. Any people that are suffering have to stick together, whether they like it or not, whether they be black, brown, or pink. ...

3   I began to see how everything was so wrong. When growers can have an intricate watering system to irrigate their crops but they can't have running water inside the houses of workers. Veterinarians tend to the needs of domestic animals but they can't have medical care for the workers. They can have land subsidies for the growers but they can't have adequate unemployment compensation for the workers. They treat him like a farm implement. In fact, they treat their implements better and their domestic animals better. They have heat and insulated barns for the animals but the workers live in beat-up shacks with no heat at all.

4   Illness in the fields is 120 percent higher than the average rate for industry. It's mostly back trouble, rheumatism, and arthritis, because of the damp weather and the cold. Stoop labor is very hard on a person. Tuberculosis is high. And now because of the pesticides, we have many respiratory diseases.

5   The University of California at Davis had

A Mexican field worker on a farm in California packs freshly harvested heads of lettuce for transportation, 1958.

GRAMMAR & USAGE

Parallel Structure
Parallel Structure is the repetition of words or phrases that have similar grammatical structures. Such repetition in writing creates rhythm and emphasizes ideas. In the first paragraph, Acuna repeats infinitive phrases—verbs with *to*: "I saw the need to change the California feudal system, to change the lives of farm workers, to make these huge corporations feel they're not above anybody." The overall impact of this repetition is to emphasize his commitment to improving farm workers' lives. Study Acuna's repetition of the verbs *can have* and *can't* in paragraph 3.

WORD CONNECTIONS

Etymology
During the Middle Ages, peasants who worked the land essentially belonged to and were protected by the lord who had been granted the land as part of a feudal system. The origin of *feudal* can be found in Medieval Latin *feudalis* ("land granted"), Old High German *fihu* ("cattle"), and Middle English *feodary* ("one who holds lands in exchange for service"). *Feudal* is not related to *feud*.

subsidies: grants or sums of money

insulated: protected from heat and/or cold

stoop labor: agricultural labor performed in a squatting position

My Notes

government experiments with pesticides and chemicals. They get a bigger crop each year. They haven't any regard as to what safety precautions are needed. In 1964 and '65, an airplane was spraying these chemicals on the fields. Spraying rigs they're called. Flying low, the wheels got tangled in the fence wire. The pilot got up, dusted himself off, and got a drink of water. He died of convulsions. The ambulance attendants got violently sick because of the pesticide he had on his person. A little girl was playing around a sprayer. She stuck her tongue on it. She died instantly.

6 These pesticides affect the farm worker through the lungs. He breathes it in. He gets no compensation. All they do is say he's sick. They don't investigate the cause.

7 There were times when I felt I couldn't take it anymore. It was 105 in the shade and I'd see endless rows of lettuce and I felt my back hurting. … I felt the frustration of not being able to get out of the fields. I was getting ready to jump any foreman who looked at me cross-eyed. But until two years ago, my world was still very small. I would read all these things in the papers about Cesar Chavez and I would denounce him because I still had that thing about becoming a first class patriotic citizen. In Mexicali they would pass out leaflets and I would throw 'em away. I never participated. The grape boycott didn't affect me much because I was in lettuce. It wasn't until Chavez came to Salinas where I was working in the fields, that I saw what a beautiful man he was. I went to this rally, I still intended to stay with the company. But something—I don't know—I was close to the workers. They couldn't speak English and wanted me to be their spokesman in favor of going on strike. I don't know—I just got caught up with it all, the beautiful feeling of solidarity.

8 You'd see the people on the picket lines at four in the morning, at the camp fires, heating up beans and coffee and tortillas. It gave me a sense of belonging. These were my own people and they wanted change. I knew this is what I was looking for. I just didn't know it before.

9 My mom had always wanted me to better myself. I wanted to better myself because of her. Now when the strikes started, I told her I was going to join the union and the whole movement. I told her I was going to work without pay. She said she was proud of me. (His eyes glisten. A long, long pause.) See, I told her I wanted to be with my people. If I were a company man, no one would like me anymore. I had to belong to somebody and this was it right here. She said, "I pushed you in your early years to try to better yourself and get a social position. But I see that's not the answer. I know I'll be proud of you."

10 All kinds of people are farm workers, not just Chicanos. Filipinos started the strike. We have Puerto Ricans and Appalachians too, Arabs, some Japanese, some Chinese. At one time they used us against each other. But now they can't and they're scared, the growers. They can organize conglomerates. Yet when we try organization to better our lives, they are afraid. Suffering people never dreamed it could be different. Cesar Chavez tells them this and they grasp the idea—and this is what scares the growers.

denounce: publicly declare to be wrong

11 Now the machines are coming in. It takes skill to operate them. But anybody can be taught. We feel migrant workers should be given the chance. They got one for grapes. They got one for lettuce. They have cotton machines that took jobs away from thousands of farm workers. The people wind up in the ghettos of the cities, their culture, their families, their unity destroyed.

12 We're trying to **stipulate** it in our contract that the company will not use any machinery without the consent of the farm workers. So we can make sure the people being replaced by the machines will know how to operate the machines.

13 Working in the fields is not in itself a degrading job. It's hard, but if you're given regular hours, better pay, decent housing, unemployment, and medical compensation, pension plans—we have a very relaxed way of living. But growers don't recognize us as persons. That's the worst thing, the way they treat you. Like we have no brains. Now we see they have no brains. They have only a wallet in their head. The more you squeeze it the more they cry out.

Grape pickers carry American flags and National Farm Workers Association banners as they march along a road from Delano to Sacramento to protest their low wages and poor working conditions, 1966.

14 If we had proper compensation we wouldn't have to be working seventeen hours a day and following the crops. We could stay in one area and it would give us roots. Being a migrant, it tears the family apart. You get in debt. You leave the area penniless. The children are the ones hurt the most. They go to school three months in one place and then on to another. No sooner do they make friends, they are uprooted again. Right here, your childhood is taken away. So when they grow up, they're looking for this childhood they have lost.

15 If people could see—in the winter, ice on the fields. We'd be on our knees all day long. We'd build fires and warm up real fast and go back onto the ice. We'd be picking watermelons in 105 degrees all day long. When people have

stipulate: demand or specify a condition

melons or cucumber or carrots or lettuce, they don't know how they got on their table and the consequences to the people who picked it. If I had enough money, I would take busloads of people out to the fields and into the labor camps. Then they'd know how that fine salad got on their table.

Making Observations
- Which part of Acuna's story creates the most powerful image for you?
- How does this text make you feel?

Returning to the Text
- Return to the texts as you respond to the following questions. Use text evidence to support your responses.
- Write any additional questions you have about the texts in your Reader/Writer Notebook.

"Who Burns for the Perfection of Paper?"

1. What can you infer about the speaker based on the details in lines 1–21?

_____

_____

_____

_____

2. How do the words in lines 14–15 affect the tone of the poem?

_____

_____

_____

_____

3. How does the poet's choice to chronologically depict the events of the day affect the meaning of the poem?

_____

_____

_____

_____

"Roberto Acuna Talks About Farm Workers"

4. According to Acuna, how should employers show respect for human farm work and workers?

_____

_____

_____

_____

5. In paragraph 3, how does Acuna use parallelism? What effect does this parallelism have?

_____

_____

_____

_____

6. What is Studs Terkel's purpose for publishing the words of Acuna?

_____

_____

_____

_____

Both Texts

7. In what way do Roberto Acuna and Martin Espada have a similar experience? Explain your answer.

_____

_____

_____

_____

8. Why does Acuna want to "take busloads of people out to the fields"? How would their realization be like that of Martin Espada?

_____

_____

_____

_____

Check Your Understanding

In a few sentences, explain how the jobs described in "Who Burns for the Perfection of Paper?" and "Roberto Acuna Talks About Farm Workers" relate to the American Dream.

Writing Prompt: Argumentative

Write a short essay developing an argument on the difference between an immigrant's and a citizen's sense of opportunity in the United States. Discuss the similarities and differences in what the United States offers immigrants and native-born Americans in terms of opportunities to achieve the American Dream and how both groups view the future. Be sure to:

- Plan effectively by choosing an appropriate audience and thinking about how to write your essay with their knowledge, concerns, and biases in mind.
- Write a thesis statement that clearly states your position.
- Paraphrase, summarize, and use direct quotations from the texts you have read to develop your claim fairly and thoroughly, acknowledging each source's strengths and limitations.
- Acknowledge potential counterclaims fairly and provide enough reasons or evidence to convince your audience that those counterclaims are incorrect or that your claim is stronger.
- Provide an effective conclusion.

The Road to Success

Learning Targets

- Analyze the structural elements and characteristics of argumentative texts, including the effects of rhetorical devices.
- Defend or challenge an author's claims using evidence from a text.

Preview

In this activity, you will read and analyze two argumentative texts. Then you will write a narrative essay in which you will imagine that the two authors are having a conversation about the American Dream.

As You Read

- Underline words and phrases that show the author's definitions of the American Dream.
- Highlight words and phrases that indicate how the writer feels about access to the American Dream.
- Circle unknown words and phrases. Try to determine the meaning of the words by using context clues, word parts, or a dictionary.

About the Author

Barack Obama (b. 1961) was the 44th president of the United States and the country's first African American president. He was awarded the Nobel Peace Prize in 2009 for "his extraordinary efforts to strengthen diplomacy and cooperation between peoples." Known as an eloquent orator, Obama has given many famous speeches. In 2004, when Obama was the junior senator from Illinois, his speech at the Democratic National Convention vaulted him to national prominence.

Speech

from Keynote Address to the 2004 Democratic Convention

by Barack Obama

1   On behalf of the great state of Illinois, crossroads of a nation, land of Lincoln, let me express my deep gratitude for the privilege of addressing this convention. Tonight is a particular honor for me because, let's face it, my presence on this stage is pretty unlikely. My father was a foreign student, born and raised in a small village in Kenya. He grew up herding goats, went to school in a tin-roof shack. His father—my grandfather—was a cook, a domestic servant to the British.

My Notes

GRAMMAR & USAGE

Precise Language
Precise language makes use of exact nouns and vivid verbs to create strong images and make writing more understandable. Precise language can also create a specific tone in a piece of writing. In paragraph 3, for example, Obama says his grandfather signed up on a specific day, "the day after Pearl Harbor." Similarly, he says his grandmother worked "on a bomber assembly line." His precise language gives us a clearer picture of events and also helps establish the down-to-earth, populist tone of the speech.

Find other examples of exact nouns and noun phrases in this address. How do they contribute to the tone of the speech?

My Notes

_____
_____
_____
_____
_____
_____
_____
_____
_____
_____
_____
_____
_____
_____
_____
_____
_____
_____

2   But my grandfather had larger dreams for his son. Through hard work and perseverance my father got a scholarship to study in a magical place, America, that shone as a beacon of freedom and opportunity to so many who had come before.

3   While studying here, my father met my mother. She was born in a town on the other side of the world, in Kansas. Her father worked on oil rigs and farms through most of the Depression. The day after Pearl Harbor he signed up for duty, joined Patton's army and marched across Europe. Back home, my grandmother raised a baby and went to work on a bomber assembly line. After the war, they studied on the G.I. Bill, bought a house through FHA, and moved west, all the way to Hawaii, in search of opportunity.

4   And they, too, had big dreams for their daughter, a common dream, born of two continents. My parents shared not only an improbable love; they shared an abiding faith in the possibilities of this nation. They would give me an African name, Barack, or "blessed," believing that in a tolerant America your name is no barrier to success. They imagined me going to the best schools in the land, even though they weren't rich, because in a generous America you don't have to be rich to achieve your potential. They are both passed away now. Yet, I know that, on this night, they look down on me with pride.

5   I stand here today, grateful for the diversity of my heritage, aware that my parents' dreams live on in my two precious daughters. I stand here knowing that my story is part of the larger American story, that I owe a debt to all of those who came before me, and that, in no other country on earth, is my story even possible. Tonight, we gather to affirm the greatness of our nation, not because of the height of our skyscrapers, or the power of our military, or the size of our economy. Our pride is based on a very simple premise, summed up in a declaration made over two hundred years ago, "We hold these truths to be self-evident, that all men are created equal, that they are endowed by their Creator with certain inalienable rights, that among these are life, liberty and the pursuit of happiness."

6   That is the true genius of America, a faith in the simple dreams, the insistence on small miracles; that we can tuck in our children at night and know they are fed and clothed and safe from harm; that we can say what we think, write what we think, without hearing a sudden knock on the door; that we can have an idea and start our own business without paying a bribe; that we can participate in the political process without fear of retribution, and that our votes will be counted—or at least, most of the time.

7   This year, in this election, we are called to reaffirm our values and our commitments, to hold them against a hard reality and see how we are measuring up, to the legacy of our forebearers, and the promise of future generations. And fellow Americans—Democrats, Republicans, Independents—I say to you tonight: we have more work to do. More to do for the workers I met in Galesburg, Illinois, who are losing their union jobs at the Maytag plant that's moving to Mexico, and now they're having to compete with

heir own children for jobs that pay seven bucks an hour; more to do for the
ather I met who was losing his job and choking back tears, wondering how
ie would pay $4,500 a month for the drugs his son needs without the health
penefits he counted on; more to do for the young woman in East St. Louis, and
housands more like her, who have the grades, have the drive, have the will, but
loesn't have the money to go to college.

8 Don't get me wrong. The people I meet in small towns and big cities,
n diners and office parks, they don't expect government to solve all their
problems. They know they have to work hard to get ahead and they want to.
Go into the collar counties around Chicago, and people will tell you: They
lon't want their tax money wasted by a welfare agency or the Pentagon. Go
nto any inner city neighborhood, and folks will tell you that government alone
an't teach kids to learn. They know that parents have to teach, that children
an't achieve unless we raise their expectations and turn off the television sets
nd eradicate the slander that says a black youth with a book is acting white.
They know those things. People don't expect government to solve all their
problems. But they sense, deep in their bones, that with just a slight change in
priorities, we can make sure that every child in America has a decent shot at
ife, and that the doors of opportunity remain open to all. They know we can do
petter. And they want that choice. … John Kerry believes in America. And he
.nows it's not enough for just some of us to prosper. For alongside our famous
ndividualism, there's another ingredient in the American saga, a belief that
ve are connected as one people. If there's a child on the south side of Chicago
vho can't read, that matters to me, even if it's not my child. If there's a senior
itizen somewhere who can't pay for their prescription drugs and has to choose
etween medicine and the rent, that makes my life poorer, even if it's not my
randmother. If there's an Arab American family being rounded up without
enefit of an attorney or due process, that threatens my civil liberties. It is that
undamental belief—it is that fundamental belief—I am my brother's keeper,
am my sister's keeper—that makes this country work. It's what allows us to
ursue our individual dreams, yet still come together as a single American
amily." "E pluribus unum," out of many, one.

9 Now even as we speak, there are those who are preparing to divide
s, the spin masters and negative ad peddlers who embrace the politics of
nything goes. Well, I say to them tonight, there's not a liberal America and
conservative America—there's the United States of America. There's not a
lack America and white America and Latino America and Asian America;
here's the United States of America. The **pundits** like to slice-and-dice our
ountry into Red States and Blue States; Red States for Republicans, Blue States
or Democrats. But I've got news for them, too. We worship an awesome God
n the Blue States, and we don't like federal agents poking around our libraries
n the Red States. We coach Little League in the Blue States and, yes, we've got
ome gay friends in the Red States. There are patriots who opposed the war in
raq and patriots who supported the war in Iraq. We are one people, all of us
ledging allegiance to the stars and stripes, all of us defending the United States
f America.

pundit: a critic who makes
comments and judgments

My Notes

10 In the end, that's what this election is about. Do we participate in a politics of cynicism or a politics of hope? John Kerry calls on us to hope. John Edwards calls on us to hope. I'm not talking about blind optimism here—the almost willful ignorance that thinks unemployment will go away if we just don't talk about it, or the health care crisis will solve itself if we just ignore it. That's not what I'm talking about. I'm talking about something more substantial. It's the hope of slaves sitting around a fire singing freedom songs; the hope of immigrants setting out for distant shores; the hope of a young naval lieutenant bravely patrolling the Mekong Delta; the hope of a mill worker's son who dares to defy the odds; the hope of a skinny kid with a funny name who believes that America has a place for him, too. Hope in the face of difficulty, hope in the face of uncertainty, the audacity of hope!

11 In the end, that is God's greatest gift to us, the bedrock of this nation; the belief in things not seen; the belief that there are better days ahead. I believe we can give our middle class relief and provide working families with a road to opportunity. I believe we can provide jobs to the jobless, homes to the homeless, and reclaim young people in cities across America from violence and despair. I believe that we have a righteous wind at our backs, and that as we stand on the crossroads of history, we can make the right choices, and meet the challenges that face us. …

Making Observations
- What details in Obama's speech stood out to you?
- What words does Obama use to describe America?

Returning to the Text

• Return to the speech as you respond to the following questions. Use text evidence to support your responses.

• Write any additional questions you have about the text in your Reader/Writer Notebook.

1. How does Obama use rhetoric in paragraph 6 to advance his point of view?

_____

_____

_____

_____

2. In paragraph 8, how does Obama address potential counterarguments?

_____

_____

_____

3. How does the Obama's choice to end the speech by stating a series of beliefs contribute to the speech's overall impact?

_____

_____

_____

4. What is the main message of Obama's speech?

_____

_____

_____

5. In paragraph 9, Obama makes the claim that the United States is not divided. Do you think this claim is correct or incorrect? Defend your answer using text evidence.

_____

_____

_____

_____

As You Read

• Underline words and phrases that show the author's definitions of the American Dream.

• Highlight words and phrases that indicate how the writer feels about access to the American Dream.

• Circle unknown words and phrases. Try to determine the meaning of the words by using context clues, word parts, or a dictionary.

My Notes

_____
_____
_____
_____
_____
_____
_____
_____
_____
_____
_____
_____
_____
_____
_____
_____
_____
_____
_____

About the Author

William Zinsser (1922–2015), American critic and writer, was born in New York and educated at Princeton. He wrote articles for many leading magazines and newspapers and authored 19 books. In perhaps his most famous book, *On Writing Well*, he preached brevity and writing concisely. He was known for his positive attitude and once deadpanned that he was "cursed with optimism."

Essay

The Right to Fail

by **William Zinsser**

1   I like "dropout" as an addition to the American language because it's brief and it's clear. What I don't like is that we use it almost entirely as a dirty word.

2   We only apply it to people under twenty-one. Yet an adult who spends his days and nights watching mindless TV programs is more of a dropout than an eighteen-year-old who quits college, with its frequently mindless courses, to become, say, a VISTA volunteer. For the young, dropping out is often a way of dropping in.

3   To hold this opinion, however, is little short of treason in America. A boy or girl who leaves college is branded a failure—and the right to fail is one of the few freedoms that this country does not grant its citizens. The American dream is a dream of "getting ahead," painted in strokes of gold wherever we look. Our advertisements and TV commercials are a hymn to material success, our magazine articles a toast to people who made it to the top. Smoke the right cigarette or drive the right car—so the ads imply—and girls will be swooning into your deodorized arms or caressing your expensive lapels. Happiness goes to the man who has the sweet smell of achievement. He is our national idol, and everybody else is our national fink.

4   I want to put in a word for the fink, especially the teen-age fink, because if we give him time to get through his finkdom—if we release him from the pressure of attaining certain goals by a certain age—he has a good chance of becoming our national idol, a Jefferson or a Thoreau, a Buckminster Fuller or an Adlai Stevenson, a man with a mind of his own. We need mavericks and dissenters and dreamers far more than we need junior vice presidents, but we paralyze them by insisting that every step be a step up to the next rung of the ladder. Yet in the fluid years of youth, the only way for boys and girls to find their proper road is often to take a hundred side trips, poking out in different directions, faltering, drawing back, and starting again.

5   "But what if we fail?" they ask, whispering the dreadful word across the Generation Gap to their parents, who are back home at the Establishment nursing their "middle-class values" and cultivating their "goal oriented society." The parents whisper back: "Don't!"

lapels: folded flaps of cloth below the collar of a formal jacket or suit coat

fink: a person strongly disliked and viewed with contempt

mavericks: independent individuals who do not conform to the group

dissenters: people who disagree in matters of opinion and belief, rebels

6   What they should say is "Don't be afraid to fail!" Failure isn't fatal. Countless people have had a bout with it and come out stronger as a result. Many have even come out famous. History is strewn with **eminent** dropouts, "loners" who followed their own trail, not worrying about its odd twists and turns because they had faith in their own sense of direction. To read their biographies is always exhilarating, not only because they beat the system, but because their system was better than the one that they beat. Luckily, such rebels still turn up often enough to prove that individualism, though badly threatened, is not extinct. Much has been written, for instance, about the fitful scholastic career of Thomas P. F. Hoving, New York's former Parks Commissioner and now director of the Metropolitan Museum of Art. Hoving was a dropout's dropout, entering and leaving schools as if they were motels, often at the request of the management. Still, he must have learned something during those unorthodox years, for he dropped in again at the top of his profession.

7   His case reminds me of another boyhood—that of Holden Caulfield in J. D. Salinger's *The Catcher in the Rye*, the most popular literary hero of the postwar period. There is nothing accidental about the grip that this dropout continues to hold on the affections of an entire American generation. Nobody else, real or invented, has made such an engaging shambles of our "goal-oriented society," so gratified our secret belief that the "phonies" are in power and the good guys up the creek. Whether Holden has also reached the top of his chosen field today is one of those speculations that delight fanciers of good fiction. I speculate that he has. Holden Caulfield, incidentally, is now thirty-six.

8   I'm not urging everyone to go out and fail just for the sheer therapy of it, or to quit college just to coddle some vague discontent. Obviously it's better to succeed than to flop, and in general a long education is more helpful than a short one. (Thanks to my own education, for example, I can tell George Eliot from T. S. Eliot, I can handle the pluperfect tense in French, and I know that Caesar beat the Helvetii because he had enough frumentum.) I only mean that failure isn't bad in itself, or success automatically good.

9   Fred Zinnemann, who has directed some of Hollywood's most honored movies, was asked by a reporter, when *A Man for All Seasons* won every prize, about his previous film, *Behold a Pale Horse*, which was a box-office disaster. "I don't feel any obligation to be successful," Zinneman replied. "Success can be dangerous—you feel you know it all. I've learned a great deal from my failures." A similar point was made by Richard Brooks about his ambitious money loser, *Lord Jim*. Recalling the three years of his life that went into it, talking almost with elation about the troubles that befell his unit in Cambodia, Brooks told me that he learned more about his craft from this considerable failure than from his many earlier hits.

10   It's a point, of course, that applies throughout the arts. Writers, playwrights, painters and composers work in the expectation of periodic defeat, but they wouldn't keep going back into the arena if they thought it was the end of the world. It isn't the end of the world. For an artist—and perhaps for anybody—it is the only way to grow.

eminent: successful and respected

My Notes

11 Today's younger generation seems to know that this is true, seems willing to take the risks in life that artists take in art. "Society," needless to say, still has the upper hand—it sets the goals and condemns as a failure everybody who won't play. But the dropouts and the hippies are not as afraid of failure as their parents and grandparents. This could mean, as their elders might say, that they are just plumb lazy, secure in the comforts of an affluent state. It could also mean, however, that they just don't buy the old standards of success and are rapidly writing new ones.

12 Recently it was announced, for instance, that more than two hundred thousand Americans have inquired about service in VISTA (the domestic Peace Corps) and that, according to a Gallup survey, "more than 3 million American college students would serve VISTA in some capacity if given the opportunity." This is hardly the road to riches or to an executive suite. Yet I have met many of these young volunteers, and they are not pining for traditional success. On the contrary, they appear more fulfilled than the average vice-president with a swimming pool.

13 Who is to say, then, if there is any right path to the top, or even to say what the top consists of? Obviously the colleges don't have more than a partial answer—otherwise the young would not be so disaffected with an education that they consider vapid. Obviously business does not have the answer—otherwise the young would not be so scornful of its call to be an organization man.

14 The fact is, nobody has the answer, and the dawning awareness of this fact seems to me one of the best things happening in America today. Success and failure are again becoming individual visions, as they were when the country was younger, not rigid categories. Maybe we are learning again to cherish this right of every person to succeed on his own terms and to fail as often as necessary along the way.

Making Observations
- What words does the author use to indicate his feelings?
- What idea captured your attention in this text?

vapid: dull or boring

Returning to the Text

- Return to the speech as you respond to the following questions. Use text evidence to support your responses.
- Write any additional questions you have about the text in your Reader/Writer Notebook.

6. How does the author address a potential counterargument in paragraph 5–6?

_____

_____

_____

_____

7. How does the author's mixture of slang, colloquialisms, and pop culture references with his formal tone and language increase the text's effectiveness?

_____

_____

_____

_____

8. The author places the sentence "Thanks to my own education, for example, I can tell George Eliot from T. S. Eliot, I can handle the pluperfect tense in French, and I know that Caesar beat the Helvetii because he had enough frumentum" in paragraph 8 within parentheses (a _parenthentical_ statement). Why does he make this text parenthetical?

_____

_____

_____

_____

_____

9. Who is the author's intended audience for this article? Provide details from the text to support your answer.

_____

_____

_____

_____

_____

_____

_____

10. Does the author's choice to consider real and fictional examples of "dropouts" have a positive or negative impact on his argument? Explain your answer using text evidence.

_____

_____

_____

_____

☑ Check Your Understanding

How do these pieces complicate, confirm, or challenge what you have learned about the American Dream? Can the American Dream be both failure and success?

Working from the Text

To write a literary analysis that compares two texts, you must first identify the claims that each author makes. Then you must evaluate whether the author is successful at supporting those claims. Complete the graphic organizer.

Passage	Author's Claim	Evaluation of Claim
from "Keynote Address to the 2004 Democratic Convention"		
"The Right to Fail"		

11. With a partner, discuss each author's claims. Then discuss if the authors have a similar or opposing viewpoint about the American Dream.

✒ Writing Prompt: Literary

Imagine Obama and Zinsser having a conversation about the American Dream. What would that conversation sound like? How would they view and respond to each other's ideas? Working in a small group, think about what ideas each of them would assert, what qualifications they would offer to the other's ideas, which of the other's ideas they would challenge or disagree with, and what responses they could have to defend their own ideas. As a group, plan and write the dialogue they might have. Be sure to:

- Write the dialogue as though it were in a play but without the stage directions.

- Develop each author's ideas based on the texts you have read and represent those ideas fairly and fully.

- Paraphrase or use direct quotations from the texts. If you use direct quotations, make sure they are accurate.

INDEPENDENT READING LINK

Read and Respond

From your independent reading, select a subject or author who is struggling to achieve what is believed to be the American Dream. Write how this character's dream may be made possible by the work of others or how his or her work may help someone else succeed.

American Dream: Real or Imagined

Learning Strategies

Drafting
Note-taking
Peer Editing
Rereading
Self-Editing
Sharing and Responding

ACADEMIC

VOCABULARY

To **defend** is to support the statement that has been made. To **challenge** is to oppose or refute the statement that has been made. To **qualify** is to consider to what extent the statement is true or untrue (i.e., to what extent you agree or disagree).

Learning Targets

- Synthesize multiple sources in order to defend, challenge, or qualify a particular position.
- Collaborate to prepare a formal academic conversation asserting a claim, presenting evidence, and coming to a decision.

Preview

In this activity, you will work with a partner to research and support an argument. Then you and your partner will discuss your position with another pair, reach consensus, and craft a group position statement.

Structured Academic Controversy

In preparation for the writing you will do on Embedded Assessment 2, you will now participate in a small-group discussion model designed to achieve three goals:

- To gain a deeper understanding of an issue
- To find common ground
- To make a decision based on evidence and logic

The Issue: Does the United States still provide access to the American Dream for everyone?

In this activity, you will research and defend one side of the argument:

Side A

No, the American Dream no longer exists.

Side B

Yes, the American Dream is still a reality.

Conducting Research

1. With your partner, review the reading and thinking that you have done so far in this unit using the lens of your assigned position. What evidence do you have to support your position fairly and thoroughly? Research and organize evidence to support your side of the argument and write a statement of your position or answer to the question.

Types of Evidence

- Facts and statistics
- Analogy (figurative or literal)
- Personal experience or anecdote
- Illustrative example
- Expert/personal testimony
- Hypothetical case

My Notes

2. To present a fair and balanced argument, you also need to research potential counterclaims and evidence that acknowledges their strengths and limitations.

3. To appeal to an audience, a writer and/or speaker uses a variety of evidence to support claims. As you research evidence, consider your audience's knowledge, concerns, values, and possible biases. Use a table like this one to organize your initial research.

Summary of Your Position	
Evidence and Support	**Type of Evidence**

Position Presentation

4. In groups of four, present your position and evidence to the groups with the opposing argument. Be sure to:

- Take notes while the other argument is being presented and prepare to ask clarifying questions and restate the opponent's position. Evaluate their reasoning and use of evidence.

- Be fair and thorough in the presentation of your claim and evidence. Respect the norms of formal presentations, giving turns and speaking in a collegial but formal style.

5. Create a graphic organizer for your note-taking during the discussion of the issue. Proceed in the following sequence:

The Side A group presents its argument and evidence, including counterclaims (concessions and refutations).

Notes from the presentation:

Side B restates Side A's argument(s).

Restate the argument:

The Side B group presents its argument and evidence, including counterclaims (concessions and refutations).

Notes from the presentation:

Side A restates Side B's argument(s).

Restate the argument:

Reaching Consensus: Discussion

6. At this stage of the discussion, each side abandons its position and the group of four begins to work together to build consensus regarding the prompt. Using evidence gathered during their initial conversation, each member of the group should offer purposeful ideas to help move the group toward a consensus. Encourage group members to ask relevant and insightful questions that will help strength the group's position. For example:

   - Who supports this opinion?
   - For what reason do you support this opinion?
   - What position do the facts and statistics support?
   - Why is this position the strongest?
   - What are the counterarguments to this position?

Publishing Your Position

7. Together, craft a position that states the group position and decide what evidence supports the consensus decision on whether the United States still provides access to the American Dream. Post all of the positions on the wall under the categories *Yes* and *No*.

Getting Ready for the Embedded Assessment

8. Begin by reading and discussing the prompt from the Embedded Assessment and then brainstorming three different ways to respond to this type of prompt: by defending, challenging, or qualifying it.

Prompt: Defend, challenge, or qualify the statement "America still provides access to the American Dream."

Response 1 (Defend):

Response 2 (Challenge):

Response 3 (Qualify):

☑ Check Your Understanding

As a group, review the texts you have read in Unit 1. Create lists of which texts you could use to defend, challenge, or qualify the prompt.

⊕ Independent Reading Checkpoint

After completing your independent readings consider how these texts connect to the question of whether the American Dream is still alive and can be achieved. Synthesize in a short written statement how you think your readings respond to this question. Note which ones best support your stated position.

Synthesizing the American Dream

 ASSIGNMENT

Your assignment is to synthesize at least three to five sources and your own observations to defend, challenge, or qualify the statement that America still provides access to the American Dream. This question requires you to integrate a variety of sources (three to five) into a coherent, well-written argumentative essay. Your argument should be central; the sources and your observations should support this argument.

Planning and Prewriting	■ What are the elements of a strong synthesis paper, and how can you use these elements as a sort of "to-do list" for your planning?
	■ What texts from this unit provide relevant evidence for your own answer to the essay prompt?
Drafting	■ How will you clearly voice your position on the topic without overlooking the nuances and complexities of the topic?
	■ What assumptions or beliefs are either spoken or unspoken in your sources?
	■ How do the ideas in your selected sources relate to your position? Do they agree with, disagree with, or offer a sort of qualification to your ideas?
Evaluating and Revising	■ Do you consistently show how each selected quote from your sources relates to your central position?
	■ How can you make sure that your syntax is sophisticated and varied, especially the openings of your sentences?
	■ Are your ideas sequenced in the best way to guide your reader through your ideas and present a convincing argument? How could reordering some of your ideas improve this?
Editing and Publishing	■ How will you check for grammatical and technical accuracy?
	■ What sort of outside resources can help you to check your draft (e.g., a style guide such as MLA, a dictionary)?
	■ How will you prepare yourself to present this essay to an audience?

Reflection

After completing this Embedded Assessment, think about how you went about accomplishing this assignment and respond to the following:

• In what ways did your various sources validate your ideas about the American Dream, and in what ways did they add new elements or depth to your thinking?

SCORING GUIDE

Scoring Criteria	Exemplary	Proficient	Emerging	Incomplete
Ideas	The essay • effectively synthesizes sources to defend, challenge, or qualify the central claim of the prompt • provides a strong thesis that anticipates audience needs • uses convincing, thorough, and relevant evidence • acknowledges and refutes counterclaims fairly and thoroughly	The essay • adequately synthesizes sources to defend, challenge, or qualify the central claim of the prompt • provides a straight forward thesis that briefly contextualizes the issue • uses support that clearly connects the various source materials to the writer's position	The essay • attempts to synthesize sources but inadequately defends, challenges, or qualifies the central claim of the prompt • provides a thesis that attempts to contextualize the issue • uses support that connects the source material but with lapses in accuracy or completeness	The essay • tries to synthesize sources but does not defend, challenge, or qualify the claim of the prompt • includes a weak thesis or one that is lost in a summary of sources • includes support that paraphrases source material with no commentary or analysis
Structure	The essay • is organized to effectively reinforce the ideas of the argument • moves smoothly with successful use of transitions that enhance coherence • concludes by going beyond the thesis, illuminating how the writers influence the reader	The essay • is organized to support the ideas of the argument • arranges ideas so they are easy to follow, using transitions to move between ideas • includes a conclusion that is logical yet may be somewhat repetitive to the thesis	The essay • follows a simplistic organization with lapses in coherence • arranges ideas in a confusing way and with an inconsistent use of transitions • includes a conclusion that may be logical yet is too close to the original thesis	The essay • shows a lack of organization that detracts from argument, making the ideas difficult to follow • may jump too rapidly between ideas and lack transitions • includes a conclusion that returns directly to the attempted thesis
Use of Language	The essay • demonstrates a mature style that advances the writer's ideas • employs precise diction and skillful use of syntax, with keen attention to varied sentence openings, which helps to create a convincing voice • follows standard writing conventions (including accurate citation of sources)	The essay • demonstrates a style that adequately supports the writer's ideas • uses logical diction and syntax, with some attention to varied sentence openings, creating a suitable voice • largely follows standard writing conventions (including accurate citation of sources); errors do not seriously impede readability	The essay • demonstrates an inconsistent style that minimally supports the writer's idea • unevenly uses diction and syntax to convey a suitable voice, with few varied sentence openings • contains errors in standard writing conventions that may impede readability; some sources are inaccurately cited	The essay • demonstrates a limited style that ineffectively supports the writer's ideas • contains lapses in diction or syntax that may not allow a suitable voice to sustain throughout the essay; sentence openings may be repetitive • contains errors that impede readability; sources may be inaccurately cited

THE POWER OF PERSUASION

I am certain that my fellow Americans expect that on my induction into the Presidency I will address them with a candor and a decision which the present situation of our people impel. This is preeminently the time to speak the truth, the whole truth, frankly and boldly. Nor need we shrink from honestly facing conditions in our country today. This great Nation will endure as it has endured, will revive and will prosper. So, first of all, let me assert my firm belief that the only thing we have to fear is fear itself ...

—from Franklin D. Roosevelt's First Inaugural Address, March 3, 1933

CONTENTS

My Independent Reading List

CONTENTS

My Independent
Reading List

Texts not included in these materials.

Previewing the Unit

Learning Targets
- Preview the big ideas for the unit.
- Create a plan for reading independently.

Preview

In this activity, you will explore the big ideas and tasks of the unit and make plans for your independent reading.

About the Unit

Imagine you are a witness to a situation you perceive as being unjust. What is your response? Do you speak out or remain silent? Now, imagine you are an author who has witnessed an unjust situation and you decide to speak out using the most influential forum you know: your writing. Songwriters, poets, dramatists, bloggers—writers and performers of all ages—use social commentary to speak out against perceived injustices every day. Using art to advance social commentary has long been a hallmark of artistic expression.

Essential Questions

The following Essential Questions will be the focus of the unit study. Respond to both questions.

1. How can artistic expression advance social commentary?

2. How is rhetoric applied to the creation and delivery of persuasive speeches?

Unpacking Embedded Assessment 1

Closely read the assignment for Embedded Assessment 1: Creating and Performing a Dramatic Scene.

Your assignment is to work with a group to write and perform an original dramatic script in which you make a statement about a conflict that faces society. By doing so, you should be able to demonstrate your understanding of how Arthur Miller spoke out about a contemporary issue (persecution of suspected Communists) while setting his drama in a time period with corresponding events (persecution of suspected witches).

Find the Scoring Guide and work with your class to paraphrase the expectations for the assignment. Create a graphic organizer to use as a visual reminder of the required skills and concepts. Copy the graphic organizer into your Reader/ Writer Notebook and revisit it after each activity to check your progress.

🕐 Planning Independent Reading

In this unit, you will read literary fiction and nonfiction that explores America's commitment to freedom of speech. Collaborate with peers and discuss the pros and cons of free speech. In what ways is free speech an essential element of democracy? In what ways might free speech be dangerous, at times, for some members of society? Based on this discussion, compile a list of works for independent reading that discuss both sides of the issue.

Learning Strategies

Graphic Organizer
Paraphrase

ACADEMIC

Social commentary is a means of speaking out about issues in a society. It may take the form of rhetoric as well as artistic forms.

My Notes

Learning Targets

- Evaluate textual details to understand key ideas presented in primary source texts.
- Synthesize information from various primary source texts to understand the historical context of a play.
- Integrate ideas from multiple texts to build knowledge and vocabulary about a religion and witchcraft in colonial New England.

Preview

Arthur Miller's play *The Crucible* is set in Puritan New England. In this activity, you will study primary source documents to build your knowledge of the historical context of the play.

Researching Historical Context

When reading a play or novel set in another time or place, researching the historical context of the setting can help you better understand its plot, characters, and themes. Researching the historical context of a piece of literature refers to learning information about aspects like the social, economic, political, and religious conditions of the text's setting. Consider the following nursery rhyme:

> Humpty Dumpty sat on a wall,
>
> Humpty Dumpty had a great fall;
>
> All the king's horses and all the king's men
>
> Couldn't put Humpty together again

If you conducted research into this nursery rhyme's historical context, you would learn that Humpty Dumpty was not the anthropomorphized egg found in most illustrated versions of this text. Instead, Humpty Dumpty was a massive siege cannon that was used by King Charles I's men during the English Civil War that lasted from 1642 to 1651. Humpty Dumpty was strategically positioned at the top of a church tower and for eleven weeks successfully kept the supporters of Parliament from advancing. Eventually, the tower was blown up by the opposition and poor Humpty Dumpty fell into the surrounding marshland and was never recovered. Researching the political aspects of this seemingly simple nursery rhyme unlocks a greater meaning for the reader. In advance of reading *The Crucible* by Arthur Miller, you will read and analyze the various primary sources in this activity to begin to learn more about the historical context of the play.

My Notes

1. Use this KWL chart to help gain an understanding of *The Crucible*'s historical context. Begin by completing the W column with your teacher's assistance.

What I Know (K) About Puritan New England	What I Want to Know (W) About Puritan New England	What I Have Learned (L) About Puritan New England

My Notes

KNOWLEDGE QUEST

Knowledge Question:

What is the connection between religion and witchcraft in colonial New England? In Activity 2.2, you will read a series of primary documents that provide historical context for *The Crucible*. While you read and build knowledge about its historical context, think about your answer to the Knowledge Question.

dominion: authority
immoderate: excessive
brimstone: sulphur

As You Read

- Circle any unknown words or phrases. Try to determine the meaning of the words by using context clues, word parts, or a dictionary.
- Underline any words or phrases that answer the research questions in the Wcolumn of your KWL chart.
- Summarize or paraphrase excerpts from the text (paragraphs, lines, etc.).

About the Author

Jonathan Edwards (1703–1758), the son of a minister, was born in Connecticut Colony and grew up steeped in the Puritan tradition. Ordained as a minister at age 23, he became a prominent leader in the Great Awakening, a movement to reconnect Christians with their faith on a personal level. Although the sermon "Sinners in the Hands of an Angry God" was delivered in 1741, almost 50 years after the Salem witch trials, it reflects the Puritan concepts and ideals of the time.

Sermon

Sinners in the Hands of an Angry God

by **Jonathan Edwards**

1 [Men] deserve to be cast into hell; so that divine justice never stands in the way; it makes no objection against God's using His power at any moment to destroy them. Yea, on the contrary, justice calls aloud for an infinite punishment of their sins.

2 The devil stands ready to fall upon them, and seize them as his own, at what moment God shall permit him. They belong to him; he has their souls in his possession, and under his **dominion**. The Scripture represents them as his goods.

3 The corruption of the heart of man is **immoderate** and boundless in its fury; and while wicked men live here, it is like fire pent up by God's restraints, whereas if it were let loose, it would set on fire the course of nature; as the heart is now a sink of sin, so, if sin was not restrained, it would immediately turn the soul into a fiery oven, or furnace of fire and **brimstone**.

4 God has laid Himself under no obligation, by any promise to keep any natural man out of hell one moment. God certainly has made no promises either of eternal life, or of any deliverance or preservation from eternal death, but what are contained in the covenant of grace, the promises that are given in Christ, in whom all the promises are yea and amen.

5 So that, thus it is that natural men are held in the hand of God, over the pit of hell; they have deserved the fiery pit, and are already sentenced to it; and God is dreadfully provoked: His anger is as great towards them as those that are actually suffering the execution of the fierceness of His wrath in hell; and they have done nothing in the least to appease or abate that anger, neither is God in the least bound by any promise to hold them up for one moment. The devil is waiting for them, hell is gaping for them, the flames gather and flash about them, and would fain lay hold on them, and swallow them up; the fire pent up in their own heart is struggling to break out.

Knowledge Quest
- What religious imagery does Edwards's words create in your mind?
- How do you think the people of colonial New England felt after hearing the sermon?

Returning to the Text
- Return to the sermon as you respond to the following questions. Use text evidence to support your responses.
- Write any questions you have about the text in your Reader/Writer Notebook.

2. KQ In paragraph 1, what does Edwards mean by *divine* when he refers to "divine justice"?

3. What support does Edwards provide for his claim that people deserve to go to hell?

wrath: anger
appease: soothe

My Notes

4. What does Edwards believe can save people from hell?

_____

_____

_____

_____

5. Summarize the points that Edwards reemphasizes in the last paragraph of the excerpt.

_____

_____

_____

_____

6. Based on details in the text, what are some examples of Puritan values and beliefs?

_____

_____

_____

_____

7. What is the purpose of Edwards's sermon, and how does he tailor his message to his audience?

_____

_____

_____

_____

8. KQ How does Edwards's sermon provide historical context about the connection between religion and witchcraft in colonial New England?

_____

_____

_____

_____

About the Document

For more than 100 years, Puritan children received their first schooling from *The New England Primer*. Because the chief purpose of education in Puritan times was to enable people to read the Bible, it was natural that the alphabet rhymes chanted by the children should be based on Bible stories. *The Primer* is believed to have been in existence by 1688. Several versions have been printed, often with different verses for the letters.

Historical Document

The New England Primer

A	In Adam's Fall, We sinned all.
B	Heaven to find; The Bible Mind.
C	Christ crucify'd For sinners dy'd.
D	The Deluge drown'd The Earth around.
E	Elijah hid, By Ravens fed.
F	The judgment made Felix afraid.

T — Time cuts down all Both great and small.

U — Uriah's beauteous Wife Made David seek his Life.

W — Whales in the Sea God's Voice obey.

X — Xerxes the great did die, And so must you & I.

Y — Youth forward slips Death soonest nips.

Z — Zacheus he Did climb the Tree His Lord to see.

KNOWLEDGE QUEST

Knowledge Question:

What is the connection between religion and witchcraft in colonial New England?

G	As runs the Glass, Our Life doth pass.
H	My Book and Heart Must never part.
J	JOB feels the Rod, Yet blesses GOD.
K	Proud Korah's troop Was swallowed up
L	LOT fled to *Zoar*, Saw fiery Shower On *Sodam* pour.
M	MOSES was he Who *Israel's* Host Led thro' the Sea.

N	NOAH did view The old world & new.
O	Young OBADIAS, DAVID, JOSIAS, All were pious.
P	PETER deny'd His Lord and cry'd.
Q	Queen ESTHER sues And saves the Jews.
R	Young pious RUTH, Left all for Truth.
S	Young SAM'L dear, The Lord did fear.

T	Young TIMOTHY Learnt sin to fly.
V	VASHTI for Pride Was set aside.
W	Whales in the Sea, GOD's Voice obey.
X	XERXES did die, And so must I.
Y	While youth do chear Death may be near.
Z	ZACCHEUS he Did climb the Tree Our Lord to see.

My Notes

_____
_____
_____
_____
_____
_____
_____
_____
_____
_____
_____
_____
_____
_____
_____
_____
_____
_____
_____
_____
_____
_____
_____
_____
_____
_____
_____
_____
_____
_____
_____

⊘ Knowledge Quest

- What words are repeated in the primer?
- How would you describe the people who lived in colonial New England based on the contents of the primer?

9. The conventions of grammar have changed dramatically since the 17th century, which can make deciphering historical documents challenging. Some of the older conventions to notice in this historical document are the use of noun capitalization and the use of apostrophes to shorten words. It was also common for students to memorize passages, so primers for children included rhyming phrases to make memorization easier. Find two examples each that contain noun capitalization, apostrophe shortening, and rhyming. Then rewrite the lines using modern grammar and phrasing. Think about the reasons behind the changes in grammar conventions over time.

_____
_____
_____
_____

About the Author

Cotton Mather (1663–1728) was born in Boston in the Massachusetts Bay Colony. Following in the footsteps of his father and both of his grandfathers, he became a Puritan minister, and he eventually wrote more than 450 books and pamphlets. He urged caution in the Salem witch trials but largely ended up supporting them and published accounts of the proceedings in Salem.

Historical Account

The Trial of Martha Carrier

by **Cotton Mather**

1   Martha Carrier was indicted for bewitching certain persons, according to the form usual in such cases, pleading not guilty to her **indictment**. There were first brought in a considerable number of the bewitched persons, who not only made the Court sensible of any horrid witchcraft committed upon them, but also **deposed** that it was Martha Carrier, or her shape, that grievously tormented them by biting, pricking, pinching, and choking of them. It was further deposed that while this Carrier was on her examination before the **Magistrates**, the poor people were so tortured that everyone expected their death upon the very spot, but that upon the binding of Carrier they were eased. Moreover, the look of Carrier then laid the **afflicted** people for dead, and her touch, if her eye at the same time were off them, raised them again: which things were also now seen upon her trial. And it was testified that upon the mention of some having their necks twisted almost round, by the shape of this Carrier, she replied, It's no matter though their necks had been twisted quite off.

2   Before the trial of this prisoner, several of her own children had frankly and fully confessed not only that they were witches themselves, but that this their mother had made them so. This confession they made with great shows of repentance, and with much demonstration of truth. They related place, time, occasion; they gave an account of journeys, meetings, and mischiefs by them performed and were very credible in what they said. Nevertheless, this evidence was not produced against the prisoner at the bar, inasmuch as there was other evidence enough to proceed upon.

3   Benjamin Abbot gave his testimony that last March was a twelvemonth, this Carrier was very angry with him, upon laying out some land near her husband's. Her expressions in this anger were that she would stick as close to Abbot as the bark stuck to the tree, and that he should repent of it afore seven years came to an end, so as Doctor Prescot should never cure him. These words were heard by others besides Abbot himself, who also heard her say she would hold his nose as close to the grindstone as ever it was held since his name was Abbot. Presently after this he was taken with a swelling in his foot, and then with a pain in his side, and exceedingly tormented. It bred into a sore, which was **lanced** by Doctor Prescot, and several gallons of **corruption** ran out of it. For six weeks it continued very bad, and then another sore bred in the groin, which was also lanced by Doctor Prescot. Another sore then bred in his groin, which was likewise cut and put him to very great misery. He was brought until

KNOWLEDGE QUEST

Knowledge Question:
What is the connection between religion and witchcraft in colonial New England?

GRAMMAR & USAGE

Sentence Types
A sentence usually begins or ends with the main idea. When the main idea begins a sentence, it is called a cumulative sentence: "Martha Carrier was indicted for bewitching certain persons ..." Here the independent clause, "Martha Carrier was indicted," is followed by details that tell more information about the person and the event. The reader's understanding grows in a cumulative way as he or she combines each new piece of information with previously stated details.

When the main idea comes at the end, a periodic sentence results: "Before the trial of this prisoner, several of her own children had frankly and fully confessed ..." A periodic sentence is usually lengthy and creates a sense of suspense about the main idea.

Find examples of these sentences and think about the effect they have on your understanding of main ideas.

indictment: official accusation of a crime
deposed: testified under oath
magistrates: judges
afflicted: anguished
lanced: cut open
corruption: decay

The trial of Martha Carrier started on May 31, 1692, when she was transported to the Salem Village Meeting House to face her accusers, many of them young girls. When Martha entered the room, the girls fell to the floor, writhing with cries of agony.

death's door and so remained until Carrier was taken and carried away by the Constable, from which very day he began to mend and so grew better every day and is well ever since.

Sarah Abbot, his wife, also testified that her husband was not only all this while afflicted in his body, but also that strange, extraordinary, and unaccountable **calamities** befell his cattle, their death being such as they could guess at no natural reason for.

4   Allin Toothaker testified that Richard, the son of Martha Carrier, having some difference with him, pulled him down by the hair of the head. When he rose again, he was going to strike at Richard Carrier, but fell down flat on his back to the ground and had not power to stir hand or foot until he told Carrier he yielded: and then he saw the shape of Martha Carrier go off his breast.

This Toothaker had received a wound in the wars and now testified that Martha Carrier told him he should never be cured. Just afore the **apprehending** of Carrier, he could thrust a knitting needle into his wound, four inches deep; but presently, after her being seized, he was thoroughly healed.

He further testified that when Carrier and he sometimes were at **variance**, she would clap her hands at him, and say he should get nothing by it; whereupon he several times lost his cattle by strange deaths, whereof no natural causes could be given.

5   John Rogger also testified that upon the threatening words of this malicious Carrier, his cattle would be strangely bewitched, as was more particularly then described.

6   Samuel Preston testified that about two years ago, having some difference with Martha Carrier, he lost a cow in a strange preternatural, unusual matter: and about a month after this, the said Carrier, having again some difference with him, she told him he had lately lost a cow and it should not be long before he lost another, which accordingly came to pass: for he had a thriving and well-kept cow, which without any known cause quickly fell down and died.

WORD CONNECTIONS

Roots and Affixes

Preternatural is formed from the root *nature*; the suffix *-al*, meaning "of" or "connected to"; and the prefix *preter-*, from the Latin *praeter*, meaning "beyond" or "more than."

Samuel Preston uses *preternatural* to say he lost his cow in a manner that is beyond the explanation of nature.

calamities: great misfortunes or disasters

apprehending: arresting or seizing

variance: difference or disagreement

⊘ Knowledge Quest

- What about Mather's account of the event stands out most to you?
- What additional knowledge about colonial New England did you gain from reading this historical account?

Returning to the Text

- Return to the account as you respond to the following questions. Use text evidence to support your responses.
- Write any additional questions you have about the text in your Reader/Writer Notebook.

10. KQ In section 1, what does Mather mean by *bewitching* when he refers the charges brought against Martha Carrier?

_____

_____

_____

_____

11. What are the charges against Martha Carrier? What is the evidence against her?

_____

_____

_____

_____

12. What evidence does Cotton Mather include in section 2 of his account that is not presented at the trial? What does the inclusion of this evidence reveal about Mather's view of Carrier?

_____

_____

_____

_____

13. What evidence do Benjamin and Sarah Abbot offer as proof that Martha Carrier is a witch? Would this evidence hold up in a court today? Why or why not?

_____

_____

_____

_____

_____

14. Whose trial testimony seems likely to result in a further investigation of someone other than Martha Carrier? Explain.

15. What insight can Edwards's ideas in "Sinners in the Hands of an Angry God" provide into the trial of Martha Carrier?

16. KQ How does Mather's historical account provide historical context about the connection between religion and witchcraft in colonial New England?

About the Illustration

Francisco Maria Guazzo was a priest who lived in Italy during the 16th and 17th centuries. The following image is from his *Compendium Maleficarum*, a guide to witch-hunting that Guazzo published in 1608. (A compendium is a collection of information about a specific topic. *Maleficarum* is a Latin word meaning "witch.") In Puritan New England, the book was considered an authoritative reference work. It was routinely consulted by clergy, lawyers, and judges alike as a guide to the detection and prevention of witchcraft.

KNOWLEDGE QUEST

Knowledge Question:

What is the connection between religion and witchcraft in colonial New England?

My Notes

Illustration

Sorcerer Exchanging Gospels for a Book of Black Magic

Knowledge Quest

- Who do you think the figures in the image represent?
- What interests you about the artist's portrayal of the connection between religion and witchcraft in colonial New England?

KNOWLEDGE QUEST

Knowledge Question:

What is the connection between religion and witchcraft in colonial New England?

My Notes

About the Document

In Salem in 1692, a frequently ill young girl named Abigail Williams was among the first to exhibit behaviors associated with oppression by witchcraft. She accused several local women of causing her troubles. At one of the seven trials at which she appeared, a local official named Joseph Hutchinson testified against her in favor of the accused. In this deposition, or sworn written testimony, Hutchinson describes to the court conversations he has had with Abigail. The document was entered into evidence at the trial.

Legal Document

The Deposition of Joseph Hutchinson

by **Joseph Hutchinson**

The deposition of Joseph Hutchinson aged 59: year doe testifie as fourth

Abigaill Williams I have heard you spake often of a booke that have bin offred to you. She Said that thare was two Books one wos a short thike book & the other wos a Long booke: I asked her w'h Coler the booke war of: she said the bookes ware as rede as blode I asked her if she had sene the booke opned: shee said that shee had sen it opned many times: I asked her if shee did see any Ritinge in the in the booke: shee said thar wos many lins Riten & at the end of Evary line thar wos a seall: I asked her whoe brought the booke to her: shee towld me that it was the blacke man I asked her whoe the blacke man was: shee towld mee it wos the devell: I asked her if shee wos not afraid to see the devell: Shee said at the first shee was and did goe from him but now shee wos not afraid but Could talke with him as well as shee Could with ~~him~~ mee

Original handwritten deposition of Joesph Hutchinson

Knowledge Quest

- What connection between religion and witchcraft does Hutchinson make in his deposition?
- What words or phrases would have stood out to a jury in colonial New England?

Returning to the Text

- Return to the legal document as you respond to the following questions. Use text evidence to support your restponses.
- Write any additional questions you have about the text in your Reader/Writer Notebook.

17. **KQ** What does the word *seall* mean in context? What connotation does it have?

18. Summarize the contents of Joseph Hutchinson's deposition accurately and in your own words.

19. How would someone familiar with the illustration and the book from which it came most likely react to Hutchinson's deposition?

20. **KQ** How does Hutchinson's deposition provide historical context about the connection between religion and witchcraft in colonial New England?

⊘ Knowledge Quest

With a partner, discuss how reading the primary sources helped deepen your understanding of the connection between religion and witchcraft in colonial New England. Be sure to:

- Refer to evidence from the primary sources.
- Take turns speaking, responding, and asking one another follow-up questions.
- Ask clarifying questions.
- Write down notes from your discussion and further questions you have about the topic.

Working from the Text

21. Look back at your notes from the five primary sources in this activity. Use what you have learned to complete the L column of the chart. Instead of adding specific details from each source, synthesize the information from multiple sources to write comprehensive and complex notes.

22. Your teacher will sort you into groups and assign each group an aspect of *The Crucible*'s historical context to examine in greater detail. Evaluate the details that you read in each primary source to understand the key ideas about your aspect of setting. After your discussion, individually write a paragraph that briefly explains your aspect of the play's setting.

⬚ INDEPENDENT READING LINK

Read and Discuss

You can continue to build your knowledge about religion and witchcraft by reading other articles at ZINC Reading Labs. Search for keywords such as *persecution* or *religion*.

🍂|ZINC

23. Your teacher will assign you to a new group to discuss your paragraph with other students. Share your insights with theirs to gain an overall understanding of *The Crucible*'s setting.

24. What additional questions do you have about the historical context of *The Crucible*? Write three or four questions that you could use to do additional research about Puritan New England. As you continue to study the context of the play, remember to modify these questions as necessary.

☑ Check Your Understanding

The setting of Arthur Miller's contemporary play *The Crucible* in Puritan New England is key to your understanding of Miller's message. With a partner, summarize what you now know about the historical context of the play. Be sure to:

- Refer to evidence from the primary sources you read.
- Take turns speaking and responding by asking follow-up questions.
- Make clarifying statements.
- Keep a list of questions you still have about the historical context of the play.

The Lessons of Salem

Learning Targets

- Use newly acquired content vocabulary about the Salem witch trials in discussion and writing.
- Evaluate details about the Salem witch trials to understand key ideas.

Preview

In this activity, you will read the article "The Lessons of Salem" by Laura Shapiro and evaluate the details to understand key ideas about the Salem witch trials.

Learning Strategies

Graphic Organizer
Marking the Text
Note-taking
Rereading
Skimming/Scanning

Vocabulary of the Salem Witch Trials

1. To discuss *The Crucible*, you will need to be familiar with vocabulary related to the Salem Witch Trials. In your small groups, conduct informal research and explain each of the terms listed in the chart in the context of the witch trials. Record as much information about the term as possible, including its meaning, part of speech, and different forms of the word. If possible, explain any Greek or Latin roots or other word parts. Then synthesize the information to write a thorough explanation of each term. In the third column, identify other forms each term can take that indicate different meanings or parts of speech.

Salem Witch Trials Vocabulary	Definition/Explanation	Different Forms of the Word
accusation		
acquit		
hysteria		
magistrate		
Puritanism		
spectral evidence		
voodoo		
convulsions		
confess		
prejudice		
theology		

As You Read

- Underline key details about the Salem witch trials.
- Circle the vocabulary words that you studied at the beginning of this activity and make sure that you understand which meanings of the multiple-meaning words make sense based on the context.
- Pause after each chunk, evaluate the details you just read, and write down a key idea in the My Notes section.

Article

The Lessons of Salem

by **Laura Shapiro**

After 300 years, people are still fascinated by the notorious Puritan witch hunts—maybe because history keeps repeating itself.

Chunk 1

1   They came for Martha Carrier at the end of May. There was plenty of evidence against her: Allen Toothaker testified that several of his cattle had suffered "strange deaths" soon after he and Carrier had an argument, and little Phoebe Chandler said that shortly before being stricken with terrible pains, she had heard Carrier's voice telling her she was going to be poisoned. Even Carrier's children spoke against her: they confessed that they, too, were witches and that it was their mother who had converted them to evil. (Their statements were not introduced in court, however—perhaps because two of her sons had to be tied up until they bled from their mouth before they would confess. A small daughter spoke more freely; she told officials that her mother was a black cat.) Most damning of all was the evidence offered by half a dozen adolescent girls, who accused Carrier of tormenting them and who fell into writhing fits as she stood before the magistrate. They shrieked that they had seen the Devil whispering into Carrier's ear. "You see you look upon them and they fall down," said the magistrate. "It is a shameful thing that you should mind these folks that are out of their wits," answered Carrier. "I am wronged." On Aug. 19, 1692, she was hanged on Gallows Hill in Salem Mass., for the crime of witchcraft.

2   Last week marked the 300th anniversary of Carrier's death, an execution carried out during the most notorious summer in Massachusetts history. Between June and September of 1692, 14 women and 5 men were hanged in Salem as witches, and 1 man was tortured to death. Scores more were named as witches and imprisoned. "What will be the issue of these troubles, God only knows," wrote Thomas Brattle, a merchant in nearby Boston who was horrified by the events. "I am afraid that ages will not wear off that **reproach** and those stains which these things will leave behind upon our land."

WORD CONNECTIONS

Multiple-Meaning Words
In casual usage, the verb mind usually means "to object to or dislike something." It can also mean "to worry about something." However, Martha Carrier, as quoted in the first paragraph, uses *mind* to say that the magistrates are listening to and seriously considering the claims of the witnesses against her.

reproach: disgrace

My Notes

_____

_____

_____

_____

_____

_____

_____

3   He was right: even now the Salem witch trials haunt the imaginations of hundreds of thousands of Americans, tourists and history buffs alike, who visit Salem for a glimpse of our Puritan past at its most chilling. This year Salem is getting more attention than ever: the city is sponsoring an array of programs commemorating the Tercentenary, including dramatizations of the trials and symposiums of the legal and medical aspects of identifying witches in the 17th century. With the participation of such organizations as Amnesty International, the Tercentenary has placed a special emphasis on human rights and the role of the individual conscience in times of terror. In 1692, those who "confessed" to witchcraft were spared; only those who insisted on their innocence were hanged. Earlier this month a memorial to the victims was unveiled and on that occasion the first annual Salem Award, created to honor a significant contribution to social justice, was presented to Gregory Allen Williams of Inglewood, Calif. In the midst of the Los Angeles riots last spring, Williams, who is black, risked his life to save an Asian-American attacked by a mob.

Chunk 2

4   At the heart of the Tercentenary is the awareness that the witch trials represent more than just a creepy moment in history: they stand for the terrible victory of prejudice over reason, and fear over courage—a contest that has been replayed with different actors, again and again since 1692. Modern witch hunts include the roundup of Japanese-Americans during World War II, the pursuit of Communists in the '50s and, according to an increasing number of critics, some of today's outbreaks of community hysteria over **purported** sex abuse in preschools. Experts say that although most child-abuse allegations are valid, the preschool cases are the flimsiest, resting as they do on a mixture of parental error and children's confusion. Just as in Salem, the evidence in these cases tends to spring from hindsight, fueled by suspicion and revulsion. Whatever the truth may be, it has little chance to surface under such conditions.

5   Like all witch hunts, the troubles of 1692 began in a community that felt torn and besieged. Salem Village, now the town of Danvers, was about eight miles from the seat of local power in Salem Town. A contentious place, chafing to pull free of Salem Town and its taxes, Salem Village had suffered bitter disputes over its first three ministers before settling on a fourth, the Rev. Samuel Parris. During the winter of 1691–92, a few girls, mostly teenagers, started gathering in Parris's kitchen. There they listened to stories, perhaps voodoo tales, told by his Western Indian slave Tituba; they also tried to discern their future husbands by fortunetelling—dropping an egg white into a glass and seeing what shape it took. For girls raised in Puritanism, which demanded lifelong discipline and self-control, these sessions with Tituba represented a rare and risky bit of indulgence in pure fancy. Too risky, perhaps.

WORD CONNECTIONS

Word Relationships

Revulsion, *repulsion*, *aversion*, and *detestation* all refer to a strong feeling of disgust, but each word has its own unique connotation. *Revulsion* might make someone pull away from the object of disgust, while *repulsion* pushes one away. *Aversion* will cause one to avoid the object, and *detestation* involves a strong hatred of the object.

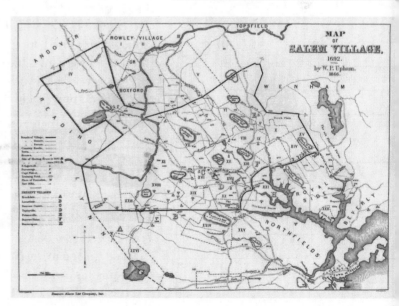

purported: said to be true but not necessarily proven

Suddenly one after another of the girls was seized with fits. Their families were bewildered: the girls raved and fell into convulsions; one of them ran around on all fours and barked. Dr. William Griggs was called in and made his diagnosis: the "evil hand" was upon them.

6   Fits identified as satanic possession had broken out among adolescent girls at earlier times in New England. Often their distress was traced to local women who, it was said, had entered into a compact with the Devil and were now recruiting new witches by tormenting the innocent until they succumbed. So the adults in Salem Village began pressing the girls with questions: "Who torments you? Who torments you?" Finally they named three women—Tituba, Sarah Good and Sarah Osborne—all of them easily recognizable as Satan's hand-maidens. Tituba was seen as a shameless pagan, Good was a poor beggar given to muttering angrily as she went from house to house and Osborne was known to have lived with her second husband before they were married. The three were arrested and jailed, but the girls' torments did not cease. On the contrary, fits were spreading like smallpox; dozens more girls and young women went into violent contortions, flailing, kicking and uttering names.

7   And the names! Rebecca Nurse was 71, the pious and beloved matriarch of a large family; she was hanged in July. George Jacobs, an old man whose servant girl was one of the afflicted, thought the whole lot of them were "bitch witches" and said so; he was hanged in August. Susannah Martin was named, but that surprised nobody; people had been calling her a witch for years. Six or seven years earlier, Barnard Peach testified, he had been lying in bed at night when Martin appeared at his window and jumped into his room; she then lay down upon him and prevented him from moving for nearly two hours. Others had similar tales; Martin was hanged in July. Nor was there much doubt about Dorcas Good, who was arrested soon after her mother, Sarah, was jailed. The afflicted girls cried out that Dorcas was biting and pinching them, and although the attacks were invisible to everyone else, the girls had the bite marks to prove it. Dorcas was jailed with the others, and a special set of chains was made for her. She was only 5, and the regular shackles were too big.

8   All along, there were townspeople who had misgivings about what was happening. Several came to the defense of some of the accused citizens, and others testified that they had heard an afflicted girl saying she had made at least one accusation "for sport." But the machinery seemed unstoppable. If a prisoner was released or a jury decided to acquit someone, the girls went into such shrieking torments that the court quickly reversed itself.

9   Spectral evidence: Finally, in October, the governor of Massachusetts stepped in. Too many citizens "of good reputation" had been accused, he wrote, including his own wife. What's more, clergy in both Boston and New York were expressing dismay over the witch trials, especially the reliance on "spectral" evidence, such as the sight of the Devil whispering in Martha Carrier's ear—otherworldly evidence invisible to everyone but the person testifying. The governor ruled out the use of spectral evidence, making it virtually impossible to convict any more of the accused. That fall the witch craze effectively ended, and by spring the last prisoners had been acquitted.

succumbed: stopped trying to resist, yielded

☑ Focus on the Sentence

Use the image and the information you have learned so far about the Salem witch trials to answer the questions that follow. Then use what you know about sentence expansion to develop the kernel sentence into an informative caption. Try to include two or three of the content vocabulary terms you learned in this activity in your caption.

Kernel: A young girl has a fit.

When? _____

Where? _____

Why? _____

Expanded Sentence:

_____

_____

Salem Society: Meet the Characters

Learning Strategies

Drama Game
Note-taking
Predicting
Previewing

My Notes

Learning Targets

- Analyze a dramatic text to determine appropriate tone and inflection to convey meaning.
- Analyze texts and make inferences based on textual evidence.

Preview

In this activity, you will play drama games as a way of meeting the characters in Arthur Miller's *The Crucible*.

About the Author

Arthur Miller (1915–2005) was born in New York to a family of Polish immigrants. He started writing plays in college and went on to win many awards for his writing. His plays *Death of a Salesman*, which won the Pulitzer Prize, and *The Crucible* have found permanent places in American culture. After writing *The Crucible*, Miller was called in front of the House Un-American Activities Committee, where he refused to name other "Communists."

The Crucible

Arthur Miller is a leader among the ranks of writers who use their art to comment on social issues. Miller created *The Crucible* to speak his conscience; he uncovered a setting, developed compelling characters through masterful characterization, created dialogue rich with metaphor and purpose, and structured a plot that transformed ideas into a drama of such persuasive appeal that it continues to speak to audiences all over the world. The most complete way to appreciate a drama of this caliber is to read it, perform it, view it, and, finally, emulate it.

1. Begin by thinking about the title and the meaning of the word *crucible*.

2. Listen closely as the text of the preface is read aloud. What can you infer about why Miller may have felt compelled to begin the play in this manner?

Introducing the Strategy: Drama Games

Drama games are a form of role-playing. Performing a role helps you make meaning of a text and understand it from the viewpoint of both a reader and a performer. Drama games require imagination, teamwork, and rehearsal. They also require a sharing of ideas to help make a text come alive in a visual way.

Drama Game

3. Follow your teacher's instructions to prepare to play the drama game. As needed, ask your teacher or peers clarifying questions to make sure that you understand the task.

Character: Reverend Parris

Line 1: You will confess yourself or I will take you out and whip you to your death, Tituba!

Line 2: How can it be the Devil? Why would he choose my house to strike? We have all manner of licentious people in the village! (to Hale)

Line 3: Rebecca, Rebecca, go to her, we're lost. She suddenly cannot bear to hear the Lord's-

Character: Tituba

Line 1: And I say, "You lie, Devil, you lie!" And then he come one stormy night to me, and he say, "Look! I have white people belong to me. And I look—and there was Goody Good."

Line 2: Mister Reverend, I do believe somebody else be witchin' these children.

Line 3: No, no, don't hang Tituba! I tell him I don't desire to work for him, sir. (to Hale)

Character: Reverend Hale

Line 1: Now let me instruct you. We cannot look to superstition in this. The Devil is precise; the marks of his presence are definite as stone. (to Putnam and Parris)

Line 2: We shall need hard study if it comes to tracking down the Old Boy.

Line 3: Tituba, you must have no fear to tell us who they are, do you understand? We will protect you. The Devil can never overcome a minister. You know that, do you not?

Character: Giles Corey

Line 1: Mr. Hale, I have always wanted to ask a learned man—what signifies the readin' of strange books?

Line 2: A fart on Thomas Putnam, that is what I say to that!

Line 3: I will not give you no name. I mentioned my wife's name once and I'll burn in hell long enough for that. I stand mute.

Character: Rebecca Nurse

Line 1: Goody Ann! You sent a child to conjure up the dead?

Line 2: This will set us all to arguin' again in the society, and we thought to have peace this year.

Line 3: I fear it, I fear it. Let us rather blame ourselves and

Character: John Proctor

Line 1: Can you speak one minute without we land in Hell again? I am sick of Hell.

Line 2: I come to see what mischief your uncle's brewin' now. Put it out of mind, Abby.

Line 3: Ah, you're wicked yet, aren't y'!

Character: Abigail Williams

Line 1: Can I have a soft word, John?

Line 2: My name is good in the village! I will not have it said my name is soiled! Goody Proctor is a gossiping liar!

Line 3: I danced for the Devil; I saw him; I wrote in his book.

Character: Mr. Putnam

Line 1: ... Mr. Hale. We look to you to come to our house and save our child.

Line 2: Why, we are surely gone wild this year. What anarchy is this? That tract is in my bounds, it's in my bounds, Mr. Proctor.

Line 3: That is a notorious sign of witchcraft afoot, Goody Nurse, a prodigious sign!

4. You will now move around the room as though you are a guest at a tea party. Introduce yourself to your classmates as if you are your assigned character and then give your line. Try to interact with as many classmates as possible. As you meet other characters, note inferences and predictions based on their lines.

5. After the activity, join the others who were assigned your character. Compare information and make inferences about your character based on the quotes you have been given.

☑ Check Your Understanding

Choose a character other than your own, and examine the predictions you made about that character in step 4. Compare your predictions to that character's quotes, and write a few sentences explaining whether the quotes support or contradict your prediction. If necessary, correct your prediction to make it accurate.

The Beginnings of Characterization

Learning Targets

- Make inferences about character motivations by analyzing actions and dialogue.
- Explain how a playwright develops a character in a script.
- Evaluate the author's use of foils to develop a main character.

Preview

In this activity, you will establish a routine for analyzing the development of characters throughout the play.

My Notes

Motivations

Characters in a work of literature act in ways that advance the plot. As is true of people in real life, fictional characters have reasons for the things they do. Those reasons are called **motivation**.

Sometimes characters react to situations in which they find themselves. Those actions are a result of external motivation. Other times characters act according to their worldviews, values, or personality traits. Those actions are prompted by internal motivation.

Often, as in *The Crucible*, character behaviors and motivations contribute to moral dilemmas. Those dilemmas further motivate characters and move the plot along.

A writer must have a clear understanding of character motivation to make those characters believable. Writers must also clearly present those motivations, either implicitly or explicitly, to make a play or other work believable.

1. Your teacher will assign you a character. Read the commentary sections in Act One that pertain to your character and try to find specific details. Use the Character Note-taking Chart to take notes on your character, writing down words and phrases from the text that describe your character's behaviors and reveal underlying motivations.

2. Use what you already know about the Salem witch trials and your character notes to participate in a class discussion. Complete notes on your chart as different character groups report to the class. Subsequently, as you continue to read the play, add information about characters to your note-taking chart.

Character Note-taking Chart

Character	Textual Evidence	Inferences about Character Motivations
Reverend Parris		
Tituba		
Abigail		
Mr. Putnam		
John Proctor		
Francis and Rebecca Nurse		
Reverend Hale		
Giles Corey		

☑ Focus on the Sentence

Choose one character from the chart and complete the following sentence frames about that character's actions and motivations using *because, but*, and *so*.

............acts/does/says .... because ....

............acts/does/says ...., but ....

............acts/does/says ...., so ....

Character Foils

A **foil** is a character who is placed in a work to provide a contrast to a more important character. This literary device stresses a main character's traits by giving an example of what the opposite of those traits looks like.

3. Return to Act One to note words and phrases that describe character traits of John Proctor, John Hale, and Giles Corey.

4. John Hale and Giles Corey can be seen as character foils to John Proctor, the main character. This juxtaposition of characters highlights key attributes of the major character. With your class, begin a class poster that lists the similarities and differences in actions and attitudes between Proctor and Hale and between Proctor and Corey. Use the table to make notes about these characters.

LITERARY

A **foil** is a secondary character who is contrasted with the main character to offer insights into facets of the main character.

VOCABULARY

Hale	Proctor	Corey

☑ Check Your Understanding

Write a few sentences that analyze how Miller develops Proctor's character in Act One by juxtaposing him against Reverend Hale or Giles Corey.

INDEPENDENT READING LINK

Read and Discuss

Discuss with classmates the types of characters or people you have encountered in your independent reading. Make notes in your Reader/Writer Notebook regarding how these characters or people fit within the setting of the work. What inferences are you able to make about characters and their motivations? What predictions are you able to make regarding these characters, and why?

Pivotal Scene 1: Considering Interpretations

VOCABULARY

LITERARY

Subtext is the underlying meaning in dialogue in a book, movie, play, or film. Not explicitly stated, subtext includes the thoughts of a character that may—or may not—coincide with his or her spoken words.

Learning Targets

- Collaborate on preparing a dramatic presentation.
- Evaluate implicit and explicit meanings of a dramatic text as a means of interpreting a scene.
- Analyze the effect of character motivation on the plot of a dramatic work.

Preview

In this activity, you will study lines from *The Crucible* to interpret the relationship between Proctor and Abigail. Then you will examine how that relationship helps shape the moral dilemmas of the play's plot.

Drama Study

1. Imagine that you are the director of a stage version of *The Crucible*. You must decide how you will portray the relationship between Proctor and Abigail. Discuss with a partner the different ways you could enact the following lines from Act One based on the **subtext,** different interpretations you may have of the nature of their relationship:

PROCTOR, *gently pressing her from him, with great sympathy but firmly*: Child—

ABIGAIL, *with a flash of anger*: How do you call me child!

PROCTOR: Abby, I may think of you softly from time to time. But I will cut off my hand before I'll ever reach for you again. Wipe it out of mind. We never touched, Abby.

ABIGAIL: Aye, but we did.

PROCTOR: Aye, but we did not.

ABIGAIL, *with a bitter anger*: Oh, I marvel how such a strong man may let such a sickly wife be—

My Notes

2. Following are three possible interpretations of the relationship between Proctor and Abigail. Reread the entire scene in which they are alone for the first time and create gestures, blocking (movements), facial expressions, and vocal delivery to match the different interpretive subtexts suggested. Be sure to identify the specific lines where the stage directions would apply.

Proctor Is in Love with Abigail				
Line	Gestures	Movements (from Stage Directions)	Facial Expressions	Vocal Delivery

3. How do the stage directions support the interpretation that Proctor is in love with Abigail and focus your understanding of this scene's staging and blocking choices?

Proctor Hates Abigail				
Line	Gestures	Movements	Facial Expressions	Vocal Delivery

4. How do the stage directions support the interpretation that Proctor hates Abigail and focus your understanding of this scene's staging and blocking choices?

Proctor Is Conflicted in His Feelings for Abigail				
Line	Gestures	Movements	Facial Expressions	Vocal Delivery

5. How do the stage directions you have added support the interpretation that Proctor is conflicted in his feelings for Abigail and focus your understanding of this scene's staging and blocking choices?

6. **Perform a Scene:** Now that your group has considered three interpretations of the scene, choose two of these interpretations to enact in a live performance. Take turns acting and observing the acting. When you play the role of actor, be sure to incorporate gestures, movements, expressions, and vocal delivery from your notes. When you play the role of director/audience, provide specific feedback to the performers about their performances. Suggest movements or expressions that you think will make the performances more convincing.

The Crucible by Arthur Miller, directed by Yael Farber, opened at The Old Vic Theatre on March 7, 2014 with Richard Armitage as John Proctor and Samantha Corley as Abigail Williams.

Moral Dilemma

7. In the scene between Proctor and Abigail, Proctor displays evidence of conflicting motivations. What are the conflicting motivations? Cite textual evidence to support your response.

8. When you have completed Act One, analyze how Proctor's behaviors and motivations create a moral dilemma and keep notes in the table about how that dilemma influences the plot and theme of *The Crucible*.

Proctor's Moral Dilemma	Influence on the Plot and Theme

INDEPENDENT READING LINK

Read and Respond

In your Reader/Writer Notebook, analyze and interpret an important scene from your independent reading. What movements, gestures, facial expressions, and words contribute to an understanding of the relationships between characters or people? In what ways might these dramatic elements be changed to shift the characters' feelings about one another?

☑ Check Your Understanding

Write a few sentences about the experience of trying out different interpretations. Which interpretation worked best? Why?

Analyzing the Elements of a Script

Learning Strategies

Graphic Organizer
Note-taking
Skimming/Scanning

My Notes

Learning Targets

- Examine how a scriptwriter uses literary elements, structure, print and graphic features, and language to develop a drama.
- Take notes to construct a checklist of elements for successful script writing.

Preview

In this activity, you will analyze the elements of a dramatic script. You will then construct a script-writing checklist addressing those elements: literary elements, structure, language, and print features.

Elements of a Dramatic Script

1. Embedded Assessment 1 will ask you to write and perform an original dramatic script. It is important that you be familiar with the elements of a script. Now that you have read Act One of *The Crucible*, take a few minutes with a partner to scan the text of *The Crucible* for the characteristics of a script.

2. On your own paper, create a four-square graphic organizer like the one shown. Use the guiding questions in the organizer to help you analyze the text for the elements of a script. For each of the areas, provide a sample from *The Crucible*.

Narrative Elements	Structure
• How do character and motivation influence the plot? • How is conflict introduced? • How does conflict advance the story? • Who speaks the most, and why? • How does the setting influence the characters and their actions?	• How does the writer develop events to create action? • How do dramatic shifts advance the plot and increase knowledge of the characters? • How does the text structure support the author's purpose? • How does the division of the play into acts create certain affects like suspense?
Language	**Print Features**
• How does the writer use diction and syntax in the dialogue to convey a particular time and place? • How does the writer develop mood, tone, and voice through language (syntax and diction)?	• What conventions of script writing are demonstrated by the play? • How do the stage directions contribute to the story? • How do the author's notations enhance understanding of the work?

☑ Check Your Understanding

Generate a script-writing checklist to use when you compose scripts. This checklist should address each element discussed here.

Illuminating Hysteria: Characters, Conflict, and Social Commentary

Learning Strategies

Graphic Organizer
Note-taking
Rereading
Skimming/Scanning
Summarizing
Word Maps

Learning Targets

- Evaluate how the motif of hysteria in *The Crucible* advances the plot and sheds light on the theme.
- Create a script for one dramatic scene.

Preview

In this activity, you will evaluate how the motif of hysteria advances *The Crucible*'s plot and illuminates its theme. Then you will write a scene that shows hysteria growing from rumor and unfounded accusations.

VOCABULARY

LITERARY
A **motif** is a recurrent thematic element—such as hysteria, a crucible, or witchcraft—or pattern—such as the Hero's Journey.

Motif

1. One **motif** in *The Crucible* is hysteria. The final scene in Act One shows the girls hysterically yelling out the names of people they have seen with the devil. While it is possible that each of the girls is simply lying, it is also possible that they, or at least some of them, are in the grip of hysteria. Eventually, much of the town succumbs to this hysteria. What reasons can you generate for the girls' hysterical behavior? Brainstorm possibilities in the margin and share your ideas with your group.

2. Use the word map to take notes during a class discussion of *hysteria*.

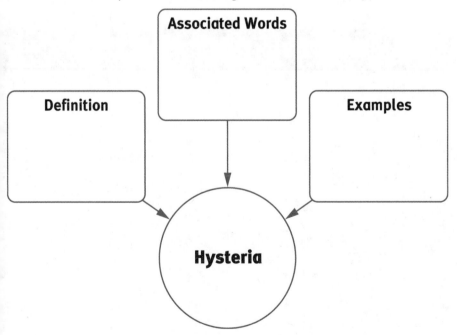

My Notes

3. To help you distinguish *rumor* from *hysteria*, reread the following excerpt from the article "The Lessons of Salem" by Laura Shapiro that you read in Activity 2.3, which provides historical information about hysteria. Mark the text for possible explanations for the girls' behavior. Be prepared to share them in a class discussion.

Today many scholars believe it was clinical hysteria that set off the girls in Tituba's kitchen. Fits, convulsions, vocal outbursts, feelings of being pinched and bitten—all of these symptoms have been witnessed and described, most often in young women, for centuries. Sometimes the seizures have been attributed to Satan, other times to God, but ever since Freud weighed in, hysteria has been traced to the unconscious. As Dr. Richard Pohl, of Salem Hospital, told a Tercentenary symposium, hysteria "can mimic all the physical diseases known to man," and occurs when repressed thoughts and emotions burst forth and take over the body. Life could be dreary for girls in 17th century Salem: their place was home and their duty was obedience; many were illiterate, and there were few outlets for youthful imagination except in the grim lessons of Puritan theology. Dabbling in magic in the reverend's own kitchen would have been wonderfully scary, perhaps enough to release psychic demons lurking since childhood.

Despite the fact that young girls made the accusations, it was the adults who lodged formal charges against their neighbors and provided most of the testimony. Historians have long believed that local feuds and property disputes were behind many of the accusations, and in *Salem Possessed* (1974), Paul Boyer and Stephen Nissenbaum uncovered patterns of social and civic antagonism that made the community fertile ground for a witch hunt …

Working from the Text

4. Consult your word map and the text of the play to track the growth of hysteria in Act One of *The Crucible*. Chart the growth.

Page Reference	Relevant Text	Part the Text Plays in "Hysteria" Motif

5. How do the girls' behaviors contribute to the moral dilemmas that influence *The Crucible*'s theme? What is the nature of those dilemmas, and who faces them the most?

☑ Focus on the Sentence

Different types of sentences are used for different purposes. Review these four sentence types.

- A statement tells someone information.
- A question asks others for a response and ends with a question mark.
- An exclamation expresses emotion and typically ends with an exclamation point.
- A command tells another person something to do.
- A command may not have a subject because it is understood that the subject is the person or thing being addressed.

Read these sample sentences about *The Crucible*.

Statement: I read *The Crucible* in 11th grade.

Question: What is the name of John Proctor's wife in *The Crucible*?

Exclamation: This is the best play I have ever seen!

Command: You must read Act Three, so we can discuss the courtroom scene.

Write four different sentences about the hysteria mounting in Salem. Use text evidence in your responses.

Statement: _____

Question: _____

Exclamation: _____

Command: _____

 Gaining Perspectives

In *The Crucible*, the townspeople accuse each other of being witches or of being possessed by the devil based on what they have seen or been told. As you have learned, clinical hysteria can present itself if many physical ways; however, the Puritans did not always investigate people's behavior fully before passing judgment. With a partner, discuss what it would be like to be accused of wrongdoing based on your actions related to a health problem. How could you effectively communicate your health issues to others? What types of communication skills might not be effective and cause people not to believe you? When you are done, summarize your discussion in your Reader/Writer Notebook.

Writing Prompt: Literary

With a partner or small group, select one of the following scenarios, or create an original scenario. Write a script to illustrate it. In your scene, show how hysteria grows out of rumor and unfounded accusations. Be sure to:

- Include a dramatic scene that illuminates the injustice of hysteria.
- Format your script using the guidelines in your script-writing checklist.
- Use purposeful dialogue and stage directions.

Scenario A: You enter math class one day to find a substitute. Classmates claim the teacher has moved suddenly without telling anyone, but specific details have not yet been provided. Consider the different perspectives students might have based on their perceived knowledge of an adult's character and imagine the rumors and accusations that might begin. How might such a situation create a context for hysteria? What role might justice (or injustice) play in this scenario?

Scenario B: The morning news carries reports of outbreaks of a disease that has affected local teens and young adults. Unusual symptoms have been reported, but there is no conclusive diagnosis from the medical community. What rumors circulate among the students as they attend morning classes? What evidence suggests that these rumors might lead to hysteria? How might students respond to this type of hysteria?

Scenario C: At an all-school assembly, students receive news that the athletic program will be cut due to lack of funding. At first, students speculate over budget cuts at the state level and complain about the injustice of financial restrictions on school programs. Later, rumors of inaccurate bookkeeping within the district begin to circulate. What unfounded accusations might fuel these rumors? How might this scenario become a context for hysteria?

Performers, directed by Wang Xiaoying, stage *The Crucible* in Beijing, China, at the National Center for the Peforming Arts on January 11, 2015.

Conflicts in Salem

Learning Strategies

Graphic Organizers
Marking the Text
Note-taking
Rereading

Learning Targets

- Analyze character motivations that cause conflict, moral and otherwise, and advance the plot.
- Analyze the role of conflict in supporting the theme of *The Crucible*.

Preview

In this activity, you will examine how *The Crucible*'s conflicts drive its action and advance one of its themes.

Conflicts Driving the Action

1. Even before the accusations of witchcraft start, the people of Salem seem to be in the middle of many different conflicts. The scene just after the commentary about Rebecca illuminates several strained relationships within the community of Salem. What motivates the characters to act as they do?

2. After reading Act One, identify who is fighting with whom as well as the reasons for the conflicts. This will be essential information to know as the community starts tearing itself apart. Reread this scene and mark the text by annotating examples of these conflicts.

Character	Versus	Character	Reasons	Effects on the Plot
	Versus			
	Versus			
	Versus			
	Versus			
	Versus			
	Versus			

INDEPENDENT READING LINK

Read and Connect

In your Reader/Writer Notebook, identify and analyze the role of conflict in important scenes in your independent reading. How do character or human motivations lead to conflict? How do these conflicts drive the action and affect the outcome of a scene or of the work? How do these character conflicts compare and contrast with those found in *The Crucible*?

My Notes

3. Choose a conflict from the chart and explain how it advances the plot of *The Crucible*.

4. How does the conflict you chose connect to the theme of the play?

 Check Your Understanding

Think about how one of these personal conflicts is also a struggle for power in the community. Briefly explain how this conflict mirrors a conflict in your local or national community.

 Writing Prompt: Informational

Select one of the conflicts you listed in the chart earlier in this activity. Write a paragraph analyzing how the conflict between these particular characters connects to a larger theme in the play, such as hysteria, intolerance, power, or reputation. Be sure to:

- Introduce and organize complex ideas by specifically stating how the conflict in the relationship relates to a theme.
- Write exploratory text that examines the connections between the characters' conflict, the plot, and the larger theme of the work.
- Use a variety of transitions and sentence structures to link the different sections of your analysis.
- Maintain a formal style and objective tone to convey your analysis.
- Provide textual evidence to support your analysis.
- End with a conclusion that follows logically from your explanation.

Speaking Like a Puritan

Learning Strategies

Diffusing
Graphic Organizer
Note-taking
Skimming/Scanning

Learning Targets

- Evaluate how an author's use of language shapes the perception of readers by immersing them in a historical setting.
- Write a scene between two characters emulating their voices.

Preview

In this activity, you will evaluate how Arthur Miller uses both archaic and figurative language to shape the perception of readers—placing them in Puritan New England. Then you will use your evaluation to write a consistently voiced scene between two characters.

My Notes

Using Language to Create a Historical Setting

In *The Crucible*, Miller uses diction to give his characters voices that are specific to Puritan New England.

1. The following words are among many that Miller chose to use in his quest to create a language that was an "echo" of the language spoken by the Puritans. What impact does this diction have on creating voice?

Act Two Vocabulary	
magistrate	quail (used as a verb)
fraud	lechery
charity	abomination
naught	blasphemy
poppet	vengeance
theology	conjure

2. With a partner or small group, write the definitions of any words you might already know in your Reader/Writer Notebook. Then, as you read Act Two, note where the words occur and how they are used. Use context to help you determine the meanings and consult a dictionary or other resource for confirmation.

3. Another way that Arthur Miller conveys the Puritan setting and mood and central thematic ideas of *The Crucible* is through the use of metaphoric language. Read the following lines and work with your group to determine the meaning behind the metaphors.

Metaphor	Meaning of the Words/Phrases and What They Reveal about the Character
Proctor: "a funeral marches round your heart"	
Elizabeth: "the magistrate sits in your heart"	
Proctor: "I will curse her hotter than the oldest cinder in Hell"	
Hale: "Theology is a fortress"	
Francis Nurse: "My wife is the very brick and mortar of the church"	
Proctor: "Vengeance is walking Salem"	

☑ Check Your Understanding

After looking at the metaphoric language Miller's characters speak, try your hand at creating a metaphor or simile to describe Mary Warren, Hale, or Abigail.

4. Find examples of character speech in the play and examine its diction. Then rephrase that speech using contemporary diction. Compare and note differences between the two.

> ### ✍ Writing Prompt: Literary
>
> Write an original scene between two characters from *The Crucible*. In this scene, emulate the language Miller creates to develop or extend a conflict related to one of the themes of the play. Be sure to:
>
> - Include appropriate language that echoes Puritan speech.
> - Write stage directions that set the context and guide the actions and vocal delivery of the speakers.
> - Provide a clear sense of a central conflict.

Elements of Plot: Rising Action

Learning Targets

- Analyze the impact of minor characters on conflict and plot.
- Analyze how two incidents complicate the conflict and move the plot inevitably to a climax.

Preview

In this activity, you will examine the plot structure of Acts One and Two of *The Crucible* in the framework of Freytag's Pyramid.

My Notes

Elements of the Plot

1. Act Two begins one week after the opening act. Once again, the action is set in a domestic context, bringing the conflict into the home of John Proctor, the protagonist. As you read, think about how Miller intensifies the level of personal and social conflict in this act.

2. Review the elements of plot as you read Act Two and think about how Miller uses them.

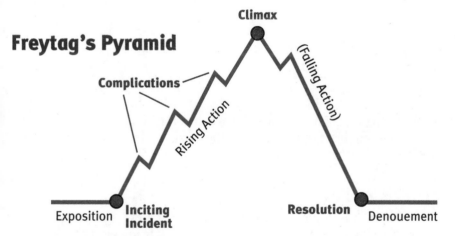

Freytag's Pyramid

Plotting the Conflict

A plot map can guide you as you think about creating a short dramatic scene. Act Two creates complications that set the plot on a path to destruction. Review the elements of effective plotting.

Exposition, or Setup

The beginning of the play must establish a little about the characters, setting, and conflict. This happens through stage directions and dialogue. Early Act One accomplished this for us in *The Crucible*. Locate a sentence or paragraph that functions as exposition in the play.

Inciting Incident

This is where our protagonist is launched into the action—like it or not. Again, both stage directions and dialogue make this happen. Review Act One of *The Crucible* for this moment in the life of John Proctor.

Rising Action

This is the long hill upward on the way to the climax of the play. Here is where the playwright builds tension by developing characters, deepening their relationships, and complicating the conflicts between them. How do the incidents in Act Two function to build this tension?

Climax

Here is the point of greatest suspense in a play. It doesn't last long, but it culminates all the conflict thus far. It is the moment in which the conflict could go either way. Like the "roller coaster" image, the climax will come close to the end of the play. Be on the lookout for the climax of *The Crucible* as you continue reading Acts Three and Four.

Falling Action

Will our antagonist be defeated? Will our protagonist fulfill his mission? Here's where we get these answers as things move quickly toward the resolution.

Resolution

The resolution of the play occurs when the protagonist solves the main problem or conflict or someone solves it for him or her.

Denouement

Think of denouement as the opposite of the exposition; the author is getting ready to end with a final explanation of any remaining secrets and questions. This section is very difficult to identify, as it is often very closely related to the resolution.

☑ Check Your Understanding

In your Reader/Writer Notebook, briefly summarize each of the elements of the plot structure in *The Crucible*. You may wish to add these elements to a diagram for future reference.

Pivotal Scene 2: Proctor and Elizabeth

Learning Targets

- Visualize different interpretations of a dramatic scene.
- Analyze implicit and explicit aspects of a fictional relationship.
- Engage in a collaborative discussion, responding thoughtfully to diverse perspectives.

Preview

In this activity, you will study lines from *The Crucible* to interpret the relationship between Proctor and Elizabeth. Then you will examine how that relationship helps shape the moral dilemma of the play's plot.

Learning Strategies

Close Reading
Diffusion
Graphic Organizer
Rereading

Drama Study

1. Imagine that you are the director of a stage version of *The Crucible*. How will you portray the relationship between Proctor and Elizabeth? Share your initial reaction to their tense conversation on pages 47–53 and be sure to consider the subtext of the spoken words.

2. Following are four possible scenarios or subtexts that could inform the relationship and interaction between Proctor and Elizabeth. After you have read the scene where they are alone for the first time, describe the gestures, movements, facial expressions, and vocal delivery actors might use at specific places in this scene to communicate the different interpretations. Be sure to identify the specific line where the stage directions might take place.

Proctor Is Cold and Distant				
Line	Gestures	Blocking (Movements)	Facial Expressions	Vocal Delivery

3. How do the stage directions you have added support the interpretation that Proctor is cold and distant and focus your understanding of this scene's staging and blocking choices?

Elizabeth Is Cold and Distant				
Line	Gestures	Blocking (Movements)	Facial Expressions	Vocal Delivery

4. How do the stage directions you have added support the interpretation that Elizabeth is cold and distant and focus your understanding of this scene's staging and blocking choices?

Proctor and Elizabeth Are in Love				
Line	Gestures	Blocking (Movements)	Facial Expressions	Vocal Delivery

5. How do the stage directions you have added support the interpretation that Proctor and Elizabeth are in love and focus your understanding of this scene's staging and blocking choices?

Select an Interpretation for Yourself				
Line	Gestures	Movements	Facial Expressions	Vocal Delivery

6. How do the stage directions you have added support this interpretation and focus your understanding of this scene's staging and blocking choices?

Richard Armitage as John Proctor and Anna Madeley as Elizabeth Proctor in *The Crucible* directed by Yael Farber in 2014.

Moral Dilemma

Skim or reread pages 47–53. Examine John Proctor's initial reaction to the news of Mary Warren's departure to Salem and how that reaction evolves as he learns more about the situation there.

7. At the scene's beginning, why does Elizabeth believe John should go to Salem?

_____

_____

_____

_____

8. What is at stake in the Salem court?

_____

_____

_____

_____

9. Why is John reluctant to talk to the Salem court even though it is obviously the right thing to do?

_____

_____

_____

_____

10. How does the return of Mary Warren intensify John's moral dilemma?

_____

_____

_____

_____

1. How does Elizabeth's insistence that John confront Abigail contribute to John's moral dilemma?

_____

_____

_____

_____

☑ Check Your Understanding

Write a few sentences about the experience of examining different interpretations. Which interpretation worked best? Why?

Courtroom Drama:
Examining Logical Fallacies

Learning Targets

- Analyze the validity of confession and evidence.
- Identify logical fallacies and examine their effects on the way the text is read and understood.
- Create an original script illuminating a conflict on an ethical issue.

Preview

In this activity, you will analyze the effects of logical fallacies in the way *The Crucible* is read and understood.

Setting the Scene

1. Think about a typical courtroom trial. What constitutes evidence in a trial? What role do eyewitness testimonials, confessions, and character witnesses play in determining guilt or innocence? What other types of proof are typically required for a conviction?

2. After a close reading of Act Three, think about the type of evidence that was used to prove someone guilty of witchcraft. List examples from Acts One, Two, and Three of the evidence that was used.

3. What is the role of confession and accusation in this courtroom? Considering the consequences, why would someone not confess?

My Notes

4. Briefly describe the consequence of Giles Corey's testimony in the courtroom.

Logical Fallacies

Logic is a type of reasoning that applies strict rules to determine whether a statement is valid. A logical fallacy is a violation of those rules. Some common logical fallacies are:

- **Ad hominem:** attacking a person instead of his or her arguments. ("You only believe that because you're undereducated.")

- **Bandwagon (appeal to popularity):** accepting a position because most people agree with it. ("Most people don't vote, so there's no point to it.")

- **Circular reasoning:** using an argument's conclusion as an assumption. ("It's alright to yell when you're angry because angry people yell.")

- **False dilemma (either/or):** presenting only two possible conclusions to a complex argument. ("If you love your country, you'll vote against this amendment.")

- **False analogy:** comparing two things that are not similar. ("People who like free samples are just like thieves who like money.")

- **Hasty generalization:** forming a general conclusion based on a few examples. ("I've been bitten by dogs, so I know that dogs usually bite people.")

- **Non sequitur:** a conclusion that does not follow from the evidence. ("Cars should be illegal because moving too fast is bad for people.")

- **Post hoc:** assuming cause and effect simply because one thing followed another. ("She ate a peanut butter sandwich yesterday, so that's what made her sick.")

- **Red herring:** a conclusion that changes the subject. ("I shouldn't have to write this paper because other people have already explored this topic.")

- **Slippery slope:** concluding that accepting something will lead to accepting something else. ("Letting children eat candy bars will lead to widespread obesity among young people.")

- **Stereotyping:** arbitrary statements about groups of people or things. ("French people don't like Americans very much.")

- **Straw man:** misrepresenting an opponent's position and then refuting that misrepresentation. ("While my opponent says she wants to lower income taxes, I support public school teachers, who are paid by our property taxes.")

> **VOCABULARY**
>
> **ACADEMIC**
>
> Logic is a type of reasoning that applies strict rules to determine whether a statement is valid. A fallacy is a false idea. Therefore, a logical fallacy is a violation of those rules; logical fallacies are by definition invalid. An example of a logical fallacy is an *ad hominem* attack, in which the opponent's character, and not the opponent's argument, is debated. Stereotyping and generalizations are also examples of logical fallacies.

Examining the Evidence

The dialogue in Act Three of *The Crucible* contains several examples of logical fallacy. Skim the text and find examples to complete the chart.

Character	Dialogue Example	Type of Fallacy	Why?
Parris	"Such a Christian that will not come to church but once in a month!"	ad hominem	Parris is attacking Proctor as a Christian rather than addressing his words.

☑ Check Your Understanding

Choose one logical fallacy from the chart you completed and write a brief explanation of how it affects the way the text is read and understood.

 Writing Prompt: Literary

Work with a small group to develop a short scene and then write a script based on one of the following scenarios, or a different scenario. Consider the role that various forms of evidence, including confession, might play in the scene. Write a script for the scene and assign roles. Rehearse the scene and perform it for another group. Be sure to:

- Include dialogue that develops the characters' traits within the setting.
- Write stage directions that set the context and guide the actions and vocal delivery of the speakers.
- Provide a clear sense of a central conflict.

Scenario A: A friend convinced you to donate money to a charity last year. You attended one of its meetings six months ago but did not get actively involved. Last week, you heard that a member of the group blew up an abandoned building in protest. The police arrested that person and want to collect the names of everyone involved in the group to prevent further violence. The police tell you that you have to give them the names of all the people at the meeting you attended. If you do not provide the names, you could be put in jail until you do.

Scenario B: You are an accountant for a large company. Your boss asks you to make some transactions that are possibly illegal. These types of transactions have been going on for some time, and the police are investigating the company and the transactions. You and a coworker are considering becoming whistle-blowers. A whistle-blower is someone with inside information who shares it with authorities. If you become known as a whistle-blower, you could be fired by the company. Other companies might also be wary about hiring you as an accountant. You have been interviewed once by the police, but you have not yet told them all that you know.

Scenario C: The school bus that you ride has been vandalized. The bus driver accuses a student sitting near you. You do not know who vandalized the bus, but you know the student in question was asleep for the entire bus ride. However, you have witnessed the student vandalizing school property in the past. The principal wants to question every student on the bus. If the person responsible is not found, the principal will ban backpacks on the bus route.

INDEPENDENT READING LINK

Read and Connect

In your Reader/Writer Notebook, construct a graphic organizer similar to the one you completed during this activity to analyze instances of irony in the work you are reading independently. Which types of irony are most prevalent, and what functions do they serve? How does irony move the plot forward, or convey an author's theme or message? What similarities and differences do you notice in how authors use irony?

Learning Targets

- Examine how characters' choices move the conflict toward a climax.
- Evaluate the use of dramatic, verbal, and situational irony to convey a social message.

Preview

In this activity, you will evaluate irony in Act Three of *The Crucible* and how it is used to convey a social message.

Character Choices

One of the key elements of characterization revolves around the choices a character makes. As you reread the scene with Proctor and Elizabeth in the courtroom, answer the following text-dependent questions in your Reader/Writer Notebook to analyze their choices and how these choices move the conflict toward a climax.

1. What secrets do both Proctor and Elizabeth have? What evidence supports your answer?

   _____

   _____

   _____

   _____

2. What choices do Proctor and Elizabeth make in this scene? Cite text evidence that demonstrates their choices.

   _____

   _____

   _____

   _____

3. For what reasons do they make their choices? Support your answer with text evidence.

   _____

   _____

   _____

   _____

4. How does Proctor's choice affect Elizabeth?

_____

_____

_____

_____

> **LITERARY**
> **Dramatic irony** occurs when the audience knows more about circumstances or events in a story than the characters within it do. **Situational irony** occurs when an event contradicts the expectations of the characters or the reader. **Verbal irony** occurs when a speaker or narrator says one thing while meaning the opposite.

Irony

5. Review the definitions of dramatic, situational, and verbal irony. With your group members, create an original graphic organizer on a separate piece of paper that demonstrates the similarities and differences between the different types of irony. Be prepared to explain your creation to the class.

6. Use the graphic organizer to identify and evaluate examples of dramatic, situational, and verbal irony in Act Three of *The Crucible*.

Type of Irony	Text Evidence	Evaluation *How does this example of irony help to convey a social message?*
Dramatic		
Situational		
Verbal		

☑ Check Your Understanding

Choose one type of irony illustrated in this scene and explain it.

My Notes

Learning Targets

- Analyze the purpose of a speech and the rhetorical devices used to achieve that purpose.
- Research the historical context in which a literary text was written to understand the social commentary it is presenting.

Preview

In this activity, you will conduct research into McCarthyism to better understand the society Arthur Miller was commenting on.

On the Spot Research

- What questions do you have about McCarthyism? Conduct research to extend your knowledge about the historical significance of the Communist "witch hunts" of the early 1950s.
- Reflect on the historical and political significance of the activities of the House Un-American Activities Committee (HUAC) during this period. What evidence from your research helps you gain insight into the plot and theme of *The Crucible*?

As You Read

- Underline or highlight portions of the text in which you find especially powerful use of language.
- Circle unknown words and phrases. Try to determine the meaning of the words by using context clues, word parts, or a dictionary.

About the Author

Margaret Chase Smith (1897–1995) was born in Maine. In 1936 her husband, Clyde, was elected to the U.S. House of Representatives, and Margaret succeeded him after he died in 1940. She went on to be elected multiple times in both the House and the U.S. Senate, the first woman to do so. She was also the first Republican senator to speak out against Senator Joseph McCarthy's anti-Communist campaign.

Speech

Declaration of Conscience

by **Margaret Chase Smith**

This is an excerpt from a speech delivered to the U.S. Senate, June 1, 1950. Smith was protesting the activities of the House on Un-American Activities Committee, which was formed by the U.S. Congress to investigate and identify Americans who were suspected of being Communists.

Mr. President:

1   I would like to speak briefly and simply about a serious national condition. It is a national feeling of fear and frustration that could result in national suicide and the end of everything that we Americans hold dear ...

2   I speak as briefly as possible because too much harm has already been done with irresponsible words of bitterness and selfish political **opportunism**.

3   I speak as briefly as possible because the issue is too great to be obscured by eloquence. I speak simply and briefly in the hope that my words will be taken to heart.

4   I speak as a Republican. I speak as a woman. I speak as a United States senator. I speak as an American.

5   The United States Senate has long enjoyed worldwide respect as the greatest **deliberative** body in the world. But recently that deliberative character has too often been debased to the level of a forum of hate and character assassination sheltered by the shield of congressional immunity. ...

6   I think that it is high time for the United States Senate and its members to do some soul-searching—for us to weigh our consciences—on the manner in which we are performing our duty to the people of America—on the manner in which we are using or abusing our individual powers and privileges.

7   I think that it is high time that we remembered that we have sworn to uphold and defend the Constitution. I think that it is high time that we remembered that the Constitution, as amended, speaks not only of the freedom of speech but also of trial by jury instead of trial by accusation.

8   Whether it be a criminal prosecution in court or a character prosecution in the Senate, there is little practical distinction when the life of a person has been ruined.

9   Those of us who shout the loudest about Americanism in making character assassinations are all too frequently those who, by our own words and acts, ignore some of the basic principles of Americanism:

The right to criticize;

The right to hold unpopular beliefs;

The right to protest;

The right of independent thought.

opportunism: taking advantage of opportunities for personal gain

deliberative: acting with careful thought

10   The exercise of these rights should not cost one single American citizen his reputation or his right to a livelihood nor should he be in danger of losing his reputation or livelihood merely because he happens to know someone who holds unpopular beliefs. Who of us doesn't? Otherwise none of us could call our souls our own. Otherwise thought control would have set in. ...

11   As an American, I am shocked at the way Republicans and Democrats alike are playing directly into the Communist design of "confuse, divide, and conquer." As an American, I don't want a Democratic Administration "whitewash" or "cover-up" any more than I want a Republican smear or witch hunt.

12   As an American, I condemn a Republican "Fascist" just as much as I condemn a Democrat "Communist." I condemn a Democrat "Fascist" just as much as I condemn a Republican "Communist." They are equally dangerous to you and me and to our country. As an American, I want to see our nation recapture the strength and unity it once had when we fought the enemy instead of ourselves.

13   It is with these thoughts that I have drafted what I call a "Declaration of Conscience."

Making Observations

- What questions do you have about the speech after reading it?
- What emotions do you feel as you read the speech?

Returning to the Text

- Reread the speech to answer these text-dependent questions. Use text evidence to support your responses.
- Write any additional questions you have about the text in your Reader/Writer Notebook.

1. What does the phrase *obscured by eloquence* mean? What does this phrase reveal about Smith's attitude toward her fellow senators?

_____

_____

_____

_____

_____

2. Identify and describe the rhetorical device Smith uses in paragraph 4. What effect does it achieve? Is it an example of strong logical argument? Explain.

_____

_____

_____

_____

_____

3. Explain Smith's use of rhetorical appeal in paragraph 5.

_____

_____

_____

_____

_____

4. What is the difference between "trial by jury" and "trial by accusation" (paragraph 7)? Which does Smith believe is a "witch hunt" (paragraph 11)? Explain.

_____

_____

_____

_____

_____

5. What does Smith believe is included among the "free speech" rights of American citizens?

_____

_____

_____

_____

_____

☑ Check Your Understanding

What part of Senator Smith's speech do you find most powerful? Explain why and give examples of her diction.

_____

_____

_____

_____

_____

As You Read

- Underline or highlight portions of the text in which you find support for the author's argument.
- Circle unknown words and phrases. Try to determine the meaning of the words by using context clues, word parts, or a dictionary.

Essay

Why I Wrote The Crucible: An Artist's Answer to Politics

by **Arthur Miller**

October 1996

1   As I watched *The Crucible* taking shape as a movie over much of the past year, the sheer depth of time that it represents for me kept returning to mind. As those powerful actors blossomed on the screen, and the children and the horses, the crowds and the wagons, I thought again about how I came to cook all this up nearly fifty years ago, in an America almost nobody I know seems to remember clearly. In a way, there is a biting irony in this film's having been made by a Hollywood studio, something unimaginable in the fifties. But there they are—Daniel Day-Lewis (John Proctor) scything his sea-bordered field, Joan Allen (Elizabeth) lying pregnant in the frigid jail, Winona Ryder (Abigail) stealing her minister-uncle's money, majestic Paul Scofield (Judge Danforth) and his righteous **empathy** with the Devil-possessed children, and all of them looking as **inevitable** as rain.

2   I remember those years—they formed *The Crucible's* skeleton—but I have lost the dead weight of the fear I had then. Fear doesn't travel well; just as it can warp judgment, its absence can diminish memory's truth. What terrifies one generation is likely to bring only a puzzled smile to the next. I remember how in 1964, only twenty years after the war, Harold Clurman, the director of "Incident at Vichy," showed the cast a film of a Hitler speech, hoping to give them a sense of the Nazi period in which my play took place. They watched as Hitler, facing a vast stadium full of adoring people, went up on his toes in ecstasy, hands clasped under his chin, a sublimely self-gratified grin on his face, his body swiveling rather cutely, and they giggled at his overacting.

3   Likewise, films of Senator Joseph McCarthy are rather unsettling—if you remember the fear he once spread. Buzzing his **truculent** sidewalk brawler's snarl through the hairs in his nose, squinting through his cat's eyes and sneering like a villain, he comes across now as nearly comical, a self-aware performer keeping a straight face as he does his juicy threat-shtick.

empathy: understanding
inevitable: impossible to avoid
truculent: easily annoyed

Senator Joseph McCarthy showing a cropped photo that he claims is evidence of American Communist infiltration at a Senate investigation in 1954.

4   McCarthy's power to stir fears of creeping Communism was not entirely based on illusion, of course; the paranoid, real or pretended, always secretes its pearl around a grain of fact. From being our wartime ally, the Soviet Union rapidly became an expanding empire. In 1949, Mao Zedong took power in China. Western Europe also seemed ready to become Red—especially Italy, where the Communist Party was the largest outside Russia and was growing. Capitalism, in the opinion of many, myself included, had nothing more to say, its final poisoned bloom having been Italian and German Fascism. McCarthy—brash and ill-mannered but to many authentic and true—boiled it all down to what anyone could understand: we had "lost China" and would soon lose Europe as well, because the State Department—staffed, of course, under Democratic presidents—was full of treasonous pro-Soviet intellectuals. It was as simple as that.

5   If our losing China seemed the equivalent of a flea's losing an elephant, it was still a phrase—and a **conviction**—that one did not dare to question; to do so was to risk drawing suspicion on oneself. Indeed, the State Department proceeded to hound and fire the officers who knew China, its language, and its **opaque** culture—a move that suggested the **practitioners** of sympathetic magic who wring the neck of a doll in order to make a distant enemy's head drop off. There was magic all around; the politics of alien conspiracy soon dominated political **discourse** and **bid fair** to wipe out any other issue. How could one deal with such enormities in a play?

6   *The Crucible* was an act of desperation. Much of my desperation branched out, I suppose, from a typical Depression-era trauma—the blow struck on the mind by the rise of European Fascism and the brutal anti-Semitism it had brought to power. But by 1950, when I began to think of writing about the hunt for Reds in America, I was motivated in some great part by the paralysis that had set in among many liberals who, despite their discomfort with the inquisitors' violations of civil rights, were fearful, and with good reason, of being identified as covert Communists if they should protest too strongly.

7   In any play, however trivial, there has to be a still point of moral reference against which to gauge the action. In our lives, in the late nineteen-forties and early nineteen-fifties, no such point existed anymore. The left could not look straight at the Soviet Union's **abrogations** of human rights. The anti-Communist liberals could not acknowledge the violations of those rights by congressional committees. The far right, meanwhile, was licking up all the cream. The days of "J'accuse[1]" were gone, for anyone needs to feel right to

---

[1] "*J'accuse*," French for "I accuse," was the title of an 1898 letter by famous writer Emile Zola protesting government anti-Semitism and miscarriage of justice—since used by many protest books and booklets, films and TV shows, articles, and speeches.

declare someone else wrong. Gradually, all the old political and moral reality had melted like a Dali watch. Nobody but a fanatic, it seemed, could really say all that he believed.

8   President Truman was among the first to have to deal with the dilemma, and his way of resolving it—of having to trim his sails before the howling gale on the right—turned out to be momentous. At first, he was outraged at the allegation of widespread Communist infiltration of the government and called the charge of "**coddling** Communists" a **red herring** dragged in by the Republicans to bring down the Democrats. But such was the gathering power of raw belief in the great Soviet plot that Truman soon felt it necessary to institute loyalty boards of his own.

9   The Red hunt, led by the House Committee on Un-American Activities and by McCarthy, was becoming the dominating **fixation** of the American psyche. It reached Hollywood when the studios, after first resisting, agreed to submit artists' names to the House Committee for "clearing" before employing them. This unleashed a veritable holy terror among actors, directors, and others, from Party members to those who had had the merest brush with a front organization.

10   The Soviet plot was the hub of a great wheel of causation; the plot justified the crushing of all nuance, all the shadings that a realistic judgment of reality requires. Even worse was the feeling that our sensitivity to this **onslaught** on our liberties was passing from us—indeed, from me. In *Timebends*, my autobiography, I recalled the time I'd written a screenplay ("The Hook") about union corruption on the Brooklyn waterfront. Harry Cohn, the head of Columbia Pictures, did something that would once have been considered unthinkable: he showed my script to the F.B.I. Cohn then asked me to take the gangsters in my script, who were threatening and murdering their opponents, and simply change them to Communists. When I declined to commit this idiocy (Joe Ryan, the head of the longshoremen's union, was soon to go to Sing Sing for racketeering), I got a wire from Cohn saying, "The minute we try to make the script pro-American you pull out." By then—it was 1951—I had come to accept this terribly serious insanity as routine, but there was an element of the marvelous in it which I longed to put on the stage.

11   In those years, our thought processes were becoming so magical, so paranoid, that to imagine writing a play about this environment was like trying to pick one's teeth with a ball of wool: I lacked the tools to illuminate miasma. Yet I kept being drawn back to it. I had read about the witchcraft trials in college, but it was not until I read a book published in 1867—a two-volume, thousand-page study by Charles W. Upham, who was then the mayor of Salem—that I knew I had to write about the period. Upham had not only written a broad and thorough investigation of what was even then an almost lost chapter of Salem's past but opened up to me the details of personal relationships among many participants in the tragedy.

12   I visited Salem for the first time on a dismal spring day in 1952; it was a sidetracked town then, with abandoned factories and vacant stores. In the

My Notes

WORD CONNECTIONS

Word Meanings
The word marvelous means miraculous or supernatural. In this use, it has the connotation of improbable or incredible as Miller goes on to associate the word with magic and paranoia.

---

coddling: treating with excessive care
red herring: distraction
fixation: unhealthy focus
onslaught: powerful attack
miasma: thick, unpleasant fog or vapor

My Notes

_____
_____
_____
_____
_____
_____
_____
_____
_____
_____
_____
_____
_____
_____
_____
_____
_____
_____
_____

gloomy courthouse there I read the transcript of the witchcraft trials of 1692, as taken down in a primitive shorthand by ministers who were spelling each other. But there was one entry in Upham in which the thousands of pieces I had come across were jogged into place. It was from a report written by the Reverend Samuel Parris, who was one of the chief instigators of the witch-hunt. "During the examination of Elizabeth Procter, Abigail Williams and Ann Putnam"—the two were "afflicted" teen-age accusers, and Abigail was Parris's niece—"both made offer to strike at said Procter; but when Abigail's hand came near, it opened, whereas it was made up, into a fist before, and came down exceeding lightly as it drew near to said Procter, and at length, with open and extended fingers, touched Procter's hood very lightly. Immediately Abigail cried out her fingers, her fingers, her fingers burned. ..."

13 In this remarkably observed gesture of a troubled young girl, I believed, a play became possible. Elizabeth Proctor had been the orphaned Abigail's mistress, and they had lived together in the same small house until Elizabeth fired the girl. By this time, I was sure, John Proctor had bedded Abigail, who had to be dismissed most likely to appease Elizabeth. There was bad blood between the two women now. That Abigail started, in effect, to condemn Elizabeth to death with her touch, then stopped her hand, then went through with it, was quite suddenly the human center of all this turmoil.

14 All this I understood. I had not approached the witchcraft out of nowhere or from purely social and political considerations. My own marriage of twelve years was teetering and I knew more than I wished to know about where the blame lay. That John Proctor the sinner might overturn his paralyzing personal guilt and become the most forthright voice against the madness around him was a reassurance to me, and, I suppose, an inspiration: it demonstrated that a clear moral outcry could still spring even from an ambiguously unblemished soul. Moving crabwise across the profusion of evidence, I sensed that I had at last found something of myself in it, and a play began to accumulate around this man.

15 But as the dramatic form became visible, one problem remained unyielding: so many practices of the Salem trials were similar to those employed by the congressional committees that I could easily be accused of skewing history for a mere partisan purpose. Inevitably, it was no sooner known that my new play was about Salem than I had to confront the charge that such an analogy was specious—that there never were any witches but there certainly are Communists. In the seventeenth century, however, the existence of witches was never questioned by the loftiest minds in Europe and America; and even lawyers of the highest eminence, like Sir Edward Coke, a veritable hero of liberty for defending the common law against the king's arbitrary power, believed that witches had to be prosecuted mercilessly. Of course, there were no Communists in 1692, but it was literally worth your life to deny witches or their powers, given the exhortation in the Bible, "Thou shalt not suffer a witch to live." There had to be witches in the world or the Bible lied. Indeed, the very structure of evil depended on Lucifer's

spelling: giving a rest, relieving

forthright: simple and honest, frank

ambiguously: doubtfully, uncertainly

skewing: changing from facts

specious: false or baseless, fallacious

eminence: rank

arbitrary: unlimited

plotting against God. (And the irony is that klatches of Luciferians exist all over the country today; there may even be more of them now than there are Communists.)

16 As with most humans, panic sleeps in one unlighted corner of my soul. When I walked at night along the empty, wet streets of Salem in the week that I spent there, I could easily work myself into imagining my terror before a gaggle of young girls flying down the road screaming that somebody's "familiar spirit" was chasing them. This anxiety-laden leap backward over nearly three centuries may have been helped along by a particular Upham footnote. At a certain point, the high court of the province made the fatal decision to admit, for the first time, the use of "spectral evidence" as proof of guilt. Spectral evidence, so aptly named, meant that if I swore that you had sent out your "familiar spirit" to choke, tickle, poison me or my cattle, or to control my thoughts and actions, I could get you hanged unless you confessed to having had contact with the Devil. After all, only the Devil could lend such powers of invisible transport to **confederates**, in his everlasting plot to bring down Christianity.

17 Naturally, the best proof of the sincerity of your confession was your naming others whom you had seen in the Devil's company—an invitation to private vengeance, but made official by the seal of the **theocratic** state. It was as though the court had grown tired of thinking and had invited in the instincts: spectral evidence—that poisoned cloud of paranoid fantasy—made a kind of lunatic sense to them, as it did in plot-ridden 1952, when so often the question was not the acts of an accused but the thoughts and intentions in his alienated mind.

18 The breathtaking circularity of the process had a kind of poetic tightness. Not everybody was accused, after all, so there must be some reason why you were. By denying that there is any reason whatsoever for you to be accused, you are implying, by virtue of a surprisingly small logical leap, that mere chance picked you out, which in turn implies that the Devil might not really be at work in the village, or, God forbid, even exist. Therefore, the investigation itself is either mistaken or a fraud. You would have to be a crypto-Luciferian to say that—not a great idea if you wanted to go back to your farm.

19 The more I read into the Salem panic, the more it touched off corresponding images of common experiences in the fifties: the old friend of a blacklisted person crossing the street to avoid being seen talking to him; the overnight conversions of former leftists into born-again patriots; and so on. Apparently, certain processes are universal. When Gentiles in Hitler's Germany, for example, saw their Jewish neighbors being trucked off, or farmers in Soviet Ukraine saw the Kulaks vanishing before their eyes, the common reaction, even among those unsympathetic to Nazism or Communism, was quite naturally to turn away in fear of being identified with the condemned. As I learned from non-Jewish refugees, however, there was often a despairing pity mixed with "Well, they must have done something." Few of us can easily surrender our

WORD CONNECTIONS

Roots and Affixes
The prefix **crypto-** comes from the Greek *kryptos* and means "hidden" or "covered." Miller suggests that only a hidden Satanist would imply that the witch investigations were a fraud. Other related words are *crypt* and *cryptic*.

confederates: allies
theocratic: governed by God or priests

belief that society must somehow make sense. The thought that the state has lost its mind and is punishing so many innocent people is intolerable. And so the evidence has to be internally denied.

20 I was also drawn into writing *The Crucible* by the chance it gave me to use a new language—that of seventeenth-century New England. The plain, craggy English was liberating in a strangely sensuous way, with its swings from an almost legalistic precision to a wonderful metaphoric richness. "The Lord doth terrible things amongst us, by lengthening the chain of the roaring lion in an extraordinary manner, so that the Devil is come down in great wrath," Deodat Lawson, one of the great witch-hunting preachers, said in a sermon. Lawson rallied his congregation for what was to be nothing less than a religious war against the Evil One—"Arm, arm, arm!"—and his concealed anti-Christian accomplices.

21 But it was not yet my language, and among other strategies to make it mine I enlisted the help of a former University of Michigan classmate, the Greek-American scholar and poet Kimon Friar (He later translated Kazantzakis.) The problem was not to the archaic speech but to try to create a new echo of it which would flow freely off American actors' tongues. As in the film nearly fifty years later, the actors in the first production grabbed the language and ran with it as happily as if it were their customary speech.

22 *The Crucible* took me about a year to write. With its five sets and a cast of twenty-one, it never occurred to me that it would take a brave man to produce it on Broadway, especially given the prevailing climate, but Kermit Bloomgarden never faltered. Well before the play opened, a strange tension had begun to build. Only two years earlier, the *Death of a Salesman* touring company had played to a thin crowd in Peoria, Illinois, having been boycotted nearly to death by the American Legion and the Jaycees. Before that, the Catholic War Veterans had prevailed upon the Army not to allow its theatrical groups to perform, first, *All My Sons*, and then any play of mine, in occupied Europe. The Dramatists Guild refused to protest attacks on a new play by Sean O'Casey, a self-declared Communist, which forced its producer to cancel his option. I knew of two suicides by actors depressed by upcoming investigation, and every day seemed to bring news of people exiling themselves to Europe: Charlie Chaplin, the director Joseph Losey, Jules Dassin, the harmonica virtuoso Larry Adler, Donald Ogden Stewart, one of the most sought-after screenwriters in Hollywood, and Sam Wanamaker, who would lead the successful campaign to rebuild the Old Globe Theater on the Thames.

23 On opening night, January 22, 1953, I knew that the atmosphere would be pretty hostile. The coldness of the crowd was not a surprise; Broadway audiences were not famous for loving history lessons, which is what they made of the play. It seems to me entirely appropriate that on the day the play opened, a newspaper headline read "ALL 13 REDS GUILTY"—a story about American Communists who faced prison for "conspiring to teach

intolerable: unbearable
archaic: no longer used in ordinary language
prevailing: commonly accepted by most people

and advocate the duty and necessity of forcible overthrow of government." Meanwhile, the remoteness of the production was guaranteed by the director, Jed Harris, who insisted that this was a classic requiring the actors to face front, never each other. The critics were not swept away. "Arthur Miller is a problem playwright in both senses of the word," wrote Walter Kerr of the Herald Tribune, who called the play "a step backward into mechanical parable." The Times was not much kinder, saying, "There is too much excitement and not enough emotion in 'The Crucible.'" But the play's future would turn out quite differently.

24 About a year later, a new production, one with younger, less accomplished actors, working in the Martinique Hotel ballroom, played with the fervor that the script and the times required, and *The Crucible* became a hit. The play stumbled into history, and today, I am told, it is one of the most heavily demanded trade-fiction paperbacks in this country; the Bantam and Penguin editions have sold more than six million copies. I don't think there has been a week in the past forty-odd years when it hasn't been on a stage somewhere in the world. Nor is the new screen version the first. Jean-Paul Sartre, in his Marxist phase, wrote a French film adaptation that blamed the tragedy on the rich landowners conspiring to persecute the poor. (In truth, most of those who were hanged in Salem were people of substance, and two or three were very large landowners.)

25 It is only a slight exaggeration to say that, especially in Latin America, *The Crucible* starts getting produced wherever a political coup appears imminent, or a dictatorial regime has just been overthrown. From Argentina to Chile to Greece, Czechoslovakia, China, and a dozen other places, the play seems to present the same primeval structure of human sacrifice to the furies of fanaticism and paranoia that goes on repeating itself forever as though imbedded in the brain of social man.

26 I am not sure what *The Crucible* is telling people now, but I know that its paranoid center is still pumping out the same darkly attractive warning that it did in the fifties. For some, the play seems to be about the dilemma of relying on the testimony of small children accusing adults of sexual abuse, something I'd not have dreamed of forty years ago. For others, it may simply be a fascination with the outbreak of paranoia that suffuses the play—the blind panic that, in our age, often seems to sit at the dim edges of consciousness. Certainly, its political implications are the central issue for many people; the Salem interrogations turn out to be eerily exact models of those yet to come in Stalin's Russia, Pinochet's Chile, Mao's China, and other regimes. (Nien Cheng, the author of "Life and Death in Shanghai," has told me that she could hardly believe that a non-Chinese—someone who had not experienced the Cultural Revolution—had written the play.) But below its concerns with justice the play evokes a lethal brew of illicit sexuality, fear of the supernatural, and political manipulation, a combination not unfamiliar these days. The film, by reaching

My Notes

parable: story that teaches a lesson
fervor: enthusiasm
regime: type of government
implications: suggestions

My Notes

a broad American audience as no play ever can, may well unearth still other connections to those buried public terrors that Salem first announced on this continent.

27   One thing more—something wonderful in the old sense of that word. I recall the weeks I spent reading testimony by the **tome**, **commentaries**, broadsides, confessions, and accusations. And always the **crucial** damning event was the signing of one's name in the Devil's book. This Faustian agreement to hand over one's soul to the dreaded Lord of Darkness was the ultimate insult to God. But what were these new inductees supposed to have done once they'd signed on? Nobody seems even to have thought to ask. But, of course, actions are as irrelevant during cultural and religious wars as they are in nightmares. The thing at issue is buried intentions—the secret allegiances of the alienated heart, always the main threat to the theocratic mind, as well as its **immemorial** quarry.

Making Observations

- What are your first thoughts about the article?
- Which of Miller's observations do you find interesting?
- What images in the essay catch your attention?

tome: large book
commentaries: texts that comment on a topic
crucial: very important
immemorial: beyond time or memory

LANGUAGE & WRITER'S CRAFT: Rhetorical Punctuation

One way to make a point in an argument is to use effective punctuation. Effective punctuation helps a reader understand how to read a sentence, often by using commas to denote a pause, a question mark to show a question, or a period to end a statement. Punctuation can also include apostrophes, colons, and semicolons.

Example: But what were these new inductees supposed to have done once they'd signed on?

Here Miller uses a question mark to pose a rhetorical question. Authors might use a rhetorical question mark in an argument to guide readers to consider a point that is being made.

PRACTICE Decide which of the following sentences are rhetorical questions and punctuate them correctly.

How are we to know what Miller's political beliefs are [ ]

Miller's political beliefs are hard to decipher [ ]

What do Miller's political beliefs have to do with *The Crucible* [ ]

☑ Check Your Understanding

Has Miller's explanation enhanced or limited your interpretation of the play? Briefly explain your answer.

📝 Explain How an Author Builds an Argument

Write an essay in which you explain how the author builds an argument to persuade the audience of the social agenda promoted in a speech or essay. Select one passage as the focus for your essay: Margaret Chase Smith's speech Declaration of Conscience or Arthur Miller's essay "Why I Wrote *The Crucible*: An Artist's Answer to Politics." In your essay, analyze how the author uses three or more of the rhetorical techniques you have studied to strengthen the logic and persuasiveness of the argument. Be sure to:

- Identify the author's claim.
- Label and provide evidence of rhetorical techniques, introducing and punctuating them correctly.
- Analyze the effects of each rhetorical technique.
- Evaluate the overall effectiveness of the passage.
- End with a conclusion that follows logically from your analysis.
- Check to make sure you have correctly used hyphens and other punctuation.

Integrity Rises to the Top: Writing Dialogue

Learning Targets

- Analyze the use of dialogue and character interactions in a dramatic text.
- Generate scripted dialogue that reveals character and propels action.

Preview

In this activity, you will study dialogue that reveals character and propels action and then use the insights you have gained to write dialogue.

My Notes

Falling Action

1. **Quickwrite:** With one more act remaining in the play and the tension at its peak, predict the outcome of the play. Use details from the text to support your prediction.

2. As you read the opening section of Act Four (until Elizabeth and Proctor are alone), mark the text for changes that have occurred in the town. Be prepared to share your observations with the class.

Analyzing Dialogue

3. Continue the exploration of foils that you began in Activity 2.5 by tracking the characteristics of Proctor, Hale, and Corey as possible representations of particular points of view in the final pages of Act Four by paying special attention to their dialogue. In the graphic organizer, record adjectives that describe each character.

Hale	Proctor	Corey

4. Cite a specific example of dialogue from one of the three characters that conveys a point of view. Explain how the dialogue does so.

5. In general, what role does dialogue play in the advancement of *The Crucible*'s plot

☑ Check Your Understanding

Briefly describe how Hale and Corey function as foils to John Proctor. Which of Proctor's traits are more apparent when comparing him with each of the other men

Creating a Dialogue

The last step in writing a script is to actually write the dialogue. This essential element functions to reveal characters' relationships and to move the action forward. As you look through the three excerpts from the play, review your writer's checklist and add any details that will help you in writing your own script.

Dialogue that reveals characters' relationships:

ACT TWO, SCENE 2

PROCTOR

(*Searching*)

I must speak with you, Abigail. (*She does not move, staring at him.*) Will you sit?

ABIGAIL

How do you come?

PROCTOR

Friendly.

ABIGAIL

(*glancing about*)

I don't like the woods at night. Pray you, stand closer. (*He comes closer to her.*) I knew it must be you. When I heard the pebbles on the window, before I opened up my eyes I knew. (*Sits on log.*) I thought you would come a good time sooner.

PROCTOR

I had thought to come many times.

Dialogue that moves the action forward:

ACT THREE

DANFORTH

Your husband—did he indeed turn from you?

ELIZABETH

(*in agony*)

My husband—is a goodly man, sir.

DANFORTH

Then he did not turn from you.

ELIZABETH

(*starting to glance at Proctor*)

He—

DANFORTH

(*reaches out and holds her face, then*)

Look at me! To your own knowledge, has John Proctor ever committed the crime of lechery? (*In a crisis of indecision she cannot speak.*) Answer my question! Is your husband a lecher!

ELIZABETH

(*faintly*)

No, sir.

A final type of speaking in a play is a **monologue**, in which a character reveals private thoughts and emotions.

MARY

(*Innocently*)

I never knew it before. I never knew anything before. When she come into the court I say to myself, I must not accuse this woman, for she sleep in ditches, and so very old and poor. ... But then ... then she sit there, denying and denying, and I feel a misty coldness climbin' up my back, and the skin on my skull begin to creep, and I feel a clamp around my neck and I cannot breathe air; and then ... (*Entranced as though it were a miracle*) I hear a voice, a screamin' voice, and it were my voice ... and all at once I remembered everything she done to me! (*Slight pause as Proctor watches Elizabeth pass him, then speaks, being aware of Elizabeth's alarm.*)

Comparing Interpretations

Listen to the audio recording of the monologue from SpringBoard Digital. In your Reader/Writer Notebook, write down your observations as you listen. What words does the actor emphasize? What emotions do you notice? After you listen to the monologue and record your notes, discuss your observations with a small group, comparing how listening to the monologue changed or confirmed your interpretation and why.

✒ Writing Prompt: Literary

With your group, reread the script from Activity 2.7 that shows how hysteria grows out of rumor and unfounded accusations. Working together, revise the script to include a monologue that reveals a character's inner thoughts. Use the monologue to convey your group's social commentary on the scene. Be sure to:

- Include dialogue that moves the action forward and reveals characters' thoughts and emotions.
- Incorporate varied syntax in the dialogue, keeping in mind that characters need to speak realistically and according to their individual traits (be sure to reference your character notes).

Rehearse the lines and act out the stage directions. Then revise the dialogue and stage directions according to your group's intended effect on the audience. Remember that stage directions are written in the present tense.

When your script is complete, perform the scene for another group in the class. Use the Scoring Guide so the other group can offer feedback on the script. Switch roles and offer suggestions to help the other group improve its script as well.

Contemporary Conflicts

Learning Targets

- Brainstorm a variety of contemporary concerns.
- Generate social commentary within a dramatic script.
- Compose a plan for a dramatic script using genre characteristics.

Preview

In this activity, you will work with a group to brainstorm a plan for a dramatic script.

Learning Strategies

Graphic Organizer
Marking the Text
Note-taking
Rereading

My Notes

Preparing for a Dramatic Scene

1. Before discussing with your group, individually jot notes that answer the following question.

   What personal and community conflicts concern you and your friends? Consider campus, local, national, and global conflicts. You may think in terms of health, families, technology, the environment, and any other area that comes to mind.

2. Gather as a small group. Choose one person to record notes. Say your ideas out loud as the recorder writes them on paper. Together, generate as many ideas as you can.

3. Reread your group's ideas. Choose one conflict from the list to use as a topic for your group's dramatic scene. If you have a hard time agreeing, conduct a silent vote using numbers (three points for your first choice, two points for your second choice, one point for your third choice). Then brainstorm and list possible historical time periods that might provide a good setting for exploring the conflict.

4. In preparing to create and perform the dramatic scene for Embedded Assessment 1, reread this passage from "Why I Wrote *The Crucible*" by Arthur Miller. Mark the text for the universal underlying issues that Miller's play exposed to help you connect personal conflicts with universal conflicts.

   I am not sure what *The Crucible* is telling people now, but I know that its paranoid center is still pumping out the same darkly attractive warning that it did in the fifties. For some, the play seems to be about the dilemma of relying on the testimony of small children accusing adults of sexual abuse, something I'd not have dreamed of forty years ago. For others, it may simply be a fascination with the outbreak of paranoia that suffuses the play—the blind panic that, in our age, often seems to sit at the dim edges of consciousness. Certainly its political implications are the central issue for many people; the Salem interrogations turn out to be eerily exact models of those yet to come in Stalin's Russia, Pinochet's Chile, Mao's China, and other regimes. (Nien Cheng, the author of Life and Death in Shanghai, has told me that she could hardly believe that a non-Chinese— someone who had not experienced the Cultural Revolution—had written the play.) But below its concerns with justice the play evokes a lethal brew of illicit sexuality, fear of the supernatural, and political manipulation, a combination not unfamiliar these days. The film, by reaching a broad American audience as no play ever can, may well unearth still other connections to those buried public terrors that Salem first announced on this continent.

5. Use the graphic organizer to help you organize your thoughts about the scene you will write. The examples provide a model for the three areas you need to identify prior to writing your script.

Contemporary Societal Conflict	Underlying, Universal Conflict	Parallel Historical Setting
Example A: McCarthy trials/political injustice due to paranoia	Political manipulation	Salem witch trials
Example B: The fastest-growing homeless group is families	People have the attitude "It's their own fault"; there is a large stigma attached to receiving charitable help	The Great Depression
Example C: Environmental issues surrounding fuel	Global economic issues; global environmental issues	The time of the invention of the automobile

6. Review the Planning steps in the Embedded Assessment 1 instructions. Use a separate paper to plan your characters, conflicts, plot lines, stage directions, and dialogue.

7. Draft your scene on a separate paper, using *The Crucible* as the model text. Be sure to use the script-writing checklist that you created earlier in the unit.

🕮 Independent Reading Checkpoint

You have read a variety of texts related to social issues, including free speech. Which text did you find most compelling? What made it more compelling than the other texts? Include comparisons of excerpts from different texts that portray similar events or present similar ideas.

Creating and Performing a Dramatic Scene

ASSIGNMENT

As a small group, choose a modern social conflict. Then write and perform a dramatic scene set in a different historical time period that makes a statement about the conflict. Your performance should demonstrate your understanding of Arthur Miller's purpose for writing *The Crucible* and how the play's historical setting supports his purpose.

Planning and Prewriting: Take time to plan, write, and rehearse your scene	■ How can you relate your social issue to a personal conflict in a way that is engaging and relevant to the audience? ■ What historical settings could best convey your group's statement on the social conflict, just as Miller did? How can you find out more information about your scene's historical context? ■ What roles will each group member play in the performance? How will the number of people in your group affect the characters and plot of your scene? ■ What is the fairest way to share the responsibilities of the assessment between group members? How can you use a program such as Google Docs to promote collaborative work on the script drafts?
Drafting: Compose a draft of your dramatic script	■ How will you use set design, stage directions, and dialogue to help your audience understand the scene's historical setting? ■ How will you engage the audience at the beginning of your scene? How can you order the events in your scene so your group's statement is clear to the audience? How do your characters and setting reveal your group's statement? ■ What role will dialogue, stage directions, and set design play in helping your audience understand the characters, conflict, and plot? ■ How will you format your text to include dialogue and stage directions?
Revising and Rehearsing: Plan time to revise and rehearse your scene	■ What dramatic props, movement, or sound effects can you use to add to the impact of your writing? ■ How can you evaluate your performance for vocal delivery, energy of performance, and overall quality? ■ How can you use the Scoring Guide to help guide your revision?
Editing for Publishing and Performance: Polish the scene and rehearse to deliver a smooth presentation	■ What resources are available to help you edit and finalize your script? ■ How will you share responsibility to ensure that all the necessary elements of your performance are ready at the assigned time?

Reflection

After completing this Embedded Assessment, reflect on your work for this assignment. Respond to the following:

- What was most challenging about taking your chosen issue and transferring it to another historical context?
- How did that process add new meaning or relevance to your intended message?

SCORING GUIDE

Scoring Criteria	Exemplary	Proficient	Emerging	Incomplete
Ideas	The scene • demonstrates a sophisticated understanding of Miller's approach to speaking his conscience about a current event through a drama set in an analogous time period • effectively provides social commentary on the chosen issue • insightfully communicates the intended effect to the audience.	The scene • demonstrates a clear understanding of Miller's approach to speaking his conscience about a current event through a drama set in an analogous time period • serves as social commentary on the chosen issue • plausibly communicates the intended effect to the audience.	The scene • demonstrates a limited understanding of Miller's approach to speaking his conscience about a current event through a drama set in an analogous time period • includes social commentary that may be unclear or confusing • somewhat communicates the intended effect to the audience.	The scene • demonstrates an unclear understanding of Miller's approach to speaking his conscience about a current event through a drama set in an analogous time period • lacks a social commentary • does not successfully communicate the intended effect to the audience.
Structure	The scene • skillfully uses various theatrical elements • strategically uses all elements of vocal delivery • effectively uses elements of visual delivery to create focus and maintain energy for the scene • demonstrates equal sharing of responsibility.	The scene • adequately uses various theatrical elements • knowledgeably uses all elements of vocal delivery • uses elements of visual delivery to create focus and maintain energy for the scene • demonstrates a mostly balanced sharing of responsibility.	The scene • attempts to use various theatrical elements and elements of vocal delivery with limited success • attempts to use elements of visual delivery with limited success • demonstrates an unequal division of responsibilities.	The scene • does not use various theatrical elements • does not use all elements of vocal delivery • does not use elements of visual delivery • demonstrates no division of responsibilities.
Use of Language	The scene • includes written materials that demonstrate a mature style that advances the group's ideas • crafts dialogue that maintains consistent character voice and propels the plot.	The scene • includes written materials that demonstrate a style that adequately supports the group's ideas • includes dialogue that largely maintains character voice and serves the plot.	The scene • includes written materials that demonstrate a limited style that ineffectively supports the group's ideas • includes dialogue that struggles to maintain consistent character voice and/or impedes the plot.	The scene • includes written materials that demonstrate little style and fail to support the group's ideas • includes dialogue that fails to maintain consistent character voice and/or impedes the plot.

Unpacking Embedded Assessment 2

Learning Strategies

Brainstorming
Discussion Groups
Graphic Organizer
Marking the Text
Quickwrite

Learning Targets

- Reflect on the big ideas for the unit.
- Create a plan for reading independently.

Preview

In this activity, you will explore the big ideas and tasks of the unit and make plans for your independent reading.

My Notes

Making Connections

The Crucible is an example of how artistic expression is a significant part of the American ideal of freedom of expression and the freedom to say what we believe. The historic guarantee was a hard-won freedom, and over time our greatest statespeople and politicians have nurtured that freedom through speeches such as Margaret Chase Smith's *Declaration of Conscience*. Public speech, as well as literary work, is still a significant forum for the expression of important ideas and ideals. You will find that your experience creating and presenting an original dramatic scene will prepare you to create and present a speech about an issue of importance.

Essential Questions

Your work with Arthur Miller has given you an idea of how social commentary can be a part of artistic expression. Now, respond to Essential Question 2: How are the components of rhetoric applied to the creation and delivery of effective speeches?

Unpacking Embedded Assessment 2

Closely read the assignment for Embedded Assessment 2: Writing and Presenting a Persuasive Speech.

Your assignment is to write and present an original, persuasive two- to three-minute speech that addresses a contemporary issue. Your speech should include a clear claim, support, counterclaim, and conclusion/call to action. Incorporate rhetorical appeals and devices to strengthen your argument and help you achieve your desired purpose.

Create a graphic organizer that demonstrates your analysis of the assignment. What knowledge must you possess and what skills must you have in order to write and deliver a persuasive speech?

Planning for Independent Reading

For outside reading, you may choose famous speeches and find audio versions for listening. As you listen to each speech, make notes in your Reader/Writer Notebook about the delivery and its effectiveness. Select one speech you find particularly effective and recommend it to classmates, including reasons for your recommendation.

Developing Speaking Skills

My Notes

Learning Targets

- Draw connections between giving successful performances and presentations, including awareness of audience and effective delivery of information.
- Collaborate and share ideas with classmates about characteristics of successful oral presentations.

Preview

In this activity, you will reflect on how your experience from writing and performing a scene can be applied to writing and presenting a persuasive speech by considering the roles of the speaker and the audience.

Comparing Performances and Presentations

1. What have you learned from writing and performing a dramatic scene that could be applied to writing and presenting a speech to persuade? How are the two experiences the same and different?

2. In small discussion groups, brainstorm characteristics of speaker and audience during a successful oral presentation. Pass a single sheet of paper and pencil around the table, with each group member writing one characteristic for either speaker or audience. Continue to pass the pencil and paper until your teacher directs you to stop.

Speaker	Audience

3. Choose one group member to stand and share your group's list with the whole class. Each team member should add cumulative list of characteristics in the chart. When your group representative has shared your group's ideas, he or she should sit and remain sitting until all groups' ideas have been shared.

Practice

4. Keep a list of the following oral presentation skills to practice. Model for each other what it looks like to do the following:

- Make eye contact while speaking
- Pause for effect
- Enunciate and speak loudly enough
- Use purposeful gestures
- Communicate ideas effectively

5. Work together to turn your list of characteristics of good oral presentations into a brief presentation on effective ways to be either a presenter or a listening audience member. As a group decide if your brief presentation will include:

- Visual elements
- Role-playing
- A multimedia component

Assign each member of your group an element of the presentation to present.

Topic	Tips	Components	Presenter

6. After organizing your presentation and its components, rehearse as a group and give each other feedback on use of eye contact, enunciation, volume, and other presentation skills.

7. Meet with another group and take turns giving your presentations. Fill out the feedback organizer during the other group's presentation and then share your feedback with each other.

Presenter	Did their presentation anticipate the needs of the audience?	How were their eye contact and speaking skills? Were they loud enough? Did they pause for effect?	Did they incorporate any other visual, role-playing, or multimedia components effectively?

☑ Check Your Understanding

As you develop ideas about successful performance and oral presentations, consider these questions: Which performance skills will transfer easily from drama to speech delivery? Which new skills will you need to develop?

Learning Strategies

Brainstorming
Shared Reading
SOAPSTone

VOCABULARY

ACADEMIC

A **rhetorical context** refers to the subject, purpose, audience, occasion, or situation in which writing occurs. Rhetorical context can help inform the reader of all the other elements that might inform a writer's argument. All these factors work together to influence what the text itself says and how it conveys its message.

Learning Targets

- Analyze the rhetorical context of a seminal U.S. speech.
- Adapt speech for a particular rhetorical context.

Preview

In this activity, you will read a seminal speech given by President Abraham Lincoln and analyze its rhetorical context using the SOAPSTone strategy.

Rhetorical Context

Like historical context, the **rhetorical context** of a speech is an important part of analyzing the ideas and evaluating the reasoning of the speaker. The reading strategy SOAPSTone is a familiar strategy that can help you analyze a speech.

As You Read

- Underline details that you will use during your SOAPSTone analysis.
- Circle unknown words and phrases. Try to determine the meaning of the words by using context clues, word parts, or a dictionary.

My Notes

About the Author

Abraham Lincoln was an American statesman and lawyer who served as the 16th President of the United States from March 1861 until his assassination in April 1865. Lincoln led the United States through the American Civil War. In his First Inaugural Address, President Lincoln had argued at length against secession and urged Americans in both the North and South to remain dedicated to the Union. The tone of his Second Inaugural Address is quite different. As you read the speech, pay attention to Lincoln's use of diction and syntax to create a somber tone that reveals the effects of four years of devastating war on both himself and the American public.

Speech

Second Inaugural Address of Abraham Lincoln

given **Saturday, March 4, 1865, one month before the end of the Civil War**

Fellow Countrymen:

1   At this second appearing to take the oath of the Presidential office there is less occasion for an extended address than there was at the first. Then a statement somewhat in detail of a course to be pursued seemed fitting and proper. Now, at the expiration of four years, during which public declarations have been constantly called forth on every point and phase of the great contest which still absorbs the attention and engrosses the energies of the nation, little that is new could be presented. The progress of our arms, upon which all else chiefly depends, is as well known to the public as to myself, and it is, I trust, reasonably satisfactory and encouraging to all. With high hope for the future, no prediction in regard to it is ventured.

2   On the occasion corresponding to this four years ago all thoughts were anxiously directed to an impending civil war. All dreaded it, all sought to avert it. While the inaugural address was being delivered from this place, devoted altogether to saving the Union without war, insurgent agents were in the city seeking to destroy it without war—seeking to dissolve the Union and divide effects by negotiation. Both parties **deprecated** war, but one of them would make war rather than let the nation survive, and the other would accept war rather than let it perish, and the war came.

3   One-eighth of the whole population were colored slaves, not distributed generally over the Union, but localized in the southern part of it. These slaves constituted a peculiar and powerful interest. All knew that this interest was somehow the cause of the war. To strengthen, **perpetuate**, and extend this interest was the object for which the insurgents would rend the Union even by war, while the Government claimed no right to do more than to restrict the territorial enlargement of it. Neither

> **deprecated:** criticized
> **perpetuate:** continue indefinitely

My Notes

party expected for the war the magnitude or the duration which it has already attained. Neither anticipated that the cause of the conflict might cease with or even before the conflict itself should cease. Each looked for an easier triumph, and a result less fundamental and astounding. Both read the same Bible and pray to the same God, and each **invokes** His aid against the other. It may seem strange that any men should dare to ask a just God's assistance in wringing their bread from the sweat of other men's faces, but let us judge not, that we be not judged. The prayers of both could not be answered. That of neither has been answered fully. The Almighty has His own purposes. "Woe unto the world because of offenses; for it must needs be that offenses come, but woe to that man by whom the offense cometh." If we shall suppose that American slavery is one of those offenses which, in the providence of God, must needs come, but which, having continued through His appointed time, He now wills to remove, and that He gives to both North and South this terrible war as the woe due to those by whom the offense came, shall we discern therein any departure from those divine **attributes** which the believers in a living God always **ascribe** to Him? Fondly do we hope, fervently do we pray, that this mighty **scourge** of war may speedily pass away. Yet, if God wills that it continue until all the wealth piled by the bondsman's two hundred and fifty years of unrequited toil shall be sunk, and until every drop of blood drawn with the lash shall be paid by another drawn with the sword, as was said three thousand years ago, so still it must be said "the judgments of the Lord are true and righteous altogether."

4   With **malice** toward none, with charity for all, with firmness in the right as God gives us to see the right, let us strive on to finish the work we are in, to bind up the nation's wounds, to care for him who shall have borne the battle and for his widow and his orphan, to do all which may achieve and cherish a just and lasting peace among ourselves and with all nations.

Making Observations
- What emotional tone does Lincoln strike in his speech?
- How might Lincoln's audience have reacted given the context?

invokes: calls forth
attributes: qualities
ascribe: think of coming from
scourge: plague or misfortune
malice: desire to cause harm

Returning to the Text

- Return to the speech as you respond to the following questions. Use text evidence to support your responses
- Write any additional questions you have about the text in your Reader/Writer Notebook.

1. Find one example of anaphora in paragraph 2 and one in paragraph 3. How does this rhetorical device contribute to the power of the speech?

_____

_____

_____

_____

_____

2. What is the effect of Lincoln telling the audience "little that is new could be presented" while giving a speech about the state of the country?

_____

_____

_____

_____

_____

3. Summarize how Lincoln describes the two sides are similar. What rhetorical appeal does he use to warn against laying blame? Why would or wouldn't it be an effective appeal for his audience?

_____

_____

_____

_____

_____

4. How might Lincoln's use of language that uses religious reasoning shape his audience's understanding of his call to end the Civil War?

_____

_____

_____

_____

_____

5. Who is Abraham Lincoln's intended audience? How does Lincoln anticipate his audience's needs and expectations?

_____

_____

_____

_____

_____

_____

6. Based on the details you underlined, what specific language does Lincoln use to invoke emotions in his audience?

_____

_____

_____

_____

_____

_____

Working from the Text

7. Review the SOAPSTone annotations you have made with your group members. As a group, discuss how the historical context of the Civil War is reflected in the speech. Complete the SOAPSTone graphic organizer as a group.

SOAPSTone	Analysis	Textual Support
Speaker What does the listener know about the speaker?		
Occasion What are the circumstances surrounding this speech?		
Audience Who is the target audience?		
Purpose Why did the speaker give this text?		
Subject What is the topic?		
Tone What is the author's tone, or attitude?		

8. The use of parallel structure has a powerful effect on a written and spoken message. Identify the examples of parallelism at work in the speech. Practice reading the paragraph as you believe it would be spoken, using parallel structure to guide your emphasis and inflection.

_____

_____

_____

_____

_____

Drafting the Embedded Assessment

Think of an issue close to home where you feel a change is warranted. Brainstorm ideas for a speech that you could give on the topic to the appropriate audience to convey your strongest message. Be sure to:

- Identify your role as speaker in this piece (concerned citizen, student).
- Convey the occasion that informs your writing (the circumstances prompting this piece).
- Identify your audience (whom you are addressing).
- Define your purpose (what you want to accomplish).
- Choose your subject (the topic of your essay).
- Establish your tone (your attitude toward the issue and the opposition).

The Power of Rhetoric

Learning Strategies

Discussion Groups
Drafting
Marking the Text
Quickwrite
Revisiting Prior Work
Shared Reading

Learning Targets

- Analyze the structure and use of rhetorical devices in an argumentative text.
- Write an analysis of how a speaker builds an argumentative speech.

Preview

In this activity, you will read and analyze a speech for its use of structure and rhetorical devices in order to explain how the author builds his argument.

Analyzing an Argument

You have analyzed the rhetorical context of an effective speech. What about the message? Where does it get its power? Powerful writers such as Lincoln use structure and rhetorical devices intentionally; effective argumentation is anything but an accident. And when you add a powerful delivery to strong writing, you move hearts, people, and sometimes whole nations.

As you prepare to read one of the most powerful speeches in our nation's history, a speech pivotal to the colonial revolution against the throne of England, you will be examining two components:

- The structure of an argument
- The use of rhetorical devices

The Structure of an Argument

a. The claim acknowledges the point of the argument.

b. The support uses logical reasoning, relevant evidence, and accurate and credible sources. It also demonstrates an understanding of the topic.

c. The counterclaim acknowledges the opposing point of view and offers reasons and evidence that reject the counterclaim.

d. The concluding statement offers a call to action that asks audience members to change their minds or actions to support the claim.

The Use of Rhetorical Devices

Rhetorical devices are literary devices that a writer uses to enhance the message and/or to create an effect. If the speech is argumentative, the effect should be to persuade for change. In Patrick Henry's speech, be prepared to see devices such as aphorism, allusion, analogy, and rhetorical questions.

As You Read

- Mark elements of the argumentative structure you see in the text.
- Highlight rhetorical devices used by the speaker and note their impact.
- Circle unknown words and phrases. Try to determine the meaning of the words by using context clues, word parts, or a dictionary.

My Notes

My Notes

_____
_____
_____
_____
_____
_____
_____
_____
_____
_____
_____
_____
_____
_____
_____
_____
_____
_____
_____
_____
_____
_____

About the Author

Patrick Henry (1736–1799) was born in Virginia. He tried several occupations before becoming a lawyer and then a politician encouraging separation from Great Britain. He served as a delegate from Virginia to the First Session of the Continental Congress in 1774 and became noted as a powerful speaker whose words helped sweep the colonists toward their declaration of independence.

About the Speech

Patrick Henry delivered his most famous speech on March 23, 1775, at the Second Virginia Convention. Henry gave a reasoned and dramatic presentation, building from calm tones to a passionate finale. A deep silence followed Henry's memorable conclusion. After the speech, the delegates voted by a narrow margin to form a Virginia militia to guard against a possible British attack. No record was made of his exact words at the time; this version was assembled in the early 1880s from accounts of several people who attended the convention.

Speech
March 23, 1775

Speech to the Virginia Convention

_by_ **Patrick Henry**

1   Mr. President: No man thinks more highly than I do of the patriotism, as well as abilities, of the very worthy gentlemen who have just addressed the House. But different men often see the same subject in different lights; and, therefore, I hope it will not be thought disrespectful to those gentlemen if, entertaining, as I do, opinions of a character very opposite to theirs, I shall speak forth my sentiments freely and without reserve. This is no time for ceremony. The question before the House is one of awful moment to this country. For my own part, I consider it as nothing less than a question of freedom or slavery; and in proportion to the magnitude of the subject ought to be the freedom of the debate. It is only in this way that we can hope to arrive at truth, and fulfill the great responsibility which we hold to God and our country. Should I keep back my opinions at such a time, through fear of giving offense, I should consider myself guilty of treason towards my country, and of an act of disloyalty toward the Majesty of Heaven, which I revere above all earthly kings.

WORD CONNECTIONS

Etymology
In Latin, _momentum_ means "movement." A _moment_ is a particle heavy enough to cause a set of scales to move. Henry calls the question before the House one of "awful moment." He suggests that the way in which the House answers the question will cause movement toward freedom or slavery for the country.

2 Mr. President, it is natural to man to indulge in the illusions of hope. We are apt to shut our eyes against a painful truth, and listen to the song of that siren[1], till she transforms us into beasts. Is this the part of wise men, engaged in a great and arduous struggle for liberty? Are we disposed to be of the number of those who, having eyes, see not and, having ears, hear not,[2] the things which so nearly concern their temporal salvation? For my part, whatever anguish of spirit it may cost, I am willing to know the whole truth; to know the worst, and to provide for it.

3 I have but one lamp by which my feet are guided, and that is the lamp of experience. I know of no way of judging the future but by the past. And judging by the past, I wish to know what there has been in the conduct of the British ministry for the last ten years to justify those hopes with which gentlemen have been pleased to solace themselves and the House. Is it that insidious smile with which our petition has been lately received? Trust it not, sir; it will prove a snare to your feet. Suffer not yourselves to be betrayed with a kiss. Ask yourselves how this gracious reception of our petition comports with those warlike preparations which cover our waters and darken our land. Are fleets and armies necessary to a work of love and reconciliation? Have we shown ourselves so unwilling to be reconciled that force must be called in to win back our love? Let us not deceive ourselves, sir. These are the implements of war and subjugation; the last arguments to which kings resort.

4 I ask gentlemen, sir, what means this martial array, if its purpose be not to force us to submission? Can gentlemen assign any other possible motive for it? Has Great Britain any enemy in this quarter of the world, to call for all this accumulation of navies and armies? No sir, she has none. They are meant for us: they can be meant for no other. They are sent over to bind and rivet upon us those chains which the British ministry have been so long forging. And what have we to oppose to them? Shall we try argument? Sir, we have been trying that for the last ten years. Have we anything new to offer upon the subject? Nothing. We have held the subject up in every light of which it is capable; but it has been all in vain. Shall we resort to entreaty and humble supplication? What terms shall we find which have not been already exhausted? Let us not, I beseech you, sir, deceive ourselves. Sir, we have done everything that could be done, to avert the storm which is now coming on. We have petitioned; we have remonstrated; we have supplicated; we have prostrated ourselves before the throne, and have implored its interposition to arrest the tyrannical hands of the ministry and Parliament. Our petitions have been slighted; our remonstrances have produced additional violence and insult; our supplications have been disregarded; and we have been spurned, with contempt, from the foot of the throne! In vain, after these things, may we indulge the fond hope of peace and reconciliation. *There is no longer any room for hope.* If we wish to be free—if we mean to preserve inviolate those inestimable privileges for which

---

[1] "Song of that siren" is an allusion to classical Greek mythology. The Sirens were three dangerous mermaid-like creatures who seduced nearby sailors with music, causing the sailors to wreck their ships.

[2] "Having eyes, see not, and having ears, hear not" is an allusion to several passages in the Bible, including Isaiah 6:10, Jeremiah 5:21, and Mark 8:18.

temporal: earthly rather than spiritual

solace: comfort

insidious: treacherous

subjugation: act of conquering and subduing

martial: warlike

interposition: intervention

slighted: disrespected

inviolate: pure

My Notes

we have been so long contending—if we mean not **basely** to abandon the noble struggle in which we have been so long engaged, and which we have pledged ourselves never to abandon until the glorious object of our contest shall be obtained—we must fight!—I repeat it, sir, we must fight! An appeal to arms and to the God of hosts, is all that is left us!

5 They tell us, sir, that we are weak; unable to cope with so formidable an adversary. But when shall we be stronger? Will it be the next week, or the next year? Will it be when we are totally disarmed, and when a British guard shall be stationed in every house? Shall we gather strength by irresolution and inaction? Shall we acquire the means of effectual resistance by lying supinely on our backs, and hugging the delusive phantom of hope, until our enemies shall have bound us hand and foot? Sir, we are not weak if we make a proper use of those means which the God of nature hath placed in our power. The millions of people, armed in the holy cause of liberty, and in such a country as that which we possess, are invincible by any force which our enemy can send against us. Besides, sir, we shall not fight our battles alone. There is a just God who presides over the destinies of nations and who will raise up friends to fight our battles for us. The battle, sir, is not to the strong alone; it is to the vigilant, the active, the brave. Besides, sir, we have no election. If we were base enough to desire it, it is now too late to retire from the contest. There is no retreat but in submission and slavery! Our chains are forged! Their clanking may be heard on the plains of Boston! The war is inevitable—and let it come! I repeat it, sir, let it come.

Peter F. Rothermel's painting titled "Patrick Henry Before the Virginia House of Burgesses" was created in 1851 and depicts Henry giving his famous speech.

6 It is in vain, sir, to **extenuate** the matter. Gentlemen may cry, Peace, Peace—but there is no peace. The war is actually begun! The next gale that sweeps from the north will bring to our ears the clash of resounding arms! Our brethren are already in the field! Why stand we here idle? What is it that gentlemen wish? What would they have? Is life so dear, or peace so sweet, as to be purchased at the price of chains and slavery? Forbid it, Almighty God! I know not what course others may take; but as for me, give me liberty, or give me death!

basely: in a lowly way
extenuate: lengthen

Making Observations

- What is the tone of Henry's speech?
- What argumentative appeals stand out to you as being effective?

Returning to the Text

- Return to the speech as you respond to the following questions. Use text evidence to support your responses.
- Write any additional questions you have about the text in your Reader/Writer Notebook.

5. The Bible says Judas kisses Jesus before delivering him to his executioners. What is the significance of Henry's use of the allusion "Suffer not yourselves to be betrayed with a kiss" in paragraph 3?

_____

_____

_____

_____

6. What central idea does Henry develop in paragraph 3 to strengthen his argument? How is or isn't it effective?

_____

_____

_____

_____

7. In paragraph 4, Henry uses five verbs to describe how the colonists have tried to avoid a confrontation with Britain: *petition*, *remonstrate*, *supplicate*, *prostrate*, and *implore*. How are their meanings related? What is their effect on the readers' perception of Henry's argument?

_____

_____

_____

_____

8. Which element of the typical structure of an argument does Henry present in paragraph 5? Explain his rhetorical response.

_____

_____

_____

_____

9. What kinds of appeals does Henry use to convince Virginia to begin to prepare for war with Great Britain?

_____

_____

_____

_____

Working from the Text

10. Review your notes about the structure of Henry's speech. What pattern do you see?

11. With your discussion group, determine the order of claim, support, counterclaim, and conclusion/call to action and create an outline of Henry's speech.

 **Check Your Understanding**

Quickwrite: If you had attended the Virginia Convention for Henry's speech, would you have sided with or against him? Why? What kinds of rhetorical devices did Henry use to persuade his audience?

 INDEPENDENT READING LINK

Read and Discuss

Using notes from your Reader/Writer Notebook, discuss with classmates a speech you have read independently. How does the author use rhetorical devices to persuade his or her audience? What do you notice about how the author builds his or her argument to a well-reasoned conclusion? Give examples to support your ideas.

Explain How an Author Builds an Argument

Write an essay in which you explain how Patrick Henry builds an argument to persuade his audience that the colonies should declare their independence from Great Britain. In your essay, analyze the three most effective rhetorical devices Henry uses to strengthen the logic and persuasiveness of his argument. Your essay should not explain whether you agree with Henry's claims, but rather it should explain how the author builds an argument to persuade his audience. Be sure to:

- Identify Henry's claim.
- Use evidence from the text to show the progression of Henry's argument.
- Explain the effect of each piece of evidence and include transitions to connect your claims, reasoning, and evidence.
- Evaluate the overall effectiveness of Henry's speech.
- Include a conclusion that supports your ideas.

The Appeal of Rhetoric

Learning Targets

- Analyze the use of rhetorical appeals in an argumentative text.
- Incorporate rhetorical appeals while generating an argument.

Preview

In this activity, you will read and analyze a speech for its rhetorical appeals and create an outline for your own argument that incorporates rhetorical appeals.

My Notes

Rhetorical Appeals

You have analyzed Abraham Lincoln's masterful use of rhetoric in his Second Inaugural Address. Next, you will analyze his use of rhetorical appeals in the Gettysburg Address. Although it is one of the shortest speeches in U.S. history, it is also one of the most recognized. Pay close attention to Lincoln's claim and appeals and what makes his conclusion convincing. Like other great orators, Lincoln swayed his audience by using the **rhetorical appeals** first identified by Aristotle as *pathos*, *ethos*, and *logos*. Writers and speakers choose their appeals based on their intended audience, purpose, and the nature of the argument itself.

Review the types of rhetorical appeals with your group members. Illustrate a representation of each type of appeal in the margin.

Pathos (emotional appeal): This appeal attempts to persuade the reader or listener by appealing to the senses and emotions. Political ads that show politicians kissing babies or shaking hands with the elderly often appeal to the emotions. Also, these appeals usually include statements with vivid sensory details, which are used to awaken the senses and perhaps manipulate the emotions of the audience. In many of Lincoln's speeches, he uses powerful emotional language to achieve his purpose. However, it can be easy for a writer or speaker to wind up using fallacies if he or she relies too heavily on emotional appeals.

Ethos (ethical appeal): This type of appeal attempts to persuade the reader or listener by focusing on the qualifications of the speaker. The speaker's credibility is paramount in an ethical appeal. Ethical appeals focus on the speaker even more than the situation. Examples of ethical appeals in advertising are expert or celebrity endorsements of products. You can increase your credibility, or your "ethos," with your authority, character, sources, fairness, and error-free presentation. Other examples of ethical appeals are a teen's argument that he or she should be allowed to do something because he or she has never been in trouble or because his or her friend is a perfect citizen, and so on. Finally, writers or speakers can enhance their ethos by acknowledging counterarguments or anticipating rebuttals.

Logos (logical appeal): This type of appeal attempts to persuade the reader or listener by leading him or her down the road of logic and causing him or her to come to his or her own conclusion. Logical appeals state the facts and show how the facts are interrelated. If/then statements are examples of logical appeals. Logical appeals are often used in courtroom situations. Compelling logic adds to the ethos of an argument.

Aristotle tells us that all three appeals are important to persuasive writing. However, he determined that logical appeals are the most persuasive. Emotional appeals often manipulate people's emotions in order to persuade, and ethical appeals rely on qualities that might not pass the truth test. Logical appeals, which present facts and evidence, focus on the truth.

As You Read

- As you read the Gettysburg Address, look for examples of pathos, ethos, and logos. Use different-color highlighters to mark the different appeals.
- Circle unknown words and phrases. Try to determine the meaning of the words by using context clues, word parts, or a dictionary.

About the Speech

On November 19, 1863, President Abraham Lincoln spoke at the dedication of the National Cemetery of Gettysburg in Pennsylvania. Lincoln was not the featured speaker. Noted orator Edward Everett spoke for two hours about the Battle of Gettysburg. Then Lincoln delivered his 272-word speech. Afterward, Everett wrote to Lincoln, "I wish that I could flatter myself that I had come as near to the central idea of the occasion, in two hours, as you did in two minutes."

Speech

The Gettysburg Address

by **Abraham Lincoln**

1   Four score and seven years ago our fathers brought forth, on this continent, a new nation, conceived in liberty, and dedicated to the proposition that all men are created equal. Now we are engaged in a great civil war, testing whether that nation, or any nation so conceived, and so dedicated, can long endure. We are met on a great battlefield of that war. We have come to dedicate a portion, of that field, as a final resting-place for those who here gave their lives, that that nation might live. It is altogether fitting and proper that we should do this. But, in a larger sense, we cannot dedicate, we cannot consecrate—we cannot hallow—this ground. The brave men, living and dead, who struggled here have consecrated it far above our poor power to add or detract. The world will little note, nor long remember what we say here, but it can never forget what they did here. It is for us the living, rather, to be dedicated here to the unfinished work which they who fought here

My Notes

conceived: begun
consecrate: dedicate as sacred

have thus far so nobly advanced. It is rather for us to be here dedicated to the great task remaining before us—that from these honored dead we take increased devotion to that cause for which they gave the last full measure of devotion—that we here highly resolve that these dead shall not have died in vain—that this nation, under God, shall have a new birth of freedom, and that government of the people, by the people, for the people, shall not perish from the earth.

Making Observations

- What is Lincoln's main argument in his speech?
- What rhetorical appeal does Lincoln appear to rely most heavily on?

INDEPENDENT READING LINK

Read and Connect

In your Reader/Writer Notebook, compare and contrast one of the speeches you have read independently with your analysis of Abraham Lincoln's use of rhetorical appeals. Consider using a Venn diagram. What makes each author's use of rhetorical appeals effective? Note especially any similarities between Lincoln's persuasive argument(s) and those you read independently. What can you learn from these authors about writing a persuasive speech?

Returning to the Text

- Return to the speech as you respond to the following questions. Use text evidence to support your responses.
- Write any additional questions you have about the text in your Reader/Writer Notebook.

1. What is the rhetorical effect of Lincoln opening his speech with "four score and seven years ago"? What type of rhetorical appeal does it represent?

_____
_____
_____
_____

2. How do Lincoln's different uses of the word *dedicate* affect the tone of the speech?

_____
_____
_____
_____
_____

3. What is Lincoln's call to action in "The Gettysburg Address?"

_____
_____
_____
_____

4. Which first-person pronoun is one of the most-repeated words in the speech? How would its use affect Lincoln's audience? What can you infer is Lincoln's reasoning for its repeated use?

_____
_____
_____
_____

5. What inferences can you make about how Lincoln considered the audience and the situation when choosing his rhetoric? Cite evidence from the text to support your inference.

_____
_____
_____
_____

☑ **Check Your Understanding**

What appeals in this speech would likely be most memorable to Lincoln's audience? Which kind of appeal is most prevalent in Lincoln's speech? What effect would it have on the audience?

Working from the Text

6. What is the structure of Lincoln's speech? How does he work to provide a convincing conclusion?

_____

_____

_____

_____

_____

7. With a partner, look through your annotations in the text for pathos, ethos, and logos. Find one example of each and analyze its effectiveness in the organizer.

	Text Evidence	Analysis
Pathos		
Ethos		
Logos		

📝 Drafting the Embedded Assessment

Revisit your notes from Activity 2.20 for the speech you have begun to plan. With these notes, you have created a rhetorical context for your speech. Now, it is time to outline the structure and incorporate rhetorical devices in the writing of the speech. Remember that an argumentative speech without a well-planned structure, rhetorical devices, and powerful syntax will not achieve its purpose.

The most effective argument uses a combination of all three rhetorical appeals. Choose places to strengthen your argument by appealing to your audience's emotions (pathos), logic (logos), and your own credibility on the topic (ethos). Be sure to:

- Discuss with a partner how you plan to use the appeals of pathos, logos, and ethos in your speech.
- Create an outline that includes the claim, support, counterclaim, concessions and rebuttals, and conclusion/call to action.
- Incorporate two or more rhetorical devices in your speech (metaphor, allusion, rhetorical questions, and imagery). Mark them in your speech.
- Choose a syntactic structure from Patrick Henry's speech to the Virginia Convention to incorporate into your argument. Mark it in your speech and in the margin and note its intended effect.
- Use a variety of rhetorical appeals in your speech. Mark them in your speech.
- Include a concluding statement with a call to action that asks audience members to change their minds or act in support of the claim.
- Practice reciting your speech to a classmate, parent, sibling, or friend. Consider how your delivery can enhance your written words.

Learning Strategies

Close Reading
Marking the Text
Revisiting Prior Work

VOCABULARY

ACADEMIC
Vocal delivery refers to the way words are expressed onstage through volume, pitch, rate or speed of speech, pauses, pronunciation, and articulation.

Learning Targets

- Identify and evaluate the elements of effective vocal delivery.
- Prepare a text for effective oral delivery.
- Integrate ideas from multiple texts to build knowledge and vocabulary about inaugural addresses.

Preview

In this activity, you will listen to President Franklin D. Roosevelt deliver an inaugural address to an audience worn out by the Great Depression, and you will analyze how you can use elements of his delivery when giving your own speech.

As You Read

- As you listen to an audio recording of Franklin D. Roosevelt's First Inaugural Address, take notes about his style of vocal delivery.
- Circle unknown words and phrases. Try to determine the meaning of the words by using context clues, word parts, or a dictionary.
- Highlight any of Roosevelt's diction that you find impactful and underline instances of varying syntax for effect.

About the Author

President Franklin D. Roosevelt (1882–1945) took office in the United States at the same time as Adolf Hitler did in Germany. Both men led countries caught in economic depressions. Roosevelt, elected in 1932, is known for his New Deal, which sought to help those Americans desperately in need by restoring jobs and supplying basic subsistence. He was the only U.S. president elected for four terms. He led the nation through World War II.

Speech

excerpt from the First Inaugural Address of Franklin D. Roosevelt

March 3, 1933

KNOWLEDGE QUEST

Knowledge Question:

How can presidents use their inaugural addresses to appeal to the country's citizens? In Activities 2.23 and 2.24, you will read President Roosevelt's and President Kennedy's first presidential addresses. While you read and build knowledge about how speakers can use rhetorical devices to persuade, think about your answer to the Knowledge Question.

1   I am certain that my fellow Americans expect that on my induction into the Presidency I will address them with a **candor** and a decision which the present situation of our people **impel**. This is preeminently the time to speak the truth, the whole truth, frankly and boldly. Nor need we shrink from honestly facing conditions in our country today. This great Nation will endure as it has endured, will revive and will prosper. So, first of all, let me assert my firm belief that the only thing we have to fear is fear itself—nameless, unreasoning, unjustified terror which paralyzes needed efforts to convert retreat into advance. In every dark hour of our national life a leadership of frankness and vigor has met with that understanding and support of the people themselves which is essential to victory. I am convinced that you will again give that support to leadership in these critical days.

2   In such a spirit on my part and on yours we face our common difficulties. They concern, thank God, only material things. Values have shrunken to fantastic levels; taxes have risen; our ability to pay has fallen; government of all kinds is faced by serious **curtailment** of income; the means of exchange are frozen in the currents of trade; the withered leaves of industrial enterprise lie on every side; farmers find no markets for their produce; the savings of many years in thousands of families are gone.

3   More important, a host of unemployed citizens face the grim problem of existence and an equally great number toil with little return. Only a foolish optimist can deny the dark realities of the moment.

4   Yet our distress comes from no failure of **substance**. We are stricken by no plague of locusts. Compared with the perils which our forefathers conquered because they believed and were not afraid, we have still much to be thankful for. Nature still offers her bounty and human efforts have multiplied it. Plenty is at our doorstep, but a generous use of it **languishes** in the very sight of the supply. Primarily this is because the rulers of the exchange of mankind's goods have failed, through their own stubbornness and their own incompetence, have admitted their failure, and **abdicated**. Practices of the unscrupulous money changers stand indicted in the court of public opinion, rejected by the hearts and minds of men.

My Notes

candor: honesty
impel: feel a strong need for
curtailment: reduction
substance: abundance
languishes: breaks down
abdicated: gave up a position of responsibility

INDEPENDENT READING LINK

Read and Respond

Paste an excerpt from one of the speeches you read independently in your Reader/Writer Notebook. Use colored ink to mark the text for volume increases or decreases (+ or –), raised pitch (^), rate increases (...), and pauses (#). You may want to read passages aloud in various ways before making these decisions. Then reflect in writing on the connections between delivery and message for this text.

My Notes

_____
_____
_____
_____
_____
_____
_____
_____
_____
_____
_____
_____
_____
_____
_____
_____
_____
_____

induce: cause or bring about
evanescent: short-lived

5 True they have tried, but their efforts have been cast in the pattern of an outworn tradition. Faced by failure of credit they have proposed only the lending of more money. Stripped of the lure of profit by which to **induce** our people to follow their false leadership, they have resorted to exhortations, pleading tearfully for restored confidence. They know only the rules of a generation of self-seekers. They have no vision, and when there is no vision the people perish.

6 The money changers have fled from their high seats in the temple of our civilization. We may now restore that temple to the ancient truths. The measure of the restoration lies in the extent to which we apply social values more noble than mere monetary profit.

7 Happiness lies not in the mere possession of money; it lies in the joy of achievement, in the thrill of creative effort. The joy and moral stimulation of work no longer must be forgotten in the mad chase of **evanescent** profits. These dark days will be worth all they cost us if they teach us that our true destiny is not to be ministered unto but to minister to ourselves and to our fellow men.

⊘ Knowledge Quest

• What is the tone of President Roosevelt's speech?
• What approach does President Roosevelt take to convince his audience that he will be a good leader?

Returning to the Text

• Return to the speech as you respond to the following questions. Use text evidence to support your responses.
• Write any additional questions you have about the text in your Reader/Writer Notebook.

1. KQ In paragraph 1, what does Roosevelt mean by using the word *endure* in this context?

_____

_____

_____

_____

2. How does the clause "the only thing we have to fear is fear itself" suggest Roosevelt's purpose for speaking?

_____

_____

_____

_____

3. How does Roosevelt use an allusion to the Bible to help people gain perspective on the economic situation?

_____

_____

_____

_____

4. What effect do the phrases "ancient truths" and "temple of our civilization" have on the tone of the speech?

_____

_____

_____

_____

5. Why does Roosevelt use the phrases "not to be ministered unto" and "to minister to ourselves and to our fellow man" in the final sentence? How do they shape the perception of the audience?

_____

_____

_____

_____

6. How does Roosevelt's understanding of his audience underscore the purpose of his speech?

_____

_____

_____

_____

7. What is the effect of hearing Roosevelt's speech in comparison to reading it? How does he use his voice for emphasis?

_____

_____

_____

8. **KQ** How does Roosevelt use his inaugural address to appeal to the citizens of the United States?

_____

_____

_____

_____

Working from the Text

9. Share with your group the annotations you made about Roosevelt's delivery of the speech. How clear and coherent is Roosevelt's message?

_____

_____

_____

_____

10. With a partner, critique one of the paragraphs in Roosevelt's speech for its use of diction and syntax. Bold the words you notice and underline the varying syntax that has an effect. What can you glean about the effect of his use of words and varying sentence structure?

Diction or Syntax	Analysis of Its Effects

☑ Focus on the Sentence

Using subordinating conjunctions, combine the following sentences from Roosevelt's speech in order to see the effect on their syntax. Read each version aloud with a partner.

The money changers have fled from their high seats in the temple of our civilization. We may now restore that temple to the ancient truths.

_____

_____

_____

_____

This is preeminently the time to speak the truth, the whole truth, frankly and boldly. Nor need we shrink from honestly facing conditions in our country today.

_____

_____

_____

_____

They know only the rules of a generation of self-seekers. They have no vision, and when there is no vision the people perish.

_____

_____

_____

_____

11. Revisit the persuasive speech you have been writing in the past few activities. Review your rhetorical context (subject, audience, occasion, etc.). What tone do you need to convey to your audience in consideration of your subject and occasion?

12. Quietly read your written speech aloud, noting your vocal delivery elements as you did in Roosevelt's speech. Be sure to consider the following elements of vocal delivery as you plan your presentation with the goal of persuading your audience:

- Eye contact
- Volume
- Pitch
- Rate
- Pauses
- Gestures
- Pronunciation (Do you know how to pronounce every word in your speech?)
- Enunciation (Practice enunciating your words so a person seated in the back of the room would have no trouble hearing your argument.)

One Last Stand with Syntax

My Notes

Learning Targets

- Analyze the use of syntax in a historical document.
- Intentionally craft sentences for persuasive effect.
- Integrate ideas from multiple texts to build knowledge and vocabulary about a inaugural speeches.

Preview

In this activity, you will read and analyze John F. Kennedy's Inaugural Address for its use of syntax and persuasion and craft sentences of your own for persuasive effect.

Syntax and Persuasion

Syntax is not a new term for you, but as you grow as a reader and writer, you will encounter increasingly complex sentences. Your ability to decipher meaning in complex syntactic structures and to purposefully use these structures to make meaning in your own texts is critical to your success.

Certain types of sentences or their arrangement affect a passage's overall meaning significantly. Sometimes, authors deliberately choose a variety of syntactical constructions for their sentences; other times, authors consciously repeat certain types of sentences to achieve the desired effect. Syntax can help shape the mood, voice, and tone of a passage.

Sentence Length	Telegraphic	sentences shorter than five words in length
	Short	sentences approximately five words in length
	Medium	sentences approximately 18 words in length
	Long	sentences 30 or more words in length

Sentence Structure	Simple	contains one independent clause	*The goalie waved to his fans.*
	Compound	contains two independent clauses joined by a coordinating conjunction or by a semicolon	*The goalie bowed to his fans, but he gave no autographs.*
	Complex	contains an independent clause and one or more subordinate clauses	*Because the goalie was tired, he went straight to the locker room.*
	Compound-Complex	contains two or more independent clauses and one or more subordinate clauses	*The goalie waved while the fans cheered, but he gave no autographs.*
	Cumulative (or Loose)	makes complete sense if brought to a close before the actual ending	*We reached New York that morning after a turbulent flight and some exciting experiences, tired but exhilarated, full of stories to tell our friends and neighbors.*
	Periodic	makes sense fully only when the end of the sentence is reached	*That morning, after a turbulent flight and some exciting experiences, we reached New York.*
	Balanced	the phrases or clauses balance each other by virtue of their likeness of structure, meaning, or length	*He makes me lie down in green pastures; he leads me beside the still waters.*

As You Read

- Put an exclamation point next to any long sentences.
- Put a star next to any sentence containing repetition.
- Circle unknown words and phrases. Try to determine the meaning of the words by using context clues, word parts, or a dictionary.

About the Author

John F. Kennedy was elected president of the United States in November 1960 and took the oath of office in January 1961. His Inaugural Address has become one of the most famous and most-often-quoted speeches for its rhetoric of both inspiration and challenge.

KNOWLEDGE QUEST

Knowledge Question:

How can presidents use their inaugural addresses to appeal to he country's citizens?

GRAMMAR & USAGE

Sentence Structure: Antithesis

At times, a speaker may create a kind of parallelism between two opposing ideas to emphasize contrast. When authors juxtapose contrasting ideas in balanced phrases or clauses, they use antithesis. Notice that Kennedy uses antithesis no fewer than three times in the very first sentence of his speech: " ... not a victory of party, but a celebration of freedom—symbolizing an end, as well as a beginning, signifying renewal, as well as change." Each phrase works to emphasize and illuminate its opposing idea.

My Notes

_____

_____

_____

_____

_____

_____

_____

mortal: human
tempered: strengthened through hardship

Speech

Inaugural Address of John F. Kennedy

January 20, 1961

1 Vice President Johnson, Mr. Speaker, Mr. Chief Justice, President Eisenhower, Vice President Nixon, President Truman, reverend clergy, fellow citizens, we observe today not a victory of party, but a celebration of freedom—symbolizing an end, as well as a beginning—signifying renewal, as well as change. For I have sworn before you and Almighty God the same solemn oath our forebears prescribed nearly a century and three quarters ago.

2 The world is very different now. For man holds in his **mortal** hands the power to abolish all forms of human poverty and all forms of human life. And yet the same revolutionary beliefs for which our forebears fought are still at issue around the globe—the belief that the rights of man come not from the generosity of the state, but from the hand of God.

3 We dare not forget today that we are the heirs of that first revolution. Let the word go forth from this time and place, to friend and foe alike, that the torch has been passed to a new generation of Americans—born in this century, **tempered** by war, disciplined by a hard and bitter peace, proud of our ancient heritage—and unwilling to witness or permit the slow undoing of those human rights to which this Nation has always been committed, and to which we are committed today at home and around the world.

4 Let every nation know, whether it wishes us well or ill, that we shall pay any price, bear any burden, meet any hardship, support any friend, oppose any foe, in order to assure the survival and the success of liberty.

5 This much we pledge—and more.

6 To those old allies whose cultural and spiritual origins we share, we pledge the loyalty of faithful friends. United, there is little we cannot do in a host of cooperative ventures. Divided, there is little we can do—for we dare not meet a powerful challenge at odds and split asunder.

7 To those new states whom we welcome to the ranks of the free, we pledge our word that one form of colonial control shall not have passed away merely to be replaced by a far more iron tyranny. We shall not always expect to find them supporting our view. But we shall always hope to find them strongly supporting their own freedom—and to remember that, in the past, those who foolishly sought power by riding the back of the tiger ended up inside.

8 To those peoples in the huts and villages across the globe struggling to break the bonds of mass misery, we pledge our best efforts to help them help

My Notes

themselves, for whatever period is required—not because the Communists may be doing it, not because we seek their votes, but because it is right. If a free society cannot help the many who are poor, it cannot save the few who are rich.

9 To our sister republics south of our border, we offer a special pledge—to convert our good words into good deeds—in a new alliance for progress—to assist free men and free governments in casting off the chains of poverty. But this peaceful revolution of hope cannot become the prey of hostile powers. Let all our neighbors know that we shall join with them to oppose aggression or **subversion** anywhere in the Americas. And let every other power know that this Hemisphere intends to remain the master of its own house.

10 To that world assembly of **sovereign** states, the United Nations, our last best hope in an age where the instruments of war have far outpaced the instruments of peace, we renew our pledge of support—to prevent it from becoming merely a forum for **invective**—to strengthen its shield of the new and the weak—and to enlarge the area in which its **writ** may run.

11 Finally, to those nations who would make themselves our adversary, we offer not a pledge but a request: that both sides begin anew the quest for peace, before the dark powers of destruction unleashed by science engulf all humanity in planned or accidental self-destruction.

12 We dare not tempt them with weakness. For only when our arms are sufficient beyond doubt can we be certain beyond doubt that they will never be employed.

13 But neither can two great and powerful groups of nations take comfort from our present course—both sides overburdened by the cost of modern weapons, both rightly alarmed by the steady spread of the deadly atom, yet both racing to alter that uncertain balance of terror that stays the hand of mankind's final war.

14 So let us begin anew—remembering on both sides that civility is not a sign of weakness, and sincerity is always subject to proof. Let us never negotiate out of fear. But let us never fear to negotiate.

15 Let both sides explore what problems unite us instead of **belaboring** those problems which divide us.

16 Let both sides, for the first time, formulate serious and precise proposal for the inspection and control of arms—and bring the absolute power to destroy other nations under the absolute control of all nations.

17 Let both sides seek to invoke the wonders of science instead of its terrors. Together let us explore the stars, conquer the deserts, **eradicate** disease, tap the ocean depths, and encourage the arts and commerce.

18 Let both sides unite to heed in all corners of the earth the command of Isaiah—to "undo the heavy burdens ... and to let the oppressed go free."

---

subversion: weakening or undermining a government
sovereign: self-governing
invective: insults or abuse
writ: written word
belaboring: discussing excessively
eradicate: completely eliminate

19 And if a beachhead of cooperation may push back the jungle of suspicion, let both sides join in creating a new endeavor, not a new balance of power, but a new world of law, where the strong are just and the weak secure and the peace preserved.

20 All this will not be finished in the first 100 days. Nor will it be finished in the first 1,000 days, nor in the life of this Administration, nor even perhaps in our lifetime on this planet. But let us begin.

21 In your hands, my fellow citizens, more than in mine, will rest the final success or failure of our course. Since this country was founded, each generation of Americans has been summoned to give testimony to its national loyalty. The graves of young Americans who answered the call to service surround the globe.

22 Now the trumpet summons us again—not as a call to bear arms, though arms we need; not as a call to battle, though embattled we are—but a call to bear the burden of a long twilight struggle, year in and year out, "rejoicing in hope, patient in tribulation"—a struggle against the common enemies of man: tyranny, poverty, disease, and war itself.

23 Can we forge against these enemies a grand and global alliance, North and South, East and West, that can assure a more fruitful life for all mankind? Will you join in that historic effort?

24 In the long history of the world, only a few generations have been granted the role of defending freedom in its hour of maximum danger. I do not shrink from this responsibility—I welcome it. I do not believe that any of us would exchange places with any other people or any other generation. The energy, the faith, the devotion which we bring to this endeavor will light our country and all who serve it—and the glow from that fire can truly light the world.

25 And so, my fellow Americans: ask not what your country can do for you—ask what you can do for your country.

26 My fellow citizens of the world: ask not what America will do for you, but what together we can do for the freedom of man.

27 Finally, whether you are citizens of America or citizens of the world, ask of us the same high standards of strength and sacrifice which we ask of you. With a good conscience our only sure reward, with history the final judge of our deeds, let us go forth to lead the land we love, asking His blessing and His help, but knowing that here on earth God's work must truly be our own.

Knowledge Quest

- What ideas from President Kennedy's speech stick out to you?
- What emotions might you feel if you were in the audience for this speech?

beachhead: foothold or staging area for an attack

Returning to the Text

- Return to the speech as you respond to the following questions. Use text evidence to support your responses.
- Write any additional questions you have about the text in your Reader/Writer Notebook.

1. **KQ** In paragraph 2, what does Kennedy mean by using the word *revolutionary* in this context?

_____

_____

_____

_____

2. Use the Grammar & Usage box to recall the definition of antithesis. What is the effect of Kennedy's use of antithesis in paragraph 6? How might it also be considered a fallacy?

_____

_____

_____

_____

3. Which clues in paragraph 11 help you identify the audience to whom Kennedy refers? What message is he sending them? Recall that Kennedy delivers this speech during the Cold War, a period of political and military strain following World War II.

_____

_____

_____

_____

4. In paragraph 16, how does Kennedy use the word *absolute* in different ways to create different effects?

_____

_____

_____

_____

5. How does Kennedy's use of repetition in paragraphs 15–18 contribute to the tone of the speech?

_____

_____

_____

6. In paragraph 19, what does Kennedy mean by the clause "a beachhead of cooperation may push back the jungle of suspicion"? What is the effect of this metaphor?

_____

_____

_____

7. What is an additional instance of antithesis in Kennedy's speech? What is its effect on voice?

_____

_____

_____

_____

_____

_____

8. How persuasive is Kennedy's speech? What different appeals does he rely on, and how effective are they?

_____

_____

_____

_____

_____

_____

_____

9. KQ How does Kennedy use his inaugural address to appeal to the citizens of the United States?

_____

_____

_____

_____

 Knowledge Quest

With a partner, discuss how you think Roosevelt's and Kennedy's audiences may have felt hearing their speeches, given your understanding of the historical contexts. Be sure to:

- Refer to evidence from the speeches.
- Take turns speaking, responding, and asking one another follow-up questions.
- Ask clarifying questions.
- Write down notes and ideas for further research.

INDEPENDENT READING LINK

Read and Discuss

You can continue to build your knowledge about inaugural speeches by reading other articles at ZINC Reading Labs. Search for keywords such as _inaugural address_ or _presidential speech_.

 ZINC

Working from the Text

10. As a class, watch the video footage of Kennedy's address. Use the chart to keep track of the different aspects and rhetorical devices used in his address, such as repetition, parallel structure, analogy, rhetorical questions, allusions, anaphora, and metaphor. Take note of the rhetorical devices or syntax choices that you find especially effective or memorable. Then discuss your observations as a group. How did Kennedy's delivery of emphasized words, repetition, and syntax affect his message? How do they effect the clarity and coherence of his message?

Use of Rhetorical Devices	Impact of Words or Phrases	Use of Syntax	Effect on Clarity and Coherence

11. Review your notes about syntax as a group. Create a poster that includes the following:

    - A syntactic structure from your chunk of reading (include length, style, and order)
    - An example sentence of this structure from the text
    - Its effect on the audience
    - Your notes on how to vocally deliver it

12. Assign every group member a responsibility and share your syntax discovery with the class. While listening to other groups, consider some syntax styles that you could intentionally incorporate into your original speech.

☑ Check Your Understanding

Quickwrite: Compare your speech to Kennedy's. How might you incorporate one of Kennedy's rhetorical devices in your own speech?

✏ Drafting the Embedded Assessment

Revise your planned speech again with careful attention to syntax. Refer to your notes on syntactical structure from Kennedy's speech. Consider which styles you can incorporate smoothly into your current draft. Be sure to:

- Read your speech from beginning to end to check for smooth syntax.
- Mark new sentences with notes for vocal delivery.
- Use varied syntax and sentence structure to add to the persuasive impact of your speech and hold audience interest.
- End with a memorable conclusion that uses rhetorical technique.
- Plan and practice inflection, facial expression, and gestures to create an engaging delivery for your audience.

LANGUAGE & WRITER'S CRAFT: Chiasmus

Chiasmus is a type of reverse parallelism in which two clauses are related through a reversal of structure. Consider how a carnival mirror reflects an image of the looker that may be structurally opposite from the original: a small person sees a large image. This type of language reversal helps an author convey a grand and memorable idea to the audience.

Examples:
Let us never negotiate out of fear. But let us never fear to negotiate.

Ask not what your country can do for you—ask what you can do for your country.

PRACTICE Revise your speech to contain at least one example of chiasmus to make a main idea more memorable.

Language Checkpoint:
Writing Logical Comparisons

- Recognize the structure of a logical comparison.
- Understand what makes a comparison illogical.
- Revise in order to maintain logical comparisons in writing.

Preview

In this activity, you will learn about the structure of logical comparisons and work to revise illogical comparisons.

Understanding Logical Comparisons

Writers frequently use comparisons to help their audience understand their ideas. Comparisons are usually made between two nouns. For example:

Life on Mars is harder than life on Earth.

Two similar things are being compared—living on Mars and living on Earth. This comparison is logical, and a reader will clearly understand what the writer is trying to say.

Writers make a couple of different mistakes when making comparisons.

Error	Example	Why It Is an Error
Illogical comparison	Life on Mars is harder than Earth.	The things being compared are not actually similar. *Life on Mars* is being compared to *Earth*.
Comparing one specific thing to all things of that type	Earth is better than any planet capable of sustaining life.	The comparison doesn't acknowledge that Earth itself is a planet.

1. Discuss the following questions with a partner:

   - Why might a writer accidentally make an illogical comparison?
   - Why might a reader be able to understand the comparison even though it is illogical?

2. What is the illogical comparison in the following sentence?

   Franklin D. Roosevelt's speech is more revered than **Truman**.

3. Revise the sentence to make the comparison logical.

4. What is the illogical comparison in the following sentence?

Franklin D. Roosevelt is better than **any president**.

5. Revise the sentence to make the comparison logical.

Fixing Illogical Comparisons

Recognizing and fixing illogical comparisons in writing is important to ensure that the meaning is clear to readers. There are a few ways that illogical comparisons can be revised and made logical.

Rewrite a sentence's noun phrases so that each is they are parallel.

Life on Mars is better than **life on Earth**.

Roosevelt's speech was better than **Truman's speech**.

When two phrases are parallel, they have a similar construction that makes clear how the phrases are alike and different. For example, in the preceding sentences, the phrases *life on Mars* and *life on Earth* are parallel, as are the phrases *Roosevelt' s speech* and *Truman' s speech*.

Rewrite the noun phrases so that each uses a possessive noun, or a noun that shows ownership.

Mars's landscape is harsher than **Earth's**.

Roosevelt's speech is better appreciated than **Truman's**.

In the first sentence, both *Mars' s* and *Earth' s* are possessive, so the sentence implies that both Mars and Earth have landscapes. In the second sentence, both *Roosevelt' s* and *Truman' s* are possessive, so the sentence implies that both Roosevelt and Truman gave a speech.

Add a determiner to the sentence.

Life on Mars is harder than <u>that</u> on **Earth**.

Roosevelt's speeches are more revered than <u>those</u> of **Truman**.

A determiner is a kind of pronoun that shows ownership. The determiner *that* agrees with a singular antecedent, and the determiner *those* agrees with a plural antecedent. In the first sentence, the antecedent of *that* is *life*, which is singular. In the second sentence, the antecedent of *those* is *speeches*, which is plural.

6. Work with a partner to make each of the following comparisons logical.

a. The audiences in New York were larger than San Francisco.

b. The president's approval ratings were lower than her opponent.

c. The United States' swim relay team was faster than the Italians.

Revising

Read the following paragraph. It includes some illogical comparisons. Mark each illogical comparison, and then rewrite it.

[1] Franklin D. Roosevelt was in office longer than any president. [2] He died while in office, however, and his vice president, Harry S. Truman, took his place. [3] Roosevelt delivered many speeches better known than Truman. [4] Truman's oratory was less vigorous than Roosevelt. [5] Despite these differences, both presidents could command great attention when they spoke. [6] Truman's legacy may never reach the stature of Roosevelt, but he was an important president.

☑ Check Your Understanding

What question(s) can you ask yourself whenever you write to be sure that your comparisons are logical? What techniques can you use to make your comparisons logical? Add the question(s) to your Editor's Checklist.

Practice

You have read speeches by Abraham Lincoln, Patrick Henry, John F. Kennedy, and Franklin D. Roosevelt. In a short explanatory text of two or three paragraphs, compare the rhetorical techniques of two of these speakers. After you complete a first draft, underline all the comparisons. Check to make sure the comparisons are logical and revise any that are not.

Explain How an Author Builds an Argument

- Read an argument and analyze how the author builds it.
- Write a timed essay that includes an introduction and conclusion, includes relevant and accurate textual evidence, and adheres to standard English conventions.

Preview

In this activity, you will practice writing an analysis of an argument in a timed setting. You will be given a passage to read, analyze, and write about. This activity will take 50 minutes, so be sure to use your time wisely. Read the prompt carefully, annotate the text, and leave yourself time to quickly review what you have written at the end.

Prompt

As you read the passage, consider how Alfred M. Green uses:

- A thesis supported by evidence and examples.
- Evidence, such as facts, to support claims.
- Reasoning to develop ideas and to connect claims and evidence.
- Stylistic or persuasive elements, such as word choice or appeals to emotion, to add power to the ideas expressed.
- Organization of ideas in order to convey a purpose.

Write an essay in which you explain how Alfred M. Green builds an argument to persuade his audience that they, African Americans, should fight for the United States even though they do not yet have equal rights. In your essay, analyze how Green uses one or more of the listed features (or features of your own choice) to strengthen the logic and persuasiveness of his argument. Be sure that your analysis focuses on the most relevant features of the passage and includes details and examples from the text.

Your essay should not explain whether you agree with Green's claims but rather explain how the author builds an argument to persuade his audience.

Vocal Delivery

Learning Strategies

Debate
Discussion Groups
Graphic Organizer
Note-taking
Rehearsing
Revising

Learning Targets

- Analyze a speaker's use of diction and syntax.
- Evaluate clarity and coherence in a speaker's message.

Preview

In this activity, you will watch or listen to two speeches in order to evaluate their delivery and use of language and structure.

My Notes

Elements of Speech

1. Read the following list of physical and rhetorical elements used commonly in effective speeches. As you watch or listen to the speeches, use the chart to take notes on the components that you see or hear. As you watch or listen, consider how the speaker's delivery affects his message.

Physical	Rhetorical	
Volume	Anaphora	Logical appeals
Smooth delivery	Aphorism	Emotional appeals
Gestures	Analogy	Ethical appeals
Speaking Rate	Allusion	Syntax
Movement	Alliteration	Parallelism
Enunciation	Rhetorical questions	Chiasmus
Eye Contact	Diction	Other rhetorical devices

Speech 1:

Physical	Rhetorical

Speech 2:

Physical	Rhetorical

2. Discuss with your classmates the similarities and differences in the vocal delivery of these two speakers. How might their vocal delivery have been affected by the climate of the nation and contemporary issues during their respective terms?

3. In small groups, debate which speaker gave a more persuasive or convincing speech. Use the notes you took earlier in the activity to point to specific physical and rhetorical examples within the speeches to back up your position. After your debate, come up with a list of criteria you decide on as a group about what physical and rhetorical qualities make up a good speech.

Physical	Rhetorical

4. Revisit the speech you have been drafting and revising. By now, you should have a speech with a clear argumentative structure, including the following:

   - Rhetorical devices
   - Rhetorical appeals
   - Intentional, convincing syntax
   - Notes about the tone and the way in which it will be delivered

5. Now it is time to practice presenting a clear, persuasive argument to your audience. Rehearse your speech while a peer critiques your speech and delivery based on the physical and rhetorical structures. Revise the speech or delivery style as necessary.

☑ Check Your Understanding

Reflection: How would you assess your performance? List your strengths and areas for improvement.

🎁 Independent Reading Checkpoint

You have read and listened to a variety of speeches and analyzed how speakers employ rhetorical devices and delivery techniques to effectively persuade audiences. What have you learned about physical and rhetorical elements that you could apply to your own presentation of a persuasive speech? Prepare your answers in the form of a brief "how-to" list for persuasive speakers.

Writing and Presenting a Persuasive Speech

ASSIGNMENT

Your assignment is to write and present an original, persuasive two- to three-minute speech that addresses a contemporary issue. It should include a clear claim, support, counterclaim, and conclusion/call to action. Incorporate rhetorical appeals and devices to strengthen your argument and to help you achieve your desired purpose.

Planning: Take time to make a plan for writing and rehearsing your speech	■ Out of the various positions that one might take on this issue, which one seems the most promising for a persuasive speech? ■ How have you made careful consideration of your purpose and audience in the planning of your speech? ■ How has your planning allowed you to incorporate the elements of effective physical and vocal delivery?
Drafting: Create a draft of your speech and ask for feedback	■ How can you anticipate and respond to questions or objections that audience members might have before they make them? ■ What outside evidence or quotations can you use to support or reinforce your ideas? ■ Who can you ask to read or listen to your speech to offer suggestions for improvement?
Revising and Rehearsing: Incorporate changes into your speech and practice delivering it	■ How can you use rehearsal of your speech as a way to determine what additional revision is needed? ■ How can you improve the variety of your syntax while crafting sentences that add to your impact on the audience? ■ How can you make sure that your performance includes an appropriate tone of voice and gestures to add to the persuasive effect?
Publishing for Performance: Make final changes and prepare your speech for delivery	■ How will you check your work for grammatical and technical accuracy? ■ Are the rhetorical devices that you have included both effective and apparent to your audience?

Reflection

After completing this Embedded Assessment, think about how you went about accomplishing this assignment, and respond to the following:

- How was writing something meant to be performed in front of an audience different from writing a traditional essay?
- What was the most challenging part about trying to anticipate the reactions of your audience?

SCORING GUIDE

Scoring Criteria	Exemplary	Proficient	Emerging	Incomplete
Ideas	The speech • presents a significant and compelling thesis on a contemporary issue • is clearly developed and supported • presents a convincing argument and adeptly uses a variety of rhetorical appeals.	The speech • presents a clear thesis on a contemporary issue • is sufficiently developed and supported • presents a plausible argument and effectively uses rhetorical appeals.	The speech • presents a thesis • is somewhat developed and weakly supported • attempts to make an argument, but it is not plausible and uses rhetorical appeals ineffectively.	The speech • presents a position that is difficult to distinguish • is insufficiently developed and supported • does not make an argument that is plausible and lacks rhetorical appeals.
Structure	The speech • sequences ideas to aptly reinforce the argument • presents an introduction that intrigues the audience while establishing the topic • concludes with a clear and convincing call to action.	The speech • sequences material to support the argument • presents an introduction that establishes the topic • concludes in a way that provides a finished feeling to the speech, possibly suggesting further action.	The speech • attempts to sequence material with a weak connection to the argument • presents an introduction that weakly established the topic • concludes abruptly or with a proposed action that is inappropriate.	The speech • organizes ideas in a manner that is difficult to follow or jumps too rapidly between ideas • does little to introduce the topic, possibly only stating the subject of the speech • lacks a conclusion or fails to propose action.
Use of Language	The speech • deliberately and effectively uses rhetorical devices for the intended purpose • uses varied syntax in a way that adds to the persuasive impact • demonstrates well placed inflection and gestures that create an engaging delivery style indicative of advance preparation.	The speech • clearly attempts to use rhetorical devices for the intended purpose • varies syntax over the course of the speech • demonstrates some use of inflection and gestures that create an appropriate delivery style indicative of advance preparation.	The speech • attempts to use rhetorical devices, but the result is ineffective for the intended purpose • attempts to vary syntax over the course of the speech with limited success • demonstrates limited use of inflection and gestures, impairing the delivery style.	The speech • does not use rhetorical devices • uses syntax that is largely repetitive and lacks variation • demonstrates minimal use of inflection and gestures.

VISUAL PROMPT
TV news, news magazines, newspapers, radio, and the Internet give us sometimes vital, and sometimes trivial, facts and opinions, creating a swirling array of often-conflicting information. How do you obtain news and other information?

AMERICAN FORUMS: THE MARKETPLACE OF IDEAS

A self-governing society, by definition, needs to make its own decisions. It cannot do that without hard information, leavened with an open exchange of views.

—George A. Krimsky from "The Role of Media in a Democracy"

American Forums: The Marketplace of Ideas

ACTIVITY	CONTENTS	

My Independent Reading List

📦 My Independent
Reading List

*Texts not included in these materials.

Previewing the Unit

Learning Strategies

Close Reading
Graphic Organizer
Marking the Text
Paraphrasing
Summarizing

Learning Targets

- Examine the key ideas for the unit.
- Identify and analyze the skills and knowledge necessary for success in completing the Embedded Assessment.

Preview

In this activity, you will explore the big ideas and tasks of the unit and make plans for your independent reading.

About the Unit

If you have ever listened to talk radio, watched cable "news" shows, or browsed the Web and social media sites, you may have seen many different versions of the same information. Some news is presented with a biased point of view, and when it comes to the expression of editorial opinions, sources often rely heavily on language and evidence that attempt to persuade through manipulation. So when you come into contact with the news, you should ask what information you are receiving and not receiving, where that information came from, and whether the purveyor of the news might have an agenda. In this unit, you will learn more about how to identify bias and how language is sometimes used as a substitute for logic. Good writers use evidence and reasoning to support their claims; the failure to do so can result in fallacies.

Essential Questions

Based on your current knowledge, respond to the Essential Questions.

1. What is the role of media in our society, and how can we become responsible consumers and producers of information in a digital age?

2. How can writers use satire to bring about change in society?

Unpacking Embedded Assessment 1

Read the assignment for Embedded Assessment 1: Creating an Op-Ed News Project.

Working in groups, your assignment is to plan, develop, write, revise, and present an informational article on a timely and debatable issue of significance to your school community, local community, or national audience. After your group completes its article, you will individually develop a variety of editorial products that reflect your point of view (agreement, alternative, or opposing) on the topic. Be creative with your editorial products and include at least two different pieces, such as cartoons, editorials, letters, posters, photos, and so on.

With your class, read closely and mark the text for the knowledge and skills you must have to successfully complete this project.

My Notes

My Notes

⬡ Planning Independent Reading

During this unit, you will read a local, national, or online newspaper every day. Create a log to keep track of what and when you read and write down the titles of significant articles that you encounter in each section. Don't just read the first page or landing page (if you are reading an online publication); navigate through all the sections. Each day, cut out, scan, copy, or photograph one article that you enjoyed reading. Choose a publication that interests you because you will be spending considerable time with it.

Rights and Responsibility

Learning Strategies

Diffusing
Marking the Text
Metacognitive Markers
Questioning the Text
Rereading

Learning Targets

- Use print or digital resources to clarify or validate the meaning of words and phrases as they are used in a text.
- Evaluate the opinion of a writer using textual details as support.
- Participate collaboratively in a Socratic Seminar.

Preview

In this activity, you will read the article "The Role of the Media in a Democracy" by George A. Krimsky, examine Krimsky's arguments, and participate in a Socratic Seminar to discuss his ideas about the role of a free press in a democracy.

Rights and the American Dream

While the American Dream is central to Americans' shared sense of identity, another defining belief of the American people is in the importance of free speech. As Supreme Court Justice Oliver Wendell Holmes famously observed in 1919, "The best test of truth is the power of the thought to get itself accepted in the competition of the market." Viewed in this way, the expression of contrasting and even conflicting ideas and opinions provides information that is crucial to our ability to make informed decisions about everything from personal beliefs to public policy. Indeed, the ways in which these ideas and voices interact with each other help us to shape, test, and revise our own perspectives on the issues that dominate our lives. This unit, with its focus on the media, begins with an in-depth examination of the constitutional amendment guaranteeing U.S. citizens their freedom of speech.

1. In Unit 1, you read the First Amendment to the United States Constitution as part of your study of the Bill of Rights. Refresh your memory of the First Amendment by rereading the text.

Historical Document

First Amendment to the United States Constitution

Congress shall make no law respecting an establishment of religion, or prohibiting the free exercise thereof; or abridging the freedom of speech, or of the press; or the right of the people peaceably to assemble, and to petition the Government for a redress of grievances.

My Notes

Vocabulary Study

2. Each of the following terms is taken verbatim from the First Amendment. Read through the list and then underline each word or term where it appears in the text of the First Amendment. Next, define each term. Note that advanced vocabulary often has multiple meanings. Use the context to determine which meaning of the term is correct. Then use a print or digital resource to clarify or validate your understanding of the term and how it is used in the text.

respecting	
establishment	
prohibiting	
free exercise	
thereof	
abridge	
the press	
peaceably	
assemble	
petition	
redress	
grievances	

3. Now transform the text by rewriting the First Amendment, replacing the vocabulary words with their definitions. In some cases, your definition may fit exactly; in others, you may need to rework the phrasing.

4. The First Amendment includes four basic rights or freedoms. What are they? Which of these will be the focus of this unit?

As You Read

- Use metacognitive markers to monitor your comprehension by noting anything that raises a question for you (?), anything you find surprising (!), and anything that connects to the First Amendment (*).
- Use print or digital resources to clarify your understanding of any unfamiliar terms, including words that have multiple meanings.

About the Author

George Krimsky (1942–2017) worked for 45 years as a journalist, author, lecturer, and media critic. His career began in 1969, when he joined the Associated Press. In 1984, he founded the International Center for Journalists (IFCJ), a group dedicated to supporting innovative and diverse voices in news coverage. He is co-author of the highly regarded *Hold the Press: The Inside Story on Newspapers*, first published in 1995. "The Role of the Media in a Democracy" was written in 1997 and placed on the U.S. Department of State's informational website in 2007.

Informational Text

The Role of the Media in a Democracy

by **George A. Krimsky**

Chunk 1

1   Volumes have been written about the role of the mass media in a democracy. The danger in all this examination is to submerge the subject under a sludge of **platitudes**. The issue of whether a free press is the best communications solution in a democracy is much too important at the close of this century and needs to be examined dispassionately.

2   Before addressing the subject, it helps to define the terminology. In the broadest sense, the media embraces the television and film entertainment industries, a vast array of regularly published printed material, and even public relations and advertising. The "press" is supposed to be a serious member of that family, focusing on real life instead of fantasy and serving the widest possible audience. A good generic term for the press in the electronic age is "news media." The emphasis in this definition is on content, not technology or delivery system, because the press—at least in developed

platitudes: clichéd statements

My Notes

GRAMMAR & USAGE

Rhetorical Devices

A **rhetorical question** is a figure of speech in the form of a question that an author asks to emphasize a point rather than elicit an answer. Rhetorical questions often occur immediately after a comment and suggest the opposite of it—the idea is to make a point more prominent. Authors often use rhetorical questioning as a persuasive device to influence the kind of response they want from an audience.

Notice the question in paragraph 8. The reader is not expected to answer this question but rather to understand that the application of constitutional theory has not proven simple at all.

Find another rhetorical question that the author uses and discuss its effect with a partner.

succinctly: briefly and accurately

subsidy: financial support

countries—can be found these days on the Internet, the fax lines, or the airwaves.

3   A self-governing society, by definition, needs to make its own decisions. It cannot do that without hard information, leavened with an open exchange of views. Abraham Lincoln articulated this concept most **succinctly** when he said: "Let the people know the facts, and the country will be safe."

4   Some might regard Lincoln's as a somewhat naive viewpoint, given the complexities and technologies of the 20th century; but the need for public news has been a cornerstone of America's system almost from the start.

5   Thomas Jefferson felt so strongly about the principle of free expression he said something that non-democrats must regard as an absurdity: "If it were left to me to decide whether we should have a government without newspapers or newspapers without a government, I should not hesitate a moment to prefer the latter." The implication of those words is that self-governance is more essential than governance itself. Not so absurd, perhaps, if you had just fought a war against an oppressive government.

Chunk 2

6   In the wake of America's successful revolution, it was decided there should indeed be government, but only if it were accountable to the people. The people, in turn, could only hold the government accountable if they knew what it was doing and could intercede as necessary, using their ballot, for example. This role of public "watchdog" was thus assumed by a citizen press, and as a consequence, the government in the United States has been kept out of the news business. The only government-owned or-controlled media in the United States are those that broadcast overseas, such as the Voice of America. By law, this service is not allowed to broadcast within the country. There is partial government **subsidy** to public television and radio in the United States, but safeguards protect it against political interference.

7   Because the Constitution is the highest law in the land, any attempts by courts, legislators and law enforcement officers to weaken protected liberties, such as free expression, are generally preventable.

8   Fairly simple in theory, but how has all this worked out?

9   Generally speaking, pretty well, although the concept of a free press is challenged and defended every day in one community or another across the land. The American press has always been influential, often powerful and sometimes feared, but it has seldom been loved. As a matter of fact, journalists today rank in the lower echelons of public popularity. They are seen as too powerful on the one hand, and not trustworthy on the other.

10   In its early days, the American press was little more than a pamphleteering industry, owned by or affiliated with competing political interests and engaged in a constant war of propaganda. Trust was not an issue. What caused the press to become an instrument for democratic decision-making was the variety of voices. Somehow, the common truth managed to

My Notes

emerge from under that chaotic pile of information and misinformation. A quest for objectivity was the result.

Chunk 3

11 Many critics have questioned whether there is such a thing as "objectivity." Indeed, no human being can be truly objective; we can only *seek* objectivity and **impartiality** in the pursuit of truth. Journalists can try to keep their personal views out of the news, and they employ a number of techniques to do so, such as obtaining and quoting multiple sources and opposing views.

12 The question is whether the truth always serves the public. At times, the truth can do harm. If the truthful report of a small communal conflict in, say, Africa, leads to more civil unrest, is the public really being served? The journalistic purists—often those sitting in comfortable chairs far from conflict—say it is not their job to "play God" in such matters, and that one should not "shoot the messenger for the message."

13 If, however, one takes the rigid view that the truth always needs to be controlled—or Lenin's dictum that truth is **partisan**—the door is wide open for enormous abuse, as history has demonstrated time and again. It is this realization (and fear) that prompted Jefferson to utter that absurdity about the supreme importance of an uncensored press.

14 What Jefferson and the constitutional framers could not have foreseen, however, was how modern market forces would expand and exploit the simple concept of free expression. While media with meager resources in most developing countries are still struggling to keep governments from **suppressing** news that Westerners take for granted, the mass media in America, Britain, Germany and elsewhere are preoccupied with their role as profitable businesses and the task of securing a spot on tomorrow's electronic superhighway. In such an environment, truth in the service of the public seems almost a quaint anachronism.

15 Is the capitalist drive an **inherent** obstacle to good journalism? In one sense, the marketplace can be the ally, rather than the enemy of a strong, free media. For the public to believe what it reads, listens to and sees in the mass media, the "product" must be credible. Otherwise, the public will not buy the product, and the company will lose money. So, profitability and public service can go hand in hand. What a media company does with its money is the key. If it uses a significant portion of its profits to improve its newsgathering and marketing capabilities and eliminate dependence upon others for its survival (e.g. state subsidies, newsprint purchases, or access to printing facilities), the product improves, and the public is served. If it uses its profits primarily to make its owners rich, it might as well be selling toothpaste.

16 The assumption in this argument is that the public overwhelmingly wants to believe its news media, and that it will use this credible information to actively and reasonably conduct its public affairs. Unfortunately, that assumption is not as valid as it was in simpler times. In affluent societies today,

impartiality: lack of support for one side or the other

partisan: supports one party over another

suppressing: holding down or back

inherent: built-in

media consumers are seeking more and more entertainment, and the news media's **veracity** (even its **plausibility**) is less important than its capacity to attract an audience.

17 But, you say, look at the new technology that can penetrate any censorship system in the world. Look at the choices people have today. Look at how accessible information is today. Yes, the choices may be larger, but a case can be made they are not deeper—that big money is replacing quality products and services with those of only the most massive appeal. The banquet table may be larger, but if it only contains "junk food," is there really more choice? Declining literacy, for example, is a real problem in the so-called developed world. That's one reason why newspapers are so worried about their future.

Chunk 4

18 Where is the relevance of all this to the emerging democracies around the world? Certainly the American experience, for all its messiness, provides a useful **precedent**, if not always a model.

19 For example, when one talks about an independent media, it is necessary to include financial independence as a prerequisite, in addition to political independence. The American revenue-earning model of heavy reliance on advertising is highly suspect in many former communist countries, but one has to weigh the alternatives. Are government and party subsidies less imprisoning? If journalists are so fearful of contamination by advertiser pressure, they can build internal walls between news and business functions, similar to those American newspapers erected earlier in this century.

20 If they are fearful of political contamination of the information-gathering process, they can build another wall separating the newsroom from the editorial department—another important concept in modern American journalism.

21 The problem in many new democracies is that journalists who once had to toe the single-party line equate independence with opposition. Because they speak out against the government, they say they are independent. But haven't they just traded one **affiliation** for another? There is little room for unvarnished truth in a partisan press.

22 Is objectivity a luxury in societies that have only recently begun to enjoy the freedom to voice their opinions? Listen to a Lithuanian newspaper editor shortly after his country gained its independence: "I want my readers to know what their heads are for." His readers were used to being told not only what to think about, but what to think. Democracy requires the public to make choices and decisions. This editor wanted to prepare citizens for that responsibility with articles that inform but do not pass judgment. His circulation increased.

23 Though nearly 60 percent of the world's nations today are declared democracies—a monumental change from a mere decade ago—most of them have nevertheless instituted press laws that prohibit reporting on a

veracity: truthfulness
plausibility: believability
precedent: prior example
affiliation: close association

whole array of subjects ranging from the internal activity and operations of government to the private lives of leaders. Some of these are well-intentioned efforts to "preserve public stability." But all of them, ALL of them, undermine self-governance.

24 The watchdog role of the free press can often appear as mean-spirited. How do the government and public protect themselves from its excesses? In the United States, it is done in a variety of ways. One, for example, is the use of "ombudsmen." In this case, news organizations employ an in-house critic to hear public complaints and either publish or broadcast their judgments. Another is the creation of citizens' councils which sit to hear public complaints about the press and then issue verdicts, which, although not carrying the force of law, are aired widely.

25 Last, and most effective, is libel law. In the United States, a citizen can win a substantial monetary award from a news organization if libel is proven in a court of law. It is much harder for a public official or celebrity than an ordinary citizen to win a libel case against the press, because the courts have ruled that notoriety comes with being in the limelight. In most cases, the complaining notable must prove "malice aforethought."

26 There is nothing in the American constitution that says the press must be responsible and accountable. Those requirements were reserved for government. In a free-market democracy, the people—that is the voters and the buying public—ultimately decide as to how their press should act. If at least a semblance of truth-in-the-public-service does not remain a motivating force for the mass media of the future, neither free journalism nor true democracy has much hope, in my opinion.

27 The nature and use of new technology is not the essential problem. If true journalists are worried about their future in an age when everyone with a computer can call themselves journalists, then the profession has to demonstrate that it is special, that it offers something of real value and can prove it to the public. There is still a need today—perhaps more than ever— for identifying sense amidst the nonsense, for sifting the important from the trivial, and, yes, for telling the truth. Those goals still constitute the best mandate for a free press in a democracy.

28 George Washington's admonition, uttered at the Constitutional Convention, still stands: "Let us raise a standard to which the wise and honest can repair."

Making Observations
- Based on your use of metacognitive markers, what connections to the First Amendment do you notice?
- Who are some historical figures Krimsky mentions in his article?

libel: publishing a false statement that hurts someone's reputation
notable: well-known person
semblance: outward appearance
mandate: authorization
repair: go back

Returning to the Text

- Reread the article as you respond to the following questions. Use text evidence to support your responses.
- Write any additional questions you have about the text in your Reader/Writer Notebook.

5. The word *passion* has at least two meanings. Use print or digital resources, along with your knowledge of context and affixes, to determine the meaning of *dispassionately* in paragraph 1.

_____

_____

_____

_____

6. What details in paragraphs 3–7 support the author's arguments in favor of the First Amendment's "free press" clause?

_____

_____

_____

_____

_____

7. How do words and phrases such as "dispassionately" (paragraph 1), "it was decided" (paragraph 6), "accountable" (paragraph 6), and "generally speaking" (paragraph 9) set a tone that contributes to Krimsky's persuasiveness?

_____

_____

_____

_____

8. In paragraph 11, how does Krimsky describe journalists' attempts to be objective? How does he himself demonstrate this technique in paragraph 12?

_____

_____

_____

_____

_____

9. In Chunk 4, Krimsky specifies two types of independence that a democracy's media must maintain. Name those two types of independence and summarize his suggestions for maintaining them.

_____

_____

_____

_____

_____

10. Examine the context of the questions "Are government and party subsidies less imprisoning?" (paragraph 19) and "But haven't they just traded one affiliation for another?" (paragraph 21). Why does the author use questions instead of statements to make his point? What is the effect?

_____

_____

_____

_____

_____

11. In paragraph 21, Krimsky suggests that journalists who oppose the government in new democracies "equate independence with opposition." How does this support his argument for a non-partisan, objective news media?

_____

_____

_____

_____

12. How does the anecdote about the Lithuanian newspaper editor in paragraph 22 support Krimsky's central idea regarding press objectivity? How does it affect the way the text is read and understood?

_____

_____

_____

_____

_____

13. Based upon the context of the article's last sentence, what is an *admonition?* Use a print or digital resource to clarify or validate your understanding of this multiple-meaning word.

_____

_____

_____

_____

_____

14. Summarize Krimsky's point of view about the importance of a free press within a democracy.

_____

_____

_____

_____

_____

☑ Focus on the Sentence

Examine the arguments and supporting statements Krimsky makes in his article. Write three or four sentences that summarize some of his views using *because*, *but*, or *so* as conjunctions between clauses. You may use the following sentence frame to help you compose your sentences, or you may construct them on your own.

The author states that _____ (because/but/so) _____.

_____

_____

_____

_____

_____

_____

_____

LANGUAGE & WRITER'S CRAFT: Diction and Tone

When writers make an argument, they choose between a subjective and an objective tone to convey information. Writers may use a subjective tone if they want to provide an opinion that contains a biased viewpoint, or they might use an objective tone if they want to convey unbiased facts that pertain to the argument. Each choice has its merits and drawbacks—when readers know an argument is subjective, it may feel more personal and contain emotions and judgment. When an argument is objective, it may feel as though the writer's opinions have been removed from the equation to produce a purely fact-based argument. Pay close attention to a writer's diction, or word choice, in order to ascertain whether the tone is subjective or objective. Subjective arguments tend to contain more emotional or opinionated language: "The American press … has seldom been loved." Objective arguments tend to contain more neutral or factual language: "The media embraces the television and film entertainment industries, a vast array of regularly published printed material, and even public relations and advertising."

How do you know which tone to take in crafting an argument? First, consider your audience. A meeting with your teacher about raising a grade might not benefit from subjective emotional language. However, if you provide objective, measurable facts about your performance, the teacher may be more likely to consider your point of view.

PRACTICE Choose one paragraph from "The Role of the Media in a Democracy" and analyze whether the tone is objective or subjective. Which clues from the writer's diction indicate objectivity or subjectivity? Then rewrite the paragraph in the opposing tone, paying close attention to diction.

Working from the Text

15. Skim Krimsky's article to analyze its characteristics and structural elements. List quotes from the text that illustrate those characteristics/elements in the chart and write a short interpretive statement for each.

Characteristic/ Element	Quote	Interpretation
Audience	"The issue of whether a free press is the best communications solution in a democracy is much too important at the close of this century and needs to be examined dispassionately."	The audience for the article is people who live in a democracy.
Thesis		
Argument		
Counterarguments/ Rebuttals/ Concessions		
Conclusion		
Call to Action		

Socratic Seminar

You will next participate in a Socratic Seminar. To prepare, review the texts in this activity. Then, in small groups, respond to the pre-seminar questions as they relate to the texts. Discuss the conflicting points of view presented in the article and measure each position against your understanding of the First Amendment. Cite specific details from each text to support your ideas and viewpoints.

Pre-seminar questions:

- How important is a free press to a democratic society? What is the balance between the freedoms guaranteed by the First Amendment and the responsibility of the individual in our society?
- Why is it important that the government is not involved with the media?
- Write one of your own open-ended questions based on the text.

Participation Remember that as you participate in the Socratic Seminar, follow the rules for a collaborative discussion:

- Offer your ideas or judgments that are purposeful in moving the class toward goals.
- Ask relevant and insightful questions.
- Be tolerant of a range of positions and ambiguity in decision making among your peers.
- Evaluate the group's work based on agreed-upon criteria.

Explain How an Author Builds an Argument

Krimsky begins his essay by defining terminology and revisiting some historical and key ideas about the founding of the U.S. government. Write an essay that explains how Krimsky continues to structure his essay to persuade readers of the vital role of free media within a democracy. How effective is this structure in conveying Krimsky's ideas in a convincing way? Be sure to:

- Revise your draft as needed to use diction and precise language that maintain an objective tone as you describe and analyze Krimsky's structure.
- Employ logical organization as you build an analysis of how Krimsky's ideas progress.
- Develop your explanation by citing significant and relevant quotations, making sure not to introduce errors of fact or understanding.

Learning Strategies

Making Inferences
Note-taking

My Notes

Learning Targets

- Read and evaluate the reasoning of a legal decision.
- Understand central ideas in a text and consider how they might be refuted.

Preview

In this activity, you will read a 1971 Supreme Court ruling and analyze it argument and central ideas.

As You Read

- Highlight details the Supreme Court uses to support its ruling.
- Underline the reasoning the Supreme Court uses in its argument.
- Circle any unknown words or phrases. Try to determine the meaning of the words by using context clues, word parts, or a dictionary.

About the Document

New York Times Co. v. United States was a case brought before the Supreme Court in 1971. The case concerned the First Amendment in regard to whether *The New York Times* and *The Washington Post* should be allowed to publish the Pentagon Papers, which were considered classified government documents. President Nixon had used his executive authority to force *The New York Times* to stop publication of any classified information it may have had, and The New York Times Co. wanted to be able to publish the papers without fear of censorship or punishment. The Supreme Court had to decide whether *The New York Times* was guaranteed the constitutional right of freedom of the press under the First Amendment or whether the government was allowed to halt publication in order to maintain the secrecy of its information. The Supreme Court ultimately ruled that *The New York Times* was protected under the First Amendment and allowed to print the classified information.

Legislation

New York Times Co. v. United States, 403 U.S. 713

by **U.S. Supreme Court**

1   MR. JUSTICE BLACK, with whom MR. JUSTICE DOUGLAS joins, concurring.

2   I adhere to the view that the Government's case against the Washington Post should have been dismissed, and that the injunction against the New York Times should have been vacated without oral argument when the cases were first presented to this Court. I believe that every moment's continuance of the injunctions against these newspapers amounts to a flagrant, indefensible, and continuing violation of the First Amendment. Furthermore, after oral argument, I agree completely that we must affirm the judgment of the Court of Appeals for the District of Columbia Circuit and reverse the judgment of the Court of Appeals for the Second Circuit for the reasons stated by my Brothers DOUGLAS and BRENNAN. In my view, it is unfortunate that some of my Brethren are apparently willing to hold that the publication of news may sometimes be enjoined. Such a holding would make a shambles of the First Amendment.

3   Our Government was launched in 1789 with the adoption of the Constitution. The Bill of Rights, including the First Amendment, followed in 1791. Now, for the first time in the 182 years since the founding of the Republic, the federal courts are asked to hold that the First Amendment does not mean what it says, but rather means that the Government can halt the publication of current news of vital importance to the people of this country.

4   In seeking injunctions against these newspapers, and in its presentation to the Court, the Executive Branch seems to have forgotten the essential purpose and history of the First Amendment. When the Constitution was adopted, many people strongly opposed it because the document contained no Bill of Rights to safeguard certain basic freedoms. They especially feared that the new powers granted to a central government might be interpreted to permit the government to curtail freedom of religion, press, assembly, and speech. In response to an overwhelming public clamor, James Madison offered a series of amendments to satisfy citizens that these great liberties would remain safe and beyond the power of government to abridge. Madison proposed what later became the First Amendment in three parts, two of which are set out below, and one of which proclaimed: "The people shall not

---

concurring: agreeing
adhere: hold closely
injunction: order
flagrant: offensive
brethren: brothers
curtail: restrict
clamor: protest
abridge: restrict

be deprived or abridged of their right to speak, to write, or to publish their sentiments, and the freedom of the press, as one of the great **bulwarks** of liberty, shall be **inviolable**." (Emphasis added.) The amendments were offered to curtail and restrict the general powers granted to the Executive, Legislative, and Judicial Branches two years before in the original Constitution. The Bill of Rights changed the original Constitution into a new charter under which no branch of government could abridge the people's freedoms of press, speech, religion, and assembly. Yet the Solicitor General argues and some members of the Court appear to agree that the general powers of the Government adopted in the original Constitution should be interpreted to limit and restrict the specific and **emphatic** guarantees of the Bill of Rights adopted later. I can imagine no greater perversion of history. Madison and the other Framers of the First Amendment, able men that they were, wrote in language they earnestly believed could never be misunderstood: "Congress shall make no law . . . abridging the freedom . . . of the press. . . ." Both the history and language of the First Amendment support the view that the press must be left free to publish news, whatever the source, without censorship, injunctions, or prior restraints.

5　In the First Amendment, the Founding Fathers gave the free press the protection it must have to fulfill its essential role in our democracy. The press was to serve the governed, not the governors. The Government's power to censor the press was abolished so that the press would remain forever free to **censure** the Government. The press was protected so that it could bare the secrets of government and inform the people. Only a free and unrestrained press can effectively expose deception in government. And **paramount** among the responsibilities of a free press is the duty to prevent any part of the government from deceiving the people and sending them off to distant lands to die of foreign fevers and foreign shot and shell. In my view, far from deserving condemnation for their courageous reporting, the New York Times, the Washington Post, and other newspapers should be commended for serving the purpose that the Founding Fathers saw so clearly. In revealing the workings of government that led to the Vietnam war, the newspapers nobly did precisely that which the Founders hoped and trusted they would do.

6　The Government's case here is based on premises entirely different from those that guided the Framers of the First Amendment. The Solicitor General has carefully and emphatically stated: "Now, Mr. Justice [BLACK], your construction of . . . [the First Amendment] is well known, and I certainly respect it. You say that no law means no law, and that should be obvious. I can only say, Mr. Justice, that to me it is equally obvious that 'no law' does not mean 'no law,' and I would seek to persuade the Court that that is true. . . . [T] here are other parts of the Constitution that grant powers and responsibilities to the Executive, and . . . the First Amendment was not intended to make it impossible for the Executive to function or to protect the security of the United States."

7　And the Government argues in its brief that, in spite of the First Amendment, "[t]he authority of the Executive Department to protect the

bulwarks: institutions
inviolable: not dishonored
emphatic: forcibly expressed
censure: disapprove of
paramount: most important

nation against publication of information whose disclosure would endanger the national security stems from two interrelated sources: the constitutional power of the President over the conduct of foreign affairs and his authority as Commander-in-Chief."

8 In other words, we are asked to hold that, despite the First Amendment's emphatic command, the Executive Branch, the Congress, and the Judiciary can make laws enjoining publication of current news and abridging freedom of the press in the name of "national security." The Government does not even attempt to rely on any act of Congress. Instead, it makes the bold and dangerously far-reaching contention that the courts should take it upon themselves to "make" a law abridging freedom of the press in the name of equity, presidential power and national security, even when the representatives of the people in Congress have adhered to the command of the First Amendment and refused to make such a law.

Making Observations
- What tone does the language emphasize?
- What details stand out to you?
- What questions does this text raise for you?

Returning to the Text

- Return to the ruling as you respond to the following questions. Use evidence from the text to support your responses.
- Write any additional questions you have about the text in your Reader/Writer Notebook.

1. In paragraph 2, what inferences can be made about how the justices arrived at their decision?

_____

_____

_____

_____

2. In paragraph 3, what premise given by the Government do the justices reject? On what grounds do they reject the Government's premise?

_____

_____

_____

_____

3. In paragraph 4, what do the justices mean by "perversion of history" in context?

_____

_____

_____

_____

4. What claims do the justices make in paragraph 5? What evidence do they provide for their claim?

_____

_____

_____

_____

5. Summarize the arguments the justices make over the course of their ruling. How do they develop their argument?

_____

_____

_____

_____

Working from the Text

6. Revisit the annotations you made of the reasoning that the justices use to support their argument. First, identify their reasons and record them in the chart. Then think about possible rebuttals for each using evidence from the text.

Reasons	Possible Rebuttals

Check Your Understanding

Quickwrite: How has the Supreme Court ruling on this case affected the freedom of the press since? How might things have turned out differently if the ruling had favored the government?

Learning Strategies

Discussion Groups
Graphic Organizer
Questioning the Text

My Notes

_____

_____

_____

_____

_____

_____

_____

_____

_____

_____

_____

_____

_____

_____

_____

_____

_____

_____

_____

_____

_____

_____

_____

_____

_____

_____

_____

_____

_____

_____

Learning Targets

- Describe the characteristics of various news sources, including multimodal and digital sources.
- Explain how those characteristics contribute to or detract from their effectiveness.

Preview

In this activity, you will analyze the effectiveness of characteristics of various news sources.

News Media Survey

1. Rank the following news media outlets in the order you would turn to them for information on a major news story. (Use 1 to indicate the outlet you would turn to most often. Write N/A to indicate you would not use that outlet.)

   _____ Newspaper   _____ Radio News

   _____ Local TV News   _____ News Magazines

   _____ Cable News Station   _____ News Podcast

   _____ Word of Mouth   _____ Social Media

   _____ Websites/Internet

2. Rank the following media outlets for accuracy and trustworthiness in how they present information. (Rank the most trustworthy outlet 1.)

   _____ Newspaper   _____ Radio News

   _____ Local TV News   _____ News Magazines

   _____ Cable News Station   _____ News Podcast

   _____ Word of Mouth   _____ Social Media

   _____ Websites/Internet

3. Think back on the past month. About how much time (in hours) did you spend receiving news (not entertainment) from the following media outlets?

   _____ Newspaper   _____ Radio News

   _____ Local TV News   _____ News Magazines

   _____ Cable News Station   _____ News Podcast

   _____ Word of Mouth   _____ Social Media

   _____ Websites/Internet

4. Rank each of the following reasons that you might give for not reading newspapers. (Write 1 next to the reason most appropriate for you. Write N/A if you disagree with the statement.)

   _____ They are boring.

   _____ They take too long to read.

_____ They don't have information that applies to me and my life.

_____ They usually focus on scandals, politics, and gossip.

_____ They are often filled with mistakes and lies.

_____ Other:

5. Do you feel that it is important to be knowledgeable about news? Explain.

Exploring News Sources

In today's world, news sources can be divided into two types: **print** and **digital**. Print news sources are defined as any news product that is produced through the traditional printing process—newspapers, magazines, newsletters, and so on. A digital news source transmits digitized news through airwaves, satellite transmissions, or the Internet (or any combination of those media).

Both print and digital news sources are frequently **multimodal**. That means they use two or more communication modes (written language, spoken language, still images, moving images, music, visual effects, sound effects, etc.) to present their content. Presenters of news shape these modes into headlines, images with captions, teasers, quotes, graphics, video images, audio snippets, and so on, in an enormous variety of combinations. Presenters can use these modes in various ways to influence the audience's perception of the content. Thus, two news sources can present the same information but with very different purposes reflected in the format and tone of the presentation.

The form and tone of any particular news presentation are influenced largely by its target audience, the group or groups of people for whom the presentation is intended. News presenters also consider their secondary audience, those who might also be exposed to the message or have some influence over the target audience.

As guided by your teacher, examine the content of a print and digital news source. Discuss the following questions as a class and write your answers in your Reader/Writer Notebook:

- What is the purpose of the content you are examining?
- Who are the target and secondary audiences for this source?
- What modes are the news presenters using to reach those audiences?
- Why are the news presenters using those particular modes?
- Is their method of presentation effective or ineffective?
- What about their method of presentation makes it effective or ineffective?

6. When you have finished, your teacher will divide the class into small groups. Repeat the activity with your group using a source assigned by your teacher, discussing the questions and presenting your agreed-upon answers to the class when you have finished.

> **LITERARY**
>
> A target audience is the intended group for which a work is designed to appeal or reach. A secondary audience is the group who may also receive the message or may influence the target audience.

VOCABULARY

News Source Analysis Chart

Select two print and two online news sources. Attempt to include sources that address a variety of topic areas, ages, and interest levels. Conduct an analysis of each of your sources using the questions and chart.

Source/items: What is the name of your source, and what are the topics/headlines of two of its news items?

Purpose: What is the news source's purpose in presenting each news item?

Target audience: To whom in particular is each presentation designed to appeal?

Modes and characteristics of source: Are the source's items multimodal? If so, what modes are used? What characteristics or features (headlines, images with captions, teasers, quotes, graphics, video images, audio snippets, etc.) do the news presenters employ?

Effectiveness: Are the choices made by the news presenters effective in achieving the item's purpose and reaching the intended audience? Explain.

Source/Items	Purpose	Target Audience	Modes and Characteristics of Source	Effectiveness
Print Source 1:				
Print Source 2:				
Online Source 1:				
Online Source 2:				

7. Compare your results to those of at least two other groups in your class. What commonalities do you notice among print and online news sources? What differences do you notice? What might explain both the commonalities and the differences?

☑ Check Your Understanding

After discussing similarities and differences in print and online news sources, write a paragraph explaining how a source's coverage of news is shaped to appeal to its target audience. Use a source you have examined in this activity as the framework for your explanation.

Learning Strategies

Discussion Groups
Marking the Text
Paraphrasing
Skimming/Scanning

VOCABULARY

ACADEMIC

An editorial is an article in a newspaper or magazine expressing the opinion of its editor or publisher. An editorial is similar to an essay in that it focuses on a specific issue or topic, offers a thesis, and provides reasons and evidence to convince its readers.

Learning Targets

• Analyze how concessions and refutations can be used as responses to an argument.

• Apply strategies of refutation to a set of claims and evidence.

• Integrate ideas from multiple texts to build knowledge and vocabulary about editorials.

Preview

In this activity, you will read and analyze two editorials, one that makes a claim about modern media consumption and another that refutes the claim.

Do You Agree?

1. Look over the following quotations about newspapers. In the space after each quote, paraphrase what the author is saying and then state whether you agree and why.

• "Were it left to me to decide whether we should have a government without newspapers, or newspapers without a government, I should not hesitate a moment to prefer the latter." —Thomas Jefferson, 1787

My Notes

• "The newspapers, especially those in the East, are amazingly superficial and ... a large number of news gatherers are either cynics at heart or are following the orders and the policies of the owners of their papers." —Franklin D. Roosevelt, May 7, 1934

• "For my part I entertain a high idea of the utility of periodical publications; insomuch as I could heartily desire, copies of ... magazines, as well as common Gazettes, might be spread through every city, town, and village in the United States. I consider such vehicles of knowledge more happily calculated than any other to preserve the liberty, stimulate the industry, and ameliorate the morals of a free and enlightened people." —George Washington, 1788

- "As people get their opinions so largely from the newspapers they read, the corruption of the schools would not matter so much if the Press were free. But the Press is not free. As it costs at least a quarter of a million of money to establish a daily newspaper in London, the newspapers are owned by rich men. And they depend on the advertisements of other rich men. Editors and journalists who express opinions in print that are opposed to the interests of the rich are dismissed and replaced by subservient ones." —George B. Shaw, Irish playwright, 1949

- "The decline of competing local daily newspaper voices diminishes not only the availability of local and regional news to consumers but also the availability of competing opinions and ideas, not just at local levels but at all levels. Social thinkers, historians, and political analysts have identified such diversity of thought—a marketplace of ideas—as essential to a functioning democracy." —Steven M. Hallock, journalism professor, 2007

My Notes

As You Read

- Highlight details Sunstein uses as reasoning and evidence to support his argument about modern media consumption.
- Underline any words with British spellings. (The *Financial Times* is a British newspaper.)
- Circle any unknown words or phrases. Try to determine the meaning of the words by using context clues, word parts, or a dictionary.

ACADEMIC

Reasoning is the thinking or logic used to make a claim in an argument. Evidence is the specific facts, examples, and other details used to support the reasoning. Evaluating an argument requires that you look closely at the writer's or speaker's evidence to determine its validity.

VOCABULARY

My Notes

About the Author

Cass Sunstein is a noted American legal scholar who has written dozens of books, essays, and newspaper and magazine articles on public policy, economics, law, and psychology. He has taught at the law schools of the University of Chicago, Harvard University, and Columbia University.

Editorial

How the Rise of the Daily Me Threatens Democracy

Financial Times, **January 10, 2008**

by **Cass Sunstein**

1 More than a decade ago the technology specialist, Nicholas Negroponte, prophesied the **emergence** of the Daily Me—a fully personalised newspaper. It would allow you to include topics that interest you and screen out those that bore or annoy you. If you wanted to focus on Iraq and tennis, or exclude Iran and golf, you could do that.

2 Many people now use the internet to create something like a Daily Me. This behaviour is reinforced by the rise of social networking forums, collaborative filtering and viral marketing. For politics, the phenomenon is especially important in campaigns. Candidates in the US presidential race can construct information cocoons in which readers are deluged with material that is, in their eyes, politically correct. Supporters of Hillary Clinton construct a Daily Me that includes her campaign's perspective but offers nothing from Barack Obama, let alone Mitt Romney.

3 What is wrong with the emerging situation? We can find a clue in a small experiment in democracy conducted in Colorado in 2005. About 60 US citizens were put into 10 groups. They **deliberated** on controversial issues, such as whether the US should sign an international treaty to combat global warming and whether states should allow same-sex couples to enter into civil unions. The groups consisted of predominantly either leftwing or rightwing members, with the former drawn from left-of-centre Boulder and the latter from Colorado Springs, which tends to be right of centre. The groups, not mixed, were screened to ensure members **conformed** to stereotypes. (If people in Boulder liked Vice-President Dick Cheney, they were cordially excused.) People were asked to state their opinions anonymously before and after the group discussion.

emergence: rise in popularity
deliberated: thought about or discussed carefully
conformed: held to

4 In almost every group, people ended up with more extreme positions. The Boulder groups favoured an international treaty to control global warming before discussion; they favoured it far more strongly afterwards. In Colorado Springs, people were neutral on that treaty before discussion; discussion led them to oppose it strongly. Same-sex unions became much more popular in Boulder and less so in Colorado Springs.

5 Aside from increasing extremism, discussion had another effect: it squelched diversity. Before members talked, many groups displayed internal disagreement. These were greatly reduced: discussion widened the rift between Boulder and Colorado Springs.

6 Countless versions of this experiment are carried out online every day. The result is group polarisation, which occurs when like-minded people speak together and end up in a more extreme position in line with their original inclinations.

7 There are three reasons for this. First is the exchange of information. In Colorado Springs, the members offered many justifications for not signing a climate treaty and a lot fewer for doing so. Since people listened to one another, they became more sceptical. The second reason is that when people find their views **corroborated**, they become more confident and so are more willing to be extreme. The third reason involves social comparison. People who favour a position think of themselves in a certain way and if they are with people who agree with them, they shift a bit to hold on to their preferred self-conception.

8 Group polarisation clearly occurs on the internet. For example, 80 per cent of readers of the leftwing blog Daily Kos are Democrats and fewer than 1 per cent are Republicans. Many popular bloggers link frequently to those who agree with them and to contrary views, if at all, only to ridicule them. To a significant extent, people are learning about supposed facts from narrow niches and like-minded others.

9 This matters for the electoral process. A high degree of self-sorting leads to more confidence, extremism and increased contempt for those with contrary views. We can already see this in the presidential campaign. It will only intensify when the two parties square off. To the extent that Democratic and Republican candidates seem to live in different political universes, group polarisation is playing a large role.

10 Polarisation, of course, long preceded the internet. Yet given people's new power to create echo chambers, the result will be serious obstacles not merely to civility but also to mutual understanding and constructive problem solving. The Daily Me leads **inexorably** also to the Daily Them. That is a real problem for democracy.

My Notes

Knowledge Quest

- What is your initial reaction to the author's claim?
- Where do you find yourself agreeing with the author?

corroborated: strengthened by evidence

inexorably: unstoppably

Returning to the Text

- Return to the editorial as you respond to the following questions. Use text evidence to support your responses.
- Write any additional questions you have about the text in your Reader/Writer Notebook.

2. **KQ** In paragraph 1, what does the word *prophesied* mean in context? What effect does it have on the tone?

_____

_____

_____

_____

_____

3. Summarize the "Daily Me" situation Sunstein describes in paragraphs 1 and 2.

_____

_____

_____

_____

_____

4. Summarize the experiment described in paragraphs 3–5. What were its results on the individuals who participated?

_____

_____

_____

_____

_____

5. What arguable thesis (claim) does Sunstein make, and how does his description of the 2005 experiment in Colorado support that thesis?

_____

_____

_____

_____

_____

6. How does the image of "echo chambers" in paragraph 10 contribute to Sunstein's thesis?

_____

_____

_____

_____

_____

7. What concession does Sunstein make in the article's final paragraph, and how does he address it to support his thesis?

_____

_____

_____

_____

_____

8. KQ How does the editorial make its claim effectively?

_____

_____

_____

_____

_____

Working from the Text

9. Revisit the annotations that you made of the reasons and evidence that Sunstein used to support his arguable thesis (claim). First, identify Sunstein's thesis and then record your annotations in the chart. Lastly, think about possible rebuttals for each using evidence from the text.

Thesis:

Reasons and Evidence	Possible Rebuttals

Refuting an Argument

To refute an existing argument, authors rely on a variety of strategies of refutation. These strategies often "attack" different elements of an opponent's position. Some of the most common "attacks" include:

- **Attack on a claim:** Is the writer's claim relevant or arguable?
- **Attack on reasoning:** Does the evidence the writer uses logically support his or her conclusions?
- **Attack on evidence:** Is the evidence timely, accurate, and unbiased? Is there counterevidence?
- **Attack on assumption:** What does the writer assume to be true, and is that assumption accurate? (A writer's assumptions are often unstated.)

As You Read

- Highlight Potter's concessions and refutations.
- Circle unknown words and phrases. Try to determine the meaning of the words by using context clues, word parts, or a dictionary.

About the Author

Andrew Potter (b. 1972) is the former editor-in-chief of *The Ottawa Citizen*, a daily newspaper published in Ontario, Canada. He has a PhD in philosophy from the University of Toronto and is an associate professor at McGill University. Andrew coauthored the international bestseller *Nation of Rebels*, which was published in 2004.

My Notes

LITERARY

VOCABULARY

A concession is an admission in an argument that the opposing side has valid points. A refutation is the reasoning used to disprove an opposing point.

KNOWLEDGE QUEST

Knowledge Question:

How do newspaper editorials make and refute claims?

My Notes

Editorial

The Newspaper Is Dying—Hooray for Democracy

Maclean's, **April 7, 2008**

by **Andrew Potter**

1 The Newspaper Audience Databank (NADbank) released its readership numbers for 2007 a couple of weeks ago, and for those of us in the industry it was grim reading: almost everywhere you look, circulation, ad revenues and page counts are down, which is why you can now fire a cannon through any given newsroom at midday and not have to worry about committing reportercide.

2 But unless you work in the business, is there any reason to be especially concerned? Each year may put another loop in the newspaper's death spiral, but the overall consumption of news is on the rise, almost entirely thanks to the myriad online sources. The Internet is eating the newspaper's lunch, but there's plenty of food on the buffet table.

3 In certain quarters, though, there is growing concern that the demise of the newspaper is a threat to democracy itself. The argument goes something like this: the economic logic of mass circulation meant a newspaper had to try to appeal to as many potential readers as possible. To do so, it brought together in one package a diverse set of voices, presenting each reader with ideas and perspectives that he or she might not otherwise have seen or sought out. This fostered the democratic values of curiosity, enlightenment and toleration, and the worry is that if the newspaper declines, so might democracy.

4 The sharpest version of this argument comes from Cass Sunstein, a law professor at the University of Chicago. In a recent column in the Financial Times, Sunstein fusses about the rise of what he calls the Daily Me, the highly personalized and customized information feeds that will allow you to "include topics that interest you and screen out those that bore or anger you." As Sunstein sees it, the Daily Me is the potential Achilles heel of democracy because of a phenomenon called group polarization: when like-minded people find themselves speaking only with one another, they get into a cycle of ideological reinforcement where they end up endorsing positions far more extreme than the ones they started with.

5 Group polarization is everywhere. It helps explain why, for example, humanities departments are so left-wing, why fraternities are so sexist, why journalists drink so much. But, for the most part, it isn't a problem (for

myriad: huge number of
ideological: beliefs-based

democracy anyway), since we routinely come into contact with so many people from so many different groups that the tendency toward polarization in one is at least somewhat **tempered** by our encounters with others.

6   Yet Sunstein is worried that group polarization on the Internet will prove far more **pernicious**. Why? Because of the image of the blogosphere as a series of echo chambers, where every viewpoint is repeated and amplified to a hysterical pitch. As our politics moves online, he thinks we'll end up with a public sphere that is partisan and extreme, and as an example, he points out that 80 per cent of readers of the left-wing blog Daily Kos are Democrats, while fewer than one per cent are Republicans. The result, he claims, "will be serious obstacles not merely to civility but also to **mutual** understanding."

7   As upside-down arguments go, this one is ingenious. For decades, **progressive** critics have complained about the anti-democratic influence of the mass media, and that newspapers present a selective and highly biased picture of the world, promoting pseudo-arguments that give the illusion of debate while preserving the status quo. (Remember that the villain in *Manufacturing Consent*, the film about Noam Chomsky, was—wait for it—the New York Times.) And now that the Internet is poised to cast these lumbering dinosaurs of black ink and dead trees into the pit of extinction, we're supposed to say hang on, what about democracy?

8   There's a basic error here, paired with an equally basic misunderstanding of how the marketplace of ideas works. There is no reason at all to be concerned that 80 per cent of Daily Kos readers are Democrats, any more than to worry that 80 per cent of the visitors to McDonald's like hamburgers. Given what each of these outlets is selling, it would be bizarre if it were otherwise. What would be worrisome was if four-fifths of Democrats read only the Daily Kos, but there is absolutely no evidence that is the case.

9   Earlier this month, the Project for Excellence in Journalism, a think tank sponsored by the Pew foundation, released its fifth annual report (at journalism. org) on the state of the news media. For the most part, its analysis of the newspaper business confirmed the trends of declining circulation, revenues and staff. But with respect to public attitudes, the PEJ found that most readers see their newspaper as increasingly biased, and 68 per cent say they prefer to get their news from sources that don't have a point of view. The PEJ also found a substantial disconnect between the issues and events that dominate the news hole (e.g., the Iraq surge, the massacre at Virginia Tech) and what the public wants to see covered—issues such as education, transportation, religion and health. What this suggests, is, aside from some failings of newspapers, that readers go online in search of less bias, not the self-absorption of the Daily Me.

10   Nothing about how people consume media online suggests they are looking for confirmation of preexisting biases. In fact, we have every reason to believe that as people migrate online, it will be to seek out sources of information that they perceive to be unbiased, and which give them news they can't get anywhere else. The newspaper may be dying, but our democracy will be healthier for it.

INDEPENDENT READING LINK

Read and Connect

As you read daily from your self-selected news source, do you find yourself creating a kind of "Daily Me" by fully reading only those stories that support your personal interests or beliefs, or do you find yourself reading stories on a variety of topics and with varying viewpoints? Why are you employing this approach? Discuss your ideas with a partner.

My Notes

_____

_____

_____

_____

_____

_____

_____

_____

_____

_____

_____

_____

_____

tempered: lessened
pernicious: quietly deadly
mutual: shared
progressive: politically liberal or left-wing
perceive: interpret

- What are your first thoughts about why the author wrote this editorial?
- Where in the editorial does the author's tone surprise you?

Returning to the Text

- Return to the editorial as you respond to the following questions. Use text evidence to support your responses.
- Write any additional questions you have about the text in your Reader/Writer Notebook.

10. **KQ** In paragraph 1, what does the word *circulation* mean in context? Why is circulation important to the newspaper industry?

_____

_____

_____

_____

_____

11. In the editorial's first two paragraphs, how does Potter use imagery and figurative language to present and refute his opponent's argument?

_____

_____

_____

_____

_____

_____

_____

_____

12. Which structural element of an argument essay is exemplified by paragraph 4? How does it set the course for the text that follows? Explain.

_____

_____

_____

_____

_____

13. What claim does Potter make about group polarization in paragraph 5? Does he provide evidence for his idea, and if so, is it convincing?

_____

_____

_____

_____

_____

14. **KQ** How does the editorial make its claim effectively by refuting the claim made in the first editorial?

_____

_____

_____

_____

_____

15. How do Potter's diction and syntax in paragraphs 4–7 create a tone that reflects his opinion of Sunstein's argument?

_____

_____

_____

_____

_____

16. In paragraphs 8 and 9, why is Sunstein concerned that 80 percent of Daily Kos readers are Democrats? In paragraph 8, why does this fact not concern Potter? What evidence does Potter cite in paragraph 9?

_____

_____

_____

_____

_____

17. In Potter's conclusion, he claims that "nothing about how people consume media online suggests they are looking for confirmation of preexisting biases." Is his statement convincing? Explain.

_____

_____

_____

_____

_____

INDEPENDENT READING LINK

Read and Discuss

You can continue to build your knowledge about editorials by reading these and other articles at ZINC Reading Labs. Search for keywords such as *editorial writing* or *opinion piece*.

 ZINC

 Knowledge Quest

With a partner, discuss how both of these editorials make claims, refutations, and concessions effectively. Be sure to:

- Refer to evidence from the editorials.
- Take turns speaking, responding, and asking one another follow-up questions.
- Ask clarifying questions.
- Write down notes and ideas about making claims, refutations, and concessions effectively.

Working from the Text

8. Most of Potter's editorial is dedicated to addressing Sunstein's claims in "How the Rise of the Daily Me Threatens Democracy." Use the chart to list and identify Potter's concessions and refutations in the form of quotations. Revisit the Refuting an Argument section to determine types of refutations (attacks).

Treatment of the Counterargument	Concession or Refutation? (If refutation, include type)

9. In a deductive argument, the author presents a thesis and then attempts to support it. In an inductive argument, the structure is reversed; evidence is examined, and then a conclusion is reached. Identify the structures of the Sunstein and Potter editorials as deductive or inductive. Cite textual evidence in your answer.

☑ Focus on the Sentence

Choose one of the two texts in this activity and write two sentences using text evidence that challenge a claim made by the article. Start the sentences with the subordinating conjunctions that follow.

While _____

_____

_____

_____

Even though _____

_____

_____

_____

Recognizing Frequently Confused Words

Many words in the English language are frequently confused with one another, especially in writing. Even though readers might be able to figure out what is meant, writers' credibility suffers when they use incorrect words. Some commonly confused words include *effect* and *affect*, *allusion* and *illusion*, and *loose* and *lose*.

1. **Quickwrite:** Why might these words be easily confused in writing?

Effect/Affect

The key to keeping *effect* and *affect* straight is to look at how they are being used in the sentence. The word *effect* is usually a noun, and the word *affect* is usually a verb. Look at these examples related to the readings in Activity 3.4.

Aside from increasing extremism, discussion had another **effect**: it squelched diversity.

Here, *effect* is a noun representing a thing; it is not doing any action in the sentence. *Effect* is the correct choice.

Sunstein believes that group polarization will negatively **affect** democracy.

In this case, *will affect* is the verb in the sentence. It is a verb meaning "will influence" or "will change."

---

2. Add *affect* or *effect* to each sentence.

Reading a newspaper or other news source could definitely _____ your view of politics.

Many teenagers want to have an _____ on the world around them.

Hearing other people's perspectives can _____ your understanding of your own culture.

Blogs are spaces where writers can express their views and have a positive _____ on others.

---

3. Write two sentences, one using *affect* and one using *effect*. Then briefly explain how you knew which word to use.

Allusion/Illusion

An allusion is an indirect reference to a person, event, or thing. Authors use allusions to help readers make connections to things they already know or to evoke certain feelings. For example, in "The Newspaper Is Dying—Hooray for Democracy," Potter makes the following allusion:

As Sunstein sees it, the Daily Me is the potential Achilles heel of democracy because of a phenomenon called group polarization…

4. Briefly describe what Potter is alluding to. (Use one or more reference sources if necessary.) Why do you think he is making this allusion?

5. Now read the following sentence.

Sunstein's overreaction to expression gives readers the illusion of living in a country where people are forced to accept the same belief system as those around them.

Use context clues to determine the meaning of the word *illusion*.

6. Use *illusion* or *allusion* to complete each sentence.

Some would say that the idea that democracy is under threat is merely an _____ .

Potter makes an _____ to classical myth.

Both authors are going to say the other's perception is an _____ and their opponent is wrong.

7. Choose one of the sentences and explain to your partner how you knew your answer was correct.

Loose/Lose

8. Use a dictionary to review the definition of the word *loose*, and then write a sentence that uses the word.

9. Use a dictionary to review the definition of the word *lose*, and then write a sentence using the word.

Revising

Read the paragraph and choose the correct word in each sentence.

Voting is a right I'm looking forward to exercising this fall. As a senior in high school, I believe my vote has an [**effect/affect**] on my future. My grandfather, who was my idol, spent hours talking to me about politics when I was a kid. I didn't care much about what he had to say then. I just wanted to be with him, hear his deep voice, watch his bottom teeth pop forward when he got excited, and then see him suck them back in again as he grinned at me. I watched in anticipation as if it were a great [**illusion/allusion**] and not a side [**effect/affect**] of [**loose/lose**] dentures and a crazy sense of humor. He instilled in me a patience to hear out both sides of an issue before jumping to a conclusion and an interest in gathering information before choosing a side. He taught me that even though my candidate may [**loose/lose**], my choosing to use my voice is a victory. So here I am today— finally ready to vote. I am going to [**effect/affect**] my country for the better! I know that my grandfather cannot be with me when I go into the voting booth; however, he would be proud of my choice to stand up for what I believe in.

☑ Check Your Understanding

What words do you commonly confuse? What question can you ask yourself about frequently confused words to make sure you've used the correct one? Identify at least three sets of words and write one question for each set. Add the questions to your Editor's Checklist. Add to your checklist as you discover more words that you frequently confuse.

Practice

Write a paragraph that explains which of Potter's arguments in " The Newspaper Is Dying—Hooray for Democracy" are most and least convincing. Include the words *effect, affect, effective,* and *ineffective* in your paragraph. You may refer to your responses to the Returning to the Text questions in Activity 3.5 as you compose your paragraph. Double-check for correct use of *effect, affect, effective,* and *ineffective.*

News or Views: A Closer Look

Learning Targets
- Examine a news story for credibility, bias, and accuracy.
- Research a timely and debatable issue.

Preview
While editorials openly present opinions, newspaper articles may appear objective until carefully examined for evidence that reveals a more subjective agenda. In this activity, you will read a news story and examine it for credibility, bias, and accuracy.

My Notes

Examining Credibility and Accuracy

Credibility and accuracy are integral to any news story you're reading. A credible news story is one that's trustworthy and believable. *Accurate* means "factually correct."

Always make sure that the writer whose work you are reading is reliable. Some sources do not name their writers. This doesn't necessarily make a story unreliable, but it does mean that the credibility and accuracy of the source itself should be established.

When trying to determine whether a story is credible and accurate, ask questions such as:

- Who exactly wrote this story?
- Have I heard of the story's author or source?
- What kind of expertise or reputation does the author or source have?
- Are there facts in the story that I can verify independently?

If you don't know the answers to these questions, do some investigating. A good search engine can help you determine the credibility of a story's author or source. If the author's name is given, determine whether he or she has a reputation for credible, accurate reporting. Do similar research on the story's website or print source. Establish whether other reliable sources have used work from the author or source of your story. If so, the information is likely credible and accurate.

Examining Bias

We tend to think that news articles are objective, which means they are based on factual information. However, all news reports are to some extent subjective—or based on feelings or opinions—because they represent the reporter's analysis of the information surrounding the story's topic. Close analysis of the text's content, structure, and publication context can reveal subtle indications of bias in terms of how the writer frames the issue.

1. You will be assigned one of the following six types of bias. In your small group, paraphrase the explanation for your assigned type of bias. Next, generate several guiding questions you can use to discern whether your assigned type of bias is present in a given text.

ACADEMIC VOCABULARY

Credibility is the quality of being believed or accepted as true, real, or honest.
Accuracy is the freedom from mistake or error.
Bias is a slanted attitude of either preferring or disliking something.

My Notes

Types of Bias

A. Bias Through Selection and Omission

- An editor can express a bias by choosing to use or not to use a specific news item. For example, the editor might believe that advertisers want younger readers—they spend more money. Therefore, news of specific interest to old people will be ignored.

- Within a given story, details can be ignored or included to give readers or viewers a different opinion about the events reported. If, during a speech, a few people boo, the reaction can be described as "remarks greeted by jeers." Or the people jeering can be dismissed as "a handful of dissidents" or perhaps not even mentioned.

- Bias through the omission of stories or details is very difficult to detect. Only by comparing news reports from a wide variety of outlets can this form of bias be observed.

- Bias in local news coverage can be found by comparing reports of the same event from different papers.

B. Bias Through Placement

- Readers of papers judge first-page stories to be more significant than those buried in the back. Television and radio newscasts run the most important stories first and leave the less significant to later. Where a story is placed, therefore, influences what a reader or viewer thinks about its importance and suggests the editor's evaluation of its importance.

- For example, a local editor might campaign against handgun ownership by giving prominent space to every shooting with a handgun and gun-related accident in his or her paper.

- Some murders and robberies receive front-page attention, while others receive only a mention on page 20.

- Similarly, where information appears within an article may also reveal evidence of bias. Because most readers only read the first few paragraphs of any given article, burying information at the end may work to suppress a particular point of view or piece of information, while placing it at the beginning emphasizes it. The opposite might be true as well; the end could reveal the writer's closing thought (and thus his or her personal bias) on the issue.

C. Bias by Headline

- Many people read only the headline of a news item. In addition, most people scan nearly all the headlines in a newspaper. As a result, headlines are the most-read part of a paper. They can summarize as well as present carefully hidden biases and prejudices. They can convey excitement where little exists, they can express approval or condemnation, and they can steer public opinion.

D. Bias by Photos, Captions, and Camera Angles

- Some pictures flatter a person; others make the person look unpleasant. A paper can choose photos to influence opinion about, for example, a candidate for election. Television can show film or videotape that praises or condemns. The choice of which visual images to display is extremely important. Newspapers run captions that are also potential sources of bias and opinion.

E. Bias Through Statistics and Crowd Counts

- To make a disaster seem more spectacular (and therefore worthy of reading), numbers can be inflated. "One hundred injured in train wreck" is more powerful than "Passengers injured in train wreck."

- Crowd counts are notoriously inaccurate and often reflect the opinion of the person doing the counting. A reporter, event sponsor, or police officer might estimate a crowd at several thousand if he or she agrees with the purpose of the assembly—or a much smaller number if he or she is critical of the crowd's purposes or beliefs. News magazines use specific numbers to enhance believability.

F. Bias by Source Control

- To detect bias, always consider where a news item "comes from." Is the information supplied by a reporter, by an eyewitness, by police or fire officials, by executives, by elected or appointed government officials? Each might have a particular bias that is presented in the story.

- Puff pieces are supplied to media outlets by companies or public relations directors—and even sometimes by the government (directly or through press conferences). The term *puff piece* comes from the word *puffery*, which means "overly flattering words about a topic." For example, the Avocado Growers Association might send a press release in the form of a news story telling of a doctor who claims that avocados are healthy and should be eaten by all. A food company might supply recipes for a newspaper's food section that recommends use of its products in the recipes. A country's tourist bureau will supply a glowing story, complete with pictures of a pleasant vacation. Recently, even government agencies have sometimes issued such releases.

- A pseudo-event is some event (demonstration, sit-in, ribbon cutting, speech, ceremony, ground breaking, etc.) that takes place primarily to gain news coverage.

- Similarly, the question of who is quoted in an article can point to bias. Be sure to consider who is quoted, what the quote seems to reveal or imply (negatively or positively) about the position, who is merely paraphrased, and what perspectives are unrepresented or remain silent in the article.

Identifying Bias

2. Use the following graphic organizer to keep track of examples of the guiding questions each group developed for identifying bias. Then apply those questions to a sample newspaper article or online news source.

Bias Type	Guiding Questions	Examples
Bias Through Selection and Omission		
Bias Through Placement		

Bias Type	Guiding Questions	Examples
Bias by Headline		
Bias by Photos, Captions, and Camera Angles		
Bias Through Statistics and Crowd Counts		
Bias by Source Control		

As You Read

- Underline any text that answers one of the guiding questions your class generated.
- Circle unknown words and phrases. Try to determine the meaning of the words by using context clues, word parts, or a dictionary.

Article

Facebook Photos Sting Minnesota High School Students

The Associated Press

1   EDEN PRAIRIE, Minn. — For 16-year-old Nick Laurent, walking out of Eden Prairie High School yesterday to protest the school's punishment of students seen partying on Facebook pages was about asking administrators to be fair.

2   More than a dozen students joined Laurent after learning of the walkout from fliers the junior handed out the day before. The students said school administrators overreacted to the **perception** that students in the photos were drinking.

3   "It's the loudest thing we could do," said Laurent, who organized the walkout but said he wasn't one of the students in the photos.

4   Laurent tried to make his point by passing out red plastic cups that were similar to those seen in some of the photos. He noted that it was impossible to see what was inside the cups, so administrators couldn't prove that students were drinking.

5   Laurent agreed that athletes and other students who sign a code of conduct to be involved in activities should face consequences if they break the rule against drinking alcohol. But he said the punishments were too harsh.

6   "They don't have (the) support of the students to hand out **arbitrary** punishments and punishments that don't fit the crime," he said.

7   Once the photos on the social-networking Web site came to the attention of administrators, 42 students were interviewed and 13 face some discipline over the pictures, school officials said.

8   School officials haven't said how the students were disciplined, but Minnesota State High School League penalties start with a two-game suspension for the first violation. Laurent and other students said they knew of classmates who were banned from their sports teams for five weeks.

9   Principal Conn McCartan did not return a call seeking comment on the walkout, but students said they expected they'd be punished.

10   In earlier statements, the school's principal said school officials did not seek out the pictures. But he didn't say who gave the school the photos.

perception: impression
arbitrary: unreasonable

My Notes

11 "We do not go out looking at student social networking sites. We do however take action when we are given **legitimate** information about school or Minnesota State High School League violations," McCartan said in an e-mail to families of his students.

12 McCartan said interviews with students suggested, however, that the pictures might have been posted on such sites, and warned of the dangers.

13 "These sites are not private places," he wrote. "Their content forms a permanent and public record of conversations and pictures."

14 In an e-mail to parents and guardians, Superintendent Melissa Krull said, "We are not legally at liberty to discuss further details of this investigation."

15 Fourteen-year-old Ali Saley said cutting class for the cause was worth it. She held signs such as, "They walk or we do," in **solidarity** with the students who were punished. A few cars honked in support of the students as they gathered on a footbridge over the road in front of the school.

16 The Eden Prairie High School students who got into trouble ran afoul of a new reality: digital cameras and social networking sites make the entire world a public space.

17 It's becoming increasingly common for schools and potential employers to check social networking sites such as Facebook and MySpace, and to penalize kids or other people for what they find, said William McGeveran, a professor at the University of Minnesota Law School and an expert on data privacy.

18 "Facebook is largely a public space. Users don't always perceive it that way, but that's what it is," McGeveran said.

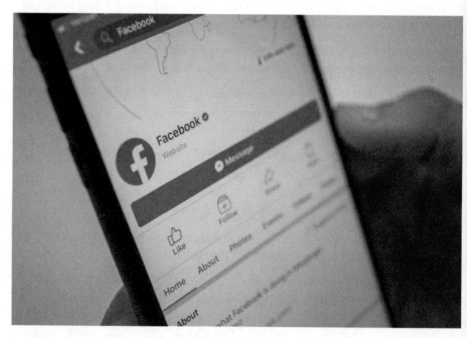

legitimate: real or true
solidarity: togetherness

My Notes

19 Even when young people are cautious about what they put on the pages, he said, friends or acquaintances can post pictures of them in questionable situations without their knowing about it.

20 McGeveran cited research by the Pew Internet & American Life Project that suggested most teens were aware of the risks of posting personal information on the Internet. A report issued last month found that most teens restrict access to their posted photos and videos at least some of the time, and that few consistently share them without any restrictions.

21 "But some students are still foolish about what they put on their pages," he said.

22 Eden Prairie High School has about 3,300 students, and Facebook lists about 2,800 members in its network for the school, including more than 500 from the current senior class. A spot check on Jan. 9 showed that some had posted dozens and even hundreds of pictures of themselves and their friends. However, most members used a privacy setting to limit access to their profiles to friends and other authorized people.

23 Schools in Minnesota have limited ability to regulate the conduct of students after hours. When students participate in sports or certain fine-arts activities, however, they must agree in writing to abide by the long-standing rules of the Minnesota State High School League, which prohibit the use of alcohol, tobacco and controlled substances, even over the summer.

24 League spokesman Howard Voigt noted that parents must sign the forms, too, certifying that they understand the rules and penalties. Still, he said, complaints are common.

25 "We run into that all the time here—parents call and accuse us of being too hard on their kid," he said.

26 Voigt said there had been several cases of students' running afoul of league rules because of potential violations posted on social-networking sites.

27 It's not safe for kids to assume what they do in small groups won't be broadcast to the entire world, McGeveran said.

28 "I don't think most of us would have liked to have lived our teen years in an era of **ubiquitous** camera phones and social networking," he said. "It really changes the perception of what places are private and which ones aren't."

Making Observations
- What details in this article feel important to you?
- What words that the students use catch your attention?
- What questions do you have after reading the article?

ubiquitous: ever-present

Returning to the Text

- Return to the article as you respond to the following questions. Use text evidence to support your responses.
- Write any additional questions you have about the text in your Reader/Writer Notebook.

3. Does the article's focus in paragraphs 1–3 make the article seem more or less objective? Why?

_____

_____

_____

_____

4. How does the structure of the first half of the article support the writer's central idea that students are being punished unfairly?

_____

_____

_____

_____

_____

_____

5. Examine the text of the student's sign in paragraph 15 of the article. What are some questions that readers might ask themselves to interpret the meaning of that text?

_____

_____

_____

6. How does the information provided by expert William McGeveran in paragraphs 17–21 and paragraphs 27–28 develop the central idea that social media sites are not private places?

_____

_____

_____

_____

7. What questions might you ask after reading the article to learn more about Eden Prairie High School students' social lives, social media, and private spaces?

_____

_____

_____

_____

Working from the Text

8. In preparation for group work, revisit the annotations that you made while you read.

9. Meet with your group to examine the article for credibility, accuracy, and bias by collaboratively answering the guiding questions you established at the start of this activity. Be prepared to discuss your findings with the rest of the class.

Guiding Question #1: _____

Response #1: _____

_____

_____

Guiding Question #2: _____

Response #2: _____

_____

_____

Guiding Question #3: _____

_____

Response #3: _____

_____

_____

Guiding Question #4: _____

_____

Response #4: _____

_____

_____

INDEPENDENT READING LINK

Read and Discuss

Review several stories in your self-selected news source. Find examples of at least two types of bias. Share these examples with your peers. Explain how each example exemplifies the bias.

My Notes

_____
_____
_____
_____
_____
_____
_____
_____
_____
_____
_____
_____
_____
_____
_____
_____
_____
_____
_____
_____
_____
_____
_____
_____
_____
_____
_____

☑ Focus on the Sentence

Write a sentence about bias (or lack of bias) in "Facebook Photos Sting Minnesota High School Students" beginning with the word *Although*.

_____

_____

_____

_____

Examining Sources

With a partner, brainstorm possible topics for a short informational article. They should be timely, debatable, and significant to your school or local community or have national importance. Then, on your own, select an issue from your brainstorm list. Examine relevant informational sources and choose two or three that are appropriately bias-free, credible, and accurate.

Why do you believe your sources are trustworthy?

✍ Writing Prompt: Informational

Use your sources to write a short informational article about your chosen issue. Be sure to:

- Introduce a topic statement that states the issue and your view on its significance.
- Develop the topic by selecting direct quotations, specific examples, and concrete details from source texts.
- Use varied transitions and sentence construction to show the relationships among ideas.

The Bias of Rhetoric

Learning Strategies

Discussion Groups
Marking the Text
Note-taking
Paraphrasing
Quickwrite
Rereading
SMELL

Learning Targets

- Analyze how language can be used to inform and shape the perception of readers or viewers.
- Analyze the effects of rhetorical devices on the way the text is read and understood.

Preview

In this activity, you will analyze an editorial to learn how its author uses language to shape readers' perspective.

Slanting Reader Perception

1. **Quickwrite:** While the previous activity focused on how writers can construct the "truth" of their subject via their choices regarding content and structure, this activity focuses on how language itself can be used to shape the reader's perception of the subject. View the advertisement selected by your instructor. Then in a Quickwrite, identify what elements from the advertisement contribute to its power. Record your response in your Reader/Writer Notebook.

2. Sometimes a writer compensates for a lack of evidence and logical argumentation by using slanted language and emotional appeals that present a prejudiced depiction of a subject. This happens so often that there are names for these various **slanters**. As you read through the following techniques, try to think of examples from the media that fit the descriptions. Determine whether the language in the examples contains figurative, connotative, or technical meanings. (Adapted from Brooke Noel Moore and Richard Parker's *Critical Thinking*, 8th ed., 2007)

VOCABULARY

LITERARY
Slanters are rhetorical devices used to present the subject in a biased way, either positively or negatively.

My Notes

Types of Slanters

A. Labeling (Euphemisms and Dysphemisms)

Labeling is the use of a highly connotative word or phrase to name or describe a subject or action, a technique also called using **loaded language** or a **question-begging epithet**. When the connotations are positive (or less negative), the writer is using **euphemism**. For example, car dealers try to sell "pre-owned vehicles" rather than "used cars." In the opposite case, when the connotations are negative, the writer is using **dysphemism**. Consider, for example, the differences between these terms: *freedom fighter, guerrilla, rebel,* and *terrorist. Freedom fighter* is a euphemism, while *terrorist* is a dysphemism.

B. Rhetorical Analogy

Rhetorical analogy is the use of a figurative comparison (sometimes a simile or a metaphor) to convey a positive or negative feeling toward the subject. For example, in the 2008 presidential race, Sarah Palin suggested (via a joke) that she was like a pit bull with lipstick.

C. Rhetorical Definition

Rhetorical definition is the use of emotionally charged language to express or elicit an attitude about something. A classic example is defining capital

My Notes

punishment as "government-sanctioned murder." A rhetorical definition stacks the deck either for or against the position it implies.

D. Rhetorical Explanation

When an opinion is expressed as if it were fact and is expressed in biased language, it is a rhetorical explanation. For example, you might say someone "didn't have the guts to fight back" when taunted by another person. This paints the person as motivated by cowardice. Or you might say the person "took the high road instead of taking a swing."

E. Innuendo

Innuendo is the use of language to imply that a particular inference is justified, as if saying "go ahead and read between the lines!" In this way, the speaker doesn't have to actually make a claim that can't be supported; instead, the audience is led to make the leap on their own. For example, a presidential candidate might say, "Think carefully about whom you choose; you want a president who will be ready to do the job on day one." The implication is that the opposing candidate is not ready.

F. Downplayers

Downplayers are qualifier words or phrases that make someone or something look less important or significant. Words like *mere* and *only* work this way, as does the use of quotation marks, to suggest a term is ironic or misleading. For example: "She got her 'degree' from a correspondence school." Often these are linked to concessions with connectors such as *nevertheless*, *however*, *still*, or *but*.

G. Hyperbole

Hyperbole is the use of extravagant overstatement that can work to move the audience to accept the basic claim even if they reject the extremes of the word choice. Many of the other slanters can be hyperbolic in how they are worded; the key element is that the statement or claim is extreme. For example, in response to a dress code, a student might say, "This school administration is fascist!"

H. Truth Surrogates

Using a truth surrogate is hinting that proof exists to support a claim without actually citing that proof. For example, ads often say "studies show," and tabloids often say things like "according to an insider" or "there's every reason to believe that ..." If the evidence does exist, the author is doing a poor job of citing it; meanwhile, the author has not actually identified any source—or made any claim—that can be easily disproven or challenged.

I. Ridicule/Sarcasm

Ridicule and sarcasm are uses of language that suggest that the subject is worthy of scorn. The language seeks to evoke a laugh or sarcastically mock the subject.

Presenting a Slanter

Your teacher will divide you into small groups. With your group, select a slanter from the list. Then work together to complete the following tasks:

- Compose a paraphrased definition of your slanter.
- Study the list's example(s) of your slanter and brainstorm at least three additional examples.
- Discuss and evaluate each brainstormed example.
- As a group, choose which examples most clearly communicate the meaning of your slanter. Narrow your examples to a single choice.
- Create a brief skit using your chosen example to demonstrate the meaning of your slanter along with one or two questions for your audience about what the slanter is and how it is used to influence an audience.
- Present your skit to the class and invite volunteer classmates to answer your question(s). Be prepared to clarify the nature of your slanter as necessary.
- Allow your classmates to evaluate the effectiveness of your skit at communicating the meaning of your slanter.

☑ Check Your Understanding

Write down the slanter example that you used in your presentation. Then rewrite it in a way that conveys the same information in literal, neutral, or straightforward language.

As You Read

- Highlight any slanters you recognize in the editorial and note what kind of slanter each one is.
- Circle unknown words and phrases. Try to determine the meaning of the words by using context clues, word parts, or a dictionary.

About the Author

Raymond A. Schroth, SJ, is a Jesuit priest, journalist, and Jesuit Community Professor of Humanities at Saint Peter's College. He is the author of six books and an award-winning media critic for the *National Catholic Reporter*. Schroth also holds the position of editor emeritus at *America*.

INDEPENDENT READING LINK

Read and Discuss

Review several stories in your self-selected news source and find examples of at least two types of slanting. Share these examples with your peers. Explain how each example exemplifies bias. Tell the group whether you think the writer's techniques are effective and explain your reasons.

My Notes

Editorial

Abolish High School Football!

NJ.com, September 20, 2007

by **Raymond A. Schroth**

1   Are you sure playing high school football is good for your son?

2   I had doubts long before I read the report in the New York Times (Sept 15) that of the 1.2 million teenagers who play high school football, an estimated 50 percent have suffered at least one concussion, 35 percent two or more. Since 1997, throughout 20 states, 50 boys have died.

3   A concussion is a blow to the head that smashes the brain against the skull. Because their brain tissues are less developed, adolescents are most **vulnerable**. The victim feels "weird," has splotchy vision, falls to the ground, vomits, goes into a coma, dies. If he survives he suffers depression, he can't concentrate, drops out, and/or develops symptoms later in life.

4   Worst of all, the young men overwhelmingly told the reporter that if they thought their heads had been damaged they would never tell the coach, because he might take them out of the game.

5   I've felt high school football did more harm than good since I taught high school in the 1960s, since I began getting an inkling of the damage done young bodies in both high school and college, where linemen are encouraged to "bulk up" to a grotesque 300 pounds in order to do more damage to the enemy—to say nothing of the damage done to their own late adolescent bodies by getting so fat.

6   Football, especially in high school, distorts the goals of the so-called educational institution that sponsors it, turns ordinary boys into bedazzled heroes, tells them they're the kings of the corridors, coddled by teachers afraid to flunk them, as their parents try to live out their glamorous dreams over the broken bodies of their children bashing their helmeted heads into one another as thousands cheer.

7   Buzz Bissinger's 1990 bestselling *Friday Night Lights*, a popular book, film, and TV series, was, in the long run, an **indictment** of the small Texas town with nothing going for it but its high school football team. If the town had a library, churches, a theater, a park—if the school had any classes—we never saw them. They were **irrelevant**.

8   The boys went to high school to play, feeding **delusions** that they would be noticed by a scout who would get them college scholarships and contracts on pro teams.

9   But, you say, if high schools drop football, that will deprive colleges and the pros of their feeder system. Right. It will also deprive colleges of many who have come for only one reason—to play—while their paid tutors ease them through the motions of an education.

vulnerable: easily hurt
indictment: strong criticism
irrelevant: not important
delusions: false beliefs

My Notes

10 But, you say, some football players are very bright. Absolutely right. I have taught three in recent years who were the best in the class, straight A's, a delight to have in the room. But they are exceptions to the rule, and few and far between.

11 Without football, how can ambitious athletes thrive? They can play soccer, basketball, baseball, tennis, lacrosse, and squash. They can run, swim, row, sail, wrestle, and bike. They can also read, write for the paper, act, sing, dance, walk, and pray. And when they graduate their brains will be enriched, not bruised.

12 The Times article quotes Kelby Jasmon, a high school student in Springfield, Ill., walking around today with two concussions, who says there is "no chance" he would tell the coach if he gets hit hard and symptoms return. "It's not dangerous to play with a concussion," he says. "You've got to sacrifice for the team. The only way I come out is on a stretcher."

13 If the school officials and his parents read that and leave him on the field, something is very, very wrong.

Making Observations

- Based on your highlights, what are some words that describe how the author feels about high school football?
- Which sentence stands out most to you?

Returning to the Text

- Return to the editorial as you respond to the following questions. Use text evidence to support your responses.
- Write any additional questions you have about the text in your Reader/Writer Notebook.

3. Is Schroth's evidence in paragraph 2 subjective or objective? How can you tell, and what purpose does the evidence serve?

_____

_____

_____

_____

_____

4. Quote and describe the slanters Schroth uses in paragraph 3. Do they make his editorial more or less convincing?

_____

_____

_____

_____

_____

5. State examples of ridicule and sarcasm in paragraphs 7 and 9. What effects do they achieve? Do they make Schroth's argument more convincing or less so?

_____

_____

_____

_____

6. Read and analyze paragraph 10. Is Schroth presenting straightforwardly objective evidence, or does he use a slanter? Explain.

_____

_____

_____

_____

7. In paragraph 12, what kind of slanter does Schroth cite from *The New York Times* article? How does his use of it impact the effectiveness of his conclusion in paragraph 13?

_____

_____

_____

_____

Gaining Perspectives

You have heard one person's opinion of why football should be banned in high school. With a partner, imagine you are a principal in a school who has a meeting with a parent regarding the safety of student football players. Compare a variety of online sources to gather information about the possible dangers. Then role-play talking with a parent in the school about your research as you negotiate and work together to reduce the safety and health risks for not only football players but all student-athletes. When you are done, summarize the outcome of the discussion in your Reader/Writer Notebook.

Working from the Text

Introducing the Strategy: SMELL

SMELL is an acronym for sender, message, emotional strategies, logical strategies, and language. This strategy is useful for analyzing persuasive texts by asking five key questions:

- **S**ender-receiver relationship—What is the sender-receiver relationship? Who are the images and language meant to attract? Describe the speaker (or writer) of the text.
- **M**essage—What is the message? Summarize the thesis of the text.
- **E**motional Strategies—What is the desired effect?
- **L**ogical Strategies—What logic is being used? How does it (or its absence) affect the message? Consider the logic of images as well as words.
- **L**anguage—What does the language of the text describe? How does it affect the meaning and effectiveness of the writing? Consider the language of images as well as words.

8. In pairs, use the SMELL strategy to analyze this editorial. You have already done some work in the language section of the strategy.

Sender–Receiver Relationship	To whom is the writer explicitly addressing his argument?	
	How does he seem to feel about that target audience?	
	What values does the sender assume readers share or argue that they should share?	

Message	What is a literal summary of the content?	
	What is the article's ultimate thesis regarding the subject?	
Emotional Strategies	What emotional appeals does the writer include?	
	What seems to be his desired effect?	
Logical Strategies	What logical arguments or appeals does the writer include?	
	What is their effect on the readers' perception?	
Language	What specific language/slanters are used in the article to support the message or characterize the opposition?	
	What is their effect on the readers' perception?	

9. Review what you have ascertained about the author's use of language (especially slanted language and rhetorical devices). Write a short paragraph in your Reader/Writer Notebook stating how that language use shapes the perception of the reader.

10. Copy two of the more slanted passages from Schroth's editorial and revise them to be more neutral and less rhetorically manipulative.

Original Passage	Revised Passage

☑ **Check Your Understanding**

Quickwrite: Respond to the Essential Question: What is the role of media in our society, and how can we become responsible consumers and producers of information in a digital age?

Putting It All Together

Learning Strategies

Graphic Organizer
Quickwrite
Predicting

Learning Targets

- Examine how the target audience affects a writer's choices in diction, syntax, and tone.
- Evaluate an author's use of print and graphic features to support an argument.

Preview

In this activity, you will read and analyze a Pultizer Prize–nominated editorial from the *Star Tribune*.

My Notes

Reading an Editorial

As you read through the following guidelines for reading editorials, paraphrase each of the points by writing a word or two in the margins that will help you to remember the point.

a. Examine the headline, sub-headline, and related cartoon (if it exists). What will this editorial be about? What guesses or assumptions can you make about the author's perspective at this point?

b. Look at the author's name and affiliation, if given. What do you know about the author's background and/or potential bias at this point? Is the author or source credible?

c. Read the first two to three paragraphs very carefully. What issue is the author discussing, and what is his or her stance on this issue?

d. Once you have determined the author's stance on the issue, stop reading for a moment or two. What is the other side to the issue? Who might think differently? What are one or two reasons that you know that might support other side of the author's stance?

e. Continue reading the editorial. What are two of the strongest pieces of evidence that the author uses to support his or her side of the issue? Why are they effective or ineffective?

f. Did the author persuade you? Did the author address or refute the main objections of the opposition? Give an example. What did he or she not address? Why might the author have chosen not to address this element? Do you think the author was fair to the other side? Why or why not?

g. Can you detect any biases? Has the author left out any important details that may have changed your perspective? Has any information been placed at the end of the editorial to deemphasize it? Who is or is not quoted in the editorial?

h. Go back through the editorial and circle slanters and other rhetorical devices. How do these words affect your feelings about the issue? About the author?

i. If the author were standing right next to you now, what would you say to him or her?

Print and Graphic Features

When reading editorials and other news articles, you might find the following print and graphic features:

- **Text divisions** such as introductions, summaries, sections with headings, footnotes or endnotes, and information about the author.
- **Graphics** that present information in a visual format, such as diagrams, charts, tables, graphs, maps, timelines, and so on. Graphics support the information and ideas presented in the text.
- **Special formatting** such as boldface, italics, numbered or bulleted text, or the use of different typefaces and sizes. For example, in this list, the types of text features are placed in boldface to draw attention to them.

Making Predictions Based on Text Features

1. Before you read, look at the title, section heads, and graphics and predict what the text is about.

As You Read

- As you read, underline examples of information that is represented in a graphic.
- Circle unknown words and phrases. Try to determine the meaning of the words by using context clues, word parts, or a dictionary.

About the Author

Jill Burcum has been a member of the Editorial Board at the *Star Tribune* since 2008. Her series of editorials highlighting the poor conditions of Bureau of Indian Education schools titled "Separate and Unequal" was a 2015 Pulitzer Prize finalist for editorial writing. Burcum started her career as a reporter for the *Rochester Post-Bulletin* after graduating from the University of Washington. She writes on a broad range of topics including health care, water quality, and American Indian issues.

Editorial

Separate and Unequal: Indian Schools, a Nation's Neglect

by **Jill Burcum** from the *Star Tribune*

Part one of four parts: Better futures aren't built by indifference, but that's how the federal government treats dilapidated tribal schools to which it owes resources. The results are tangible.

1   LEECH LAKE INDIAN RESERVATION, MINN.—"Watch. This is the coolest moment of my day," science teacher Allison Barta says, unlocking the door to her classroom at the Bug-O-Nay-Ge-Shig High School.

2   Inside, a freshwater aquarium takes up much of the back wall, providing the only light in the windowless space. For a moment, the room resembles an environmental science lab. Then Barta flips on the lights.

3   This is what years of federal neglect look like at schools such as Bug-O-Nay-Ge-Shig—part of the 183-school federal Bureau of Indian Education system (BIE).

4   Barta's classroom is housed in a rodent-infested building with a shockingly long list of problems: a roof that caves in under heavy snowfall, a failing heating system that has many students wearing coats and blankets in class as soon as the weather turns and a sewer system that backs up during extreme cold—all adding to the discomforts and indignities of an aging, metal "pole barn" that has to be evacuated when wind gusts top 40 miles per hour.

5   In an era when educators emphasize science, technology, engineering and mathematics as keys to students' future success, Barta's science room has no lab tables and few microscopes, and no storage for hazardous materials needed for basic lessons. The ventilation and electrical systems are antiquated.

6   At Bug-O-Nay-Ge-Shig in northern Minnesota—and on reservations across the country—the educational promises this nation made to tribes are being broken. It is a policy of disgraceful **indifference**, leaving generation after generation of American Indian children struggling to build better lives.

7   The decrepit conditions at Bug-O-Nay-Ge-Shig are not unusual in the BIE system, which sprawls over 23 states and 64 reservations. Many of the schools serve some of the nation's poorest and most remote communities. Test scores for the system's 49,079 students lag those of both Indians and non-Indians in

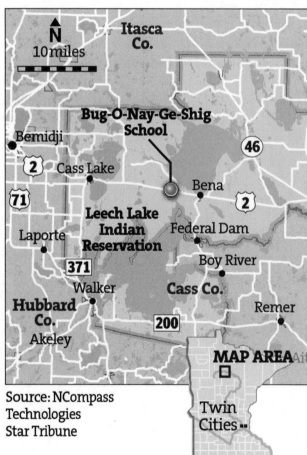

Source: NCompass
Technologies
Star Tribune

antiquated: outdated
indifference: lack of interest

public schools. Yet the estimated $1.3 billion needed to put all BIE schools into good condition has long failed to materialize.

8 For more than a decade, school officials and leaders of the Leech Lake Band of Ojibwe have tried to convince federal officials that Bug-O-Nay-Ge-Shig needs to be rebuilt. Plans for a project with a price now estimated at $27 million were completed four years ago. Hopes rose across the reservation in August when U.S. Interior Secretary Sally Jewell toured the school. Jewell, whose Department of the Interior is the parent agency for the BIE and the Bureau of Indian Affairs, came just two months after President Obama traveled to North Dakota's Standing Rock Reservation and repeatedly underscored his commitment to tribal relations and education.

9 But at Bug-O-Nay-Ge-Shig, the cold reality for the 100 students is that no date has been set—or likely is close to being set—for replacing the school building. Nor does it appear that improvements will come soon enough to spare another generation from having to endure the 62 other BIE schools rated in poor condition.

10 They are not the only schools in America in disrepair—about 3 percent of public school facilities are in similarly poor condition, according to the National Center on Education Statistics—but a far greater share of BIE schools has been ignored.

11 Funding for replacement schools, improvements and repairs to BIE schools has fallen by 76 percent over the past decade. Despite its rhetoric about various tribal relations initiatives, the Obama administration has ignored the system's fundamental need for safe, functional schools. Even more frustrating, the administration is standing by while BIE learning environments fall drastically behind those of the other federal K-12 system: Department of Defense (DOD) schools serving children of military families and civilian employees.

12 The DOD launched a $5 billion construction surge in 2010 to renovate or replace 134 of its 181 schools by 2021. Seventeen new schools have been completed, 23 are under construction and 37 are in the design phase.

13 In contrast, the Interior Department has requested just $3.2 million in replacement school construction funding for one Indian school in 2015. Funding for new BIE schools over the past four years totaled $39 million—less than the cost of one large DOD elementary school that will open next year in Virginia.

14 The Interior Department also zeroed out its budget requests for BIE school replacement construction in 2013 and 2014—more evidence that the agency and the Obama administration's Office of Management and Budget view the BIE system as nothing more than a place to find savings.

15 No American should begrudge the investment in DOD schools: Our military families deserve the best. But under the watch of Obama, Jewell and Education Secretary Arne Duncan, the BIE system has increasingly and inexcusably become what advocates for Indian schools and U.S. Rep. Betty McCollum, D-Minn., have described as "separate and unequal."

16 On South Dakota's Pine Ridge Indian Reservation, which has four deteriorating BIE schools, former tribal President Cecilia Fire Thunder summed up what many tribal students, educators and leaders are wondering about federal officials: "Why aren't they fighting for us?"

Culture in education

17 The BIE school system enrolls about 10 percent of Indian students nationally—with the remainder generally attending local public schools. But the slender enrollment figures belie the essential role these schools play in Indian education. Because of the remote locations of reservations, BIE schools are the only hope for many students. Indian languages and history also typically play a more central role in BIE school curricula, helping to preserve valued traditions nearly eradicated by decades of misguided U.S. government policies.

18 The culture-at-the-core approach is critical for students like Charles Raisch, 17, who felt out of place at the sports-focused public high school near his home in Deer River, Minn. So Raisch, who hopes to become a car mechanic, transferred to Bug-O-Nay-Ge-Shig, where a school day that includes tanning hides, learning to speak Ojibwe or harvesting wild rice helps him make friends and focus on his regular classwork.

19 The smaller school—named for Chief Hole-In-The-Day—and the focus on Raisch's culture has helped him deal with stress and has made him appreciate his heritage. He now often starts his day by walking into the woods near his home to offer tobacco, a sacred plant, to the Creator. He also likes working with younger kids during cultural activities. On a recent trip to nearby Mud Lake to harvest wild rice, Raisch was one of the older boys helping elementary school students in and out of canoes.

20 Knowing that the younger kids look up to him inspires Raisch to work harder at school. At what is affectionately known as the Bug school, he said, "I feel better and more positive overall."

21 Indian leaders believe a culture-rich education can help combat social ills plaguing their communities, such as high rates of drug and alcohol use, crime and suicide.

22 "By going back to our ceremonies and sweat and purification lodges and moving back to the reservation, many people are finding balance again," Pine Ridge's Fire Thunder said. "Our culture is what grounds us, and this is what is going to save us."

My Notes

GRADUATION RATES

Graduation rates for ethnic groups from 1999 through 2010.

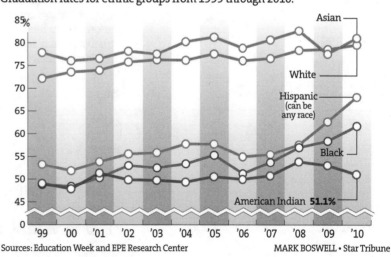

Sources: Education Week and EPE Research Center

MARK BOSWELL • Star Tribune

A national disgrace

23 Federal neglect is handicapping learning at BIE schools nationwide, according to a 2014 report commissioned by Jewell and Duncan. But students in the Upper Midwest and the Southwest may be suffering the most.

24 Those two regions have the nation's largest clusters of BIE schools—the legacy of being home to large, influential Indian nations that ceded land and signed treaties with the U.S. government as settlers pushed west in the mid-1800s. The federal government assumed educational obligations as part of this exchange for tribes' ancestral lands. The government's ongoing trust responsibilities are recognized in modern law and unchanged by the advent of tribal casinos. In any case, there aren't enough profitable casinos to fund the BIE system's construction needs.

25 As deplorable as the conditions are at Bug-O-Nay-Ge-Shig, Minnesota is fortunate that it's the only one of the state's four BIE schools currently in poor condition. The others are in Onamia, Cloquet and White Earth.

26 Twenty-eight of Arizona's 54 BIE schools are listed in poor condition, and two—Cove Day School and Little Singer Community School—have been on the BIE's priority replacement list for a decade. BIE officials who oversee the Arizona schools say there's little they can do.

27 "They keep telling us that Congress doesn't have the money," said Deborah Belone, who oversees Cove as well as Red Rock Day School, another school in such disrepair that it needs replacement. In addition to mold, a faulty roof, a failing cooling system, asbestos and an inadequate number of classrooms for a growing student body, Red Rock's dated electrical system is so overloaded that teachers can't use their classroom "smartboards," the modern equivalent of a chalkboard, all at the same time.

CONSTRUCTION FUNDING FALTERS

Replacement school construction funding for schools in the Bureau of Indian Education system has dropped sharply over the past decade. Funding for construction is handled by the deputy assistant secretary for management in the assistant secretary for Indian Affairs department.

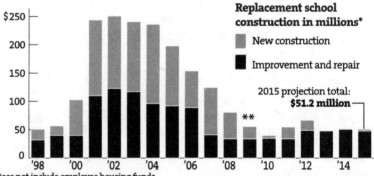

Replacement school construction in millions*

■ New construction
■ Improvement and repair

2015 projection total: **$51.2 million**

*Does not include employee housing funds.
**2009 figures exclude federal stimulus dollars for school replacement.
Source: Department of the Interior

MARK BOSWELL • Star Tribune

Schools without books

28 Ten of South Dakota's 22 BIE facilities, and four of North Dakota's 11 schools, are also considered in poor condition, generally meaning that the backlog of needed repairs or renovations is so extensive that it's more economical to put up a new structure.

29 At the Little Wound K-12 school in Kyle, S.D., part of the elementary school still in use was built in 1939. The nurse's office for a school serving about 800 kids is on an auditorium stage; there's no other place for it.

30 The middle school is housed in two structures, one of which is a pole barn that was supposed to be temporary but is now 21 years old. To get to classes in the barn, eighth-graders like Shadow Red Owl, George Killsback and Ryder Tobacco pass through a covered walkway frequented by bats and draped with hanging electrical cables. School officials aren't sure if a nearby portable classroom—which has boarded-up windows, a rotted foundation and an obscenity spray-painted on it—has been condemned yet.

31 But elementary Principal Ardis Iron Cloud doesn't dream of a fancy new facility or high-tech computer labs. She simply wants her students to have access to books. "If you want to raise reading scores," Iron Cloud said, "you have to have a library."

Blaming Congress

32 Asked how the inaction on BIE school construction squares with the Obama administration's commitment to Indian education, Interior Secretary Jewell blamed Congress.

33 "I will not promise what I cannot deliver, and tribal leaders and educators have heard me say this, because I've had conversations with them about the budget atmosphere in which we work in Washington, D.C.," Jewell said. "We have a huge problem on our hands, a problem that is not easily solved. But I want to do what I can administratively, and that means I will continue working with my colleagues in the Cabinet and working with leaders and tribes to see what we can do with the hand that we're dealt right now to begin to make a real difference for Indian children."

34 Jewell's frustration with Congress is fair. Interior belongs to the part of the federal budget hit hard by automatic spending reductions made as part of Washington's 2011 debt ceiling deal. In 2013, these cuts to BIE totaled $58 million.

35 Congress funded BIE school replacement construction at more robust levels during the administration of former President George W. Bush—hitting a high-water mark of $140 million in 2004.

36 Minnesota's Democratic U.S. Sen. Al Franken, who has held field hearings on BIE schools' plight, has publicly urged Jewell to ask for additional funding in fiscal 2016, the budgetary details of which are being worked out right now and are not yet public. Sen. Jon Tester, D-Mont., chairman of the U.S. Senate Committee on Native Affairs, has held hearings on deteriorating schools.

That Jewell hasn't been before the committee in 18 months, while her agency is tardy in replies to inquiries from members, has been noticed.

37   Tester's message to Jewell couldn't be clearer: Get going and give us a plan. "The BIE must work with tribes to develop a comprehensive long-term plan to address the education needs of Native students. The **infrastructure** needs at BIE schools are incredibly serious, and it is critical that the BIE's next budget proposal include a plan to address the dismal state of so many BIE schools across Indian Country," he said.

"A better future"

38   Even with a plan, getting funding approved is a daunting challenge, which is why Jewell needs to personally sell it once it's developed. She'll need help from Education Secretary Duncan, whose agency is larger and more influential. The two also need to forcefully advocate for other funding solutions, including one devised by a Minneapolis banker that has already been partly passed by Congress. It would allow tribes to tap into private financing to replace school buildings.

39   If Duncan is serious about addressing educational **disparities**, which has been a focus of his, he can't be absent without leave on the buildings in which some of the nation's most disadvantaged students are trying to learn.

40   It isn't just Indian nations that have placed their trust in Jewell's agency. States that are home to large Indian populations, like Minnesota with its seven reservations and four Indian communities, are depending on BIE schools to educate a new generation of citizens and workers with skills critical for the future.

41   Kids shivering in thin-walled classrooms or studying under leaky roofs year after year aren't getting the education they need or deserve. With the larger community's visible neglect all around them, they receive the wrong message about the value of education.

42   During his June visit to North Dakota, Obama inspired the crowd when he said, "We can break old cycles. We can give our children a better future." Providing BIE students with adequate schools is the place to start.

INDEPENDENT READING LINK

Read and Connect

Read an editorial from your self-selected news source. Use the Working from the Text questions in this activity to write an analysis of the editorial.

Making Observations

- What print and graphic features did you notice in the text?
- What is one detail from the graphs and map you noticed that someone else might have missed?
- What questions do you have after reading the editorial?

infrastructure: system of public works

disparities: fundamentally different qualities

Returning to the Text

- Return to the editorial as you respond to the following questions. Use text evidence to support your responses.
- Write any additional questions you have about the text in your Reader/Writer Notebook.

2. Reread paragraphs 1–16 and summarize the conditions of BIE schools across the United States. How do you feel about the conditions of these schools? What words and phrases does the author use to make you feel this way?

_____

_____

_____

_____

3. Why does Burcum choose to include the personal story of student Charles Raisch in her editorial? What is the intended effect on readers perceptions of BIE schools?

_____

_____

_____

_____

4. What can a reader learn from the bar graph titled "Construction Funding Falters"? What effect is achieved by the inclusion of the graphic feature?

_____

_____

_____

5. What is the claim being made in this editorial, and what evidence is used to support it?

_____

_____

_____

_____

6. How do the author's examples about individuals contribute to her claim over the course of the text?

_____

_____

_____

_____

7. What events does the author describe in order to support her claim?

_____

_____

_____

_____

Working from the Text

8. Use the questions in the Reading an Editorial section to guide your responses to the editorial.

Title: Author:

Issue:

Question	Response
a	
b	
c	
d	
e	

Question	Response
f	
g	
h	
i	

Using the notes you have generated, be prepared to participate in a class discussion addressing the following questions (as well as any others inspired by the text):

- What does the author seem to assume the audience is feeling about the issue?
- How does the author tailor language and argument to his or her audience?
- Does the author use slanters? If so, what is their effect?

☑ Check Your Understanding

Quickwrite: How is an editorial different from a news story?

✍ Writing Prompt: Rhetorical Analysis

Now independently analyze another editorial of your choice. Then write a text explaining how the writer tailors the language and argument to a target audience. Be sure to:

- Include a clear summary of the argument.
- Cite specific examples from the text.
- Comment on the effect the author's language has on the intended audience.

How to Write an Editorial

Learning Strategies

Brainstorming
Drafting
RAFT
Sharing and Responding
SOAPStone

Learning Targets

• Craft an editorial of your own, carefully considering audience and context.

Preview

In this activity, you will draft, write, and revise an editorial about a contemporary issue.

My Notes

How to Write an Editorial

1. You have had the opportunity to read and analyze a couple of editorials. Now you will walk through the steps of writing your own editorial.

Before You Write

• **Brainstorm for topics:** Choose topics in which you have a genuine interest and some prior knowledge. Be sure the topics are issues that are debatable. Do not, for example, argue for school violence because it would be difficult to find anyone in favor of such a thing. Many editorials are written as responses to news articles or other editorials, so be alert for interesting ideas while reading your news sources each day.

• **Research your topic:** Ask opinions, conduct interviews, and locate facts. While editorials are opinion pieces, those opinions must still be supported with evidence.

• **Get both sides:** In addition to having support for your position, be certain that you have information about the other side of the issue. You will need this soon.

• **Consider your audience:** Use SOAPSTone as a prewriting strategy to consider details of your audience. What does your audience currently believe about this issue? Why? How will they respond to you? Why? What can you do to persuade them to change their minds? How will using slanted language affect your credibility and persuasiveness with them?

• **Write a thesis:** Before writing your draft, you must have a clearly stated position on this issue with a strongly worded reason for your position.

• **Write out your topic sentences and/or main ideas:** This preparation will help you organize your thoughts as you draft your editorial.

• **Decide on a structure:** Consider ways of organizing your essay and choose the one that seems most useful. Remember you can change your mind during the writing process if you like.

Writing a Draft

• **Get to the point:** Your first paragraph should immediately bring the reader's attention to the seriousness of the issue. Create a "hook" that will sell the piece to the reader: a current event or imminent danger, for example. You should then provide a concise summary of what you're going to tell the reader and include your thesis statement.

• **Provide context:** Give your readers important background information about the issue. This background should not be common knowledge (e.g., "drugs are dangerous") but should frame the issue and define any key terms that your reader will need to understand in order to consider your argument.

- **Make your point:** Give your strongest two or three reasons why the reader should agree with you. Use relevant and appropriate evidence to support your reasons. State the source of your information and be sure that your argument is clear and organized.

- **Address your opposition:** Reasonable people may think differently than you do on the subject. State at least one or two of the most credible reasons why someone might object to your point of view. Then refute their positions by explaining why their assumptions, claims, logic, and/or evidence are wrong.

- **Wrap it up:** Briefly summarize the main points of your argument and think of a powerful way to end your piece. Often this means giving your reader one last thought to consider.

Revising, Editing, and Publishing Your Draft

- **Check your evidence:** As you look back through your draft, consider whether you have included enough evidence to convince someone who thinks differently than you. Also, is that evidence relevant to your position?

- **Check your rhetoric:** Where is your language slanted? What words or phrases could you modify to "tone down" your voice and appeal to more people?

- **Check your grammar and style:** Nothing will make dismissing your ideas easier than misspelled or misused words or phrases. Triple-check your editorial for mistakes. Print or online style guides can be very useful at this stage. Your computer's spell-check feature can be useful, but it won't catch *has* when you meant *had* because it is spelled correctly. Reread your text to make certain that your words are both correctly spelled and the ones you want.

- **Publish your work:** Make your work available to your target audience. You may do it by printing and distributing copies, putting it on a bulletin board, or including it in a class newsletter or website. Ask your teacher which publication method you should use.

✍️ Writing Prompt: Argumentative

With a partner, co-write a brief editorial on the subject of the Eden Prairie High School suspensions or another contemporary issue of your choice. Use the steps outlined in the How to Write an Editorial section to guide your writing. Be sure to:

- Introduce and establish the significance of your claim.
- Make use of rhetorical devices, such as appeals to emotion, logic, or ethics, to support your argument.
- Use language and varied sentence structures to establish relationships among reasons and evidence.
- Establish and maintain a formal style and objective tone.

As You Read

- Underline each writer's position and key reasons for his position.
- Circle unknown words and phrases. Try to determine the meaning of the words by using context clues, word parts, or a dictionary.
- Highlight any words or phrases that illustrate the writer's tone.

GRAMMAR & USAGE

Diction

Diction, or the words a writer chooses, plays an important role in establishing tone and credibility. A writer may choose to use formal or informal words, abstract or concrete words, and emotional or clinical words, all to create an overall effect. Notice how O'Connell uses formal diction in his editorial to reflect his position as the state superintendent of schools. He chooses words such as *remediation, rigorous,* and *perform* to establish his credibility on the subject of education.

Find two more examples of the author's diction that reinforce the overall tone of the argument and explain their impact to a partner.

My Notes

_____
_____
_____
_____
_____
_____
_____
_____
_____
_____

rigors: strict requirements
remediation: help
vocational: job-related
socioeconomically: related to money and social status
bound: moving toward

Editorial

Pro and Con: Raising Graduation for High School Students: Time to Raise the Bar in High Schools

by Jack O'Connell

1   The most important challenge we face in public education today is to improve high schools so that all California students graduate prepared to succeed in either college or the workplace. Today, far too many of our 1.7 million high school students are prepared for neither the demands of skilled employment nor the **rigors** of higher education. Employers consistently complain of graduates who lack critical problem-solving and communications skills. More than half of students entering California State University need **remediation** in reading or math. It is clearly time for us to reexamine high school in California, to raise the level of rigor we expect of all of our students and begin preparing every high school student to reach higher expectations.

2   How we meet the challenge of improving high school student achievement will determine the futures of our children and their ability to compete and succeed in the decades to come. Moreover, how we respond to this challenge will significantly affect the economic and social future of our state.

3   Research shows that students who take challenging, college-preparatory courses do better in school, even if they started out with poor test scores and low expectations. Students who take rigorous courses are also less likely to drop out, and they perform better in **vocational** and technical courses.

4   Our high schools today struggle with an achievement gap that leaves African-American, Latino and **socioeconomically** disadvantaged students lagging behind their peers. A failure to provide and expect all students to take demanding academic coursework has also created a high school "reality gap": While more than 80 percent of high school students say they intend to go to college, only about 40 percent actually take the rigorous coursework required for acceptance at a four-year university. The numbers are even lower for African-American graduates (24 percent) and Latinos (22 percent).

5   Many students are not aware that the "minimum requirement" courses they are taking aren't providing the rigorous foundation that will prepare them to fulfill their dreams after high school. In some cases, students are steered away from tough courses or find them overenrolled. The result is thousands of students who must spend significant, unnecessary time and money after high school if they are ever to fulfill their dreams.

6   To reverse this trend, we must make rigorous courses available to all of our students. We must redefine high schools as institutions that provide all students with a strong academic foundation, whether they are **bound** for college or the workplace after graduation.

My Notes

7 I am proposing a High Performing High Schools Initiative that will raise expectations for our high schools and high school students. It will provide better training and support for high school principals. And it will establish a state "seal of approval" process for high school instructional materials, giving districts guidance in choosing materials that are standards-**aligned**, and therefore more rigorous than many used in high schools today.

8 It is simply wrong to decide for students as young as age 15 whether or not they are "college material" and capable of challenging courses in high school. Guiding students to an easier academic pathway, even if they show little early motivation or curiosity about possibilities beyond high school, **virtually** guarantees they won't be prepared with important foundational skills. It limits their opportunities for years to come. Years ago, this was called "tracking." Students facing childhood challenges such as poverty or the need to learn English—the description of fully well over a quarter of California's students today—would be tracked to less-challenging courses and denied opportunities after high school as a result.

9 By advocating for tougher curriculum in high schools, I am not in any way suggesting vocational education programs should be eliminated. In fact, legislation I introduced to improve high school achievement would reward schools that collaborate with businesses or labor unions to expand such successful programs as career partnership academies. These academies have been successful where they have provided rigorous academic instruction geared toward a career pathway.

10 The truth is that we can no longer afford to hold high expectations only for our college-bound students. Today, all of our students need the skills and knowledge contained in the curriculum that was once reserved only for the college-bound. Strong communications skills, knowledge of foreign language and culture, higher-level math and problem-solving skills are needed in technical trades as well as white-collar professions. The job of K-12 education in California must be to ensure that all of our students graduate with the ability to fulfill their potential—whether that takes them to higher education or directly to their career.

aligned: supported
virtually: almost completely

Making Observations

- What words and phrases does the author enclose in quotation marks?
- Based on the words or phrases you highlighted, what is a detail that feels important to you?

Returning to the Text

- Return to the editorial as you respond to the following questions. Use text evidence to support your responses.
- Write any additional questions you have about the text in your Reader/Writer Notebook.

2. Describe O'Connell's diction and the tone it creates. How do his word choice and syntax reflect his position as California State Superintendent of Public Instruction?

_____

_____

_____

_____

_____

3. Find an example of a counterargument in O'Connell's editorial. How does he respond to it?

_____

_____

_____

_____

_____

4. What text evidence addresses O'Connell's claim that minorities are disproportionately underserved by the low difficulty level of their academic coursework? Is the evidence objective and valid or subjective and unconvincing? Explain.

_____

_____

_____

_____

_____

Editorial

New Michigan Graduation Requirements Shortchange Many Students

by **Nick Thomas**

1 Imagine waking up in the morning to find the electricity is out, or a pipe has burst or your car won't start. As you look though the Yellow Pages for a technician, do you really care if that person has a working knowledge of matrices, oxidation numbers, and Kepler's laws of planetary motion?

2 Apparently the state of Michigan does. Its new high school graduation requirements will assure that every graduate, regardless of their career choice, will have taken advanced math and science classes.

3 Among the new requirements are one credit each of algebra I, geometry and algebra II and an additional math class in the senior year. Also required is one credit of biology, one credit of physics or chemistry and one additional year of science.

4 This new curriculum may be helpful for a student who plans to go on to college, but it seems excessive for vocational students.

5 Plumbers, mechanics, construction workers, hairdressers and many other positions do not need an advanced math and science background. Math needed for vocational jobs could be learned through an "applied math" class, or on-site learning.

6 I'm concerned that when students are forced to take classes that are unnecessary for their chosen careers, they'll feel discouraged and put little effort into their classes. And if they can't take the classes they want, I'm afraid that more of them will drop out.

Advanced classes becoming basic classes

7 One of my biggest concerns with all students taking advanced classes is that the pace of the courses will slow down. Some students will undoubtedly not try to learn the material, and some will be incapable of learning as fast as others, leaving the teacher compelled to dumb down the class. In effect, advanced classes will become basic classes. This will have no additional benefit for vocational students and will hamper college prep students.

8 There's yet another way college-bound students might suffer from the new requirements. A very gifted English student who lacks ability in math could have their grade point average lowered significantly when required to take advanced math classes. And of course, when applying to college, high school grades are important.

9 A well-rounded education is ideal but can be achieved in many ways, not just through academics. Our economy depends on a variety of jobs. We need carpenters as well as engineers. We need hairdressers as well as doctors, and we need heavy equipment operators as well as lawyers.

10 All jobs are important, and students deserve to pursue their choice of a career without being forced to take unnecessary classes.

Making Observations

- How does the question in the introduction make you feel?
- Where does the author use the first-person point of view?

Returning to the Text

- Return to the editorial as you respond to the following questions. Use text evidence to support your responses.
- Write any additional questions you have about the text in your Reader/Writer Notebook.

5. How does Thomas's diction compare with O'Connell's? Which writer's approach do you feel is more engaging and convincing, and why?

_____

_____

_____

_____

_____

6. Locate the subhead Thomas uses in his editorial. Why does he use it, and how does it support his argument?

_____

_____

_____

_____

_____

_____

7. Describe a key idea on which O'Connell and Thomas agree.

_____

_____

_____

_____

_____

 Gaining Perspectives

You have read two editorials about education. The right to an education and the right to express your opinion are part of the Universal Declaration of Human Rights created by the United Nations. With a partner, research other human rights mentioned in the document. Are these rights protected in the United States? What about other countries around the world? Why is it important to uphold human rights? Summarize you findings and present them to the class.

Working from the Text

8. Use the chart to organize the annotations you made while you read each editorial.

Author	Reasons For	Reasons Against	Strongest Statement of Position
Jack O'Connell			
Nick Thomas			
You			
A Person You Know			

9. Use the chart to compare the key ideas the two writers present. In your opinion, which of the two writers made the stronger case? Explain.

> ### ✒ Writing Prompt: Argumentative
>
> You have co-written a brief editorial, and you have read two editorials with opposing views. Now, compose an editorial that responds to your original editorial. Write from an alternate perspective. Be sure to:
>
> - Introduce and establish the significance of your claim.
> - Develop the claim and respond to counterclaims with relevant evidence.
> - Establish and maintain a formal style and an objective tone.

Where's Your Proof?

Learning Targets

- Evaluate the effectiveness of different types of evidence.
- Revise writing to incorporate appropriate evidence.

Preview

In this activity, you will analyze the effectiveness of evidence in this unit's editorials. Then you will revise your own editorial by strengthening the effectiveness of your evidence.

The Art of Evidence

1. To support the claims they make, authors use a variety of types of evidence. With a partner or small group, revisit one of the editorials you have read in this unit and fill in the chart.

Type of Evidence: What is it used for? What are its limitations? "They X, but they Y."	Example from an Editorial in This Unit	Evaluation: What kind of appeal does it make: logos, ethos, or pathos? Does the evidence logically support the author's claim in this case? Why or why not?
Illustrative Examples (Personal Experience/Anecdotal/Media Example). They add reality to the claim but may not be generalizable.		
Hypothetical Cases. They challenge the reader to consider possible circumstances or outcomes, but there's no reason they will definitely happen.		
Analogies/Comparison. They make the unfamiliar or abstract more accessible, but they need to be more similar than different in order to be persuasive.		
Expert/Testimony. They provide expert support for causal claims, predictions of outcomes, or possible solutions, but they're still just opinions—and the source needs to be checked carefully!		

Type of Evidence: What is it used for? What are its limitations? "They X, but they Y."	Example from an Editorial in This Unit	Evaluation: What kind of appeal does it make: logos, ethos, or pathos? Does the evidence logically support the author's claim in this case? Why or why not?
Statistics/Surveys. They support generalized claims and make strong logical appeals, but they must be reliable and unbiased.		
Causal Relationships. They suggest possible positive or negative outcomes, but there needs to be a clear link between the cause and the effect.		

2. Once you have recorded your observations in the graphic organizer, be prepared to discuss those observations. You will want to make sure to address both the types and effectiveness of each technique the author has used. Make sure you reference specific examples from the text. With a partner, discuss why using a wide variety of evidence might be more persuasive or effective than using only one kind of evidence.

☑ Check Your Understanding

Select one of the editorials you have written in this unit and revise one paragraph in it by adding at least one of the types of evidence from this activity. Share your revision with a partner and ask your partner to identify the type of evidence you used in your writing.

Reading and Writing a Letter to the Editor

Learning Targets

- Evaluate the effectiveness of multiple editorial letters according to specific criteria.
- Write an editorial letter using the criteria for effectiveness.

Preview

In this activity, you will analyze several letters to the editor and then write your own.

My Notes

How to Write a Letter to the Editor

Letters that are intended for publication should be drafted carefully. Here are some tips to keep in mind:

- Make one point (or at most two) in your letter. Be sure to identify the topic of your letter. State the point clearly, ideally in the first sentence.
- Make your letter timely. If you are not addressing a specific article, editorial, or letter that recently appeared in the paper you are writing to, try to tie the issue you want to write about to a recent event.
- Familiarize yourself with the coverage and editorial position of the paper to which you are writing. Refute or support specific statements, address relevant facts that are ignored, offer a completely different perspective on the issue, but avoid blanket attacks on the media in general or the newspaper in particular.
- Consider your audience (the newspaper's editors and readers):
  - What does your audience currently believe about the issue? Why?
  - How will they respond to you? Why?
  - What can you do to persuade them to change their minds?
  - How will using slanted language affect your credibility and persuasiveness?
- Check the letter specifications of the newspaper to which you are writing. Length and format requirements vary from paper to paper. (Generally, roughly two short paragraphs are ideal.) You also must include your name, signature, address, and phone number.
- Look at the letters that appear in your paper. Is a certain type of letter usually printed?
- Support your facts. If the topic you address is controversial, consider sending documentation along with your letter. But don't overload the editors with too much information.
- Keep your letter brief. Type and spell-check it. Have a peer edit it.
- When possible, find others in the community to write letters to show concern about the issue. If your letter doesn't get published, perhaps someone else's on the same topic will.
- If your letter has not appeared within a week or two, follow up with a call to the newspaper's editorial department.

As You Read

- Jot down any questions you have about the letters to the editor in the My Notes area.
- Highlight any words or phrases that indicate the writers' tone.

Letters to the Editor

Letters: The NYC Subway Is Not "Beyond Repair"

From **The Atlantic**

June 13, 2018

Last weekend, Peter Wayner advocated for a radical overhaul of the city's current subway system, proposing instead a network of subterranean highways filled with hoverboards, scooters, and autonomous vehicles.

Letter 1

1   After reading "The New York City Subway Is Beyond Repair," I felt compelled to respond to what I see as basic inaccuracies that undermine the piece as a whole. I have a degree in infrastructure engineering and am an engineer-in-training in the field, but the inaccuracies in question are not nearly so arcane as to require such credentials.

2   The respective capacities of free-flowing vehicular lanes and subway transit are well established. Generously, a freeway lane might carry 2,000 vehicles per hour, which—again, generously—might each carry somewhere between one and two travelers, on average. This gives us a high-end estimate of moving 2,000 to 4,000 people per hour in a single direction.

3   An MTA subway track, such as Mr. Wayner effectively proposes to replace with a single lane of traffic, is capable of carrying in excess of 30,000 people per hour. This is not a small difference and makes one wonder whether the author has considered it.

4   This is the simplest critique, as it relies on simple math, but the challenges with Mr. Wayner's proposal are legion. For the geometry alone, there are a number of difficulties with using passenger vehicles rather than trains.

5   Vastly larger stations would be required to accommodate all the spaces for cars picking up and dropping off pedestrians. In order to prevent delays for vehicles not stopping, additional bypass tunnels would need to be excavated at every station. To permit safe operation, much of the signaling equipment that

My Notes

Mr. Wayner wanted to rip out would instead need to be replaced with much more sophisticated and expensive Intelligent Transportation Systems (ITS) to coordinate a far larger number of vehicles.

6 These are all massive challenges, with huge price tags, that would, again, result in a tremendous decrease in capacity for the system as a whole. It's a pleasant fantasy to believe that innovation and a Silicon Valley mindset are all that's necessary to solve one of America's most intractable infrastructure challenges. The truth, much less attractive, is that it requires massive and consistent funding, collaboration across a range of stakeholders, and time.

Patrick Zerr
North Vancouver, Canada

Letter 2

1 Peter Wayner proposed that we should replace trains in the New York City subway with autonomous cars and hoverboards. He sounds like a modern-day Robert Moses, obsessed with automobiles as a replacement for public transit, proclaiming that cars will be more convenient and efficient for us all. Robert Moses built a system of roads on which only cars and trucks may travel—which are and have always been notoriously congested, especially during the rush hours. Subway riders must tolerate stops at stations they will not get off at because other passengers might be boarding or exiting the train, but automobile passengers must tolerate stops for traffic jams that serve no purpose for anyone.

2 The New York City subway is not broken beyond repair; for all its faults, for all the mismanagement, the subway remains the lifeline of this city. Mr. Wayner suggests that modern technology—autonomous cars, personal transit devices— can replace trains, but it is not as if trains have not benefited from modern technology as well. Computers, artificial intelligence, robotics—all these things are being applied to railroads, improving efficiency and reducing costs for both passenger and freight systems. There is a lot of potential in the subway; unlike most other metro systems that are double-tracked, the New York City system has numerous triple—and quadruple—tracked lines, which are currently used to allow express trains to pass local trains but which could be used to even greater effect with more modern control systems (for example, to allow a super-express service that skips more stops).

3 It is also important to remember that the subway system provides service to neighborhoods that are currently underserved by taxis, and which would almost certainly be underserved by autonomous cars operated by competing, for-profit companies. The most profitable places to serve will be in the city center where there are always people waiting to ride the vehicles; but the people most in need of subway service tend to live far from the city center, and to pick them up the vehicles will be forced to make long and unprofitable trips without passengers, just like subway trains. The reason the government took over the subway and commuter railroads was to maintain a vital but unprofitable service.

My Notes

Benjamin Kreuter
Jersey City, N.J.

Several readers responded on Facebook:

Isaac Brumer wrote: For all its problems, the NYC transit system is not "beyond repair." It safely serves millions of people every day, 24/7. How will those people get around while you're ripping out the tracks, repairing the tunnels, then retrofitting them for the transportation system you've dreamed up? And all transportation systems need costly maintenance over time. Does the author believe the new system will be maintenance-free?

Andrea Abarca Coutts wrote: What ever happened to all the flying cars and buses I was promised by movies and TV? Eight year old me definitely thought we'd be hovering around cities by now.

Peter Wayner replies:

1   Mr. Zerr and Mr. Kreuter make the same mistake that many do by assuming that the autonomous vehicles will flow like human-driven cars. Consider as a thought experiment a line of hoverboards a mile long with 10 feet of empty space behind each one. That's 528 people. If they move 15 miles an hour, the tunnel will carry 7,290 people per hour.

2   Hoverboards are slim and we can slice the tunnel into three, four, or maybe five lanes and carry 23,760, 31,680 or 39,600 people per hour. Thinner lanes are a big advantage because a mishap or planned maintenance in one slim lane wouldn't block everything. That speaks to Mr. Brumer's point.

3   Interested readers can repeat the same experiment with two lanes of five-foot-wide autonomous cars spaced 20 feet apart, carrying four passengers and going 30 miles an hour. These can offer airbags and other safety features missing from trains. These are just two hypothetical models that could deliver the same throughput as the one train—when it can follow its official rush hour schedule of approximately sixteen trains per hour.

4   Why can these autonomous vehicles compete with one train that can carry 2,000 people? Local trains need large gaps because the stops take so long. Autonomous vehicles will stop only at their destination, when they zip out of the flow. They can use the large gap.

5   As to Mr. Kreuter's point about the outer boroughs, the competing fleets may still be owned by the city or heavily regulated. We can have both plenty of choices and a differential pricing model with room to help whomever the politicians favor.

6   I agree that we need to sweat many details, but there's plenty of opportunity. The hoverboards might zip over to the next line or carry the passenger to the street. The corridors and roads upstairs are fair game. They could give the handicapped more time to board than the subway at rush hour.

My Notes

7   There's also plenty of room. The platforms are 600 feet long and Disney loads their rides in much less space.

8   And there's also plenty of budget. We're already being asked to shoulder a $19 billion bill. We can either redesign the signaling and everything else for the last generation or aim for the future.

Making Observations

- Based on words and phrases you highlighted in Letters 1 and 2, how does each writer feel about Peter Wayner's proposal?
- Which letter to the editor do you respond to most strongly?

Returning to the Text

- Return to the letters as you respond to the following questions. Use text evidence to support your responses.
- Write any additional questions you have about the text in your Reader/Writer Notebook.

1. Based on paragraph 1 of Patrick Zerr's letter to the editor, what is his purpose for writing?

_____

_____

_____

_____

2. Summarize the evidence that Zerr provides in paragraphs 3 and 4 to rebut Wayner's proposal.

_____

_____

_____

_____

3. How does Zerr conclude his letter? Is it convincing?

_____

_____

_____

_____

4. In the second letter, Kreuter compares Wayner to Robert Moses. What is the effect of this comparison?

_____

_____

_____

_____

5. Summarize Wayner's claim that Kreuter rebuts in paragraph 2. What reasoning and evidence does Kreuter present in his rebuttal?

_____

_____

_____

_____

6. What is the rebuttal Isaac Brumer is making in this Facebook post?

_____

_____

_____

_____

7. Describe the tone Peter Wayner uses to respond to the letters to the editor. Cite examples of diction and syntax in your response.

_____

_____

_____

_____

8. What is Wayner's purpose for including paragraph 6?

_____

_____

_____

_____

Exploring Additional Letters to the Editor

9. Your teacher will provide an editorial and several letters written in response to the editorial. Fill in the chart for each of the letters to the editor. The last box is for your opinion on the editorial.

Letter Number	Agree or Disagree with Original Editorial?	Reasons/Evidence
1		
2		

Letter Number	Agree or Disagree with Original Editorial?	Reasons/Evidence
3		
4		
Your Opinion		

☑ Check Your Understanding

Quickwrite: Which of the letters to the editor makes the strongest argument? What makes that argument compelling?

_____

_____

_____

_____

_____

✒ Writing Prompt: Argumentative

Write a letter to the editor in response to one of the editorials you have read in this unit. Use the steps outlined in the How to Write a Letter to the Editor section to guide your writing. Be sure to:

- Utilize an organizational structure that follows the specifications of your local newspaper and logically sequences your claim, reasons, evidence, and response to counterclaims.
- Use a variety of rhetorical techniques, including anecdotes, case studies, or analogies.
- Provide a concluding statement that follows logically from your argument.

Fallacies 101

Learning Strategies

Discussion Groups
Graphic Organizer
Questioning the Text
Quickwrite
Rereading
Self-Editing

Learning Targets

- Analyze the effects of logical fallacies on the way a text is read and understood.
- Use logical fallacies and refute the fallacies of others in a debate.

Preview

In this activity, you will analyze news articles to test your knowledge of the logical fallacies that you learned about in Unit 2. As you spot these fallacies, you will determine their likely effect on the reader.

Identifying Fallacies

1. You will be given a set of card manipulatives, some of which will contain the names of specific types of fallacies and others of which will contain the definitions. In your small group, you will need to match the fallacies with their definitions.

2. Next, read through the following informational text and check your answers.

Types of Fallacies

Fallacies are commonplace in advertising, political discourse, and everyday conversations—and they will continue to be as long as they work to persuade.

By learning to recognize them when you see them, you can strip away their power. There are many different ways to categorize fallacies, and many different names for the various types. The following 11 fallacies (adapted from Brooke Noel Moore and Richard Parker's *Critical Thinking*, 8th ed., 2007) are divided into the different types of offense they represent. Learn these, and you'll be ready to see through many of the rhetorical scams that come your way each day.

A. Logical Fallacies: Errors in Reasoning

- **Hasty generalization:** The leap to a generalized conclusion based on only a few instances. For example, on a trip to Paris you meet several rude Parisians, leading you to conclude that French people are rude.

- **Post hoc:** Literally meaning "after this," it's a causal fallacy in which a person assumes one thing caused another simply because it happened prior to the other. For instance, the high school soccer team loses an important game the day after they start wearing new uniforms. The coach blames the loss on the new uniforms.

B. Emotive Fallacies: Replacing Logic with Emotional Manipulation

- **Ad populum:** Literally meaning "appeal to the people"; arguing that something is true because other people think so; refers to a variety of appeals that play on the association of a person or subject with values that are held by members of a target group (think of images of the flag in ads playing on patriotism) or the suggestion that "everybody knows" that something is true (as with bandwagoning).

My Notes

WORD CONNECTIONS

Foreign Words

Although the study of logic began in Ancient Greece, most terms used today for logical fallacies derive from Latin. Two terms frequently used in the names of logical fallacies are **post** ("after") and **ad** ("for" or "to"). Other words include:

antiquitatem = tradition

baculum = club (weapon)

hoc = this

hominem = person

ignorantium = ignorance

misericordiam = pity

populum = the people

ridiculum = ridicule

Because Latin forms the basis of so much of our own language, you can sometimes guess the English meanings of terms such as *populum, antiquitatem, ignorantium*, and *ridiculum* simply by looking at them closely.

My Notes

- **"Argument" from outrage:** Aristotle said that if you understand what makes a person angry, you can use that anger to persuade him or her to accept a position without critically evaluating it. This fallacy is the backbone of talk radio and of political rhetoric on both extremes of the political spectrum. It often employs loaded language and labels. It also includes scapegoating—blaming a certain group of people or even a single person.

- **Ad misericordiam, or appeal to pity:** If you have ever asked a teacher to give you a better grade or a second chance because things have been tough recently or because you worked so hard, you're guilty of this one! It refers to an attempt to use compassion or pity to replace a logical argument.

- **Ad baculum, or scare tactics:** An appeal to fear in place of logic. If a candidate for office says, "Electing my opponent will open the door for new terrorist attacks," it represents an attempt to scare people into rejecting the person despite providing no evidence to justify the claim.

C. Rhetorical Fallacies: Sidestepping Logic with Language

- **Straw man:** Erecting a distorted or exaggerated representation of a position that is easily refuted. For example, Schroth says, "But, you say, if high schools drop football it will deprive colleges and the pros of their feeder system," an argument that is, of course, a ridiculous attempt to justify high school football—and one that is thus easy to refute.

- **Ad hominem/genetic fallacy:** Literally meaning "to the man," ad hominem refers to attacks against a person himself- or herself rather than the ideas the person presents. This is a dominant feature in political campaigns, where sound-bite 30-second advertisements attack a candidate's character, often with mere innuendo, instead of his or her policy positions. When this extends to criticizing or rejecting a general type of something simply because it belongs to or was generated by that type, it is a genetic fallacy. For example, to say an idea comes from the "media elite" makes it sound like it should be rejected—but who are the media elite?

- **Red herring/smokescreen:** Answering the question by changing the subject. For example, when pulled over for speeding, a person might respond to the officer's question "Why were you speeding?" by saying, "The school no longer offers driver's education classes."

- **Slippery slope:** Half appeal to fear and half a causal fallacy, a person uses a slippery slope when they suggest one action will lead to an inevitable and undesirable outcome. To say legalizing voluntary euthanasia paves the way for forced euthanasia is a slippery slope argument.

- **Either/or (or false dilemma):** This is a conclusion that oversimplifies the argument by suggesting that there are only two possible sides or choices. It is very common in debates of policy, where issues are always complex but are reduced by politicians to simplistic binaries (either/or) for rhetorical purposes.

Analyzing the Effects of Fallacies

Review the editorials you have read in this unit. In the chart, list some logical fallacies from the editorials, the editorial in which you found each, and the fallacy's possible effect on the reader.

Editorial/Quote	Type of Logical Fallacy	Possible Effect
Potter: "[Sunstein's] worry is that if the newspaper declines, so might democracy."	straw man (nowhere in his editorial does Sunstein assert this) and slippery slope (decline of newspapers does not inevitably mean the decline of democracy)	The reader may be taken in by Potter's refutation of his misstatement of Sunstein's argument. By arguing how important newspapers are to democracy, the slippery slope may seem more likely.

Fallacy Face-Off

3. Now that you have been introduced to the concept of fallacious appeals, take up the challenge to use as many as possible in a **Fallacy Face-Off**. As a class, select a current, high-profile, controversial issue. Feel free to pull this topic from some of your recent newspaper readings. You will use this topic in a **mock debate**.

4. Next, split into teams. Each team member will select or be assigned a fallacious appeal to use regarding the selected topic.

5. When the teams are ready, they will use these fallacious appeals in a mock debate. Each team will take turns presenting their appeals to the class as if presenting at a public rally, televised debate, or other venue of the class's choosing.

6. As other teams present their arguments, you will be responsible for identifying and challenging the nature of the fallacy being used by the speaker. All discourse and interaction will be conducted courteously and respectfully. Be sure to evaluate each speaker's reasoning and use of evidence.

7. After exploring these fallacies in class, discuss the following questions with your team:

   • Why are fallacies so common in our political discourse? Which ones are most common, and why?

   • Why are fallacies so powerful—and so dangerous?

   • Why might you choose to use a fallacy—or rhetorical slanters—in a letter or speech? What would be the pros and cons of doing so?

   • How does the use of fallacies affect the ethos of a writer or speaker?

   • What is the relationship between considering your audience and deciding whether to use fallacious appeals or slanters?

   • How can a speaker or writer's use of fallacies influence an audience's sense of trust in their argument?

📝 Writing Prompt: Argumentative

Review the letter to the editor that you wrote in Activity 3.11 and revise it using at least one of the types of fallacies from this activity. Share your revision with a partner and ask him or her to identify the type of fallacy you used. Be sure to:

• Revise your letter to clearly state your position, if needed.

• Incorporate at least one fallacy into your letter.

• Prepare your letter in final draft, checking that it is grammatically and technically accurate. As needed, consult references to ensure that you are spelling and using words correctly.

How to Read and Write an Editorial Cartoon

Learning Strategies

Brainstorming
Sketching
Skimming/Scanning
Visualizing

Learning Targets

- Analyze the effectiveness of characteristics of editorial cartoons.
- Apply knowledge from this analysis to create an editorial cartoon.

Preview

In this activity, you will delve into the world of editorial cartoons. Once you have studied the genre and analyzed some examples, you will have an opportunity to create your own cartoon.

As You Read

- Circle unknown words and phrases. Try to determine the meaning of the words by using context clues, word parts, or a dictionary.
- Put a question mark next to anything that raises a question for you.
- Put an exclamation point next to anything that you have a strong response to or surprises you.

Informational Text

An Inside Look at Editorial Cartoons

by **Bill Brennen**

1   A few weeks ago, Joy Utecht, the journalism teacher at Grand Island Senior High, asked if I could visit with some of her students about editorial cartoons.

2   The invitation was exciting because editorial cartoons are one of my favorite subjects. Very few items are as unique to a newspaper as editorial cartoons.

3   A very brief history lesson: Editorial cartoons first appeared in the United States on single-page broadsheets during the colonial times. The first popular cartoon is a snake severed into 13 parts with the names of each colony by each piece. The caption is simple, "Divided we die."

4   Such a theme helped the colonies, with their diverse locations and interests, unite under a common cause.

5   Flash forward to the years in New York City after the Civil War, when Tammany Hall[1] became such a powerful political machine that it nearly sucked the life out of its residents. In addition, William Tweed stole millions from the taxpayers.

My Notes

WORD CONNECTIONS

Etymology
Broadsheets, also called *broadsides*, were originally large pieces of paper printed on one side, often used for announcements. They later evolved into the modern newspaper. Newspapers considered broadsheets are larger and tend to cover serious stories, as opposed to *tabloids*, which are smaller and tend to cover more sensational stories.

---

[1] Tammany Hall was the name given to the Democratic political machine that dominated New York City politics from the 1790s until the 1960s.

6   Eventually, *The New York Times* and eventually law enforcement officials began investigations of the Tweed Ring, but it was the powerful cartoons of Nast that brought the politicians to their knees. At one point, Nast, who worked for *Harper's Weekly*, turned down a bribe of $500,000 to discontinue his cartoons.

7   Instead, Nast made Tweed the most recognizable face in America. When Tweed tried to flee conviction, he was arrested in Spain, because authorities recognized his face from Nast's cartoons.

8   By the way, Nast deserves partial credit for another icon, one that has stood the test of time. Along with an artist named Clement Moore, Nast drew the first Santa Claus.

9   Photography became a part of American newspapers and magazines as early as the Civil War, but the process was difficult and illustrations remained a part of American newspapers until early into the 20th Century.

10   But the sketches known as editorial cartoons are as popular today as they ever have been. People love the humor, simplicity and caricatures of politicians of the day. Caricatures, I told the students at Senior High, are exaggerations of one's physical features.

11   In recent years, there have been the JFK haircut, the LBJ ears, the Nixon eyebrows, the Carter teeth and the Clinton jaw. Of course, each cartoonist has his or her own style, but it is amazing how they reach out to the same features to identify a politician.

12   A good editorial cartoon must have five basic features.

   • It must be simple. ...

   • People must understand it. The cartoon must make sense to those who read the particular paper. A school newspaper might run a cartoon about cafeteria food that includes an inside joke and isn't readily understood by the general public. The cartoon would only make sense in the school newspaper.

   • The cartoon must be timely. ...

   • It must evoke emotion. A good cartoon should make people laugh or make them mad.

   • Always, the cartoon must give a point of view. The cartoon may be looking at the truth, but it usually is coming from a specific viewpoint. When we look down at an object, the viewpoint is very different when we look up at the object. Editorial cartoons are the same way.

13   The *Independent* doesn't always agree with the viewpoint of each cartoon in the paper. Most certainly the readers don't always agree with them. But we all should agree that political cartoons are thought provoking. Just like a photograph, a well-illustrated editorial cartoon can be worth a thousand words.

14 There probably are about 100 newspapers, give or take a few, that employ full-time cartoonists. Unfortunately, it is a luxury that only metropolitan-sized newspapers can afford. Smaller newspapers subscribe to syndicated features for the right to reprint some of the better cartoons that have been published.

15 The next time you look at an editorial cartoon in the newspaper, try to look at it a new way. Instead of thinking about just whether you agree or disagree with the message, see if the cartoons have the five basic components to it[*sic*]. Then you can determine whether the message is getting through.

Making Observations

- What print features did you notice in the text?
- Based on your question marks and exclamation points, what most surprises or interests you in the text?

Returning to the Text

- Return to the informational text as you respond to the following questions. Use text evidence to support your responses.
- Write any additional questions you have about the text in your Reader/Writer Notebook.

1. What details in paragraphs 5–7 indicate that editorial cartoons can be agents of change?

_____

_____

_____

_____

_____

2. What are some questions you might research in preparation for an informational report on editorial cartoons?

_____

_____

_____

_____

_____

3. What explanation is given in paragraphs 10–12 for why photographs have never replaced editorial cartoons?

_____

_____

_____

_____

_____

Reading Editorial Cartoons

4. Because there is so little space for an editorial cartoonist to make his or her point, the cartoonist often uses symbols and allusions as shorthand for the meaning of the cartoon. Examine each of the cartoons your teacher supplies and identify the symbols and allusions. Why might the cartoonist have chosen these symbols or allusions?

5. What is there about editorial cartoons that make them particularly suited to publication in newspapers?

6. Most editorial cartoons present a specific political perspective. Do the cartoons you are examining have an identifiable point of view? Examine and describe the author's use of print and graphic features in expressing his or her perspective.

7. Editorial cartoons are designed to evoke emotion—humor, anger, or outrage, for example. What emotions are evoked in the cartoons you are analyzing?

8. Based on your responses to the other questions here, what does the messages of your assigned cartoons seem to be, and what can you infer about their intended purpose?

Creating Your Own Editorial Cartoons

9. Now that you have had some experience reading and analyzing political cartoons, try to create some of your own.

   • Brainstorm topic ideas by thinking about current events in your school, your hometown, or the world. List a few ideas.

   • Choose one of your ideas and describe a point that you might want to make about that event. Perhaps you agree and want to show your support, or perhaps you would like to ridicule those who might feel differently.

   • What symbols, sayings, pop culture allusions, or other easily recognizable references might be appropriate for this topic?

   • Sketch a very rough draft of what your cartoon might look like.

Independent Reading Checkpoint

Review your self-selected news source. Which articles have you read? Create a portfolio of these articles by printing copies or writing brief summaries. Add commentary after each article, including the writer's claim or topic, a description of rhetorical organization or strategies, and an analysis of effectiveness.

Creating an Op-Ed News Project

 ASSIGNMENT

Working in groups, your assignment is to plan, develop, write, revise, and present an informational article on a timely and debatable issue of significance to your school community, your local community, or a national audience. After your group completes its article, you will individually develop a variety of editorial products that reflect your point of view (agreement, alternative, or opposing) on the topic. Be creative with your editorial products and include at least two different pieces, such as cartoons, editorials, letters, posters, photos, and so on.

Planning and Prewriting: Take time to plan all the texts that you will include.	■ How can you build a list of potential issues that are both interesting to your group and debatable and timely? ■ What format will your opinion pieces take (e.g., editorials by newspaper staff, letters to the editor, editorial cartoon)? ■ How will you split the various tasks and roles among your group members so that everyone is doing a fair amount of work?
Drafting: Decide how you will incorporate support and organize texts.	■ How will you gather evidence to support your positions? ■ How can you use models of argumentative writing from this unit to help you add rhetorical elements that will appeal to your audience? ■ What sort of organizational patterns do the kinds of pieces you are writing tend to follow? How can you emulate these so that your pieces read like a real informational or editorial publication?
Evaluating and Revising: Create opportunities to review and revise.	■ What sort of strategies can you use to provide feedback to each other on the quality of your pieces (e.g., SMELL, SOAPSTone)? ■ What kinds of feedback from peers and the Scoring Guide can help guide your revision? ■ How will you ensure that your product as a whole represents multiple perspectives on your topic?
Checking and Editing for Publication: Be sure your work is the best it can be.	■ How can you use examples of either print or online newspapers to create a realistic layout for your articles? ■ How will you check your own or each other's work for grammatical and technical accuracy? What references will you consult?

Reflection

After completing this Embedded Assessment, think about how you went about accomplishing the assignment, and respond to the following:

- How do newspapers affect public opinion or public perception?
- Which of the rhetorical techniques that your group used do you think were the most effective in appealing to your audience? Why?

SCORING GUIDE

Scoring Criteria	Exemplary	Proficient	Emerging	Incomplete
Ideas	The project • explicitly represents multiple and varied editorial perspectives • is extremely persuasive throughout every piece, demonstrating a thorough understanding of persuasive techniques • provides evidence of thorough and original research throughout; each piece demonstrates appropriate and ample evidence to support the thesis.	The project • represents various perspectives that are implied throughout the work as a whole • demonstrates a clear intention to persuade in most pieces, showing an adequate understanding of persuasive techniques • demonstrates that research has been conducted to support the positions; the majority of pieces demonstrate sufficient evidence supporting the thesis.	The project • represents a limited range of perspectives • demonstrates an intention to persuade in a few of the pieces; some of the pieces may be descriptive or expository rather than persuasive • demonstrates that some research has been conducted to support the positions with lapses in completeness to adequately support the thesis.	The project • lacks a range of perspectives • offers pieces that may be descriptive or expository rather than persuasive • does not demonstrate adequate research; the majority of the pieces demonstrate insufficient evidence to adequately support the thesis and/or opinions remain unsupported.
Structure	The project • is organized exceptionally, so that ideas move smoothly and comfortably • accurately follows the organizational pattern of the article type, whether informational or editorial.	The project • is organized in a way that is clear and easy to follow • largely follows the organizational pattern of the article type, whether informational or editorial.	The project • is unevenly organized with lapses in coherence • attempts to follow the organizational pattern of the article type, whether informational or editorial, with some lapses.	The project • is difficult to follow and may jump too rapidly between ideas • struggles to follow the organizational pattern of the article type, whether informational or editorial.
Use of Language	The project • demonstrates purposeful use of rhetoric designed to appeal to the target audience(s) • contains few or no errors in grammar or conventions.	The project • demonstrates functional use of rhetoric but may not directly appeal to the target audience • may include minor errors in grammar and conventions that do not interfere with understanding.	The project • attempts to use rhetoric with limited appeal to the target audience • includes some errors in grammar and conventions that interfere with the meaning.	The project • inconsistently demonstrates rhetoric • includes many errors in grammar and conventions that seriously interfere with the meaning.

Previewing Embedded Assessment 2 and Introducing Satire

Learning Targets

- Reflect on concepts, Essential Questions, and vocabulary.
- Identify and analyze the knowledge and skills needed to complete Embedded Assessment 2 successfully.
- Generate examples of satirical writing.

Preview

In this activity, you will review the Essential Questions, preview the assignments for Independent Reading and Embedded Assessment 2, and learn about the literary genre of satire.

Making Connections

The op-ed page is an important forum for the exchange of ideas in our society, but the conversation does not stop there. Not everyone who contributes to the conversation means exactly what they say. Satire may be the tool of choice for some writers (and cartoonists) who prefer to use irony and a range of tones to make statements about the issues of the day. If you have ever enjoyed watching late-night comedy shows, you know how effective—and how much fun—this approach can be when it comes to changing perception of the subjects being lampooned. Immersing yourself in the art of satire, you will explore how writers use a range of genres and techniques to present their messages in indirect ways. In this way, satirists can make powerful contributions to the marketplace of ideas.

Essential Questions

Based on your study of the first part of the unit, review and revise your answers to the Essential Questions.

1. What is the role of media in our society, and how can we become responsible consumers and producers of information in a digital age?

2. How can writers use satire to bring about change in society?

Unpacking Embedded Assessment 2

Closely read the assignment for Embedded Assessment 2: Writing a Satirical Piece.

You have been studying how opinions are expressed and perceived in a democratic society through a variety of rhetorical formats including satire. Your assignment is to develop a satirical piece critiquing some aspect of our society.

In your own words, summarize what you will need to know to complete this assessment successfully. With your class, create a graphic organizer to represent the skills and knowledge you will need to complete the tasks identified in the Embedded Assessment.

My Notes

My Notes

🗂 Planning Independent Reading

In this unit, you will have the opportunity to further explore the entertaining genre of satire. Satire is a poplar genre for news outlets, television shows, and websites. Many famous works of literature utilize satire as well. Satire is an entertaining way for readers to critically analyze a topic, often in a humorous way.

Collaborate with peers to discuss satirical authors and texts. Include both modern and historical texts and authors. Based on this discussion, compile a list of works for independent reading based on your interests.

3. As you read the following text, use your metacognitive markers to indicate anything that provokes a question (?), anything about which you wish to comment or make a connection (*), and anything you find surprising (!). Be prepared to discuss your response.

Introduction to Satire

Satire is a literary genre that uses irony, wit, and sometimes sarcasm to expose humanity's vices and foibles, giving impetus to change or reform through ridicule. Types of direct satire include Horatian satire and Juvenalian satire, named after the Roman writers Horace and Juvenal, who made the genre famous. As you read satire, look for these characteristic techniques of satiric writing.

Irony: A mode of expression that uses words (verbal irony) or events (situational irony) to convey a reality different from and usually opposite to appearance or expectation. The surprise recognition by the audience often produces a comic effect. When a text intended to be ironic is not seen as such, the effect can be disastrous. To be an effective piece of sustained irony, there must be some sort of audience tip-off through style, tone, use of clear exaggeration, or other device.

Hyperbole: Deliberate exaggeration to achieve an effect; overstatement.

Litotes: A form of understatement that involves making an affirmative point by denying its opposite. Example: "The grave's a fine and private place, / But none, I think, do there embrace." (Andrew Marvell, "To His Coy Mistress")

Caricature: An exaggeration or other distortion of an individual's prominent features or characteristics to the point of making that individual appear ridiculous. The term is applied more often to graphic representations than to literary ones.

Wit: Most commonly understood as clever expression—whether aggressive or harmless, that is, with or without derogatory intent toward someone or something in particular. We also tend to think of wit as being characterized by a mocking or paradoxical quality, evoking laughter through apt phrasing.

Sarcasm: Intentional derision, generally directed at another person and intended to hurt. The term comes from a Greek word meaning "to tear flesh like dogs" and signifies a cutting remark. Sarcasm usually involves obvious verbal irony, achieving its effect by jeeringly stating the opposite of what is meant so as to heighten the insult.

VOCABULARY

LITERARY

Satire is a manner of writing that mixes a critical attitude with wit and humor in an effort to improve humankind and human institutions. Editorial cartoons are often rather satirical. You will learn more about satire in the second half of this unit.

Horatian satire pokes fun at human foibles and folly with a witty, gentle, and even indulgent tone.

Juvenalian satire denounces, sometimes harshly, human vice and error in dignified and solemn tones.

WORD CONNECTIONS

Roots and Affixes

Denounce begins with the Latin prefix *de-*, which means "remove from" or "do the opposite of." The root of *denounce* is from the Latin *nuntiare,* meaning "to report." Adding *de-* creates the meaning of reporting in a negative way. Determine the meaning of derision using the meaning of the Latin prefix *de-* and the Latin root *ride ̄re,* meaning "to laugh."

Ridicule: Words intended to belittle a person or idea and arouse contemptuous laughter. The goal is to condemn or criticize by making the thing, idea, or person seem laughable and ridiculous.

Parody: An imitation of a work or of an author with the idea of ridiculing the author, ideas, or work. The parodist exploits the peculiarities of an author's expression: his or her propensity to use too many parentheses, certain favorite words, or other elements of the author's style.

Invective: Speech or writing that abuses, denounces, or attacks. It can be directed against a person, cause, idea, or system. It employs a heavy use of negative emotive language. Example: "I cannot but conclude the bulk of your natives to be the most pernicious race of little odious vermin that nature ever suffered to crawl upon the surface of the earth." (Jonathan Swift, *Gulliver's Travels*)

Characteristics of Satire Poster

Create a poster that includes text and visual elements to illustrate the different types of satire explained in the Introduction to Satire section. You may create your own examples or use examples from books, newspapers, or other print or online publications. Present your poster to the class.

My Notes

Identifying the Elements of Satire

Learning Strategies

Diffusing
Marking the Text
Quickwrite

My Notes

Learning Targets

- Analyze the author's message embedded in the satire.
- Evaluate the author's use of satire to achieve a specific purpose.

Preview

In this activity, you will read a satirical article and analyze and explain the elements of satire in the article.

As You Read

- Highlight words, phrases, or sentences you find funny.
- Circle unknown words and phrases. Try to determine the meaning of the words by using context clues, word parts, or a dictionary.

About the Author

David Bouchier is a British writer who has lived in the United States since 1986. He has written fiction, nonfiction, commentaries, and humor columns for newspapers, literary journals, and magazines. He is also an award-winning essayist for National Public Radio.

Satire

Let's Hear It for the Cheerleaders

by **David Bouchier**

1   Strange things happen on college campuses in summer. I was nearly trampled to death the other day by a horde of very young women wearing very short red skirts and chanting something that sounded like "A fence! A fence!"

2   A fence might be a very good idea, perhaps with some razor wire and a warning sign saying "Danger: Cheerleaders Ahead." Long Island is host to more than a dozen cheerleader camps. For the educationally gifted, Hofstra and Adelphi Universities even offer cheerleading scholarships ("Give me an A! Give me an A!").

3   But I think there is some intellectual work to be done here. Cheerleading needs a history, a philosophy and, above all, a more sophisticated theory of communications.

4   The cheerleading phenomenon is almost unknown in the rest of the world. British soccer fans do their own cheerleading, with a medley of traditional songs, bricks and bottles. In less civilized parts of the world, fans express their enthusiasm by running onto the field and beating up the opposing

eam. Only in America do we have professional partisans to do the jumping and yelling for us.

5   Strange as it may seem to foreigners, the cheerleading industry has many ardent supporters. It is said to build self-confidence, positive attitudes and a mysterious quality called spirit, which seems to involve smiling a lot. Cheerleading also teaches the value of teamwork, something that women have often despised in the past as a male excuse for mindless violence and idiotic loyalties. "Be 100 percent behind your team 100 percent of the time" is a slogan that would be heartily endorsed by Slobodan Milosevic, the Orange Order and the Irish Republican Army.

6   Young cheerleaders also acquire valuable practical skills: impossible balancing tricks, back flips and the brass lungs they will need for child raising or being heard at the departmental meeting. Above all, they learn to compete in hundreds of local and national events. Cheerleaders are clearly the corporate leaders and the political stars of the future.

7   Cheerleader culture is much broader and shallower than I had imagined. There are glossy magazines and webzines featuring the essential equipment: deodorants, contact lenses, Cheer Gear, makeup, party dresses and miracle diets. Novices can learn how to create a successful cheer routine with hot music, unique moves, fab formations, and multiple levels. They can also learn to make their own pom poms (called just "Poms"). There are international stars out there you've never heard of, and even a few anonymous muscular cheerleading males, whose job it is to support the base of the feminine pyramid.

8   Despite cheerleaders' obsession with pyramids, my research suggests that cheerleading began in ancient Greece, rather than in Egypt. The first cheerleaders were called Maenads, female attendants of the god Bacchus. Their task was to encourage the crowds to have a good time, with frenzied rites and extravagant gestures. The opposing squad, the Furies, were merciless goddesses of vengeance who would swing into violent action if their team was losing. The ancient Greeks must get the credit for being the first to give young women these important career opportunities.

9   So many teams were decimated by the Furies or led astray by the Maenads that cheerleading fell into disrepute for 2,000 years, until it was revived in a kinder, gentler form in the United States. But it's still a dangerous activity. In an average year, high school footballers lose 5.6 playing days to injuries, according to the January 1998 Harper's Index, a compilation of statistics. Cheerleaders lose 28.8 days. These accidents are blamed on excessive acrobatics and the passion for building taller and taller pyramids.

10   But all enthusiasm is dangerous, especially when it takes a physical form. If cheerleading is part of education, let's use it to educate by focusing on the message. Surely we can do better than waving our poms, doing somersaults and chanting:

novices: beginners
compilation: collection

My Notes

Champs take it away

Now Play by Play

Move that ball

Win win win.

11 Let's face it, this is not exactly a stellar example of the sophisticated use of the English language. To reduce the risk of injury and make the sport more educational and less distracting for the fans, I propose to substitute verbal skills for physical high jinks. Routines should become more static, and chants should become more grammatical, more literary and more **conducive** to the kinder, gentler society we all hope for in the next century.

Why don't you fellows

Pick up that ball

And move it carefully

To the other end of the field?

12 If we really want to teach good social values, let's chant this famous verse from Grantland Rice:

For when the one great Scorer comes

To write against your name

He writes not that you won or lost

But how you played the game.

13 Now there's a catchy message for the millennium!

14 And why not bring that youthful spirit and those brilliant visuals out of the stadium and into the workplace? Cheerleaders should be in every office, with a chant for every corporate game. In a lawyer's office, for example, a spirited cry of "Rule of Law! Rule of Law! Sue! Sue! Sue!" accompanied by some eyepopping dance steps, would give courage and purpose to desk-bound drones. On Wall Street, a simple chant of "Go Greenspan! Low Interest! Never mind the Asians!" would create a positive environment for investment. And cheerleaders would share their boundless enthusiasm with the rest of us who, in the game of life, so often find ourselves on the losing team.

Making Observations

- Based on words or phrases you highlighted, which ones do you find funny?
- What new words do you find unfamiliar?

conducive: likely to bring about

eturning to the Text

Return to the satire as you respond to the following questions. Use text evidence to support your responses.

Write any additional questions you have about the text in your Reader/Writer Notebook.

1. In paragraph 1, what information does the reader understand that Bouchier's persona does not? What is the effect on the tone of the text?

2. In paragraph 5, what rhetorical devices does the author use to shape the readers' perception of cheerleading? What effects do these rhetorical devices have?

3. What are two examples of Bouchier's use of diction to create a specific tone in paragraph 7? Is the author successful in creating the desired tone?

4. What does Bouchier parody in paragraph 11? For what purpose does the author include the parody?

5. For what purpose does the author write this satire about cheerleading? Is the author successful in achieving this purpose?

_____

_____

_____

_____

_____

Working from the Text

6. Use the graphic organizer to identify the type of satire used in each quote. Then analyze and evaluate the purpose of each quote. An example has been provided to get you started.

Satirical Passage	Type of Satire	Purpose
"I was nearly trampled to death the other day by a horde of very young women…"	hyperbole	successfully builds humor and sets tone
"The opposing squad, the Furies, were merciless goddesses of vengeance who would swing into violent action if their team was losing."		
"… the brass lungs they will need for child raising or being heard at the departmental meeting.		
"Why don't you fellows Pick up that ball And move it carefully To the other end of the field?"		

☑ Check Your Understanding

Quickwrite: In your Reader/Writer Notebook, explain how Dave Bouchier's article fits the definition of satire. Support your answer with evidence from the text.

Determining the Meaning of Unknown Words

When you are reading a text and find a word you do not know, there are several ways to determine the word's meaning.

First of all, look for **context clues** and use the reading strategy of diffusing. What meanings and **connotations** do surrounding words and sentences provide?

> Example: What does the word *ardent* mean in the following text?

> The cheerleading industry has many **ardent** supporters. It is said to build self-confidence, positive attitudes, and a mysterious quality called spirit, which seems to involve smiling a lot. Cheerleading also teaches the value of teamwork, something that women have often despised in the past as a male excuse for mindless violence and idiotic loyalties. "Be 100 percent behind your team 100 percent of the time" is a slogan that would be heartily endorsed by Slobodan Milosevic, the Orange Order and the Irish Republican Army.

Here, *ardent* is clearly modifying *supporters*. The second sentence tells you that people believe many good things about cheerleading, so you can probably tell that *ardent* means "enthusiastic" or "passionate." But you need to analyze the connotation of the word to properly analyze the author's word choice. The paragraph goes on to shed a negative light on other people and organizations who had "ardent" supporters. Because of this, the imagery and connotations created here are of supporters who are frenzied and blindly support the cause.

☑ Check Your Understanding

Read the following text and use context clues to determine the meaning of *brass*.

> Young cheerleaders also acquire valuable practical skills: impossible balancing tricks, back flips and the **brass** lungs they will need for child raising or being heard at the departmental meeting.

First, jot notes based on context clues. Then look up the word in a good dictionary or dictionary of usage. What was the word's original, literal meaning? Is it still used that way? What connotations and imagery are created by the word's use in this context?

7. Based on your observations, place the text on the continuum. Be prepared to justify your answer.

1 —— 2 —— 3 —— 4 —— 5 —— 6 —— 7 —— 8 —— 9 —— 10
Horatian   **Juvenalian**

Analyzing Satirical Cartoons

Learning Strategies

Discussion Groups
Graphic Organizer
Think-Pair-Share

My Notes

Learning Targets

- Analyze cartoons for satirical content and techniques.
- Compare and contrast cartoons to determine purposes for satire.

Preview

In this activity, you will analyze cartoons for their satirical content and techniques.

Setting a Purpose for Viewing

1. You may want to review the satirical techniques you already know as you examine the cartoon. How does the visual content contribute to the cartoon's overall tone? As you examine the cartoon, consider the following questions and record your answers.

   - What elements of satire are present in the cartoon? _____
   _____

   - What is the implied message of the artist? _____
   _____

   - Is the cartoon effective in presenting the implied message? _____
   _____

   - Where does the cartoon fit in the Horatian to Juvenalian continuum? Justify your placement. _____
   _____

About the Author

Jen Sorensen (b. 1974) is an American cartoonist and illustrator. Her cartoons appear in alternative newsweeklies around the country, including her local paper, *The Austin Chronicle*. In 2014, she became the first woman to win the Herblock Prize, and in 2017 she was named a Pulitzer Prize finalist in Editorial Cartooning. The cartoon featured in this activity was part of the submission that made her a finalist. The cartoon was created in response to the public health disaster in Flint, Michigan, where 100,000 residents were exposed to toxic water.

Editorial Cartoon

Analyzing Cartoons as a Group

Your teacher will assign you an additional cartoon to analyze with your group. Use the same questions as before to guide your viewing. Record your answers in your Reader/Writer Notebook.

> ## ✍ Writing Prompt: Informational
>
> Review the sample cartoons and consider the artist's purpose for satire in each cartoon. Then, in an essay, explain how each cartoon seeks to affect the reader's perception of the subject. Be sure to:
>
> - Introduce the artist's purpose in a topic statement.
> - Include concrete details and examples from the cartoon to support your claim.
> - Use precise language, including metaphor, simile, or analogy, to explain your ideas.

Learning Strategies

Drafting
Graphic Organizer
Marking the Text

My Notes

Learning Targets

- Explore the impact of ridicule on the reader's perception of a writer's subject.
- Analyze and evaluate the author's use of satire to achieve a specific purpose.
- Evaluate how the author's diction contributes to the tone of the text.

Preview

In this activity, you will read and analyze an article from the satirical publication *The Onion*. Then you will write a literary analysis that reviews the satirical techniques used in the article.

As You Read

- Highlight words, phrases, or sentences you find funny.
- Circle unknown words and phrases. Try to determine the meaning of the words by using context clues, word parts, or a dictionary.
- Put a star next to text that shows the author is parodying the form of a news article.

About the Author

The Onion calls itself "America's Finest News Source," and its motto, *Tu stultus es*, is Latin for "You are a fool/idiot." Once a print publication available in select Midwest cities, *The Onion* moved online and is now solely available online. Its history is steeped in being a satirical "news" source. It rarely breaks character and presents its satirical articles as if they were serious news content. *The Onion*'s satire reaches the "About" section of its website, where it touts that it "enjoys a daily readership of 4.3 trillion." (At last count, the world population was only about 7.4 billion.) For the uninformed, *The Onion* often fools readers who do not realize that it is a satirical publication.

INDEPENDENT READING LINK

Read and Discuss

Discuss with a group what one of your independent reading texts is satirizing. Discuss the author's purpose and the primary mode of the satire.

Satire

Girl Moved to Tears by Of Mice and Men Cliffs Notes

from The Onion

1 CHARLOTTESVILLE, VA—In what she described as "the most emotional moment" of her academic life, University of Virginia sophomore communications major Grace Weaver sobbed openly upon concluding Steinbeck's **seminal** work of American fiction *Of Mice And Men*'s Cliffs Notes early last week.

2 "This book has changed me in a way that only great literature summaries can," said Weaver, who was so shaken by the experience that she requested an extension on her English 229 essay. "The humanity displayed in the Character Flowchart really stirred something in me. And Lennie's childlike innocence was beautifully captured through the simple, ranch-hand slang words like 'mentally handicapped' and 'retarded.'"

3 Added Weaver: "I never wanted the synopsis to end."

4 Weaver, who formed an "instant connection" with Lennie's character-description paragraph, said she began to suspect the novel might end tragically after reading the fourth sentence which suggested the gentle giant's strength and fascination with soft things would "lead to his untimely **demise**."

5 "I was amazed at how attached to him I had become just from the critical **commentary**," said Weaver, still clutching the yellow-and-black-striped study guide. "When I got to the last sentence—'George shoots Lennie in the head'—it seemed so abrupt. But I found out later that the '**ephemeral** nature of life' is a major theme of the novel."

6 Weaver was assigned *Of Mice And Men*—a novel scholars have called "a masterpiece of **austere** prose" and "the most skillful example of American naturalism under 110 pages"—as part of her early twentieth-century fiction course, and purchased the Cliffs Notes from a cardboard rack at her local Barnes & Noble. John Whittier-Ferguson, her professor for the class, told reporters this was not the first time one of his students has expressed interest in the novel's plot summary.

7 "It's one of those universal American stories," said Ferguson after being informed of Weaver's choice to read the Cliffs Notes instead of the pocket-sized novel. "I look forward to skimming her essay on the importance of following your dreams and randomly assigning it a grade."

8 Though she completed the two-page brief synopsis in one sitting, Weaver said she felt strangely drawn into the plot overview and continued on, exploring the more fleshed-out chapter summaries.

GRAMMAR & USAGE

Dash

Writers use dashes to force readers to pay attention to a particular part of a sentence. A dash interrupts the flow of the sentence and signals for the reader to slow down and get ready for what he or she is going to read next. Dashes also tend to create more dramatic tension in a sentence than commas do.

Notice how the writer uses dashes effectively in this text to heighten the irony and humor. In paragraph 5, the writer sets the line *George shoots Lennie in the head* between dashes to emphasize the clash between what the student expects to read and what she is surprised to read.

Find another example in the text of a dash and practice saying the sentence aloud with a partner to note how the punctuation changes the pacing and emphasis of the sentence.

seminal: very original
demise: death
commentary: explanations
ephemeral: short-lived
austere: plain, simple

9 "There's something to be said for putting in that extra time with a good story," Weaver said. "You just get more out of it. I'm also going to try to find that book about rabbits that George was always reading to Lennie, so that I can really understand that important allusion."

10 Within an hour of completing the Cliffs Notes, Weaver was already telling friends and classmates that Steinbeck was her favorite author, as well as reciting select quotations from the "Important Quotations" section for their benefit.

11 "When I read those quotes, found out which characters they were attributed to, and inferred their context from the chapter outlines to piece together their significance, I was just blown away," said a teary-eyed Weaver. "And the way Steinbeck wove the theme of hands all the way through the section entitled 'Hands'—he definitely deserved to win that Nobel Prize."

12 Weaver's roommate, Giulia Crenshaw, has already borrowed the dog-eared, highlighted summary of the classic Depression-era saga, and is expecting to enjoy reading what Weaver described as "a really sad story about two brothers who love to farm."

13 "I loved this book so much, I'm going to read all of Steinbeck's Cliffs Notes," said Weaver. "But first I'm going to go to the library to check out the original version *Of Mice And Men* starring John Malkovich and Gary Sinise."

Making Observations
- What words, phrases, or sentences do you find funny?
- Based on the words you circled, which ones do you find confusing and have to look up?
- How does the headline set your expectations of the article's tone?

Returning to the Text

- Return to the satire as you respond to the following questions. Use text evidence to support your responses.
- Write any additional questions you have about the text in your Reader/Writer Notebook.

1. How does the authors' diction in paragraph 2 help establish the tone of the article?

_____

_____

_____

_____

_____

2. In paragraph 7, how does the author's use of the term *pocket-sized novel* shape the reader's opinion about people who choose to read Cliffs Notes?

_____

_____

_____

_____

_____

3. In paragraph 12, what is ironic about Weaver's description of the story? What is the purpose of this irony? Is the author successful in this use of irony?

_____

_____

_____

_____

_____

Working from the Text

4. Select three satirical words or phrases from the article. Identify the type of satire each quote uses and explain the purpose.

Satirical Passage	Type of Satire	Purpose

☑ Check Your Understanding

Is the tone of the piece objective or subjective?

🖉 Writing Prompt: Rhetorical Analysis

As a group, review the satirical techniques in Activity 3.14. Then write a group analysis of the author's purpose for writing the satire "Girl Moved to Tears by *Of Mice and Men* Cliffs Notes." Evaluate whether the author achieved the purpose. Be sure to:

- State the purpose of the satire in a topic statement. What is the author criticizing?
- Select relevant examples of satire from the text. Analyze and evaluate the purpose of each.
- Evaluate how the author's use of diction contributed to tone and shaped the perception of readers.
- Include a conclusion that summarizes your analysis and evaluation.

Writing a Parody

Learning Strategies

Drafting
Marking the Text
Oral Reading

Learning Targets

- Examine and evaluate how an author uses parody to critique a subject.
- Plan, compose, and publish an original parody of a mass-media program.

Preview

In this activity, you will read a parody by Dave Barry and create one of your own about some aspect of television programming.

Introducing Parody

Parody is a specific technique that imitates an author or a work for the purpose of humor. The parodist exploits the peculiarities of an author's expression or the characteristics of a typical format.

1. Based on your discussion of this definition, brainstorm a list of parodies you're familiar with. Think of popular music, television, movies, print sources, etc.

2. As you watch the news excerpt provided by your teacher, make a list of things in the show that might be ripe for parody. Think about the people you see, the show's style, the graphics used, the stories reported, etc., that are typical of this show and of news broadcasts in general.

As You Read

- Highlight words, phrases, or sentences you find particularly funny.
- Circle unknown words and phrases. Try to determine the meaning of the words by using context clues, word parts, or a dictionary.
- In the My Notes section, keep a running list of the different elements of television news shows Barry is parodying.

About the Author

Dave Barry (b. 1947) is a writer and journalist who made a career out of humorous writing. He wrote a weekly humor column for the *Miami Herald* for more than 20 years, but his work was syndicated around the country. Barry won a Pulitzer Prize for commentary in 1988 and is the only humor writer to win this prestigious award, given to him because of "his consistently effective use of humor as a device for presenting fresh insights into serious concerns."

My Notes

Parody

In Depth, but Shallowly

by **Dave Barry**

1   If you want to take your mind off the troubles of the real world, you should watch local TV news shows. I know of no better way to escape reality, except perhaps heavy drinking.

2   Local TV news programs have given a whole new definition to the word *news*. To most people, *news* means *information* about events that affect a lot of people. On local TV news shows, news means anything that you can take a picture of, especially if a local TV News Personality can stand in front of it. This is why they are so fond of accidents, burning buildings, and crowds: these are good for standing in front of.

3   On the other hand, local TV news shows tend to avoid stories about things that local TV News Personalities cannot stand in front of, such as budgets and taxes and the economy. If you want to get a local TV news show to do a story on the budget, your best bet is to involve it in a car crash.

4   I travel around the country a lot, and as far as I can tell, virtually all local TV news shows follow the same format. First you hear some exciting music, the kind you hear in space movies, while the screen shows local TV News Personalities standing in front of various News Events. Then you hear the announcer:

5   ANNOUNCER: From the On-the-Spot Action Eyewitness News Studios, this is the On-The-Spot Action Eyewitness News, featuring Anchorman Wilson Westbrook, Co-Anchor-person Stella Snape, Minority-Group Member James Edwards, Genial Sports Personality Jim Johnson, Humorous Weatherperson Dr. Reed Stevens, and Norm Perkins on drums. And now, here's Wilson Westbrook.

6   WESTBROOK: Good evening. Tonight from the On-the-Spot Action Eyewitness News Studios we have actual color film of a burning building, actual color film of two cars after they ran into each other, actual color film of the front of a building in which one person shot another person, actual color film of another burning building, and special reports on roller-skating and child abuse. But for the big story tonight, we go to City Hall, where On-the-Spot Reporter Reese Kernel is standing live.

7   KERNEL: I am standing here live in front of City Hall being televised by the On-the-Spot Action Eyewitness News minicam with Mayor Bryce Hallbread.

My Notes

8 MAYOR: That's "Hallwood."

9 KERNEL: What?

10 MAYOR: My name is "Hallwood." You said "Hallbread."

11 KERNEL: Look, Hallbread, do you want to be on the news or don't you?

12 MAYOR: Yes, of course, it's just that my name is—

13 KERNEL Listen, this is the top-rated news show in the three-county area, and if you think I have time to memorize every stupid detail, you'd better think again.

14 MAYOR: I'm sorry. "Hallbread" is just fine, really.

15 KERNEL: Thank you, Mayor Hallbread. And now back to Wilson Westbrook in the On-the-Spot Action Eyewitness News Studios.

16 WESTBROOK: Thank you, Reese; keep us posted if anything further develops on that important story. And now, as I promised earlier, we have actual color film of various objects that either burned or crashed, which we will project on the screen behind me while I talk about them. Here is a building on fire. Here is another building on fire. Here is a car crash. This film was shot years ago, but you can safely assume that objects just like these crashed or burned in the three-county area today. And now we go to my Co-Anchorperson, Stella Snape, for a Special Report on her exhaustive three-week investigation into the problem of child abuse in the three-county area. Well, Stella, what did you find?

17 SNAPE: Wilson, I found that child abuse is very sad. What happens is that people abuse children. It's just awful. Here you see some actual color film of me standing in front of a house. Most of your child abuse occurs in houses. Note that I am wearing subdued colors.

18 WESTBROOK (reading from a script): Are any efforts under way here in the three-county area to combat child abuse?

19 SNAPE: Yes.

20 WESTBROOK: Thank you, Stella, for that informative report. On the lighter side, On-the-Spot Action Eyewitness Reporter Terri Tompkins has prepared a three-part series on roller-skating in the three-county area.

21 TOMPKINS: Roller-skating has become a major craze in California and the three-county area, as you can see by this actual color film of me on roller skates outside the On-the-Spot Action Eyewitness News Studio. This certainly is a fun craze. Tomorrow, in Part Two of this series, we'll see actual color film of me falling down. On Wednesday we'll see me getting up.

22 WESTBROOK: We'll look forward to those reports. Our next story is from Minority-Group Reporter James Edwards, who, as he has for the last 324 consecutive broadcasts, spent the day in the minority-group sector of the three-county area finding out what minorities think.

23 EDWARDS: Wilson, I'm standing in front of a crowd of minority-group members, and as you can see, their mood is troubled. (*The crowd smiles and waves at the camera.*)

24 WESTBROOK: Good report, James. Well, we certainly had a sunny day here in the three-county area, didn't we, Humorous Weatherperson Dr. Reed Stevens?

25 STEVENS: Ha ha. We sure did, though I'm certainly troubled by that very troubling report Stella did on child abuse. But we should see continued warm weather through Wednesday. Here are a bunch of charts showing the relative humidity and stuff like that. Ha ha.

26 WESTBROOK: Ha ha. Well, things weren't nearly as bright on the sports scene, were they Genial Sports Personality Jim Johnson?

27 JOHNSON: No, Wilson, they certainly weren't. The Three-County Community College Cutlasses lost their fourth consecutive game today. Here you see actual color footage of me watching the game from the sidelines. The disgust is evident on my face. I intended to have actual color film of me interviewing the coach after the game, but the team bus crashed and everyone was killed.

28 WESTBROOK: Thank you, Jim. And now, here is Basil Holp, the General Manager of KUSP-TV, to present an Editorial Viewpoint:

29 HOLP: The management of KUSP-TV firmly believes that something ought to be done about earthquakes. From time to time we read in the papers that an earthquake has hit some wretched little country and knocked houses down and killed people. This should not be allowed to continue. Maybe we should have a tax or something. What the heck, we can afford it. The management of KUSP-TV is rolling in money.

30 ANNOUNCER: The preceding was the opinion of the management of KUSP-TV. People with opposing points of view are probably in the vast majority.

31 WESTBROOK: Well, that wraps up tonight's version of the On-the-Spot Action Eyewitness News. Tune in tonight to see essentially the same stories.

Making Observations

- Based on the list you created, what familiar elements of a television news show does Barry parody?
- How does the parody make you feel?

Returning to the Text

- Return to the parody as you respond to the following questions. Use text evidence to support your responses.
- Write any additional questions you have about the text in your Reader/Writer Notebook.

3. In paragraph 5, what is the purpose behind the titles and names of the imagined news team during the announcer's introduction? Does the author's choice of names and titles achieve that purpose?

_____

_____

_____

_____

4. During the exchange between Snape and Westbrook in paragraphs 17–20, what is Barry parodying with Stella Snape's report on child abuse? How does his choice of language shape the perception readers have on the way local news reports handle this kind of story?

_____

_____

_____

_____

_____

_____

5. In the exchange between Westbrook and Edwards in paragraphs 22–23, what evidence in Edwards's minority-group report reveals Barry's message regarding this type of report?

_____

_____

_____

_____

6. Near the end of the broadcast, how does Barry use hyperbole in Holp's editorial viewpoint to critique the practices of local TV news shows?

_____

_____

_____

_____

7. Does the author's choice to structure the text as a transcript of a new broadcast help or hurt the author's purpose? Explain your answer.

_____

_____

_____

_____

Working from the Text

8. Read the following lines of text from Barry's "In Depth, but Shallowly." Evaluate how each line of text informs or shapes the perception of readers.

Text	How Text Informs or Shapes Readers' Perception
KERNEL: Listen, this is the top-rated news show in the three-county area, and if you think I have time to memorize every stupid detail, you'd better think again.	
Here is a building on fire. Here is another building on fire. Here is a car crash. This film was shot years ago, but you can safely assume that objects just like these crashed or burned in the three-county area today.	
The Three-County Community College Cutlasses lost their fourth consecutive game today. Here you see actual color footage of me watching the game from the sidelines. The disgust is evident on my face.	

☑ Check Your Understanding

Rank Barry's satirical intent on the scale. Justify your ranking.

1 ——— 2 ——— 3 ——— 4 ——— 5 ——— 6 ——— 7 ——— 8 ——— 9 ——— 10

**Just plain silly
(Horatian)**

**Biting sarcasm/criticism
(Juvenalian)**

✐ Writing Prompt: Literary

Write a parody of some aspect of TV programming. Choose a partner and a subject (a genre like soap operas, sports broadcasts, reality shows, children's television programs or a specific show). Next, write your parody using the format of a script. Be sure to:

- Plan the tone, purpose, and audience by brainstorming and discussing with your partner.
- Organize your script in a way that best suits the purpose of your parody.
- Compose your script using appropriate formatting and grammar.
- Publish your finished script for your classmates to read.

Use the following questions as a basis for planning your parody.

Details: What images should you include? What images should you avoid? Put your subject in the middle of a circle, and then brainstorm a list of conventions and features that might be good parody material. Think about what things in the show are just a little annoying.

Tone/purpose: How critical should you be? Is it time for brutal sarcasm or playful wit? Is the show an offense to good taste or just a silly waste of time? Are you out to destroy or merely to tease?

Audience: How familiar is your audience with the show? What is their attitude toward the show? How will these answers affect what you should and should not do in your script? How will the use of irony, overt sarcasm, or ridicule affect your audience's response to your parody? You will present your script to your classmates in a reader's theater, so keep that audience in mind.

Organization: Focusing on the formulas of your subject, how should you start, develop, and end your script?

Diction: What patterns of speech can you identify that would be easy to parody? How stupid or cliché do you want to make your characters/personalities appear?

Syntax: What about the pacing of the script? Where should it read the most quickly? Where should the reader hang on every word? How can you accomplish this?

Need Some Advice?

Learning Targets

- Infer the meaning of a satire and evaluate details to understand key ideas.
- Examine and analyze how satirical techniques and syntax are used for comedic effect.
- Write a satirical lecture of advice using syntax for comedic effect.
- Integrate ideas from multiple texts to build knowledge and vocabulary about the art of satire.

Preview

In this activity, you will read a satirical essay by Mark Twain called "Advice to Youth."

As You Read

- Put a star next to any places where the text takes a surprising departure from where it seems to be going.
- Put a question mark next to any parts that you can tell are supposed to be funny but you don't quite get the joke.
- Circle unknown words and phrases. Try to determine the meaning of the words by using context clues, word parts, or a dictionary.

About the Author

Samuel Clemens, whose pen name was Mark Twain, was born in 1835 in Missouri. His most famous novel, *The Adventures of Huckleberry Finn*, caused a revolution in American literature. During his life, he was also famous for his humorous lectures, essays, and sayings.

KNOWLEDGE QUEST

Knowledge Question:

What makes satire effective? Across Activities 3.19 and 3.20, you will read two pieces of satire by the author Mark Twain. While you read and build knowledge about the topic, think about your answer to the Knowledge Question.

didactic: that teaches moral values

Satire

Advice to Youth

by **Mark Twain**

1   Being told I would be expected to talk here, I inquired what sort of talk I ought to make. They said it should be something suitable to youth—something didactic, instructive, or something in the nature of good advice. Very well. I have a few things in my mind which I have often longed to say for the instruction of the young; for it is in one's tender early years that such things will best take root and be most enduring and most valuable. First, then. I will say to you my young friends—and I say it beseechingly, urgingly—

2   Always obey your parents, when they are present. This is the best policy in the long run, because if you don't, they will make you. Most parents think they know better than you do, and you can generally make more by humoring that superstition than you can by acting on your own better judgment.

3   Be respectful to your superiors, if you have any, also to strangers, and sometimes to others. If a person offends you, and you are in doubt as to whether it was intentional or not, do not resort to extreme measures; simply watch your chance and hit him with a brick. That will be sufficient. If you shall find that he had not intended any offense, come out frankly and confess yourself in the wrong when you struck him; acknowledge it like a man and say you didn't mean to. Yes, always avoid violence; in this age of charity and kindliness, the time has gone by for such things. Leave dynamite to the low and unrefined.

4   Go to bed early, get up early—this is wise. Some authorities say get up with the sun; some say get up with one thing, others with another. But a lark is really the best thing to get up with. It gives you a splendid reputation with everybody to know that you get up with the lark; and if you get the right kind of lark, and work at him right, you can easily train him to get up at half past nine, every time—it's no trick at all.

5   Now as to the matter of lying. You want to be very careful about lying; otherwise you are nearly sure to get caught. Once caught, you can never again be in the eyes of the good and the pure, what you were before. Many a young person has injured himself permanently through a single clumsy and ill finished lie, the result of carelessness born of incomplete training. Some authorities hold that the young ought not to lie at all. That of course, is putting it rather stronger than necessary; still while I cannot go quite so far as that, I do **maintain**, and I believe I am right, that the young ought to be temperate in the use of this great art until practice and experience shall give them that confidence, elegance, and precision which alone can make the accomplishment graceful and profitable. Patience, diligence, painstaking attention to detail— these are requirements; these in time, will make the student perfect; upon these, and upon these only, may he rely as the sure foundation for future **eminence**. Think what tedious years of study, thought, practice, experience, went to the equipment of that **peerless** old master who was able to impose upon the whole world the lofty and sounding maxim that "Truth is mighty and will prevail"—the most majestic compound fracture of fact which any of woman born has yet achieved. For the history of our race, and each individual's experience, are sewn thick with evidences that a truth is not hard to kill, and that a lie well told is immortal. There is in Boston a monument of the man who discovered anesthesia; many people are aware, in these latter days, that that man didn't discover it at all, but stole the discovery from another man. Is this truth mighty, and will it prevail? Ah no, my hearers, the monument is made of hardy material, but the lie it tells will outlast it a million years. An awkward, feeble, leaky lie is a thing which you ought to make it your unceasing study to avoid; such a lie as that has no more real permanence than an average truth. Why, you might as well tell the truth at once and be done with it. A feeble, stupid, **preposterous** lie will not live two years—except it be a **slander** upon somebody. It is indestructible, then, of course, but that is no merit of yours. A final word: begin your practice of this gracious and beautiful art early— begin now. If I had begun earlier, I could have learned how.

maintain: declare strongly
eminence: success
peerless: without equal
preposterous: silly
slander: harmful statement
about someone

WORD CONNECTIONS

Roots and Affixes
The word **inestimable** is formed from the prefix *in-*, meaning "not"; the root *estim*, meaning "to value"; and the suffix *-able*, meaning "able to be." Thus, something *inestimable* is impossible to put a value on. The words *estimate* and *esteem* also derive from the same Latin root.

My Notes

6 Never handle firearms carelessly. The sorrow and suffering that have been caused through the innocent but heedless handling of firearms by the young! Only four days ago, right in the next farm house to the one where I am spending the summer, a grandmother, old and gray and sweet, one of the loveliest spirits in the land, was sitting at her work, when her young grandson crept in and got down an old, battered, rusty gun which had not been touched for many years and was supposed not to be loaded, and pointed it at her, laughing and threatening to shoot. In her fright she ran screaming and pleading toward the door on the other side of the room; but as she passed him he placed the gun almost against her very breast and pulled the trigger! He had supposed it was not loaded. And he was right—it wasn't. So there wasn't any harm done. It is the only case of that kind I ever heard of. Therefore, just the same, don't you meddle with old unloaded firearms; they are the most deadly and unerring things that have ever been created by man. You don't have to take any pains at all with them; you don't have to have a rest, you don't have to have any sights on the gun, you don't have to take aim, even. No, you just pick out a relative and bang away, and you are sure to get him. A youth who can't hit a cathedral at thirty yards with a Gatling gun in three quarters of an hour, can take up an old empty musket and bag his grandmother every time, at a hundred. Think what Waterloo would have been if one of the armies had been boys armed with old muskets supposed not to be loaded, and the other army had been composed of their female relations. The very thought of it makes one shudder.

7 There are many sorts of books; but good ones are the sort for the young to read. Remember that. They are a great, an inestimable and unspeakable means of improvement. Therefore be careful in your selection, my young friends; be very careful; confine yourselves exclusively to Robertson's Sermons, Baxter's Saint's Rest, The Innocents Abroad, and works of that kind.

8 But I have said enough. I hope you will treasure up the instructions which I have given you, and make them a guide to your feet and a light to your understanding. Build your character thoughtfully and painstakingly upon these **precepts**, and by and by, when you have got it built, you will be surprised and gratified to see how nicely and sharply it resembles everybody else's.

⌀ Knowledge Quest
- What lines do you find funny?
- What jokes do you not fully understand?

precepts: rules

Returning to the Text

- Return to the satire as you respond to the following questions. Use text evidence to support your responses.
- Write any additional questions you have about the text in your Reader/Writer Notebook.

1. **KQ** In paragraph 1, what does the word *nature* mean in context? What effect does it have on the tone?

_____

_____

_____

_____

2. How does Twain satirize typical advice about obeying one's parents in paragraph 2? How does this advice shape the reader's perception? Use text evidence to support your answer.

_____

_____

_____

_____

_____

_____

3. Does Twain successfully change the meaning of *get up with the lark* in paragraph 4 to create humor? Explain your answer.

_____

_____

_____

_____

4. Which words and phrases in paragraph 5 express the likelihood of learning to tell the perfect "immortal" lie? What is Twain's real message?

_____

_____

_____

_____

_____

_____

5. What is the effect of the paradox Twain presents in the line "A feeble, stupid, preposterous lie will not live two years—except it be a slander upon somebody. It is indestructible, then"?

_____

_____

_____

_____

6. How does the last sentence suggest Twain's purpose for the satire?

_____

_____

_____

_____

_____

_____

7. KQ How is Twain's use of satire effective?

_____

_____

_____

_____

Working from the Text

8. _Didactic_ (Greek, _didaktikos_: "apt at teaching") is a term often used to describe a speaker's or writer's tone when that speaker or writer is attempting to educate or inform an audience. Provide an example of textual evidence for why Twain's piece could be described as didactic.

☑ Check Your Understanding

Quickwrite: Where does "Advice to Youth" fall on the Horatian to Juvenalian continuum? Identify textual support to justify your answer.

LANGUAGE & WRITER'S CRAFT: Cumulative or Loose Sentence Patterns

Cumulative (or **loose**) sentences are a type of diction in which sentences have a main idea that is followed by a series of phrases that supply further details about a person, place, event, or idea. Writers tend to use this style of diction to establish an informal or conversational tone to their writing. Consider this example in which the main idea or clause is in italics followed by a series of phrases.

> "*We reached New York that morning* after a turbulent flight and some exciting experiences, tired but exhilarated, full of stories to tell our friends and neighbors."

In "Advice to Youth," Mark Twain uses cumulative sentences to establish a comedic tone. Notice how this works in the second sentence of his speech:

> "*They said it should be something suitable to youth*—something didactic, instructive, or something in the nature of good advice."

By listing out the "suitable" qualities that "they" suggest, Twain seems to wink knowingly at the audience in a conversational way. This establishes his desired comedic tone.

PRACTICE In the graphic, identify at least three pieces of advice Twain renders to his audience. Write the main clause in the first column. Then write the main or modifying phrase or clause in the second column. Finally, in the third column, evaluate how the loose sentence pattern affects the tone.

Main Clause 1	Main Clause 2 or Modifying Phrase/Clause	Effect on Meaning

Writing Prompt: Literary

Write your own lecture of advice to a particular audience. Use a RAFT to select a role for you to play and an audience to whom to impart your great wisdom about your topic. Be sure to:

- Select a topic that is specific to your audience.
- Use an appropriate format in which to deliver your message to your audience (e.g., an editorial, a letter, etc.) and follow the format's conventions.
- Use loose sentence patterns to create a humorous effect.

Learning Strategies

Graphic Organizer
Marking the Text
SOAPSTone

Learning Targets

- Compare and contrast two satirical texts and write responses that analyze the purpose of the satirical devices the authors use.
- Evaluate how an author's diction and syntax contribute to the tone.
- Integrate ideas from multiple texts to build knowledge and vocabulary about the art of satire.

Preview

In this activity, you will read another satirical piece by Mark Twain to analyze how the master of American humor used tone to appeal to an audience.

As You Read

- Highlight words, phrases, or sentences you find particularly funny.
- Identify and keep notes about the satirical techniques Twain uses.
- Circle unknown words and phrases. Try to determine the meaning of the words by using context clues, word parts, or a dictionary.

🧭 KNOWLEDGE QUEST

Knowledge Question:
What makes satire effective?

WORD CONNECTIONS

Word Relationships
The verb invoke, meaning "to ask for help," usually from a god, is derived from the Latin word *invocare*, meaning "to call." Other words based on *invocare* are *invoker*, *invocation*, and *invocatory*.

martial: military
sabers: heavy cavalry swords with curved blades
tumult: noise and confusion

Satire

The War Prayer

by **Mark Twain**

1 It was a time of great and exalting excitement. The country was up in arms, the war was on, in every breast burned the holy fire of patriotism; the drums were beating, the bands playing, the toy pistols popping, the bunched firecrackers hissing and spluttering; on every hand and far down the receding and fading spread of roofs and balconies a fluttering wilderness of flags flashed in the sun; daily the young volunteers marched down the wide avenue gay and fine in their new uniforms, the proud fathers and mothers and sisters and sweethearts cheering them with voices choked with happy emotion as they swung by; nightly the packed mass meetings listened, panting, to patriot oratory which stirred the deepest deeps of their hearts, and which they interrupted at briefest intervals with cyclones of applause, the tears running down their cheeks the while; in the churches the pastors preached devotion to flag and country, and invoked the God of Battles beseeching His aid in our good cause in outpourings of fervid eloquence which moved every listener. It was indeed a glad and gracious time, and the half dozen rash spirits that ventured to disapprove of the war and cast a doubt upon its righteousness straightway got such a stern and angry warning that for their personal safety's sake they quickly shrank out of sight and offended no more in that way.

2 Sunday morning came—next day the battalions would leave for the front; the church was filled; the volunteers were there, their young faces alight with **martial** dreams—visions of the stern advance, the gathering momentum, the rushing charge, the flashing **sabers**, the flight of the foe, the **tumult**, the

nveloping smoke, the fierce pursuit, the surrender! Then home from the war, bronzed heroes, welcomed, adored, submerged in golden seas of glory! With the volunteers sat their dear ones, proud, happy, and envied by the neighbors and friends who had no sons and brothers to send forth to the field of honor, there to win for the flag, or, failing, die the noblest of noble deaths. The service proceeded; a war chapter from the Old Testament was read; the first prayer was said; it was followed by an organ burst that shook the building, and with one impulse the house rose, with glowing eyes and beating hearts, and poured out that tremendous invocation—"God the all-terrible! Thou who ordainest! Thunder thy clarion and lightning thy sword!"

3   Then came the "long" prayer. None could remember the like of it for passionate pleading and moving and beautiful language. The burden of its supplication was, that an ever-merciful and benignant Father of us all would watch over our noble young soldiers, and aid, comfort, and encourage them in their patriotic work; bless them, shield them in the day of battle and the hour of peril, bear them in His mighty hand, make them strong and confident, invincible in the bloody onset; help them to crush the foe, grant to them and to their flag and country imperishable honor and glory—

4   An aged stranger entered and moved with slow and noiseless step up the main aisle, his eyes fixed upon the minister, his long body clothed in a robe that reached to his feet, his head bare, his white hair descending in a frothy cataract to his shoulders, his seamy face unnaturally pale, pale even to ghastliness. With all eyes following him and wondering, he made his silent way; without pausing, he ascended to the preacher's side and stood there waiting. With shut lids the preacher, unconscious of his presence, continued with his moving prayer, and at last finished it with the words, uttered in fervent appeal, "Bless our arms, grant us the victory, O Lord our God, Father and Protector of our land and flag!"

5   The stranger touched his arm, motioned him to step aside—which the startled minister did—and took his place. During some moments he surveyed the spellbound audience with solemn eyes, in which burned an uncanny light; then in a deep voice he said:

6   "I come from the Throne—bearing a message from Almighty God!" The words smote the house with a shock; if the stranger perceived it he gave no attention. "He has heard the prayer of His servant your shepherd, and will grant it if such shall be your desire after I, His messenger, shall have explained to you its import—that is to say, its full import. For it is like unto many of the prayers of men, in that it asks for more than he who utters it is aware of—except he pause and think.

7   "God's servant and yours has prayed his prayer. Has he paused and taken thought? Is it one prayer? No, it is two—one uttered, the other not. Both have reached the ear of Him Who heareth all supplications, the spoken and the unspoken. Ponder this—keep it in mind. If you would beseech a blessing upon yourself, beware! lest without intent you invoke a curse upon a neighbor at the same time. If you pray for the blessing of rain upon your crop which needs

supplication: plea
cataract: waterfall
smote: struck hard

_____

_____

_____

_____

_____

_____

_____

_____

_____

_____

_____

_____

_____

_____

_____

_____

_____

_____

_____

_____

_____

_____

INDEPENDENT READING LINK

Read and Respond

Select an independent reading text. Explain how the author's tone helps achieve a specific purpose and support your analysis with evidence from the text.

commissioned: assigned the task

unavailing: useless

protract: prolong

beset: troubled

contrite: remorseful or apologetic

it, by that act you are possibly praying for a curse upon some neighbor's crop which may not need rain and can be injured by it.

8 "You have heard your servant's prayer—the uttered part of it. I am **commissioned** of God to put into words the other part of it—that part which the pastor—and also you in your hearts—fervently prayed silently. And ignorantly and unthinkingly? God grant that it was so! You heard these words: 'Grant us the victory, O Lord our God!' That is sufficient. The whole of the uttered prayer is compact into those pregnant words. Elaborations were not necessary. When you have prayed for victory you have prayed for many unmentioned results which follow victory—must follow it, cannot help but follow it. Upon the listening spirit of God fell also the unspoken part of the prayer. He commandeth me to put it into words. Listen!

9 "O Lord our Father, our young patriots, idols of our hearts, go forth to battle—be Thou near them! With them—in spirit—we also go forth from the sweet peace of our beloved firesides to smite the foe. O Lord our God, help us to tear their soldiers to bloody shreds with our shells; help us to cover their smiling fields with the pale forms of their patriot dead; help us to drown the thunder of the guns with the shrieks of their wounded, writhing in pain; help us to lay waste their humble homes with a hurricane of fire; help us to wring the hearts of their unoffending widows with **unavailing** grief; help us to turn them out roofless with little children to wander unfriended the wastes of their desolated land in rags and hunger and thirst, sports of the sun flames of summer and the icy winds of winter, broken in spirit, worn with travail, imploring Thee for the refuge of the grave and denied it—for our sakes who adore Thee, Lord, blast their hopes, blight their lives, **protract** their bitter pilgrimage, make heavy their steps, water their way with their tears, stain the white snow with the blood of their wounded feet! We ask it, in the spirit of love, of Him Who is the Source of Love, and Who is the ever-faithful refuge and friend of all that are sore **beset** and seek His aid with humble and **contrite** hearts. Amen.

(After a pause.)

10 "Ye have prayed it; if ye still desire it, speak! The messenger of the Most High waits!"

11 It was believed afterward that the man was a lunatic, because there was no sense in what he said.

🖋 Knowledge Quest

- What parts of this story made you laugh?
- What ideas about satire do you have as you read the story?

Returning to the Text

- Return to the satire as you respond to the following questions. Use text evidence to support your responses.
- Write any additional questions you have about the text in your Reader/Writer Notebook.

1. KQ In paragraph 1, what does the word *oratory* mean in context? What effect does it have on the tone?

_____

_____

_____

_____

2. How do Twain's descriptions create a caricature in paragraph 1? What is the purpose of this paradox?

_____

_____

_____

_____

3. In paragraph 2, what are the townspeople's expectations for the war? What evidence supports this analysis?

_____

_____

_____

_____

4. In paragraph 4, how does the author's diction in the description of the messenger affect the mood of the story?

_____

_____

_____

_____

5. Summarize the man's message to the townspeople as stated in his prayer in paragraph 9. How does this prayer affect the reader?

_____

_____

_____

_____

6. What can you infer about human nature from the town's reaction to the messenger in paragraph 11?

_____

_____

_____

7. **KQ** How is Twain's use of satire effective? How is its satire different from "Advice to Youth"?

_____

_____

_____

_____

INDEPENDENT READING LINK

Read and Discuss

You can continue to build your knowledge about satire by reading these and other articles at ZINC Reading Labs. Search for keywords such as *satire*.

 ZINC

⊘ Knowledge Quest

With a partner, discuss how both of these satires are effective in making a point and how they represent different kinds of satire. Be sure to:

- Refer to evidence from both satires.
- Take turns speaking, responding, and asking one another follow-up questions.
- Ask clarifying questions.
- Write down notes and ideas about how satire can be effective and which kind of satire is most effective for different kinds of topics.

Working from the Text

8. Once you have finished reading the piece, conduct a comparative SOAPSTone, looking at the different ways in which Twain treats these drastically different topics. To help you organize your thoughts, complete the graphic organizer. Be prepared to discuss your responses.

	"Advice to Youth"	"The War Prayer"
Speaker		
Occasion		
Audience		
Purpose		
Subject		
Tone		

9. As a follow-up to the comparative SOAPSTone activity, discuss the following questions:

- How is the type of satire being used appropriate for the subject and purpose?
- How do the terms *Horatian satire* and *Juvenalian satire* apply to the two satires by Twain?

10. Write a paragraph that compares an element of satire in both texts.

☑ Check Your Understanding

Transfer your answers to a poster and include a visual element that symbolizes the differences between the texts. Present your poster to the class.

Learning Strategies

Brainstorming
Marking the Text

My Notes

Learning Targets

- Analyze and evaluate how writers use diction and syntax to create a tone that helps achieve a specific purpose.
- Plan, organize, compose, revise, and edit a satirical narrative on a controversial topic.

Preview

In this activity, you will read two satirical pieces and use them as guides to begin work on your own.

As You Read

- Highlight words, phrases, or sentences you find particularly funny.
- Underline words, phrases, and sentences that contribute to the satiric tone and purpose of each essay.
- Circle unknown words and phrases. Try to determine the meaning of the words by using context clues, word parts, or a dictionary.

Satire

Gambling in Schools

by **Howard Mohr**

1   [When Minnesota jumped into legalized gambling, it was off the deep end without a lifeguard. First it was Canterbury Downs, a clean, well-lighted horse track that seemed more like a Lutheran church with betting windows. Then came Powerball, Daily Three, Gopher Five (named after the official state rodent), and Scratch-Offs. At the same time Native American casinos were springing up in the land of sky blue waters, raking it in with blackjack and slot machines and high-stakes bingo. What could possibly be next?]

2   Parents and teachers who have been worried sick about finding enough money just to maintain public schools at a **minimal** level, worry no more. The Minnesota Legislature last week approved the Education Gambling Bill. The bill allows Video Gaming Devices (VGDS) in K-12 classrooms. Only two machines per classroom will be permitted, unless the class size exceeds thirty, in which case one additional VGD machine will be permitted for each additional ten students. Class size, however, will not be a problem once the gambling revenue begins pouring in.

3   Students in math classes will be instructed in probability, statistics, and hot streaks. The VGDs in kindergarten classrooms will operate with nickels only. All students will be expected to do their assignments and homework before gambling, unless they're on a roll.

minimal: basic

4 Powerball and Gopher Five tickets will be sold only in the lunchroom during the noon hour. But the attractive neon Minnesota lottery signs will be permitted at the main entrance of the school and near the scoreboard at games.

5 Pulltabs and Scratch-Offs are specifically outlawed in the bill because they make a big mess, according to the powerful Janitor's Lobby.

6 Off-track horse betting will be handled in the Principal's office, with a $2 and $5 window initially, but with the option of a $100 window after the first year. Race results will be available in convenient locations. The first half hour of the school day will be a "handicapping homeroom," but students will be encouraged to arrive early if they are psyched up and have the feeling that this is the day.

7 Each school system may publish and sell its own Tip Sheet or it can hire a professional tipster, such as "Gimp" Gordon or "Fast-Forward" Freddy, to be a counselor and role model.

8 Betting on high school sports will be forbidden, but the morning line for collegiate and professional sports will be broadcast on Channel One and posted in the principal's office near the sports betting window. As a safeguard, students will not be allowed to bet on sporting contests unless they have successfully passed Math II, "Point Spreads and Injuries."

9 Poker games will be operated as an extracurricular activity from the final bell until four a.m. The School will be the "house" and provide the dealers. There will be a 10 percent rakeoff for each pot up to a maximum of $10 per hand. Only Five-Card Draw, Stud, and Hold-Em will be permitted. Midnight Baseball, Spit in the Ocean, or Mission Impossible will not be permitted because they are silly games of chance and would send the wrong message to students.

10 Gambling will obviously bring new life and big money to the schools, but there are other advantages:

1: Students will be prepared for jobs in the gambling industry after graduating.

2: Part-time jobs will be created in the schools for change walkers, dealers, security officers, and so on.

3: A wider variety of people will be attracted to the teaching profession.

4: Discipline will be better because the hope of getting something for nothing is one of the oldest drives for excellence.

11 A bigger gambling issue faces the Legislature soon: Should gaming be permitted in hospitals and medical centers? And if so, how much and what kind? Would patients be able to bet the ponies from their beds? Could nurses deal blackjack in the sunroom? Could you go double or nothing with your physician?

Making Observations
- What phrases or sentences make you laugh?
- How do you feel about gambling in schools?

lobby: group that works to influence lawmakers

handicapping: picking which horse will win a race

3.21

Returning to the Text

- Return to the satire as you respond to the following questions. Use text evidence to support your responses.
- Write any additional questions you have about the text in your Reader/Writer Notebook.

1. What kind of tone does the phrase "off the deep end without a lifeguard" set for the text?

   _____

   _____

   _____

   _____

   _____

2. How is the last sentence in paragraph 9 ironic? How does this irony shape the reader's perception of the text?

   _____

   _____

   _____

   _____

   _____

3. How does the shift to hospitals and medical centers in paragraph 11 convey Mohr's message on gambling as a means of financial support for public services?

   _____

   _____

   _____

   _____

   _____

Satire

How to Poison the Earth

by **Linnea Saukko**

1   Poisoning the earth can be difficult because the earth is always trying to cleanse and renew itself. Keeping this in mind, we should generate as much waste as possible from substances such as uranium-238, which has a half-life (the time it takes for half of the substance to decay) of one million years, or plutonium, which has a half-life of only 0.5 million years but is so toxic that if distributed evenly, ten pounds of it could kill every person on the earth. Because the United States generates about eighteen tons of plutonium per year, it is about the best substance for long-term poisoning of the earth. It would help if we would build more nuclear power plants because each one generates only 500 pounds of plutonium each year. Of course, we must include persistent toxic chemicals such as polychlorinated biphenyl (PCB) and dichlorodiphenyltrichloroethane (DDT) to make sure we have enough toxins to poison the earth from the core to the outer atmosphere. First, we must develop many different ways of putting the waste from these nuclear and chemical substances in, on, and around the earth.

2   Putting these substances in the earth is a most important step in the poisoning process. With deep-well injection we can ensure that the earth is poisoned all the way to the core. Deep-well injection involves drilling a hole that is a few thousand feet deep and injecting toxic substances at extremely high pressures so they will penetrate deep into the earth. According to the Environmental Protection Agency (EPA), there are about 360 such deep injection wells in the United States. We cannot forget the groundwater aquifers that are closer to the surface. These must also be contaminated. This is easily done by shallow-well injection, which operates on the same principle as deep-well injection, only closer to the surface. The groundwater that has been injected with toxins will spread contamination beneath the earth. The EPA estimates that there are approximately 500,000 shallow injection wells in the United States.

3   Burying the toxins in the earth is the next best method. The toxins from landfills, dumps, and lagoons slowly seep into the earth, guaranteeing that contamination will last a long time. Because the EPA estimates there are only about 50,000 of these dumps in the United States, they should be located in areas where they will leak to the surrounding ground and surface water.

4   Applying pesticides and other poisons on the earth is another part of the poisoning process. This is good for coating the earth's surface so that the poisons will be absorbed by plants, will seep into the ground, and will run off into surface water.

GRAMMAR & USAGE

Verbal Phrases

A **gerund** is a verb ending with *-ing* and functioning as a noun. For example, the gerund of the verb *poison* is *poisoning*. A **gerund phrase** consists of a gerund, its object, and its modifiers. Notice the gerund phrase functioning as the subject in the first sentence of this text: "*Poisoning the earth can be difficult ...*"

A **participle** is a word formed from a verb that can also be used as an adjective. For example, the verb *rise* may be used as a past adjective (*the risen sun*) or a present adjective (*the rising sun*). A **participial phrase** consists of a participle and any modifiers. Notice this participial phrase from the text: "*Keeping this in mind*, we should generate ..."

Find two more examples of gerund phrases and participial phrases in the text.

POISON

5   Surface water is very important to contaminate because it will transport the poisons to places that cannot be contaminated directly. Lakes are good for long-term storage of pollutants while they release some of their contamination to rivers. The only trouble with rivers is that they act as a natural cleansing system for the earth. No matter how much poison is dumped into them, they will try to transport it away to reach the ocean eventually.

6   The ocean is very hard to contaminate because it has such a large volume and a natural buffering capacity that tends to neutralize some of the contamination. So in addition to the pollution from rivers, we must use the ocean as a dumping place for as many toxins as possible. The ocean currents will help transport the pollution to places that cannot otherwise be reached.

7   Now make sure that the air around the earth is very polluted. Combustion and evaporation are major mechanisms for doing this. We must continuously pollute because the wind will disperse the toxins while rain washes them from the air. But this is good because a few lakes are stripped of all living animals each year from acid rain. Because the lower atmosphere can cleanse itself fairly easily, we must explode nuclear tests bombs that shoot radioactive particles high into the upper atmosphere where they will circle the earth for years. Gravity must pull some of the particles to earth, so we must continue exploding these bombs.

8   So it is that easy. Just be sure to generate as many poisonous substances as possible and be sure they are distributed in, on, and around the entire earth at a greater rate than it can cleanse itself. By following these easy steps we can guarantee the poisoning of the earth.

Making Observations

* How does this text make you feel about pollution?
* What form of pollution mentioned in the text is a problem that you had not thought of before?

Returning to the Text

- Return to the satire as you respond to the following questions. Use text evidence to support your responses.
- Write any additional questions you have about the text in your Reader/Writer Notebook.

4. What effect does Saukko's objective tone have in the sentence "we should generate as much waste as possible from substances such as uranium-238, which has a half-life ... of one million years"?

_____

_____

_____

_____

5. At the end of paragraph 1, the author says, "First, we must develop many different ways of putting the waste from these nuclear and chemical substances in, on, and around the earth." How does this language shape the reader's perception of the text?

_____

_____

_____

_____

6. How is the phrase "poisoned all the way to the core" in paragraph 2 an example of hyperbole? What effect does it have on the reader?

_____

_____

_____

_____

_____

_____

7. How does Saukko use irony throughout the text to convey her message?

_____

_____

_____

_____

Working from the Text

8. Which satire is more effective in making its point? Why?

_____

_____

_____

_____

_____

_____

_____

_____

_____

_____

9. Meet with others who chose the same essay. Be prepared to debate with a member of the group who chose the other essay, using effective reasoning and evidence from the text to prove your claim. Be able to point to satirical techniques and purpose.

_____

_____

_____

_____

_____

_____

_____

_____

_____

_____

_____

_____

_____

Writing a Satire

The first task of writing a satire is to choose a topic you are informed and passionate about. Think of some of the topics written about in this unit: shallowness, football, war, gambling, and pollution.

Imagine that your school has a persistent problem with students being late to class. Evaluate how the steps that follow can get you started on a satirical piece of writing.

Step 1: Plan and Organize the Satire

Generate ideas by utilizing a planning strategy, such as brainstorming, journaling, reading, or discussing. Organize your satire in a way that is appropriate to the purpose, audience, topic, and context. See the sample satire planning that follows.

- *Identify the topic.*
  Students being late to class (tardiness)

- *State the problem in hyperbolic terms.*
  The staggering lack of students at the beginning of class leaves teachers paralyzed. (The diction overstates the severity of the problem: *paralyzed* and *staggering*.)

- *Propose an ironic solution.*
  If students are late, they must stand outside the door for 20 minutes. (This action does not solve the problem because students are still outside the classroom instead of being in class learning.) 1st offense: Students will carry around a 40-pound clock for the remainder of the day. 2nd offense: Students will receive jail time.(The punishment does not fit the "crime.")

Step 2: Revise the Satire

Revise your satire to improve clarity, development, organization, style, diction, and sentence fluency, both within and between sentences. At this step, you can focus on revising sentences to include specific elements of satire that you may not have been able to work during your original draft.

- *Revise to add wit (wordplay, clever language, or rhetorical analogy).*
  Punishment will be doled out in a *timely* manner. (word play)
  This problem is a *ticking time bomb*! (rhetorical analogy)

- *Revise to downplay the severity of the punishment using litotes.*
  Missing class and being ridiculed is a *small price to pay* to promote punctuality.

Step 3: Edit the Satire

Edit the satire to ensure that the spelling, grammar, and punctuation are all correct. Use a style guide as needed.

Step 4: Publish the Satire

Publish the finished satire for your intended audience to enjoy.

Sample paragraph using the preceding process:
It has come to my attention that students have been late to class at an alarming level. The staggering lack of students at the beginning of class leaves teachers paralyzed. To address this problem, we are adopting a new tardy policy. Following the first offense, students will carry around a 40-pound clock for the remainder of the day. Following the second offense, students will receive a night in jail, during which time they will be able to think about what they have done wrong. We promise to dole out this punishment in a timely manner because we have identified this issue as a ticking time bomb!

☑ Check Your Understanding

Brainstorm a list of controversial public issues you could satirize.

✍ Writing Prompt: Literary

Choose one controversial topic from your brainstorm to develop. Compose a satirical narrative paragraph about the topic. Be sure to:

- Plan the setting, characters, problem, and narrative point of view of the satire.
- Organize the satire so that it states the problem in hyperbolic terms and proposes an ironic solution.
- Revise the satire to ensure that it includes fun, precise words; telling details; and sensory language to create vivid images.
- Publish the finished product.

⊕ Independent Reading Checkpoint

Which independent reading text did you have the best personal connection to? Did you connect to the text because of the topic or purpose of the satire? Did you connect to the text because of the language and style of the satire? Write a paragraph telling which text and explaining why you had a personal connection to it.

Writing a Satirical Piece

 ASSIGNMENT

You have been studying how opinions are expressed and perceived in a democratic society through a variety of rhetorical formats including satire. Your assignment is to develop a satirical piece critiquing some aspect of our society.

Planning and Prewriting: Take time to create a plan for choosing a topic and audience.	■ What has guided your choice of topics? Do you have the information to sustain a satiric treatment? ■ Will your piece be more Horatian or Juvenalian? What techniques of satire apply well to that form (hyperbole, parody, irony, ridicule, etc.)? ■ If you use parody, what typical conventions of the format do you plan to use as part of the satire? ■ To whom will you address your satire and why? What is your satirical purpose—what effect do you hope to have on this audience?
Drafting: Decide how you will incorporate elements of satire.	■ How will you demonstrate the flaws or foibles of your satire's subject? ■ As you draft your essay, how will you stick to the conventions that you identified for your satire in your prewriting? ■ What sort of tone is appropriate for the audience and purpose you identified?
Evaluating and Revising: Create opportunities to review and revise.	■ How can you revise to add additional satirical language elements (loose and cumulative sentences, irony, hyperbole, and litotes)? ■ What sort of strategies could you and a peer use to provide each other with feedback (e.g., evaluate with the Scoring Guide, use the SOAPSTone strategy)?
Checking and Editing for Publication: Be sure your work is the best it can be.	■ How will you check for grammatical and technical accuracy? ■ What sort of outside resources can help you to check your draft (e.g., a format guide, a dictionary, etc.)?

Reflection

After completing this Embedded Assessment, think about how you went about accomplishing this assignment, and respond to the following:

• Satire requires a sort of balancing act, mixing humor that draws in your audience with criticism that points out a particular flaw. How did you approach the challenge of balancing these two different elements?

SCORING GUIDE

Scoring Criteria	Exemplary	Proficient	Emerging	Incomplete
Ideas	The satire • offers insight into a topic that is relevant, current, and debatable • argues a convincingly persuasive position • skillfully demonstrates techniques of satire that are ideal for the topic.	The satire • presents a topic that is generally relevant, current, and debatable • argues a clear position • demonstrates techniques of satire that are suitable for the topic.	The satire • presents a topic that is not fully relevant, current, or debatable • argues a position • demonstrates techniques of satire that are somewhat suitable for the topic.	The satire • presents a topic that is irrelevant • includes a vague or unclear position • fails to demonstrate techniques of satire that are somewhat suitable for the topic.
Structure	The satire • presents ideas in an arrangement that is most conducive to the writer's position • is aptly organized using typical conventions of the format.	The satire • logically arranges ideas to support the writer's position • is organized appropriately using typical conventions of the format.	The satire • arranges ideas to somewhat support the writer's position • is mostly organized using typical conventions of the format.	The satire • arranges ideas in a way that detracts from the writer's position or may be irrelevant • is organized in a way that does not match the typical conventions of the format.
Use of Language	The satire • uses language elements (e.g., skillfully incorporating loose and cumulative sentences, irony, hyperbole, and litotes, etc.) extremely effectively • insightfully matches tone and satirical effect to the intended audience and purpose • contains almost no errors in standard writing conventions.	The satire • uses language elements (e.g., incorporating loose and cumulative sentences and satirical techniques) appropriately • applies appropriate tone and satirical effect for the intended audience and purpose • may contain minor errors in writing conventions that do not interfere with understanding.	The satire • uses language elements less effectively • struggles to match tone and satirical effect to the intended audience and purpose • includes some errors in conventions that interfere with the meaning.	The satire • does not use language elements • does not match tone and satirical effect to the intended audience and purpose • includes errors in writing conventions that seriously interfere with its meaning.

VISUAL PROMPT
Duke Ellington was a major presence in the Harlem Renaissance. He was famous for playing jazz, although he played other genres as well, such as classical, blues, and gospel. How does the music of an era influence writers?

AN AMERICAN JOURNEY

Like jars of ginger we are sealed
By nature's heritage.
But let us break the seal of years
With pungent thrusts of song,
For there is joy in long-dried tears
For whetted passions of a throng.

—from "To Usward" by Gwendolyn B. Bennett

ACTIVITY	CONTENTS	

Texts not included in these materials.

My Independent Reading List

Previewing the Unit

Learning Strategies

Marking the Text
Paraphrasing
Skimming/Scanning
Summarizing
Think-Pair-Share

Learning Targets
- Preview the big ideas for the unit.
- Create a plan for independent reading.

Preview

In this activity, you will begin thinking about your first Embedded Assessment, a research project about the Harlem Renaissance.

My Notes

About the Unit

Ever since the Pilgrims traveled to America, the concept of the "journey" has been part of the American experience. In this unit, you will take two journeys. First, you will experience a cultural journey by exploring the voices of the Harlem Renaissance. Your research will culminate in a multimedia research presentation. You will then study one voice of the Harlem Renaissance in depth by reading *Their Eyes Were Watching God* by Zora Neale Hurston. You will use your new knowledge of the predominant philosophies, values, and beliefs of the Harlem Renaissance to analyze how Hurston's novel is both a reflection of and a departure from this literary movement.

Essential Questions

Based on your current knowledge, respond to the following Essential Questions:

1. How do cultural movements such as the Harlem Renaissance reflect and create people's attitudes and beliefs?

2. How is one writer's work both a natural product of and a departure from the ideas of a specific literary movement in American literature?

Unpacking Embedded Assessment 1

Closely read the assignment for Embedded Assessment 1: Presenting a Literary Movement: The Harlem Renaissance.

Your assignment is to work in pairs or a small group to create an interactive multimedia research presentation about a topic related to the Harlem Renaissance. This presentation to your classmates should include a variety of media and must also include an annotated bibliography. Your presentation should focus on some aspect of the era that presents the values and ideas of the Harlem Renaissance, such as historical context, philosophy and beliefs, the arts, or daily life.

With your class, create a graphic organizer that details the knowledge and skills you must have to create an interactive, multimedia research presentation about a topic related to the Harlem Renaissance.

Independent Reading Plan

For your independent reading during this unit, select a novel, memoir, collection of short stories, or book of poetry from the Harlem Renaissance literary movement. Do some research to find a selection that interests you. Most bookshops and libraries have websites with reviews and comments, and some social media sites cater to book lovers.

The Research Process

3. Embedded Assessment 1 requires you to complete a formal research project about a topic related to the Harlem Renaissance and then present the results of your research to your class. How familiar are you with the research process? Turn and talk to your partner about a research project you completed in the past. Take notes on your conversation in your Reader/Writer Notebook.

4. Read and paraphrase each step in the graphic organizer. Then try to think of any resources (Internet, librarian, your teacher, family or neighbors, historical societies or museums, books, documentaries, and so on) that you might use during each step.

Research Process Steps	Paraphrase	Resources You Might Use
1. Identify the topic to be researched.		
2. Prepare questions that will guide you toward the information you want to include in your presentation.		
3. Develop a plan for how and where you will conduct your research.		
4. Locate and evaluate sources for credibility and accuracy and to ensure that they are free from bias and faulty reasoning.		
5. Gather evidence; write additional questions to narrow or broaden research.		
6. Synthesize information from a variety of sources, making sure to include academic citations.		
7. Use an appropriate mode of delivery, whether written, oral, or multimodal, to present results.		

5. Throughout the next few activities, you will go through each step of the research process first as a class and then with your presentation groups. As you complete each step, you will critique the process to implement changes as needs occur and are identified. Before you begin, write down any questions that you may have and discuss them with a small group.

Developing Research Questions

Learning Targets

- Analyze the characteristics and structural elements of an informational text.
- Develop research questions about the Harlem Renaissance.

Preview

In this activity, you will read an informational text about the Harlem Renaissance and use it to generate potential research questions.

What Do You Know About the Harlem Renaissance?

Asking questions to gain information is a useful practice before, during, and after reading a source. Asking before reading helps you determine the points you want to explore. Asking questions as you read and after you read you helps analyze the text and refine your research focus.

1. Your teacher will show you some images to help you recall what you already know about the Harlem Renaissance. Note your impressions of the images and the facts they bring to mind.

_____

_____

_____

_____

_____

_____

_____

_____

_____

_____

_____

_____

2. Next, structure your notes into short, one-sentence statements and place your statements into the **K** column of the KWL chart that follows.

VOCABULARY

ACADEMIC

A renaissance is a rebirth or revival. The word is derived from the French *re*, meaning "again" and *naitre*, meaning "to be born." When spelled with a capital *R*, the word refers to a revival in art, literature, and learning of a historical period.

INDEPENDENT READING LINK

Read and Discuss

Use the definitions of the three types of questions that you reviewed for this activity to create questions for your independent reading selection. Read your questions to a small group. If anyone in the group disagrees with your designated question level, work together to reformulate the question.

What I Know (K) About the Harlem Renaissance	What I Want to Know (W) About the Harlem Renaissance	What I Have Learned (L) About the Harlem Renaissance

3. Use what you have written in the **K** column as a basis for creating questions that will lead you to gain more information about the Harlem Renaissance. Write those questions in the KWL chart's **W** column. It may be helpful to review the levels of questions strategy before you begin writing your questions to make sure that you are asking level 2 questions.

Making Predictions Using Text Features

4. To increase your knowledge about the Harlem Renaissance, you are going to read an informational text titled "The Harlem Renaissance" by Kathleen Drowne and Patrick Huber. Writers of informational texts often use text features such as subtitles, section heads, and footnotes to help their readers know what is going to be discussed in the text. Before you begin reading, skim the text and note the text features used by the authors and use them to predict what you will learn about the Harlem Renaissance from the article. Write your predictions in your Reader/Writer Notebook.

My Notes

- Put an exclamation point next to any information you want to investigate further.
- Circle unknown words and phrases. Try to determine the meaning of the words by using context clues, word parts, or a dictionary.
- Write additional questions that occur to you about the information in the text in the **W** column of your KWL chart.

About the Authors

Kathleen Drowne and Patrick Huber teach English and U.S. history, respectively, at the Missouri University of Science and Technology. They are co-authors of *The 1920s* volume of the *American Popular Culture Through History* series. Drowne's other works include *Spirits of Defiance*, a study of Prohibition-era American literature. Huber is co-author of *A&R Pioneers: Architects of American Roots Music on Record*, a study of the origins of recorded music production in the United States.

Informational Text

The Harlem Renaissance

adapted from *The 1920s* by **Kathleen Drowne and Patrick Huber**

Historical Context

1   Between 1915 and 1918, approximately half a million African Americans left the South for northern urban-industrial centers like Harlem, Chicago, St. Louis, and Detroit as part of the Great Migration. ... Most of these migrants moved north to find higher-paying jobs and to carve out better lives for themselves and their families. They also sought to escape segregation, sharecropping, and racial violence common in the South. The flood of African-American newcomers heightened competition with white workers for jobs, housing, and public facilities, and set off an unprecedented surge of race riots in northern and Midwestern cities.

2   For the most part, southern black migrants were disappointed by what they found in the North. Not only were well-paying jobs scarce for black workers in northern and Midwestern cities, but racist practices also forced these new arrivals to suffer the indignities of segregated schools, theaters, housing, and other facilities. Although the 1920s saw a tremendous flowering of African-American arts, particularly in Harlem and other northern cities,

the decade overall was one of tense, turbulent, and sometimes violent relations between black and white Americans. (9–10)

3 Although the phrase "New Negro" dates to the late nineteenth century, it was not until the 1920s that this label gained currency as a description for middle-class African Americans who advocated a new sense of **militancy** and racial pride. Indeed, Alain Locke, an African-American philosopher, critic, and editor, titles his Harlem Renaissance literary anthology *The New Negro* (1925) in order to signal these powerful currents of black artistic consciousness, renewed civil rights advocacy, and racial **solidarity**. The National Association for the Advancement of Colored People (NAACP) and other organizations waged court battles in an attempt to secure African Americans' civil and political rights. Black writers, musicians, and artists, especially those who resided in Harlem, the so-called "Mecca[1] of the New Negro," used their work to celebrate African-American culture and challenge damaging racist stereotypes. Above all, "New Negroes" attempted to assert their own **agency** and participate fully in American culture, while resisting white America's attempts to cast them as a "problem" that somehow needed to be solved. Many critics, in hindsight, see the New Negro movement as overly optimistic and even naïve, but at the time this impulse toward self-expression, self-assertiveness, and self-determination was a driving force among some middle-class African Americans. (12–13)

Literature

4 The Harlem Renaissance, sometimes called the Negro Renaissance or the New Negro Movement, describes the period roughly between the end of World War I and the onset of the Great Depression, during which African Americans produced a vast number of literary, musical, and artistic works. The artists associated with the Harlem Renaissance attempted to promote racial consciousness and black pride by creating new images of African Americans and by celebrating their blues and folklore traditions, in order ultimately to destroy old racist stereotypes. The works they created were, for the most part, confident, positive, and optimistic about the future of black America.

5 ... Thousands of black families crowded into Harlem, a large neighborhood in upper Manhattan loosely defined in the 1920s as the area between 110th and 155th Streets. This dramatic population shift transformed Harlem into the capital of African-American culture during the 1920s. ... Black people from the American South, the West Indies, and even Africa crowded into the neighborhood, competing for jobs and living space. Harlem became an important cultural crossroads, and talented writers such as Langston Hughes, Countee Cullen, Claude McKay, Jessie Fauset, and Zora Neale Hurston were only a few of the hundreds of young African Americans who flocked to Harlem to join the growing colony of black intellectuals fueling the Harlem Renaissance. (186–187)

---

[1] **Mecca:** a city in Saudi Arabia that is sacred to Islam; pilgrims travel there as part of their spiritual journey

---

WORD CONNECTIONS

Multiple-Meaning Words
The word **currency** has multiple meanings. Use a print or digital resource to clarify the correct meaning of the word *currency* in this context.

My Notes

---

militancy: aggressive behavior in support of a cause
solidarity: sense of togetherness
agency: ability to do things for oneself

4.2

WORD CONNECTIONS

Content Connections

A **colloquialism** is a word or phrase used when speaking informally. One example of such a phrase is *the blues*, meaning a feeling of deep sadness. In music, this sadness is expressed by minor harmonies, slow rhythms, and melancholy lyrics.

My Notes

Music

6 Although initially considered little more than a passing musical fad when it was first recorded in 1917, jazz became the most influential form of American popular music in the 1920s. Jazz combined elements of a wide range of music, including ragtime compositions, brass-band marches, minstrel numbers, and to a lesser degree, blues songs. ...

7 The enormous popularity of jazz provided new opportunities for African-American musicians to make records, occasionally perform on radio, and find work playing for live audiences. ...

8 With the advent of National Prohibition, Harlem nightclubs and cabarets, located above 125th Street in Manhattan, began to attract wealthy white partygoers and tourists who wanted to drink, dance, and hear "exotic" African-American music. In 1929, Variety listed 11 major nightclubs in Harlem that catered to predominately white crowds, including Small's Paradise, Connie's Inn, and the Cotton Club. These swanky nightclubs and cabarets employed hundreds of African-American jazz musicians during the late 1920s, including bandleader Edward "Duke" Ellington. ... (199–200)

The Duke Ellington Orchestra performs "Take the A Train" with singer Bette Roche in the film *Reveille with Beverly*, released in January 1943.

9 By far the greatest jazz musician of the 1920s was Louis Armstrong, a New Orleans born cornetist and trumpeter whose inventive solos and technical brilliance marked the pinnacle of hot jazz. ... (200)

10 Another influential form of African-American music that rose to prominence during the 1920s was the blues. Although it remains difficult to pinpoint an exact origin, the blues emerged sometime around the turn of the twentieth century and evolved from a variety of traditional black musical forms, including field hollers, work songs, ballads, and rags. ... Early folk blues reflected a variety of experiences of African-American life during segregation

and often spoke of work, gambling, crime, alcohol, imprisonment, disasters, and hard times. Above all, the blues commented on the universal themes of troubled love relationships and sexual desires. ... (205)

11 One of the most influential vaudeville blues singers of the 1920s was Gertrude "Ma" Rainey, a flamboyant dresser who flaunted expensive beaded gowns, a necklace made of $20 gold pieces, and ostentatious diamond earrings and rings. ... Billed as "the Mother of the Blues," she recorded more than 100 songs over five years. ... Rainey's young protégé, Bessie Smith, emerged as an even greater vaudeville star. Smith's first record, "Gulf Coast Blues," coupled with "Downhearted Blues," made in 1923 for Columbia, sold 780,000 copies in its first six months. ... With her expressive, soulful phrasing, she remained the biggest blues star of the 1920s, and today she is unquestionably considered by music historians to be the greatest vaudeville blues singer of all times. (205–206)

Art

12 One serious problem that plagued African-American artists during the 1920s was a lack of opportunity to study art and to show their work. Some museums refused to exhibit the work of black artists, and some art schools declined to consider black applicants for scholarships. In 1923, sculptor Augusta Savage brought this discrimination against black artists to the attention of the American public when, after being rejected for a summer school in France because of her race, she appealed to the press. After her story appeared in newspapers, many editorials and letters followed, and while she never did receive the scholarship, she did other black artists a great service by focusing public scrutiny on the problem. ...

13 Perhaps the best-known African-American painter of the Harlem Renaissance was Aaron Douglas. Douglas was a student of the German artist Winold Reiss, who painted African Americans neither as crude stereotypes nor as white people with dark complexions, but rather as dignified, unique individuals. Reiss encouraged Douglas to incorporate African imagery into his paintings, which he did with great success. His May 1927 cover for the Urban League's magazine *Opportunity*, for example, depicts the proud profile of a long-neck Magbetu woman with an elaborate African hairstyle. ... In 1928, Douglas became the first president of the Harlem Artists Guild, an organization that helped black artists secure federal funding from the Works Progress Administration during the Great Depression. (274)

My Notes

_____

_____

_____

_____

_____

_____

_____

_____

Aaron Douglas painted "The Judgment Day" in 1939, more than a decade after creating the book illustration on which the painting is based. The illustration was one of seven created for a collection of poems titled *God's Trombones: Seven Negro Sermons in Verse* by James Weldon Johnson.

Making Observations

- What text features do you notice in this text?
- Were the predictions you made before reading the informational text correct?

Returning to the Text

- Return to the informational text as you respond to the following questions. Use text evidence to support your responses.
- Write any additional questions you have about the text in your Reader/Writer Notebook.

5. What details in paragraph 1 help explain how social conditions of the time contributed to the development of the Harlem Renaissance?

_____

_____

_____

_____

_____

6. Which sentence in paragraph 4 states the thesis of "The Harlem Renaissance"? Why was the thesis placed there and not at the beginning of the essay?

_____

_____

_____

_____

_____

7. What can you conclude about the authors' purpose, audience, and message from paragraphs 4 and 5 of "The Harlem Renaissance"?

_____

_____

_____

_____

_____

8. How does the way the text is organized help the reader understand it? What textual evidence supports your answer?

_____

_____

_____

_____

_____

9. What universal themes are reflected in blues music? How do they reflect the Harlem Renaissance? Cite text evidence in your response.

_____

_____

_____

_____

_____

10. Revisit the section on art in the text and explain the relationship among discrimination, racial stereotypes, and African American art during the Harlem Renaissance?

_____

_____

_____

_____

_____

11. Why was Harlem called the "Mecca of the New Negro"? How does the author show this over the course of the text?

_____

_____

_____

_____

_____

Gaining Perspectives

In the years between 1915 and 1918, Northern and Midwestern cities saw an influx of African American residents. People wanted a progressive life in a democracy—one where all people's rights were truly respected as well as protected by laws. With a partner, think about the social conditions that caused African Americans to move north. Then consider which cultural areas and communities began to flourish after the residential influx. Apply what you learn about the years between 1915 and 1918 as you research two other countries where signs of democratization helped communities flourish. Create a brief media presentation to share your findings with the class.

Working from the Text

12. Look back at the article "The Harlem Renaissance" and identify each area of artistic accomplishment addressed by the authors. Then write two or three descriptive sentences about each area, including two examples of Renaissance figures from the article and one from print or online sources. Maintain a formal register and informative tone in your writing and construct your sentences in an active voice.

Area of Accomplishment	Description and Examples
Literature	Harlem Renaissance writing was noteworthy for its confidence and optimism about the future of black America. Noted writers of the period include Langston Hughes, Zora Neale Hurston, and James Weldon Johnson.

13. Return to the KWL chart at the start of the activity and complete the **L** column ("What I have Learned (**L**) About the Harlem Renaissance"). You may draw upon information you collected in the previous task along with any other evidence from the article that you find significant.

☑ Check Your Understanding

Turn back to "The Harlem Renaissance" and find one text feature the author used in the text. Why do you think the author chose to use this feature?

Participating Collaboratively

14. For the remainder of the activity, you will begin working in groups to prepare for your multimedia presentation. Before you and your group members review your KWL charts and the text you just read, review the following guidelines for effective collaboration.

Collaboration Guidelines

All group members should:

- Be prepared for collaborative discussions by reading your assigned sources and taking notes ahead of time.
- Be alert; use appropriate eye contact and engage with your group.
- Speak up so that the other group members can hear.
- Take turns speaking and listening; everyone should have the opportunity to share ideas.
- Agree upon criteria in which to evaluate the work of the group.
- Keep the goals of your collaboration in mind; stay on topic and watch the time.
- Ask relevant and insightful questions that build on other students' ideas and help the discussion.
- Offer ideas or judgments that are purposeful in moving the group toward your goals.
- Paraphrase comments from other group members to ensure understanding.
- Tolerate a range of positions and ambiguity in decision making.

15. Paraphrase the preceding points by writing the actions you will take in group collaborations as both a speaker and a listener.

As a speaker, I will ...	As a listener, I will ...

16. Now, practice participating collaboratively following the guidelines for collaboration you just reviewed. With your group members, you will choose a research topic and start generating research questions for your multimedia presentation on the Harlem Renaissance.

Choosing a Research Topic

17. Brainstorm possible research topics for your multimedia Harlem Renaissance presentation. Begin your brainstorming by considering the questions in the **W** column of your KWL chart ("What I **W**ant to Know About the Harlem Renaissance") that went unanswered or were refined after reading the text. Write down the topic ideas you have. Work with your group to choose one research topic, following the guidelines for collaboration.

Writing a Research Question

A research question is a clear, focused, concise, and complex question that drives your research. Research questions help you focus your research by providing a path through the research process. Creating research questions will help you work toward supporting a clear thesis.

To write a research question:

> Think about your general topic. What do you want to know?

> Consider your audience. Keep your audience in mind when developing your question. Would that particular audience be interested in this question?

> Start asking questions. Ask open-ended "how" and "why" questions about your general topic to help you think of different areas of your topic.

> Evaluate your possible questions. Research questions should not be answerable with a simple "yes" or "no" or by easily found facts. They should, instead, require both research and analysis on the part of the researcher.

> Hypothesize possible answers. After you have written your research question, use what you already know to think of possible answers or explanations. This will help guide your research.

18. Which of these questions can be considered effective research questions?

Is watching television good for you?

How do peers influence one's political opinions?

How many moons orbit the planets in our solar system?

What connection is there between childhood eating habits and adult obesity?

19. Practice writing research questions about the Harlem Renaissance. Write at least five possible questions. Then share your ideas with your group and use the flowchart to evaluate your questions.

Research Topic:

Research Questions:

20. With your group, come to a consensus about your major research question and record it. Then generate secondary questions to focus your research.

Major Research Question: _____

_____

Secondary Research Questions: _____

_____

_____

_____

_____

☑ **Check Your Understanding**

Critique this part of the research process. Do you need to change your approach?

The Historical Context of the Harlem Renaissance

INDEPENDENT READING LINK

Read and Respond

Think about how your independent reading text discusses the context of the Harlem Renaissance. What aspects of the Harlem Renaissance does your text deal with? How does it deal with them? Record your ideas using a graphic organizer similar to the one you will complete for this activity. Then share your graphic organizer with a peer.

My Notes

Learning Targets

- Work in groups to develop and revise a plan for researching the historical context of the Harlem Renaissance.
- Identify the philosophy, values, and beliefs of the Harlem Renaissance and write an informational text to articulate your understanding.
- Integrate ideas from multiple texts to build knowledge and vocabulary about communities.

Preview

In this activity, you will collaborate with a group to develop a research plan for Embedded Assessment 1.

Developing a Research Plan

A research plan is a road map that will help your group maximize your time researching your topic. For example, if you wanted to purchase a car, you wouldn't waste your time going to every dealership or looking through all the auto sale ads until you found the right one, would you? No, you would read reviews to find the car that has all the features you want at the right price, and then you would find out which dealership nearby had that car for sale. There are millions of sources in the library and on the Internet. If you do not take the time to plan your research, you could become overwhelmed by the excess of information available. A research plan includes your topic, major and secondary research questions, a list of sources that are likely to include the information that you need to answer those questions, and a timeline for reading and synthesizing those sources.

1. You already have your topic and major and secondary research questions. In this activity, you will begin to refine those aspects of your plan by conducting guided research about the Harlem Renaissance.

Historical Context

Understanding the historical context of a literary work can be essential to understanding the text. For example, understanding the historical context of McCarthyism in America provides essential background knowledge for the reader to fully comprehend Arthur Miller's social commentary in *The Crucible*. When researching a literary period like the Harlem Renaissance, it is important to draw information from both primary and secondary sources to support your understanding. As you study the works included in this activity, try to answer your research questions.

2. Your class will view a documentary film together. Then your teacher will assign your discussion group one set of additional sources to investigate. Mark the text for evidence that helps you infer information, and then take notes on the graphic organizer in the Working from the Text section.

3. Be sure to mark the vocabulary that is essential to understanding the text as you take notes. If needed, include definitions to clarify what you read.

SOURCE 1: DOCUMENTARY FILM

You will begin building understanding of the Harlem Renaissance by watching a segment of a film that your teacher will share with you. Your purpose for watching this film is to help you develop an answer to Essential Question 1: How do cultural movements such as the Harlem Renaissance reflect and create people's attitudes and beliefs? Take notes on this film and the rest of the research sources provided.

SOURCE 2: ART

Your group's research will focus on the art created during the Harlem Renaissance. Descriptions of primary artists follow, but you may also choose to add others to this list. Your cooperative group should share the artwork, noting textual evidence from the art and explaining what this information tells you about the Harlem Renaissance. For the reading of the visual texts, consider using the OPTIC strategy.

About the Artist: Augusta Savage

Augusta Savage (1892–1962)—artist, activist, and educator—was born in Green Cove Springs, Florida. An important African American artist, Savage began making art as a child using the natural clay found in her community. She liked to sculpt animals and other small figures. But her father, a Methodist minister, did not approve of this activity and did whatever he could to stop her. Savage once said that her father "almost whipped all the art out of me."

Art to Research: *Lift Every Voice and Sing*, sculpture by Augusta Savage

About the Artist: Lois Mailou Jones

In the 1930s, the art of Lois Mailou Jones (1905–1998) reflected the influences of African traditions. She designed African-style masks and in 1938 painted *Les Fétiches*[1], which depicts masks in five distinct ethnic styles. During a year in Paris, she produced landscapes and figure studies, but African influences reemerged in her art in the late 1960s and early 1970s, particularly after two tours of Africa.

Art to Research: *Les Fétiches* by Lois Mailou Jones

About the Artist: Aaron Douglas

Aaron Douglas (1899–1979) was an African American painter and graphic artist who played a leading role in the Harlem Renaissance of the 1920s and 1930s. His first major commission, to illustrate Alain Locke's book *The New Negro*, prompted requests for graphics from other Harlem Renaissance writers. By 1939, Douglas started teaching at Fisk University, where he remained for the next 27 years.

Art to Research: *Rise, Shine for Thy Light Has Come!* by Aaron Douglas

About the Artist: Palmer C. Hayden

Palmer C. Hayden (1890–1973) was born Peyton Hedgeman in Wide Water, Virginia. He took his artistic name from the corrupted pronunciation of Peyton Hedgeman by a commanding sergeant during World War I. Hayden was among the first African American artists to use African subjects and designs in his painting.

Art to Research: *Midsummer Night in Harlem* by Palmer Hayden

---

[1] **Les Fétiches:** related to the English word *fetish*, an object believed to have magical powers

My Notes

_____
_____
_____
_____
_____
_____
_____
_____
_____
_____
_____
_____
_____
_____
_____
_____

SOURCE 3: INFORMATIONAL TEXT

As You Read

- Refer to the chart in the Working from the Texts section to guide your notes.
- Underline words and phrases that indicate the author's feelings about the Harlem Renaissance.
- Circle unknown words and phrases. Try to determine the meaning of the words by using context clues, word parts, or a dictionary.

About the Author

Alain Leroy Locke (1885–1954) was an American writer, philosopher, educator, and patron of the arts. In *The Black 100*, Locke ranks as the 36th most influential African American ever, past or present. Distinguished as the first African American Rhodes Scholar in 1907, Locke was the philosophical architect—the acknowledged "Dean"—of the Harlem Renaissance, a period of growth connected with the "New Negro" movement from 1919 to 1934.

Informational Text

Introduction to *The New Negro*

by **Alain Locke, 1925**

1   In the last decade something beyond the watch and guard of statistics has happened in the life of the American Negro and the three *norns*[2] who have traditionally presided over the Negro problem have a changeling in their laps. The Sociologist, the Philanthropist, the Race-leader are not unaware of the New Negro, but they are at a loss to account for him. He simply cannot be swathed in their formulæ. For the younger generation is vibrant with a new psychology; the new spirit is awake in the masses, and under the very eyes of the professional observers is transforming what has been a perennial problem into the progressive phases of contemporary Negro life.

2   Could such a metamorphosis have taken place as suddenly as it has appeared to? The answer is no; not because the New Negro is not here, but because the Old Negro had long become more of a myth than a man. The Old Negro, we must remember, was a creature of moral debate and historical controversy. ...

---

[2] **norns:** three Norse goddesses of fate, comparable to the Greek Fates, who ensured that what was meant to happen to each person did happen

3   In the very process of being transplanted, the Negro is becoming transformed.

4   The tide of Negro migration, northward and city-ward, is not to be fully explained as a blind flood started by the demands of war industry coupled with the shutting off of foreign migration, or by the pressure of poor crops coupled with increased social terrorism in certain sections of the South and Southwest. Neither labor demand, the bollweevil, nor the Ku Klux Klan is a basic factor, however contributory any or all of them may have been. The wash and rush of this human tide on the beach line of the northern city centers is to be explained primarily in terms of a new vision of opportunity, of social and economic freedom, of a spirit to seize, even in the face of an extortionate and heavy toil, a chance for the improvement of conditions. With each successive wave of it, the movement of the Negro becomes more and more a mass movement toward the larger and the more democratic chance—in the Negro's case a deliberate flight not only from countryside to city, but from medieval America to modern.

5   Take Harlem as an instance of this. Here in Manhattan is not merely the largest Negro community in the world, but the first concentration in history of so many diverse elements of Negro life. It has attracted the African, the West Indian, the Negro American; has brought together the Negro of the North and the Negro of the South; the man from the city and the man from the town and village; the peasant, the student, the business man, the professional man, artist, poet, musician, adventurer and worker, preacher and criminal, exploiter and social outcast. Each group has come with its own separate motives and for its own special ends, but their greatest experience has been the finding of one another. Proscription and prejudice have thrown these dissimilar elements into a common area of contact and interaction. Within this area, race sympathy and unity have determined a further fusing of sentiment and experience. So what began in terms of segregation becomes more and more, as its elements mix and react, the laboratory of a great racewelding. Hitherto, it must be admitted that American Negroes have been a race more in name than in fact, or to be exact, more in sentiment than in experience. The chief bond between them has been that of a common condition rather than a common consciousness; a problem in common rather than a life in common. In Harlem, Negro life is seizing upon its first chances for group expression and self-determination. It is—or promises at least to be—a race capital. That is why our comparison is taken with those nascent centers of folk-expression and self-determination which are playing a creative part in the world today. Without pretense to their political significance, Harlem has the same role to play for the New Negro as Dublin has had for the New Ireland or Prague for the New Czechoslovakia.

WORD CONNECTIONS

Multiple-Meaning Words
The meaning of the word concentration varies greatly depending on its use. In some uses, it means "mental focus." The word can also mean "many people or things in one place," as in this passage. In cooking or science, the *concentration* is the amount of an ingredient in a mixture.

extortionate: excessive or harsh
proscription: legal restraint
nascent: beginning

Ⓐ Knowledge Quest
- What change in the community stands out to you most?
- How is Harlem a community of people?

Returning to the Text

- Return to the informational text as you respond to the following questions. Use text evidence to support your responses.
- Write any additional questions you have about the text in your Reader/Writer Notebook.

4. **KQ** What metaphor does Locke use in paragraph 4 to describe the movement that led to the Harlem Renaissance? How does the metaphor help explain the concept of a community at this time in history?

_____

_____

_____

_____

_____

5. What additional elements of diversity does Locke note in the population of Harlem that were not mentioned in the text in Activity 4.2? How does his expanded description develop the main idea of this text?

_____

_____

_____

_____

_____

_____

6. How does the author's definition of "race" in paragraph 5 contribute to a greater understanding of the larger context and movement of the Harlem Renaissance?

_____

_____

_____

_____

_____

7. Review both "The Harlem Renaissance" in Activity 4.2 and Locke's piece. How does each piece explain the reasons for the Great Migration? How do these reasons support each piece's theme?

_____

_____

_____

_____

8. **KQ** Using a print or digital source, determine and list possible meanings of the word *concentration*. Which meaning is applicable to the word's use in the second sentence of paragraph 5? Explain.

_____

_____

_____

_____

_____

My Notes

As You Read

- Highlight and label sound devices (such as assonance, consonance, alliteration, and rhyme) used by the writer.
- Mark references to the community.
- Refer to the chart in the Working from the Text section to guide your notes.

About the Author

Gwendolyn B. Bennett (1902–1981) was an African American writer who contributed to *Opportunity*, a magazine that chronicled cultural advancements in Harlem. Though often overlooked, she was an accomplished writer in poetry and prose. Her heritage is a main theme in her poetry, and her works reflect the shared themes and motifs of the Harlem Renaissance. Racial pride, rediscovery of Africa, recognition of African music, and dance are common themes in Bennett's works. Bennett read the following poem on March 21, 1924, at a gathering of writers. Some historians say that this night was the official beginning of the Harlem Renaissance.

KNOWLEDGE QUEST

Knowledge Question:
What makes up a community?

Poetry

To Usward

by **Gwendolyn B. Bennett (1924)**

> Let us be still
>
> As ginger jars[3] are still
>
> Upon a Chinese shelf.
>
> And let us be contained
>
> 5   By entities of Self. ...
>
> Not still with lethargy and sloth,
>
> But quiet with the pushing of our growth.
>
> Not self-contained with smug identity
>
> But conscious of the strength in entity.

WORD CONNECTIONS

Roots and Affixes

The root *ent* comes from Latin and means "being." The suffix *-ity* means "a quality or state." Words using this suffix with this root include *nonentity* and *identity*.

---

[3] **ginger jar:** a large porcelain container with a wide mouth, a spherical shape, and a domed lid

My Notes

10 If any have a song to sing
That's different from the rest,
Oh let them sing
Before the urgency of Youth's **behest**!
For some of us have songs to sing

15 Of jungle heat and fires,
And some of us are solemn grown
With pitiful desires,
And there are those who feel the pull
Of seas beneath the skies,

20 And some there be who want to croon
Of Negro lullabies.
We claim no part with racial **dearth**;
We want to sing the songs of birth!
And so we stand like ginger jars

25 Like ginger jars bound round
With dust and age;
Like jars of ginger we are sealed
By nature's heritage.
But let us break the seal of years

30 With pungent thrusts of song,
For there is joy in long-dried tears
For whetted passions of a throng.

🖉 Knowledge Quest

- Based on what you highlighted, what do you notice about the words of the poem?
- What references or imagery about the community stand out to you?
- What emotions does the poem suggest to you?

---

behest: desire or request
dearth: lack

Returning to the Text

- Return to the poem as you respond to the following questions. Use text evidence to support your responses.
- Write any additional questions you have about the text in your Reader/Writer Notebook.

9. **KQ** How do lines 7–9 of the poem support Alain Locke's descriptions in "Introduction to *The New Negro*" of a community's growth?

_____

_____

_____

_____

10. How does the poem reflect themes similar to those expressed in "The Harlem Renaissance"?

_____

_____

_____

_____

11. Does Bennett use a single rhyme scheme or multiple rhyme schemes in her poem? Explain and describe the effect that choice creates.

_____

_____

_____

_____

12. What sound device does Bennett use in lines 10–14, and what is its effect?

_____

_____

_____

_____

13. How does the author use the word *pungent* in line 30 to support the symbolism of a human experience?

_____

_____

_____

_____

As You Read

- Make mental images as you read the poem.
- Circle unknown words and phrases. Try to determine the meaning of the words by using context clues, word parts, or a dictionary.
- Refer to the chart in Working from the Texts to guide your note-taking.

About the Author

James Weldon Johnson (1871–1938) was an American author, lawyer, politician, and activist. He is remembered largely for his leadership within the NAACP, the oldest and largest civil rights organization in the United States. His writing included novels, poems, and collections of folklore. His poem "Lift Every Voice and Sing" was first performed publicly by 500 schoolchildren on Lincoln's birthday in 1900. It was later set to music by Johnson's brother and adopted by the NAACP as its official song. It is often referred to as "The Black National Anthem."

KNOWLEDGE QUEST

Knowledge Question:
What makes up a community?

Poetry

Lift Every Voice and Sing

by **James Weldon Johnson**

Lift every voice and sing

Till earth and heaven ring,

Ring with the harmonies of Liberty;

Let our rejoicing rise

5   High as the listening skies,

Let it resound loud as the rolling sea.

Sing a song full of the faith that the dark past has taught us,

Sing a song full of the hope that the present has brought us,

Facing the rising sun of our new day begun

In 1939, Augusta Savage was commissioned to create a sculpture for the New York World's Fair. Titled "The Harp," the work was strongly influenced by Weldon's poem.

WORD CONNECTIONS

Etymology
The word **chastening** originally meant "punishment" in old French. In Middle English this meaning changed to "correcting someone's behavior." The term *chastening rod* elicits images of punishments that enslaved people endured, so it still carries the idea of correction. *Chastening* may also mean "causing someone to feel sad or embarrassed."

My Notes

10 Let us march on till victory is won.

Stony the road we trod,

Bitter the chastening rod,

Felt in the days when hope unborn had died;

Yet with a steady beat,

15 Have not our weary feet

Come to the place for which our fathers sighed?

We have come over a way that with tears has been watered,

We have come, treading our path through the blood of the slaughtered,

Out from the gloomy past,

20 Till now we stand at last

Where the white gleam of our bright star is cast.

God of our weary years,

God of our silent tears,

Thou who has brought us thus far on the way;

25 Thou who has by Thy might

Led us into the light,

Keep us forever in the path, we pray.

Lest our feet stray from the places, our God, where we met Thee,

Lest, our hearts drunk with the wine of the world, we forget Thee;

30 Shadowed beneath Thy hand,

May we forever stand.

True to our God,

True to our native land.

⊘ Knowledge Quest

- How would you describe the poet's feelings toward his community?
- How does this poem build on your knowledge of what makes a community?

Returning to the Text

- Return to the lyrics as you respond to the following questions. Use text evidence to support your responses.
- Write any additional questions you have about the text in your Reader/Writer Notebook.

14. **KQ** How does the poem support statements in this section's previous text and poem about the Harlem Renaissance?

_____

_____

_____

_____

15. What poetic technique(s) does the poet use to add meaning and beauty to the poem? How does this engage the reader?

_____

_____

_____

_____

16. How do the first six lines of the poem establish themes that are carried throughout the remainder of the poem?

_____

_____

_____

_____

_____

17. **KQ** Explain the poet's use of the phrase rising sun as a metaphor in lines 9–10 of the poem. What message is being conveyed, and what is the tone of that message?

_____

_____

_____

_____

SOURCES 5: POETRY AND LITERARY CRITICISM

As You Read

- Summarize the main idea of each paragraph in the My Notes section.
- Circle unknown words and phrases. Try to determine the meaning of the words by using context clues, word parts, or a dictionary.
- Refer to the chart in the Working from the Text section to guide your notes.

About the Author

Eugenia W. Collier (b. 1928) is an African American writer and critic best known for her 1969 short story "Marigolds." She was born in Baltimore, Maryland. The former English Chair at Morgan State University, Collier has also taught at Coppin State College (now University), the University of Maryland, and Howard University. She graduated magna cum laude from Howard University in 1948 and was awarded an MA from Columbia University two years later. In 1976, she earned a PhD from the University of Maryland. Since retiring in 1996, Collier continues to live in Baltimore and occasionally visits classes to discuss writing and her stories.

Literary Criticism

Excerpt from "On 'From the Dark Tower'"

by **Eugenia W. Collier**

College Language Association Journal 11.1 (1967)

1   It seems to me that a poem which effectively expresses the spirit of Harlem Renaissance poetry is "From the Dark Tower," by Countee Cullen. It is a restrained, dignified, poignant work, influenced in form by Keats and Shelley rather than by the moderns.

2   Incidentally, The Dark Tower was actually a place on 136th Street in Harlem, where a number of the poets used to gather. Perhaps Cullen knew he was speaking for the others, too, when he wrote:

> We shall not always plant while others reap
> The golden increment of bursting fruit,
> Not always countenance, abject and mute
> That lesser men should hold their brothers cheap;
> Not everlastingly while others sleep
> Shall we beguile their limbs with mellow flute,
> Not always bend to some more subtle brute;
> We were not made eternally to weep.

The night whose sable breast relieves the stark
White stars is no less lovely being dark,
And there are buds that cannot bloom at all
In light, but crumple, piteous, and fall;
So in the dark we hide the heart that bleeds,
And wait, and tend our agonizing seeds.

3 Let us examine the symbolism contained in the poem. Here we have the often-used symbol of planting seeds and reaping fruit. This symbol invariably refers to the natural sequence of things—the hope eventually realized, or the "just deserts" finally obtained. The sowing-reaping symbol here effectively expresses the frustration that inevitably falls to the individual or group of people caught in an unjust system. The image of a person planting the seeds of his labor, knowing even as he plants that "others" will pluck the fruit, is a picture of the frustration which is so often the Negro's lot. The image necessarily (and perhaps unconsciously) implies certain questions: What must be the feelings of the one who plants? How long will he continue to plant without reward? Will he not eventually stop planting, or perhaps begin seizing the fruit which is rightfully his? In what light does he see himself? How does he regard the "others" who "reap the golden increment of bursting fruit"? What physical and emotional damage results to the laborer from this arrangement to which obviously he never consented?

4 In his basic symbol then, Cullen expresses the crux of the protest poem which so flourished in the Harlem Renaissance. In poem after poem, articulate young Negroes answered these questions or asked them again, these questions and many more. And in the asking, and in the answering, they were speaking of the old, well-worn (though never quite realized) American ideals.

5 In the octave[4] of the poem, Cullen answers some of these questions. The grim promise "not always" tolls ominously like an iron bell through the first eight lines. "We shall not always plant while others reap," he promises. By degrees he probes deeper and deeper into the actual meaning of the image. In the next two lines he points out one of many strange paradoxes of social injustice: that the "abject and mute" victim must permit himself to be considered inferior by "lesser men"—that is, men who have lost a measure of their humanity because they have degraded their brothers. This image is a statement of a loss of human values—the "abject and mute" victim of an unjust social system, bereft of spirit, silently serving another who has himself suffered a different kind of loss in robbing his fellow man of his potential—that is, the fruit of his seed. Perhaps this destruction of the human spirit is the "more subtle brute" of which the poet speaks. The last line of the octave promises eventual change in the words, "We were not made eternally to weep." Yet it implies that relief is still a long way off. It is in the sestet[5] that the poem itself blossoms into full-blown dark beauty. With the skill of an impressionistic

[4] **octave:** an eight-line stanza or section of a sonnet characterized by a specific rhyme scheme and setting out the problem of the sonnet

[5] **sestet:** a six-line stanza or section of a sonnet with a specific rhyme scheme that usually answers the problem set out in the octave

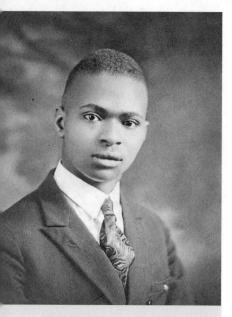

Countee Cullen was an American poet, novelist, children's writer, and playwright during the Harlem Renaissance.

My Notes

painter, the poet juxtaposes black and white into a canvas of brilliant contrasts. The night is pictured as being beautiful because it is dark—a welcome relief from the stark whiteness of the stars. The image suggests the pride in Negritude which became important in the Harlem Renaissance—the pride in the physical beauty of black people, the Negro folk culture which has enriched America, the strength which the Negro has earned through suffering. Cullen describes the night as being not only a lovely thing, but also a sheltering thing. The image of the buds that cannot bloom in light suggests that the Negro's experience has created a unique place for him in American culture: there are songs that he alone can sing.

6   The final couplet combines the beautiful and sheltering concept of darkness with the basic symbol of futile planting. The poet now splashes a shocking red onto his black and white canvas. The dark becomes not only a shelter for developing buds, but also a place to conceal gaping wounds. These two lines are quiet but extremely disturbing:

"So in the dark we hide the heart that bleeds, / And wait, and tend our agonizing seeds." And the reader cannot help wondering, what sort of plant will grow from these "agonizing seeds"?

Knowledge Quest

- What is your impression of the poem being analyzed?
- How was the Dark Tower a community?

Returning to the Text

- Return to the literary criticism as you respond to the following questions. Use text evidence to support your responses.
- Write any additional questions you have about the text in your Reader/Writer Notebook.

18. KQ In paragraph 1, what does the word *spirit* mean in context? How does this word connect to the idea of a community?

_____

_____

_____

_____

_____

19. How does Collier classify "From the Dark Tower"? What evidence does she give to support her classification?

_____

_____

_____

_____

_____

20. What structure does the author use to discuss her interpretation of the poem? How does her choice affect the reader's understanding of the poem and its interpretation?

_____

_____

_____

_____

_____

21. According to Collier, what does the dark night represent? How does the historical context support her interpretation?

_____

_____

_____

_____

_____

22. What analysis does Collier apply to the imagery of planting seeds and reaping fruit, and how does she argue that it supports the central message of "From the Dark Tower"?

_____

_____

_____

_____

_____

23. **KQ** How does the text help define what makes the Harlem Renaissance a community?

_____

_____

_____

_____

INDEPENDENT READING LINK

You can continue to build your knowledge about communities by reading other articles at ZINC Reading Labs. Search for keywords such as *unity* or *community*.

Knowledge Quest

After reading these texts about communities, think about what makes up a community and why. With a partner, write an informative text about the makeup of a community. Respond to the following questions: *What is a community you know? Who is in this community? Is it big, small, or somewhere in between? How else can you describe your community? How do you feel about the ways in which you belong to this community?* Be sure to:

- Develop the topic with concrete details that give facts, not opinions, about your community.
- Use precise language to manage the complexity of your topic.

Working from the Text

24. As you examine the preceding sources, make notes about your understanding of these readings by completing the following graphic organizer or by creating your own graphic organizer in your Reader/Writer Notebook. Note each category in the graphic organizer and write notes as to what you can infer from the text about the literary and artistic movement known as the Harlem Renaissance. Be sure to cite textual evidence to support your understanding.

	Documentary Film	Art	Informational Text	Poetry
Historical Context				
Values and Beliefs				
Genres and Style				
Significant Authors and Works				

☑ Focus on the Sentence

Examine the observations and information you have placed in the graphic organizer. Write four different sentences that combine ideas from the sources you have analyzed using the sentence structures indicated.

Statement: _____

_____

Question: _____

_____

Exclamation: _____

_____

Command: _____

_____

✍ Writing Prompt: Informational

Select one aspect of the Harlem Renaissance, such as its history, values and beliefs, authors and works, or genres and styles. Write an informational text that describes your understanding of that aspect. Use the information you have read in both primary and secondary sources for reference. Develop your text by using the most significant and relevant facts and details from these references. Be sure to:

- Begin your paragraph with a well-stated topic sentence.
- Provide lead-ins to cite textual evidence, using transition words and phrases to connect ideas and create a cohesive paragraph.
- End with a conclusion that follows logically from the points presented and refers to your topic.

Revising Your Plan and Modifying Your Major Research Question

25. Now that you have conducted research from a variety of sources, it's time to look again at your major research question. Does it need to be modified based on what you have learned? Do you have additional secondary research questions? Record updates to your research questions and plan in your Reader/Writer Notebook.

Synthesizing Facts, Interpretations, and Media Formats

My Notes

Locating Relevant Sources

Before continuing your group work with the creation of your multimedia informational presentation, your teacher will guide you through an exercise in locating relevant sources.

Remember that a relevant, or usable, source is:

- accurate: consists of truthful, verifiable information.
- credible: from a source known to be trustworthy.
- free of bias: factual and presented without an attempt to support an opinion.
- free of faulty reasoning: logically sound and free of fallacies like those you learned about in Unit 3.

1. For this exercise, your teacher and your class will locate a relevant source in response to the question *What was the role of visual artists during the Harlem Renaissance?* Create a research plan by:

   - listing the types of visual arts common during the time of the Harlem Renaissance (approximately 1918–1937).

   - constructing online searches designed to locate informative sources about these Harlem Renaissance art types.

2. Execute your research plan with the guidance of your teacher. Then, as a class, construct secondary online searches to help you find a relevant source. Once everyone has agreed on the choice of a relevant source, discuss whether the source is primary or secondary and how you know it is accurate, credible, and free of bias and faulty reasoning.

Presenting Your Results

For a multimedia presentation, you must begin to consider how you will present this information to your audience and what information you will share.

3. Consult this list of some possible media formats. When you meet with your group members, discuss which media formats will best provide the vehicles for your presentations. What other multimedia formats can you add? Add them to the list.

presentation slides	social media	chart, map, or diagram
music	blog	brochure
video	billboard	timeline
poster	photographs	board game
scene from a play	advertisement	newspaper article
letter	review of a performance	interview

Other possible media formats:

_____

_____

4. Listen as your teacher reads aloud the information in the first three rows of the table. Then work together as a class to complete the row for the class research question.

Synthesizing Facts, Interpretations, and Media Formats			
Research Facts	**Reflection**	**Possible Media Formats**	**Possible Commentary**
Record pertinent information from the source and include page numbers. Be sure to use quotation marks for a direct quotation.	_Include questions and comments on the facts presented._	_Consider possible media resources to convey the facts (i.e., the best media resource to share this information with my classmates)._	_Note ideas for content to include in the media resource (i.e., commentary that will support my understanding of the research information)._
Class Research Question: What was the role of visual artists during the Harlem Renaissance?			
Your Research Question:			

Your Turn

My Notes

5. Locate at least two relevant sources—one print, one electronic—that you can share with your group as support for the major research question. Read the sources and examine them for credibility, bias, accuracy, and faulty reasoning. Then, for each source, complete the first column of the Synthesizing Facts, Interpretations, and Media Formats graphic organizer; you will complete the remaining columns later with your presentation group. Make enough copies of both sources for everyone in your presentation group.

☑ Check Your Understanding

Why do you think it is important to draw information from more than one source? What could happen if you use a source that is not credible? How does having more than one source help you check the validity of a document? Record your thoughts in your Reader/Writer Notebook and then discuss with a partner.

Documenting Your Sources

Learning Strategies

Discussion Groups
Marking the Text
Note-taking

My Notes

Learning Targets

- Summarize and evaluate research sources in an annotated bibliography.
- Understand the use of academic citations and annotations as a means of avoiding plagiarism.

Preview

In this activity, you will consult print or online references as a guide to create an annotated bibliography for your multimedia informational presentation.

Sharing Research Information

1. You will now read and analyze the information that other members of your group have provided. Each of you should share copies of research information. For each source, take notes on a Synthesizing Facts, Interpretations, and Media Formats graphic organizer or another effective note-taking format.

Using Source Materials Ethically

To do something **ethically** means to do it in a way that does not violate principles of honesty or integrity. When writing, this means not only using the most relevant, accurate, and credible sources possible but also avoiding intentional or unintentional **plagiarism**, the uncredited use of someone else's words or ideas.

Plagiarism can be avoided by:

- paraphrasing, or rephrasing text into your own words.
- quoting, or copying a text word for word, placing it within quotation marks, and clearly stating the source of the quote.
- citing, or using established formatting guidelines to indicate the source and author of the material you are using.

Citing Sources

2. Consult a reference such as the *MLA Handbook* or another reference that your teacher specifies to find the proper methods of citation for your research. You may also search the web using a search term such as "MLA style sheet" to get information about citation methods.

3. After you decide on the sources that your writing group will use, prepare an annotated bibliography that you will include in your presentation. Remember that anything coming from an outside source must be cited, including paraphrased and quoted text. Note the following elements of annotated bibliographies:

- After each documentation of source, a note explains the content of the source and its value.
- It gives readers information on the sources and provides proof of the validity and reliability of the sources.
- Notes are written in third-person objective academic voice.

VOCABULARY

ACADEMIC
An **annotated bibliography** cites complete information about sources, provides a critical review of each source, and provides notes about the informational value of each source.

The following are examples of entries from an annotated bibliography.

Bessie Smith, 31 March 2012. *www.redhotjazz.com/bessie.html*.

This informative website offers a summary of Bessie Smith's contribution to the development of jazz music and her relationships with other great jazz performers. It also provides an alphabetized listing of her recordings along with recording date, place of recording, and production company. Two other helpful sections are the names of the musicians who accompanied her recordings and a bibliography. For anyone exploring the musical aspect of the Harlem Renaissance, this is a helpful resource.

Drowne, Kathleen, and Patrick Huber. *The 1920s*. Ed. Ray B. Browne. Westport, CT: Greenwood Press, 2004.

The book is part of a series titled *American Popular Culture Through History*. It provides information to build background knowledge of the 1920s with such topics as "Everyday America," "Leisure Activities," "Food and Drink," and "Visual Arts." It is a helpful resource for understanding the philosophy, historical context, arts, and daily life of the 1920s.

Ford, Nick Aaron. "A Study in Race Relations—a Meeting with Zora Neale Hurston," *Zora Neale Hurston*. Ed. Harold Bloom. Philadelphia, PA: Chelsea House Publishers, 1986. 7–10.

Ford divides this essay into two parts. Part I relates a casual encounter between the writer and Zora Neale Hurston, who told him, "I have ceased to think in terms of race; I think only in terms of individuals." Part II provides readers an explanation of the traditional portrayal of to in literature up to the Harlem Renaissance. He then explains why Hurston's beliefs are in conflict with her contemporaries. This essay and others in this book outline the varying attitudes toward Hurston's writing, from her contemporaries to modern scholars.

Continuing Research

4. Continue to research so that you gather well-documented information that will support an accurate and detailed presentation. You might find that additional sources will lead to secondary questions that lead from the major question. As you gather information, complete a Synthesizing Facts, Interpretations, and Media Formats graphic organizer for sources that you consider supportive of your research question.

5. After your writing group has analyzed the sources, prepare an annotated bibliography entry for each source that you find most informative and supportive of your major research question. Ensure equal participation within your group by distributing the writing to each member of your group. Remember:

   • Use an appropriate bibliographic format.
   • Explain why the source supports your research question.
   • Use the appropriate point of view.

☑ Check Your Understanding

Describe the importance of proper citation in one sentence by using the following stem:

Using an annotated bibliography is a way to make certain that _____.

Finalizing Research and Organizing Your Presentation

My Notes

Learning Targets

- Construct a thesis statement that answers a research question.
- Collaboratively plan and organize research to create an informational multimedia presentation.
- Practice giving a formal presentation and revising it as needed.

Preview

In this activity, you will synthesize your research, write a thesis, and organize your presentation.

Synthesizing Your Research

Collaborate with your group to complete the construction and polishing of your group's informational multimedia presentation. Review the procedures you established in the Participating Collaboratively task in Activity 4.2 before continuing. Then follow these steps to synthesize your research:

1. Conduct a group review and revision of your research plan.

2. Write your agreed-upon major research question and secondary research questions.

Major research question: _____

_____

Secondary research questions: _____

_____

3. Distribute your chosen sources among individuals or pairs of group members. Each person/pair should conduct a final examination of an assigned source to make certain it is relevant and adequately addresses your group's research questions. Collaborate to organize your pieces of information using a chart similar to the one that follows. Use separate writing paper or a flipchart, if available.

Source	Relevant Information in Source	Information's Location in Source

Keep your chart as a resource to consult as you organize your presentation. As you proceed, remember that your group's goal is to present your information in a way that suits your topic, audience, and purpose.

LANGUAGE & WRITER'S CRAFT: Writing a Thesis Statement

A thesis statement usually appears at the beginning of the introductory paragraph of an essay, and it offers a specific summary of the main point or claim of the essay. The thesis statement fulfills the following criteria:

- It answers the major research question.
- It reflects an opinion that can be argued with reasoning and evidence from your source.
- It provides the organization of ideas.

Study these sample research questions and the thesis statement that answers each question. Analyze how each statement meets the requirements of an effective thesis statement.

Research Question	Thesis Statement
How did Alain Locke contribute to the Harlem Renaissance movement?	Alain Locke, an influential leader of the Harlem Renaissance, instilled purpose and responsibility into the young writers of the time with his essays and leadership.
Why was jazz music such an influential art form during the Harlem Renaissance?	Reflecting the historical context and daily life of the Harlem Renaissance, jazz music gave musicians a new outlet of expression.
Major question: Why were Jessie Redmon Fauset's novels viewed with dismissive criticism during the Harlem Renaissance? Secondary question: Why is her work being revisited today?	Jessie Redmon Fauset, whose Harlem Renaissance novels were received with mixed reviews when they were first released, is now viewed as one of America's first black feminist writers for her portrayal of race relations and black women.

PRACTICE Now that you have collected sources that support your major research question, create a thesis statement for your presentation.

Organizing Your Presentation

4. Now that you have your thesis statement, you will need to organize your research so that it supports your thesis. Divide your topic into subtopics and sort your individual pieces of information into those subtopics. Since this is going to be a multimedia presentation, planning will also include making decisions about which type of media you will use to present each subtopic. Create a chart similar to the one that follows to sort your information into subtopics and organize the use of media in your presentation.

Subtopic	Pieces of Information Contained in the Subtopic	Media to Be Used in Presentation of Subtopic

5. Next, distribute your subtopics among individuals or pairs. Each person/pair is to write a "script" according to the following Writing Prompt.

📝 Drafting the Embedded Assessment

Each group member will select one subtopic from the information the group has gathered. Generate a draft of a script for that section of your presentation. As you draft your section, consider the media that you will use. Be sure to:

- Begin with a thesis statement that answers the major research question and clearly states your opinion.
- Include commentary that directly explains the connection between the research and the thesis statement. Provide in-text documentation of the research through the use of details and examples.
- Make effective use of rhetorical devices.
- Smoothly transition from one topic and media type to another.

---

6. Reassemble your group and have the author(s) of each script present it orally, reading aloud both the informational text and descriptions of how the chosen media will be used. Use a chart like the following to assess each script as it is read.

Name of Subtopic and Subtopic Presenter(s):

Does the subtopic presentation...	Observations, Examples, and Comments
... exhibit a logical structure?	
... exhibit smooth transitions?	
... contain clear, accurate evidence?	
... contain well-chosen details?	
... make good use of rhetorical devices?	

7. Once every subtopic has been analyzed, collaborate on assembling the final draft for your presentation including writing an effective introduction that is engaging and informative and a conclusion that follows from the thesis and the ideas developed. Place notes in the text of your script with suggestions about the effective use of eye contact, pauses, enunciation, gestures, and other oratorical devices as appropriate.

8. Finally, give the script for your multimedia presentation one last review as a group.

Presenting Your Research

As your group presents your work to the class, your teacher will offer suggestions on effectively using eye contact, speaking style, gestures, and word choice to better communicate your group's ideas. Take notes on this feedback in your Reader/Writer notebook. Afterward, discuss with your group how to integrate your teacher's guidance and recommendations into your presentation. Revisit and repeat relevant portions of your presentation to practice the suggested improvements.

Providing for Audience Note-Taking

During your presentation, you will want your audience to take notes to capture your main idea and the evidence you present in support of that idea. As you think about ways to provide for note-taking, keep these questions in mind:

- What type of note-taking graphic organizer could you create for your classmates to use in taking effective notes on your presentation?
- What information do you need to provide on your graphic organizer?

☑ Check Your Understanding

Write a short reflection on the experience you have had conducting this research. What was it like to work in your group? What went well, and what was difficult?

🛈 Independent Reading Checkpoint

Review the independent reading you have completed so far. Review any notes you took about how the texts relate to the Harlem Renaissance. Look for information in the texts that you can use as source material for your multimedia presentation.

My Notes

Presenting a Literary Movement:
The Harlem Renaissance

 ## ASSIGNMENT

Your assignment is to work in pairs or a small group to create an interactive multimedia research presentation about a topic related to the Harlem Renaissance. This presentation to your classmates should include a variety of media and must also include an annotated bibliography. Your presentation should focus on some aspect of the era that represents the values and ideas of the Harlem Renaissance, such as historical context, philosophy and beliefs, the arts, or daily life.

Planning: Make a plan to conduct research to gather relevant and engaging resources.	▪ Is the research that you have done sufficient for your presentation? What questions still need to be answered? ▪ Have you sufficiently critiqued and revised your research plan? ▪ Have you examined and modified your major research question as new information is introduced? ▪ How will you collaborate on the tasks that remain? Consider both the preparation and the delivery of each section of your group's presentation. ▪ What resource will you provide your audience so they can take notes that emphasize the main idea and the evidence of your presentation?
Drafting: Be sure you organize and showcase a variety of multimedia.	▪ How will you ensure that your presentation has an engaging introduction and a reflective conclusion? ▪ Are you making sufficient and appropriate use of rhetorical devices, details, examples, and commentary? ▪ How can group members who are working on separate elements check in to make sure you avoid omission or repetition of ideas? ▪ How can you structure your presentation to take advantage of the different media types you are using so that the content is engaging to the audience?
Evaluating and Revising: Create time to review, reflect upon, and revise drafts.	▪ Do all of your details and commentary support your thesis? ▪ Do you provide transitions that allow smooth shifts from one element to the next? ▪ Are all sources correctly referenced and/or cited?
Rehearsal and Presentation: Take time to rehearse so the presentation moves smoothly and creates clear connections for the listeners.	▪ How can you use the speaking and performing guidelines from Unit 2 as a resource? ▪ How can group members provide each other with helpful and constructive feedback? ▪ How can you use the Scoring Guide as a resource before the final presentation?

Reflection

After completing this Embedded Assessment, think about how you went about accomplishing this assignment and respond to the following:

This assessment required incorporating multiple media types into one coherent presentation. How was that task challenging, and what advantages did it bring over a presentation that uses one media type?

SCORING GUIDE

Scoring Criteria	Exemplary	Proficient	Emerging	Incomplete
Ideas	The presentation • provides an extensive, well-researched response to the topic • includes substantial support for the ideas presented about the subject • includes interaction by providing an appropriate note-taking tool for the audience.	The presentation • provides a researched response to the topic • provides adequate support for the ideas presented about the subject • includes interaction by providing a note-taking tool for the audience.	The presentation • attempts to respond to the topic with research but has a weak or uneven focus • provides partial support for the ideas presented about the subject • provides a note-taking tool for the audience but does not use it.	The presentation • does not address all aspects of the topic • provides inadequate support for the ideas presented about the subject • does not provide a note-taking tool for the audience.
Structure	The presentation • provides an engaging thesis and sophisticated context • uses appropriate and effective transitional devices to move from one point to the next • concludes with an in-depth reflection that brings closure • includes a complete annotated bibliography with correct citations, summaries, and source evaluations.	The presentation • introduces the topic, contains a thesis and sets the context • uses transitional devices to move the reader from one point to the next • concludes with an adequate reflection and brings closure • includes an annotated bibliography with citations, summaries, and source evaluations.	The presentation • introduces the topic, contains a thesis, and attempts to set the context • attempts to use transitional devices to move the reader with uneven results • concludes with some reflection and attempts to bring closure • includes an incomplete annotated bibliography.	The presentation • does not appropriately introduce the topic, contains an unclear thesis, and/or does not adequately explain the context • does not use transitions • does not provide sufficient reflection and/or bring closure • lacks an annotated bibliography with citations, summaries, and source evaluations.
Use of Language	The presentation • effectively addresses the intended audience • seamlessly integrates research • shows a command of grammar, punctuation, and conventions.	The presentation • accurately addresses the intended audience • clearly integrates research • shows an appropriate use of conventions; some minor errors are evident.	The presentation • does little to address the intended audience • attempts to integrate research • contains errors in conventions, many of which interfere with meaning.	The presentation • does not address the intended audience • contains very little integration of research • contains extensive errors in grammar, punctuation, and conventions.

Unpacking Embedded Assessment 2

Learning Targets

- Preview the knowledge and skills needed to be successful on the EA.
- Create a plan for independent reading.

Preview

In this activity, you will begin preparing to write an essay about the writing of Zora Neale Hurston.

My Notes

Making Connections

One of the great literary discoveries after the Harlem Renaissance has been Zora Neale Hurston's novel *Their Eyes Were Watching God*. It was unappreciated by some of Hurston's male contemporaries in the literary and artistic movement. Upon its first publication in 1937, the novel slipped out of print until Alice Walker, the author of *The Color Purple*, brought it back to the public eye in the 1970s. Since then, Hurston's story of Janie Crawford, a woman on a journey of self-discovery, has received wide acclaim by diverse readers and has made its own journey into the canon of American literature.

Essential Questions

Respond to the Essential Questions based on your study of the first part of the unit:

1. How do cultural movements such as the Harlem Renaissance reflect and create people's attitudes and beliefs?

2. How is one writer's work both a natural product of and a departure from the ideas of a specific literary movement in American literature?

Unpacking Embedded Assessment 2

Read closely and mark the text for the skills and knowledge you will need to accomplish the assignment for Embedded Assessment 2: Writing an Analytical Essay.

Write an analytical essay in which you discuss how Zora Neale Hurston's writing is both a reflection of and a departure from the ideas of the Harlem Renaissance. Include aspects of the Harlem Renaissance that you see reflected in Hurston's writing as well as characteristics of Hurston's writing that are departures from selected aspects of the Harlem Renaissance.

As you unpack the Embedded Assessment, create a graphic organizer that details the skills and knowledge required to complete the assignment successfully.

Independent Reading Plan

For your independent reading during this part of the unit, continue reading novels, memoirs, short stories, or books of poetry from the Harlem Renaissance literary movement. Take notes or mark the text with sticky notes when you find information that directly relates to the Harlem Renaissance. Share your observations with a small group.

'A Unity of Opposites'

Learning Targets

- Understand the historical context of a text.
- Analyze how an author's diction and syntax contribute to the voice of a text.
- Make inferences by synthesizing and finding evidence in a primary and secondary source.
- Integrate ideas from multiple texts to build knowledge and vocabulary on different perspectives about self-awareness and the understanding of self.

Preview

American author Alice Walker once said of Zora Neale Hurston, "[She] became an orphan at nine, a runaway at fourteen, maid and manicurist before she was twenty, and with one dress and a dream—managed to become Zora Neale Hurston, author and anthropologist." In this activity, you will read an essay written by Hurston in 1928 to better understand the historical context of her work.

As You Read

- Underline words and phrases that the author uses to describe herself.
- While you read, jot down questions you have about the essay in the My Notes section.
- Circle unknown words and phrases. Try to determine the meaning of the words by using context clues, word parts, or a dictionary.

About the Author

Zora Neale Hurston (1891–1960) was a novelist, essayist, anthropologist, and vibrant part of the Harlem Renaissance. She grew up in the small town of Eatonville, Florida—the first incorporated black township. Hurston's idyllic childhood was interrupted by the death of her mother when Hurston was only 9. She struggled to finish high school, which she still had not accomplished by age 26. Despite her early struggles, Hurston went on to graduate from Barnard College in 1928. *Their Eyes Were Watching God* is considered her master work. "How It Feels to Be Colored Me," originally published in the May 1928 edition of *The World Tomorrow*, was a contentious essay. It obviously did not fit with the ideologies of racial segregation, but it also did not completely mesh with the flowering of black pride associated with the Harlem Renaissance.

My Notes

WORD CONNECTIONS

Cognates

The English word **proscenium** means "the part of a stage that is in front of the curtain." The Spanish word *proscenio* has the same root and also describes the part of the stage closest to the audience: the part of the stage that is between the curtain and the orchestra.

first-nighter: person who attends an opening performance

oleanders: evergreen shrubs with fragrant flowers

Essay

How It Feels to Be Colored Me

by **Zora Neale Hurston**

1   I am colored but I offer nothing in the way of extenuating circumstances except the fact that I am the only Negro in the United States whose grandfather on the mother's side was *not* an Indian chief.

2   I remember the very day that I became colored. Up to my thirteenth year I lived in the little Negro town of Eatonville, Florida. It is exclusively a colored town. The only white people I knew passed through the town going to or coming from Orlando. The native whites rode dusty horses; the Northern tourists chugged down the sandy village road in automobiles. The town knew the Southerners and never stopped cane chewing when they passed. But the Northerners were something else again. They were peered at cautiously from behind curtains by the timid. The more venturesome would come out on the porch to watch them go past and got just as much pleasure out of the tourists as the tourists got out of the village.

3   The front porch might seem a daring place for the rest of the town, but it was a gallery seat for me. My favorite place was atop the gatepost. Proscenium box for a born **first-nighter**. Not only did I enjoy the show, but I didn't mind the actors knowing that I liked it. I usually spoke to them in passing. I'd wave at them and when they returned my salute, I would say something like this: "Howdy-do-well-I-thank-you-where-you-goin'?" Usually the automobile or the horse paused at this, and after a queer exchange of compliments, I would probably "go a piece of the way" with them, as we say in farthest Florida. If one of my family happened to come to the front in time to see me, of course, negotiations would be rudely broken off. But even so, it is clear that I was the first "welcome-to-our-state" Floridian, and I hope the Miami Chamber of Commerce will please take notice.

4   During this period, white people differed from colored to me only in that they rode through town and never lived there. They liked to hear me "speak pieces" and sing and wanted to see me dance the parse-me-la, and gave me generously of their small silver for doing these things, which seemed strange to me, for I wanted to do them so much that I needed bribing to stop. Only they didn't know it. The colored people gave no dimes. They deplored any joyful tendencies in me, but I was their Zora nevertheless. I belonged to them, to the nearby hotels, to the county—everybody's Zora.

5   But changes came in the family when I was thirteen, and I was sent to school in Jacksonville. I left Eatonville, the town of the **oleanders**, as Zora. When I disembarked from the riverboat at Jacksonville, she was no more. It

eemed that I had suffered a sea change. I was not Zora of Orange County any more, I was now a little colored girl. I found it out in certain ways. In my heart as well as in the mirror, I became a fast brown—warranted not to rub nor run.

6   But I am not tragically colored. There is no great sorrow dammed up in my soul, nor lurking behind my eyes. I do not mind at all. I do not belong to the sobbing school of Negrohood who hold that nature somehow has given them a lowdown dirty deal and whose feelings are all hurt about it. Even in the helter-skelter skirmish that is my life, I have seen that the world is to the strong regardless of a little **pigmentation** more or less. No, I do not weep at the world—I am too busy sharpening my oyster knife.[1]

7   Someone is always at my elbow reminding me that I am the granddaughter of slaves. It fails to register depression with me. Slavery is sixty years in the past. The operation was successful and the patient is doing well, thank you. The terrible struggle that made me an American out of a potential slave said, "On the line!" The Reconstruction said, "Get set!" and the generation before said, "Go!" I am off to a flying start and I must not halt in the stretch to look behind and weep. Slavery is the price I paid for civilization, and the choice was not with me. It is a bully adventure and worth all that I have paid through my ancestors for it. No one on earth ever had a greater chance for glory. The world to be won and nothing to be lost. It is thrilling to think—to know that for any act of mine, I shall get twice as much praise or twice as much blame. It is quite exciting to hold the center of the national stage, with the spectators not knowing whether to laugh or to weep.

GRAMMAR & USAGE

Dashes

Writers use **dashes** to amplify a point or to further explain. Notice the author's use of a dash in this sentence to amplify her point: "I belonged to them, to the nearby hotels, to the country—everybody's Zora".

Commas, parentheses, or colons can provide a similar effect, but in this instance the dash slows the reader down enough to understand that the author is further emphasizing to whom she belongs.

Try revising another sentence from this essay by replacing a dash with a colon, a comma, or parentheses. How does your revision change the way you read the sentence?

My Notes

Zora Neale Hurston and friend at a recording site, Belle Glade, Florida. This photograph was taken by Alan Lomax in 1935 as part of the Library of Congress's effort to record the sights and sounds of the diverse cultures of Florida, including those of working-class black Americans, struggling with Jim Crow segregation and racial discrimination.

pigmentation: natural coloring

[1] **oyster knife:** a reference to the saying "The world is my oyster"

8 The position of my white neighbor is much more difficult. No brown specter pulls up a chair beside me when I sit down to eat. No dark ghost thrusts its leg against mine in bed. The game of keeping what one has is never so exciting as the game of getting.

9 I do not always feel colored. Even now I often achieve the unconscious Zora of Eatonville before the Hegira.[2] I feel most colored when I am thrown against a sharp white background.

10 For instance at Barnard.[3] "Beside the waters of the Hudson" I feel my race. Among the thousand white persons, I am a dark rock surged upon, and overswept, but through it all, I remain myself. When covered by the waters, I am; and the ebb but reveals me again.

11 Sometimes it is the other way around. A white person is set down in our midst, but the contrast is just as sharp for me. For instance, when I sit in the drafty basement that is The New World Cabaret with a white person, my color comes. We enter chatting about any little nothing that we have in common and are seated by the jazz waiters. In the abrupt way that jazz orchestras have, this one plunges into a number. It loses no time in circumlocutions, but gets right down to business. It constricts the thorax and splits the heart with its tempo and narcotic harmonies. This orchestra grows rambunctious, rears on its hind legs and attacks the tonal veil with primitive fury, rending it, clawing it until it breaks through the jungle beyond. I follow those heathen—follow them exultingly. I dance wildly inside myself; I yell within, I whoop; I shake my assegai[4] above my head, I hurl it true to the mark *yeeeeooww!* I am in the jungle and living in the jungle way. My face is painted red and yellow and my body is painted blue. My pulse is throbbing like a war drum. I want to slaughter something— give pain, give death to what, I do not know.

12 But the piece ends. The men of the orchestra wipe their lips and rest their fingers. I creep back slowly to the veneer we call civilization with the last tone and find the white friend sitting motionless in his seat, smoking calmly.

13 "Good music they have here," he remarks, drumming the table with his fingertips.

14 Music. The great blobs of purple and red emotion have not touched him. He has only heard what I felt. He is far away and I see him dimly across the ocean and the continent that have fallen between us. He is so pale with his whiteness then and I am *so* colored.

15 At certain times I have no race. I am *me*. When I set my hat at a certain angle and saunter down Seventh Avenue, Harlem City, feeling as snooty as the lions in front of the Forty-Second Street Library, for instance. So far as my feelings are concerned, Peggy Hopkins Joyce on the Boule Mich with

circumlocutions: the use of many words to say something that could be simplified

veneer: attractive but superficial appearance

[2] **Hegira:** Mohammed's flight from Mecca to Medina in AD 622; hence, any trip or journey, especially one made to escape a dangerous or undesirable situation

[3] **Barnard:** the college in New York City from which Hurston graduated in 1928

[4] **assegai (*n.*):** a slender spear or javelin with an iron tip, used in southern Africa

My Notes

her gorgeous raiment, stately carriage, knees knocking together in a most aristocratic manner, has nothing on me. The cosmic Zora emerges. I belong to no race nor time. I am the eternal feminine with its string of beads.

16 I have no separate feeling about being an American citizen and colored. I am merely a fragment of the great Soul that surges within the boundaries. My country, right or wrong.

17 Sometimes, I feel discriminated against, but it does not make me angry. It merely astonishes me. How can *any* deny themselves the pleasure of my company? It's beyond me.

18 But in the main, I feel like a brown bag of miscellany propped against a wall. Against a wall in company with other bags, white, red, and yellow. Pour out the contents, and there is discovered a jumble of small things priceless and worthless. A **first-water** diamond, an empty spool, bits of broken glass, lengths of string, a key to a door long since crumbled away, a rusty knife blade, old shoes saved for a road that never was and never will be, a nail bent under the weight of things too heavy for any nail, a dried flower or two still a little fragrant. In your hand is a brown bag. On the ground before you is the jumble it held—so much like the jumble in the bags, could they be emptied, that all might be dumped in a single heap and the bags refilled without altering the content of any greatly. A bit of colored glass more or less would not matter. Perhaps that is how the Great Stuffer of Bags filled them in the first place—who knows?

⊘ Knowledge Quest

• What details about Hurston's experience stand out to you?

• What details tell you about Hurston's awareness of self?

first-water: of the best quality

Returning to the Text

- Return to the essay as you respond to the following questions. Use text evidence to support your responses.
- Write any additional questions you have about the text in your Reader/Writer Notebook.

1. KQ What happened to change Hurston's perspective of herself and her race? Why was this significant given the time period in which she lived? Support your answer.

_____

_____

_____

_____

2. KQ How does the author's use of the word *fast* in paragraph 5 relate to her self-awareness?

_____

_____

_____

_____

3. Why does Hurston choose to use the word *circumlocutions* in paragraph 11? How does this word contribute to the tone of the text?

_____

_____

_____

_____

4. What role does the author's use of figurative language play in developing the theme? What evidence from the text supports your answer?

_____

_____

_____

_____

5. How does the metaphor in the last paragraph relate to Hurston's statements earlier in the essay? How do the themes of the essay reflect those of the Harlem Renaissance?

_____

_____

_____

_____

Appreciating the Author's Craft

Voice is an author's style, the quality that makes his or her writing unique and that conveys his or her attitude, personality, or character in a text. Authors deliberately use specific diction and syntax to create a unique voice in their writing. Return to the text and underline all the words and phrases that Hurston places in quotations or italicizes. Then answer the following question.

6. How do Hurston's diction and syntax contribute to the voice of the text? How would you describe her voice?

_____

_____

_____

_____

Secondary Source Reading

In his essay "Zora Neale Hurston: 'A Negro Way of Speaking,'" Henry Louis Gates Jr. says of Hurston:

> Virtually ignored after the early fifties, even by the Black Arts movement in the sixties, an otherwise noisy and intense spell of black image- and myth-making that rescued so many black writers from remaindered oblivion, Hurston embodied a more or less harmonious but nevertheless problematic unity of opposites. It is this complexity that refuses to lend itself to the glib categories of 'radical' or 'conservative,' 'black' or 'Negro,' 'revolutionary' or 'Uncle Tom'—categories of little use in literary criticism. It is this same complexity, embodied in her fiction, that, until Alice Walker published her important essay ("In Search of Zora Neale Hurston") in Ms. magazine in 1975, had made Hurston's place in black literary history an ambiguous one at best.

7. With a small group, discuss and analyze Gates's interpretation of Hurston's contribution to black literary history. Discuss what evidence he provides for his interpretation and its validity.

_____

_____

_____

_____

_____

_____

Working from the Text

8. Review your notes about the ideas and values of Harlem Renaissance. Then review your responses to the text-dependent questions associated with Hurston's essay. Use this two-column note organizer to consider Hurston's philosophy and to identify why Gates described Hurston as a "unity of opposites." Enter inferences that you make from her text and cite textual evidence that supports your inferences.

What philosophies and beliefs did Hurston share with the Harlem Renaissance?	In what ways did Hurston follow her own path?

9. Use the evidence and inferences you made in the chart to write a brief analysis of the ways in which the Harlem Renaissance shaped Hurston's philosophy and the ways in which Hurston trod her own path.

☑ Check Your Understanding

Quickwrite: How did the historical context of the Harlem Renaissance shape and influence writers such as Hurston?

The Tradition of Dialect

Learning Targets

- Explore how writers use dialogue and dialect to bring their stories to life.
- Identify how Hurston's style distinguished her as a unique voice during the Harlem Renaissance.
- Integrate ideas from multiple texts to build knowledge and vocabulary on different perspectives about self-awareness and the understanding of self.

Preview

In this activity, you will examine the way in which an author uses dialogue and dialect to capture how characters speak.

LITERARY

Dialect is the distinctive language, including the sounds, spelling, grammar, and diction, of a specific group or class of people at a certain time period and in a certain geographical region.

VOCABULARY

An Introduction to Dialect

Hurston is noted for her gifted storytelling and for honoring oral tradition, including **dialect**. An author's use of dialect validates the oral traditions of a people, a time, and a place. It also contributes to the voice of a text, shaping the perceptions of the reader about the characters and setting. Through their choice of dialect, authors create a representation of the spoken language, which helps record the history of language as it evolves over generations. Your reading of "Sweat" introduces you to Hurston's entertaining use of the oral tradition.

1. Preview one of Hurston's most famous short stories, "Sweat," by scanning Chunk 1 and underlining unfamiliar words. Listen carefully as your teacher reads aloud the first section of "Sweat." You will hear that Hurston reproduces the actual speech of the characters.

2. Next, work with a small group to formulate some "pronunciation rules" for pronouncing the words. Use the following graphic organizer to guide your work. Some examples have been provided for you.

Dialect	Conventional English
dat, wid	that, with (*th* is often replaced by *d*)
skeer	
ah	
fuh	

3. Practice reading the dialogue in paragraphs 5–8 out loud in your group, taking turns to read each sentence in dialect. Take time to discuss how hearing the dialect spoken creates a particular voice and what perception it gives you about the characters and setting.

As You Read

- Highlight the story's details to create a mental image of the characters and setting.
- Underline words and phrases that are allusions to Christianity and the Bible.
- Circle unknown words and phrases. Try to determine the meaning of the words by using context clues, word parts, or a dictionary. and try rereading, using background knowledge, asking questions, or annotating to deepen your understanding.

My Notes

 KNOWLEDGE QUEST

Knowledge Question:

How can a person's sense of self affect the outcome of a situation?

My Notes

_____

_____

_____

_____

_____

_____

_____

_____

_____

_____

_____

galvanized: made of metal covered with zinc

Short Story

Sweat

by **Zora Neale Hurston**

Chunk 1

1   It was eleven o'clock of a Spring night in Florida. It was Sunday. Any other night, Delia Jones would have been in bed for two hours by this time. But she was a wash-woman, and Monday morning meant a great deal to her. So she collected the soiled clothes on Saturday when she returned the clean things. Sunday night after church, she sorted them and put the white things to soak. It saved her almost a half day's start. A great hamper in the bedroom held the clothes that she brought home. It was so much neater than a number of bundles lying around.

2   She squatted in the kitchen floor beside the great pile of clothes, sorting them into small heaps according to color, and humming a song in a mournful key, but wondering through it all where Sykes, her husband, had gone with her horse and buckboard.

3   Just then something long, round, limp and black fell upon her shoulders and slithered to the floor beside her. A great terror took hold of her. It softened her knees and dried her mouth so that it was a full minute before she could cry out or move. Then she saw that it was the big bull whip her husband liked to carry when he drove.

4   She lifted her eyes to the door and saw him standing there bent over with laughter at her fright. She screamed at him.

5   "Sykes, what you throw dat whip on me like dat? You know it would skeer me—looks just like a snake, an' you knows how skeered Ah is of snakes."

6   "Course Ah knowed it! That's how come Ah done it." He slapped his leg with his hand and almost rolled on the ground in his mirth. "If you such a big fool dat you got to have a fit over a earth worm or a string, Ah don't keer how bad Ah skeer you."

Chunk 2

7   "You aint got no business doing it. Gawd knows it's a sin. Some day Ah'mgointuh drop dead from some of yo' foolishness. 'Nother thing, where you been wid mah rig? Ah feeds dat pony. He aint fuh you to be drivin' wid no bull whip."

8   "You sho is one aggravatin' nigger woman!" he declared and stepped into the room. She resumed her work and did not answer him at once. "Ah done tole you time and again to keep them white folks' clothes outa dis house."

9   He picked up the whip and glared down at her. Delia went on with her work. She went out into the yard and returned with a galvanized tub and set

t on the washbench. She saw that Sykes had kicked all of the clothes together again, and now stood in her way **truculently**, his whole manner hoping, *praying*, for an argument. But she walked calmly around him and commenced to re-sort the things.

10 "Next time, Ah'm gointer kick 'em outdoors," he threatened as he struck a match along the leg of his corduroy **breeches**.

11 Delia never looked up from her work, and her thin, stooped shoulders sagged further.

12 "Ah aint for no fuss t'night, Sykes. Ah just come from taking sacrament at the church house."

13 He snorted scornfully. "Yeah, you just come from de church house on a Sunday night, but heah you is gone to work on them clothes. You ain't nothing but a hypocrite. One of them amen-corner Christians—sing, whoop, and shout, then come home and wash white folks clothes on the Sabbath."

14 He stepped roughly upon the whitest pile of things, kicking them helter-skelter as he crossed the room. His wife gave a little scream of dismay, and quickly gathered them together again.

15 "Sykes, you quit grindin' dirt into these clothes! How can Ah git through by Sat'day if Ah don't start on Sunday?"

16 "Ah don't keer if you never git through. Anyhow, Ah done promised Gawd and a couple of other men, Ah aint gointer have it in mah house. Don't gimme no lip neither, else Ah'll throw 'em out and put mah fist up side yo' head to boot."

17 Delia's habitual meekness seemed to slip from her shoulders like a blown scarf. She was on her feet; her poor little body, her bare knuckly hands bravely defying the strapping hulk before her.

18 "Looka heah, Sykes, you done gone too fur. Ah been married to you fur fifteen years, and Ah been takin' in washin' for fifteen years. Sweat, sweat, sweat! Work and sweat, cry and sweat, pray and sweat!"

19 "What's that got to do with me?" he asked brutally.

20 "What's it got to do with you, Sykes? Mah tub of suds is filled yo' belly with **vittles** more times than yo' hands is filled it. *Mah* sweat is done paid for this house and Ah reckon Ah kin keep on sweatin' in it."

21 She seized the iron skillet from the stove and struck a defensive pose, which act surprised him greatly, coming from her. It cowed him and he did not strike her as he usually did.

22 "Naw you won't," she panted, "that ole **snaggle-toothed** black woman you runnin' with aint comin' heah to pile up on *mah* sweat and blood. You aint paid for nothin' on this place, and Ah'm gointer stay right heah till Ah'm toted out foot foremost."

truculently: angrily
breeches: short pants
vittles: food and drink
snaggle-toothed: with an irregular, broken, or projecting tooth

WORD CONNECTIONS

Multiple-Meaning Words
The most common meaning of the word **pass** is "to move past." It can mean to cause something to move in a specified way or to give something to someone using the hands. Something that *passes* can happen, take place, end, or go away. The author uses the word in the context of an idiom, meaning a situation is very bad.

My Notes

23 "Well, you better quit gittin' me riled up, else they'll be totin' you out sooner than you expect. Ah'm so tired of you Ah don't know whut to do. Gawd how Ah hates skinny wimmen!"

24 A little awed by this new Delia, he sidled out of the door and slammed the back gate after him. He did not say where he had gone, but she knew too well. She knew very well that he would not return until nearly daybreak also. Her work over, she went on to bed but not to sleep at once. Things had come to a pretty pass!

25 She lay awake, gazing upon the debris that cluttered their **matrimonial** trail. Not an image left standing along the way. Anything like flowers had long ago been drowned in the salty stream that had been pressed from her heart. Her tears, her sweat, her blood. She had brought love to the union and he had brought a longing after the flesh. Two months after the wedding, he had given her the first brutal beating. She had the memory of his numerous trips to Orlando with all of his wages when he had returned to her penniless, even before the first year had passed. She was young and soft then, but now she thought of her knotty, muscled limbs, her harsh knuckly hands, and drew herself up into an unhappy little ball in the middle of the big feather bed. Too late now to hope for love, even if it were not Bertha it would be someone else. This case differed from the others only in that she was bolder than the others. Too late for everything except her little home.

26 She had built it for her old days, and planted one by one the trees and flowers there. It was lovely to her, lovely.

27 Somehow, before sleep came, she found herself saying aloud: "Oh well, whatever goes over the Devil's back, is got to come under his belly. Sometime or ruther, Sykes, like everybody else, is gointer reap his sowing." After that she was able to build a spiritual **earthworks** against her husband. His shells could no longer reach her. *Amen.* She went to sleep and slept until he announced his presence in bed by kicking her feet and rudely snatching the cover away.

28 "Gimme some kivah heah, an' git yo' damn foots over on yo' own side! Ah oughter mash you in yo' mouf fuh drawing dat skillet on me."

29 Delia went clear to the rail without answering him. A triumphant indifference to all that he was or did.

Chunk 3

30 The week was as full of work for Delia as all other weeks, and Saturday found her behind her little pony, collecting and delivering clothes.

31 It was a hot, hot day near the end of July. The village men on Joe Clarke's porch even chewed cane listlessly. They did not hurl the cane-knots as usual. They let them dribble over the edge of the porch. Even conversation had collapsed under the heat.

32 "Heah come Delia Jones," Jim Merchant said, as the shaggy pony came 'round the bend of the road toward them. The rusty buckboard was heaped with baskets of crisp, clean laundry.

matrimonial: relating to marriage
earthworks: a raised bank or wall made of soil

33 "Yep," Joe Lindsay agreed. "Hot or col', rain or shine, jes ez reg'lar ez de weeks roll roun' Delia carries 'em an' fetches 'em on Sat'day."

34 "She better if she wanter eat," said Moss. "Sykes Jones aint wuth de shot an' powder hit would tek tuh kill 'em. Not to *huh* he aint."

35 "He sho' aint," Walter Thomas chimed in. "It's too bad, too, cause she wuz a right pritty li'l trick when he got huh. Ah'd uh mah'ied huh mahseff if he hadnter beat me to it."

36 Delia nodded briefly at the men as she drove past.

37 "Too much knockin' will ruin any 'oman. He done beat huh 'nough tuh kill three women, let 'lone change they looks," said Elijah Moseley. "How Sykes kin stommuck dat big black greasy Mogul he's layin' roun' wid, gits me. Ah swear dat eight-rock couldn't kiss a sardine can Ah done throwed out de back do' 'way las' yeah."

38 "Aw, she's fat, thass how come. He's allus been crazy 'bout fat women," put in Merchant. "He'd a' been tied up wid one long time ago if he could a' found one tuh have him. Did Ah tell yuh 'bout him come sidlin' roun' *mah* wife—bringin' her a basket uh pee-cans outa his yard fuh a present? Yessir, mah wife! She tol' him tuh take 'em right straight back home, cause Delia works so hard ovah dat washtub she reckon everything on de place taste lak sweat an' soapsuds. Ah jus' wisht Ah'd a' caught 'im 'roun' dere! Ah'd a' made his hips ketch on fiah down dat shell road."

39 "Ah know he done it, too. Ah sees 'im grinnin' at every 'oman dat passes," Walter Thomas said. "But even so, he useter eat some mighty big hunks uh humble pie tuh git dat lil' 'oman he got. She wuz ez pritty ez a speckled pup! Dat wuz fifteen yeahs ago. He useter be so skeered uh losin' huh, she could make him do some parts of a husband's duty. Dey never wuz de same in de mind."

40 "There oughter be a law about him," said Lindsay. "He aint fit tuh carry guts tuh a bear."

41 Clarke spoke for the first time. "Taint no law on earth dat kin make a man be decent if it aint in 'im. There's plenty men dat takes a wife lak dey do a joint uh sugar-cane. It's round, juicy an' sweet when dey gits it. But dey squeeze an' grind, squeeze an' grind an' wring tell dey wring every drop uh pleasure dat's in 'em out. When dey's satisfied dat dey is wrung dry, dey treats 'em jes lak dey do a cane-chew. Dey throws 'em away. Dey knows whut dey is doin' while dey is at it, an' hates theirselves fuh it but they keeps on hangin' after huh tell she's empty. Den dey hates huh fuh bein' a cane-chew an' in de way."

42 "We oughter take Sykes an' dat stray 'oman uh his'n down in Lake Howell swamp an' lay on de rawhide till they cain't say 'Lawd a' mussy.' He allus wuz uh ovahbearin' niggah, but since dat white 'oman from up north done teached 'im how to run a automobile, he done got too biggety to live—an' we oughter kill 'im," Old Man Anderson advised.

43 A grunt of approval went around the porch. But the heat was melting their civic virtue and Elijah Moseley began to bait Joe Clarke.

My Notes

44 "Come on, Joe, git a melon outa dere an' slice it up for yo' customers. We'se all sufferin' wid de heat. De bear's done got *me*!"

45 "Thass right, Joe, a watermelon is jes' whut Ah needs tuh cure de eppizudicks," Walter Thomas joined forces with Moseley. "Come on dere, Joe. We all is steady customers an' you aint set us up in a long time. Ah chooses dat long, bowlegged Floridy favorite."

46 "A god, an' be dough. You all gimme twenty cents and slice way," Clarke retorted. "Ah needs a col' slice m'self. Heah, everybody chip in. Ah'll lend y'll mah meat knife."

47 The money was quickly **subscribed** and the huge melon brought forth. At that moment, Sykes and Bertha arrived. A determined silence fell on the porch and the melon was put away again.

48 Merchant snapped down the blade of his jackknife and moved toward the store door.

49 "Come on in, Joe, an' gimme a slab uh sow belly an' uh pound uh coffee—almost fuhgot 'twas Sat'day. Got to git on home." Most of the men left also.

50 Just then Delia drove past on her way home, as Sykes was ordering magnificently for Bertha. It pleased him for Delia to see.

51 "Git whutsoever yo' heart desires, Honey. Wait a minute, Joe. Give huh two bottles uh strawberry soda-water, uh quart uh parched ground-peas, an' a block uh chewin' gum."

52 With all this they left the store, with Sykes reminding Bertha that this was his town and she could have it if she wanted it.

53 The men returned soon after they left, and held their watermelon feast.

54 "Where did Sykes Jones git da 'oman from nohow?" Lindsay asked.

55 "Ovah Apopka. Guess dey musta been cleanin' out de town when she lef'. She don't look lak a thing but a hunk uh liver wid hair on it."

56 "Well, she sho' kin squall," Dave Carter contributed. "When she gits ready tuh laff, she jes' opens huh mouf an' latches it back tuh de las' notch. No ole grandpa alligator down in Lake Bell ain't got nothin' on huh."

Chunk 4

57 Bertha had been in town three months now. Sykes was still paying her room rent at Della Lewis'—the only house in town that would have taken her in. Sykes took her frequently to Winter Park to "stomps." He still assured her that he was the swellest man in the state.

58 "Sho' you kin have dat lil' ole house soon's Ah kin git dat 'oman outa dere. Everything b'longs tuh me an' you sho' kin have it. Ah sho' 'bominates uh skinny 'oman. Lawdy, you sho' is got one portly shape on you! You kin git *anything* you wants. Dis is *mah* town an' you sho' kin have it."

INDEPENDENT READING LINK

Read and Connect

Browse through your independent reading selection for this unit. Find examples of each level of diction that you studied in this activity. Mark the text by color-coding the examples.

subscribed: paid

59 Delia's work-worn knees crawled over the earth in Gethsemane and up the rocks of Calvary many, many times during these months. She avoided the villagers and meeting places in her efforts to be blind and deaf. But Bertha **nullified** this to a degree, by coming to Delia's house to call Sykes out to her at the gate.

60 Delia and Sykes fought all the time now with no peaceful interludes. They slept and ate in silence. Two or three times Delia had attempted a timid friendliness, but she was repulsed each time. It was plain that the breaches must remain agape.

* * *

61 The sun had burned July to August. The heat streamed down like a million hot arrows, **smiting** all things living upon the earth. Grass withered, leaves browned, snakes went blind in shedding and men and dogs went mad. Dog days!

62 Delia came home one day and found Sykes there before her. She wondered, but started to go on into the house without speaking, even though he was standing in the kitchen door and she must either stoop under his arm or ask him to move. He made no room for her. She noticed a soap box beside the steps, but paid no particular attention to it, knowing that he must have brought it there. As she was stooping to pass under his outstretched arm, he suddenly pushed her backward, laughingly.

63 "Look in de box dere Delia, Ah done brung yuh somethin'!"

64 She nearly fell upon the box in her stumbling, and when she saw what it held, she all but fainted outright.

65 "Sykes! Sykes, mah Gawd! You take dat rattlesnake 'way from heah! You *gottuh*. Oh, Jesus, have mussy!"

66 "Ah aint gut tuh do nuthin' uh de kin'—fact is Ah aint got tuh do nothin' but die. Taint no use uh you puttin' on airs makin' out lak you skeered uh dat snake—he's gointer stay right heah tell he die. He wouldn't bite me cause Ah knows how tuh handle 'im. Nohow he wouldn't risk breakin' out his fangs 'gin *yo*' skinny laigs."

67 "Naw, now Sykes, don't keep dat thing 'roun' heah tuh skeer me tuh death. You knows Ah'm even feared uh earth worms. Thass de biggest snake Ah evah did see. Kill 'im Sykes, please."

68 "Doan ast me tuh do nothin' fuh yuh. Goin' roun' tryin' tuh be so damn astorperious. Naw, Ah aint gonna kill it. Ah think uh damn sight mo' uh him dan you! Dat's a nice snake an' anybody doan lak 'im kin jes' hit de grit."

69 The village soon heard that Sykes had the snake, and came to see and ask questions.

nullified: made to have no effect
smiting: hitting, afflicting

70 "How de hen-fire did you ketch dat six-foot rattler, Sykes?" Thomas asked.

71 "He's full uh frogs so he caint hardly move, thass how Ah eased up on 'm. But Ah'm a snake charmer an' knows how tuh handle 'em. Shux, dat aint nothin'. Ah could ketch one eve'y day if Ah so wanted tuh."

72 "Whut he needs is a heavy hick'ry club leaned real heavy on his head. Dat's de bes' way tuh charm a rattlesnake."

73 "Naw, Walt, y'all jes' don't understand dese diamon' backs lak Ah do," said Sykes in a superior tone of voice.

Chunk 5

74 The village agreed with Walter, but the snake stayed on. His box remained by the kitchen door with its screen wire covering. Two or three days later it had digested its meal of frogs and literally came to life. It rattled at every movement in the kitchen or the yard. One day as Delia came down the kitchen steps she saw his chalky-white fangs curved like **scimitars** hung in the wire meshes. This time she did not run away with averted eyes as usual. She stood for a long time in the doorway in a red fury that grew bloodier for every second that she regarded the creature that was her torment.

75 That night she broached the subject as soon as Sykes sat down to the table.

76 "Sykes, Ah wants you tuh take dat snake 'way fum heah. You done starved me an' Ah put up widcher, you done beat me an Ah took dat, but you done kilt all mah insides bringin' dat varmint heah."

77 Sykes poured out a saucer full of coffee and drank it deliberately before he answered her.

78 "A whole lot Ah keer 'bout how you feels inside uh out. Dat snake aint goin' no damn wheah till Ah gits ready fuh 'im tuh go. So fur as beatin' is concerned, yuh aint took near all dat you gointer take ef yuh stay 'roun' *me*."

79 Delia pushed back her plate and got up from the table. "Ah hates you, Sykes," she said calmly. "Ah hates you tuh de same degree dat Ah useter love yuh. Ah done took an' took till mah belly is full up tuh mah neck. Dat's de reason Ah got mah letter fum de church an' moved mah membership tuh Woodbridge—so Ah don't haftuh take no sacrament wid yuh. Ah don't wantuh see yuh 'roun' me a-tall. Lay 'roun' wid dat 'oman all yuh wants tuh, but gwan 'way fum me an' mah house. Ah hates yuh lak uh suck-egg dog."

80 Sykes almost let the huge wad of corn bread and collard greens he was chewing fall out of his mouth in amazement. He had a hard time whipping himself up to the proper fury to try to answer Delia.

81 "Well, Ah'm glad you does hate me. Ah'm sho' tiahed uh you hangin' ontuh me. Ah don't want yuh. Look at yuh stringey ole neck! Yo' rawbony laigs an' arms is enough tuh cut uh man tuh death. You looks jes' lak de devvul's doll-baby tuh *me*. You cain't hate me no worse dan Ah hates you. Ah been hatin' *you* fuh years."

scimitars: swords with a curved blade

82 "Yo' ole black hide don't look lak nothin' tuh me, but uh **passle** uh wrinkled up rubber, wid yo' big ole yeahs flappin' on each side lak uh paih uh buzzard wings. Don't think Ah'm gointuh be run 'way fum mah house neither. Ah'm goin' tuh de white folks bout *you*, mah young man, de very nex' time you lay yo' han's on me. Mah cup is done run ovah." Delia said this with no signs of fear and Sykes departed from the house, threatening her, but made not the slightest move to carry out any of them.

Chunk 6

83 That night he did not return at all, and the next day being Sunday, Delia was glad she did not have to quarrel before she hitched up her pony and drove the four miles to Woodbridge.

84 She stayed to the night service—"love feast"—which was very warm and full of spirit. In the emotional winds her domestic trials were borne far and wide so that she sang as she drove homeward,

Jurden water, black an' col'

Chills de body, not de soul

An' Ah wantah cross Jurden in uh calm time.

85 She came from the barn to the kitchen door and stopped.

86 "Whut's de mattah, ol' satan, you aint kickin' up yo' racket?" She addressed the snake's box. Complete silence. She went on into the house with a new hope in its birth struggles. Perhaps her threat to go to the white folks had frightened Sykes! Perhaps he was sorry! Fifteen years of misery and suppression had brought Delia to the place where she would hope *anything* that looked towards a way over or through her wall of inhibitions.

87 She felt in the match safe behind the stove at once for a match. There was only one there.

88 "Dat niggah wouldn't fetch nothin' heah tuh save his rotten neck, but he kin run thew whut Ah brings quick enough. Now he done toted off nigh on tuh haff uh box uh matches. He done had dat 'oman heah in mah house, too."

89 Nobody but a woman could tell how she knew this even before she struck the match. But she did and it put her into a new fury.

90 Presently she brought in the tubs to put the white things to soak. This time she decided she need not bring the hamper out of the bedroom; she would go in there and do the sorting. She picked up the pot-bellied lamp and went in. The room was small and the hamper stood hard by the foot of the white iron bed. She could sit and reach through the bedposts—resting as she worked.

passle: large number

Language Change

Our world is vast, and throughout the world, dialect and speech have varied from place to place and over time. For this reason, authors sometimes use their own experiences to light up a story with language that may be considered complex. For example, phrases in "Sweat" may include nonconventional variations in spelling, grammar, punctuation, and meaning, such as:

- "... Mah *sweat is done paid for this house* ..." (paragraph 20)
- "... *jez ez reg' lar ez de weeks roll roun'* ..." (paragraph 33)
- "*Too much knockin'* ..." (paragraph 37)

These words give a more accurate account of the story as it plays out in the author's mind.

Find two examples in the text of phrases that include variations in dialect and work with a partner to discuss the literal meaning of the phrases.

As a group, evaluate why an author might choose to use a nonconventional word or phrase in a story.

91 "Ah wantah cross Jurden in uh calm time." She was singing again. The mood of the "love feast" had returned. She threw back the lid of the basket almost gaily. Then, moved by both horror and terror, she sprang back toward the door. *There lay the snake in the basket!* He moved sluggishly at first, but even as she turned round and round, jumped up and down in an insanity of fear, he began to stir vigorously. She saw him pouring his awful beauty from the basket upon the bed, then she seized the lamp and ran as fast as she could to the kitchen. The wind from the open door blew out the light and the darkness added to her terror. She sped to the darkness of the yard, slamming the door after her before she thought to set down the lamp. She did not feel safe even on the ground, so she climbed up in the hay barn.

92 There for an hour or more she lay sprawled upon the hay a gibbering wreck.

93 Finally, she grew quiet, and after that, coherent thought. With this, stalked through her a cold, bloody rage. Hours of this. A period of introspection, a space of retrospection, then a mixture of both. Out of this an awful calm.

94 "Well, Ah done de bes' Ah could. If things aint right, Gawd knows taint mah fault."

95 She went to sleep—a twitchy sleep—and woke up to a faint gray sky. There was a loud hollow sound below. She peered out. Sykes was at the wood-pile, demolishing a wire-covered box.

96 He hurried to the kitchen door, but hung outside there some minutes before he entered, and stood some minutes more inside before he closed it after him.

97 The gray in the sky was spreading. Delia descended without fear now, and crouched beneath the low bedroom window. The drawn shade shut out the dawn, shut in the night. But the thin walls held back no sound.

98 "Dat ol' scratch is woke up now!" She mused at the tremendous whirr inside, which every woodsman knows, is one of the sound illusions. The rattler is a ventriloquist. His whirr sounds to the right, to the left, straight ahead, behind, close under foot—everywhere but where it is. Woe to him who guesses wrong unless he is prepared to hold up his end of the argument! Sometimes he strikes without rattling at all.

99 Inside, Sykes heard nothing until he knocked a pot lid off the stove while trying to reach the match safe in the dark. He had emptied his pockets at Bertha's.

100 The snake seemed to wake up under the stove and Sykes made a quick leap into the bedroom. In spite of the gin he had had, his head was clearing now.

101 "Mah Gawd!" he chattered, "ef Ah could on'y strack uh light!"

102 The rattling ceased for a moment as he stood paralyzed. He waited. It seemed that the snake waited also.

103 "Oh, fuh de light! Ah thought he'd be too sick"—Sykes was muttering to himself when the whirr began again, closer, right underfoot this time. Long before this, Sykes' ability to think had been flattened down to primitive instinct and he leaped—onto the bed.

104 Outside Delia heard a cry that might have come from a maddened chimpanzee, a stricken gorilla. All the terror, all the horror, all the rage that man possibly could express, without a recognizable human sound.

105 A tremendous stir inside there, another series of animal screams, the intermittent whirr of the reptile. The shade torn violently down from the window, letting in the red dawn, a huge brown hand seizing the window stick, great dull blows upon the wooden floor punctuating the gibberish of sound long after the rattle of the snake had abruptly subsided. All this Delia could see and hear from her place beneath the window, and it made her ill. She crept over to the **four-o'clocks** and stretched herself on the cool earth to recover.

106 She lay there. "Delia, Delia!" She could hear Sykes calling in a most despairing tone as one who expected no answer. The sun crept on up, and he called. Delia could not move—her legs were gone flabby. She never moved, he called, and the sun kept rising.

107 "Mah Gawd!" She heard him moan, "Mah Gawd fum Heben!" She heard him stumbling about and got up from her flower-bed. The sun was growing warm. As she approached the door she heard him call out hopefully, "Delia, is dat you Ah heah?"

108 She saw him on his hands and knees as soon as she reached the door. He crept an inch or two toward her—all that he was able, and she saw his horribly swollen neck and his one open eye shining with hope. A surge of pity too strong to support bore her away from that eye that must, could not, fail to see the tubs. He would see the lamp. Orlando with its doctors was too far. She could scarcely reach the Chinaberry tree, where she waited in the growing heat while inside she knew the cold river was creeping up and up to extinguish that eye which must know by now that she knew.

⌀ Knowledge Quest
- When do you notice Delia's sense of self starts to change?
- What language does the author use to describe Delia's self-awareness?

GRAMMAR & USAGE

Sentence Fragments
In paragraph 105, Hurston uses three **sentence fragments**, or incomplete sentences, to describe what Delia sees and hears. The first two fragments focus on sound and lack the verbs necessary to make them complete sentences. The third focuses on movement. The fragments in this paragraph are deliberate snapshots of sounds, actions, and colors that work together to create a vivid scene. Write your own series of three fragment sentences in Hurston's style to describe a scene from your day.

four-o'clocks: a flower that opens in the cool of the evening

Returning to the Text

- Return to the short story as you respond to the following questions. Use text evidence to support your responses.
- Write any additional questions you have about the text in your Reader/Writer Notebook.

4. What role does dialect play in the development of the tone of the story?

_____

_____

_____

_____

5. How do the words and actions of Sykes in paragraphs 46 foreshadow possible events in the story? Why might Sykes be "hoping, *praying*, for an argument" in paragraph 9? How does it shape your perception of him?

_____

_____

_____

_____

_____

6. How does the author describe Delia's character? Why is establishing this important to the story?

_____

_____

_____

_____

7. How does the author choose to give exposition about the characters? How does this choice contribute to the meaning of the story?

_____

_____

_____

_____

_____

8. Why does Delia reflect in paragraph 25 that "debris ... cluttered their matrimonial trail"? What is the significance of this in relation to the overall theme and to the story's placement as part of the Harlem Renaissance?

_____

_____

_____

_____

_____

9. **KQ** What role do Delia's memories have in creating a sense of self-awareness? How do these memories eventually cause her to change her character?

_____

_____

_____

_____

_____

10. Why are the neighborhood men against Sykes? How do their views contribute to a theme of the story?

_____

_____

_____

_____

_____

11. What point of view does the author use to tell the story? How does her choice contribute to the effectiveness of the story? How would the story change if it were told from a different point of view?

_____

_____

_____

_____

_____

12. What figurative language does the author use to describe Delia's response to Bertha living in town? In what ways is this consistent or inconsistent with what the reader knows of Delia's character?

_____

_____

_____

_____

13. KQ Why might the author use the word *pouring* to describe the snake's action in paragraph 91?

_____

_____

_____

_____

14. How is the story structured overall? How does this structure build meaning for the reader?

_____

_____

_____

_____

_____

15. How does the end of the story affect the reader? In what ways does the outcome reflect one or more of the themes in the story and its historical context?

_____

_____

_____

_____

16. Which common themes of the times does the story reflect? In what ways does the story differ from those themes and ideals?

_____

_____

_____

_____

_____

Knowledge Quest

After reading Hurston's works, think about how Delia's self-awareness helped her to focus on a higher purpose. With a partner, discuss how self-awareness can create hope for a positive outcome out of a negative situation. Answer these questions: *What is self-awareness? How can a person's self-awareness help him or her make the right decisions? Why is it important to "check in" with your feelings about a subject?* After your discussion, write down your thoughts and opinions in the space. Be sure to:

- Respond thoughtfully to diverse perspectives.
- Determine any additional information needed to propel the discussion.
- Promote a civil, democratic discussion.

 INDEPENDENT READING LINK

You can continue to build your knowledge about this theme by reading related fiction at ZINC Reading Labs. Select the **fiction** filter and type keywords such as *self* or *perception* in the **Search all ZINC articles** field.

 ZINC

Working from the Text

17. "Sweat" is steeped in Christian symbolism, a sign of the culture Hurston was raised in and was writing for. Work with a partner to find allusions to the Bible and Christian symbols in the story. Explain how the literary device of allusions creates meaning in the text.

Allusions	Effect on the Text

18. Look back over the chart you filled out in order to discuss and write a brief analysis of what specific purpose Huston's use of allusions achieves in the text.

LANGUAGE & WRITER'S CRAFT: Levels of Diction

An author can choose to use a variety of diction and syntax in order to shape the mood, voice, or tone of their writing. Huston is known for using different levels of diction, including dialect, in her writing. Review the levels of diction summarized and the following examples.

Formal or high diction usually contains words that make the tone sound educated. It uses complicated syntax and effective and impressive word choices. Unlike informal diction, formal diction avoids slang, contractions, and other informal expressions.

Example: *In Zora Neale Hurston's short story "Sweat," she alternates between a neutral narrative voice and the specific Floridian dialect of her characters in dialogue, revealing sociological context about the setting and the background cultural influences that shape their lives.*

Neutral diction uses ordinary words and syntax without complicated words. It can include some elements of informal diction, such as contractions.

Example: *In Zora Neale Hurston's short story "Sweat," she switches between a narrator's voice and the dialect of her characters in dialogue. The difference shows the setting and context of the characters' lives.*

Informal or low diction is the type of relaxed language people use in typical conversations. Contractions, slang, and idioms are some typical markers of this type of diction.

Example: *In "Sweat," Hurston flips between a narrator's voice and characters talking in dialect. It's hard to understand the dialect sometimes, but it shows where the characters are from.*

Dialect is regional language, which has its own syntax, words, and grammar. In literature, dialect often divides characters into different sectors of society.

Example: *Well, Ah done de bes' Ah could. If things aint right, Gawd knows taint mah fault.*

PRACTICE Find one example of each level that Hurston uses in "Sweat." Choose one sentence and revise it into a different level of diction. Compare your revision with a partner's and discuss how it changes the voice of text.

Literary Analysis

The purpose of a response-to-literature essay is to demonstrate thoughtful understanding of a literary passage. Writing a literary analysis begins with planning what aspects you will analyze through brainstorming, outlining, and finding textual evidence to support your analysis. With the information you've gathered, you can then craft an analysis of the text and the author's stylistic technique and support it with textual evidence to convey meaning to the reader. A literary analysis includes the following:

- a well-crafted thesis statement that demonstrates understanding of the literary element being analyzed
- body paragraphs that cite textual evidence to support the thesis
- effective transitions that connect ideas and move smoothly through the essay
- original commentary on the writer's response to the literature
- concluding statements that follow from the ideas introduced in the thesis and developed in the essay

Writing Prompt: Literary Analysis

Analyze the extent to which Hurston's story is a tribute to the lives of ordinary African American people. Choose a method of prewriting and then draft a response to this story. In your analysis, address the literary elements you have studied, including Hurston's use of diction, and explain how her use of diction and syntax shapes the mood, voice, and tone of the story. Your writing should be composed using only formal diction. Be sure to:

- Choose a writing structure that conveys your purpose, audience, topic, and context.
- Include a thesis statement that analyzes the author's use of diction and syntax.
- Cite textual evidence and give commentary to support your analysis.
- Provide a conclusion that restates your claim and supports the ideas developed in the argument.

Revising and Editing with Peer Review

After you have completed your draft, pair with a writing partner and read your partner's essay. You'll be reading each other's essays to help improve clarity, development of ideas, organization, style, word choices, and sentence structure. Provide peer response by giving the following feedback:

- Underline the thesis statement. Does the thesis give direction to the essay?
- Underline the topic sentence in each body paragraph.
- Put a wavy line under any sentence that feels unclear or out of place.
- Place a box around any language that doesn't seem formal or academic or where another word might be more appropriate.
- If you find textual evidence not followed by documentation, write a suggestion in the margin for either a lead-in or a parenthetical method of citing the source.
- Place a * on commentary sentences that precede or follow the textual evidence.
- If commentary is missing, make a note in the margin indicating the need to add it.
- Mark the explanation about Hurston's use of diction with a +.
- Highlight the sentences that clearly discuss how the literary elements add meaning to the text.
- Note any places where syntax is choppy or overly wordy or where standard English conventions are not being used properly.
- Circle the conclusion.

Learning Targets

- Understand how different types of clauses combine to form complete sentences.
- Analyze the use of sentence fragments for effect.
- Apply an understanding of sentence boundaries and punctuation when revising writing.

Preview

In this activity, you will analyze different types of clauses in order to create complete sentences as well as how sentence fragments can be used for literary effect.

Analyzing Types of Clauses

Knowing the difference between types of clauses can help writers identify complete and incomplete sentences when revising their work. For a sentence to be considered complete, it must contain at least one **independent clause**. At a minimum, an independent clause includes a subject and a verb, and it expresses a complete idea.

1. Look at these examples from "Sweat" by Zora Neale Hurston. How many independent clauses does each sentence contain?

> She peered out.
>
> The sun had burned July to August.
>
> Grass withered, leaves browned, snakes went blind in shedding, and men and dogs went mad.
>
> She picked up the pot-bellied lamp and went in.

In addition to at least one independent clause, a sentence may contain dependent clauses. Like an independent clause, a **dependent clause** contains a subject and a verb. However, a dependent clause cannot stand alone as a complete sentence because it does not express a complete idea. Dependent clauses often include a word such as *as, because, before, if, since, unless, when,* or *while,* which shows that the clause needs more information.

2. Read the following sentences from "Sweat." Mark any words that introduce a dependent clause. Then identify the independent and dependent clauses in each sentence.

> She wondered, but started to go on into the house without speaking, even though he was standing in the kitchen door and she must either stoop under his arm or ask him to move.
>
> As she was stooping to pass under his outstretched arm, he suddenly pushed her backward.
>
> That night she broached the subject as soon as Sykes sat down to the table.

Using Sentence Fragments for Effect

If a group of words written as a sentence lacks at least one independent clause, it is a sentence fragment. In academic contexts, writers typically avoid sentence fragments because fragments can make writing seem informal or unclear. However, fragments are often used by literary writers—especially in works of fiction—to create effect.

3. Read the excerpt from "Sweat" and mark any sentence fragments. Then discuss with a partner why the author might have chosen to use fragments in this passage.

> Finally, she grew quiet, and after that, coherent thought. With this, stalked through her a cold, bloody rage. Hours of this. A period of introspection, a space of retrospection, then a mixture of both. Out of this an awful calm.

Using Complete Sentences in Formal Writing

While writers sometimes make intentional choices to use sentence fragments for effect, it is important to be able to recognize and correct the unintentional use of incomplete or incorrectly punctuated sentences in your own writing. More often than not, following the conventions of academic writing will help you communicate clearly with your audience.

4. Read the descriptions of common sentence errors and the examples of each in the chart. Revise each example sentence into a complete, conventional sentence with conventional punctuation.

Common Sentence Errors	Example	Conventional Sentence
Sentence fragment: a group of words that lacks an independent clause	"All the terror, all the horror, all the rage that man possibly could express..."	
Run-on sentence: two or more independent clauses joined by short connector words—such as *and, but, or*—without necessary punctuation (usually a comma or semicolon)	The author uses many allusions in the story but the snake is the most obvious symbol and it carries both literal and metaphorical significance.	

Common Sentence Errors	Example	Conventional Sentence
Comma splice: two or more independent clauses joined with only a comma	Delia deserves respect, the neighborhood men think Sykes is worthless.	
Fused sentence: two or more independent clauses joined without punctuation or connector words	Delia looked over Sykes looked at the ground.	

Revising

Read the following paragraph from an article about Zora Neale Hurston's hometown of Eatonville, Florida. Identify sentences that need to be revised in order to be considered complete sentences with correct punctuation. Annotate the paragraph to show how you would revise it.

[1] It may be small and hard to find but Eatonville is important for two reasons, it was the first all-black incorporated town in the United States, it was the childhood home of Zora Neale Hurston. [2] Much of Hurston's writing is set here, many of her characters are thinly disguised versions of actual residents. [3] Eatonville gave Hurston her best material and a few years ago the favor was returned. [4] The Hurston connection gave Eatonville an argument; to save itself from being paved over. [5] Hurston and Eatonville have always been closely linked. To understand one. You have to understand the other.

☑ Check Your Understanding

Looking at the paragraph you just revised, think about what questions you might ask the writer to help her revise sentences that are incomplete or that need different punctuation. Add these questions to your Editor's Checklist as a reminder to check your own work for complete, correctly punctuated sentences.

Practice

In Activity 4.9, you reviewed a peer's response to the Writing Prompt about the story "Sweat." Exchange your draft again—with the same peer or a different partner—and examine the writing specifically for correct use of complete sentences with correct punctuation. Put an exclamation point next to any incomplete or incorrectly punctuated sentences and work with your partner to revise them.

My Notes

Learning Targets

- Discuss explicit and implicit meaning of a text.
- Identify and analyze direct and indirect characterization.
- Analyze how foreshadowing shapes the author's portrayal of the plot.

Preview

In this activity, you will begin reading the novel *Their Eyes Were Watching God* in order to make predictions, discuss meaning, analyze the author's use of characterization, and evaluate the use of foreshadowing.

The Double-Entry Journal

1. As you read *Their Eyes Were Watching God*, you will take notes in a double-entry journal. Copy or summarize passages from the book on the left side (textual evidence) and write your response to each passage on the right side (commentary). Draw a horizontal line under each entry. For reference, record the page number of each quote.

   Responses could include the following:

   - **questions** that will help you clarify what is happening in the novel
   - **details** about characters or plot events
   - **connections** you make to personal experiences, ideas in other texts, and society
   - **predictions** about how characters will react to events
   - **inferences** (logical conclusions) about why characters are saying or doing things and the evidence that supports your inference

2. Create a double-entry journal in your Reader/Writer Notebook to use as you read and discuss the first chapter together as a class. Try to use a variety of responses (questions, detail, connection, prediction, inference). As you read the novel independently, you will continue to use the double-entry journal to note the connection between the research that has been presented about the Harlem Renaissance and the events and ideas of the novel. In your notes, cite textual evidence. Include commentary that shows how Hurston's work is characteristic of the Harlem Renaissance as well as elements that illustrate Hurston's departure from the Harlem Renaissance and its philosophy/beliefs, historical context, relation to the arts, and daily life.

Predicting Using Text Features

3. Authors choose novel titles for many reasons. For example, the protagonist in the novel *Gone with the Wind* refers to her town being overtaken by the Yankees and wonders whether her home was "also gone with the wind which had swept through Georgia." Predict the meaning of the title *Their Eyes Were Watching God*.

Beginning the Novel: Men and Women

4. Read the first two paragraphs of Chapter 1. What distinction do the first two paragraphs make between men and women?

5. What questions do these paragraphs raise for you?

6. *Male students*: Interpret and analyze the first paragraph. Note your findings and be prepared to present them to the female students in your class.

   Female students: Interpret and analyze the second paragraph. Note your findings and be prepared to present them to the male students in your class.

7. **Collaborative Conversation:** As a class, discuss the first two paragraphs of Chapter 1 and compare your interpretations of them. Take turns pointing out sentences that contain explicit meaning and sentences that contain implicit meaning and discuss their differences and how each kind of sentence aids in helping you understand the meaning of these paragraphs. Record your notes from the conversation in your Reader/Writer Notebook.

Characterization in Chapter 1

The way an author portrays characters also influences the relationship between them and the themes, setting, and plot of a text. However, authors need to find ways to create a well-rounded depiction of their characters by both telling about them and showing their actions, thoughts, and relationships. An author uses **direct characterization** to tell the audience who and what the character is:

- *So the beginning of this was a woman and she had come back from burying the dead.*

Sentences like this help the reader create a visual picture of the character in their mind. Yet just as in real life, people also gather information and first impressions about others indirectly—the way a person treats other people or behaves. An author uses indirect characterization to show things that reveal the personality of a character.

Methods of indirect characterization include the following:

- **the character's appearance:** *The women took the faded shirt and muddy overalls and laid them away for remembrance.*
- **what the character says:** *"Ah' m tryin' to soak some uh de tiredness and de dirt outa mah feet."*
- **what the character thinks:** *Seeing the woman as she was made them remember the envy they had stored up from other times.*
- **what the character does:** *Her speech was pleasant enough, but she kept walking straight to her gate.*
- **what other characters say about a character:** *"Humph. Y' all let her yuh. If she ain' t got manners enough to stop and let folks know how she been makin' out, let her g' wan."*

LITERARY

Indirect characterization is any method—except for direct characterization—that a writer uses to develop characters other than simply telling the reader what to think of the character.

VOCABULARY

---

8. Complete the following chart using evidence from Chapter 1.

Janie Mae Crawford		
Character Detail	How does the reader learn this?	Direct or Indirect?

9. Continue using a chart like the one you just completed for Janie and the other characters you meet as you continue to read the novel.

he Porch Sitters

the novel, upon her return, Janie is greeted by the "porch sitters": townspeople
tting on porches and discussing their thoughts on ideas on where she's been
d the kind of person she is. Huston uses the porch sitters as a kind of **chorus:**
group that serves to provide commentary about the action that is taking place.
ancient Greece, many playwrights used a chorus to serve as an extra narrative
ice that would provide key information about everything that happened
offstage." In *Their Eyes Were Watching God*, the porch sitters fill in the blanks
ith conjecture about where Janie might have been and what happened before she
ft, helping provide the reader with context.

0. In paragraph 4, what does the author mean by saying of the porch sitters
that "they sat in judgment"? What does this tell you about them and their
relationship with Janie?

1. Revisit the role of the porch sitters in "Sweat" in Chunk 3. How do they
compare to the porch sitters in Chapter 1 of *Their Eyes Were Watching God*?

☑ Focus on the Sentence

fter reading Chapter 1, reflect on how Janie is characterized. Write two
entences about how Hurston characterizes Janie starting with the subordinating
onjunctions.

/hile _____

_____

lthough _____

_____

My Notes

Plot Development

When a writer presents the events of a story the way events happen in real life—in time order—it is called *linear plot development*. Sometimes, though, a writer needs to tell about an event from the past or hint about an event in the future. To share an event that happened at a point in time before the time of the story, a writer uses flashback. To hint at a future event, a writer uses foreshadowing. The use of such techniques is called *nonlinear plot development*.

12. Reread Janie's conversation with Pheoby in Chapter 1. Identify examples of foreshadowing and use them to make inferences. Write your evidence and inferences in the following graphic organizer.

Evidence of Foreshadowing in the Novel	Inference About What Is Being Foreshadowed

13. Continue to look for additional examples of flashbacks and foreshadowing as you read the novel and add them to your double-entry journal. Evaluate how these different literary elements shape the author's portrayal of the plot.

Comparing Different Mediums: Film

14. A novel and its accompanying film may or may not follow an identical storyline. As you watch the film *Their Eyes Were Watching God*, think about Janie Mae Crawford's character in the novel. Copy the following chart in your Reader/Writer Notebook to help you evaluate how the film interprets Janie Mae Crawford's internal traits in the novel.

Janie Mae Crawford		
Internal Trait		
How the Film Interprets This Trait		

Nanny's Story

Learning Targets

- Evaluate how Hurston's use of varying points of view shape the reader's understanding of the plot.
- Make comparisons about the message of a poem and a speech.
- Analyze how the historical, social, and economic contexts of the setting influence the plot, characterization, and theme.

Preview

In this activity, you will compare a poem by Langston Hughes and Chapter 2 of *Their Eyes Were Watching God*.

My Notes

Point of View in Chapter 2

One of the hallmarks of Hurston's writing style is her use of narrative voice. She uses a variety of narrative points of view to tell the story, offer characterization, and convey a message. Authors usually choose to primarily use one point of view to tell their story:

First-person point of view comes directly from a character's perspective and uses the pronoun *I*.

Third-person omniscient point of view comes from a narrator who can see into every character's thoughts and observe their actions. It uses pronouns such as *he, she,* or *they*.

Third-person limited point of view also comes from a narrator with more distance, but he or she can only see into one character's thoughts.

Note all the points of view you find in Chapter 2. As you continue to read *Their Eyes Were Watching God*, pay attention to the way Hurston skillfully shifts between different narrative voices, or points of view.

1. In the following chart, identify the different points of view in the excerpts and describe the effect or purpose of each type.

Point of View	Example	Effect or Purpose
	"And, Janie, maybe it wasn't much, but Ah done de best Ah kin by you. Ah raked and scraped and bought dis lil piece uh land so you wouldn't have to stay in de white folks' yard and tuck yo' head befo' other chillun at school."	

Point of View	Example	Effect or Purpose
	"The people all saw her come because it was sundown. The sun was gone, but he had left his footprints in the sky. It was the time for sitting on porches beside the road. It was the time to hear things and talk. These sitters had been tongueless, earless, eyeless conveniences all day long."	
	"It was a spring afternoon in West Florida. Janie had spent most of the day under a blossoming pear tree in the back-yard. She had been spending every minute that she could steal from her chores under that tree for the last three days. That was to say, ever since the first tiny bloom had opened. It had called her to come and gaze on a mystery."	

2. What theme does Hurston introduce with Janie's story about playing with the Washburn children?

3. At the paragraph that begins, "Pheoby's hungry listening helped Janie to tell her story," the narrative point of view begins to change. How does moving to this third-person narration affect your understanding of Janie?

As You Read

- Underline words that relate to emotions.
- Circle unknown words and phrases. Try to determine the meaning of the words by using context clues, word parts, or a dictionary.

Poetry

Mother to Son

by **Langston Hughes**

Well, son, I'll tell you:

Life for me ain't been no crystal stair.

It's had tacks in it,

And splinters,

5 And boards torn up,

And places with no carpet on the floor—

Bare.

But all the time

I'se been a-climbin' on,

10 And reachin' landin's,

And turnin' corners,

And sometimes goin' in the dark

Where there ain't been no light.

So, boy, don't you turn back.

15 Don't you set down on the steps.

'Cause you finds it's kinder hard.

Don't you fall now—

For I'se still goin', honey,

I'se still climbin',

20 And life for me ain't been no crystal stair.

My Notes

Making Observations

- What are you first thoughts about the poem?
- Based on the words you underlined, what emotions stand out to you in the poem?

Returning to the Text

- Return to the poem as you respond to the following questions. Use text evidence to support your responses.
- Write any additional questions you have about the text in your Reader/Writer Notebook.

4. Who is the speaker in the poem? Who is the speaker speaking to? What is the situation?

_____

_____

_____

_____

5. What is the mood created by the diction Hughes uses in the line "And reachin' landin's, / And turnin' corners, / And sometimes goin' in the dark / Where there ain't been no light."?

_____

_____

_____

_____

6. How does Hughes use the metaphor of the staircase? What purpose does it achieve? What message does the poem ultimately convey?

_____

_____

_____

_____

_____

7. What is the effect of Hughes's use of repetition and line breaks in the poem?

_____

_____

_____

_____

☑ Focus on the Sentence

Choose the correct placement for the commas in this sentence and underline the appositive.

Hughes's use of line breaks and repetition which mimics the struggle of climbing stairs is able to convey a message of continuing in the face of struggle.

_____

_____

Making Text-to-Text Comparisons

8. As Nanny becomes the narrator of her story in Chapter 2, she says to Janie:

"Ah was born back due in slavery so it wasn't for me to fulfill my dreams of whut a woman oughta be and to do. Dat's one of de hold-backs of slavery. But nothing can't stop you from wishin'. Ah didn't want to be used for a work-ox and a brood-sow and Ah didn't want mah daughter used dat way neither. It sho wasn't mah will for things to happen lak they did. Ah even hated de way you was born. But, all de same Ah said thank god, Ah got another chance. Ah wanted to preach a great sermon about colored women sittin' on high, but they wasn't no pulpit for me. Freedom found me wid a baby daughter in mah arms, so Ah said Ah'd take a broom and a cook-pot and throw up a highway through de wilderness for her. She would expound what Ah felt. ...

"Ah wouldn't marry nobody, though. Ah could have uh heap uh times, cause Ah didn't want nobody mistreating mah baby. So Ah got with some good white people and come down here in West Florida to work and make de sun shine on both sides of de street for Leafy.

"Mah Madam help me wid her just lak she been doin' wid you. Ah put her in school when it got so it was a school to put her in. Ah was 'spectin to make a school teacher outa her."

Explain the differences in Janie's desires and Nanny's plans for her.

9. Make a text-to-text comparison between the voice and advice in "Mother to Son" and Nanny's voice and concerns in her speech to Janie.

Historical, Social, and Economic Context of Setting

The setting a writer uses in a text informs the context of the story, according to its time and place. A story that takes place in an impoverished New York City neighborhood in the 19th century will lend itself differently to a plot than a story that takes place in a medieval castle. Authors may even choose to incorporate historical events into a fictional text. But where characters live, when they live, and how they live will shape the story they are in as well as the ways in which they act.

Their Eyes Were Watching God takes place in the South, in an era in which African Americans had few rights and even less in the way of economic equality with whites. This context influences the decisions that the characters in the story make about where to live and how to live.

10. With a small group, research some facts about the historical, social, and economic context of *Their Eyes Were Watching God*. Aim to find a mix of facts from primary and secondary sources.

Historical Context	Social Context	Economic Context

11. With your group, return to Chapter 2 of the text and reread Nanny's story. As you read, record details about how the context of her life affects Janie as well as how it influences the plot and theme of the novel.

Evidence from Nanny's Story	How It Affects Janie	How It Affects the Plot	How It Affects the Theme

Evidence from Nanny's Story	How It Affects Janie	How It Affects the Plot	How It Affects the Theme

12. What connections can you make between the historical, social, and economic context that you researched about the novel and Nanny and Janie's experience? How might Hurston's experience have influenced the novel and its characters?

Making Connections to the Harlem Renaissance

13. As you revisit Chapter 2, use your double-entry journal to take notes. As you make your journal entries, keep in mind how the values, beliefs, history, arts, and concerns with daily life that characterize the Harlem Renaissance are embodied in Hurston's work.

A Moral Dilemma

Learning Strategies

Close Reading
Discussion Groups
Double-Entry Journal
Drafting
Predicting
Quickwrite

Learning Targets

• Analyze the behavior of characters in order to understand their underlying motivations and moral dilemmas.
• Make connections between the themes of the Harlem Renaissance and the text.

Preview

In this activity, you will analyze a character's behavior, motivations, and moral dilemmas and how they influence the plot.

My Notes

_____
_____
_____
_____
_____
_____
_____
_____
_____
_____

A Moral Dilemma: Chapters 3 and 4

What drives people to make decisions? Authors must consider this question when directing the actions of their characters, and underlying motivations often drive a person's behavior—whether they want something, are hiding something, or are torn between right and wrong. Underlying motivations can cause moral dilemmas that influence the plot and theme of a story. Consider the story of a person who covets an important object that doesn't belong to them—what actions might they take? How might it compromise their beliefs about themselves? What would they learn?

1. As you read Chapters 3 and 4, record notes about Janie's behaviors and underlying motivations. Then think about what moral dilemmas are created as a result and ultimately how Janie's choices about the moral dilemma influence the plot.

Janie's Behaviors and Motivations	What moral dilemmas occur as a result?	How do Janie's choices about the moral dilemma influence the plot?

2. Explain how Janie's moral dilemma influences the theme.

☑ Focus on the Sentence

Use what you have observed about Janie's moral dilemma so far to complete the following sentences.

Janie faces a moral dilemma because _____

_____

Janie wants to believe she will love Logan after they are married, but _____

_____

Joe is different than Logan, so _____

_____

Making Connections to the Harlem Renaissance

3. Discuss the questions that follow and take notes in your double-entry journal.

- As Janie evaluates her marriage to Logan Killicks, Hurston presents the recurring image of the horizon: "The familiar people and things had failed her so she hung over the gate and looked up the road towards way off. She knew now that marriage did not make love. Janie's first dream was dead, so she became a woman." Discuss how Janie's frustration helps her growing self-awareness.

- What other images add meaning to the text and define Hurston's style as a Harlem Renaissance writer?

☑ Check Your Understanding

What symbolic act does Janie perform when she leaves Logan? At the end of Chapter 4, examine the paragraph that begins, "The morning road air ..." How does Hurston's word choice echo the optimism of the Harlem Renaissance?

My Notes

My Notes

Writing Prompt: Argumentative

Scholar Robert E. Hemenway wrote *Zora Neal Hurston: A Literary Biography*. This excerpt from the biography explains that Nanny represents a belief from which Hurston departed in her writing. Read the excerpt and make a text-to-text connection to *Their Eyes Were Watching God*.

> People erred because they wanted to be above others, an impulse which eventually led to denying the humanity of those below. .... Janie's grandmother ... thinks that freedom is symbolized by achieving the position on high. Zora Hurston had always known, just as Janie discovers, that there was no air to breathe there. She had always identified with what she called 'the poor Negro, the real one in the furrows and the cane breaks.' She bitterly criticized black leaders who ignored this figure...

Review Chapters 2 and 3. Think about Nanny's desires for Janie to have a life far different from her own and Leafy's as well as Nanny's belief "that freedom is symbolized by achieving the position on high." Write a paragraph explaining how these ideas are contrary to Hurston's own ideas. Include information about how Nanny represents ideas held during the Harlem Renaissance and if and how Hurston departs from those. Be sure to:

- Include a thesis statement that defines your opinion and gives direction to your writing.
- Clarify the relationships among your thesis statement, reasons, and supporting evidence from the text.
- Write a strong conclusion that follows from your claim and supports the argument you presented.

Janie's New Life

Learning Targets

- Evaluate how an author's use of language informs and shapes the perception of readers.
- Defend or challenge an author's claims using relevant text evidence.

Preview

In this activity, you will identify characteristics of folktales that are evident in the novel and evaluate how they shape the perception of the reader.

Questioning the Text: Chapter 5

1. Read Chapter 5 and then write three questions for each of the following levels of questions to help you gain a deeper understanding of the text. Use the following examples as models.

Literal	Interpretive	Universal
What does Joe Starks say when the audience requests that Janie speak?	Based on Joe Starks's statements about women, what can the reader infer about Joe's attitude toward women?	How does society define male and female roles?

2. Share your questions with your classmates. With your class, choose three questions that best identify the central issues of Chapter 5. Write those questions here.

1. _____

    _____

2. _____

    _____

3. _____

    _____

4.13

VOCABULARY

LITERARY

A **folktale** is a story without a known author that has been preserved through oral retelling and is part of the oral tradition in literature.

Oral Tradition: Chapter 6

A **folktale** has many or all of the following characteristics.

- It is generally handed down to a group orally.
- It is characteristic of the time and place in which it is told.
- It speaks to universal and timeless themes.
- It tries to explain human life and how people deal with life or the origin of something.
- It often contains a story about about a common person.
- The characters struggle with natural events.
- The stories validate elements of a culture.
- It may entertain with exaggerated characters, conflicts, or dialogue.

3. As an anthropologist, Hurston collected stories, conversations, and other aspects of oral tradition that she then infused into her writing. In Chapter 6, Hurston presents two layers of the oral tradition: her omniscient narrator tells the readers a story of the porch sitters, and their conversations carry the stories of Matt's mule. As you read Chapter 6, track the elements of the oral tradition in the following graphic organizer and think about how these elements contribute to the effects on the reader.

Elements of the Oral Tradition and the Folktale	Example from the Chapter	Effects on the Perception of the Reader
Folktales, myths, fairy tales		
Reflection of time and place in which they are told, especially the use of dialect		
Exaggerated characters or situations for the sake of humor or glorification of deeds		

Elements of the Oral Tradition and the Folktale	Example from the Chapter	Effects on the Perception of the Reader
Humans coping with the world in which they live		
Common people as characters		
Characters struggle with nature		
Validates aspects of a culture		
Universal and timeless themes		

4. Think about the characters, setting, and conflicts in Chapters 5 and 6. Then write analytical responses to the interpretive questions that follow.

• How has Joe enslaved Janie? What comments does he make that illustrate his view of husbands and wives? Do you see any parallels between Joe's treatment of the mule and his treatment of Janie?

• Hurston often used Eatonville, her real-life childhood home, as a setting in her work. Describe Eatonville as it is presented in *Their Eyes Were Watching God*. What effect is the young town having on Joe, Janie, and their marriage?

• "She had an inside and an outside now and suddenly she knew how not to mix them." When have you seen evidence of the two sides of Janie in Chapters 5 and 6? What is the reason for this disparity?

Making Text-to-Text Connections

In his essay "One of the New Realists" (Chelsea House Publishers, 1986), Benjamin Brawly describes Zora Neale Hurston:

> She would get together a group of men in a railroad or turpentine camp or in a phosphate mining village, talk informally until they were no longer self-conscious, and then see which could outdo the other with his yarn. ... Like some others who have dealt in folk-lore, Miss Hurston has not escaped criticism at the hands of those who frowned upon her broad humor and the lowly nature of her material. Her interest, however, is not in solving problems, the chief concern being with individuals. As for the untutored Negro, she presents him without apology, a character as good as other characters but different.

☑ Check Your Understanding

Briefly summarize Brawly's description of Hurston.

📝 Writing Prompt: Argumentative

Review the characteristics of folktales and the portions of Chapter 6 that reflect folktale characteristics. Write a paragraph in which you agree or disagree with critics who "frowned upon [Hurston's] broad humor and the lowly nature of her material." Be sure to:

- Include a clear statement of your claim that either agrees or disagrees with the critic in the topic sentence.
- Demonstrate your understanding of the folktale elements of the mule story by including examples of the elements in your claim. Embed any quotations using correct conventions.
- Use varied syntax and edit your draft to demonstrate command of the conventions of Standard English.

Janie's "Route of Tradition"

Learning Strategies

Double-Entry Journal
Marking the Text
Predicting

INDEPENDENT READING LINK

Read and Connect

Choose a chunk of text from your independent reading selection. Complete a chart like the one you used for this activity. Show important plot developments and assign adjectives to describe the main character's emotional response to these developments. Then compare and contrast your main character's responses with Janie's responses.

Learning Targets

- Use textual evidence to track key actions and characters' emotional responses.
- Analyze how Hurston's writing reflects and departs from the ideas of the Harlem Renaissance.

Preview

In this activity, you will read Chapters 7, 8, and 9 and analyze how characters respond to developments in the plot.

Character Study: Chapters 7, 8, and 9

1. Review the ending of Chapter 6, beginning with "Janie did what she had never done before ..." Think about what this action means to Janie's character development. Turn to a partner and share your ideas.

2. As you read Chapters 7 and 8, give close attention to the rising actions and the conflicts that compound Janie's feelings of being "a rut in the road."

3. After reading the first two paragraphs of Chapter 7, describe how the author's use of imagery expresses Janie's sense of her marriage. How does her behavior at the beginning of this chapter compare with her actions at the end of Chapter 6?

4. As you read Chapters 7 and 8, use this graphic organizer to record characters' actions and emotional responses.

Important Plot Developments	Adjectives to Describe Janie's Emotional Response
Chapter 7	Chapter 7

Important Plot Developments	Adjectives to Describe Janie's Emotional Response
Chapter 8	Chapter 8

5. How are Hurston's beliefs in the power of the individual reflected in Janie's character?

6. How does Janie's character reflect and depart from the Harlem Renaissance? Again, note the words in the right-hand column.

7. Think about the critical commentaries that are provided in the graphic organizer that follows. Identify textual evidence from Chapters 7, 8, and 9 and complete the columns of the graphic organizer.

Aspects of the Harlem Renaissance	Examples from Chapters 7, 8, or 9	Is it a natural product of the ideas of a specific historical period in American literature?	Is it a departure from the ideas of a specific historical period in American literature?
Historical Context "*The conflict which Janie represents, between freedom or passion and restraint or reserve, has a special quality in black fiction. ... The condition in slavery was the ultimate restriction in which freedom to be oneself is out of the question.*" —from "Their Eyes Were Watching God" by Roger Rosenblatt			

Aspects of the Harlem Renaissance	Examples from Chapters 7, 8, or 9	Is it a natural product of the ideas of a specific historical period in American literature?	Is it a departure from the ideas of a specific historical period in American literature?
Philosophy/Beliefs "*Some believed that it was the duty of black artists to picture their race in the 'best' possible light, thereby implying that only middle-class blacks were worthy of being depicted in art. ...* [James Weldon] *Johnson shows his acceptance of the lower social classes ... as a source for literary materials.*" —from "Zora Neale Hurston's America" by Theresa R. Love			
The Arts "*Their Eyes Were Watching God, a novel of intense power, evidences the strength and power of African-American culture. ... Here characters were outsiders in America because they were the inheritors of a culture different from that of others.*" —from "The Outsider" by Addison Gayle Jr.			
Daily Life "*In rebelling against the definition of black women and moving to assert her own individuality, Janie must travel the route of tradition.*" from "The Outsider," by Addison Gayle, Jr.			

☑ Check Your Understanding

After you have completed the graphic organizer, choose one aspect of the Harlem Renaissance and write a paragraph to support the claim that Zora Neal Hurston's work is both a natural product of and a departure from the ideas of the Harlem Renaissance.

Discussion Groups

Learning Targets

- Prepare for discussion though the use of levels of questions and collecting information from notes and other sources.
- Work collaboratively to synthesize information and develop an understanding of *Their Eyes Were Watching God*.

Preview

In this activity, you will read the remaining chapters of the novel in groups using collaborative group guidelines.

Novel Study: The Remaining Chapters

You have approached the first half of *Their Eyes Were Watching God* in a variety of ways, such as shared reading, oral reading, and guided reading. For the second half of the novel, you will move to greater independence, reading on your own and participating in student-led discussion groups.

The remaining chapters of the novel can be divided into these broad chunks:

- Chapters 10–13 (Janie and Tea Cake in Eatonville)
- Chapters 14–19 (Janie and Tea Cake on the Muck)

You will read Chapter 20 with your class in the next activity.

1. For each chapter from Chapter 10 to 19, you will write literal, interpretive, and universal questions to help guide your group discussions and deepen your understanding of the text.

2. You will meet with your discussion group to create a schedule for reading, making sure that your schedule reflects the timeline provided by your teacher. Make sure that each group member writes down the reading schedule in his or her calendar; it is imperative that each member of the group maintain the reading schedule in order for discussions to be effective.

3. A model of a note-taking guide is provided for you. You may copy this guide into your Reader/Writer Notebook or modify it to fit your discussions; just be sure to take good notes during each discussion. These notes will help you understand the novel and prepare for writing an analytical essay.

Discussion Group Reading

4. To guide your discussion group's reading, consider these aspects of the Harlem Renaissance to trace throughout the novel:

- historical context
- philosophy/beliefs
- the arts
- daily life

As you discover textual evidence that connects to each of these aspects, write your levels of questions. Be prepared to discuss these points by identifying how the text illustrates Hurston's reflections of the Harlem Renaissance and her departures from its common themes.

My Notes

5. You might use the following note-taking guide as a model for your notes, continue your double-entry journal, or create something similar to capture your discussions. Complete your notes before meeting with your discussion group.

Today's date:	Reading assignment:
Interpretive questions based on the reading assignment	Universal questions based on the reading assignment

After-Reading Discussions

6. As you meet with your discussion group, share your questions and discuss potential answers. To maintain order and ensure that all group members participate cooperatively, appoint one member as the timer. The timer should limit each member's comments to one or two minutes. Proceed to rotate around the group and follow the time limit. Take notes from your group members' comments to collect information to help you with Embedded Assessment 2.

Use a graphic organizer like this or your Reader/Writer Notebook to take notes during the group's discussion.

Today's topics:	
Topic 1:	Topic 2:
Notes:	Notes:

☑ Check Your Understanding

At the end of each discussion group meeting, write a summary of what you have learned in the meeting and reflect on the group process.

The End of a Long Journey

Learning Targets

- Identify and evaluate the images and motifs that create the plot structure and thematic design of the novel.
- Participate in a collaborative discussion that synthesizes insights and interpretations.

Preview

In this activity, you will read the last chapter of *Their Eyes Were Watching God* and evaluate how Hurston's use of literary elements such as plot, character, setting, and point of view develops the theme and supports the author's purpose.

Novel Study: Completing the Book

1. Chapter 20 provides the final "frame" of Janie's story. Hurston chose to organize this novel by having Chapters 1 and 20 frame Janie's telling of her story to Pheoby. By the end of the novel, if you return to the first scene, you have a much clearer understanding of Janie's perception of her life and her "grand journey."

   Your purposes for reading this last chapter include:

   - to evaluate the organizational structure of the frame story
   - to mark the text for evidence of images and motifs that you recognize as being repeated throughout the novel (use sticky notes)

2. Mark the text and make your final entries into your double-entry journal. Be prepared to share these entries with your discussion group.

Thematic Development

Writing a Thematic Statement: Now that you have read the novel and discussed it at length, think about the major themes presented. Write a thematic statement in which you synthesize your understanding of the novel's literary elements and how they informed your interpretation of the author's purpose.

Keep in mind the guidelines for writing the thematic statement:

- It is one sentence that states the text's universal meaning about life, its central insight into life.
- It avoids summarizing the story, stating a moral, or reducing the story to a cliché.
- It can be supported by the imagery, characters, and events in the story.

My Notes

Reviewing the Reviews

Learning Strategies

Socratic Seminar

VOCABULARY

LITERARY
A **book review** is a formal assessment or examination of a book.

Learning Targets

- Evaluate multiple critical reviews in light of the ideas of the Harlem Renaissance.
- Identify and evaluate multiple thematic interpretations of a novel.

Preview

In this activity, you will read and evaluate multiple critical reviews of the novel you just finished and choose one to defend or challenge.

Reading Reviews

1. Much has been written in response to *Their Eyes Were Watching God*. Henry Louis Gates explains, "The curious aspect of the widespread critical attention being shown to Hurston's texts is that so many critics embracing such a diversity of theoretic approaches seem to find something new at which to marvel in her texts." Look at the back cover of the novel. It most likely has quotes from people who have written **reviews** of the book. Read and discuss the quotes with a partner.

2. Read the book review excerpts that follow and annotate in the margins, comparing each one to your understanding of the themes of *Their Eyes Were Watching God*. Ask yourself, "How does this interpretation help me understand how Hurston is a product of and a departure from the ideas of the Harlem Renaissance?"

Book Review 1

"It is folklore fiction at its best, which we gratefully accept as an overdue replacement for so much faulty local color fiction about Negroes. But when will the Negro novelist of maturity, who knows how to tell a story convincingly—which is Miss Hurston's cradle gift, come to grips with motive fiction and social document fiction? Progressive southern fiction has already banished the legend of these entertaining pseudo-primitives whom the reading public still loves to laugh with, weep over and envy. Having gotten rid of condescension, let us now get over oversimplification!"
—Alain Locke, *Opportunity*, June 1, 1938

Book Review 2

"Miss Hurston can write; but her prose is cloaked in that facile sensuality that has dogged Negro expression since the days of Phyllis Wheatley. Her dialogue manages to catch the psychological movements of the Negro folk-mind in their pure simplicity, but that's as far as it goes. Miss Hurston *voluntarily* continues in her novel the tradition which was forced upon the Negro in the theater, that is, the minstrel technique that makes the 'white folks' laugh. Her characters eat and laugh and cry and work and kill; they swing like a pendulum eternally in that safe and narrow orbit in which America likes to see the Negro live: between laughter and tears. [...] The sensory sweep of her novel carries no theme, no message, no thought. In the main, her novel is not addressed to the

My Notes

Negro, but to a white audience whose chauvinistic tastes she knows how to satisfy. She exploits the phase of Negro life which is 'quaint,' the phase which evokes a piteous smile on the lips of the 'superior' race."
—Richard Wright, "Between Laughter and Tears," *New Masses*, 5 October 1937, p. 25

Book Review 3

"In a rich prose (which has, at the same time, a sort of nervous sensibility) she tells the tale of a girl who 'wanted things sweet with mah marriage, lak when you sit under a pear tree and think.' Janie did not get sweetness when her Grandma married her to Mister Killicks with his sixty acres of West Florida land, and his sagging belly, and his toenails that looked like mules' foots; and she didn't get it when she ran off with Joe Starks and got to be the Mayor's wife, and sat on her own store porch. But when Tea Cake came along with his trampish clothes and his easy ways and his nice grin that made even a middle-aged woman like Janie sort of wishful the minute she sets eyes on him, he handed her the keys of the kingdom, and their life together (what there was of it) was rapture and fun and tenderness and understanding—the perfect relationship of man and woman, whether they be black or white."
—Sheila Hibben, *The New York Herald Tribune Weekly Book Review*, September 26, 1937

Book Review 4

"The story of Janie's life down on the muck of Florida Glades, bean picking, hunting and the men shooting dice in the evening and how the hurricane came up and drove the animals and the Indians and finally the black people and the white people before it, and how Tea Cake, in Janie's eyes the 'son of Evening Son,' and incidentally the best crap shooter in the place, made Janie sing and glitter all over at last, is a little epic all by itself. Indeed, from first to last this is a well nigh perfect story—a little **sententious** at the start, but the rest is simple and beautiful and shining with humor."
—Lucille Tompkins, *The New York Times Book Review*, September 26, 1937

Making Observations

- Which reviews do you immediately agree or disagree with?
- What questions do you have after reading each review?

GRAMMAR & USAGE

Quoted Text

Notice how Hurston's words are enclosed in single quotation marks in the first sentence of Book Review 3. When quoting a critic who is quoting a part of a text, you must use double quotation marks around the critic's words and single quotation marks around the words of the text to distinguish them.

In Book Review 2, the review leaves out a part of the quote and lets the reader know by using ellipses […] to signify that some text has been omitted.

Try shortening a quote from either book review. Use the proper quotation marks and substitute ellipses for the parts you want to omit.

WORD CONNECTIONS

Etymology

The word **chauvinistic** first described someone who had an exaggerated patriotism that could be seen as more of a vice than a virtue. The term came from the last name of a soldier who served in Napoleon's army, who was known for his fanatical patriotism. Today the meaning is similar: believing, with disapproval or contempt for others, that your country or gender is superior.

sententious: self-righteous

Returning to the Text

- Return to the book reviews as you respond to the following questions. Use text evidence to support your responses.
- Write any additional questions you have about the book reviews in your Reader/Writer Notebook.

3. What is the main idea in Locke's review? What does he applaud or criticize about the novel and/or Hurston's writing? What evidence from the text supports your answer?

_____

_____

_____

_____

_____

_____

4. How does the structure of Tompkins's review reflect her opinion? How might this also reflect the artistic voices of the Harlem Renaissance? Support your answer with evidence from the text.

_____

_____

_____

_____

_____

_____

_____

_____

5. How does Wright's opinion of Hurston's novel compare to the "psychological movements of the Negro folk-mind" and the themes and goals of the Harlem Renaissance? What textual evidence supports your answer?

_____

_____

_____

_____

_____

_____

6. How does Tompkins's review expand on Hibben's ideas? Taken together, how do these reviews contribute to an understanding of Hurston's possible goals in writing the novel?

_____

_____

_____

_____

_____

_____

_____

_____

Socratic Seminar

7. Craft three or four interpretive and universal questions about each of the four critical reviews. Then use these questions in a Socratic Seminar to connect these reviews to your understanding the Harlem Renaissance.

☑ Check Your Understanding

Summarize a point made by one of your classmates.

✍ Writing Prompt: Argumentative

Once you have discussed the critical reviews, choose one and defend or challenge. Connect your understanding of the critical review to the values, historical context, arts, or daily life championed by the movement known as the Harlem Renaissance. Be sure to:

- Begin your argument with a thesis sentence that introduces a precise claim.
- Establish the significance of the claim, distinguishing it from opposing claims.
- Continue to develop the claim and counterclaim fairly and thoroughly.
- Supply relevant text evidence, including quotations and commentary from the review and novel, to support your thesis.
- Establish and maintain a formal style as you write.
- Provide a conclusion that supports your argument and thesis.

🕮 Independent Reading Checkpoint

Review your independent reading. Suppose you were going to write a critical review for it. Using the book reviews in this activity as a model, identify at least two thematic interpretations of the selection. Think about how you might use this information in a critical review. Share your ideas with a group.

Writing an Analytical Essay

 ASSIGNMENT

Write an analytical essay in which you discuss how Zora Neale Hurston's writing is both a reflection of and a departure from the ideas of the Harlem Renaissance. Include aspects of the Harlem Renaissance that you see reflected in Hurston's writing as well as characteristics of Hurston's writing that are departures from selected aspects of the Harlem Renaissance.

Planning and Prewriting: Take time to make a plan for your essay.	■ What resources on the Harlem Renaissance can you use to help you plan your work? ■ What writings by Zora Neale Hurston will you refer to? ■ What elements of the Harlem Renaissance do you recognize in Hurston's writing, and what elements of her writings seem to be departures from those aspects?
Drafting: Determine the structure and how you will incorporate your evidence.	■ How can you state your claim as a single thesis statement so that it captures your thinking? ■ What organizational pattern will best allow you to compare Hurston's work to aspects of the Harlem Renaissance? How will you use textual evidence from your sources to support your ideas? How will you use commentary to explain how this evidence relates to your thesis? ■ Is the evidence that you use cited in a way that will allow your audience to know which source is being used every time? Does your works cited page provide all the information necessary for your audience?
Evaluating and Revising the Draft: Make your work the best it can be.	■ How can you use transitions so that one idea moves smoothly to the next? ■ How will you use the Scoring Guide and peer responses to help guide your revision?
Checking and Editing for Publication: Confirm that your final draft is ready for publication.	■ How will you ensure that your essay maintains an academic, formal tone; that it seamlessly embeds quotations within the text; and that it uses varied syntax? ■ How will you check for grammatical and technical accuracy?

Reflection

After completing this Embedded Assessment, think about how you went about accomplishing this assignment and respond to the following question:

- How did the use of both primary and secondary sources help you examine how writers' works can be a product of both their time and their own personal perspective?

SCORING GUIDE

Scoring Criteria	Exemplary	Proficient	Emerging	Incomplete
Ideas	The essay • presents a convincing, thorough, and perceptive understanding of Hurston's writings as well as aspects of the Harlem Renaissance • contains analysis that demonstrates an exceptional insight into Hurston's writings and the Harlem Renaissance • uses clear and effective specific and well-chosen examples that yield detailed support for the analysis.	The essay • demonstrates a solid understanding of Hurston's writing and the Harlem Renaissance and provides a convincing text • contains analysis that demonstrates a general insight into Hurston's writings and the Harlem Renaissance • uses appropriate examples to support the position.	The essay • demonstrates an uneven understanding of Hurston's writing and/or the Harlem Renaissance and does not create a convincing text • attempts to analyze Hurston's writings and the Harlem Renaissance, but the analysis may be simplistic or replaced by summary • uses evidence to support the position with a weak or unclear connection to the claim.	The essay • demonstrates a superficial understanding of Hurston's writings and the Harlem Renaissance and provides an underdeveloped text • lacks an analysis of Hurston's writings and the Harlem Renaissance • uses evidence to support the position that may be weak or provides too few examples.
Structure	The essay • is exceptionally well organized • moves smoothly and comfortably between ideas • uses clear and effective transitions to enhance the essay's coherence.	The essay • is clearly organized • sequences ideas in a way that is easy to follow • uses transitions to move between ideas.	The essay • is organized with some lapses in structure or coherence • sequences ideas in a way that may be confusing at times • inconsistently uses transitions.	The essay • is organized in a way that impedes the ideas presented • sequences ideas in a way that is difficult to follow • jumps too rapidly between ideas and lacks transitions.
Use of Language	The essay • employs stylistic choices in language that are exceptional • successfully weaves textual evidence from the novel into its own prose • demonstrates strong control and mastery of standard writing conventions.	The essay • employs stylistic choices in language that are clear and appropriate • weaves textual evidence from the novel into its own prose accurately • demonstrates control of standard writing conventions, and though some errors may appear, they do not seriously impede readability.	The essay • uses stylistic choices in language that are uneven • attempts to incorporate textual evidence from the novel into its own prose yet may do so awkwardly or inaccurately • contains errors in standard writing conventions that interfere with the meaning.	The essay • uses stylistic choices in language that are not appropriate for the topic • does not incorporate textual evidence from the novel • contains frequent errors in standard writing conventions that severely interfere with the meaning.

Resources

Independent Reading

Learning Strategies

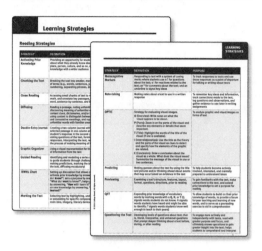

Graphic Organizers

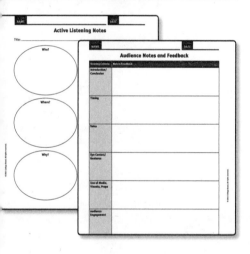

English-Spanish Glossary

Index of Skills

Index of Authors and Titles

Suggestions for Independent Reading

This list, divided into the categories of **Literature** and **Nonfiction/Informational Text,** comprises titles related to the themes and content of the unit. For your independent reading, you can select from this wide array of titles, which have been chosen based on complexity and interest. You can do your own research and select titles that intrigue you.

Unit 1 Independent Reading List: The American Dream

Literature		
Author	**Title**	**Lexile**
Avi	*Nothing but the Truth*	N/A
Azuela, Mariano	*Los de abajo*	810L
Beatty, Patrica	*Lupita Mañana*	760L
Erdrich, Louise	*Love Medicine*	780L
Flores-Scott, Patrick	*American Road Trip*	HL550L
Gansworth, Eric	*If I Ever Get Out of Here*	N/A
Hamil, Pete	*Snow in August*	N/A
Jen, Gish	*Who's Irish?*	840L
Kadohata, Cynthia	*Kira-Kira*	740L
Ryan, Pam Munoz	*Esperanza Rising*	750L
Ryan, Pam Munoz	*Esperanza renace*	740L
Restrepo, Bettina	*Illegal*	540L
Smith, Betty	*A Tree Grows in Brooklyn*	810L
Steinbeck, John	*Of Mice and Men*	630L
Taylor, Mildred D.	*Roll of Thunder Hear My Cry*	920L
Wells, Ken	*Meely LeBauve*	N/A

Nonfiction/Informational		
Author	**Title**	**Lexile**
Benson, Kathleen and James Haskins	*Space Challenger: The Story of Guion Bluford*	980L
Bissinger, H.G.	*Friday Night Lights: A Town, a Team, and a Dream*	1220L
Brown, Daniel James	*Boys in the Boat*	1260L
Dillard, Annie	*An American Childhood*	1040L
Doherty, Craig A. and Katherine M.	*Building America: Statue of Liberty*	1160L
Ebrahim, Zak	*The Terrorist's Son: A Story of Choice*	N/A
Ehrenreich, Barbara	*Nickel and Dimed*	1340L
Finkel, Michael	*The Stranger in the Woods: The Extraordinary Story of the Last True Hermit*	N/A
Gladwell, Malcolm	*Outliers: The Story of Success*	1080L
Guerrero, Diane	*In the Country We Love: My Family Divided*	HL780L
Guerrero, Diane	*En el país que amamos: Mi familia dividida*	
Haley, Alex and Malcolm X	*Autobiography of Malcolm X: As Told to Alex Haley*	1120L
Hillenbrand, Laura	*Seabiscuit: An American Legend*	990L

Hillenbrand, Laura	Unbroken	1010L
Jemison, Mae	Find Where the Wind	960L
Junger, Sebastian	The Perfect Storm: A True Story of Men Against the Sea	1140L
Kurlanksky, Mark	Frozen in Time	1220L
Levitt, Steven	Freakonomics	N/A
Maclean, Normal	A River Runs Through It	1160L
McBride, James	The Color of Water: A Black Man's Tribute to His White Mother	1240L
McBride, James	Kill 'Em and Leave: Searching for James Brown and the American Soul	N/A
Nasar, Sylvia	A Beautiful Mind	N/A
Ngai, Mae	The Lucky Ones: One Family and the Extraordinary Invention of Chinese America	N/A
Peralta, Dan-el Padilla	Undocumented: A Dominican Boy's Odyssey from a Homeless Shelter to the Ivy League	930L
Saedi, Sara	Americanized: Rebel Without a Greencard	N/A
Sheinkin, Steve	Undefeated: Jim Thorpe and the Carlisle Indian School Football Team	980L
Vance, Ashlee	Elon Musk	1200L
Wolff, Tobias	This Boy's Life	N/A

Unit 2 Independent Reading List: The Power of Persuasion

Literature

Author	Title	Lexile
Alcott, Louisa May	Little Women	750L
Baldwin, James	Go Tell It on the Mountain	970L
Didion, Joan	Democracy	1130L
Forbes, Esther	Johnny Tremain	840L
Hamid, Moshin	The Reluctant Fundamentalist	N/A
Hentoff, Nat	The Day They Came to Arrest the Book	890L
Kent, Katherine	The Heretic's Daughter: A Novel	N/A
Kingsolver, Barbara	Animal Dreams	790L
Lawrence, Jerome and Robert E. Lee	Inherit the Wind	850L
Lewis, Sinclair	It Can't Happen Here	N/A
Meyers, Anna	Assassin	790L
O'Brien, Tim	The Things They Carried	880L
Paterson, Katherine	Lyddie	860L
Petry, Ann	Tituba of Salem Village	840L
Potok, Chiam	The Promise	N/A
Rinaldi, Ann	Or Give Me Death: A Novel of Patrick Henry's Family	610L
Roth, Philip	The Human Stain	N/A
Tan, Amy	The Joy Luck Club	930L
Vonnegut, Kurt	Slaughterhouse Five	850L

Nonfiction/Informational		
Author	**Title**	**Lexile**
Alexander, Michelle	*The New Jim Crow*	1450L
Arbinger Institute	*Anatomy of Peace: Resolving the Heart of Conflict*	N/A
Benoit, Peter	*Salem Witch Trials*	1020L
Bromwich, Jonah Engel	*Memorable Inaugural Speeches: Washington, Lincoln, Jackson, Kennedy and Reagan*	990L
Corey, Shana and R. Gregory Christie	*Es hora de actuar: El gran discurso de John F. Kennedy*	870L
Daley, James (Editor)	*Great Speeches by African Americans*	N/A
Fitzgerald, Stephanie	*McCarthyism: The Red Scare (Snapshots in History)*	N/A
Furedi, Frank	*On Tolerance: A Defense of Moral Independence*	N/A
Garton Ash, Timothy	*Free Speech: Ten Principles for a Connected World*	N/A
Hudak, Heather	*McCarthyism and the Red Scare (Uncovering the Past: Analyzing Primary Sources)*	1070L
Kennedy, Rick	*The First American Evangelical: A Short Life of Cotton Mather*	N/A
Klebold, Sue	*A Mother's Reckoning: Living in the Aftermath of a Tragedy*	N/A
Montefiore, Simon Sebag (Editor)	*Speeches That Changed the World*	N/A
Morcan, James	*Arruinando al Tercer Mundo (Bankrupting the Third World)*	N/A
Neier, Aryeh	*Defending My Enemy: American Nazis, the Skokie Case, and the Risks of Freedom*	N/A
Patterson, Kerry	*Crucial Conversations*	N/A
Safire, William (Editor)	*Lend Me Your Ears: Great Speeches in History*	N/A
Schiff, Stacy	*The Witches: Salem, 1692*	N/A
Stewart, Gail B.	*The Salem Witch Trials*	1260L
Stevenson, Bryan	*Just Mercy*	1130L
Tanaka, Shelley	*A Day That Changed America: Gettysburg*	930L
Wallace, Patricia Ward	*Politics of Conscience: A Biography of Margaret Chase Smith*	1590L
Warburton, Nigel	*Free Speech: A Very Short Introduction*	N/A
Widmer, Ted (Editor)	*American Speeches: Political Oratory from Patrick Henry to Barak Obama*	N/A
Various	*American Sermons: The Pilgrims to Martin Luther King Jr.*	N/A

Unit 3 Independent Reading List: American Forums: The Marketplace of Ideas

Literature

Author	Title	Lexile
Anderson, Sherwood	*Winesburg, Ohio*	1050L
Caldwell, Ian	*The Rule of Four*	N/A
Capote, Truman	*In Cold Blood*	1040L
Cather, Willa	*O Pioneers!*	930L
Freeman, Kathie	*Pasos de la gata*	N/A
Heller, Joseph	*Catch-22*	1140L
Miller, Jennifer	*The Year of the Gadfly*	N/A
Pratchett, Terry	*Going Postal*	760L
Sierra i Fabra, Jordi	*El extraordinario ingenio parlante del profesor Palermo*	NA
Stockett, Kathryn	*The Help*	930L
Vonnegut, Kurt	*Breakfast of Champions*	930L
Waugh, Evelyn	*Scoop*	830L
Yep, Lawrence	*Dragonwings*	870L

Nonfiction/Informational

Author	Title	Lexile
Amar, Akhil Reed	*American's Constitution: A Biography*	1490L
Anderson, Bonnie	*News Flash*	N/A
Craig, Terrance and Mary E. Ludloff	*Privacy and Big Data: The Players, Regulators, and Stakeholders*	N/A
Dakers, Diane	*Information Literacy and Fake News*	1020L
Dentith, Simon	*Parody*	1460L
Donovan, Sandy	*Media: From News Coverage to Political Advertising*	1150L
Edge, Marc	*Greatly Exaggerated: The Myth of the Death of Newspapers*	N/A
Herman, Edwards S. and Noam Chomsky	*Manufacturing Consent: The Political Economy of the Mass Media*	N/A
Kaplan, Fred	*The Singular Mark Twain: A Biography*	N/A
National Children's Book & Literacy Alliance	*Our White House: Looking In, Looking Out*	1110L
Parks, Gordon	*Choice of Weapons*	N/A
Riis, Jacob	*How the Other Half Lives*	N/A
Rudel, Anthony	*Hello Everybody!: The Dawn of American Radio*	N/A
Schlosser, Eric	*Fast Food Nation: The Dark Side of the All-American Meal*	1240L
Sedaris, David	*Me Talk Pretty One Day*	N/A
Sheppard, Alice	*Cartooning for Suffrage*	1430L
Vaidhyanathan, Siva	*Antisocial Media: How Facebook Disconnects Us and Undermines Democracy*	N/A
Various	*Perder es poder (Losing is Power)*	N/A

Unit 4 Independent Reading List: An American Journey

Literature

Author	Title	Lexile
Bolden, Tonya	*Wake Up Our Souls*	1190L
Borges, Jorge Luis	*El Aleph*	940L
Brown, Daniel	*Boys in the Boat*	1000L
Chestnutt, Charles Waddell	*Stories of the Color Line*	N/A
Cofer, Judith Ortiz	*Una isla como tú: Historias del barrio An Island Like You: Stories of the Barrio)*	830L
Cullen, Countee	*Countee Cullen: Collected Poems*	N/A
Curtis, Christopher Paul	*The Watsons Go to Birmingham*	1000L
Denenberg, Barry	*The Journal of Ben Uchida*	850L
Fleischman, Paul	*Bull Run*	810L
Guy, Rosa	*The Friends*	730L
Hughes, Langston	*The Weary Blues*	N/A
Hurston, Zora Neale	*Dust Tracks on a Road*	930L
Hurston, Zora Neale	*Mules and Men*	960L
Johnson, Helene	*This Waiting for Love: Helene Johnson, Poet of the Harlem Renaissance*	N/A
Johnson, James Weldon	*The Autobiography of an Ex-Colored Man*	1100L
Larson, Erik	*The Devil in White City*	1170L
Larson, Nella	*Quicksand*	N/A
Mackay, Claude	*Home to Harlem*	860L
Martinez, Victor	*Parrot in the Oven: Mi vida*	1000L
Mosely, Walter	*47*	860L
Rock, Peter	*My Abandonment*	N/A
Thurman, Wallace	*The Blacker the Berry ...*	1070L
Toomer, Jean	*Cane*	HL660
Wright, Richard	*Native Son*	700L

Nonfiction/Informational

Author	Title	Lexile
Avery, Laurence G. (Editor)	*A Southern Life: Letters of Paul Green: 1916-1981*	1260L
Bernstein, Patricia	*The First Waco Horror: The Lynching of Jesse Washington and the Rise of the NAACP*	N/A
Bloom, Harold (Editor)	*Black American Women Fiction Writers*	1290L
Close, Ellis	*The End of Anger: A New Generation's Take on Race and Rage*	N/A
Davis, Kenneth C.	*In the Shadow of Liberty: The Hidden History of Slavery, Four Presidents, and Five Black Lives*	1110L
Douglass, Frederick	*Narrative of the Life of Frederick Douglass: An American Slave*	920L
DuBois, W.E.B.	*The Souls of Black Folk*	1280L

Dwyer, Jim	*102 Minutes: The Unforgettable Story of the Fight to Survive Inside the Twin Towers*	N/A
Hauser, Brooke	*The New Kids: Big Dreams and Brave Journeys at A High School for Immigrant Teens*	1140L
Houston, Jeanne Wakatsuki and James D. Houston	*Farewell to Manzanar*	1040L
Hughes, Langston	*The Big Sea: An Autobiography*	1090L
King, Martin Luther	*A Time to Break Silence: The Essential Works of Martin Luther King, Jr., for Students*	N/A
Kramer, Victor A.	*Harlem Renaissance Re-examined: A Revised and Expanded Edition*	1440L
McKissack, Lisa Beringer	*Women of the Harlem Renaissance*	960L
McPhee, John	*Assembling California*	N/A
Moody, Anne	*Coming of Age in Mississippi*	870L
Oppenheimer, Joanne	*Dear Miss Breed*	1040L
Philbrick, Nathaniel	*In the Heart of the Sea: The Tragedy of the Whaleship Essex*	1210L
Steinbeck, John	*Travels with Charley in Search of America*	1010L
Thorpe, Helen	*Just Like Us: The True Story of Four Mexican Girls Coming of Age in America*	1100L
Uchida, Yoshiko	*Desert Exile: The Uprooting of a Japanese-American Family*	1280L
Welch, Diana	*The Kids Are All Right*	N/A

Independent Reading Log

Directions: This log is a place to record your progress and thinking about your independent reading during each unit. Add your log pages to your Reader/Writer Notebook or keep them as a separate place to record your reading insights.

Unit _____

Independent Reading Title _____

Author(s) _____ Text Type _____

Pages read: from _____ to _____

_____
_____
_____
_____
_____

Independent Reading Title _____

Author(s) _____ Text Type _____

Pages read: from _____ to _____

_____
_____
_____
_____
_____
_____
_____

Independent Reading Title _____

Author(s) _____ Text Type _____

Pages read: from _____ to _____

_____
_____
_____
_____
_____
_____
_____

Unit _____

Independent Reading Title _____

Author(s) _____ Text Type _____

Pages read: from _____ to _____

_____
_____
_____
_____
_____
_____

Independent Reading Title _____

Author(s) _____ Text Type _____

Pages read: from _____ to _____

_____
_____
_____
_____
_____
_____

Independent Reading Title _____

Author(s) _____ Text Type _____

Pages read: from _____ to _____

_____
_____
_____
_____
_____
_____

Independent Reading Title _____

Author(s) _____ Text Type _____

Pages read: from _____ to _____

_____
_____
_____
_____
_____

Learning Strategies

Reading Strategies

STRATEGY	DEFINITION	PURPOSE
Activating Prior Knowledge	Providing an opportunity for students to think about what they already know about a concept, place, person, culture, and so on, and share their knowledge with a wider audience	To prepare students to encounter new concepts, places, persons, cultures, and so on, prior to reading a text; an Anticipation Guide and a Quickwrite can be used to activate and assess prior knowledge
Chunking the Text	Breaking the text into smaller, manageable units of sense (e.g., words, sentences, paragraphs) by numbering, separating phrases, drawing boxes	To reduce the intimidation factor when encountering long words, sentences, or whole texts; to increase comprehension of difficult or challenging text
Close Reading	Accessing small chunks of text to read, reread, mark, and annotate key passages, word-for-word, sentence-by-sentence, and line-by-line	To develop comprehensive understanding by engaging in one or more focused readings of a text
Diffusing	Reading a passage, noting unfamiliar words, discovering meaning of unfamiliar words using context clues, dictionaries, and/or thesauruses, using context to distinguish between denotative and connotative meanings, and replacing unfamiliar words with familiar ones	To facilitate a close reading of text, the use of resources, an understanding of synonyms, and increased comprehension of text
Double-Entry Journal	Creating a two-column journal with a student-selected passage in one column and the student's response in the second column (e.g., asking questions of the text, forming personal responses, interpreting the text, reflecting on the process of making meaning of the text)	To assist in note-taking and organizing key textual elements and responses noted during reading in order to generate textual support that can be incorporated into a piece of writing at a later time
Graphic Organizer	Using a visual representation for the organization of information from the text	To facilitate increased comprehension and discussion
Guided Reading	Identifying and modeling a series of strategies to guide students through challenging text (e.g., making predictions, marking the text, skimming the text, diffusing vocabulary)	To model for students the use of multiple strategies to make meaning of challenging texts and help them learn to apply the strategies independently
KWHL Chart	Setting up discussion that allows students to activate prior knowledge by answering, "What do I **know**?"; sets a purpose by answering, "What do I **want** to know?"; helps preview a task by answering, "**How** will I learn it?"; and reflects on new knowledge by answering, "What have I **learned**?"	To organize thinking, access prior knowledge, and reflect on learning to increase comprehension and engagement
Marking the Text	Selecting text by highlighting, underlining, and/or annotating for specific components, such as main idea, imagery, literary devices, and so on	To focus reading for specific purposes, such as author's craft, and to organize information from selections; to facilitate reexamination of a text

STRATEGY	DEFINITION	PURPOSE
Metacognitive Markers	Responding to text with a system of cueing marks where students use a ? for questions about the text; a ! for reactions related to the text; an * for comments about the text; and an underline to signal key ideas	To track responses to texts and use those responses as a point of departure for talking or writing about texts
Note-taking	Making notes about a text to use in a written response	To remember key ideas and information, track connections made to the text, log questions and observations, and gather evidence to use later in writing assignments
OPTIC	Strategy for evaluating visual images. **O** (Overview): Write notes on what the visual appears to be about. **P** (Parts): Zoom in on the parts of the visual and describe any elements or details that seem important. **T** (Title): Highlight the words of the title of the visual (if one is available). **I** (Interrelationships): Use the title as the theory and the parts of the visual as clues to detect and specify how the elements of the graphic are related. **C** (Conclusion): Draw a conclusion about the visual as a whole. What does the visual mean? Summarize the message of the visual in one or two sentences.	To analyze graphic and visual images as forms of text
Predicting	Making guesses about the text by using the title and pictures and/or thinking ahead about events that may occur based on evidence in the text	To help students become actively involved, interested, and mentally prepared to understand ideas
Previewing	Examining a text's structure, features, layout, format, questions, directions, prior to reading	To gain familiarity with the text, make connections to the text, and extend prior knowledge to set a purpose for reading
QHT	Expanding prior knowledge of vocabulary words by marking words with a **Q**, **H**, or **T** (Q signals words students do not know; H signals words students have heard and might be able to identify; T signals words students know well enough to teach to their peers)	To allow students to build on their prior knowledge of words, to provide a forum for peer teaching and learning of new words, and to serve as a prereading exercise to aid in comprehension
Questioning the Text	Developing levels of questions about text; that is, literal, interpretive, and universal questions that prompt deeper thinking about a text before, during, or after reading	To engage more actively and independently with texts, read with greater purpose and focus, and ultimately answer questions to gain greater insight into the text; helps students to comprehend and interpret

STRATEGY	DEFINITION	PURPOSE
Paraphrasing	Restating in one's own words the essential information expressed in a text, whether it be narration, dialogue, or informational text, while maintaining the original text's meaning	To encourage and facilitate comprehension of challenging text
RAFT	Primarily used to generate new text, this strategy can also be used to analyze a text by examining the role of the speaker (R), the intended audience (A), the format of the text (F), and the topic of the text (T)	To initiate reader response; to facilitate an analysis of a text to gain focus prior to creating a new text
Rereading	Encountering the same text with more than one reading	To identify additional details; to clarify meaning and/or reinforce comprehension of texts
SIFT	Analyzing a fictional text by examining stylistic elements, especially symbol, imagery, and figures of speech in order to show how all work together to reveal tone and theme	To focus and facilitate an analysis of a fictional text by examining the title and text for symbolism, identifying images and sensory details, analyzing figurative language, and identifying how all these elements reveal tone and theme
Skimming/Scanning	Skimming by rapid or superficial reading of a text to form an overall impression or to obtain a general understanding of the material; scanning focuses on key words, phrases, or specific details and provides speedy recognition of information	To quickly form an overall impression prior to an in-depth study of a text; to answer specific questions or quickly locate targeted information or detail in a text
SMELL	Analyzing a persuasive speech or essay by asking five essential questions: • **S**ender-receiver relationship—What is the sender-receiver relationship? Who are the images and language meant to attract? Describe the speaker of the text. • **M**essage—What is the message? Summarize the statement made in the text. • **E**motional Strategies—What is the desired effect? • **L**ogical Strategies—What logic is operating? How does it (or its absence) affect the message? Consider the logic of the images as well as the words. • **L**anguage—What does the language of the text describe? How does it affect the meaning and effectiveness of the writing? Consider the language of the images as well as the words.	To analyze a persuasive speech or essay by focusing on five essential characteristics of the genre; analysis is related to rhetorical devices, logical fallacies, and how an author's use of language achieves specific purposes

STRATEGY	DEFINITION	PURPOSE
SOAPSTone	Analyzing text by discussing and identifying **S**peaker, **O**ccasion, **A**udience, **P**urpose, **S**ubject, and **Tone**	To facilitate the analysis of specific elements of nonfiction, literary, and informational texts, and show the relationship among the elements to an understanding of the whole
Summarizing	Giving a brief statement of the main points or essential information expressed in a text, whether it be narration, dialogue, or informational text	To facilitate comprehension and recall of a text
Think Aloud	Talking through a difficult passage or task by using a form of metacognition whereby the reader expresses how he/she has made sense of the text	To reflect on how readers make meaning of challenging texts and to facilitate discussion
TP-CASTT	Analyzing a poetic text by identifying and discussing **T**itle, **P**araphrase, **C**onnotation, **A**ttitude, **S**hift, **T**heme, and **T**itle again	To facilitate the analysis of specific elements of a literary text, especially poetry. To show how the elements work together to create meaning
Visualizing	Forming a picture (mentally and/or literally) while reading a text to deepen understanding	To increase reading comprehension, deepen understanding, and promote active engagement with text
Word Maps	Using a clearly defined graphic organizer such as concept circles or word webs to identify and reinforce word meanings	To provide a visual tool for identifying and remembering multiple aspects of words and word meanings
Word Sort	Organizing and sorting words into categories designated by the teacher or selected by the student and providing a written or oral justification for the classifications	To solidify understanding of word meanings by considering the multiple uses, meanings, and relationships of word parts, words, and groups of words

Writing Strategies

STRATEGY	DEFINITION	PURPOSE
Adding `	Enhancing a text by finding areas to add facts, details, examples, and commentary; smoothing out transitions; and clarifying and strengthening ideas and assertions	To improve, refine, and clarify the writer's thoughts during drafting and/or revision
Brainstorming	Using a flexible but deliberate process of listing multiple ideas in a short period of time without excluding any idea from the preliminary list	To generate ideas, concepts, or key words that provide a focus and/or establish organization as part of the prewriting or revision process
Deleting	Enhancing a text by eliminating words, phrases, sentences, or ideas that inhibit clarity and cohesiveness	To improve, refine, and clarify the writer's thoughts during drafting and/or revision
Drafting	Composing a text in its initial form before developing it	To incorporate brainstormed or initial ideas into a written format
Freewriting	Writing freely without constraints in order to generate ideas and capture thinking	To generate ideas when planning a piece of writing, or to refine and clarify thoughts, spark new ideas, and/or generate content during drafting and/or revision
Generating Questions	Clarifying and developing ideas by asking questions of the draft. May be part of self-editing or peer editing	To clarify and develop ideas in a draft; used during drafting and as part of writer response
Graphic Organizer	Organizing ideas and information visually (e.g., Venn diagrams, flowcharts, cluster maps)	To provide a visual system for organizing multiple ideas, details, and/or textual support to be included in a piece of writing
Guided Writing	Modeling the writing that students are expected to produce by guiding students through the planning, generation of ideas, organization, drafting, revision, editing, and publication of texts before students are asked to perform the same process; coconstructing texts with students as part of guided writing	To demonstrate the writing process

Speaking and Listening Strategies

STRATEGY	DEFINITION	PURPOSE
Choral Reading	Reading text lines aloud in student groups and/or individually to present an interpretation	To develop fluency; differentiate between the reading of statements and questions; practice phrasing, pacing, and reading dialogue; show how a character's emotions are captured through vocal stress and intonation
Debate	Engaging in a structured argument to examine both sides of an issue	To provide students with an opportunity to collect and orally present evidence supporting the affirmative and negative arguments of a proposition or issue
Drama Games	Participating in creative dramatics (e.g., pantomime, tableau, role-playing) to reinforce an oral literacy skill or develop a deeper understanding of a concept	To engage students in the reading and presenting of text and to create meaning through a kinesthetic approach
Fishbowl (Inner/outer circles)	Discussing specific topics within groups; some students will form the inner circle and model appropriate discussion techniques while an outer circle of students listens to and evaluates the discussion process of the inner circle in order to respond effectively	To provide students with an opportunity to engage in a formal discussion and to experience roles both as participant and active listener; students also have the responsibility of supporting their opinions and responses using specific textual evidence
Note-taking	Creating a record of information while listening to a speaker or reading a text	To facilitate active listening or close reading; to record and organize ideas that assist in processing information
Oral Reading	Reading aloud one's own text or the texts of others (e.g., echo reading, choral reading, paired readings)	To share one's own work or the work of others; build fluency and increase confidence in presenting to a group
Rehearsal	Encouraging multiple practices of a piece of text prior to a performance	To provide students with an opportunity to clarify the meaning of a text prior to a performance as they refine the use of dramatic conventions (e.g., gestures, vocal interpretations, facial expressions)
Role-Playing	Assuming the role or persona of a character	To develop the voice, emotions, and mannerisms of a character to facilitate improved comprehension of a text
Socratic Seminar	Tying a focused discussion to an essential question, topic, or selected text in which students ask questions of each other; questions initiate a conversation that continues with a series of responses and additional questions	To help students formulate questions that address issues (in lieu of simply stating their opinions) to facilitate their own discussion and arrive at a new understanding; students also have the responsibility of supporting their opinions and responses using specific textual evidence

Collaborative Strategies

STRATEGY	DEFINITION	PURPOSE
Discussion Groups	Engaging in an interactive, small-group discussion, often with an assigned role; to consider a topic, text, or question	To gain new understanding of or insight into a text from multiple perspectives
Jigsaw	In groups, students read different texts or passages from a single text, then share and exchange information from their reading with another group. They then return to their original groups to share their new knowledge.	To summarize and present information to others in a way that facilitates an understanding of a text (or multiple texts) without having each student read the text in its entirety
Literature Circles	Groups of students read the same text to participate in a mutual reading experience; based on the objective(s) of the lesson, students take on a variety of roles throughout the reading experience; texts may be selected based on individual preferences or on the demands of the text.	To provide opportunities for students to interact with one another as they read, respond to, and interpret a common text
Think-Pair-Share	Pairing with a peer to share ideas before sharing ideas and discussion with a larger group	To construct meaning about a topic or question; to test thinking in relation to the ideas of others; to prepare for a discussion with a larger group

Graphic Organizer Directory

Contents

Active Listening Feedback

Presenter's name: _____

Content

What is the presenter's purpose? _____

What is the presenter's main point? _____

Do you agree with the presenter? Why or why not? _____

_____

_____

Form

Did the presenter use a clear, loud voice? ☐ yes ☐ no

Did the presenter make eye contact? ☐ yes ☐ no

One thing I really liked about the presentation:

_____

_____

_____

One question I still have:

_____

_____

_____

Other comments or notes:

Active Listening Notes

Title: _____

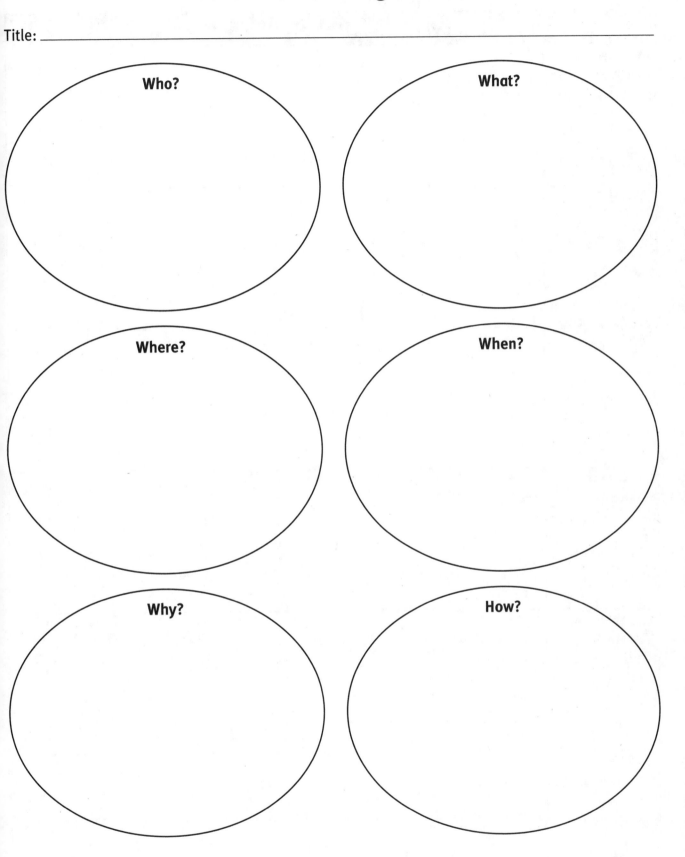

Who?

What?

Where?

When?

Why?

How?

Audience Notes and Feedback

Scoring Criteria	Notes/Feedback
Introduction/ Conclusion	
Timing	
Voice	
Eye Contact/ Gestures	
Use of Media, Visuals, Props	
Audience Engagement	

Cause and Effect

Title: _____

Cause: What happened?

➤ **Effect:** An effect of this is

Cause: What happened?

➤ **Effect:** An effect of this is

Cause: What happened?

➤ **Effect:** An effect of this is

Cause: What happened?

➤ **Effect:** An effect of this is

Character Map

Character name: _____

What does the character look like?

How does the character act and feel?

What do other characters say or think about the character?

Collaborative Dialogue

Topic: _____

Use the space below to record ideas.

"Wh-" Prompts
Who?   What?   Where?   When?   Why?

Speaker 1

Speaker 2

Conclusion Builder

Evidence

Evidence

Evidence

Based on this evidence, I can conclude

Conflict Map

Title: _____

What is the main conflict in this story?

What causes this conflict?

How is the conflict resolved?

What are some other ways the conflict could have been resolved?

Conversation for Quickwrite

1. Turn to a partner and restate the prompt in your own words.

2. Brainstorm key words to use in your quickwrite response.

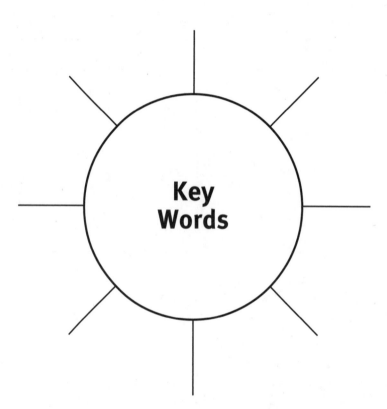

3. Take turns explaining your ideas to your partner. Try using some of the key words you brainstormed.

4. On your own, write a response to the quickwrite.

Definition and Reflection

Academic Vocabulary Word
Definition in own words
Illustration (literal or symbolic)

My experiences with this concept:

- I haven't really thought about this concept.

_____

- I have only thought about this concept in English Language Arts class.

_____

- I have applied this concept in other classes.

_____

- I have applied this concept outside of school.

_____

My level of understanding:

- I am still trying to understand this concept.

_____

- I am familiar with this concept, but I am not comfortable applying it.

_____

- I am very comfortable with this concept and I know how to apply it.

_____

- I could teach this concept to another classmate.

_____

Discourse Starters

Questioning and Discussing a Text

One question I have is _____.

Could this mean _____?

Why do you think the author _____?

I understand _____, but I wonder _____.

I notice that _____.

I think this (word/sentence/paragraph) means _____.

I think _____ because the text says _____.

In paragraph _____, the author says _____.

According to the text, _____.

One way to interpret _____ is _____.

Summarizing

The main events that take place are _____.

The major points of the text are _____.

The main idea of _____ is _____.

One central idea of this text is _____.

Another central idea is _____.

All in all, the message is _____.

The author's main purpose is to _____.

Basically, the author is saying that _____.

Comparing and Contrasting

_____ and _____ are similar because _____.

_____ and _____ are similar in that they both _____.

_____ is _____. Similarly, _____ is _____.

One thing _____ and _____ have in common is _____.

_____ and _____ are different because _____.

_____ and _____ are different in that _____.

_____ is _____. On the other hand, _____ is _____.

One difference between _____ and _____ is _____.

Clarifying

I'm not sure I understand the instructions.

Could you repeat that please?

I have a question about _____.

I am having trouble with _____.

Will you explain that again?

Could you clarify _____?

Would you mind helping me with _____?

Which (page/paragraph/section) are we reading?

How do you spell/pronounce _____?

Discourse Starters

Agreeing and Disagreeing

I agree with the idea that _____ because _____.

I share your point of view because _____.

You made a good point when you said _____.

I agree with (a person) that _____.

Although I agree that _____, I also think _____.

I understand where you're coming from, but _____.

I disagree with the idea that _____ because _____.

I see it a different way because _____.

You have a point, but the evidence suggests _____.

Arguing and Persuading with Evidence

I believe that _____ because _____.

It is clear that _____ because _____.

One reason I think _____ is _____.

Based on evidence in the text, I think _____.

Evidence such as _____ suggests that _____.

An example to support my position is _____.

This is evident because _____.

What evidence supports the idea that _____?

Can you explain why you think _____?

Evaluating

This is effective because _____.

The evidence _____ is strong because _____.

This is convincing because _____.

I see why the author _____, but I think _____.

This is not very effective because _____.

The evidence _____ is weak because _____.

This would have been better if _____.

What do you think about the writer's choice to _____?

Why do you think _____ (is/isn't) effective?

Giving Feedback and Suggesting

The part where you _____ is strong because _____.

What impressed me the most is how you _____.

This is a good start. Maybe you should add _____.

I like how you _____, but I would try _____.

You might consider changing _____.

I would suggest revising _____ so that _____.

One suggestion would be to _____.

Why did you choose _____?

A better choice might be _____.

This would be clearer if _____.

Editor's Checklist

Over the course of the year with SpringBoard, customize this Editor's Checklist as your knowledge of language conventions grows. The three examples below show you how to write a good checklist item.

	Are all the sentences complete?
	Do the subject and verb of each sentence agree?
	Do all the sentences have correct punctuation?

Writer's Checklist

Ideas

	Does your first paragraph hook the reader?
	Is the purpose of your writing clear (to inform, to make an argument, etc.)?
	Is the genre of writing appropriate for your purpose?
	Is your main idea clear and easy to summarize?
	Does your text contain details and information that support your main idea?
	Are the ideas in the text well organized?
	Do you connect your ideas by using transitions?
	Do you use parallel structure to keep your ideas clear?
	Does each paragraph have a conclusion that transitions to the next paragraph?
	Does your writing end with a strong conclusion that restates the original purpose of the text?

Language

	Do you keep a consistent point of view throughout?
	Do you use the present tense when writing about a text?
	Are any shifts in verb tense easy to follow and necessary?
	Have you removed unnecessary or confusing words?
	Do you use vivid verbs and descriptive adjectives when appropriate?
	Do you use different styles of language (like figurative or sensory) when appropriate?
	Do you use a variety of sentence types?
	Do you vary the way you begin your sentences?
	Did you split up run-on sentences?
	Are your pronoun references clear?

Evaluating Online Sources

The URL
- What is its domain?
    - .com = a for-profit organization
    - .gov, .mil, .us (or other country code) = a government site
    - .edu = affiliated with an educational institution
    - .org = a nonprofit organization
- Is this URL someone's personal page?
- Do you recognize who is publishing this page?

Sponsor:
- Does the website give information about the organization or group that sponsors it?
- Does it have a link (often called "About Us") that leads you to that information?
- What do you learn?

Timeliness:
- When was the page last updated (usually this is posted at the top or bottom of the page)?
- Is the topic something that changes frequently, like current events or technology?

Purpose:
- What is the purpose of the page?
- What is its target audience?
- Does it present information, opinion, or both?
- Is it primarily objective or subjective?
- How do you know?

Author:
- What credentials does the author have?
- Is this person or group considered an authority on the topic?

Links
- Does the page provide links?
- Do they work?
- Are they helpful?
- Are they objective or subjective?

Fallacies 101

Ad Baculum (Scare Tactics)	If you don't support the party's tax plan, you and your family will be reduced to poverty. Chairman of the Board: "All those opposed to my arguments for the opening of a new department, signify by saying, 'I resign.'"
Ad hoc	Person 1: I should have gotten an A on that test. Person 2: You didn't study for that test at all. Person 1: That class is useless!
Ad Hominem (Against the Man)/ Genetic Fallacy	"My opponent, a vicious and evil person, should absolutely never be elected to office." The Volkswagen Beetle is an evil car because it was originally designed by Hitler's army.
Ad Populum	You should turn to channel 6. It's the most watched channel this year. There is always a long line at that restaurant, so the food must be really good.
Appeal To Pity	"Jonathan couldn't have cheated! He's such a nice boy and he tries so hard."
Argument from Outrage	The airline cancelled my flight an hour before takeoff and wouldn't tell me why. This is an outrage! We should all boycott the company.
Circular Reasoning	Emotional support animals should be allowed on airplanes, so the airline should change its policy. The policy should be changed because emotional support animals should be allowed on planes!
Either/Or (False Dilemma)	We can either stop using cars or destroy Earth. We must drill now or we'll remain dependent on foreign oil suppliers.
Faulty Analogies	Buying into the stock market is the same as betting on a horse race.
Hasty Generalization	They hit two home runs in the first inning of the season. This team is going all the way to the World Series!
Non-sequitur	I always see her with a book in her hands. She must hate watching TV.
Post Hoc	I ate a turkey sandwich and now I feel tired, so the turkey must have made me tired.
Red Herring	The new dress code banning t-shirts isn't fair. Students have the right to free speech just like anyone else.
Slippery Slope Fallacy	"If I don't study for the test, then I'm going to get a bad grade. If I get a bad grade on the test, I'll get a bad grade in the class, and I won't get into a good college. Getting into a good college is the most important part of getting a good job; so if I don't study for the test, I won't get a good job!"
Straw Man	People say that Mark Twain was a good author, but I disagree. If he was such a good author, why didn't he write using his own name?

Idea and Argument Evaluator

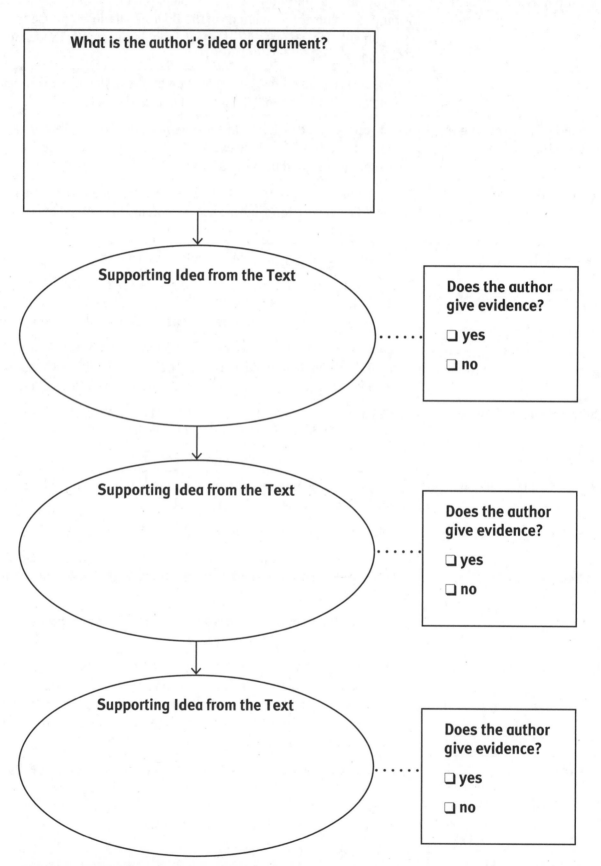

What is the author's idea or argument?

Supporting Idea from the Text

Does the author give evidence?

❑ yes

❑ no

Supporting Idea from the Text

Does the author give evidence?

❑ yes

❑ no

Supporting Idea from the Text

Does the author give evidence?

❑ yes

❑ no

Idea Connector

Directions: Write two simple sentences about the same topic. Next, write transition words around the Idea Connector. Then, choose an appropriate word to connect ideas in the two sentences. Write your combined sentence in the space below.

Sentence One

Sentence Two

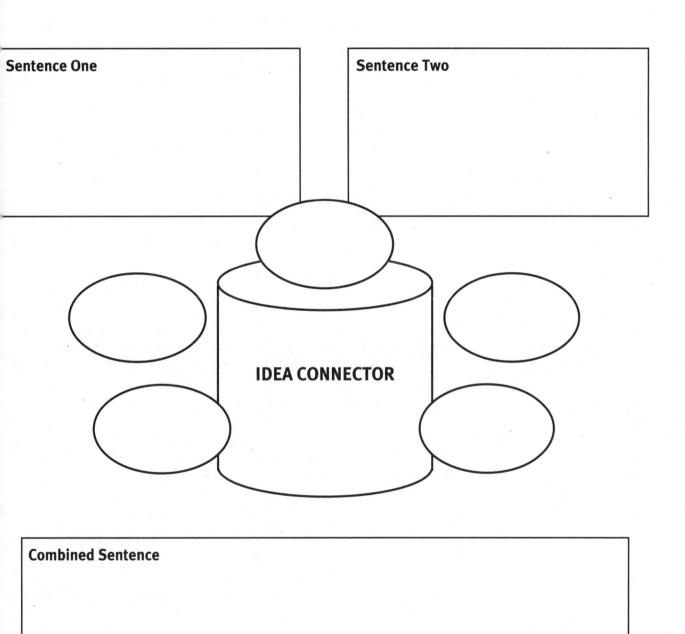

IDEA CONNECTOR

Combined Sentence

Key Idea and Details Chart

Title/Topic _____

Key Idea _____
_____
_____

Supporting detail 1 _____
_____
_____

Supporting detail 2 _____
_____
_____

Supporting detail 3 _____
_____
_____

Supporting detail 4 _____
_____
_____

Restate topic sentence: _____
_____

Concluding sentence: _____
_____
_____

Narrative Analysis and Writing

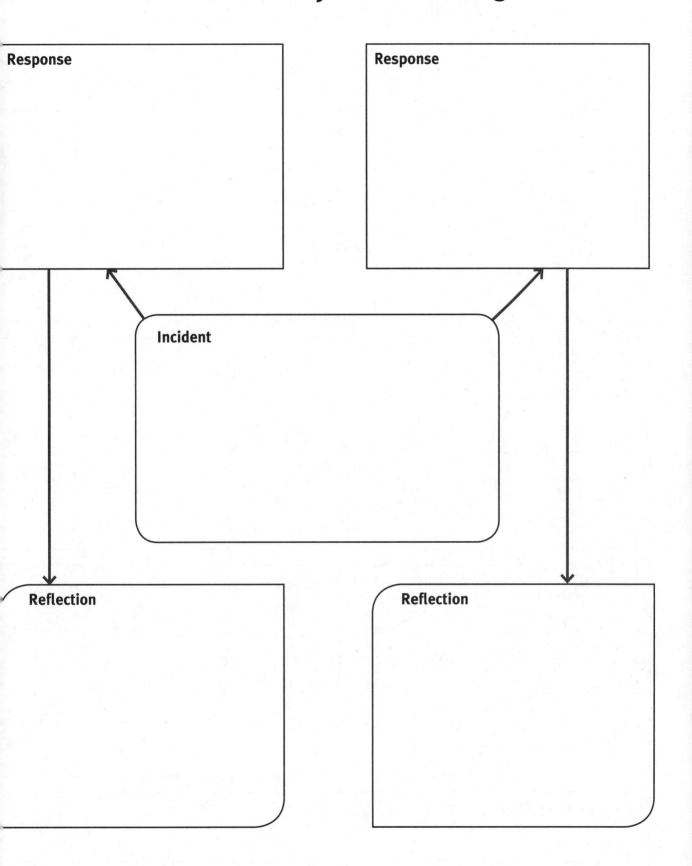

Response

Response

Incident

Reflection

Reflection

Notes for Reading Independently
Fiction

Title: _____

Author: _____

Something interesting I noticed:	**A question I have:**

Summary:

Illustration:

Connections to my life/other texts I've read:

How challenging this text was:

Easy   1   2   3   4   5   6   7   8   9   10   _Challenging_

Notes for Reading Independently
Nonfiction

Title: _____

Author: _____

Main idea:	Facts I learned:

Summary:

Questions I still have:

Connections to my life/other texts I've read:

How challenging this text was:

Easy   1   2   3   4   5   6   7   8   9   10   *Challenging*

Opinion Builder

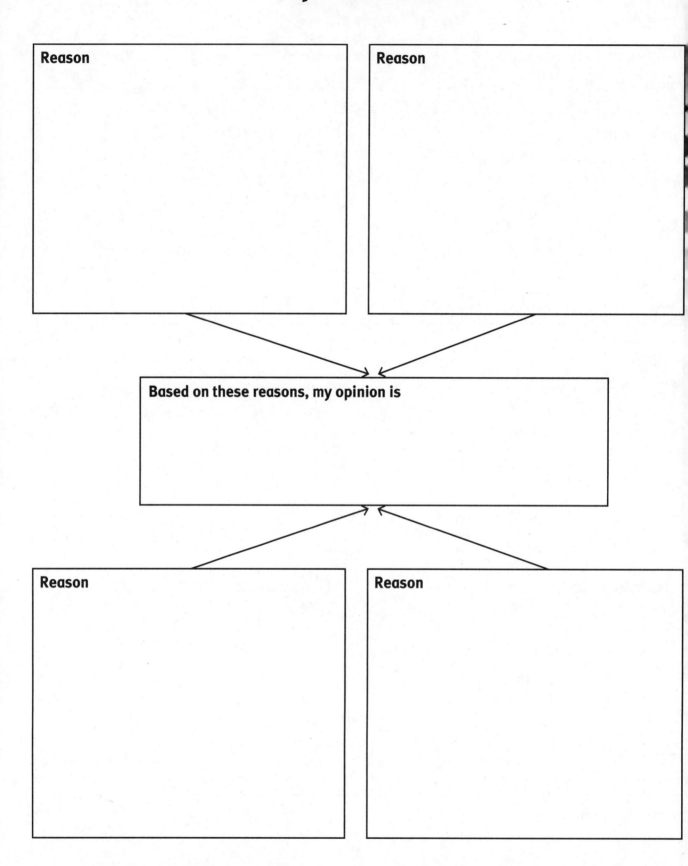

Reason

Reason

Based on these reasons, my opinion is

Reason

Reason

OPTIC

Title of Piece:

Artist: _____   **Type of artwork:** _____

Overview	Look at the artwork for at least 10 seconds. Generate questions; e.g., What is the subject? What strikes you as interesting, odd, etc.? What is happening?
Parts	Look closely at the artwork, making note of important elements and details. Ask additional questions, such as: Who are the figures? What is the setting and time period? What symbols are present? What historical information would aid understanding of this piece?
Title	Consider what the title and any written elements of the text suggest about meaning. How does the title relate to what is portrayed?
Interrelationships	Look for connections between and among the title, caption, and the parts of the art. How are the different elements related?
Conclusion	Form a conclusion about the meaning/theme of the text. Remember the questions you asked when you first examined it. Be prepared to support your conclusions with evidence.

Paragraph Frame for Conclusions

Conclusion Words and Phrases

shows that

based on

suggests that

leads to

indicates that

influences

The _____ (story, poem, play, passage, etc.)

shows that (helps us to conclude that) _____

_____

_____

There are several reasons why. First, _____

_____

_____

_____

_____

A second reason is _____

_____

_____

_____

_____

Finally, _____

_____

_____

_____

_____

In conclusion, _____

_____

_____

_____

_____

Paragraph Frame for Sequencing

Sequence Words and Phrases

at the beginning

in the first place

as a result

later

eventually

in the end

lastly

In the _____ (story, poem, play, passage, etc.)

there are three important _____

(events, steps, directions, etc.)

First, _____

_____

_____

_____

_____

Second, _____

_____

_____

_____

_____

Third, _____

_____

_____

_____

_____

Finally, _____

_____

_____

_____

_____

Paraphrasing and Summarizing Map

What does the text say?	How can I say it in my own words?

How can I use my own words to summarize the text?

Peer Editing

Writer's name: _____

Did the writer answer the prompt? ☐ yes ☐ no

Did the writer use appropriate details or evidence to develop their writing? ☐ yes ☐ no

Is the writing organized in a way that makes sense? ☐ yes ☐ no

Did the writer use a variety of sentence types to make the writing more interesting? ☐ yes ☐ no

Are there any spelling or punctuation mistakes? ☐ yes ☐ no

Are there any grammar errors? ☐ yes ☐ no

Two things I really liked about the writer's story:

1. _____
   _____
   _____

2. _____
   _____
   _____

One thing I think the writer could do to improve the writing:

1. _____
   _____
   _____

Other comments or notes:

Persuasive/Argument Writing Map

Thesis

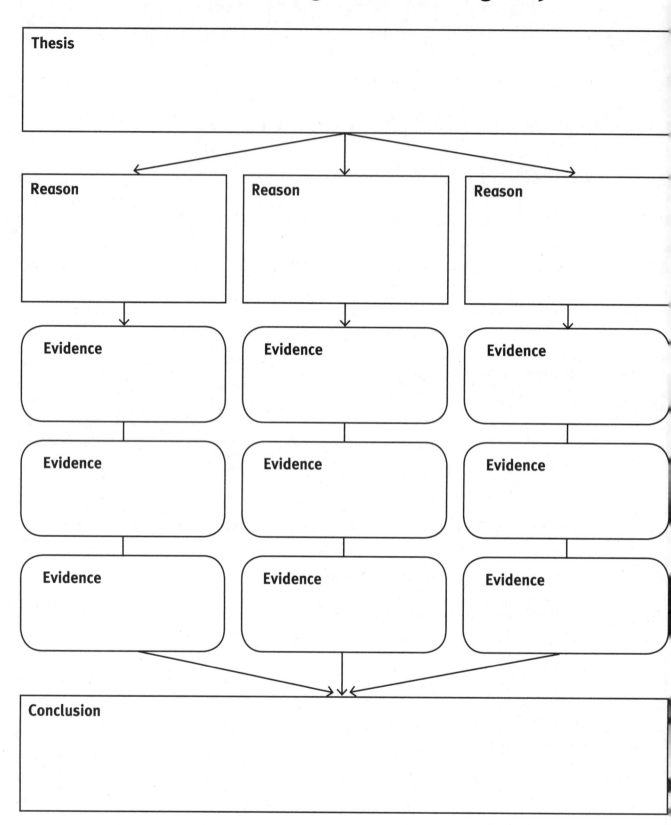

Reason

Reason

Reason

Evidence

Evidence

Evidence

Evidence

Evidence

Evidence

Evidence

Evidence

Evidence

Conclusion

Presenting Scoring Guide

Scoring Criteria	Exemplary	Proficient	Emerging	Incomplete
Introduction / Conclusion	The presentation • provides a clear, engaging, and appropriate introduction to the topic or performance • provides a clear, engaging, and appropriate conclusion that closes, summarizes, draws connections to broader themes, or supports the ideas presented.	The presentation • provides a clear and appropriate introduction to the topic or performance • provides a clear and appropriate conclusion that closes, summarizes, draws connections to broader themes, or supports the ideas presented.	The presentation • provides an adequate introduction to the topic or performance • provides an adequate conclusion that closes, summarizes, draws connections to broader themes, or supports the ideas presented.	The presentation • does not provide an introduction to the topic or performance • does not provide a conclusion that closes, summarizes, draws connections to broader themes, or supports the ideas presented.
Timing	The presentation • thoroughly delivers its intended message within the allotted time • is thoughtfully and appropriately paced throughout.	The presentation • mostly delivers its intended message within the allotted time • is appropriately paced most of the time.	The presentation • delivers some of its intended message within the allotted time • is sometimes not paced appropriately.	The presentation • does not deliver its intended message within the allotted time • is not paced appropriately.
Voice (Volume, Enunciation, Rate)	The presentation • is delivered with adequate volume enabling audience members to fully comprehend what is said • is delivered with clear enunciation.	The presentation • is delivered with adequate volume enabling audience members to mostly comprehend what is said • is delivered with mostly clear enunciation.	The presentation • is delivered with somewhat adequate volume enabling audience members to comprehend some of what is said • is delivered with somewhat clear enunciation.	The presentation • is not delivered with adequate volume, so that audience members are unable to comprehend what is said • is delivered with unclear enunciation.
Eye Contact/ Gestures	The presentation • is delivered with appropriate eye contact that helps engage audience members • makes use of natural gestures and/or body language to convey meaning.	The presentation • is delivered with some appropriate eye contact that helps engage audience members • makes use of gestures and/or body language to convey meaning.	The presentation • is delivered with occasional eye contact that sometimes engages audience members • makes some use of gestures and/or body language to convey meaning.	The presentation • is not delivered with eye contact to engage audience members • makes little or no use of gestures and/or body language to convey meaning.
Use of Media, Visuals, Props	The presentation • makes use of highly engaging visuals, multimedia, and/or props that enhance delivery.	The presentation • makes use of visuals, multimedia, and/or props that enhance delivery.	The presentation • makes use of some visuals, multimedia, and/or props that somewhat enhance delivery.	The presentation • makes use of few or no visuals, multimedia, and/or props that enhance delivery.
Audience Engagement	The presentation • includes thoughtful and appropriate interactions with and responses to audience members.	The presentation • includes appropriate interactions with and responses to audience members.	The presentation • includes a few interactions with and responses to audience members.	The presentation • does not include interactions with and responses to audience members.

RAFT

Role	Who or what are you as a writer?
Audience	As a writer, to whom are you writing?
Format	As a writer, what format would be appropriate for your audience (essay, letter, speech, poem, etc.)?
Topic	As a writer, what is the subject of your writing? What points do you want to make?

Roots and Affixes Brainstorm

Directions: Write the root or affix in the circle. Brainstorm or use a dictionary to find the meaning of the root or affix and add it to the circle. Then, find words that use that root or affix. Write one word in each box. Write a sentence for each word.

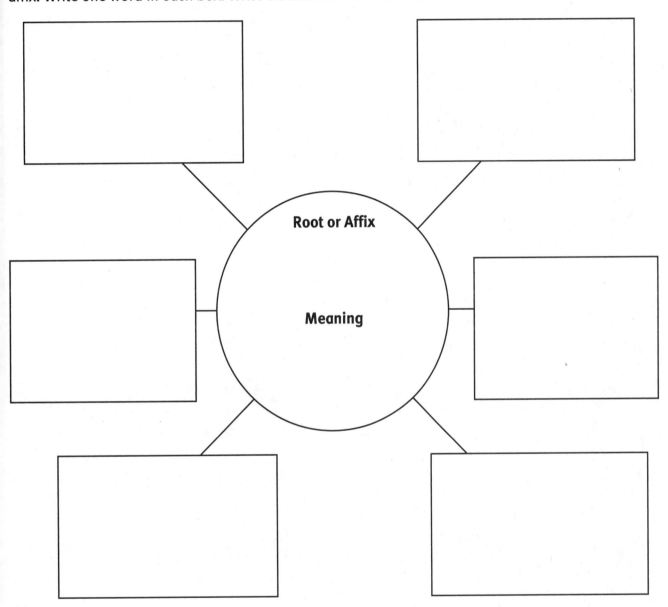

Round Table Discussion

Directions: Write the topic in the center box. One student begins by stating his or her ideas while the student to the left takes notes. Then the next student speaks while the student to his or her left takes notes, and so on.

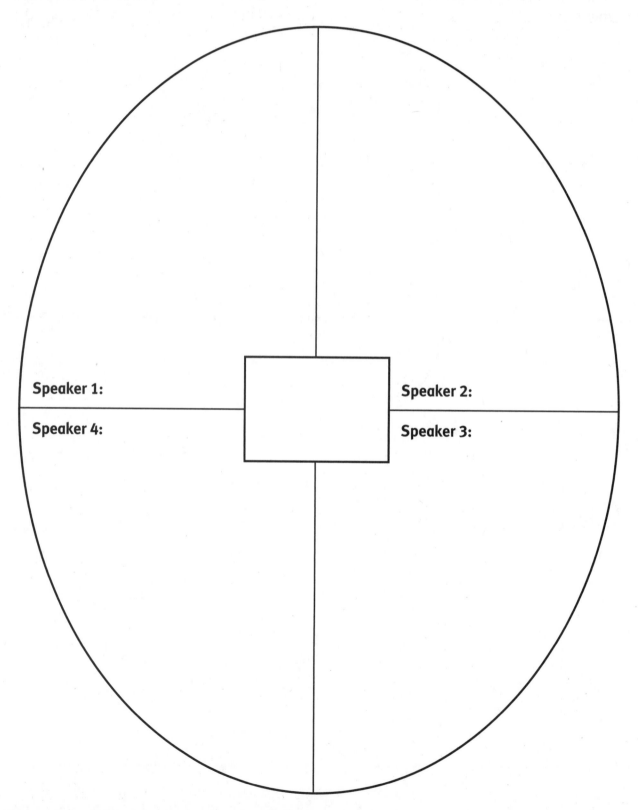

Speaker 1:

Speaker 2:

Speaker 4:

Speaker 3:

Sequence of Events Time Line

Title: _____

What happened first?

Next?

Beginning

Middle

End

Then?

Finally?

SMELL

Sender-Receiver Relationship—Who are the senders and receivers of the message, and what is their relationship (consider what different audiences the text may be addressing)?

Message—What is a literal summary of the content? What is the meaning/significance of this information?

Emotional Strategies—What emotional appeals (*pathos*) are included? What seems to be their desired effect?

Logical Strategies—What logical arguments/appeals (*logos*) are included? What is their effect?

Language—What specific language is used to support the message? How does it affect the text's effectiveness? Consider both images and actual words.

SOAPSTone

SOAPSTone	Analysis	Textual Support
Subject What does the reader know about the writer?		
Occasion What are the circumstances surrounding this text?		
Audience Who is the target audience?		
Purpose Why did the author write this text?		
Subject What is the topic?		
Tone What is the author's tone, or attitude?		

Text Structure Stairs

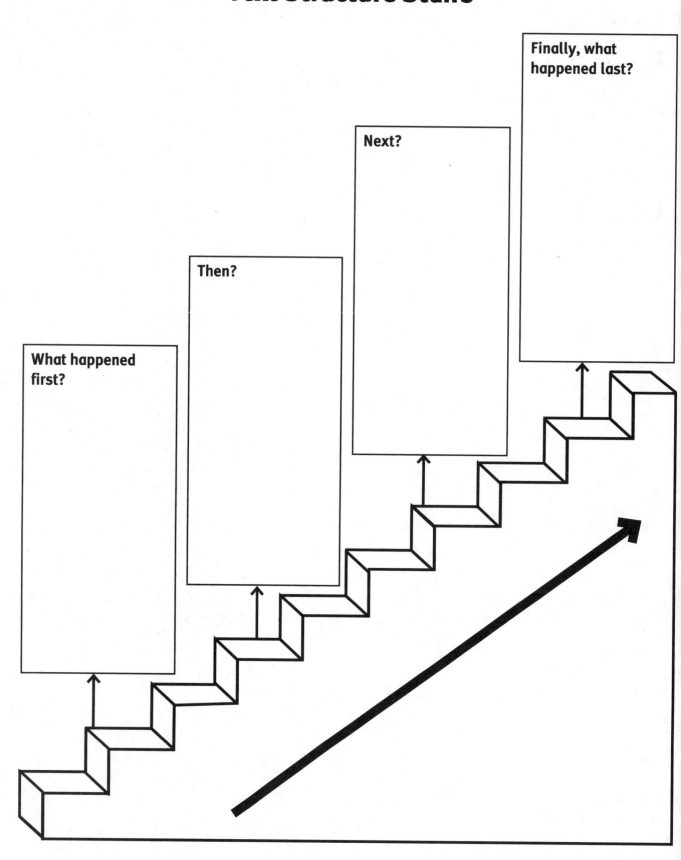

Finally, what happened last?

Next?

Then?

What happened first?

TP-CASTT Analysis

Poem Title:

Author:

Title: Make a Prediction. What do you think the title means before you read the poem?

Paraphrase: Translate the poem in your own words. What is the poem about? Rephrase difficult sections word for word.

Connotation: Look beyond the literal meaning of key words and images to their associations.

Attitude: What is the speaker's attitude? What is the author's attitude? How does the author feel about the speaker, about other characters, about the subject?

Shifts: Where do the shifts in tone, setting, voice, etc., occur? Look for time and place, keywords, punctuation, stanza divisions, changes in length or rhyme, and sentence structure. What is the purpose of each shift? How do they contribute to effect and meaning?

Title: Reexamine the title. What do you think it means now in the context of the poem?

Theme: Think of the literal and metaphorical layers of the poem. Then determine the overall theme. The theme must be written in a complete sentence.

TP-CASTT

Poem Title:

Author:

Title		
Paraphrase		
Connotation		
Attitude		
Shifts		
Title		
Theme		

Unknown Word Solver

Unknown Word

Can you find any context clues? List them.

Do you recognize any word parts?

Prefix:

Root Word:

Suffix:

Do you know another meaning of this word that does not make sense in this context?

Does it look or sound like a word in another language?

What is the dictionary definition?

How can you define the word in your own words?

Venn Diagram for Writing a Comparison

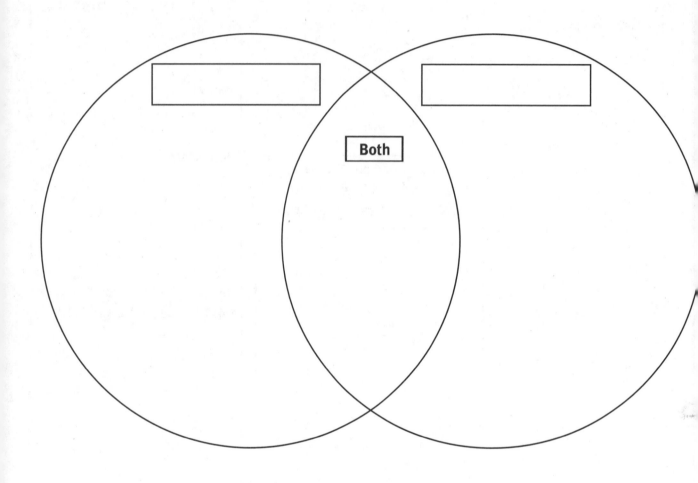

| Both |

| They are similar in that _____ | They are different in that _____ |

Verbal & Visual Word Association

Definition in Your Own Words	Important Elements

Academic Vocabulary Word

Visual Representation	Personal Association

Web Organizer

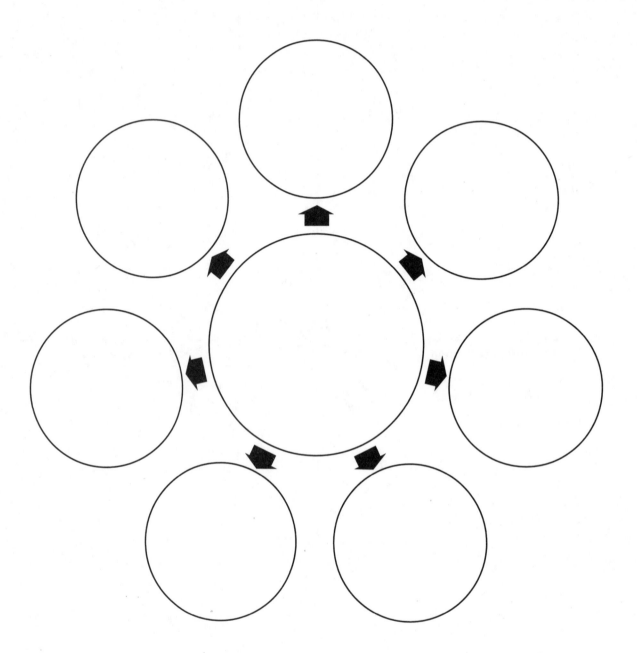

Word Choice Analyzer

Word or phrase from the text	Definition of word or phrase	How can I restate the definition in my own words?	What effect did the author produce by choosing these words?

Explain Your Analysis

The author uses the word or phrase _____ , which means

_____

Another way to say this is _____

_____

I think the author chose these words to _____

_____

_____

One way I can modify this sentence to add detail is to _____

_____

Word Map

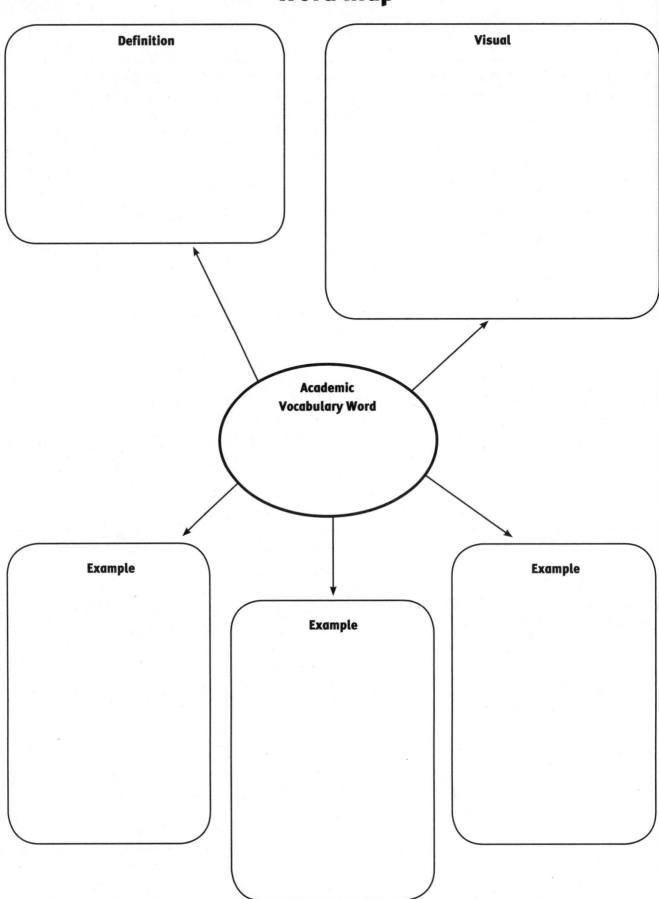

Definition

Visual

Academic
Vocabulary Word

Example

Example

Example

Glossary/Glosario

A

active-voice verbs: verbs for which the subject performs the action
verbos en voz activa: forma verbal que indica que el sujeto realiza la acción

advertising techniques: specific methods used in print, graphics, or videos to persuade people to buy a product or use a service
técnicas publicitarias: métodos específicos usados en impresos, gráfica o videos para persuadir a las personas a comprar un producto o usar un servicio

agenda: a secret plan or motivation that causes someone to act in a certain way
agenda: motivación o plan secreto que lleva a alguien a actuar de determinado modo

allegory: a story in which the characters, objects, or actions have a meaning beyond the surface of the story
alegoría: cuento en el que los personajes, objetos o acciones tienen un significado que va más allá de la superficie de la historia

alliteration: the repetition of initial consonant sounds in words that are close together
aliteración: repetición de sonidos consonánticos iniciales en palabras cercanas

allusion: a reference made to a well-known person, event, or place from history, music, art, or another literary work
alusión: referencia a una persona, evento o lugar muy conocidos de la historia, música, arte u otra obra literaria

analogy: a comparison between two things for the purpose of drawing conclusions on one based on its similarities to the other
analogía: comparación entre dos cosas con el propósito de sacar conclusiones sobre las semejanzas que una cosa tiene a otra

anaphora: the repetition of the same word or group of words at the beginnings of two or more clauses or lines
anáfora: repetición de la misma palabra o grupo de palabras al comienzo de una o más cláusulas o versos

anecdotal evidence: evidence based on personal accounts of incidents
evidencia anecdótica: evidencia basada en relatos personales de los hechos

annotated bibliography: a list of sources used in research along with comments or summaries about each source
bibliografía anotada: lista de fuentes utilizadas en la investigación, junto con comentarios o resúmenes acerca de cada fuente

antagonist: the character who opposes or struggles against the main character
antagonista: personaje que se opone o lucha contra el personaje principal

aphorism: a short statement expressing an opinion or general truth
aforismo: afirmación corta que expresa una opinión o verdad general

appeals: the efforts to persuade an audience that a certain concept is true by directing statements toward reasoning or logic, character, or senses and emotions
llamados: serie de esfuerzos que alguien realiza con el fin de convencer a una audiencia de que determinado concepto es verdadero, persuadiéndola de ello mediante el uso del razonamiento o la lógica o bien apelando a su carácter, sentidos o emociones

Archetypal Criticism: criticism that deals with symbols and patterns that recur in the literature of widely diverse cultures
crítica de arquetipos: examinación de la literatura basada en símbolos y diseño

archetypes: universal symbols—images, characters, motifs, or patterns—that recur in the myths, dreams, oral traditions, songs, literature, and other texts of peoples widely separated by time and place
arquetipos: símbolos universales—imágenes, personajes, motivos o patrones—reiterativos en los mitos, el arte y la literatura alrededor del mundo

archival footage: film footage taken from another, previously recorded, source
cortometraje de archivo: fragmento de película tomada de otra fuente grabada previamente

argument: a form of writing that presents a particular claim or idea and supports it with evidence
argumento: forma de redacción que presenta una opinión o idea particular y la apoya con evidencia

GLOSSARY/ GLOSARIO

argumentation: the act or process of arguing that includes the *hook* (quotation, example, or idea that catches readers' attention), *claim* (the opinion or thesis statement), *support* (evidence in the form of facts, statistics, examples, anecdotes, or expert opinions), *concession* (the writer's admission that the other side of the argument has a valid point), *refutation* (a well-reasoned denial of an opponent's point, based on solid evidence), and *call to action* (a request of readers)
argumentación: la estructura de una argumentación incluye el *gancho* (cita, ejemplo o idea que capta la atención del lector), *afirmación* (declaración de opinión o tesis), *apoyo* (evidencia en forma de hechos, estadísticas, ejemplos, anécdotas u opiniones de expertos), *concesión* (admisión por parte del escritor de que la otra parte del debate tiene un punto válido), *refutación* (negación bien razonada de una opinión del oponente, basada en evidencia sólida) y *llamado a la acción* (petición inspirada de lectores)

argument by analogy: a comparison of two similar situations, implying that the outcome of one will resemble the outcome of the other
argumento por analogía: comparación de dos situaciones semejantes, infiriendo que el resultado de será parecido al resultado de la otra

artistic license: the practice of rewording of dialogue, alteration of language, or reordering of the plot of a text created by another artist
licencia artística: la costumbre de reformular un diálogo, aliteración de palabras, o arreglo de la trama de un texto creado por otro artista

aside: a short speech spoken by an actor directly to the audience and unheard by other actors on stage
aparte: alocución breve dicha por un actor directamente al público y que no escuchan los demás actores que están en el escenario

assonance: the repetition of similar vowel sounds in accented syllables, followed by different consonant sounds, in words that are close together
asonancia: repetición de sonidos vocálicos similares en sílabas acentuadas, seguida de diferentes sonidos consonánticos, en palabras que están cercanas

audience: the intended readers, listeners, or viewers of specific types of written, spoken, or visual texts
público: lectores objetivo, oyentes o espectadores de tipos específicos de textos escritos, hablados o visuales

audience analysis: determination of the characteristics and knowledge of the people who will read a work or hear a speech

análisis del público: determinar las características y conocimiento de las personas que leen una obra o escuchan un discurso

author's purpose: the specific reason or reasons for the writing; what the author hopes to accomplish
propósito del autor: razón específica para escribir; lo que el autor espera lograr

autobiography: an account written by a person about his or her own life
autobiografía: narración de una vida escrita por el propio sujeto del relato

B

balanced sentence: a sentence that presents ideas of equal weight in similar grammatical forms to emphasize the similarity or difference between the ideas
oración balanceada: oración que representa ideas de igual peso en formas gramaticales similares para enfatizar la semejanza o diferencia entre las ideas

bias: an inclination or mental leaning for or against something; prevents impartial judgment
sesgo: inclinación o tendencia mental a favor o en contra de algo, lo que impide una opinión imparcial

bibliography: a list of the sources used for research
bibliografía: lista de fuentes primarias en la preparación de un texto

biography: a description or account of events from a person's life, written by another person
biografía: descripción o narración de la vida de una persona o los sucesos importantes de su vida escritos por otra persona

blank verse: unrhymed verse
verso libre: verso que no tiene rima

block: to create the plan for how actors will position themselves on the stage in relation to one another, the audience, and the objects on the stage
ensayar: establecer un plan para determinar la posición que los actores deberán ocupar en un escenario en relación a sí mismos, a la audiencia, al escenario y a los objetos del mismo

blocking: in drama, the way actors position themselves in relation to one another, the audience, and the objects on the stage
bloqueo: en drama, el modo en que los actores se sitúan entre sí, con el público y los objetos en el escenario

book review: a formal assessment or examination of a book
reseña de libro: evaluación o examinación formal de un libro

C

cacophonous: harsh and unpleasant sounding
cacofónico: sonidos molestos y desagradables

call to action: a restatement of the claim and what the writer wants the reader to do
llamado a la acción: repetición de la afirmación y lo que el escritor quiere que el lector responda

caricature: a visual or verbal representation in which characteristics or traits are exaggerated or distorted for emphasis
caricatura: representación visual o verbal en la que las características o rasgos se exageran o se distorsionan para dar énfasis

catalog poem: a poem that uses repetition and variation in the creation of a list, or catalog, of objects or desires, plans, or memories
lista en poema: poema que usa repetición y variación en la creación de una lista o catálogo, de objetos o deseos o planes o memorias

cause: an action, event, or situation that brings about a particular result
causa: acción, suceso o situación que produce un resultado particular

caveat: a cautionary detail to be thought through carefully when analyzing something
exhortación: advertencia o consejo a tener muy en cuenta a la hora de interpretar o analizar algo

censor: to examine materials for objectionable content
censurar: examinar materiales por contenido desagradable

censorship: the act of suppressing public speech or publication of materials deemed to be offensive by the censor
censura: acto de suprimir un discurso público o publicación de materiales considerados ofensivos por un censor

challenge: to oppose or refute a statement that has been made
poner en duda: oponerse a algo o refutar una declaración que alguien ha hecho

characterization: the methods a writer uses to develop characters
caracterización: métodos que usa un escritor para desarrollar personajes

characters: people, animals, or imaginary creatures that take part in the action of a story. A short story usually centers on a *main character* but may also contain one or more *minor characters*, who are not as complex, but whose thoughts, words, or actions move the plot along. A character who is *dynamic* changes in response to the events of the narrative; a character who is *static* remains the same throughout the narrative. A *round* character is fully developed—he or she shows a variety of traits; a *flat* character is one-dimensional, usually showing only one trait.
personajes: personas, animales o criaturas imaginarias que participan en la acción de un cuento. Un cuento corto normalmente se centra en un *personaje principal*, pero puede también contener uno o más *personajes secundarios*, que no son tan complejos, pero cuyos pensamientos, palabras o acciones hacen avanzar la trama. Un personaje que es *dinámico* cambia según los eventos del relato; un personaje que es *estático* permanece igual a lo largo del relato. Un personaje *complejo* está completamente desarrollado: muestra una diversidad de rasgos; un personaje *simple* es unidimensional, mostrando normalmente sólo un rasgo.

character foil: a character whose actions or thoughts are juxtaposed against those of a major character in order to highlight key attributes of the major character
antagonista: personaje cuyas acciones o pensamientos se yuxtaponen a los de un personaje principal con el fin de destacar atributos clave del personaje principal

character sketch: a brief description of a literary character
reseña del personaje: breve descripción de un personaje literario

chorus: in traditional or classic drama, a group of performers who speak as one and comment on the action of the play
coro: en el drama tradicional o clásico, grupo de actores que hablan al unísono y comentan la acción de la obra teatral

cinematic elements: the features of cinema—movies, film, video—that contribute to its form and structure: *angle* (the view from which the image is shot), *framing* (how a scene is structured), *lighting* (the type of lighting used to light a scene), *mise en scène* (the composition, setting, or staging of an image, or a scene in a film), and *sound* (the sound effects and music accompanying each scene)
elementos cinematográficos: las características del cine—películas, filmaciones, video—que contribuyen a darle forma y estructura: *angulación* (vista desde la cual se toma la imagen), *encuadre* (cómo se estructura una escena), iluminación (tipo de *iluminación* que se usa para una escena), y *montaje* (composición, ambiente o escenificación de una imagen o escena en una película), y *sonido* (efectos sonoros y música que acompañan cada escena)

cinematic techniques: the methods a director uses to communicate meaning and to evoke particular emotional responses from viewers
técnicas cinematográficas: métodos que emplea un director para comunicar un significado y evocar cierta respuesta emocional de los videntes

claim: a thesis statement describing the position the writer is taking on an issue
afirmación: declaración de opinión (o tesis) que asevera una idea o establece un debate hacia una posición específica

cliché: an overused expression or idea
cliché: expresión o idea que se usa en exceso

climax: the point at which the action reaches its peak; the point of greatest interest or suspense in a story; the turning point at which the outcome of a conflict is decided
clímax: punto en el que la acción alcanza su punto culminante; punto de mayor interés en un cuento; punto de inflexión en el que se decide el resultado del conflicto

coherence: the quality of unity or logical connection among ideas; the clear and orderly presentation of ideas in a paragraph or essay
coherencia: calidad de unidad o relación lógica entre las ideas; presentación clara y ordenada de las ideas en un párrafo o ensayo

commentary: the expression of opinions or explanations about an event or situation
comentario: expresión oral o escrita de opiniones o explicaciones sobre una situación, tema o suceso

commentary: explanations about the significance or importance of supporting details or examples in an analysis
comentario: explicaciones acerca de la importancia de los detalles que tienen apoyo o ejemplos en un análisis

complementary: combined in a way that enhances all elements combined
complementario: combinar dos o más elementos de una manera que mejora los dos

complex character: a character that has multiple or conflicting motivations
personaje complejo: personaje que tiene motivaciones multiples o conflictivas

complex sentence: a sentence containing one independent clause and one or more subordinate clauses
oración compleja: oración que contiene una cláusula independiente y una o más cláusulas subordinadas

complications: the events in a plot that develop a conflict; the complications move the plot forward in its rising action

complicaciones: sucesos de una trama que desarrollan el conflicto; las complicaciones hacen avanzar la trama en su acción ascendente

components: the parts or elements of a whole
componentes: partes o elementos que conforman un todo

compound sentence: a sentence containing two independent clauses
oración compuesta: oración que contiene dos cláusulas independientes

concession: an admission in an argument that the opposing side has valid points
concesión: admitir en un debate que el lado opositor tiene opiniones válidas

concluding statement: a statement that follows from and supports the claim made in an argument
declaración concluyente: declaración que sigue de la afirmación, o la apoya, en un argumento

conflict: a struggle or problem in a story. An *internal conflict* occurs when a character struggles between opposing needs or desires or emotions within his or her own mind. An *external conflict* occurs when a character struggles against an outside force. This force may be another character, a societal expectation, or something in the physical world.
conflicto: lucha o problema en un cuento. Un *conflicto interno* ocurre cuando un personaje lucha entre necesidades o deseos o emociones que se contraponen dentro de su mente. Un *conflicto externo* ocurre cuando un personaje lucha contra una fuerza externa. Esta fuerza puede ser otro personaje, una expectativa social o algo del mundo físico.

connotation: the associations and emotional overtones attached to a word beyond its literal definition, or denotation a connotation may be positive, negative, or neutral
connotación: asociaciones y alusiones emocionales unidas a una palabra más allá de su definición literal o denotación; una connotación puede ser positiva, negativa, o neutra

consonance: the repetition of final consonant sounds in stressed syllables with different vowel sounds
consonancia: repetición de sonidos consonánticos finales en sílabas acentuadas con diferentes sonidos vocálicos

context: the circumstances or conditions in which something exists or takes place
contexto: circunstancias o condiciones en las que algo ocurre

conventions: standard features, practices, and forms associated with the way something is usually done
convenciones: prácticas y formas usuales asociadas con las costumbres de hacer algo

counterarguments: the arguments that can be made to oppose a viewpoint
contraargumentos: argumentos que se presentan para debatir un punto de vista

counterclaim: a position taken by someone with an opposing viewpoint
contrareclamación: posición que toma una persona con un punto de vista contrario

couplet: two consecutive lines of verse with end rhyme; a couplet usually expresses a complete unit of thought
copla: dos líneas de versos consecutivos con rima final; una copla normalmente expresa una unidad de pensamiento completa

credibility: the quality of being trusted or believed
credibilidad: calidad de ser confiable o creíble

critical lens: a particular identifiable perspective as in Reader Response Criticism, Cultural Criticism, etc., through which a text can be analyzed and interpreted
ojo crítico: punto de vista particular identificable como por ejemplo Teoría de la recepción, Crítica sociocultural, etc., por medio del que se puede analizar e interpretar un texto

cultural conflict: a struggle that occurs when people with different cultural expectations or attitudes interact
conflicto cultural: lucha que ocurre cuando interactúan personas con diferentes expectativas o actitudes culturales

Cultural Criticism: criticism that focuses on the elements of culture and how they affect one's perceptions and understanding of texts
crítica cultural: analizar un texto basándose en elementos culturales y como ellos afectan la percepción y lacomprensión de textos

culture: the shared set of arts, ideals, skills, institutions, customs, attitude, values, and achievements that characterize a group of people, and that are passed on or taught to succeeding generations
cultura: conjunto de artes, ideas, destrezas, instituciones, costumbres, actitud, valores y logros compartidos que caracterizan a un grupo de personas, y que se transfieren o enseñan a las generaciones siguientes

cumulative (or loose) sentence: a sentence in which the main clause comes first, followed by subordinate structures or clauses
oración acumulativa (o frases sueltas): oración cuya cláusula principal viene primero, seguida de estructuras o cláusulas subordinadas

D

deductive reasoning: a process of drawing a specific conclusion from general information
razonamiento deductivo: proceso en que se usa información general para sacar una conclusión específica

defend: to support a statement that has been made
defender: dar apoyo a una declaración que alguien ha hecho

denotation: the precise meaning of a word
denotación: significado literal de una palabra

detail: a specific fact, observation, or incident; any of the small pieces or parts that make up something else
detalle: hecho, observación o incidente específico; cualquiera de las pequeñas piezas o partes que constituyen otra cosa

dialect: the distinctive language—including the sounds, spelling, grammar, and diction—of a specific group or class of people
dialecto: lenguaje distintivo, incluyendo sonidos, ortografía, gramática y dicción, de un grupo o clase específico de personas

dialogue: the words spoken by characters in a narrative or film
diálogo: palabras que dicen los personajes en un relato o película

dialogue tags: the phrases that attribute a quotation to the speaker, for example, *she said* or *he bellowed*
marcas del diálogo: frases que atribuyen la cita de un hablante, por ejemplo, *dijo ella* o *bramó él.*

diction: a writer's word choices, which often convey voice and tone
dicción: selección de palabras por parte del escritor; elemento estilístico que ayuda a transmitir voz y tono

diegetic sound: any sound that can logically be heard by characters on screen
sonido diegético: sonidos lógicos que los personajes pueden oír en una escena en la pantalla

direct characterization: specific information about a character provided by the narrator or author
caracterización directa: información específica sobre un personaje creada por un narrador o autor

discourse: the language or speech used in a particular context or subject
discurso: lenguaje o habla usada en un contexto o tema en particular

documentary or nonfiction film: a genre of filmmaking that provides a visual record of actual events using photographs, video footage, and interviews
documental o película de no-ficción: género cinematográfico que realiza un registro visual de sucesos basados en hechos por medio del uso de fotografías, registro en videos y entrevistas

dominant group: a more powerful group that may perceive another group as marginalized or subordinate
grupo dominante: un grupo más poderoso que puede percibir a otro grupo como maginado o subordinado

drama: a play written for stage, radio, film, or television, usually about a serious topic or situation
drama: obra teatral escrita para representar en un escenario, radio, cine o televisión, normalmente sobre un tema o situación seria

dramatic irony: a form of irony in which the reader or audience knows more about the circumstances or future events than the characters within the scene
ironía dramática: una forma de la ironía en que los lectores o el público sabe más sobre las circunstancias o sucesos futuros que los personajes en la escena

dramaturge: a member of an acting company who helps the director and actors make informed decisions about the performance by researching information relevant to the play and its context
dramaturgo: socio de una compañía teatral que ayuda al director y a los actores tomar decisiones informadas sobre la interpretación investigando información relevante a la obra teatral y su contexto

dynamic (or round) character: a character who evolves and grows in the story and has a complex personality
personaje dinámico: personaje complejo que evoluciona a lo largo de la trama literaria

E

editorial: an article in a newspaper or magazine expressing the opinion of its editor or publisher
editorial: artículo de periódico o revista, que expresa la opinión de su editor

effect: the result or influence of using a specific literary or cinematic device; a result produced by a cause
efecto: resultado o influencia de usar un recurso literario o cinematográfico específico; resultado o producto de una causa

elaborate: to expand on or add information or detail about a point and thus to develop the point more fully

elaborar: extender o agregar información o detalles sobre un asunto, y asi desarrollar el asunto de manera más completa

empirical evidence: evidence based on experiences and direct observation through research
evidencia empírica: evidencia basada en experiencias y en la observación directa por medio de la investigación

emulate: to imitate an original work or person
emular: imitar una obra original

enfranchisement: having the rights of citizenship, such as the right to vote
emancipación: tener los derechos de la ciudananía, tales como el derecho al voto

epigram: a short, witty saying
epigrama: dicho corto e ingenioso

epigraph: a phrase, quotation, or poem that is set at the beginning of a document or component
epígrafe: frase, cita, o poema que aparece al comienzo de un documento o componente

epithet: a descriptive word or phrase used in place of or along with a name
epíteto: palabra o frase descriptiva usada en lugar de o junto con un nombre

ethos: (ethical appeal) a rhetorical appeal that focuses on the character or qualifications of the speaker
ethos: (recurso ético) recurso retórico centrado en la ética o en el carácter o capacidades del orador

euphonious: a harmonious or pleasing sound
eufónico: un sonido armonioso y agradable

evaluate: to make a judgment based on an analysis about the value or worth of the information, idea, or object
evaluar: dar una opinión basándose en un análisis sobre el valor o mérito de la información, idea, u objeto

evidence: the information that supports a position in an argument; forms of evidence include facts, statistics (numerical facts), expert opinions, examples, and anecdotes; *see also* anecdotal, empirical, and logical evidence
evidencia: información que apoya o prueba una idea o afirmación; formas de evidencia incluyen hechos, estadística (datos numéricos), opiniones de expertos, ejemplos y anécdotas; ver también evidencia anecdótica, empírica y lógica

exaggeration: a statement that represents something as larger, better, or worse than it really is
exageración: representar algo como más grande, mejor o peor que lo que realmente es

exemplification: the act of defining by example by showing specific, relevant examples that fit a writer's definition of a topic or concept
ejemplificación: definir por ejemplo mostrando ejemplos específicos y relevantes que se ajustan a la definición de un tema o concepto del escritor

explanatory writing: a form of writing whose purpose is to explain, describe, or give information about a topic in order to inform a reader
escrito explicativo: forma de la escritura cuyo propósito es explicar, describir o dar información sobre un tema para informar al lector

explicit theme: a theme that is clearly stated by the writer
tema explícito: tema que está claramente establecido por el escritor

exposition: events that give a reader background information needed to understand a story (characters are introduced, the setting is described, and the conflict begins to unfold)
exposición: sucesos que dan al lector los antecedentes necesarios para comprender un cuento. Durante la exposición, se presentan los personajes, se describe el ambiente y se comienza a revelar el conflicto.

extended metaphor: a comparison between two unlike things that continues throughout a series of sentences in a paragraph or lines in a poem
metáfora extendida: metáfora que se extiende por varios versos o a través de un poema completo

external coherence: unity or logical connection between paragraphs with effective transitions and transitional devices
coherencia externa: unidad o conexión lógica entre párrafos con transiciones efectivas y recursos transitionales

eye rhymes: words that appear to rhyme because of identical spelling patterns but do not actually rhyme, for example, *cough* and *through*
falsas rimas: palabras, en inglés, que poseen una terminación idéntica y, por tanto, nos llevan erróneamente a pensar que riman, tales como *cough* y *through*

F

fallacy: a false or misleading argument
falacia: argumento o poema falso o engañoso

falling action: the events in a play, story, or novel that follow the climax, or moment of greatest suspense, and lead to the resolution

acción descendente: sucesos de una obra teatral, cuento o novela posteriores al clímax, o momento de mayor suspenso, y que conllevan a la resolución

faux pas: an embarrassing act or remark in a social situation (borrowed from French)
metedura de pata: comportamiento o comentario embarazoso en el marco de una situación social

Feminist Criticism: criticism that focuses on relationships between genders and examines a text based on the patterns of thought, behavior, values, enfranchisement, and power in relations between and within the sexes
crítica feminista: se enfoca en la relación entre los sexos y examina un texto basándose en el diseño de pensamiento, comportamiento, valores, emancipación, y poder en las relaciones entre los sexos

figurative: symbolic or emblematic; not literal
figurativo: simbólico o emblemático, no literal

figurative language: the use of words to describe one thing in terms of another
lenguaje figurativo: lenguaje imaginativo o figuras retóricas que no pretenden ser tomados literalmente; el lenguaje figurativo usa figuras literarias

film techniques: the methods a director uses to communicate meaning and to evoke particular emotional responses in viewers
técnicas cinematográficas: metodos que usa un director en la comunicación del significado y evocar una respuesta emocional específica en los videntes

fixed form: a form of poetry in which the length and pattern are determined by established usage of tradition, such as a sonnet
forma fija: forma de poesía en la que la longitud y el patrón están determinados por el uso de la tradición, como un soneto

flashback: an interruption or transition to a time before the current events in a narrative
flashback: interrupción en la secuencia de los sucesos para relatar sucesos ocurridos en el pasado

flat (or static) character: a character who is uncomplicated and stays the same without changing or growing during the story
personaje estático: personaje no complicado que permanence del mismo caracter y que no cambia a lo largo de una historia

folktale: a story without a known author that has been preserved through oral retellings
cuento folclórico: cuento sin autor conocido que se ha conservado por medio de relatos orales

footage: literally, a length of film; the expression is still used to refer to digital video clips
metraje: literalmente, la longitud de una película; la expresión aún se usa para referirse a video clips digitales

foreshadowing: the use of hints or clues in a narrative to suggest future action
presagio: uso de claves o pistas en un relato para sugerir una acción futura

form: the particular structure or organization of a work
forma: estructura o organización particular de una obra

found poem: a poem consisting of words, phrases, and/or lines that come directly from another text
poema encontrado: poema compuesto de palabras, frases o pasajes sacados directamente de otros textos

free verse: poetry without a fixed pattern of meter and rhyme
verso libre: poesía que no sigue ningún patrón, ritmo o rima regular

G

genre: a kind or style of literature or art, each with its own specific characteristics. For example, poetry, short story, and novel are literary genres. Painting and sculpture are artistic genres.
género: tipo o estilo de literatura o arte, cada uno con sus propias características específicas. Por ejemplo, la poesía, el cuento corto y la novela son géneros literarios. La pintura y la escultura son géneros artísticos.

genre conventions: the essential features and format that characterize a particular genre, or style of literature or art
convenciones genéricas: características básicas y el formato que caracterizan un género específico

graphic novel: a book-length narrative, or story, in the form of a comic strip rather than words
novela gráfica: narrativa o cuento del largo de un libro, en forma de tira cómica más que palabras

graphics: images or text used to provide information on screen
gráfica: imágenes o texto que se usa para dar información en pantalla

H

hamartia: a tragic hero's fatal flaw; an ingrained character trait that causes a hero to make decisions leading to his or her death or downfall
hamartia: error fatal de un héroe trágico; característica propia de un personaje que causa que un héroe tome decisiones que finalmente llevan a su muerte o caída

hero: the main character or protagonist of a play, with whom audiences become emotionally invested
héroe: personaje principal o protagonista de una obra teatral, con el que el público se involucra emocionalmente

historical context: the circumstances or conditions in which something takes place
contexto historico: circuntancias o condiciones en las cuales algo sucede o pasa

Historical Criticism: criticism used to uncover meaning in a literary text by examining the text in the context of the time period in which it was created
historicismo: método crítico que se usa para revelar el significado de un texto literario mediante el examen de dicho texto en el contexto de la época en que fue escrito

hook: an opening in an argument or a piece of writing that grabs the reader's attention
gancho: cita, anécdota o ejemplo interesante al comienzo de un escrito, que capta la atención del lector

Horatian satire: satire that pokes fun at human foibles and folly with a witty, gentle, even indulgent tone
sátira de Horacio: sátira en que se burla de las debilidades y locuras con un tono suave, ingenioso, hasta indulgente

humor: the quality of being amusing
humor: calidad de ser divertido

hyperbole: exaggeration used to suggest strong emotion or create a comic effect
hipérbole: exageración que se usa para sugerir una emoción fuerte o crear un efecto cómico

I

iamb: a metrical foot that consists of an unstressed syllable followed by a stressed syllable
yambo: pie métrico que consta de una sílaba átona seguida de una sílaba acentuada

iambic pentameter: a rhythmic pattern of five feet (or units), each consisting of one unstressed syllable followed by a stressed syllable

pentámetro yámbico: patrón rítmico de cinco pies (o unidades) de una sílaba átona seguida de una sílaba acentuada

image: a word or phrase that appeals to one of more of the five senses and creates a picture

imagen: palabra o frase que apela a uno o más de los cinco sentido y crea un cuadro

imagery: the verbal expression of sensory experience; descriptive or figurative language used to create word pictures; imagery is created by details that appeal to one or more of the five senses

imaginería: lenguaje descriptivo o figurativo utilizado para crear imágenes verbales; la imaginería es creada por detalles que apelan a uno o más de los cinco sentidos

imperialism: a policy of extending the rule or influence of a country over other countries or colonies; the political, military, or economic domination of one country by another

imperialismo: política de extender el dominio o la influencia de un país sobre otros países o colonias; dominio político; militar o económico de un país sobre otro(s)

implied theme: a theme that is understood through the writer's diction, language construction, and use of literary devices

tema implícito: tema que se entiende a través de la dicción del escritor, construcción lingüística y uso de recursos literarios

indirect characterization: a narrator's or author's development of a character through the character's interactions with others, thoughts about circumstances, or speaking his or her thoughts aloud

caracterización indirecta: el desarrollo de un personaje según un narrador o autor por las interacciones del personaje con otros, pensamientos sobre las circunstancias, o su habilidad de enunciar sus pensamientos en voz alta

inductive reasoning: a process of looking at individual facts to draw a general conclusion

razonamiento inductivo: proceso de observación de hechos individuales para sacar una conclusión general

inference: a conclusion about ideas or information not directly stated

inferencia: conclusión sobre las ideas o información no presentadas directamente

interior monologue: a literary device in which a character's internal emotions and thoughts are presented

monólogo interior: recurso literario en el que se presentan las emociones internas y pensamientos de un personaje

interpretation: the act of making meaning from something, such as a text

interpretación: acto de interpretar un significado de algo, tal como un texto

internal coherence: unity or logical connection within paragraphs

coherencia interna: unidad o conexión lógica entre párrafos

irony: a literary device that exploits readers' expectations; irony occurs when what happens turns out to be quite different from what was expected. *Dramatic irony* is a form of irony in which the reader or audience knows more about the circumstances or future events in a story than the characters within it; *verbal irony* occurs when a speaker or narrator says one thing while meaning the opposite; *situational irony* occurs when an event contradicts the expectations of the characters or the reader.

ironía: recurso literario que explota las expectativas de los lectores; la ironía ocurre cuando lo que se espera resulta ser bastante diferente de lo que realmente ocurre. La *ironía dramática* es una forma de ironía en la que el lector o la audiencia saben más acerca de las circunstancias o sucesos futuros de un cuento que los personajes del mismo; la *ironía verbal* ocurre cuando un orador o narrador dice una cosa queriendo decir lo contrario; la *ironía situacional* ocurre cuando un suceso contradice las expectativas de los personajes o del lector.

J

justice: the quality of being reasonable and fair in the administration of the law; the ideal of rightness or fairness

justicia: calidad de ser razonable e imparcial en la administración de la ley; ideal de rectitud o equidad

Juvenalian satire: satire that denounces, sometimes harshly, human vice and error in dignified and solemn tones

sátira de Juvenal: sátira de denuncia, a veces con aspereza, los vicios y errores humanos con tonos dignos y solemnes

juxtaposition: the arrangement of two or more things for the purpose of comparison

yuxtaposición: ordenamiento de dos o más cosas con el objeto de compararlas

L

lede: an alternative spelling of lead; the opening of a news article or a single sentence that describes the main point of the article

entradilla: comienzo de una información periodística que resume lo más importante de ella

lining out: the process of creating line breaks to add shape and meaning in free verse poetry

llamada y respuesta: proceso de crear rupturas de lineas para dar forma y significado en la poesía del verso libre

literal: explicitly stated in a text; exact

literal: algo expresado de modo explícito y exacto en un texto

literal language: the exact meanings, or denotations, of words

lenguaje literal: los signficados y denotaciones exactos de las palabras

Literary Criticism: the formal practice of interpreting, evaluating, and explaining the meaning and significance of literary works

crítica literaria: práctica formal de interpretar, evaluar y explicar el significado y el valor de obras literarias

literary theory: a systematic study of literature using various methods to analyze texts

teoría literaria: intento de establecer principios para interpretar y evaluar textos literarios

logical evidence: evidence based on facts and a clear rationale

evidencia lógica: evidencia basada en hechos y una clara fundamentación

logical fallacy: a statement that is false because it is based on an error in reasoning

argumento falaz: afirmación de carácter falso por el hecho de estar basada en un error de razonamiento

logos: (logical appeal) a rhetorical appeal to reason or logic

logos: (apelación lógica) apelación retórica que usa la evidencia factual y la lógica para apelar al sentido de la razón

M

main idea: a statement (often one sentence) that summarizes the key details of a text

idea principal: declaración (con frecuencia una oración) que resume los detalles claves de un texto

marginalize: to relegate or confine a person to a lower or outer limit

marginar: relegar o confinar a una persona a un límite bajo o ajeno

Marxist Criticism: criticism that asserts that economics provides the foundation for all social, political, and ideological reality

crítica marxista: ver un text a través de la perspectiva en que la economía proporciona la fundación de toda realidad social, política, e ideológica

media: collectively refers to the organizations that communicate information to the public

medios de comunicación: colectivamente refiere a las organizaciones que comunican información al público

media channel: a method an organization uses to communicate, such as radio, television, website, newspaper, or magazine

canales mediaticos: método que usa una organización en la comunicación como radio, televisión, sitios de web, periódico, o revista

metacognition: the ability to know and be aware of one's own thought processes; self-reflection

metacognición: capacidad de conocer y estar consciente de los propios procesos del pensamiento; introspección

metaphor: a comparison between two unlike things in which one thing is spoken of as if it were another, for example, the moon was a crisp white cracker

metáfora: comparación entre dos cosas diferentes en la que se habla de una cosa como si fuera otra, por ejemplo, la luna era una galletita blanca crujiente

meter: a pattern of stressed and unstressed syllables in poetry

métrica: patrón de sílabas acentuadas y átonas en poesía

mise en scène: the composition, or setting, of a stage

puesta en escena: la composición o el lugar de un escenario

monologue: a dramatic speech delivered by a single character in a play

monólogo: discurso dramático que hace un solo personaje en una obra teatral

montage: a composite picture that is created by bringing together a number of images and arranging them to create a connected whole

montaje: cuadro compuesto que se crea al reunir un número de imágenes y que al organizarlas se crea un todo relacionado

mood: the atmosphere or predominant emotion in a literary work, the effect of the words on the audience

carácter: atmósfera o sentimiento general en una obra literaria

motif: a recurrent image, symbol, theme, character type, subject, or narrative detail that becomes a unifying element in an artistic work or text

motivo: imagen, símbolo, tema, tipo de personaje, tema o detalle narrativo recurrente que se convierte en un elemento unificador en una obra artística

motive: a character's reason for behaving in a certain way
motivación: razón esgrimida por un personaje para obrar de determinado modo

musical (or sound) device: the use of sound to convey and reinforce the meaning or experience of poetry
aparatos musicales: uso del sonido para transmitir y reforzar el significado o experiencia de la poesía

myth: a traditional story that explains the actions of gods or heroes or the origins of the elements of nature
mito: cuento tradicional que explica las acciones de dioses o héroes, o los orígenes de los elementos de la naturaleza

N

narration: the act of telling a story
narración: acto de contar un cuento

narrative: a story about a series of events that includes character development, plot structure, and theme; can be a work of fiction or nonfiction
narrativa: narración sobre una serie de sucesos que incluye el desarrollo de personajes, estructora del argumento, y el tema; puede ser una obra de ficción o no ficción

narrative arc: the story line of a text, including a beginning (*exposition*), a middle (the *rising action*), a high point (*climax*), and an end (the *falling action* and *resolution*)
arco narrativo: línea argumental de un texto, que consta de un comienzo (*exposición*), una parte media (*acción creciente*), un punto culminante (*clímax*) y un final (*acción decreciente* y *resolución*)

narrative pacing: the speed at which a narrative moves
compás de la narrativa: la rapidez en que una narrativa pasa

narrator: the person telling the story
narrador: persona que cuenta una historia

non-diegetic sound: sound that cannot logically be heard by the characters on screen; examples include mood music and voice-overs
sonido no diegético: voces y comentarios superpuestos; sonidos que no provienen de la acción en pantalla.

nut graf: an abbreviation of the expression *nutshell paragraph*; a statement that tells readers of a news article why they should care about what happened
epítome: texto introductorio que hace entender a los lectores por qué debería importarles la noticia que se relata a continuación

O

objective: based on factual information
objetivo: basado en información de hechos

objective tone: a tone that is more clinical and that is not influenced by emotion
tono objetivo: tono que es mas aséptico y que no se deja influir por la emoción

objectivity: the representation of facts or ideas without injecting personal feelings or biases
objetividad: representación de los hechos o ideas sin agregar sentimientos o prejuicios personales

ode: a lyric poem expressing feelings or thoughts of a speaker, often celebrating a person, event, or thing
oda: poema lírico que expresa sentimientos o pensamientos de un orador, que frecuentemente celebra a una persona, suceso o cosa

omniscient narrator: a narrator who knows all and tells a story from the perspective of multiple characters
narrador omnisciente: narrador que conoce todo lo sucedido sobre un determinado acontecimiento y relata la historia desde la perspectiva de varios personajes

onomatopoeia: the occurrence of a word whose sound suggests its meaning
onomatopeya: palabras cuyo sonido sugiere su significado

oral interpretation: a planned oral reading that expresses the meaning of a written text
interpretación oral: lectura oral planeada que interpreta el signficado de un text escrito

oral tradition: the passing down of stories, tales, proverbs, and other culturally important ideas through oral retellings
tradición oral: traspaso de historias, cuentos, proverbios y otras historias de importancia cultural por medio de relatos orales

oxymoron: words that appear to contradict each other; for example, cold fire
oxímoron: palabras que parecen contradecirse mutuamente; por ejemplo, fuego frío

P

paradox: a statement that contains two seemingly incompatible points
paradoja: declaración que contiene dos asuntos aparentemente incompatibles

parallel structure (parallelism): refers to a grammatical or structural similarity between sentences or parts of a sentence, so that elements of equal importance are equally developed and similarly phrased for emphasis

estructura paralela (paralelismo): se refiere a una similitud gramatical o estructural entre oraciones o partes de una oración, de modo que los elementos de igual importancia se desarrollen por igual y se expresen de manera similar para dar énfasis

paraphrase: to briefly restate ideas from another source in one's own words

parafrasear: volver a presentar las ideas de otra fuente en nuestras propias palabras

parenthetical citations: used for citing sources directly in an essay

citas parentéticas: usadas en citas de fuentes primarias en un ensayo

parody: a literary or artistic work that imitates the characteristic style of an author or a work for comic effect or ridicule

parodia: obra literaria o artística que imita el estilo característico de un autor o una obra para dar un efecto cómico o ridículo

passive-voice verbs: verb form in which the subject receives the action; the passive voice consists of a form of the verb *be* plus a past participle of the verb

verbos en voz pasiva: forma verbal en la que el sujeto recibe la acción; la voz pasiva se forma con el verbo *ser* más el participio pasado de un verbo

pathos: (emotional appeal) a rhetorical appeal to the reader's or listener's senses or emotions

pathos: (apelación emocional) apelación retórica a los sentidos o emociones de los lectores u oyentes

patriarchal: having the male as head of the household and with authority over women and children

patriarcal: sociedad en que el varón es jefe del hogar en el cual mantiene autoridad sobre las mujeres y niños

perception: one person's interpretation of sensory or conceptual information

percepción: interpretación de una persona en cuanto a información sensorial o conceptual

periodic sentence: a sentence that makes sense only when the end of the sentence is reached, that is, when the main clause comes last

oración periódica: oración que tiene sentido sólo cuando se llega al final de la oración, es decir, cuando la cláusula principal viene al final

persona: the voice assumed by a writer to express ideas or beliefs that may not be his or her own

personaje: voz que asume un escritor para expresar ideas o creencias que pueden no ser las propias

personification: a figure of speech that gives human qualities to an animal, object, or idea

personificación: figura literaria que da características humanas a un animal, objeto o idea

perspective: a way of looking at the world or a mental concept about things or events, one that judges relationships within or among things or events

perspectiva: manera de visualizar el mundo o concepto mental de las cosas o sucesos, que juzga las relaciones dentro o entre cosas o sucesos

persuasive argument: an argument that convinces readers to accept or believe a writer's perspective on a topic

argumento persuasivo: argumento que convence a los lectores a aceptar o creer en la perspectiva de un escritor acerca de un tema

photo essay: a collection of photographic images that reveal the author's perspective on a subject

ensayo fotográfico: recolección de imágenes fotográficas que revelan la perspectiva del autor acerca de un tema

plagiarism: the unattributed use of another writer's words or ideas

plagio: usar como propias las palabras o ideas de otro escritor

plot: the sequence of related events that make up a story

trama: secuencia de sucesos relacionados que conforman un cuento o novela

poetic structure: the organization of words, lines, and images as well as ideas

estructura poética: organización de las palabras, versos e imágenes, así como también de las ideas

poetry: language written in lines and stanzas

poesía: género literario que se concreta en un poema y está sujeto a medida o cadencia

point of view: the perspective from which a narrative is told, that is, first person, third-person limited, or third-person omniscient

punto de vista: perspectiva desde la cual se cuenta un relato, es decir, primera persona, tercera persona limitada o tercera persona omnisciente

precept: a rule, instruction, or principle that guides a person's actions and/or moral behavior

precepto: regla, instrucción o principio que guía las acciones de una persona y/o conducta moral de alguien

primary footage: film footage shot by the filmmaker for the text at hand
metraje principal: filmación hecha por el cineasta para el texto que tiene a mano

primary source: an original document or image created by someone who experiences an event first hand
fuente primaria: documento original que contiene información de primera mano acerca de un tema

prologue: the introduction or preface to a literary work
prólogo: introducción o prefacio de una obra literaria

prose: ordinary written or spoken language, using sentences and paragraphs, without deliberate or regular meter or rhyme; not poetry or song
prosa: forma común del lenguaje escrito o hablado, usando oraciones y párrafos, sin métrica o rima deliberada o regular; ni poesía ni canción

prosody: the pattern and rhythm of sounds in poetry, including stress and intonation
prosodia: rasgos fónicos de la métrica de la poesía, incluidos el énfasis y la entonación

protagonist: the central character in a work of literature, the one who is involved in the main conflict in the plot
protagonista: personaje central de una obra literaria, el que participa en el conflicto principal de la trama

proverb: a short saying about a general truth
proverbio: dicho corto sobre una verdad general

Q

qualify: to consider to what extent a statement is true or untrue (to what extent you agree or disagree)
calificar: consider hasta qué punto una declaración es verdadera o falsa

quatrain: a four-line stanza in a poem
cuarteta: en un poema, estrofa de cuatro versos

R

rationale: an explanation for a belief, statement, or behavior
fundamento: cimientos o bases en los que se apoya una creencia, afirmación o comportamiento

Reader Response Criticism: criticism that focuses on a reader's active engagement with a piece of print or nonprint text; shaped by the reader's own experiences, social ethics, moral values, and general views of the world

crítica de reacción del lector: análisis de un texto basado en las experiencias, ética social, valores, y percepciones generales del mundo

reasoning: the thinking or logic used to make a claim in an argument
razonamiento: pensamiento o lógica que se usa para hacer una afirmación en un argumento

rebuttal: a reason why a counterargument is wrong
refutación: razón por la cual un contraargumento es erróneo

refrain: a regularly repeated line or group of lines in a poem or song, usually at the end of a stanza
estribillo: verso o grupo de versos que se repiten con regularidad en un poema o canción, normalmente al final de una estrofa

refutation: the reasoning used to disprove an opposing point
refutación: razonamiento que se usa para rechazar una opinión contraria

reliability: the extent to which a source provides quality and trustworthy information
confiabilidad: grado en el que una fuente da información confiable y de buena calidad

renaissance: a rebirth or revival
renacimiento: un volver a nacer o una reanimación

repetition: the use of any element of language—a sound, a word, a phrase, a line, or a stanza—more than once
repetición: uso de cualquier elemento del lenguaje—un sonido, una palabra, una frase, un verso o una estrofa—más de una vez

resolution (denouement): the end of a text, in which the main conflict is finally resolved
resolución (desenlace): final de una obra teatral, cuento o novela, en el que el conflicto principal finalmente se resuelve

résumé: a document that outlines a person's skills, education, and work history
currículum vitae: documento que resume las destrezas, educación y experiencia laboral de una persona

retrospective: looking back to analyze the events in one's past
retrospectiva: mirar atrás en el tiempo para analizar los acontecimientos del pasado de una persona

revise: to rework or reorganize a piece of writing to improve its logic and flow after completing a first draft
revisar: rehacer o reorganizar un escrito para mejorar su lógica y fluidez tras haber terminado un primer borrador

rhetoric: the art of using words to persuade in writing or speaking

retórica: arte de usar las palabras para persuadir por escrito o de manera hablada

rhetorical appeals: emotional, ethical, and logical arguments used to persuade an audience to agree with the writer or speaker

recursos retóricos: uso de argumentos emocionales, éticos y lógicos para persuadir por escrito o de manera hablada

rhetorical context: the subject, purpose, audience, occasion, or situation in which writing or speaking occurs

contexto retórico: sujeto, propósito, audiencia, ocasión o situación en que ocurre el escrito

rhetorical devices: specific techniques used in writing or speaking to create a literary effect or enhance effectiveness

dispositivos retóricos: técnicas específicas que se usan al escribir o al hablar para crear un efecto literario o mejorar la efectividad

rhetorical question: a question that is asked for effect or one for which the answer is obvious

pregunta retórica: pregunta hecha para producir un efecto o cuya respuesta es obvia

rhetorical slanters: rhetorical devices used to present a subject in a biased way

sesgos retóricos: recursos retóricos que se usan para presentar un determinado asunto de un modo tendencioso

rhyme: the repetition of sounds at the ends of words
rima: repetición de sonidos al final de las palabras

rhyme scheme: a consistent pattern of rhyme throughout a poem

esquema de la rima: patrón consistente de una rima a lo largo de un poema

rhythm: the pattern of stressed and unstressed syllables in spoken or written language, especially in poetry

ritmo: patrón de sílabas acentuadas y no acentuadas en lenguaje hablado o escrito, especialmente en poesía

rising action: the movement of a plot toward a climax or moment of greatest excitement; the rising action is fueled by the characters' responses to the conflict

acción ascendente: movimiento de una trama hacia el clímax o momento de mayor emoción; la acción ascendente es impulsada por las reacciones de los personajes ante el conflicto

dynamic (or round) character: a character who evolves and grows in the story and has a complex personality

personaje dinámico: personaje que evoluciona y crece en la historia y que tiene una personalidad compleja

S

sarcasm: deliberate, often ironic ridicule
sarcasmo: burla deliberada, de carácter generalmente irónico

satire: a manner of writing that mocks social conventions, actions, or attitudes with wit and humor

sátira: manera de escribir en que se burla de convenciones sociales, acciones, o actitudes con ingenio y humor

scenario: an outline, a brief account, a script, or a synopsis of a proposed series of events

escenario: bosquejo, relato breve, libreto o sinopsis de una serie de sucesos propuestos

secondary audience: a group that may receive a message intended for a target audience

audiencia secundaria: grupo que puede recibir un mensaje orientado a una audiencia específica

secondary source: a discussion about or commentary on a primary source; the key feature of a secondary source is that it offers an interpretation of information gathered from primary sources

fuente secundaria: discusión o comentario acerca de una fuente primaria; la característica clave de una fuente secundaria es que ofrece una interpretación de la información recopilada en las fuentes primarias

sensory details: details that appeal to or evoke one or more of the five senses—sight, sound, smell, taste, and touch

detalles sensoriales: detalles que apelan o evocan uno o más de los cinco sentidos—vista, oído, gusto, olfato, y tacto

sensory images: images that appeal to the reader's senses—sight, sound, smell, taste, and touch

imágenes sensoriales: imágenes que apelan a los sentidos del lector—vista, oído, olfato, gusto, y tacto

sequence of events: the order in which things happen in a story

secuencia de eventos: orden en que los sucesos de una historia pasan:

setting: the time and place in which a story happens
ambiente: tiempo y lugar en el que ocurre un relato

simile: a comparison of two different things or ideas using the words *like* or *as*, for example, the moon was as white as milk

símil: comparación entre dos o más cosas o ideas diferentes usando las palabras *como* o *tan*, por ejemplo, la luna estaba tan blanca como la leche

situational irony: a form of irony that occurs when an event contradicts the expectations of the characters or the reader
ironía situacional: ocurre cuando un evento contradice las espectativas de los personajes o el lector

slanters: rhetorical devices used to present the subject in a biased way
soslayo: recursos retóricos para presentar el tema de modo sesgado

slogan: a short, catchy phrase used for advertising by a business, club, or political party
eslogan: frase corta y tendenciosa que usa como publicidad para un negocio, club o partido político

social commentary: an expression of an opinion with the goal of promoting change by appealing to a sense of justice
comentario social: expresión de una opinión con el objeto de promover el cambio al apelar a un sentido de justicia

soliloquy: a long speech delivered by an actor alone on the stage; represents the character's internal thoughts
soliloquio: discurso largo realizado por un actor sobre el escenario que representa sus pensamientos internos

sonnet: a 14-line lyric poem, usually written in iambic pentameter and following a strict pattern of rhyme
soneto: poema lírico de catorce versos, normalmente escrito en un pentámetro yámbico y que sigue un patrón de rima estricto

sound bite: a short excerpt from the recording of a speech or piece of music which captures the essence of the longer recording
cuña: corto fragmento de una grabación o de una pieza musical que capta la esencia de la grabación completa

speaker: the imaginary voice or persona of the writer or author
orador: voz o persona imaginaria del escritor o autor

stage directions: instructions written into the script of a play that indicate stage actions, movements of performers, or production requirements
direcciones escénicas: instrucciones escritas en un guión o drama que indican acción, movimiento de actors, o requisitos de la producción

stakeholder: a person motivated or affected by a course of action
participante: persona motivada o afectada por el curso de una acción

stanza: a group of lines, usually similar in length and pattern, that form a unit within a poem

estrofa: grupo de versos, normalmente similares en longitud y patrón, que forman una unidad dentro de un poema

static (or flat) character: a character who is uncomplicated and remains the same without changing or growing throughout a narrative
personaje estático: personaje que no cambia a lo largo de una narrativa

stereotype: an oversimplified, generalized conception, opinion, and/or image about particular groups of people
estereotipo: concepto generalizado, opinión y/o imagen demasiado simplificada acerca de grupos específicos de personas

stichomythia: in drama, the delivery of dialogue in a rapid, fast-paced manner, with actors speaking emotionally and leaving very little time between speakers
esticomitia: en el drama, es la rendición del diálogo de una manera rápida con actores que hablan con emoción, dejando espacio muy breve entre los hablantes

storyboard: a tool to show images and sequencing for the purpose of visualizing a film or a story
guión gráfico: método de mostrar imágenes y secuencias con el propósito de visualizar una película o historia

strategize: to plan the actions one will take to complete a task
estrategizar: planear las acciones de uno para complir una tarea

structure: the way a literary work is organized; the arrangement of the parts in a literary work
estructura: manera en que la obra literaria está organizada; disposición de las partes en una obra literaria

style: the distinctive way a writer uses language, characterized by elements of diction, syntax, imagery, organization, and so on
estilo: manera distintiva en que un escritor usa el lenguaje, caracterizada por elementos de dicción, sintaxis, lenguaje figurado, etc.

subculture: a smaller subsection of a culture, for example, within the culture of a high school may be many subcultures
subcultura: subsección más pequeña de una cultura, por ejemplo, dentro de la cultura de una escuela secundaria puede haber muchas subculturas

subjective: based on a person's point of view, opinions, values, or emotions
subjetivo: basado en el punto de vista, las opiniones, los valores o las emociones de alguien

subjective tone: a tone that is obviously influenced by the author's feelings or emotions

tono subjetivo: tono obviamente influído por los sentimientos o emociones del autor

subjectivity: judgment based on one's personal point of view, opinion, or values

subjetividad: en base en nuestro punto de vista, opinión o valores personales

subordinate: a person or group that is perceived as having a lower social or economic status

subordinado: persona o grupo percibido de ser de rango social o estado económico bajo

subplot: a secondary or side story that develops from and supports the main plot and usually involves minor characters

argumento secundario: una historia secundaria o periférica que apoya el argumento principal y que suele involucrar a personajes secundarios o menores

subtext: the underlying or implicit meaning in dialogue or the implied relationship between characters in a book, movie, play, or film; the subtext of a work is not explicitly stated

subtexto: significado subyacente o implícito en el diálogo o la relación implícita entre los personajes de un libro, película, u obra teatral. El subtexto de una obra no se establece de manera explícita.

survey: a method of collecting data from a group of people; it can be written, such as a print or online questionnaire, or oral, such as an in-person interview

encuesta: método para recolectar datos de un grupo de personas; puede ser escrita, como un impreso o cuestionario en línea, u oral, como en una entrevista personal

symbol: anything (object, animal, event, person, or place) that represents itself but also stands for something else on a figurative level

símbolo: cualquier cosa (objeto, animal, evento, persona o lugar) que se representa a sí misma, pero también representa otra cosa a nivel figurativo

symbolic: serving as a symbol; involving the use of symbols or symbolism

simbólico: que sirve como símbolo; que implica el uso de símbolos o simbolismo

synecdoche: a figure of speech in which a part is used to represent the whole or vice versa

sinécdoque: figura retórica en que una parte se usa para representar el todo, o vice-versa

syntax: the arrangement of words and the order of grammatical elements in a sentence; the way in which words are put together to make meaningful elements, such as phrases, clauses, and sentences

sintaxis: disposición de las palabras y orden de los elementos gramaticales en una oración; manera en que las palabras se juntan para formar elementos significativos como frases, cláusulas y oraciones

synthesis: the act of combining ideas from different sources to create, express, or support a new idea

síntesis: acto de combinar ideas de diferentes fuentes para crear, expresar o apoyar una nueva idea

synthesize: to combine ideas from different sources to create, express, or support a new idea or claim

sintetizar: combinar ideas procedentes de distintas fuentes para crear, expresar o sustentar una nueva idea o afirmación

T

target audience: the intended group for which a work is designed to appeal or reach

público objetivo: grupo al que se pretende apelar o llegar con una obra

tenor: the intent, tone, or attitude conveyed by the words in a text

tenor: intención, tono o actitud transmitida por las palabras de un texto

textual evidence: the details, quotations, and examples from a text that support the analysis or argument presented

evidencia textual: detalles, citas, y ejemplos de un texto que apoyan el análisis o la argumentación presentada

theatrical elements: elements used by dramatists and directors to tell a story on stage. Elements include *costumes* (the clothing worn by actors to express their characters), *makeup* (cosmetics used to change actors' appearances and express their characters), *props* (objects used to help set the scene, advance a plot, and make a story realistic), *set* (the place where the action takes place, as suggested by objects, such as furniture, placed on a stage), and *acting choices* (gestures, movements, staging, and vocal techniques actors use to convey their characters and tell a story).

elementos teatrales: elementos utilizados por los dramaturgos y directores para contar una historia en el escenario. Los elementos incluyen *vestuario* (ropa que usan los actores para expresar sus personajes), *maquillaje* (cosméticos que se usan para cambiar la apariencia de los actores y expresar sus personajes), *elementos* (objetos que se usan para ayudar a montar la escena, avanzar la trama y crear una historia realista), *plató* (lugar donde tiene lugar la acción, según lo sugieren los objetos, como muebles, colocados sobre un escenario), y *opciones de actuación* (gestos, movimientos, representación y técnicas vocales que se usan para transmitir sus personajes y narrar una historia).

thematic statement: an interpretive statement articulating the central meaning or message of a text
oración temática: afirmación interpretativa que articula el significado o mensaje central de un texto

theme: a writer's central idea or main message; *see also* explicit theme, implied theme
tema: idea central o mensaje principal acerca de la vida de un escritor; *véase también* tema explícito, tema implícito

thesis: the main idea or point of an essay or article; in an argumentative essay the thesis is the writer's position on an issue
tesis: idea o punto principal de un ensayo o artículo; en un ensayo argumentativo, la tesis es la opinión del autor acerca de un tema

thumbnail sketch: a small drawing made to plan the composition of a more detailed or finished image that will be created later
boceto en miniatura: pequeño dibujo realizado para planificar la composición de una imagen más amplia o detallada que será posteriormente creada

tone: a writer's (or speaker's) attitude toward a subject, character, or audience
tono: actitud de un escritor u orador acerca de un tema

topic sentence: a sentence that states the main idea of a paragraph; in an essay, the topic sentence also makes a point that supports the thesis statement
oración principal: oración que establece la idea principal de un párrafo; en un ensayo, la oración principal también establece una proposición que apoya el enunciado de la tesis

tragedy: a dramatic play that tells the story of a character, usually of a noble class, who meets an untimely and unhappy death or downfall, often because of a specific character flaw or twist of fate

tragedia: obra teatral dramática que cuenta la historia de un personaje, normalmente de origen noble, que encuentra una muerte o caída imprevista o infeliz, con frecuencia debido a un defecto específico del personaje o una vuelta del destino

tragic hero: an archetypal hero based on the Greek concept of tragedy; the tragic hero has a flaw that makes him or her vulnerable to downfall or death
héroe trágico: héroe arquetípico basado en el concepto griego de la tragedia; el héroe trágico tiene un defecto que lo hace vulnerable a la caída o a la muerte

transcript: a written copy or record of a conversation that takes place between two or more people
transcripción: copia escrita de una conversación que sucede entre dos o más personas

U

unconventional: eccentric; unusual; original
no convencional: excéntrico; inusual; original

understatement: the representation of something as smaller or less significant than it really is; the opposite of exaggeration or hyperbole
subestimación: representación de algo como más pequeño o menos importante de lo que realmente es; lo opuesto a la exageración o hipérbole

V

valid: believable or truthful
válido: creíble o verídico

validity: the quality of truth or accuracy in a source
validez: calidad de verdad o precisión en una fuente

verbal irony: a form of irony that occurs when a speaker or narrator says one thing while meaning the opposite
ironía verbal: ocurre cuando un hablante o narrador dice una cosa mientras quiere decir lo opuesto

verbatim: in the exact words of a source
textualmente: palabras citadas exactamente como fueron expresadas

verify: to prove or confirm that something is true
verificar: probar o confirmar que algo es verdadero

vignette: a picture or visual or a brief descriptive literary piece
viñeta: ilustración o representación visual o pieza literaria descriptiva breve

visual delivery: the way a performer on stage interprets plot, character, and conflict through movement, gestures, and facial expressions

presentación visual: manera en que un actor en un escenario interpreta trama, carácter, y conflicto a través de movimiento, gestos, y expresiones de la cara

visual rhetoric: an argument or points made by visuals such as photographs or by other visual features of a text

retórica visual: argumentos o asuntos representados en visuales como fotos u otros rasgos visuales de un texto

visualize: to form a mental picture of something

visualizar: formarse una imagen mental de algo

vocal delivery: the way a performer on stage expresses the meaning of a text through volume, pitch, rate or speed of speech, pauses, pronunciation, and articulation

presentación vocal: manera en que se expresan las palabras en el escenario, por medio del volumen, tono, rapidez o velocidad del discurso, pausas, pronunciación y articulación

voice: a writer's (or speaker's) distinctive use of language to express ideas as well as his or her persona

voz: manera en que el escritor u orador usa las palabras y el tono para expresar ideas, así como también su personaje o personalidad

Index of Skills

Literary Skills

Ad baculum (scare tactics), 412

Ad hominem (genetic fallacy), 235, 412

Ad misericodism (appeal to pity), 412

Ad populum (bandwagon), 235, 411

Alliteration, 310

Allusion, 41, 275, 279, 291, 293, 302, 359, 360, 361, 419, 525, 539, 540

Analogy, 172, 275, 302, 310, 373, 401–402, 410, 433

Analytical essay, 308, 576

Anaphora, 271, 302, 310

Anecdote, 41, 172, 410

Annotated bibliography, 472, 508–509, 514

Appeal to pity (ad misericodism), 412

Arguable thesis, 104, 348, 350

Argument
    audience of, 117, 332, 379
    author's, 257
    clear and organized, 393
    compelling, 391, 399, 400, 410
    deductive, 357
    developing, 257, 308, 333, 338, 392, 400
    elements and characteristics of, 104, 111, 275, 280, 310–311, 354
    fallacy's effect on, 319
    focus of essay, 101, 118, 175, 257, 370
    inductive, 357
    key terms for, 392
    logical, 243, 379
    objective tone, 224, 331, 333, 393, 400
    refuting, 104, 111, 121, 172, 176, 351, 354, 355, 356, 357, 393, 403
    ridicule and sarcasm's effect on, 378
    structure of, 103–104, 111, 117, 118, 119, 121, 175, 275, 280, 286, 312, 332, 333, 354, 357
    subjective tone, 331
    supporting, 101, 104, 111, 113, 119, 170, 172, 175, 185, 244, 275, 279, 287, 313, 314, 328, 330, 348, 357, 381, 389–390, 393, 399, 400, 401–402, 403, 421
    tone of, 118, 268, 270, 331

Argument from outrage, 412
    argumentative text. See also Editorial

Assonance, 492

Attitude (See also Tone (attitude))

of author/speaker, 13, 14, 84, 89, 91, 141, 142, 143, 152, 154, 161, 165, 243, 255, 273, 274, 523

of characters, 213, 561

of narrator, 25, 26

of readers/listeners, 509

Audience, 50, 59, 81, 92, 104, 111, 117, 160, 169, 173, 176, 205, 239, 272, 273, 299, 332, 379, 391, 392, 403, 414, 445, 457, 465, 467, 468, 480, 541

Author's craft, 26, 118, 523

Author's purpose, 49, 50–51, 57, 58, 66, 89, 90, 91, 92, 109, 118, 119, 126, 159, 186, 205, 208, 218, 253, 263, 282, 291, 408, 429–430, 433, 434, 438, 450, 480, 571, 575

Autobiographies, 6

Bandwagon (ad populum), 235, 411

Bias
    of authors, 331, 381
    defined, 363
    by headlines, 364, 366
    identifying, 365–366, 371, 372, 375, 381
    by photos, captions, and camera angles, 364, 366, 389
    of rhetoric, 373–375
    by source control, 365, 366
    through placement, 364, 365, 381
    through selection and omission, 364, 365, 381, 389
    through statistics and crowd count, 364–365, 366, 401
    types of, 363, 365–366

Big ideas, 5, 33

Biographies, 6

Book reviews, 572–573, 574–575

Call to action, 104, 111, 122, 127, 265, 271, 275, 280, 285, 287, 313, 314, 332

Camera angles, bias by, 364, 366

Captions, bias by, 364, 366, 389

Caricature, 424, 455

Case studies, 410

Causal relationships, 401, 412

Cause-and-effect text structure, 31, 91

Central conflict, 237

Central idea, 25, 90, 225, 255, 279, 370

Central image, 74

Central message, 165, 502

Characterization, 135, 149, 150, 208, 211–213, 238, 536, 547–549, 551

Characters, 6, 27, 75, 145, 263, 466, 525, 537–538, 547–548, 550, 556–557, 562, 563, 564, 571

    actions of, 211, 213, 217, 218, 220, 223, 224, 226, 237, 536, 547, 558, 566

    analyzing, 210, 211, 212, 213, 217, 224, 229, 232, 236, 238, 258, 537

    changes of, 139, 141, 142, 217, 218, 537

    choices of, 238, 558

    descriptions of, 211

    development of, 226, 227, 228, 237, 281, 566

    direct characterization, 547, 548

    dramatic elements of, 145, 217

    dramatic presentations, 145

    emotional responses of, 260, 566–567

    foil, 213, 258

    historical context of, 182

    hysteria, 260

    indirect characterization, 226, 547, 548

    mental images of, 525

    moral dilemmas of, 217, 220, 232–233, 558, 559

    motivation of, 211, 212, 213, 217, 218, 223, 224, 558

    note taking chart, 211, 212, 213, 217

    study of, 566–568

    tone affecting, 13

    uniqueness of, 75

    voice developing, 225, 226

Character study, 566–568

Chiasmus, 303, 310

Chorus, 549

Chronological text structure, 31, 91, 158

Claim, 45, 83, 104, 111, 117, 119, 120, 121, 160, 165, 170, 173, 176, 185, 257, 265, 275, 280, 281, 282, 287, 313, 338, 349, 350, 351, 355, 356, 358, 389–390, 393, 400, 401–402, 410, 420, 464, 511, 541, 565, 568, 575, 576

Classification definition strategy, 41, 42, 43, 45, 70

Climax, 145, 227, 228, 238

Colloquialisms, 169

Commentary, 567

Reading Skills

Writing Skills

citing, 29, 176, 393, 473, 508–509, 514, 515, 541

credibility and accuracy of, 363, 371, 392, 394, 473, 505, 507

documentary films as, 486–487

evaluating, 97, 175, 372, 515

fallacies, 319, 505

informational texts as, 472, 475, 479, 481, 482, 487, 488, 495, 502, 503

locating relevant, 473, 505, 507, 510

organizing, 510, 511–512

primary, 97, 486, 504, 505, 556, 576

relevance of, 97, 175, 505, 507, 510

reliability of, 97, 372

secondary, 97, 341, 486, 505, 576

synthesizing information from, 100, 101, 175–176, 197, 199, 473, 505–507, 510

using materials ethically, 508

validity of, 97

State problems in hyperbolic terms, 465, 466

Structure, 100, 175, 176, 263, 264, 280, 287, 312, 314, 333, 370, 392, 410, 422, 467, 468, 480, 514, 515, 541, 576, 577

Summarizing, 28, 29, 40, 54, 58, 59, 71, 94, 98, 110, 160, 221, 228, 379, 391, 392, 393, 399, 438, 511, 515, 570, 575

Synthesizing information, 60, 100, 101, 174, 175–176, 197, 199, 473, 505–507, 510, 571

Text structure, 31, 263, 264, 280, 370, 422, 576

Textual evidence, 29, 45, 92, 100, 160, 174, 176, 224, 281, 285, 431, 450, 454, 487, 541, 575, 576, 577

Thematic statement, 571

Thesis statement, 28, 60, 83, 92, 93, 99, 100, 112, 121, 138, 160, 176, 314, 392, 422, 480, 484, 511, 512, 513, 514, 515, 541, 560, 575, 576

Timed prompt, 28

Topic selection, 97, 392, 419, 421, 451, 465, 472, 473, 483, 484

Topic sentences, 45, 93, 392, 403, 433, 438, 504, 541, 565

Transitions, 28, 60, 83, 99, 100, 112, 121, 176, 224, 281, 372, 504, 512, 514, 515, 541, 576, 577

Use of language, 100, 176, 226, 264, 314, 333, 393, 422, 433, 449, 467, 468, 515, 577

Writing prompt

argumentative letter, 410, 414

argumentative text, 121, 160, 174, 175–176, 393, 400, 410, 414, 560, 565, 575

editorial, 393, 400

explanatory text, 307

informational text, 60, 71, 83, 112, 224, 372, 433, 504

lecture of advice, 451

literary analysis, 28, 138, 151, 541

observation statements, 44

opening, 14

parody, 445

rhetorical analysis, 45, 257, 307, 391, 438

satirical narrative paragraph, 466

scripts, 222, 226, 237, 260, 445, 512–513

Writing with partners, 32, 50, 51, 64, 65, 287, 393, 445, 502

Media Skills

Art, as historical sources, 472, 479, 481, 482, 487, 495, 502, 503

Camera angles, bias by, 364, 366

Captions, bias of, 364, 366, 389

Create a poster, 213, 302, 457

Crowd counts, bias through, 364–365, 366

Documentary films, as historical sources, 486–487

Evaluating sources, 97, 175, 372, 515

Examining cartoons, 381, 432–433

Graphics, 382, 388, 389, 419

Headlines, bias of, 364, 366

Illustrations, 8, 193

analyzing, 193

Images, analyzing, 48, 53–54, 96, 207, 379

Interactive multimedia presentation (See Multimedia presentation)

Media formats, 341, 382, 403, 415, 421, 445, 451, 505–506, 511, 512, 514

MLA style sheet, 175, 508

Multimedia presentation, 472, 481, 509–515

generating research questions, 473, 474, 475, 483, 484–485, 506, 509, 510

organizing, 511, 514

presenting, 505–507

topic selection, 472, 473, 483, 484

Murals, analyzing, 10, 11

News sources, 319, 340

accuracy and trustworthiness of, 340, 363

analyzing bias of, 371, 375

bias of, 319, 363–364, 371, 372

characteristics of, 341, 342

credibility and accuracy of, 363, 371, 372

digital, 341

multimodal, 341, 342

print features, 382, 388, 417, 419

secondary audience, 341

target audience, 341, 342, 343, 379

Omission, bias through, 364, 365, 381

Online resources, 13, 68, 97, 320, 323, 330, 341, 342, 356, 379, 473, 482, 491, 505

Photographs, analyzing, 9, 96

Photos, bias by, 364, 366

Placement, bias through, 364, 365, 381

Political cartoons, analyzing, 8

Presenting poster, 457

Print and graphic features, analyzing, 382, 419

Publishing, 393

Puff pieces, 365

Reading and creating editorial cartoon, 415–419

Researching images, 97, 98

Satirical cartoons, analyzing, 432–433

Sculptures, analyzing, 487, 495

Selection, bias through, 364, 365, 381, 389

Setting purpose for viewing, 96, 432, 486–487

Source control, bias by, 365, 366

Special formatting, 382

Statistics, bias through, 364, 366, 401

Text divisions, 382

Video footage, analyzing, 302

Visual presentations, 12, 98

Visual prompt, 1, 177, 315, 469

Visual text

analyzing, 7–12, 487

creating, 12

Index of Authors and Titles

Credits

"Girl Moved to Tears by *Of Mice and Men* Cliffs Notes" from *The Onion*, August 18, 2008. Copyright © 2009, by Onion, Inc. Reprinted with permission of The Onion. HYPERLINK "http://www.theonion.com" http://www. theonion.com

"In Depth, but Shallowly" from *Bad Habits: A 100% Fact Free Book* by Dave Barry, humorist. Used by permission.

"Gambling in Schools" by Howard Mohr, from *Mirth of a Nation: The Best Contemporary Humor* compiled by Michael J. Rosen, Harper Paperbacks, 2000. Used by permission.

"How to Poison the Earth" by Linnea Saukko from *Student Writers at Work and in the Company of Other Writers*. Copyright © 1984 by Bedford/St. Martin's and used with permission of the publisher.

"The Harlem Renaissance" adapted from *The 1920s* by Kathleen Drowne and Patrick Huber. Copyright © 2004 by Kathleen Drowne and Patrick Huber. *American Popular Culture Through History Series*, Greenwood.

From *The New Negro* by Alain Locke. Copyright © 1925 by Albert and Charles Boni. Touchstone.

"To Usward" by Gwendolyn B. Bennett from *Shadow Dreams: Women's Poetry of the Harlem Renaissance*, edited by Maureen Honey. Copyright © 1989 by Rutgers University Press.

"From 'On a Dark Tower'" by Eugenia W. Collier, *College Language Association Journal* 11.1 (1967).

"Sweat" by Zora Neale Hurston, from *The Complete Stores of Zora Neale Hurston*, edited by Henry Louis Gates, Jr., and Sieglinda Lemke. Introduction copyright © 1995 by Henry Louis Gates, Jr. and Sieglinde Lemke. HarperCollins Publishers. Compilation copyright © 1995 by Vivian Bowden, Lois J. Hurston Gaston, Clifford Hurston, Lucy Ann Hurston, Winifred Hurston Clark, Zora Mack Goins, Edgar Hurston, Sr., and Barbara Hurston Lewis.

"Mother to Son" from *The Collected Poems of Langston Hughes* by Langston Hughes, edited by Arnold Rampersad with David Roessel, Associate Editor, copyright © 1994 by the Estate of Langston Hughes. Used by permission of Alfred A. Knopf, a division of Random House, Inc.

Image Credits

n/a mariakraynova / iStock; 1 Photo courtesy of Ellen Moses; 8 PRO-IMMIGRATION CARTOON 'Welcome to All!' An 1880 American cartoon by Joseph Keppler in favor of unrestricted immigration. / Granger / Bridgeman Images; 9 World's Highest Standard of Living...', 1937 (litho), Bourke-White, Margaret (1904-71) / Private Collection / Peter Newark American Pictures / Bridgeman Images; 10 Stepping into the American Dream (acrylic on canvas), Cortada, Xavier / Private Collection / Bridgeman Images; 15 Pictorial Press Ltd / Alamy Stock Photo; 24 Library of Congress/Prints and Photographs Division; 34 © Teresa M. Bejan; 35 Steven Senne/ASSOCIATED PRESS; 48 The Signing of the Constitution of the United States in 1787, 1940 (oil on canvas), Christy, Howard Chandler (1873-1952) / Hall of Representatives, Washington D.C., USA / Bridgeman Images; 53 Everett Collection, Inc / Alamy Stock Photo; 55 Granger Historical Picture Archive / Alamy Stock Photo; 56 Andrew_Howe/iStock; 65 By [Daderot] [Public domain], via Wikimedia Commons; 66 Colonial farmer, 2002 (w/c on paper), Frey, Matthew (b.1974) / Private Collection / Wood Ronsaville Harlin, Inc. USA / Bridgeman Images; 73 Stocktrek Images, Inc./Alamy Stock Photo; Pilotenschlaeger by Franz Koeck, 1933-1945 (b/w photo) / © SZ Photo / Bridgeman Images; 76 Everett Collection; 77 Harlem Jig, 2001 (oil on board), Bootman, Colin / Private Collection / Bridgeman Images; 77 Ramon Espinosa/AP Photo; 78 Ka_Li/Shutterstock; 84 © Kesaya E. Noda; 96 Joe Rosenthal/ Library of Congress; 108 World History Archive / Alamy Stock Photo; 113 Ann Johansson/Corbis Entertainment/ Getty Images; 124 Builders #1, 1972 (w/c, gouache & graphite), Lawrence, Jacob (1917-2000) / Saint Louis Art Museum, Missouri, USA / Eliza McMillan Trust / Bridgeman Images; 128 Joseph Bruchac (b/w photo) / © Chris Felver / Bridgeman Images; 129 Postcard of the Immigration receiving station, Ellis Island, New York City, 1940 (colour litho), American School, (20th century) / Private Collection / Peter Newark American Pictures / Bridgeman Images; 131 Photograph by LaVerne Harrell Clark 02/17/1971, courtesy of The University of Arizona Poetry Center. Photograph copyright © 2011 Arizona Board of Regents.; 133 © 2017 Shevaun Williams; 133 Fiona Osbaldstone © 2018 College Board; 146 David Attie/Getty Images; 148 Image by Kevin Berne; 152 © Bryce Richter; 154 Raoul Benavides/Getty Images; 155 The Granger Collection; 157 Ted Streshinsky/ Corbis/Getty Images; 161 Official portrait of President-elect Barack Obama/Pete Souza/Library of Congress/Prints and Photographs Division; 164 Jim Rogash/WireImage/ Getty Images; 177 Sarin Images/The Granger Collection; 184 North Wind Picture Archives / Alamy Stock Photo; 187 GRANGER / GRANGER — All rights reserved.; 188 By Peter Pelham [Public domain], via Wikimedia Commons; 190 Witches of Salem - a girl bewitched at a trial in 1692 (colour litho), American School / Private Collection / Peter Newark American Pictures / Bridgeman Images; 193 Charles Walker Collection / Alamy Stock Photo; 195 Courtesy of the "Salem Witch Trials Documentary Archive" <salem.lib.virginia.edu>; 201 Courtesy of the "Salem Witch Trials Documentary Archive" <salem.lib.virginia.edu>; 203 Everett Collection Inc / Alamy Stock Photo; 207 Salem Witch Trials (litho), English School, (20th century) / Private Collection / © Look and Learn / Bridgeman Images; 208 Alfred Eisenstaedt/The LIFE Picture Collection/Getty Images; 216 Geraint Lewis / Alamy Stock Photo; 222 Xinhua / Alamy Stock Photo; 231 Geraint Lewis / Alamy Stock Photo; 240 Margaret Chase Smith/Library of Congress/Prints and Photographs Division; 246 Everett Collection Inc / Alamy Stock Photo; "I have here in my hand--" / Herblock/ Library of Congress/ Prints and Photographs Division; 268 ClassicStock / Alamy Stock Photo; 269 Abraham Lincoln delivering his second inaugural address as President of the United States, Washington, D.C./Library of Congress/ Prints and Photographs Division; 276 North Wind Picture Archives / Alamy Stock Photo; 278 By http://www.patrickhenrylibrary.org/islandora/object/islandora%3A308] [Public domain], via Wikimedia Commons; 284 Universal History Archive / UIG / Bridgeman Images; 290 Everett Collection Inc / Alamy Stock Photo; 295 Associated Press; 315 Solstock / iStock; 323 Jessica Hill/AP Photo; 346 Jamie McCarthy/ Getty Images; 351 © Andrew Potter; 368 Johannes Berg/ Bloomberg/Getty Images; 377 TerryJ/iStockphoto; 382 © The Star Tribune; 395 Sam Edwards/Caiaimage/OJO+/ Getty Images; 397 Monkeybusinessimages/iStockphoto; 407 Kristina Blokhin / Alamy Stock Photo; 426 Courtesy of David Bouchier; 427 XonkArts/DigitalVision Vectors/ Getty Images; 432 © Jen Sorensen; 433 © Jen Sorensen; 439 WENN Rights Ltd / Alamy Stock Photo; 441 Tetiana Yurchenko/Shutterstock; 446 Hulton Archive/Getty Images; 461 CSA Images/Getty Images; 469 © Mario Burger; 478 Bettmann/Getty Images; 479 B Christopher / Alamy Stock Photo; 488 Portrait of Portrait of Alain LeRoy Locke as a young man(photo) / Private Collection / Prismatic Pictures / Bridgeman Images; 493 Ginger jar and cover, Kangxi Period, 1661-1722 (porcelain), Chinese School, Qing Dynasty (1644-1912) / Private Collection / Photo © Christie's Images / Bridgeman Images; 495 James Weldon Johnson, half-length portrait at desk with telephone/Library of Congress/ Prints and Photographs Division; 495 Manuscripts and Archives Division, The New York Public Library. "Art - Sculpture - Harp (Augusta Savage) - Harp" The New York Public Library Digital Collections. 1935 - 1945. http://digitalcollections.nypl.org/items/5e66b3e9-03a1-d471-e040-e00a180654d7; 500 Portrait of Countee Cullen (1903–46) (photo) / Private Collection / Prismatic Pictures / Bridgeman Images; 517 Everett Collection Historical / Alamy Stock Photo; 519 Zora Neale Hurston and an unidentified man probably at a recording site, Belle Glade, Florida/Library of Congress/ Prints and Photographs Division; 521 African American children outdoors, Eatonville, Florida; Zora Neale Hurston and three boys in Eatonville, Florida; Children playing singing game and dancing outdoors, Eatonville, Florida/ Library of Congress/ Prints and Photographs Division; 526 Woman hanging laundry on the line, Eatonville, Fla., taken during the Lomax, Hurston, Barnicle 1935 expedition to Georgia, Florida and the Bahamas/Library of Congress/ Prints and Photographs Division; 535 Chinaberry tree in yard of Joseph LaBlanc. Crowley, Louisiana. These trees grow quickly and produce ample shade in two years/Library of Congress/ Prints and Photographs Division; 553 Mother and son in Harlem / Mario De Biasi per Mondadori Portfolio / Bridgeman Images